PSYCHOLOGY
FOR THE
CLASSROOM

PSYCHOLOGY
FOR THE
CLASSROOM

JANICE T. GIBSON
University of Pittsburgh

Prentice-Hall, Inc., Englewood Cliffs, New Jersey

To Professor George L. Fahey
my colleague and friend,
who contributed greatly for so many years
to my professional and personal development,
and who, in so many ways,
is what a professor should be.

Library of Congress Cataloging in Publication Data

Gibson, Janice T.
Psychology for the classroom.

Bibliography: p.
Includes index.
1. Educational psychology. 2. Child development.
3. Teaching. I. Title.

LB1051.G484   370.15   75-33076
ISBN 0-13-733287-4

Printed in the United States of America

10 9 8 7 6 5 4 3 2 1

PRENTICE-HALL INTERNATIONAL, INC., London
PRENTICE-HALL OF AUSTRALIA, PTY. LTD., Sydney
PRENTICE-HALL OF CANADA, LTD., Toronto
PRENTICE-HALL OF INDIA PRIVATE LIMITED, New Delhi
PRENTICE-HALL OF JAPAN, INC., Tokyo

Credits and acknowledgments may be found on p. 556.

CONTENTS

What Makes A Successful Teacher?   1

Attributes of the Successful Teacher   2
  Knowledge of Subject Matter Content / Applying Psychological
  Principles / The Teaching-Learning Process / Adapting to
  New Situations

THE DEVELOPING INDIVIDUAL   7   **PART ONE**

Socializing the Young Child: The Preschool Years   11   **Chapter 1**

What Is Socialization?   12
The Family: Primary Transmitter and Interpreter of Culture   13
  Variations in Child-Rearing Practices / Systems of
  Caretaking / Effects of Parental Deprivation
Preschool Education Programs: Formal Transmitters and
Interpreters of Culture   25
  Preschool Education in the U.S.S.R. / Kibbutz Education in
  Israel / Preschool Education in China / Day Care in the
  United States
The Peer Group and Play: Informal Transmitters and
Interpreters of Culture   32
Modeling, Imitation, and Television   33
The Effects of Culture on Socialization   35
  Socioeconomic Status / Sex Typing and Identity
Common Behaviors Generated by Socialization   38
  Dependency and Attachment / Trust / Altruism and
  Cooperation / Anger and Aggression / Jealousy and
  Rivalry / Fear
Problem Behaviors and Socialization   42
Summary and Suggested for Further Reading   43

Developing Thought Processes: The Early School Years   45   **Chapter 2**

The Relationship Between Language and Cognitive
Development   46
  Theories of Language and Cognition
Theories of Cognitive Development   49
  Stage-Dependent Theory: Piaget / Learning-Environmental
  Theories

Planning for Cognitive Development   58
Stage-Dependent Approaches / Learning-Environmental
Approaches / Preschool Education Programs / Elementary
School Programs
Summary and Suggested for Further Reading   71

Developing Identity and Values: The Adolescent Years   73   **Chapter 3**

Adolescence: The Search for Identity and Values   74
Theories of Identity Development   76
Stage-Dependent Theories / Learning-Environmental Theories
Theories of Value Development   79
Stage-Dependent Theories / Learning-Environmental
Theories / Comparison of Two Approaches to Identity and
Value Development
Planning for Development of Identity and Values   87
Child Rearing and the Family / The Peer Group /
The School / Choosing A Vocation
Adolescence: A Time of Conflict   95
Adolescent-Adult Conflict / Drugs, Delinquency, and Alienation
Adolescents and Society: Suggestions for the Future   98
Summary and Suggested for Further Reading   100

PRINCIPLES OF LEARNING AND TEACHING   103   **PART TWO**

Explaining Behavior: Associationist Theories   107   **Chapter 4**

Introduction   108
Contiguity Theory   109
Classical (Respondent) Conditioning   109
The Law of Effect   111
Operant (Instrumental) Conditioning   113
Components of Operant Conditioning / Operant Conditioning
and Higher-Order Learning / Schedules of Reinforcement
The Significance of Associationist Theories in Learning   125
Classical Conditioning / Operant Conditioning: The Effects of
Reinforcement
Behavior Management in the Classroom: What the Teacher
Can Do   128
Select Desirable Behavior / Select Proper Reinforcers / Use
Extinction / Problems in Classroom Behavior Management
Programmed Instruction   134
Varieties of Programming / Thinking and Programmed
Instruction / Developing Teacher-Made Programs
The Science of Behavior: Implications for the Classroom and
Everyday Life   139
The Myth of Freedom / The Use of Behavioral Technology /
The Ethics of Behavior Management
Summary and Suggested for Further Reading   143

Building Understanding: Cognitive-Field Theories   144   **Chapter 5**

What Are Cognitive-Field Theories?   145
The Foundations of Cognitive-Field Theories / Differences

Between Cognitive-Field and Associationist Theories

Gestalt Theories of Learning   148
The Laws of Organization / Insight Learning / Productive
Thinking / Topological or Vector Theory of Learning (Lewinian
Field Theory)

Bruner's Theories of Learning   162
Introduction / Structure / Transfer / Cognitive
Development / Insight / The Problems of Teaching

Applications of Cognitive-Field Theory to the Classroom   175
Teaching Perceptual Skills / The Discovery Method of Teaching

Summary and Suggested for Further Reading   182

Motivating the Student in the Classroom   184   **Chapter 6**

What Is Motivation Theory?   185

Theories of Need Systems and Motivation   189
Maslow's Hierarchy of Needs / Achievement Motivation /
Competence Motivation / Stimulation and Exploration as
Needs and Motivations / The Need for Identity / The Need
for Equilibrium / Fear and Anxiety as Drives

Motivating Students: What the Teacher Can Do   203
The Hierarchy of Needs and Classroom Learning / Develop
Achievement Motivation / Promote Group Reinforcement and
Competition as Sources of Classroom Motivation / Promote
Creativity / Reduce Anxiety and Its Effects / Different Kinds
of Classroom Motivation / Plan the Curriculum for Motivation

Summary and Suggested for Further Reading   221

Specific Types, Outcomes, and Styles of Learning   223   **Chapter 7**

Types of Learning   224
Perceptual Learning / Motor Learning / Language
Learning / Concept Learning and Problem-Solving /
Attitude Learning

Outcomes of Learning   249
A Rationale for a Taxonomy of Learning Objectives /
Preparing Learning Objectives

Styles of Learning   259
Variables Affecting Learning Style / Planning for Different
Learning Styles

Summary and Suggested for Further Reading   264

Remembering, Forgetting, and Transferring Learning   267   **Chapter 8**

Introduction   268
Three Types of Memory

Why We Remember and Forget   271
Associationist Theories / Motivation Theories / Gestalt
Theories / Cybernetic Theory or Information-Processing
Approach

How to Increase Long-Term Memory   277
What the Classroom Teacher Can Do / What the Student
Can Do / Methods for Measuring Remembering in the
Classroom

Transfer of Learning   289
  What Is Transfer? / Early Development of the Concept of
  Transfer / Theories of Transfer
How to Increase Positive Transfer in Classroom Learning   296
Summary and Suggested for Further Reading   303

Alternative Instructional Designs for the Classroom   305   **Chapter 9**

Introduction   306
Alternative Instructional Designs for Preschool Education   307
  Montessori Programming / Public Educational Television for
  the Preschool Audience
Alternative Instructional Designs for Traditional Public
Elementary and High School Programs   312
  The Open Classroom / Instruction Individually Prescribed for
  the Student / The Use of Technology in Classroom
  Instruction / Programs That Reorganize Traditional Student and
  Teacher Roles
Alternative Instructional Designs for Untraditional Elementary
and High School Programs   330
  The Free School Movement
Alternative Instructional Designs for Higher Education   339
Summary and Suggested for Further Reading   341

**DIFFERENCES AMONG INDIVIDUALS: EFFECTS ON
LEARNING AND TEACHING**   345   **PART THREE**

Teaching the Socially Disadvantaged   349   **Chapter 10**

Who Are the Socially Disadvantaged?   350
  Backgrounds of the Socially Disadvantaged / Health of the
  Socially Disadvantaged / Behavior and Attitudes of the Socially
  Disadvantaged / Poverty: A Vicious Cycle
Why Are We Failing?   356
  What Are the Issues? / What Have We Accomplished So Far?
Some Solutions and Programs   362
  Changing Our Traditional Programs / Early Childhood
  Intervention Programs / Programs for School-Age Children /
  Compensatory Programs for Older Students
Summary and Suggested for Further Reading   375

Identifying and Teaching Students with Special Needs   377   **Chapter 11**

Who Are the Students with Special Needs?   378
  Special Needs and the Normal Curve / The Handicapped
  Student / The Gifted Student
Identifying Students with Special Needs   385
  Identifying the Handicapped / Identifying the Gifted
Programming for Students with Special Needs   389
  Mainstreaming: A Rationale / Mainstreaming: Services to
  Students in Heterogeneous Classes / Special Education:
  Services to Students with Special Needs in Homogeneous
  Classes / Programs and Services for Students with Special
  Needs Outside the School
Summary and Suggested for Further Reading   402

Identifying and Teaching Students with Problem Behaviors 404 **Chapter 12**

What Are Personality and Problem Behaviors? 405
  Average and Problem Behavior: A Statistical Model / Well-Adjusted and Poorly Adjusted Personalities: A Clinical Model / Problem Behaviors
Factors Related to Problem Behaviors in Schoolchildren 408
  Family-Related Factors / School-Related Factors / Society-Related Factors
Common Problem Behaviors in the Classroom 415
  Withdrawal / Violence and Other Forms of Aggression / Hyperactivity / Severe Anxiety / Adolescent Problem Behaviors
What Can Be Done 424
  Mainstreaming: The Teacher's Role in the Regular Classroom / Calling in the Specialist
Summary and Suggested for Further Reading 431

Teacher Behavior and Classroom Achievement 433 **Chapter 13**

The Role and Importance of the Teacher in the Public School System 434
  Conflicting Roles of the Teacher / The Importance of the Teacher in Affecting Classroom Achievement
The Teacher as a Human Being 437
  The Teacher's Participation as a Citizen and a Community Member / Some of the Major Dissatisfactions with Teaching / The Impact of Unionization
The Teacher as a Leader 448
  Factors in Effective Leadership / Problems Stemming from Poorly Used Leadership / Some Solutions for the Teacher
Teacher Accountability 455
  What Is Teacher Accountability? What Does It Really Mean for the Teacher? / Effects of Accountability: Implications for Education / Special Problems and Issues in Accountability / Accountability to Oneself
Summary and Suggested for Further Reading 460

USES AND METHODS OF EVALUATION 463 **PART FOUR**

Evaluating Classroom Learning 465 **Chapter 14**

Testing: A Means of Evaluation 466
  Purposes of Classroom Testing / Social Implications of Testing / Criteria of Good Tests and Their Evaluation
Developing Classroom Tests 473
Alternative Approaches to Classroom Testing 484
  Criterion-Referenced Testing and Competency-Based Instruction / Cooperative Planning / Self-Paced Evaluation
Grading: A Means of Recording Evaluation 489
  Purposes of Grading / Types of Grading / Problems of Grading: What the Teacher Can Do / Management of School Grades and Records / Grading and Teacher Accountability
Summary and Suggested for Further Reading 495

Standardized Tests of Ability and Achievement 497 **Chapter 15**

What Is a Standardized Test? 498
Types of Standardized Tests / How Standardized Tests Are Developed / Advantages and Disadvantages of Standardized Tests

Standardized Tests of Ability: The IQ Test 507
What Is the IQ? / The IQ Test as a Predictor of Future Ability / Advantages and Disadvantages of IQ Testing in the Schools

Standardized Tests of Achievement 516
What Are the Purposes of Standardized Achievement Tests? / Advantages and Disadvantages of Standardized Achievement Tests / Standardized Achievement Tests and Accountability

Summary and Suggested for Further Reading 521

Appendixes 523
Appendix 1: Averages / Appendix 2: The Normal Curve and Other Frequency Distributions / Appendix 3: Correlation / Appendix 4: Scores Often Used on Standardized Tests / Appendix 5: A Simple Item Analysis That the Teacher Can Use

Glossary 532

References and Author Index 540

Subject Index 557

PREFACE

In the past, educational psychology courses have been criticized for their failure to prepare teachers for actual classroom experiences. Most educational psychology texts have merely presented a string of disjointed theories without demonstrating how and why they are relevant to the teacher.

Psychology for the Classroom is designed to make clear the link between theory and classroom—to tie our knowledge of psychological principles to the real world of teaching. To that end, we have provided up-to-date coverage of research as well as current educational, social, and economic controversies that affect student and teacher behavior. Chapter 9, for example, discusses and evaluates the many instructional innovations at the primary, elementary, high school, and college levels that have been developed to better cope with individual differences and needs of students. Chapter 13 deals with such controversies as busing, sex discrimination, and teacher unionization, which ultimately affect the behavior of teachers as human beings and as leaders. The specific effects of different styles of teaching on classroom achievement are also discussed in this chapter.

Designed for introductory educational psychology courses, *Psychology for the Classroom* presents many points of view, since each preparing teacher should determine for himself what is most effective in his classroom for each individual student, and the style of instruction that works best for him and for his students. *Psychology for the Classroom* attempts, through the use of classroom examples, to explain the many relevant psychological theories that can be generalized to a wide range of practical situations.

Part I, "The Developing Individual," describes theories that can be used to predict and interpret behavior patterns of children at different ages. Part II, "Principles of Learning and Teaching," explains specific theories of learning and instruction and shows how they can be applied in the classroom. Part III, "Differences among Individuals: Effects on Learning and Teaching," explains the differences in abilities, interests, attitudes, and expectations among students, as well as the current political and economic situations that ultimately affect teacher behavior. Part IV, "Uses and Methods of Evaluation," describes the ways in which tests and other means of evaluation can be used by teachers and students alike as an aid in further learning and instructional design.

Psychology for the Classroom attempts to put to use many of the theories and methods it explains. In Chapter 7, for example, the use and design of learning objectives are discussed. Such objectives introduce each chapter in this book, to guide the student in reading the chapter and to help him determine if he has learned and understood the material. Similarly, within each chapter, Questions for Thought pose problems that test the student's ability to apply what he has learned. Such questions have been shown to facilitate retention of both specific and general text material. As an aid in bringing theory closer to the classroom, boxed-off areas within each chapter describe current situations as reported in news items, magazines, and journals. Suggestions for further reading, which can be used to supplement the text, appear at the end of each chapter, and a complete list of references appears at the end of the book. Finally, a glossary at the end of the book will help the student to understand terms that are new to him.

As a further aid to the student, Ronald D. Zellner and Michael J. Ash have prepared a supplemental study guide and workbook. For each chapter they have written a detailed outline and selected key terms and concepts. They have also designed a short pre-test, which can be used to test the student's knowledge of the chapter after a first reading; a review test, which summarizes the chapter; and a post-test, which can be used as a final test. Useful additions to the text for the course instructor are provided in an instructor's manual, written by Phyllis Blumberg.

ACKNOWLEDGMENTS   To help prepare this material I have relied on my own programmed text, *Educational Psychology*, and on the help of a team of specialists. They have included market specialists, who have helped clarify the major concerns of instructors in colleges and universities, a research assistant, who has done the groundwork and provided the working materials from which each chapter was written, professional writers and editors, who have prepared readable manuscript, designers, photographers, and photo researchers. I would like to express my gratitude for the effort expended by all these specialists in producing a text that, I believe, deals with often highly complex issues in a clear and concise fashion. In particular, I would like to thank Alice Greenwald, Development Editor, who managed in an amazingly short period of time, under difficult conditions, to turn an incomplete and untidy manuscript into a meaningful teaching instrument. I would also like to thank C. Thomas Gooding, David Johnson, William Roweton, and Dennis Warner, who read and commented on portions of the manuscript.

Timeliness (unusual in a textbook of this length) was acquired also, largely through the coordinated efforts of many specialists working simultaneously with up-to-date information. Several colleagues at the University of Pittsburgh have worked with me and contributed their expertise to the total effort. Phyllis Blumberg did the background research, provided data from which the manuscript was prepared, and compiled the glossary. Dr. Lorna Farrington researched and prepared the boxed-off items of interest to remind the reader of the relationship between psychological principles and actual classroom situations. Dr. Vernell Lillie supervised and coordinated the work of three student photographers from the University of Pittsburgh Alternative Curriculum, whose photographs appear in this text: Robin Gibson, Mitchell Mandell, and Greg Winokur. The Alternative Curriculum photography project not only provides evidence that alternative curricula can be exciting and meaningful, it affords us the opportunity to glimpse today's urban classrooms through the eyes—and photographs—of students.

J. T. G.

WHAT MAKES A SUCCESSFUL TEACHER?

We all know that some teachers unquestionably are more effective professionally than others—regardless of the particular philosophies of education they follow, the particular modes of instruction they use, or the particular environments in which they teach. Some teachers are able to make classroom learning exciting. Others, even though they may have accumulated advanced degrees in specific subject matters or in education, have difficulty providing students with learning experiences that are meaningful and that can be applied directly to real life. Unfortunately, these less successful teachers frequently tend to outnumber the better ones, not only in elementary and high schools but also in institutions of higher learning. (How many really excellent teachers can you recall today from your elementary and high school years?)

Historically, educators and psychologists have described the difference between successful and unsuccessful teachers in terms of what was considered at the time the "art of teaching." The assumption that teaching is an "art" is important because it rules out the importance of teacher education. The successful teacher, according to this assumption, simply has a "knack for teaching." The unsuccessful teacher does not. According to this view, there is little to be done to change the situation—a pessimistic assumption indeed!

Psychology for the Classroom is based on an entirely different and much more optimistic set of assumptions: (1) that good teaching is due not to a "knack" but rather to the acquisition of teaching skills, and (2) that these skills can be defined and taught.

The skills required of teachers are as varied and complex as the environment in which teachers work. To outline all the behaviors

This chapter contains excerpts from "Goals of Educational Psychology in Teacher Preparation: A Discipline Approach to Educational Psychology," a paper the author delivered at the American Educational Research Association Meeting, Washington, D.C., March, 1975.

needed in each specific teaching situation is hardly possible. And even if it could be done, as we shall see later, it would actually be detrimental to the teacher. What is needed is to learn the general categories of skills that are related to good teaching. Let us therefore begin by examining the major attributes or skills of the successful teacher. Then we will discuss the role that educational psychology can play in strengthening these attributes, and, more specifically, what *Psychology for the Classroom* can do to help prepare you, the prospective teacher, for a meaningful and exciting career.

ATTRIBUTES OF THE SUCCESSFUL TEACHER

Subject Matter Content   The first attribute of a successful teacher, skill in *subject-matter content*, is so critical to good teaching that it hardly needs comment. No teacher can perform well without a solid background in the subject he is teaching. But knowledge of subject matter is not in itself enough to make a successful teacher. Really good teachers, the ones students remember later in their lives, have acquired a variety of related skills in order to make learning a valuable experience for their students.

Applying Psychological Principles   Skill in *applying psychological principles* to the teaching process constitutes another important attribute of the successful teacher. Two kinds of research experiences form the basis of these psychological principles. First, psychologists have identified through research conducted under *controlled (regulated) conditions* and often in laboratory settings principles that can be applied to educational practice and often can be used to explain man's behavior in other contexts as well. Second, educational psychologists have identified through research in *classroom settings* principles that can be put to practical use by teachers.

This book emphasizes the practical application of psychological principles and theories discovered in both laboratory and classroom. The work of developmental and child psychologists, for example, is critical to predicting the behavior of schoolchildren of different experience, backgrounds, and ages. The skills that teachers need to predict and understand the reasons for behavior at each age level and for each background are described in Part 1, "The Developing Individual."

Part 2, "Principles of Learning and Teaching," provides useful tools for predicting how these same students will respond in given situations to specific types of instruction and, more generally, how children respond to the teacher's manipulation of the teaching-learning environment. The teaching-learning process can be viewed from a variety of theoretical positions, and the choice of any given viewpoint by a teacher is very likely to affect his behavior in the classroom. For this reason, many points of view are discussed throughout this text.

Psychologists and educators have long known that differences exist among people in abilities, interests, attitudes, and expectations. Part 3, "Differences among Individuals: Effects on Teaching and Learning," explores these differences as well as the methods that have been found most effective in dealing with them.

Principles of measurement provide tools for evaluating both student and teacher progress; without evaluating our progress, we have little direction for furthering instruction. Part 4, "Uses and Methods of Evaluation," explores the potentials of our measurement and evaluation expertise.

A familiarity with the *teaching-learning process* is also essential to good teaching. Too frequently new teachers enter classrooms unprepared for what they will find there. This lack of preparation leads to teacher apathy and disenchantment and to the large number of teacher dropouts during the first year in the classroom. It also leads to poor teaching. To prepare new teachers for actual classroom experience, most schools of education have designed classroom-observation and practice-teaching programs for their students. But to be prepared for the "real world" of education, the prospective teacher must become aware of many more types of experience than can be encountered through relatively brief observations in nearby schools. The teacher must also become aware of the psychological, sociological, political, and economic forces acting on the teaching-learning process.

For this reason, in recent years many teacher-preparation programs have given students the opportunity to study and participate in school and community activities, thereby focusing on significant issues in the communities where they will be employed. Such programs have been added most often on urban campuses, where many students anticipate teaching in the inner city. One innovative program initiated at the University of Pittsburgh has included such diverse experiences as examination of food distribution, health facilities, housing, educational programs, and job opportunities and rehabilitation for unskilled and semiskilled laborers (J. Gibson, 1973a). But again, the difficulty of educating through community participation lies in the amount of experience that can be made available in a limited time.

This book has been designed to help you become familiar with teaching-learning situations. Study of actual situations and problems as well as theoretical principles is critical in this context. The

The Teaching-Learning Process

emphasis for the classroom teacher should be on the classroom and all the forces acting on it that affect the teaching-learning process. Accordingly, this book has concentrated on the reality of the classroom situation, from relevant news items describing what is happening now to case histories of what has already happened. Besides examples discussed in the text, there are in each chapter a number of boxed-off items of interest selected because of their meaningfulness and timeliness in light of today's school issues.

Adapting to New Situations

A truly successful teacher is skillful in *adapting to new situations.* In recent years teachers have been bombarded with instructional innovations — individually prescribed instruction, competency-based teaching, and open classroom methods, among many others. They have been inundated as well with new teaching devices — teaching machines, computer-assisted instruction, and so on. At the same time, vast political, social, and economic changes within the United States have led to rapid and often unpredictable changes in planning and policy making in our schools. It is impossible to judge with accuracy today what will be the specific problems of tomorrow. One thing, however, remains clear: Teachers with narrow expertise in instruction cannot be effective in all the situations they are likely to meet. We know neither how long any particular mode of instruction will be effective nor how feasible it will prove to be in tomorrow's schools.

In actual practice, teachers must be *prepared to adapt to sudden innovations.* Teachers sometimes are unaware that curriculum or methodology changes will take place in their classrooms until the very day these changes occur. In West Virginia in 1974, for example, teachers victimized by community problems outside their control were suddenly required without prior notice to remove a large number of disputed textbooks from their shelves and to make sudden and major changes in their curricula, and yet still had to meet their basic obligation to teach skills to their students.

The teacher must be able to adapt to new situations as they occur. Psychologists have long been aware of the fact that the ability to use appropriately the techniques learned in one situation when new situations and problems are introduced occurs when principles rather than specific methods are taught (Judd, 1908). This book is meant to help the prospective teacher gain such skill by providing general principles that may be applied in different types of classroom situations, rather than by teaching specific behaviors that can be used only in given situations.

Individual students respond to different approaches, methods, and materials, and different teachers teach effectively with different approaches, methods, and materials. This may seem obvious, but it is crucial to the teaching-learning process and has been borne out by research (Clark, 1970). It would be wasteful to try to force either teachers or students into any one mold. This book therefore presents each instructional approach in terms of both its advantages and disadvantages, in order to allow teachers to select the approach best suited to them individually.

The successful teacher of the 1970s clearly must approach teaching as more than an "art" or a "knack." He must also be more than just a technician whose specialty lies in the details of a particular subject. The successful teacher must, instead, be capable of adapting whatever instructional procedure is available to the particular learning situation and to the particular and highly individual needs, goals, interests, aptitudes, and developmental stages of students. He must be prepared for what Toffler (1970) has called "the unknown society of tomorrow." Knowledge of the principles of educational psychology can provide the skills that make such adaptation possible and that can make teaching one of the most rewarding careers a person can pursue. *Psychology for the Classroom* was designed to be part of the program that teaches those skills.

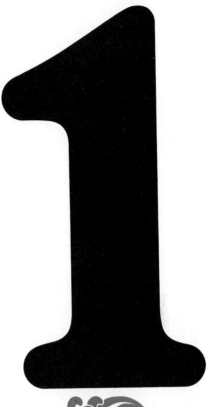

THE
DEVELOPING
INDIVIDUAL

Development refers to many kinds of changes that take place in people as time passes. The source of these changes can be physiological, environmental, or both. Development that takes place independent of interaction with the environment is called *maturation*. Other changes that take place depend, all or in part, on the interaction between the individual and the environment. We call this learning.

We can speak of many different kinds of development: physical (increases in height, weight, and motor coordination), social (changes in the ways the individual relates to other people in society), cognitive (increased ability to think and understand), and personality (changes in people that enable them to cope more effectively and realistically with their environments).

Many developmental psychologists are interested in the generalizations they can make about growth and development that are characteristic of the typical child at a given age level. This information is used to help parents, teachers, and other concerned individuals to predict the kinds of change they can expect to take place at different ages, and to plan accordingly. In addition, knowing the kinds of change to be expected in the average child serves as a useful yardstick for recognizing behavior patterns that are noticeably different. For example, as children grow older, their vocabularies increase, and they learn to use their expanded word knowledge in increasingly complex ways; if they don't, there is something wrong.

Generalizations about development are thus very useful, but they do not tell the whole story, since no two children are identical. The rate at which children change and develop—physically, mentally, emotionally, and socially—not only varies from child to child, but from age to age for any given child. Development is an extremely complex process.

Growth and development do not stop with the end of childhood, but continue throughout life. Even though height and weight tend to become stabilized by midadolescence or earlier, interaction with the environment continues and provides many opportunities for growth and development—in knowledge, personality, and attitudes toward others—throughout the adult years.

Psychologists have taken two different approaches to the study of development. The first is called the *stage-dependent* approach; it views development primarily as a function of maturation. Advocates of this viewpoint maintain that all children pass through a clearly defined sequence of developmental stages, which invariably occur in a fixed and predictable order at specific ages. Physical growth, development of cognitive processes, and personality and social development have all been described in terms of stage-dependent theories.

One well-known psychologist who has taken this approach is Arnold Gesell. A specialist in the behavior of infancy and early childhood, Gesell described the sequential stages for many different areas of development, including motor functioning, adaptive behavior, language, and personal-social behavior. Gesell's approach to cognitive development will be considered briefly in Chapter 2. Other stage-dependent theorists who will be discussed in Part 1 include Jean Piaget (cognitive development), Erik Erikson and Sigmund Freud (social and personality development), and Lawrence Kohlberg (moral development).

The second approach to the study of development is called the *learning-environmental* approach; it is based on the premise that in order to understand changes in behavior one should understand the effects of the environment on the growing individual. Harry Harlow was a pioneer in this field with his studies of the development of affectionate behavior in infant monkeys. He demonstrated that for long-term healthy development, close physical contact with a live mother or mother-surrogate is necessary at an early age. Other learning-environmental theorists who will be discussed in this text are Urie Bronfenbrenner, Jerome Kagan, Albert Bandura, and Jerome Bruner.

Perhaps the most important environmental variable is society. To a large extent, society dictates the kinds of behavior patterns a person exhibits at a given age level. At each period of our lives, we are confronted with different kinds of tasks that society expects us to master, increasing in complexity as we grow older. Robert Havighurst divided the life span into six distinct periods and defined what he called the "developmental tasks" expected of people in our culture for each particular period. According to Havighurst, successful accomplishment of each of the designated tasks at the appropriate age level leads to a positive response from others and to happiness and success with later tasks. Failure leads to a negative response from others and to unhappiness and difficulty with later tasks. The specific tasks involved vary from one society to another. In our own society, two important developmental tasks of early childhood are walking and talking. One of the tasks of middle childhood is to engage in activities without supervision, and one of the tasks of adolescence is to adjust to the changes taking place in one's body.

The notion of developmental tasks is important for teachers if they are to offer programs that are meaningful and appropriate in terms of the child's age, intelligence, and achievement level. Efforts at teaching which would be largely wasted if they occurred either too early or too late can be highly productive when they occur at the proper "teachable moment."

The first chapters of this book are arranged according to the developmental concerns of greatest importance to teachers and parents at each of three age levels—early childhood, middle childhood, and adolescence. At each age level, developmental processes are described, problems unique to that age level are discussed, and suggestions are made as to how teachers and parents can best contribute to the development of children.

Chapter 1 deals with socialization, that is, learning socially acceptable behavior, which deeply concerns parents and teachers of preschool children. Since socialization necessarily involves interaction of children with their environments, the views of the learning-environmental theorists are considered. The concerns of the school-age child revolve mainly around thinking and school learning; Chapter 2, therefore, deals with the development of the cognitive processes. In this chapter, implications of both stage-dependent and learning-environmental theories are discussed, in order to describe how thinking develops as the child grows older. Special programs designed to increase the rate of cognitive development in early childhood are carefully examined; a case is made for the preschool education program as well as for improved reading programs in elementary school.

 As the school-age child grows into adolescence, other concerns become increasingly important. Chapter 3 deals with the development of identity and values, a process that goes on from very early childhood but frequently presents major crises at the time of adolescence. The causes of these crises are examined from several points of view, and at the end of the chapter some suggestions for dealing with them are presented, which students, parents, and teachers all might use effectively.

SOCIALIZING THE YOUNG CHILD: THE PRESCHOOL YEARS

After completing this chapter, the reader should be able to:

1 Define the term *socialization* and explain its importance to both the developing individual and society.

2 Describe the variables within the home, school, and society at large that are critical to the socialization of young children; explain how each affects socialization.

3 Compare and contrast the various roles of mother, mother substitute, father, and teacher in the development of young children.

4 Propose and justify a preschool curriculum to facilitate the socialization of young children.

CHAPTER 1

WHAT IS SOCIALIZATION?

Man is a social animal, and he learns to become such by adapting to his environment in the process we call *socialization.* How we grow up, the kind of person we become, the ways in which we act are largely determined by the culture in which we are reared. Socialization begins at the moment we are born, and it has its strongest influence during our formative years as young children.

The essence of socialization is learning. A child learns what behavior is socially acceptable: what to eat, how to dress, how to treat property, how to deal with other people. He learns what religious and moral beliefs and value systems are acceptable to his society: for example, that a premium is placed on education in middle-class American society. He learns his role as a member of a group: what, by common consent of the group, is considered correct and necessary, and how to behave in accordance with accepted principles (Hartley and Hartley, 1952).

Through socialization certain patterns of behavior characteristic of a commonly shared culture are transmitted from one generation to the next (Caudill and Weinstein, 1969; Harrington and Whiting, 1972), with both universal and specific effects (Caudill and Weinstein, 1969). The effects are universal in the sense that each developing child learns to behave in a way common to all people—using a spoken language, for example. They are specific in the sense that children from different parts of the world adopt patterns of behavior unique to their society and characteristically different from those of other societies. Thus, the language American children learn to speak is different from that of South American children, which is in turn different from that of Masai children in Africa.

Imagine for a moment a society that failed to teach its young the behaviors, values, and so forth, on which it is built. That society as such would cease to exist. Socialization, therefore, is not only a way for an individual to adapt to his environment; it is also the process by which society perpetuates itself. For a society to survive, it must pass on its economic, political, and social foundations.

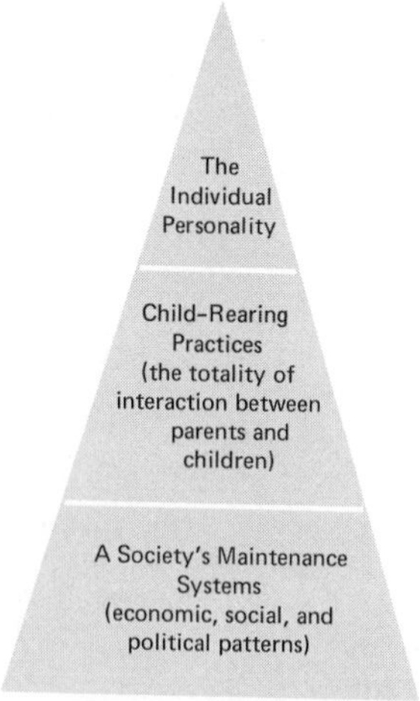

A conceptual model, such as the pyramid in Figure 1-1, can help us to better understand how the process of socialization works (Harrington and Whiting, 1972; Whiting, 1963; Whiting and Child, 1953). At its base are forces known as *maintenance systems.* These are the economic, political, and social patterns necessary to keep a society going. They determine how its members are nourished, sheltered, protected, transported, educated, employed, and so on. The structure of a household (a single parent, a nuclear family, an extended family) is an example of a maintenance system. Another is the manner in which labor is divided, as, for example, by age. As we shall see, a society's maintenance system gives rise to its particular child-rearing patterns, higher up on the pyramid, an important aspect of so-

The
Individual
Personality

Child-Rearing
Practices
(the totality of
interaction between
parents and
children)

A Society's Maintenance
Systems
(economic, social, and
political patterns)

**Figure 1-1. A model of
socialization.**

(Adapted from Harrington and
Whiting, 1972)

cialization because of the strong impact these patterns have on personality development. How we are reared determines our religious views, our relationships with parents or parental figures and with peers of the same sex and the opposite sex—even which games we prefer to play. The top of the pyramid is the human personality. This, the final cultural product, is dependent on the complex and interrelated factors below it on the pyramid.

How a child is enculturated in any society depends on the interaction of various factors. Parents and other family members, peer groups, schools, day-care centers, mass media (especially television), all transmit and interpret the culture for the developing young child. The relative importance of any one or combination of these influences to a child will vary according to the cultural environments in which he is reared. Thus, the impact of a child's biological parents on his socialization is probably greater for an American child reared in a nuclear household than for a child reared in a children's center on a kibbutz in Israel. Furthermore, socialization is greatly influenced by variables such as the child's sex and race and the educational level and socioeconomic status of his family.

In this chapter we will examine the various factors on which the young child depends for his enculturation—that is, his adaptation to a culture and his adoption of its values. Bear in mind that no factor is completely independent of the others. Rather, these factors interact, and it is this interaction that produces the unique socialization of one child in a particular culture.

THE FAMILY: PRIMARY TRANSMITTER AND INTERPRETER OF CULTURE

The family is generally considered the most important transmitter of a culture. In the United States, the term *family* usually means the *nuclear family*, consisting of the two biological parents and their offspring. In other parts of the world (indeed, for Americans in past generations), the term refers to the *extended family*, which consists of parents, children, and close relatives living together. In all societies, many children are forced to grow up, or at least attempt to grow up, with an incomplete family or no family at all. And as we shall see, parental deprivation can have a strong impact on socialization. But let us first look at how socialization develops in an intact family unit.

When we speak of child-rearing practices, we mean all the interactions between parent and child, including caretaking behavior (feeding, cleaning, protecting); training for socialization; parental expression of attitudes, values, interests, and beliefs; and various

Variations in Child-Rearing Practices

manifestations of affection and concern (love, annoyance, pride). Taken together, these help to prepare the child for life in society.

Child rearing is a dynamic process that begins the instant a child is born. Each of the ongoing interactions between parent and child can affect not only a child's present behavior but his future behavior as well. Thus, although any one interaction by itself might seem incidental (for example, parents refusing to let a child ride a bicycle), the repetition of similar interactions over several years has a lasting impact on a child's development.

A major study of child-rearing practices was conducted in 1957 by the Laboratory of Human Development at Harvard University (Sears, Maccoby, and Levin). It was limited in that it included only American middle-class or upper-working-class mothers. Nevertheless, it is significant because of the pioneering contribution it made and because it serves, in many respects, as a basis of comparison for later studies. The study sought first to establish the most important dimensions of child-rearing practices, and then to determine to what extent these dimensions were present in child-rearing behavior patterns of the mothers they interviewed. They found the following dimensions to be most important in the development of children:

1. *Permissiveness-strictness.* Pertains to such aspects of behavior as play, table manners, noise, neatness, toilet training.
2. *General family adjustment.* Mother's self-esteem, her degree of satisfaction with her husband and the marriage, her desire for children, and so on.
3. *Warmth of mother-child relationship.* Affection, demonstrativeness, relaxed attitude, use of praise, and so on.
4. *Particular training method.* Types of rewards and punishments selected to bring about desired behavior changes.
5. *Tolerance for aggressiveness.* Importance of a child's aggressiveness toward other children, use of punishment for aggression toward parents, and so on.

An important result of the study is that, when compared with other studies of mothers in many other cultures, these American mothers tended to be more strict, less warm, more punitive, and generally less satisfied with their family status than their counterparts elsewhere, all of which affect child behavior.

The main emphasis in the Sears et al. study was on the nature and outcome of the interactions between mother and child. Although no one denies the importance of the mother in the socialization of the child, other influences also affect the development of personality. One of these is the prevailing ideas of the culture at any one time as to the "best" method of rearing children. Since the study was conducted, our culture has begun to broaden its outlook

A book dealing with child rearing that has gained great popularity among parents is Haim Ginott's *Between Parent and Child: New Solutions to Old Problems* (1965). Ginott combines friendly advice with realistic and often humorous dialogue relating to specific situations. Here is an example (pp. 94–95):

THE NEW APPROACH: DIFFERENT HANDLING OF FEELINGS AND ACTS

Most discipline problems consist of two parts: angry feelings and angry acts. Each part has to be handled differently. Feelings have to be identified and expressed; acts have to be limited and redirected. At times, identification of the child's feelings may in itself be sufficient to clear the air.

Mother: It looks as if you are angry today.
   Son: I sure am!
Mother: You feel kind of mean inside.
   Son: You said it!
Mother: You are angry at someone.
   Son: Yes. You.
Mother: Tell me about it.
   Son: You didn't take me to the Little League Game, but you took Steve.
Mother: That made you angry. I bet you said to yourself, "She loves him more than she loves me."
   Son: Yes.
Mother: Sometimes you really feel that way.
   Son: I sure do.
Mother: You know, dear, when you feel that way, come and tell me.

Some basic principles to guide parents in their interactions with their children are stated outright here. Some are implicit. Can you identify them?

and to regard many different kinds of child-rearing patterns as acceptable. For example, parents and teachers today do not condemn so readily children's modes of coping that seem atypical. Personality traits that were formerly thought to be undesirable are now being recognized as manifestations of individual needs for self-expression. Sibling rivalry, feelings of jealousy, and anger and ambivalence toward parents, for example, are tolerated to a greater extent and are not considered deviant behavior (Margolin, 1974).

One of the major changes that has come about concerns who is responsible for rearing the child. Most literature on child rearing has traditionally been addressed to the mother, reflecting the general view that the father could, or should, contribute little to the care of an infant or young child. In recent years, however, particularly with the upsurge of the feminist movement, there is an awakening to the fact that the father should participate much more actively in the child's socialization. Indeed, in many families, the mother and father now share equally the responsibilities associated with bringing up a child.

Questions for Thought

In this country today, increasing numbers of women with young children are entering the labor market or going to school. And with the breakdown of the extended family, there are fewer adults in the home. Do you think these two factors are bringing about a change in child-rearing practices?

What are these changes, and are they likely to have long-term effects on the personality development of American children?

The view of the father's role in child rearing varies from one society and social class to another and, in Western society, from one era to another. According to the psychologist D. B. Lynn (1974), the social changes of the past decade or so have had important implications for the father-child relationship. "There is a resurgence of humanism accompanied by greater self-awareness, increased sophistication concerning interpersonal relationships, a desire for affectionate interaction, and much good will" (p. 11). In terms of the father-child relationship this means that many fathers today have a genuine desire to think about what each of their children needs and to try to meet these needs rather than to impose their own ambitions on them. Fathers today are generally less authoritarian, less arbitrary, and less distant from their children than fathers of the recent past. However, certain social forces—absence because of work demands or divorce, for example—often sabotage the best intentions of fathers. Lynn concludes: "Perhaps these underlying positive values, coupled with anguish over failure to actualize them, can be developed as motivating forces for discovering more compatible social structures from which satisfactory father-child relationships could emerge" (p. 11).

Systems of Caretaking   CARETAKING IN THE HOME.   The structure of the household is one of the maintenance systems of a society and can have an important bearing on child-rearing practices. Much research has compared different types of households in terms of parental behavior, including measures of indulgence, independence, and discipline training. Data gathered so far on patterns of infant indulgence in different cultures, for example, suggest that the amount of kindness and attention shown to the child varies directly with the number of adults in the home. That is, the larger the number of adults in the household, the greater the attention given to the children there. There is a greater tendency to treat the young indulgently in extended families than in households with only one or two parental figures (Whiting, 1961).

The child's personality, conceptions, and expectations reflect the amount of kindness and attention he receives from the adults in the family. And the indulgence shown by the adults reflects, in turn, the religious attitudes of the society. Societies in which parents mete out harsh treatment to their children tend to have religions in which the gods are punitive. Societies in which more indulgent parental treatment exists tend to have religions in which the gods are more benevolent (Lambert, Triandis, and Wolf, 1959; Spiro and D'Andrade, 1958; Whiting, 1959).

Child-rearing patterns and early personality development are also linked to household structure in terms of the severity of early childhood training. By severity we mean the amount of pressure placed on the child to conform to the expected standards of behavior for his age (Harrington and Whiting, 1972). Children in nuclear families have been found to be subject to more pressure to modify their behavior quickly (in toilet training, for example) than children in extended families. Possibly with more adults to help, there is more patience in waiting to see the child become independent.

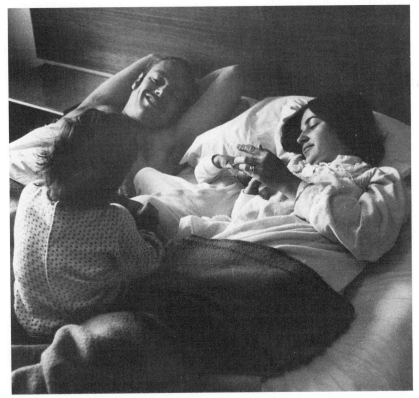

A child's personality will be determined to a large extent by the amount and quality of the attention given him by his parents.

(Joanne Leonard, Woodfin Camp & Associates)

MULTIPLE CARETAKING OUTSIDE THE HOME.   Regardless of whether a child grows up in a nuclear family or in an extended family, the primary issue in socialization is whether he is given adequate care and attention. Extensive comparisons between American children and those Israeli children raised on kibbutzim provide ample evidence on this point.*

Each kibbutz in Israel—one survey put the number of kibbutzim at about 200 (Gewirtz and Gewirtz, 1971)—has a colony of special houses in which children are grouped according to age. All children from infancy through adolescence spend most of their time in these houses with their peers. On some kibbutzim, children live in these houses apart from their parents except for visiting hours. On others, children remain in these houses only during the hours their parents are working, and they go home with them afterward.

In either case, on all kibbutzim, the responsibility for the care and discipline of youngsters over long periods of time belongs not to the biological parents but to a professional caretaker called a *metapelet* (pl., *metaplot*). As a child becomes older, however, his teacher, his peer group, his parents, and the parents of other children all assume important roles in his socialization. The child continues to visit and have close contact with his own parents on a regular basis (Devereux et al., 1974).

Questions for Thought

Consider the average American homemaker and mother who does not work outside the home in contrast to the mother on the kibbutz. How much time do you think that the American mother spends interacting with her child—talking, touching, playing, and so on—in comparison with her counterpart on a kibbutz?
What effect, if any, do you think this will have on the development of the children in each case?

The nature of child-rearing practices on the kibbutz and their effects on the children were examined by Devereux et al. (1974). Although the children participating in the study were preadolescents (ages 11 and 12), the data are significant in what they reveal about *multiple mothering*. A sample of 314 schoolchildren from a cross section of Israeli kibbutzim was compared with a sample of 287 children from three schools in Tel Aviv who lived in nuclear households. All the children were issued questionnaires on which they were asked to rate their parents, teachers, and peers on several dimensions of behavior. In addition, the kibbutz children were asked to give similar types of ratings for their metaplot.

*It should be noted that "kibbutzniks," individuals reared on collective-farm settlements in Israel, represent a very small proportion of the total Israeli population. Thus when we refer to the results of child rearing on kibbutzim, we must be careful not to generalize our conclusions to child-rearing practices elsewhere in Israel.

Lunchtime in a kibbutz. There are about 200 of these communal centers in Israel, where children spend most of their time apart from their parents.

(Louis Goldman, Rapho/Photo Researchers)

The study showed that kibbutz parents were regarded by their children as being less involved in discipline activities than the parents in the more typical nuclear households; however, they were seen as just as supportive and nurturant. Teachers and peer groups, on the other hand, were reported as more directly involved in discipline by the kibbutz children than by the Tel Aviv children. These different responses suggest that the responsibility for discipline usually assumed by the parents in the nuclear family is largely assumed by other agents—metaplot, teachers, and peer groups—on the kibbutz. However, children on the kibbutzim did not seem to find these altered roles confusing. Furthermore, the kibbutz children did not feel that the metapelet rivaled their parents for their affection. Evidently, a child growing up on a kibbutz does not encounter the problems ordinarily linked to maternal deprivation or to childhood in an institution.

Another study separated kibbutz children and American children of nuclear households from their mothers and then compared their behavior in the following situation (Rheingold, 1956). The subjects, all 2½-year-old children, were brought individually into an unfamiliar room along with their mother, a stranger, and some toys. It was hypothesized that once the mother left the room the kibbutz child would be less upset than the American child, since the former was accustomed to daily separation from his mother. But what the experiment in fact showed was that children from both groups were equally upset when their mothers left them; the incidence of crying was the same in each group. Thus, despite the differences between child-rearing practices for kibbutz children and American children in nuclear families, the attachment of the very young child to his mother, as indicated in this case by his concern at her leaving him in an unfamiliar situation, does not appear to be significantly affected by the communal child-rearing techniques of the kibbutz.

Other observations of kibbutz children (Bronfenbrenner, 1969) have shown that children reared on kibbutzim have warm, close relationships with their parents. Although experts do not agree unanimously on this point, most do feel that the affectional ties between kibbutz children and their parents have not been adversely affected by their upbringing. One expert who does disagree is Bruno Bettelheim (1969), who has suggested that kibbutz children and their parents do in fact experience difficulties in their relations. However, it should be noted that these difficulties were relatively minor.

The studies mentioned thus far tend to support the view that multiple-caretaking systems when carefully planned do not have harmful effects on the child. In fact, these systems serve certain useful functions. The extended family and the collective society have a unique advantage absent in the typical nuclear household: They offer the child the availability of several caretakers who can take turns responding to his needs. In such arrangements—when the child's mother is pregnant, for example, or busy taking care of a new baby—the older children stand less chance of being neglected. In the nuclear family, on the other hand, a mother with several children simply may not have enough time or energy to care adequately for all of them (Margolin, 1974). Furthermore, should the child lose his mother, the experience might be less traumatic for a child accustomed to other caretakers than for a child who has related to his mother exclusively (Ainsworth, 1967).

American families are becoming more aware of these advantages of multiple caretaking. When death or divorce separates a young child from a parent early in life, the child needs a viable substitute. In addition, and probably even more widespread, economic necessity and the desire for an independent identity are bringing an increasingly large percentage of mothers of young children into the labor force. When a mother works, other competent people must be available, whether in home care or in day-care centers, to help care for the young child.

As strong as arguments in support of multiple caretaking are, the position that no group can adequately take the place of the single caretaker or the child's real mother still holds force. One study of children's attachment behavior revealed that even at 4 months of age, most infants are already responding differentially to their mother, as compared with other people, and that this first interpersonal relationship is the "foundation stone" of the infant's personality

(Bowlby, 1969). The presence of the mother or mother-surrogate is a very important factor in creating a sense of security in a child. Children reared in institutions during their early years have been found to suffer detrimental, sometimes irreversible, effects. This has been related, in part, to the lack of any person who is clearly defined as a mother figure in their lives. In the typical institutional or hospital setting, many people participate in the care of the child. Their time with a child is limited to the duration of their work shifts, and the child has no opportunity—or reason—to build a lasting attachment with any of them. Moreover, the caretakers assume responsibility for so many children that they would be unique individuals indeed if they were able to show special sensitivity to the particular needs of each individual child (Ainsworth, 1967).

The procedures of these institutions contrast sharply to the practices in most kibbutzim, where metaplot are chosen for their interest in children and attentiveness, and where these caretakers remain for long periods of time with the same children. It is not surprising, then, that the findings on child development for institutionalized children run counter to the situation we described earlier on the kibbutzim. Also, findings on nonliterate societies, described by Margaret Mead, in which extended families predominate, refute the view that a single, continually present mother-figure is a prerequisite for healthy social development. Thus, these two examples indicate that not all multiple-caretaking systems are detrimental to child development.

CHARACTERISTICS OF THE MOTHER OR MOTHER-SUBSTITUTE. What characteristics of the mother or mother-substitute are most important in the development of the child's personality? A study of the patterns of interaction between 36 mothers and their firstborn children, ranging in age from 9 to 18 months, sought to answer this question (Clarke-Stewart, 1973). Direct observation of the behavior of both mother and child in spontaneous and structured situations provided data indicating that the child's social behavior corresponded significantly to that of the mother. For example, mothers who were observed to be highly affectionate and responsive tended to have smiling, affectionate children.

It is not simply the *presence* of the mother but her *reaction* to her child that is the most important factor in his personality development. In some nuclear families, the mother provides a constant physical presence yet she rarely interacts with her children in a playful, affectionate, and stimulating manner. Others who do interact may not be *consistently* responsive to their children. On the other hand, the ideal mother or mother-substitute, according to many psychologists, is one who is warm, loving, consistent, and nonrejecting. This type of mother is sensitive to her child's needs and distress signals and responds promptly and appropriately. She spends considerable time in the same room with her child, looking at him, stimulating him, and playing with him. She is free from emotional problems like anxiety and depression and thus is able to attend to her child's needs. The interactions she has with her child are mutually pleasurable (Ainsworth, 1967; Clarke-Stewart, 1973).

Overall, then, the mother or mother-substitute should be more than just "available" to her child; she must interact with him in specific and direct ways and have general maternal competence.

Effects of Parental Deprivation

Having looked into cases of child rearing in which either one or several mothers guided the socialization, let us now examine what happens to the child who is deprived of contact with a parent.

In experiments with infant rhesus monkeys, psychologists have shown that the effects of maternal deprivation vary under different conditions (Harlow, 1958; Harlow and Zimmermann, 1959). The investigators were interested in the degree to which an artificial substitute mother was capable of satisfying a young monkey's need for affection. To observe this, they reared monkeys in isolation from their real mothers, but substituted two "laboratory mothers." One artificial "mother" was constructed entirely of wire mesh; the other was covered with terrycloth.

Each infant monkey was then placed in a cage that contained both surrogate mothers. Only one mother, however, served as the source of food; a nursing bottle was attached to the chest of either the wire mother or the cloth mother. When the monkey wasn't taking milk, he was free, if he wished, to climb on top of either one of his mothers. The cloth mother was obviously much softer, and Harlow found that regardless of which mother provided the milk, the infant monkeys would much rather cling to the soft, terrycloth mother than to the wire mother. Only the cloth mothers provided the necessary contact and comfort to induce an affectionate response in the infant monkeys.

However, in a later experiment Harlow and Harlow (1966) showed that for long-term healthy development and adjustment even a soft cloth mother-substitute is inadequate. Monkeys used in this study, even those reared with a cloth mother-substitute, tended to display abnormal heterosexual and maternal behavior as adults. In order for these behaviors to develop normally, the monkey needed the contact-comfort experience that comes from interaction with other live monkeys.

In human infants, too, close physical contact with a mother or mother-substitute is necessary to social development. During World War II, babies institutionalized under crowded, understaffed conditions were seriously affected by being deprived so early in life of

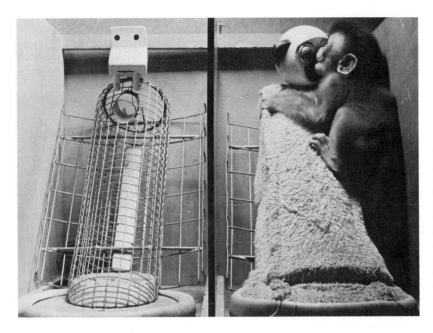

In Harlow's now-classic experiments, infant monkeys were taken away from their mothers and offered the choice of a wire or a cloth-covered mother-substitute. Even when the wire mother provided their food, the monkeys preferred the cloth mother for protection.

(Harry F. Harlow, University of Wisconsin Primate Laboratory)

adequate contact with biological or substitute parents (Freud and Burlingham, 1943, 1944; Spitz, 1945, 1946). Spitz, for example, reported that infants who had been institutionalized since birth soon began to exhibit unusual behavior. At first they would cry continuously, and later simply stared vacantly into space, totally uninterested in their surroundings or the people who approached them. They became retarded in every aspect of development—physical, intellectual, and social.

The fact that these infants were observed under extreme conditions limits the conclusions that can be drawn about parental deprivation. They were deprived not only of social contacts but also of virtually all forms of sensory stimulation. Under such conditions, it is therefore not clear which kind of deprivation contributed most to their maladaptive behavior. Furthermore, because these studies dealt only with infants who had been institutionalized and "motherless" since birth, the findings cannot be generalized to youngsters who have been separated from their mothers after having lived with them and become attached to them.

More recent studies on the subject have been better controlled, and they suggest that the effects of early parental deprivation are not necessarily as permanent as the earlier research implied. In one experimental study (Rheingold and Bayley, 1959), 14 infants who spent the first 9 months of their lives in an institution were subsequently cared for at home (either by their natural parents or by

BIG BROTHERS AND SISTERS: FILLING THE GAP

The growth of modern social welfare organizations has reflected humanistic impulses to help meet specific social needs that are currently unmet elsewhere. One such organization, Big Brothers of America, founded in 1946, is composed of male volunteers who, under professional supervision of trained social workers, offer friendship on an individual basis to boys between the ages of 8 and 17 who lack a father's companionship and guidance. A similar, sectarian group is Catholic Big Brothers, which helps mainly fatherless boys between ages 8 and 15 with the purpose of preventing and controlling juvenile delinquency. Big Sisters, Inc., at work only in the borough of Manhattan in New York City, provides casework services and enlists volunteers to help girls under 16 and boys under 10. The efforts of these groups and others attest to the importance our society places on parental guidance in socialization. If children lack such guidance, humanitarian organizations attempt to provide them with viable substitutes.

adoptive parents). They showed no measurable long-term effects from their institutional experience. Half the infants had received extra attention from the experimenter while in the institution. Although initial tests did show this group to be more socially responsive than the group that was not provided with special attention, follow-up tests a year later revealed that there were no significant differences between the groups on tests of social responsiveness and developmental progress. The sample as a whole appeared to be "normal," both intellectually and socially. The children did not exhibit any of the symptoms of emotional disturbance or blatant retardation shown by children such as those discussed previously who were reared in institutions. Apparently, hope still exists for deprived infants if stimulation is provided after the first 9 months.

Most published studies on the effects of parental deprivation on young children, including those described thus far, have focused on *maternal* deprivation, since generally it is the mother who bears the greatest responsibility for child rearing. A few recent studies, however, have dealt with the effects of *paternal* deprivation, especially in regard to the development of appropriate sex-typed behavior in boys.

One such study (Biller, 1969) compared masculine behavior in kindergarten age boys who had fathers living at home with that in boys whose fathers were absent. The father-absent boys were found to be less masculine in terms of projective sex-role orientation (that is, how masculine they felt), but not in terms of overt masculinity (that is, the specific behaviors they exhibited). The extent to which masculine behavior was encouraged by the mother was an important variable for the father-absent boys, although not for the father-present boys. This leads us to believe that mothers and, later, teachers as well can serve as sources of reinforcement for masculine behavior in fatherless boys.

The degree to which the absence of a father will affect male sex-typed behavior is dependent upon the boy's age at the time he loses his father. It was found that the effects of father absence, such as increased withdrawal and avoidance of participation in sports and other activities, were greatest when the loss occurred in the preschool years, before the teacher has an opportunity to exert an influence (Biller, 1969; Hetherington, 1966).

There are, of course, many intervening variables that can determine what effects, if any, parental deprivation can have on the development of a given child. Clearly, our conclusions at this point are merely tentative, and additional research involving both larger samples and proper experimental control is needed in this area.

Questions for Thought
In what ways can the preschool, kindergarten, or elementary teacher of a fatherless boy increase masculine behavior in this child?
What specific kinds of behavior can—or should—be reinforced?

PRESCHOOL EDUCATION PROGRAMS: FORMAL TRANSMITTERS AND INTERPRETERS OF CULTURE

In our society, the primary transmitter and interpreter of culture to the young child is the family. But as the child gets older, the time he spends in the protective environment of his home with his parents decreases and the time he spends with new people in less familiar surroundings increases. One of the first new experiences encountered by many children today is the preschool, whether a nursery school or a day-care center. Through their educational programs, these institutions contribute to socialization, as well as to cognitive development, as we shall see in Chapter 2.

What a preschool offers a child and how the preschool offers it vary among societies. The design of a preschool program will reflect the child-rearing patterns and in turn the maintenance systems (see earlier discussion) of each society. To better understand just how important a preschool program can be in the socialization of young children, we will discuss such programs in the U.S.S.R., Israel, and Communist China, for these three countries have given extremely high priority to such programs. Then, we will focus on preschool programs in the United States to examine their implications for the socialization of young children here.

Preschool Education in the U.S.S.R.

The purpose of Soviet education, according to Urie Bronfenbrenner (1970), is "to provide the child, from early infancy onward, with the physical, psychological, and social conditions regarded as necessary for his full development but not readily available in his own home" (p. 17). The areas in which Soviet schools have established objectives for the socialization of children include Communist morality, a responsible attitude toward learning, social etiquette, a basic appreciation of esthetics, and physical development and sports.

The Soviet educational system emphasizes a long-term goal called *Vospitanie*, which translates roughly as "character education." More specifically, it refers to the development of "Communist morality and upbringing" (see Table 1-1). It is in the preschool education program that the basic groundwork for this general principle of *Vospitanie* lies. Also, the U.S.S.R. gives high priority to its school programs in terms of provision of personnel, facilities, and overall care. Expense is not spared in providing for all the child's needs and also for research to develop new teaching techniques.

This priority is extremely important, since for most Soviet children the preschool supplants the home as the prime source of security and vehicle of socialization. Learning by imitation is stressed. Desirable behavior is elicited and undesirable behavior is thwarted through reinforcements meted out on a group basis. That is, rewards are given to groups who meet the goals of the programs. If their behavior falls short of the expected standards in meeting group goals, the children are made to feel guilty. In this fashion

Table 1-1
Objectives of Soviet Education for Ages 7 to 11

Communist Morality	Cultured Conduct
Sense of good and bad behavior	Care, accuracy, and neatness
Truthfulness, honesty, kindness	Courtesy and cordiality
Atheism: science vs. superstition	Proper behavior on the street and
Self-discipline	in public places
Diligence in work and care of	Cultured speech
possessions	
Friendship with classmates	Bases of Esthetic Culture
Love of one's own locality and	
the Motherland	Understanding of the beautiful in
Interest and striving for knowledge	nature, in the conduct of people,
and skill	and in creative art
Industry in study	Artistic creativity
Organizing intellectual and	
physical work	Physical Culture and Sport
Striving to apply one's knowledge	
and ability in life and work	Concern for strengthening and
	conditioning one's body
	Sanitary hygienic habits
	Preparation for sport and athletics

Source: Bronfenbrenner (1970, pp. 30–31).

Vospitanie, which is the essence of Soviet collective education, is taught.

In keeping with the objective of "full development," children whose families are incomplete or whose parents work during hours that would prevent them from spending time with their children are given first consideration for preschool admission. The child is not to be deprived of adequate stimulation; if he cannot receive it at home, he can receive it through the state-controlled preschool.

Soviet preschools are not merely preparatory programs for elementary school; their influence is much broader, overlapping every aspect of the child-rearing process. Unlike American nursery schools, which are usually open only a few hours during the day, preschools in the Soviet Union are complete day-care centers, open from morning until evening (Jacoby, 1971).

Although Soviet children can enter a preschool program as early as 3 months of age, in fact not all do so. Some parents are reluctant to place their infants and toddlers in a state nursery and rely instead on a *babushka* (grandmother) or a neighbor to help out as needed when the parents are away from home. Also, due to a shortage of space, not every child whose parents seek admission for him can be enrolled. However, because of the large number of Russian women in the labor force, the government has given top priority to new preschools, which are now being built at a rapid rate. And for the growing number of children in preschools, the experience is pervasive and powerful, exerting a strong influence on their developing personalities (Jacoby, 1971).

The basic characteristics of preschool education in Russia were reported by Bronfenbrenner (1970) in *Two Worlds of Childhood: U.S. and U.S.S.R.* I have visited, together with American graduate students of education, a cross section of Soviet preschools in Russia, Armenia, Georgia, and the Ukraine on four separate occasions from 1970 to 1973. In addition, I have visited preschools and interviewed teachers in Serbia, Croatia, and Macedonia, individual republics of Yugoslavia, a country with preschools similar in many aims to those of Russia, but designed somewhat differently for the teaching of "self-management." My own personal impressions of the schools in both countries, and their important effects on the development of young children, coincide with Bronfenbrenner's descriptions.

As soon as infants and toddlers are enrolled in Soviet preschools, they are exposed to the responsibilities of collective living. Each child is placed with about six or seven other children of his own age in a communal playpen, which is raised off the floor to facilitate face-to-face contact with the caretaking staff. Within this small, cohesive group setting, youngsters are taught to share toys and games and to engage in cooperative activity in both work and play. They learn the expression *Moe eto nashe; nashe moe*, which means "Mine is ours, ours is mine," stating in a few words the goal of such collective living.

Learning to become self-reliant is emphasized, and by the time the children have reached the age of 18 months, they are expected to have completed toilet training and to be learning how to dress themselves. And in a few years, they start to receive thorough discipline training, which enables them to criticize and correct each other independently of adult guidance. In time, the teacher ceases to play an active role in leading the group, and the children supervise themselves in much of their activity.

Play activities organized by teachers often take the form of role playing, in which real-life situations are enacted (taking care of the baby, shopping for food, going to the doctor). In addition, as the children approach kindergarten age, they are expected to assume more responsibility for everyday chores such as housekeeping and gardening.

How does the Soviet system of collective education affect personality and social development? According to Bronfenbrenner, and from what I myself have seen, the effect has been generally desirable, due to the amount of consistent warm attention given youngsters. Soviet children do, indeed, exhibit behavior we normally consider happy and honest; they exhibit few behaviors normally associated with emotional problems. A notable characteristic of Soviet youngsters is their extremely good behavior in terms of politeness, attentiveness, and interest in learning; they are friendly toward their elders and obedient. Rebellious, antisocial behavior is rare.

Although these traits appear at first glance to be desirable (how many American teachers dream of students like these!), it must also be noted that a reduction in individuality and original thinking due to the prescribed group reinforcement may be a possible negative consequence of the Soviet educational system (Jacoby, 1971).

Questions for Thought

Both Bronfenbrenner's and my own observations of the preschool education of Soviet children indicate that certain kinds of behavior are desired and rewarded by Soviet teachers. Are these behaviors the same as those rewarded by American teachers?
If not, how do they differ, and how does this difference affect the development of children in these two societies?

Kibbutz Education in Israel Education on the kibbutzim of Israel is another example of collective education. In contrast to the Soviet system, however, the kibbutz education is not centralized by the government, and therefore it varies from one kibbutz to the next.

Kibbutz education is based on the premise that socialization can be carried out most effectively in a situation of collective living. All of kibbutz life thus centers on teaching and reinforcing the values, skills, and ideals of Israeli culture. Indeed, education on the kibbutz is not confined to the classroom—it takes place in every part of the child's environment. Play, meals, classes, and so on are carried out with a group, for cooperation and good interpersonal relationships are basic parts of what the child is expected to learn.

The metapelet and peer group, as well as the classroom teacher, exert a strong influence on the child's development. In the classroom itself, a relaxed, noncompetitive atmosphere prevails. The teacher is a source of guidance and support to the child, offering help not only with schoolwork but with personal problems as well. The teacher also disciplines the child.

Socialization in a kibbutz, then, is the result of the interaction of different influences in varied environments. Its goal is to teach the child to live in a group situation.

In Communist China, as in the Soviet Union and on the Israeli kibbutzim, children are socialized largely in the school system. Chinese mothers are typically part of the labor force, which results

Preschool Education in China

Chinese children typically enter day-care centers at a very young age, because their mothers work.

(Henri Cartier-Bresson, Magnum Photos)

in their leaving their very young children in day-care centers. Although day-care staffs toilet-train, bathe, and teach children their basic skills, interaction with parents is strongly encouraged. Mothers are allowed time off from work to nurse their babies, and youngsters spend evenings and weekends with their families, but the early experience in the basics of group living teaches the child the prime importance of peer approval, which will influence him throughout his life ("Coming of Age in Communist China," *Newsweek*, 1972).

Day Care in the United States

The structure of a particular society does not always make it practicable for parents to assume the total responsibilities for child care, and we have seen how the educational programs in three collective systems have attempted to deal with this problem. Western societies have faced and have attempted to solve this problem, too. France, for example, began providing free preschools for children of working mothers as long ago as 1887 ("Day Care? In France It's a Science," *The New York Times*, 1970). In our own country, which has generally not kept pace with these other nations in the provision of day-care services, more and more people—both educators and laymen—are now recognizing the need for greatly expanded preschool educational facilities. Unfortunately, day care in our country is less than adequate. There are too few day-care centers to meet the growing demand. The pressures brought by the increasing proportion of mothers in the labor force who need day care for their young have made the situation acute. Facilities for infants and toddlers are in particular need, since many states have laws that do not permit their licensed centers to accept children at early ages.

A report by M. D. Keyserling, *Windows on Day Care* (1972), summarized the results of a study into the extent and quality of the existing day-care facilities in the United States. The report noted that approximately 6 million American children under age 6 have mothers who work. The quality of our nation's day-care centers was found to vary considerably, and only 25 percent offered what was described in the report as superior quality "developmental care." Approximately two thirds of the centers observed provided only custodial care, and one in seven was rated either "poor" or "very poor." In general, the best care was provided by the federally funded (free or low-cost) centers and the worst by the private centers.

One of the centers described in the report as "superior" was a public facility in a mid-Atlantic state. About 56 children were enrolled, most of them black. The staff included at least nine full-time professionals and five part-time helpers, several of whom were college graduates with special training in early childhood education. In addition, the center had a nutritionist, nurse, and social worker, and several mothers served as volunteers. Besides a carefully structured educational program (for which the children were grouped according to age), all the children received free transportation in the morning and meals and snacks during the day. The parents were not charged for any of the services provided.

Some of the poorer centers, which "can be found in virtually every city in the country," are described by those investigators who observed them (Keyserling, 1972, p. 64):

> If ever there was a way to close a day-care center, this one should be the first to go. The proprietor is not interested in child care but only in making a profit. She wants to get out of the business and will sell to anyone who wants to buy it. Back in a dark room, a baby was strapped in an infant's seat inside a crib and was crying pitifully.

Another made this observation about a day-care center for babies:

> They were kept in "cages"—cribs of double-decker cardboard—in one room with open gas heaters.

Still another investigator reported:

> This is an abominable center. Couldn't be much worse. One worker washed every child's face with a cloth dipped in a bucket of water one-tenth full. No decent toys. The center was run by high school girls without any adults present. The children were not allowed to talk. . . . Rat holes were apparent.

A major problem with centers judged inadequate was the inferior quality of the staff. In addition, the size of the staff was insufficient, leading to a ratio of children to adults far less than ideal, and far less than that of the programs in other societies described earlier. These two problems are due in part to a lack of adequate financing, which results from the low priority given preschools in the United States.

However, this report does not indict day-care centers; rather, it provides a persuasive commentary on the urgent need in this country for developmental day-care services that meet all the basic needs of our society's children. On the basis of its findings, the *Windows on Day Care* report made the following recommendations:

1. The opportunity for developmental day care should be made available to any family that wants it. However, priority should be given to economically disadvantaged preschool children whose mothers are the head of the household.
2. Day care should be provided free of charge to families at the poverty level and on a sliding scale based on income for other families.

Standing in the way of attempts to implement these recommendations in America is the lack of funds. For example, federal funds for day care were recently available to less than 5 percent of the economically disadvantaged preschool children who qualified. High-quality day care that is not publicly subsidized runs about $2,000 or more a year per child, way beyond what most families can afford (Garskof, Garskof, and Faragher, 1973; Keyserling, 1972).

In addition to the financial problems, the conflict many mothers face between the traditionally high value assigned to motherhood in our society and the basic economic and psychological needs that compel them to seek employment also stands in the way of adequate day care. Garskof and his colleagues (1973) have proposed an alternative to the traditional day-care center that might alleviate both problems. They suggest the creation of child-care cooperatives in which small, rotating groups of parents, aided by nonparent volunteers, share all the caretaking responsibilities. The operating expenses would also be shared, but on a sliding scale based on income. The annual cost to the parent would be much less than at a nonsubsidized day-care center of comparable quality.

Questions for Thought

What conflicts do parents have over entering their children in preschool programs?

How might they resolve their conflicts on a personal level?

How might they work together with other parents to create programs that would resolve their conflicts?

THE PEER GROUP AND PLAY: INFORMAL TRANSMITTERS AND INTERPRETERS OF CULTURE

Peer approval and play are important in developing skills for adulthood.

(Greg Winokur, Alternative Curriculum)

It is generally acknowledged that the child's peer group is one of the factors that contribute to the personality and social development of the young child. Let us look now at its role in socialization. Two trends in American society should be kept in mind here: first, that parents today are spending significantly less time with their children than did parents of the previous generation (Bronfenbrenner, 1970); second, that there is an increasing tendency, among people of all ages in our country, to spend a greater proportion of their time in the company of their peers.

Peer interaction during the preschool years consists primarily of what we call "play." *Parallel play*, in which children perform the same activities at the same time, aware of one another and, at the same time, independent of one another, is the first stage. Later, but still during preschool years, *imitative play* and *role play* begin. Preschool children in the Soviet Union use role play to act out common situations they might expect to encounter in their everyday lives,

Which game did you prefer as a child? Parcheesi? Checkers? Ring toss? From your answer to this question experts can estimate the child-training patterns in your upbringing. Anthropologist John Roberts and psychologist Brian Sutton-Smith (1962, 1966) have found that games of chance, such as Parcheesi, occur in societies that offer high rewards in child rearing for responsibility. Games of strategy, such as checkers, are found in societies that emphasize obedience in child rearing; such games enable a child to express aggression and other disobedient acts in play. Games of practical skill, like ring toss, are found in societies that offer high rewards for achievement; they provide a means for individuals to act out conflicts over achievement. Each of these games reflects anxieties brought about by the particular child-rearing practices of the society.

WHAT'S YOUR GAME?

and American children, when they play house, for example, do the same thing (Hurlock, 1971). Role play contributes to socialization by providing children with an opportunity to see their relationships to other people.

Peer play among preschoolers may also involve *model building,* which is most prominent between ages 4 and 8 (Blumberg, 1974b). Children incorporate toys, costumes, and other props into their play to make it more realistic and meaningful. This imaginative aspect of model play can be a useful outlet for self-expression. According to some researchers, model play may also help the child to establish and reaffirm his self-image. The child is, in effect, rehearsing for a particular role he may actually assume later on in life. In addition, model play aids the child in developing a system of values and morals, including a basic sense of what is right and wrong (Blumberg, 1974b).

Play is a very individual activity, but it reflects the attitudes and values characteristic of a particular culture. Although play in the general sense is a universal phenomenon, the specific activities that children select for their play tend to vary among cultures (Sutton-Smith, 1971).

MODELING, IMITATION, AND TELEVISION

Without doubt, one of the most potent influences on socialization in young children, particularly in the United States, is television. Among the mass media available to the young, this predominates. American preschool children watch television for an average of 54 hours a week, more time than they spend in any other activity except sleep (Brozan, 1975). This means that the average 3-year-old will watch more than 2800 hours of television, almost the equivalent of 4 months, 24 hours a day—all in only one year of his short life!

Television is so popular among American children that parents, other adults, and even peers may be given second priority to a favorite television program. Psychologists and laymen alike question the effects of this huge amount of television viewing on the part of impressionable children, particularly in light of the increasingly violent nature of our society. The relationship between violence depicted on television and the behavior and values of children is an area much studied today.

An analysis of the content of prime-time commercial television programs in the late 1960s showed that physical violence occurred in 80 percent of the programs, with an average of five violent episodes every hour. Children's cartoons had an even greater proportion of violence—25 episodes per hour (Gerbner, 1972).

An attempt to determine what effects violence on television has on children's behavior was made in an experiment (Friedrich and Stein, 1973) in which nursery-school children were shown one of three types of television programs: aggressive cartoons; prosocial programs providing examples of positive, nonaggressive behavior; and neutral films. The children viewed these programs over a four-week period. In order to evaluate the effect the experience had on the children, they were observed in free play before, during, and after their exposure to the programs. The results showed that the children who were exposed to the television programs depicting violence tended to increase their aggressive behavior. Much of this increased aggression was interpersonal in nature, indicating that the children did not simply imitate what they had seen; rather, they generalized their aggression to fighting among themselves. The children exposed to the prosocial programs increased their cooperation and exhibited other positive behaviors, again on an interpersonal basis.

Clearly, exposure to violence on television affects the behavior of some children. Moreover, when changes in behavior have been observed, they seem to be the result of something other than mere imitation. The children in this study exhibited symbolic equivalents of the behavior of the television model, rather than an exact replication. In addition, they generalized their behavior to situations other than the exact ones they had viewed on television. The term *modeling* is used to describe this phenomenon (Bandura, Ross, and Ross, 1963).

Television, of course, is not the only source of violence in a child's environment. Children are surrounded by other models of aggressive behavior. The effects of continued exposure to violence on the socialization of children have been interpreted in terms of what is called *imitation* (Bandura, 1969). In Bandura's experiments, preschool children were brought individually into a playroom where another person (either another child or an adult model) was already engaged actively in aggressive play. As the child entered the room he saw the model hitting dolls, throwing and breaking objects in the room, and employing aggressive language. Later, the child was brought into another room and allowed to play freely with any of the toys there. Some of the toys resembled those he had seen being used previously in an aggressive manner. In this second situation, however, no one was present to influence the child. Bandura found that the play of the children in this part of the experiment matched the aggressive behavior of the model they had watched earlier. Presumably, these children learned aggression through *imitating* the behavior model. It can be assumed that these same children will later internalize their behavior so that they will respond similarly in other situations. Then imitation will have changed to modeling.

Other experimental studies of aggression have replicated Bandura's findings. However, in most of these experiments, the children's behavior was measured under artificial laboratory conditions immediately after exposure to the aggressive stimulus. Thus, the extent to which the findings could be generalized and the long-term effects of exposure to violence on children's behavior were not entirely clear.

THE EFFECTS OF CULTURE ON SOCIALIZATION

Up to this point, our concern has been with how the child is socialized by the family, formal educational programs, the peer group, and television. Let us look now at the influences that culture exerts on socialization.

The socioeconomic status of a mother was found to influence her child-rearing patterns (Sears, Maccoby, and Levin, 1957). Using the terms "middle class" and "lower class" to describe socioeconomic status, they found that middle-class mothers generally were more permissive with their children, more inclined to be warm and affectionate, and less inclined to use physical punishment than lower-class mothers. The disciplinary techniques used by middle-class mothers were love and love-oriented. For example, they tended to use praise for good behavior, and reasoning, isolation, and appeals to guilt for bad behavior. Working-class mothers, on the other hand, preferred object-oriented discipline, such as tangible rewards, deprivation of privileges, and physical punishment. These different types of discipline clearly have a strong effect on child development and socialization.

Socioeconomic Status

A study by Kamii and Radin (1967) examined the influence of social-class differences in mothers' socialization practices. Comparing 20 lower-class black mothers with 20 middle-class black mothers on a number of dimensions of behavior, they found that middle-class mothers, to a much greater extent than lower-class mothers, initiated conversations with their children that were based on the children's implicit needs for companionship and affection. In addition, the middle-class mothers were more likely to use a larger variety of techniques to influence their children, as, for example, requesting and consulting, whereas the lower-class mothers had a more limited repertoire, consisting primarily of commanding. This reliance of lower-class mothers on "unilateral" coercive techniques, such as commanding, as opposed to "bilateral" ones, such as consulting, might explain the behavior that has been described by some psychiatrists as caused by a "lack of inner control" and often is reported in what are called "socially disadvantaged" children. (This will be discussed at some length in Chapter 10.)

The influence of social class is, of course, often determined by another factor—ethnic group. Consequently, we cannot generalize about the socialization practices of any particular American social class without taking into account as well the subcultures—black, Hispanic-American, Italian-American, and so on—each of which socializes its children differently.

Sex Typing and Identity The way in which children learn to feel and act the role of a particular sex is known as *sex-role identification*. Children normally start to learn sex-appropriate behavior very early in life. Two things contribute to this process: rewards that the parents provide and the processes of imitation and modeling discussed earlier. We see these rewards all around us: Little boys are praised for learning how to throw a ball and frowned upon for playing with dolls; for little girls, the situation is reversed. Children are most likely to imitate a model who appears to be nurturant and/or has power or status. For toddlers, this figure is most apt to be the mother, but as the child gets older, the father becomes an influential model, too (Thompson and McCandless, 1970). (We have already discussed the problems of developing what is considered by most as appropriate sex-typed behavior in young, fatherless boys.)

In our society, masculinity and femininity are associated with one's degree of aggressive behavior. Boys at any age, starting as early as 18 months, are expected to be and, in fact, are more aggressive than girls of the same age (Maccoby, 1974). The difference cuts across many behavioral situations—in free play as well as in the laboratory, in verbal aggression as well as in physical aggression.

Compliance, too, is generally sex-typed in American children. Boys are expected to have, and indeed do have, a greater tendency than girls to resist giving in to immediate demands. Usually, boys need greater pressure to obey orders than is necessary for girls (Maccoby, 1974).

When children do not exhibit the behavior considered appropriate for their sex, our society looks upon them as deviant or immature. This view transcends even what is learned in the family, and is the result of cultural stereotypes. Until recently, sex-role stereotypes were generally accepted. What was inside or outside the boundaries was clearly defined. However, today our views are broadening somewhat. The women's liberation movement, as well as an overall raising of the consciousness of men and women, has caused our society to reevaluate the older traditional notions about sex-typed behavior. The old stereotypes are giving way to new ideas of what is appropriate. Diehard views toward sex differences in clothing, hobbies, and occupational choices are being modified. Many children today are brought up in an environment of what we might call unisexuality. For example, girls as well as boys of all ages wear dungarees, and if a girl prefers a truck to a doll, or a boy finds a stove more interesting than a football, this behavior is not regarded as peculiar (Margolin, 1974).

Not long ago it would have been thought inappropriate by many for little boys to be interested in such "feminine" activities as cooking, but these stereotypes of sex roles are changing.

(Charles Gatewood, Magnum Photos)

Psychologists have not ignored these changing views. A 1972 study (Selcer and Hilton) compared the play behavior of two groups of 24 preschool children, each of 12 boys and 12 girls, one from a culture that is traditionally male-oriented (Orthodox Judaism) and the other from a subculture whose views on sex-role typing are less traditional. In the preschool attended by the first group, sex roles were clearly established. In the cooperative nursery school attended by a majority of children in the second group, a concerted effort was made not to stress sex roles that reflected the views of the parents and teachers.

The investigators observed both groups at free and then at specific tasks. In the first task the children were shown pictures of 24 toys that varied in degree of what traditionally was considered masculine or feminine. Next they were asked to select the 8 toys they liked best. They were shown photographs of children at play and asked to make up stories about them. Lastly, they were asked to tell in their own words what they considered to be the differences between boys and girls.

Significant differences were found between the groups in all three activities. The children brought up to follow the traditional sex roles displayed more sex-typed behavior than the children whose parents and teachers had been careful not to define sex roles. Similarly, the first group had much less difficulty than the second in describing sex differences.

What this study clearly shows is that *cultural differences* in child-rearing practices do indeed influence the acquisition of sex-typed behavior. This should be considered in light of what we have already said, that family, schools, peer groups, and mass media all serve as powerful models for children in this area of development.

Questions for Thought
Some feminists and certain educators have attacked publishers of textbooks used in elementary schools because it has been asserted that these textbooks teach little girls to be submissive, little boys to be dominant, little girls to like "feminine" subjects like art and music, little boys to like "masculine" subjects like science.
How much importance do you attribute to the style and content of textbooks—or of teaching—in the elementary school in the development of sex typing?

 COMMON BEHAVIORS GENERATED BY SOCIALIZATION

We now shift our attention from the factors influencing the socialization process to the children themselves and to the social behavior they exhibit at early stages of development.

Because our society is a competitive one, it is considered particularly important that children develop such qualities as initiative, independence, and properly channeled aggression. Furthermore, in our culture, adaptation to society is based more on achieved status (characteristics developed by the individual such as talents, skills, and a likable personality) than on ascribed status (characteristics predetermined at birth, such as sex, race, and religion). Consequently, children brought up in the United States are often encouraged to develop self-reliance and to become independent and assertive. Even so, the "model" child must also learn to exercise self-control

---

PRIVATE ENTERPRISE IN SOCIALIZATION

One of the most widespread and influential private enterprises participating in the socialization of children in the United States has been the Boy Scouts of America, founded in 1910, and today including boys from 8 through 15 in 63,000 Cub Scout Packs, 73,000 Scout Troops, and 25,000 Explorer Units. The principles and values that this organization seeks to instill in the young are exemplified in the following:

CUB SCOUT PROMISE
I, _____ PROMISE
to DO MY BEST
to DO MY DUTY
to God and My Country
to BE SQUARE, and
to OBEY the Law of the Pack

LAW OF THE PACK
the Cub Scout FOLLOWS Akela (Leader)
the Cub Scout HELPS the Pack go
the Pack HELPS the Cub Scout grow
the Cub Scout GIVES Goodwill

How is this enculturation specifically American?

and restraint. A delicate balance exists between the popular ideal of developing one's potential, on the one hand, and accepting and conforming by virtue of one's position in the social structure, on the other (Margolin, 1974). The ways in which parents and, later, teachers guide the socialization process are central to the development of the individual—socially, intellectually, and morally—as we will see in the chapters ahead.

Dependency and Attachment

Two types of behavior that psychologists are interested in in young children are dependency and attachment. An *attachment* is a durable tie of affection oriented toward one particular person, and is seen in such behaviors as clinging, following, smiling, and crying, which change with the age of the child. *Dependency*, on the other hand, consists of such behaviors as seeking help, attention, and approval from another person.

Neither type of behavior necessarily indicates helplessness. The child who is dependent may be attempting to secure attention, express affection, and obtain assistance through his behavior. The ways in which dependency is expressed vary with the child's age, so that although chronic and persistent crying episodes are common in infants, they are a sign of a possible problem in preschool children. Also, as the child gets older, his dependency becomes two-sided; that is, he gives as well as receives. As his world grows beyond the environment of his home, his dependency broadens to include people other than family—teachers and peers, for example.

We can never separate behavior from the variables determining it. Thus, when we see a high level of childhood dependency, we must recognize that it often reflects the attitudes and behavior patterns of the parents, particularly the mother. Specifically, dependency tends to be greatest among children with permissive-indulgent parents whose use of discipline is love-oriented, but who give little firm direction (Smart and Smart, 1972).

Trust

Another type of behavior manifested early in life, which is probably learned in the first year or two, is *trust*. Overprotective parents interfere with the normal development of trust in their youngsters. First, their behavior gives the child reason not to trust himself, since it seems to imply that, in their view, the child is incompetent. Second, children whose parents' overprotection is inconsistent come to mistrust their environment. Physical abuse also causes a lack of trust.

Too much trust on a child's part can, of course, be dangerous. A child needs a degree of trust that is realistic, that is, that will enable him to cope with an unpredictable world. (For example, most children are taught not to accept gifts and rides from strangers.) On the other hand, a child whose parents raise him to fear everything will be as severely damaged as one who is taught to blindly trust everyone and everything. To prepare their children to deal realistically with potential dangers in the environment, parents should teach them not only what to avoid but also what to do if danger does occur. But it is only through his own experience that a child will learn that there are many people in his environment he can count on, not least of all himself. And a parent should neither inhibit him needlessly in his exploration of his environment nor expose him to unnecessary danger.

Altruism and Cooperation

Kindly, unselfish behavior that has no apparent reward other than the intrinsic one of feeling good is what we call *altruism* (McCandless and Evans, 1973). Only when children have developed some ability to appreciate the attitudes, feelings, and experiences of other people do they exhibit this trait. Thus, truly altruistic behavior is rarely seen in preschool children (Hartup, 1970). However, its foundations are often laid early in life. This can be accomplished by providing the child with appropriate models, with opportunities to practice altruistic behavior himself, and with rewards, such as praise, when the altruistic behavior occurs (Hartup, 1970; Hoffman, 1970b; Rosenhan, 1969).

Cooperation, like altruism, is an important component of moral development, but, unlike altruism, it begins much earlier in life, often in infancy (McCandless and Evans, 1973; Bronfenbrenner, 1970). For example, infants learn to "help hold" their own bottles at an early age. Toddlers in Soviet preschools learn to cooperate and share in games and play. In all societies, children who wish to play with their peers must conform to the rules of the group—namely, cooperate.

As with altruistic behavior, parents can help to develop cooperative tendencies in children by providing appropriate models, clear instructions, and opportunities for practice.

Anger and Aggression

Two behavioral traits with important consequences for later development are anger and aggression. *Anger* is a feeling of distress that surfaces when you are restrained or blocked in your effort to accomplish something. Toddlers and preschool children at first have little control over their anger and typically display it by crying, kicking, and throwing things. Through *aggression* the individual attempts to cope with his anger, by increasing his power or status. At certain times, it is productive and useful; at other times it is destructive and dangerous (Smart and Smart, 1972).

The development of the child involves learning the necessary controls of both anger and aggression. Caretakers can aid a child in learning such controls if they follow certain guidelines. For example, in order to forestall a child's distress from becoming acute, basic needs like food and rest should be provided in a regular but flexible routine. A child's call for assistance should be answered promptly. As the child gets older, his opportunities for decision-making and doing things on his own should be increased. Finally, when a child does exhibit hostile aggression, caretakers should quickly express disapproval and insist that it be stopped.

Jealousy and *rivalry* are feelings of anger based on a person's belief that someone else is receiving the love, attention, or success he would like for himself. A young child will often experience feelings of jealousy when there is a new baby in the family. The infant receives a good part of the attention formerly reserved for the older child. Behavior patterns in this case vary. The child might inform his mother that she should get rid of the baby, and when she doesn't, he might start crying; or he might lash out physically, hitting the baby or his mother.   **Jealousy and Rivalry**

In conjunction with the jealousy, there is a feeling of *sibling rivalry*. The child must now compete with the new baby for his parents' time. Likewise, the baby, as he grows up, will come to feel that he is not given all the privileges accorded the older child.

If parents make an effort to prepare their children for the arrival of a new infant, they can help to control, to a degree, the feelings of jealousy that arise. For example, children who are sufficiently mature can be given opportunities to play with or help care for the baby. Despite parental effort, however, it is inevitable that the older child, who was formerly the only recipient of his parents' love and attention, will manifest some jealousy. But overall, parents must try to assure the child of their continuing love and affection for him.

No child is free from fears, and parents and educators should understand this. But a recognition of the child's fears will better equip the caretakers to assist the child in learning how to cope with them.   **Fear**

Different types of fear appear at different stages of development. Infants' fears are basic ones related to their needs for food, protection, and so on. However, an infant's fear that he will be deprived of these necessities will rapidly disappear as the mother or mother-substitute satisfies the needs. In the process of need satisfaction, the young child develops new fear. He becomes increasingly attached to his mother and is afraid of losing her, and at the same time he becomes very fearful of strangers and unfamiliar stimuli. A child of preschool age, however, who has positive experiences with new situations becomes better able to cope with them.

Many childhood fears emerge as the result of conditioning and modeling (which we will discuss at length in later chapters). Pre-school children in our culture most commonly fear animals and the dark. Children may develop a fear of dogs, for example, simply by hearing their parents talking about a child who was bitten by a dog. Coincidence accounts in only small measure for the fact that children's fears parallel those of their parents. Constant exposure to parental apprehensiveness in certain situations affects the child. Violent episodes on television and the child's own exploration and discoveries can lead to fears as well.

Parents can help reduce irrational fears in their children by gently reasoning with them and by showing them that in realistic situations no harm will come to them. Instead of being forced to encounter things they fear, children should be encouraged to talk about their fears and also to act them out in play and fantasy. Also, because children fear a loss of a loved one, separation from people to whom children are attached should be done gradually. When children are ill, their fears may magnify; therefore, loved ones should be available to provide comfort and reassurance (Smart and Smart, 1972). But again, as we discussed in the section on trust, parents must avoid overprotecting their children, so that they can develop confidence in their own capabilities.

 ## BEHAVIOR DISTURBANCES AND SOCIALIZATION

Sometimes socialization goes astray. The role of the family in the development of children's personalities concerns psychologists both as it contributes to socialization as it *should* take place and as a source of behavior *pathology* among children. Personality and behavior problems can range from mild behavior problems in specific situations, expressed through neuroses, all the way to severe psychotic reactions, such as schizophrenia, which sometimes require hospitalization.

Psychologists want to know in particular how the mother contributes to the development of childhood behavior problems. Research on influences in the family related to childhood schizophrenia, for example, has led to the concept of the "schizophrenogenic mother," who is defined as being aggressive, domineering, overanxious, and oversolicitous, yet basically rejecting. Some studies suggest that approximately 50 percent of schizophrenic children have mothers who fit this description (Frank, 1965).

Neurotic behavior in children has been linked to such conditions in the home as maternal domination and overprotection. However, other studies have implicated entirely different causes, such as maternal rejection. Neurotic behavior in parents, broken homes, and maternal rejection, among other factors, have been hypothesized and investigated with no definitive results. The research thus far

HYPERACTIVE CHILDREN

Some children can't seem to sit still for a minute, concentrate on anything, or sleep through the night. Their behavior is driven, uncontrolled, and often uncontrollable. According to recent estimates, some 2 million children fall into this behavior category, which is called hyperactive. Many doctors prescribe drugs to suppress its symptoms, whereas others are violently opposed to this kind of treatment (Walker, 1974). Still others prescribe psychotherapy in the belief that the source of the problem is to be found in the child's personal and family life. One report (Snider, 1974) describes "dramatic new evidence" that hyperactive behavior in children can be controlled by eliminating foods with artificial colors and flavors from their diet. Dr. Ben Feingold (1973) tested 25 children using this dietary approach and found that children who were on medication could discontinue it within a few days after their diets were changed. However, if they went off their diets the hyperactivity recurred. In a later experiment on 100 children, 40 displayed a complete reversal of symptoms, together with marked scholastic improvement, when their diets were changed.

has been inconclusive in identifying the familial correlates of antisocial behavior in children. And even when significant correlations are seemingly found between a certain behavior problem in a child and a particular variable in his family, we do not know for sure that that variable caused the problem. Psychologists still don't know why, when children are raised under identical family conditions, one develops normally, and another exhibits a behavior problem.

SUMMARY

The socialization of a child—that is, the way in which he adapts to his environment and learns the behavior patterns and values of his culture—is a complex process, and many different interrelated factors play a part in it. The process is vital to the individual, since it determines his personality, and to the culture itself, which sustains itself through socializing its young.

Among the variables in socialization, probably the most significant one in transmitting the culture to the child is the family. Child-rearing practices include caretaking, emotional interactions, teaching of values, discipline, and so on. Trends in child rearing are changing today—for example, in the view of the father's role in raising the child.

The kind of caretaking system and its structure also influence the socialization of the child. The nuclear family, the extended family, multiple caretaking, institutionalization, and parental deprivation, all have differential effects on child development.

Preschools are significant too. Preschool education in the U.S.S.R. follows certain objectives aimed at self-reliance and character development. The kibbutzim of Israel, also part of a collective system, seek to foster cooperation and dedication to group goals. Communist China's preschools are likewise group-oriented. The preschool system in the United States today is inadequately developed, but social pressure is being brought to bear to provide such services, especially for the children of working mothers.

The peer group influences the child principally through play activities. Television, especially as a model of aggressive behavior, influences the child's social behavior also. Social class and ethnic group are two closely related factors with an impact on child development. And certain sex-role stereotypes in the culture socialize children. However, the traditional attitudes toward sex-typed behavior are changing.

Among the behaviors generated in young children by the socialization process are dependency and attachment, trust, altruism and cooperation, anger and aggression, jealousy and rivalry, and fear. Sometimes socialization does not take place in a manner most beneficial to the child and society, and the child will manifest behavior problems.

Human behavior is extremely complicated, and the reader should thus interpret sociological and psychological data, such as we have presented in this chapter, with caution and remember that the complexity of the human personality reflects the complexity of the cultural environment in which we move.

SUGGESTED FOR FURTHER READING

Bronfenbrenner, U. *Two worlds of childhood: U.S. and U.S.S.R.* New York: Basic Books, 1970 (also available from Pocket Books).
This short text compares and contrasts Soviet socialization and early education methods with those in the United States. Implications for child rearing are discussed.

Feshbach, N. Cross-cultural studies of teaching styles in four-year-olds and their mothers. In A. Pick (Ed.), *Minnesota symposium on child psychology* (Vol. 7). Minneapolis: University of Minnesota Press, 1972.
This article discusses the relationship between parental socialization practices and child development. The function of reinforcement is stressed in relation to socialization.

Keyserling, M. *Windows on day care.* New York: National Council of Jewish Women, 1972.
This informative book provides good coverage of what is taking place in day-care centers in the United States. It provides excellent advice for parents who need to decide on day-care facilities for their children.

Lynn, D. *The father: His role in child development.* Monterey, Calif.: Brooks-Cole, 1974.
The effect on the child of the changing role of parents in today's society.

"Play." *Natural History* (special edition), 1971, *80*, whole issue.
A journal issue devoted to various aspects of play, with particular applications to early education of children.

DEVELOPING THOUGHT PROCESSES: THE EARLY SCHOOL YEARS

CHAPTER 2

After completing this chapter, the reader should be able to:

1 Describe the relationship between the development of language and the development of cognition in young children, and the impact of this relationship on both advantaged and disadvantaged children.

2 Describe and evaluate the two major theoretical approaches taken in the study of cognitive development, and the important concepts implicit in these theories.

3 Compare and contrast the positions taken by major theorists as to roles of both maturation and learning in effecting cognitive development.

4 Give examples of teacher or parent behavior conducive to the increase of cognitive development in both preschool and school-age children, taking into consideration individual differences between children both in level of maturation and in previous experience.

5 Propose educational curricula to increase cognitive and language development of both advantaged and disadvantaged children, justifying these curricula according to the major theories of cognitive development.

THE RELATIONSHIP BETWEEN LANGUAGE AND COGNITIVE DEVELOPMENT

The process of socialization—how the child learns to behave in his culture—was the subject of the preceding chapter. Now we shall turn to the development of thinking and understanding, which we call the *cognitive processes.*

Before we discuss cognition itself, we must mention several important ideas regarding language. A basic characteristic distinguishing humans from other animals is that we communicate our thoughts through language. Through language we obtain a great deal of our data about the nature of our world. And, according to some theories, language is, at the same time, the major determinant of our thought processes.

The quantitative and qualitative changes in language ability that children undergo as they increase in chronological age are intrinsic to the development of the cognitive processes. For example, as children get older they develop abilities to deal with a larger number of concepts and to use more and more words easily in everyday speech; that is, they develop language ability quantitatively. They also become capable of coping with more complex and different kinds of concepts; that is, they develop language ability qualitatively. Language and intellectual development are interrelated—one cannot be fully achieved without the other.

The socialization process is of utmost importance to the development of language and thinking. A child makes sounds, learns to repeat sounds, makes words from the sounds, and combines words into more meaningful units. He is learning to communicate with those around him in his environment. These surroundings—which we might call the child's linguistic environment—and the unique experiences he has in them have a profound effect on his language development. The level of language skills of the people in his own social class (in relation to standard middle-class English) bears a distinct relationship to what Bernstein (1958) describes as "the mode of cognitive expression"; that is, how we speak mirrors the environment in which we are socialized. A poor linguistic environment can have dramatic consequences for the child later in life in terms of not only social development but academic achievement as well. Thus, whether language develops or is learned (an issue about which psychologists argue), a child's linguistic environment is most significant with respect to his rate of language development and, it follows, his thinking, or cognition.

We have been looking at the implications of language for the cognitive processes, thinking and understanding. But this concept of language has included two parts: words and syntactical units that are internalized, that is, thought, and words and syntactical units that are vocalized, that is, speech. We must now separate them (conceptually, at least) and ask ourselves: What is the connection between thought and speech? Are the two inseparable?

In the words of John B. Watson (1913), the father of American behaviorist psychology, "Thought processes are really motor habits in the larynx." That is, thought is no more than covert speech. Thought and speech are one and the same.

Theories of Language and Cognition

Lev Vygotsky (1934/1962), a Russian psychologist, carried this theory a step further. For him, thought is not merely expressed words; it actually comes into existence through them. This established the truly functional importance of speech in the development of cognition. The implications of this theory are important to parent and teacher: If we have not learned a word or words for a concept, then we cannot think about it. In this context, the teaching of language becomes extraordinarily important!

Jean Piaget, the influential Swiss psychologist, saw the relationship between language and cognitive development in a different way. For him, cognitive development proceeds on its own, generally followed by linguistic development or reflected in the child's language. Whereas Watson and later Vygotsky emphasized language as an aid to cognitive growth, Piaget took the reverse position and emphasized cognitive growth as an aid to the development of language skills.

Piaget's interest lay in the functions of language and the manner in which it affects the development of children. In his studies of the spontaneous speech of kindergarten children, for example, he determined that they exhibited two major classes of utterances: what he called "egocentric speech" (undirected speech, not aimed at others for the purposes of communication), and what he called "socialized speech" (speech directed toward communication). Piaget further hypothesized that egocentric speech precedes socialized speech. This concept of the necessary order of stages can be found throughout his work on cognitive development, and we will discuss it at length later in this chapter.

Jerome Bruner's approach differs from the theories we have just noted; because of its importance, it is discussed at length in Chapter 5. Bruner is close to Vygotsky in his basic view that language clearly plays an important role in the development of cognition. For Bruner (1964), language makes possible certain properties of the thinking process, for it "provides a means, not only for representing experience, but also for transforming it." According to Bruner, linguistic symbols—words, phrases, sentences—can be used in a variety of ways in helping us to think. Their versatility far exceeds that of actions or images. Linguistic symbols allow us, for example,

PLAY: PATHWAY TO LANGUAGE

When watching a mother and her child playing "peek-a-boo" we always smile to ourselves and think how cute they are. We seldom realize, however, the significance such play has on the child's development. Jerome Bruner (1975) calls such interactions "exchange games" and suggests that they are significant for a child's first mastery of language. Through them, "young children learn to signal and recognize certain expectancies . . . . And they learn to manipulate features of language that they must later put together in complicated ways" (p. 83).

Bruner provides an example. Nan, a child of 9 months, learns to play an exchange game with her mother, but she has not yet learned the adult language code for giving and receiving. Thus she says "Kew" (her version of "Thank you"), as she hands an object to her mother, although she might not say "Kew" when her mother hands it to her. Later, at 12 months, "Look" replaces "Kew" in the giving phase of the game and "Kew" has moved to its proper position in the receiving phase. Says Bruner: "Nan has used the order of steps in the game to sort out the proper order for the language she uses now in play and will use later to communicate" (p. 83).

In short, play, while amusing for a child, is also serious business. It is an important pathway to the acquisition of language.

to draw inferences, make deductions, find or eliminate alternatives—the many kinds of thought manipulations that increase the child's ability to think and solve problems.

According to Bruner, the words a child hears in his daily life largely determine how he in turn will use language; they are crucial to his perception of the world and his interactions with it. Language is, in this sense, culture-bound; nevertheless, Bruner contends that children can be trained to use language appropriate to the demands of cognitive tasks. (This concept of learned techniques has important implications for education: If we don't teach students the terms that will help them to solve the tasks we give them in the classroom, we can anticipate learning problems.)

On this issue of learned techniques, Piaget strongly disagrees with Bruner. The reasons for this disagreement become clear when we remember that, for Piaget, language reflects cognitive development; it does not cause it. According to Piaget, teaching students appropriate terms can aid in increasing their cognitive development, but it will not help children whose level of cognitive development has not yet reached the point where they can comprehend the relevant concepts represented by the words. This is important to remember as we consider Piaget's views of the development of cognition and the implications of his theories for educators.

Questions for Thought
What is the connection between thought and speech? Can you have one without the other?
Lack of language communication can occur in the homes of deaf-mute parents. It can also occur in the homes of so-called disadvantaged children whose parents are too busy—or uninterested—to provide them with adequate stimulation. Would this deprivation affect the development of thinking ability of children in such homes? If so, how?

THEORIES OF COGNITIVE DEVELOPMENT

Stage-Dependent Theory: Piaget

A child's development consists of a series of progressively more complex stages. His advancement from one stage to the next occurs through an interaction of biological maturation and experiences with the environment (objects, people, events). Stage-dependent theories rest on this basic concept, although they may vary in the emphasis they place on maturation or external factors in the learning process. *Maturation* refers to the development of the body, regardless of outside influences. It is the process that makes all human beings similar in some respects and different from other living organisms. Whatever its environment, a puppy will grow to be a dog, a baby to an adult human being. Everything in the environment—both inside and outside the body—affects development; for example, the amount of food we eat, the books we read.

The concept of *developmental* stages of the child grew out of studies conducted by Arnold Gesell with infants and young children. Each stage, Gesell maintained, can be characterized by specific traits, and from his explorations of certain broad aspects of behavior he was able to generalize about what to expect at any age level. The behaviors that concerned him at each developmental stage were motor functioning, adaptive behavior, language, and personal-social behavior (Gesell and Amatruda, 1947). (Questions that would be of concern here would be, for example: At what age can we expect a child to begin responding socially to his parents? Or, at what age can we expect a child to play in parallel fashion with his peers?)

The stages of cognitive development in the child interested Piaget, another stage-dependent theorist. Piaget's concepts are based on an integration of the disciplines of biology and epistemology (the study of knowledge). For him, intelligence is "a particular instance of biological adaptation" (1936/1952) and "a system of living and action operations" (1950). We can see from this that the biological concepts of adaptation and organization (the development of systems) are basic to Piaget's views.

According to Piaget, the development of thinking proceeds in a clearly defined, fixed sequence of stages, each relevant to a specific chronological age. For example, we can expect that a child whose chronological age is 7 to 11 would have difficulties conceptualizing certain kinds of problems if the teacher has not first aided him by providing concrete stimuli. Such a child would find that learning the concepts in algebra is very hard, unless he is given concrete models of the concepts. Only when a child is older (according to Piaget, age 11 to maturity) can he perform these formal operations without the use of concrete aids. A child will not attain a new level of development until he has mastered the tasks of earlier levels; more mature methods of problem-solving presuppose earlier methods.

Piaget emphasized the fact that a child acts on his environment and that therefore experience affects his movement from lower to higher levels of cognitive development. That is, environmental stimulation increases the development of the ability to solve problems. A parent or teacher who provides stimulation that is appropriate to the child's cognitive level is indeed helping the child to learn to solve problems at his level of thinking; and therefore the child can proceed to the next level. In selecting classroom activities, the teacher is playing an exceedingly important role in influencing the cognitive development of the child, as is the parent, in selecting games, toys, and storybooks.

The concepts of organization and adaptation, called "functional

The home is the first learning environment.

(Robin Gibson, Alternative Curriculum)

invariants" by Piaget, are essential to his theory of the development of human intelligence. They are constants in the functioning of human intelligence and cause the development of cognition to proceed in the manner that it does. These mechanisms operate continuously. Through *organization* we arrange and systematize perceptual and cognitive data into units and patterns that have meaning for us. When, for example, we see a rectangle at the far end of a room, we perceive a door, and know by which route we can leave. Through *adaptation* we can alter the ways in which we deal with the needs of the environment by changing ourselves or by changing the environment.

Adaptation, according to Piaget, involves two processes: assimilation and accommodation. We *assimilate* when we take in a new stimulus from the environment and respond to it with a behavior we have already used for a familiar, and in some way similar, stimulus. For example, when a child encounters an orange for the first time and rolls it like a ball, he is assimilating. He ascribes ball-like traits to the orange because it resembles a ball to him. He fits the orange into his concept of "ball" without regard for its important non-"ball-like" attributes.

We *accommodate* when we add a new activity to what we already know or when we modify an old behavior. Using the same example: A child knows that a ball rolls; when he learns to bounce it, he has added a new behavior. Thus, his concept (of ball) matures as he adds new information (it bounces) to his preexisting idea (it is round and it rolls). This new response to a stimulus to which he has been exposed in the past increases the number of responses the child can make to the old stimulus and later to new and different stimuli (Flavell, 1963).

Piaget stresses that assimilation and accommodation occur only when an environmental stimulus (the ball in our example) is appropriately matched with the particular level of cognitive development attained by the child. Bouncing a ball in front of a newborn, for example, would not increase cognitive development, since he could not respond to it. And presenting a series of abstract mathematical problems to kindergarten children would be equally inappropriate. We will consider the implications of matching in respect to education later in this chapter.

Furthermore, to Piaget, a child's interaction with his environment will be most meaningful to his development only when assimilation and accommodation occur equally and continually. If at any time a teacher or parent ceases to provide new stimuli in the child's environment, both processes would stop, and the development of the thinking processes would thus be curtailed. In addition, a balance must exist between the two processes; they must be in *equilibrium*, as Piaget calls this balance. He suggests that development is a pro-

Table 2-1
Piaget's Stages
of Cognitive Development

Stage	Age
Sensorimotor	Birth–2 yrs
Preoperational	2–7 yrs
Preconceptual	2–4 yrs
Intuitive	4–7 yrs
Concrete operations	7–11 yrs
Formal operations	11 yrs on

gressive equilibration from one plateau, as it were, to another. Each stage of cognitive development has a particular form of equilibrium as a function of the problem-solving abilities of that stage. Equilibration allows the transformation from simpler to more complex conceptual thinking to the final equilibrium represented by the mature adult mind.

THE STAGES OF COGNITIVE DEVELOPMENT.   What are Piaget's stages of cognitive development? Initially, he distinguished between two: sensorimotor mental functioning (birth to 2 years of age) and conceptual mental functioning (age 2 to maturity). This latter stage was further subdivided into three periods: preoperational (2 to 7), concrete operations (7 to 11), and formal operations (11 through maturity). The rate at which a child completes these stages is dependent upon his biological maturation and his experiences in his environment. Some children, of course, will advance faster than others because of differences in both these factors. Thus, the chronological ages ascribed to each stage vary somewhat. Each advance to a new stage of cognitive development integrates and transforms the acquisitions of the previous stages.

The *sensorimotor stage* consists of several substages in which the child's intellectual development consists largely of action-schemas, since he cannot as yet use language. During the first month of life, he goes through the *reflexive stage*, in which his innate responses (reaching, grasping, sucking) become efficient. He later begins to perform more and more complex behaviors through a series of *circular (repetitive) reactions*. First he repeats actions for their own sake; then he repeats actions to watch the results. The coordination of these actions is evident later in means-end behavior, where he uses his responses to achieve a goal, and motivation becomes a factor in his responses. Still later a child uses active *trial and error* (11 to 18 months); he also becomes aware that objects can be hidden and attempts to find them. *Mental combinations* (18 months on) occur when the child is able to think before he acts, that is, when he can represent to himself the outcome of actions before he takes them. At this period, he also develops what Piaget calls the "object concept." He realizes that objects have a permanence and identity of their own, that they exist even when he cannot see them. And he begins to use language, first to imitate and then to represent reality.

The next stage of development, the *preoperational stage*, includes two substages: preconceptual and intuitive thought. In the *preconceptual stage* (ages 2 to 4), stimuli begin to take on symbolic meaning to a child. A little girl, for example, will treat her doll as a "real" baby.

In the *intuitive stage* of intellectual development (ages 4 to 7), direct perceptions still dominate thought. A child cannot yet under-

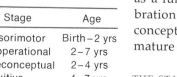

In the preoperational stage, a child cannot understand that a volume of liquid poured from a short wide container into a tall narrow one remains the same.

(Mimi Forsyth from Monkmeyer)

stand that a given quantity remains the same regardless of changes in its shape or position in relation to other objects. According to Piaget, the child focuses on one quality of an object at a time. A child who wants two cookies is satisfied that he has gotten them when he sees his mother break a cookie in half and present him with the two halves. At this stage, the child's reasoning is *egocentric*; he has difficulty in seeing viewpoints other than his own. Abstract relationships present a problem, yet the child is constructing more complex images and more elaborate concepts by which he comes to think about and understand the world around him. The use of language, as we discussed earlier, facilitates this.

At the stage of *concrete operations*, the next stage of development, the child is in school, where he is expected to "pay attention." And he does. Or, rather, he can. He is aided in this ability by his development, at this time, of reasoning and logic in respect to concrete objects. A child of this age treats an abstraction such as "God," for example, as a real—that is, concrete—person. At this time, the child develops the concept of quantity based on many dimensions; he is thus able to differentiate between part and whole,

CONCRETE OPERATIONS AND ABSTRACTIONS

"Kids say the darndest things," says Art Linkletter. And they certainly do. Part of the pleasure we derive from observing how a child's mind works comes from watching the child make abstractions "real" by describing them as concrete objects. This is an aspect of the concrete operations stage of development of 7- to 11-year-olds.

Juliet Lowell (1960) includes these two delightful examples of "concrete abstractions" in her book, *Dear Folks*.

> *Dear Aunt Fannie,*
>
> *We are riding home in a plane tomorrow. The plane is going to ride very high. I hope we wont hit the cloud God's sitting on and bump him off.*
>
> *Love,*
> *Babs*

> *Dear Aunt Renée,*
>
> *We had a nice time flying in the plane back to France. All the way I keep looking out of the window for angels. I did want to see them, they would have looked so pretty floating through the air with their little pink wings. Maybe it was just to windy for them to be out.*
>
> *Marie*

between greater and lesser. He will no longer accept a cookie broken in half as two cookies; he will recognize that they are two parts of the same cookie. He also learns *conservation*, that is, that mass remains constant regardless of its changes in form. At this stage, he first understands that a ball of clay smashed flat on the table takes up as much space as when it was round. Thus, he can think about concrete things in systematic ways, although he cannot yet think abstractly.

In the stage of *formal operations*, a child is ready to learn abstract concepts. He now develops the capacity to reason through the use of hypotheses. When he is given data, he can make logical deductions from them. He no longer needs concrete stimuli to help him solve problems in subjects such as algebra, because at this stage abstractions match his level of mental development.

The concept of *matching* is extremely important, as previously stated. The child goes through a fixed sequence of stages in cognitive development, and the teacher or parent must plan experiences and stimuli consistent with his maturational level. Such things as sophisticated mathematical and symbolic concepts cannot be taught at an early age, that is, before a child reaches the stage of formal operations (Piaget, 1964). (In this respect Piaget differs from Bruner. The views of both men have strong implications for decisions made regarding educational approaches, and these will be discussed later in this chapter.)

Questions for Thought

If it is true that each child in a class of 30 has reached his own unique and quite possibly different stage of cognitive development, should the teacher provide only one set of textbooks for the entire class?

How might the teacher match teaching aids in the classroom to the cognitive level of each child?

Piaget distinguishes between learning and cognitive development. Cognitive development is a spontaneous process that occurs as a function of total development (Piaget, 1964). As we have seen, according to this theory, a child goes through a series of developmental stages during which he gradually achieves a more sophisticated level of cognition. Maturation, experience, social transmission in the broad sense (the teaching of language, formal education, etc.), and equilibration are all parts of the process.

PIAGET'S CRITICS.   Piaget's theories were first popularized for American readers by John H. Flavell (1963) in *The Developmental Psychology of Jean Piaget*. Flavell stressed that Piaget does not consider the describing of developmental stages an end in itself. Classification is simply a means to achieve a better understanding of the developmental process.

In his description of Piaget, Flavell was quick to see the fundamental drift and focus of Piaget's critics, who have objected to his research methods and certain points made in his theoretical interpretation.

Piaget's observational methods have been challenged by psychologists both in the United States and abroad. One aspect of methodology for which he has been criticized is his use of language in the interviews he conducted in his observational studies. Some critics felt that his results might have been due to language development and not intellectual development. We might ask ourselves: Does a word mean the same thing to a child as to an adult? Going back to the example we used earlier: When a child says he wants two cookies, does he really mean two cookies or does he mean two pieces? Can we tell simply by asking him? If a child cannot find the words to express himself logically to an adult, does it mean his conceptualization is faulty? Or merely that he doesn't have the language skills necessary? These were some of the questions Piaget's critics asked.

Piaget has been criticized as well for being too dogmatic about age norms in developmental stages. Experimental psychologists (for example, Miller, Cohen, and Hill, 1970) have conducted studies that suggest that the ages at which children reach certain stages in cognitive development sometimes vary more than is suggested in Piaget's classification. In answer to this, Flavell notes that Piaget's theory is built on stages and stage differences, not on age and age differences. Flavell does point out, however, that Piaget's theory underplays somewhat the differences among children who fall within the same developmental stage and the similarities among children who fall within different stages.

Other psychologists, applying rigorous controls in experiments to test Piaget's conclusions, have found support for his theory of developmental stages. Their studies suggest that even though the ages at which children reach the different stages do vary, children tend to go through the stages of cognitive development in the same order as did Piaget's subjects (see, for example, Carlson, 1969; Elkind, 1962; Furth, Youniss, and Ross, 1970; and Lovell and Ogilvie, 1960). Piaget's developmental sequence has been tested internationally, in fact, and found to be the same in other cultures (Proscura, 1969).

On the matter of individual variations Piaget is also criticized—mainly because he does not concern himself with this subject. On the other hand, measurement psychologists, particularly those in the United States, have conducted thorough studies on the differences between individuals in cognitive development, social growth, learning abilities, and maturation, and have devised extensive means by which these differences can be measured.

Environmental differences do not concern Piaget either, although in his theory environment does play a role in cognitive development. First, he admits that lack of environmental stimulation will affect cognitive growth. Second, he suggests that unless stimuli are matched to a child's cognitive capacities, cognitive growth will be hampered. However, Piaget has not made clear how appropriate matches should be brought about, nor has he discussed at any length the educational implications following his assumptions.

That Piaget has made tremendous contributions to the field of developmental psychology is incontestable. However, other aspects of development also affect how people learn. And it is to the work of some psychologists who have done much significant research in other areas of development that we now turn.

Learning-Environmental Theories

Learning-environmental theories maintain that to properly understand cognitive development, one should focus directly on the environmental stimulation and learning experiences that are possible.

Jerome Bruner, one of the foremost learning-environmental psychologists, views development as proceeding through a hierarchy of stages, as did Piaget, but he does not view these stages as fixed and critical, as did Piaget. In a statement that refutes Piaget's concept of fixed developmental stages, Bruner (1960) has put forth what seems an astounding hypothesis: "Any subject can be taught effectively in some intellectually honest form to any child at any stage of development." Piaget would agree that you can teach a child at any age by using stimuli appropriately matched to the child's level of cognitive development; in such a manner, assimilation and then accommodation can occur. But for Bruner, what is most important is that the stage of cognitive development of a child be noted and then a curriculum arranged around it. By providing the proper curriculum, the teacher can increase the child's ability to think. (We will discuss Bruner's theory and his approach to curriculum design in detail in Chapter 5.)

Robert Gagné, another highly respected learning-environmental psychologist, is also disturbed by what he considers Piaget's indifference to the role of learning in developmental change. According to Gagné, Piaget is not interested in the contribution of learning to intellectual development. Gagné, on the other hand, believes a child develops because he learns an ordered set of abilities. As learning moves along, these abilities build upon each other in progressive fashion. Thus, a child who learns to solve simple problems improves his ability to solve more complex problems at a later time (Gagné, 1968). Abilities may also expand through self-initiated thinking activity. The implication of this for the teacher is that activities do not necessarily have to be organized for learning to take place; the child may reach a higher level of problem solving by himself. According to Gagné, stages of development are not correlated with chronological age, except in the sense that learning takes time.

Sidney Bijou and Donald Baer (1961) have also constructed a learning-environmental theory of development. They define development as behavior change and state that learning procedures are instrumental in behavior-changing processes. They believe that age differences are irrelevant to the developmental process. In his environment, a child is exposed to many learning procedures, but the sequence of these procedures is often inefficient. By constructing efficient learning procedures, a teacher can help a child to advance significantly in his development. In the view of Bijou and Baer, if a particular learning procedure is unavailable in the natural environment, it is possible to provide a behavioral alternative, and thus to "program" for a good outcome. The socially deprived child can, through routes made available to him in compensatory educational programs, increase dramatically in his cognitive development.

The work of the Russian psychologist Lev Vygotsky (1934/1962) provides a social-historical perspective for learning–environment relationships. He maintained that thinking processes change in a manner that is complex, dynamic, and interrelated with environmental phenomena, these phenomena being determined by social-historical forces. Vygotsky made a distinction between elementary levels of thinking (such as in Piaget's sensorimotor stage) and higher levels. The level of thinking of an individual, he said, reflects his particular environment, and significant changes in that environment can be expected to change the thinking patterns of the individual.

The following description (Luria, 1971) of conditions in certain isolated villages in Soviet Central Asia, where a psychological expedition was carried out in the 1930s, is illustrative of Vygotsky's theory:

The non-technical economy (gardening, cotton-raising, animal husbandry) was replaced by more complex economic systems; there was a sharp increase in the communication with the cities; new people appeared in the villages; collective economy with joint planning and joint organization of production radically changed the previous economic activity; extensive educational and propaganda work intruded on the traditional views which previously had been determined by the simpler life of the village; a large network of schools designed to liquidate illiteracy was introduced to a large portion of the population and, in the course of a few years, the residents of these villages were included in a system of educational institutions, and at the same time were introduced to a kind of theoretical activity which had previously not existed in those areas. . . . (pp. 266, 267)

Psychologists were interested in whether there were any differences between the traditional nonliterate villagers and the newly educated, actively participating residents in their patterns of thinking; for example, in how they formed concepts and drew logical conclusions from verbal syllogisms. Their findings:

> Not the abstract significance of words but concrete-practical ties reproduced from the experience of the subject play a direct role (among the nonliterate villagers); not abstract thought, but visual-motor recollection determines the course of thinking. . . . (These facts) are a completely social-historical feature of psychological activity—it is only necessary for the social-historical conditions to change in order for these features of cognitive activity to change and disappear. (Luria, 1971, p. 269)

The importance Vygotsky places on literacy as well as the social-historical conditions of the villagers is quite obvious. Vygotsky, it can be seen, is very much in the mainstream of learning-environmental theories.

PLANNING FOR COGNITIVE DEVELOPMENT

Thus far in our discussion we have hinted at the ways in which teachers can aid their students in cognitive development. We now leave the realm of theoretical approaches to cognition per se and enter the area of practical application of these theories. How can educators plan specifically for cognitive development?

Stage-Dependent Approaches

Piaget's theoretical work can be linked to actual classroom practices. First, Piaget stressed interaction with the environment, for the processes of assimilation and accommodation can occur only in a stimulating environment. Educators today are aware that children from different backgrounds do not solve problems in the same ways. Some may come from environments that do not provide sufficient or appropriate types of stimulation. Programs such as Head Start have been developed to compensate for this lack.

Second, Piaget's work is relevant to education in the concept of matching. Educational programs today seek to provide subject matter that corresponds to a child's level of cognitive development. For example, a child in the sensorimotor stage of development is provided with experiences that are action-linked; a child in the formal operations stage is provided with more theoretical experiences that match his ability to cope with complex and abstract problems.

Compensatory preschool education programs, whose aim is to better prepare a child for later school experiences, place a special

Educational programs should be matched to the child's level of cognitive development.

(Alice Kandell, Rapho/Photo Researchers)

emphasis on giving a child the opportunity to act directly on concrete objects. This preparation has a particular connection with the development of language. As one psychologist has pointed out: "Language derives from a coordination between object construction and vocal imitation, with the knowledge that is symbolized coming from object construction and the vocal signs for the objects and events of that knowledge acquired through vocal imitation" (Hunt, 1973). As the child is developing his ability to use language, a teacher must be aware of the child's level of thinking and verbalization and speak with him at this level. Thus, matching, as it relates to providing concrete experiences and the concomitant development of language, has an importance that cannot be overestimated. A teacher who does not invoke the principle of matching—by selecting stimuli that his students can use and understand—will find that the performance of his students is likely to be poor and to be accompanied by feelings of frustration, on the one hand, or apathy and boredom, on the other.

**INDIVIDUALIZED
INSTRUCTION:
PROJECT PLAN**

Would you like to learn "on your own"? To be judged by your own work instead of having your performance compared with that of others? Some students today are being given such options.

One such innovative program (Klaus, 1971) that has been developed in individualized education is called Project PLAN. Begun in 1967, it is a system of programmed learning for language arts, science, social studies, and mathematics for grades 1 through 12. Behaviorally oriented objectives are built into "teaching-learning units," or TLU's, modules of instruction representing 10 to 15 hours of instruction for an average student, each designed to be used over a two-week period.

The materials in the TLU's vary; they are tailored to each student's particular background, aptitude, and interests. Before a student begins to use the modules, he is tested extensively to determine his abilities, interests, and previously acquired knowledge. Each student proceeds at his own pace, with the teacher supplying aid only to help him to overcome specific difficulties and to check his progress on complex assignments. The student is tested to be sure that remedial steps are taken if necessary, and also to provide each student and his teacher with a flow of information—feedback—about his accomplishments and aspirations. Project PLAN also uses a computer, which collects, organizes, and analyzes the information from the tests to assess the performance of each student on each module.

An aspect of environmental stimulation that educators have learned to take into account in planning programs is that new events interest children. When a new event is both familiar enough so that it may be assimilated without distortion into the student's current cognitive level, and novel enough so that it produces some degree of conflict, then interest and learning are promoted. The child is "ready" to learn. Since, as we have mentioned, children of the same chronological age may be behaving on different cognitive levels, some educators feel that children should be given the freedom to work individually at tasks of their own choosing. This does not mean, however, that the learning situation should be unstructured; the teacher must provide the materials of interest that suit each one individually.

Piaget's basic idea of a progression through specific cognitive stages also has relevance to educational planning. Teachers must design curricula that will take a child through a logical sequence of steps so that his cognitive development may advance from one stage to the next. The course of growth in this system is one of progressive equilibration from one stage to the next by assimilation and accommodation. Growth proceeds with spurts and plateaus of achievement, and a curriculum must be designed with this in mind (Sigel, 1969).

Along with recognizing the importance of the Piagetian concepts of environmental stimulation, matching, and cognitive stages, the curriculum planner must incorporate appropriate teaching strategies in order to aid cognitive development effectively. Educators now understand that a child is not a miniature adult; he is qualitatively different, with a distinctive mental structure. And teaching strategies must take this into account. One object of education, then, is to help the child develop his full intellectual potential, to become an adult.

As Piaget (1972) has noted, however, not all children achieve the most complex level of formal operational thinking. Why? Learning-environmental psychologists would attribute it to environmental factors — cultural deprivation, poor, insufficient, or inappropriate environmental stimulation — and would point out that proper learning procedures could assist the development of skills, thus raising the otherwise low levels of cognition of some children. In this emphasis on the effects of learning, in and of itself, learning-environmental psychologists differ fundamentally from stage-dependent psychologists.

Learning-Environmental Approaches

For the learning-environmental psychologists, learning is totally dependent on interaction with the environment. One way to effect development is to alter the nature of that environment so that efficient learning can take place. To this end, they stress the importance of early stimulation. Timing here is of prime consideration.

We might ask: Is formal education prior to age 5 appropriate? A learning-environmental psychologist would answer yes. On the evidence of research on the development of IQ (Bloom, 1964), some psychologists regard intelligence (in Piagetian terms, the level of development of mental operations, or cognition) as particularly malleable during the years prior to age 5 and argue that the basic foundations for later development are established by this time. Based on this, supplying systematized programs, where necessary, in the preschool years so as to aid the development of intelligence is crucial. This intervention would be particularly vital for socially disadvantaged children who live in relatively restricted environments (Glaser and Resnick, 1972).

Robert Gagné would concur that the rate of cognitive development can be influenced by educational programs. To Gagné, learning is cumulative; a child develops because he learns an ordered set of abilities that are built one upon the other. The implication of his position is that a child would develop as soon and as fast as he

ELEMENTARY SCHOOL PHILOSOPHERS

Traditionally, philosophy has been a subject reserved for college students. But this is no longer true ("Grade School Philosophers," *Time*, 1974, p. 74). In Newark, New Jersey, children in an elementary school took part in an experimental class in philosophy. First-graders learned to categorize: "Four stores and three men make seven things in the world we can touch." Sixth-graders learned to make distinctions between things and beings: "If you have a friend who is only your friend when you are lonely, then you are using your friend as a thing." The class also covered deductive reasoning (for example: all birds are warm-blooded; robins are birds; therefore, robins are warm-blooded), universal and particular sentences, logic, differences of degree, relationships, and styles of thought.

The object was to teach young children (grades 1 through 6) to *reason*. One teacher reported that "by the end of the course . . . [the children] were going to the library and taking volumes of the encyclopedia home." The class was so successful that it is being introduced for fifth- and sixth-graders in other schools.

What do you think Piaget's response would be to such an approach to cognitive development? How would Bruner's response differ from that of Piaget?

could be taught. His readiness to learn depends not on internal, biological factors but on the availability of a sequence of learning experiences that capitalize on his emerging cognitive capacity. If a child cannot perform a particular skill, such as reading, his teacher must go back, identify the prior ability that he has not yet mastered, develop an educational sequence that leads to its acquisition, and then begin to teach him reading again. This is similar in one way to the Piagetian approach, in which a teacher might first identify the signs of potential competency in the child and then arrange a curriculum that capitalizes on it and leads him to higher levels of cognitive development.

LANGUAGE ACQUISITION. Perhaps the most striking instance of the emphasis learning-environmental psychologists place on the role of training and instruction in cognitive development is in respect to language acquisition. Bruner has said that language is culture-bound; Bernstein has suggested that an individual's thinking is directly related to his social class. For these psychologists, the use of language in the child's environment is all-important.

Bruner has suggested that children must be trained through formal instruction to use language symbolically and abstractly. His cross-cultural studies (Bruner et al., 1966) suggest that the specific language a child speaks is not as important a factor in cognitive growth as the training he receives in the uses of it. If a child lives in a cultural setting that hinders his cognitive growth because his language skills are poorly developed in this setting, then formal language programs can be used to unlock his cognitive capacities and release his full potential.

Children have relatively little trouble in grasping the concepts inherent in words for simple concrete objects (e.g., bottle, table, ball) at the age at which they usually learn these words—because they can manipulate these objects. But it is much more difficult for them to grasp the concepts in abstractions such as time (before, after), direction (underneath, between), and relative judgments (warmer, heavier). Here an extremely articulate and well-trained teacher is needed to offer the necessary elaboration, corroboration, or negation of a child's emerging ideas.

PARENTAL ROLE.   The preschool child's teacher is usually his mother. Her social class, education, intelligence, general experience, and attitudes all affect his cognitive development. A study categorizing mothers as (in the researchers' terms) either "middle class" or "lower class" shows marked differences between the two groups in the ways mothers teach their children (Hess and Shipman, 1967). Middle-class mothers generally teach through encouragement and support of their children, giving them specific information and instruction. Lower-class mothers tend to teach more through control and criticism, "showing" their children rather than leading them to reason solutions to problems.

not necessary so any more

In homes that provide instruction and support, the child's development of abstract thinking is facilitated. In the case of the socially disadvantaged child, the development of this kind of thinking is hindered because the child has not been given the essential language experience necessary to develop it. The lack of an ongoing, elaborated dialogue, more often available in the middle-class home, is the major experiential deficit of such a child (Bernstein, 1960). A study of the effects of teaching language skills to disadvantaged children on a tutorial one-to-one basis (Blank and Solomon, 1968) concluded that these children will develop a firm language base for thinking when they are given consistent guidance and frequent reinforcement of new skills. Studies of this kind reflect the recognition that language holds a central position in the process of cognitive growth.

In order to meet the problems of the disadvantaged preschool child, educators have developed two basic kinds of programs. One is *child-centered:* The child is given compensatory training at centers outside the home. The other is *parent-centered:* The parents are taught skills to use in educating their children. The programs can,

PARENTS AS TEACHERS In a study of how mothers teach their children, Hess and Shipman (1967, p. 10) found that mothers' techniques differ widely by social class. The following are typical examples of mothers' strategies. Which column represents a more helpful learning situation? Why do you think these differences occur?

Teaching Techniques

MIDDLE-CLASS MOTHERS

LOWER-CLASS MOTHERS

1a. "I've got another game to teach you."

1b. "There's another thing you have to learn here, so sit down and pay attention."

2a. "Now listen to Mommy carefully and watch what I do because I'm going to show you how we play the game."

2b. "Pay attention now and get it right, 'cause you're gonna have to show the lady how to do it later."

3a. "No, Johnny. That's a big one. Remember we're going to keep the big ones separate from the little ones."

3b. "No, that's not what I showed you! Put that with the big ones where it belongs."

4a. "Wait a minute, Johnny. You have to look at the block first before you try to find where it goes. Now pick it up again and look at it—is it big or small? . . . Now put it where it goes."

4b. "That doesn't go there— you're just guessing. I'm trying to show you how to do this and you're just putting them any old place. Now pick it up and do it again and this time don't mess up."

5a. "No, we can't stop now, Johnny. Mrs. Smith wants me to show you how to do this so you can do it for her. Now if you pay close attention and let Mommy teach you, you can learn how to do it and show her, and then you'll have some time to play."

5b. "Now you're playing around and you don't even know how to do this. You want me to call the lady? You better listen to what I'm saying and quit playing around or I'm gonna call the lady in on you and see how you like that."

of course, be combined. An evaluation of the parent-centered type of program suggests not only the need for early and continuing education of the child, but also the need for early and continuing support for parents in their roles as educators of their own children (Schaefer, 1972). Educators clearly understand and readily admit that parents have a tremendous influence on their children's cognitive development.

THE CASE FOR PRESCHOOL EDUCATION. In recent years, interest in preschool programs in the United States has grown enormously. The reasons for this include the changing economic and sociological patterns in our culture, among other things. Alterations in the consciousness and life-style of women constitute one of the major reasons for this surge of interest. More women than ever before are engaged in part-time or full-time work outside their homes; and many of these women have young children. This departure from what had been considered the traditional role of women has brought up many questions: If a mother works, who is to assume her teaching role in the child's early years? In the absence of a mother's constant presence in the home, what kinds of programs can be instituted that will help the child develop his cognitive capacities?

Interest in preschools also reflects the growing realization that the traditional methods of education have scarcely tapped a child's capacity to learn, whereas so-called modern techniques have produced dramatic effects in increasing a child's rate of mental development and in expanding his abilities. For example, with certain new techniques, preschoolers have learned the strategies necessary to solve algebraic problems and spell complex words, as well as to read and write. Many of the innovative techniques were tried first in preschools operating as research centers or in preschools for the children of relatively affluent parents.

A growing concern for the cognitive development of the children of the poor is still another reason why interest in preschool programs has grown. It has often been the case that a disadvantaged child, upon entering elementary school, is unable to keep up with the work of the class. Frequently, as we have noted, the child's home environment is deficient in the stimulation necessary for cognitive growth of the sort required by the classroom teacher. The preschool has been suggested as a source for such early stimulation when it is lacking in the home. In many instances, too, the child's mother must work to support the family or supplement its income. Thus a substitute is needed for the mother-as-teacher role. It is hoped that the preschool can help fill this gap.

The movement for the creation of day-care centers in the United States has been led in large measure by working mothers themselves. Along with this has come the realization on the part of industrial executives and government officials that, for their own purposes, preschools are both necessary and advantageous. For example, a working mother who does not have to worry about the care her children are receiving in her absence is likely to be more productive on the job. Day-care centers were instituted during World War II, when due to a labor shortage many women joined the

Preschool Education Programs

labor force; but with the war's end, the government withdrew funding and such centers were discontinued. In the 1960s, the issue was again brought to public attention—but with a shift in focus: Not only did mothers want federally funded day-care centers reinstituted, they also wanted to assure that the quality of care and training that the preschoolers would receive in these centers would be high. Mothers demanded something more than free babysitting programs; they wanted well-supervised experiential environments in which their children could learn.

Basic to the thoughts of educators when they seek to establish preschool programs has been the all-important understanding that a child's needs differ from those of adults. Facilities and programs in the past focused on the physical, social, and emotional development of the child. Today, although these factors are still very much taken into account, the focus has shifted to the cognitive development of the child.

Questions for Thought

How can the cognitive needs of the young child best be met? Through interaction with his mother at home? Or in a national system of preschool programs in which teachers have received special training to meet the needs of the child?

MONTESSORI METHOD.   Once we accept the concept of preschool education as a whole, we must proceed to determine what developmental materials to include in such a program and the proper method of using them.

As early as the turn of the century, Maria Montessori (1909/1964), an Italian educator whose theories have since been implemented all over the world, used sensorimotor materials and reality-oriented experiences to accelerate early cognitive development. She also suggested effective attitudes as well as a free and open atmosphere for learning. In schools that follow the Montessori method, preschoolers are not segregated by age; instead, each child develops at his own individual pace. The children are encouraged to use the materials at their disposal to, in effect, teach themselves. The role of the teacher (whom Montessori called a "directress") is to skillfully manipulate and supervise the overall learning environment so as to promote activities and experiences helpful to the total development of the child.

Under the Montessori method, children as young as 4 have demonstrated the ability to read and write. Children may be urged to handle letters and shapes cut out of sandpaper, with the teacher stating the name of each one as the children touch it. This active manipulation of the materials helps the children to differentiate between sizes and shapes, a perceptual task that must be accomplished before beginning to read. Once the teacher feels that the children know the names and sounds of letters, they are encouraged to begin to try to spell words on the blackboard. Montessori called this "spontaneously bursting into reading and writing."

Although Piaget and Bruner differ in their emphases, we can find the rationale for schools such as these, designed for optimal cognitive development, in both their theories. In Bruner's theory, you will recall, learning begins as soon as a child shows any signs of being able to understand the concept involved in learning a specific task. In Piaget's theory, learning activities must be matched to a child's stage of cognitive development.

STAGE-DEPENDENT CURRICULUM.   An outline has been formulated of a preschool curriculum based specifically on Piaget's stage-dependent theories (Kamii, 1972). Each phase of the program is planned so as to advance the child from one set of mental operations to the next. The curriculum is designed to develop the child's internal processes (rather than external behavior) of cognitive growth and to increase his opportunities to eventually attain the formal operations stage of thinking. This is to be accomplished by promoting his natural curiosity and initiative through active exploration, experimentation, and questioning. By providing curriculum materials that cover physically observable knowledge, social knowledge, and logicomathematical knowledge, and by encouraging the use of such materials, it is hoped that the teacher will enhance the child's creativity and his confidence in his growing capabilities.

As this projected curriculum indicates, in order for cognitive potential to develop, a learning environment must be rich in stimuli. If, however, a child doesn't have such an environment, what would be the optimal time to begin an enrichment program to provide this stimulation. According to one study (Caldwell, 1968), the best time is during the first 3 years of life. The goal for the enrichment program that was set up with disadvantaged children from 6 months to 3 years of age was to teach them the skills for future development that advantaged children of the same age would have achieved. Specific learning activities were programmed in (1) personal-social attributes; (2) sensory, perceptual, and cognitive functions; and (3) culturally relevant knowledge.

At the end of the program, the children had increased several points on the IQ tests that had been administered at the start of the program. Furthermore, those who remained in the program for the longest period showed the greatest gains, as did those from the most disadvantaged and disorganized homes. Thus, it does seem likely that providing an enriched environment at an early age can facilitate development that would not otherwise occur, although further tests and studies are still being made to complete the data.

DIRECT INSTRUCTION.   A different approach to preschool programs whose aim is to increase cognitive development in disadvantaged children is taken by Bereiter and Engelmann (1966). Their program is designed to provide direct instruction in cognitive areas only, rather than a total environment, and it deals specifically with highly structured drills and practice in language, arithmetic, and reading. The learning procedures move at a rapid pace, especially in language learning, and rely heavily on imitation and reinforcement. Although some critics argue that social and personality development are not given consideration in this program, its supporters note that IQ gains of 10 to 30 points in one year justify it sufficiently. (This program as well as Head Start are discussed at length in Chapter 10.)

HEAD START.   Probably the best-known enrichment program for disadvantaged children is Head Start, created by the federal government in 1964 and federally funded. Since that time millions of preschool children have been enrolled in various programs designed to prepare them to enter first grade on a cognitive level at a par with that of middle-class children. The programs have not been standardized throughout the country; rather, each community determines for itself which needs are most important and then devises its own materials and methods to meet these needs. For example, some Head Start educational centers have stressed cognitive growth through programs that develop language skills, reading, and number concepts; others have concentrated on cultural aspects of development by means of planned trips, art projects, and creative play. In this sense, Head Start is considered child-centered; but it is also parent-centered in its efforts to teach parents the importance of later educational and intellectual stimulation.

Assessments of the effectiveness of Head Start programs have been mixed. Some studies conclude that although children in Head Start programs have achieved cognitive gains, the gains have not been long-lasting (Cicirelli et al., 1969; Rosensweet, 1971). The main problem appears to be that the short-term gains the children make while in the program are not followed through when the children enter the regular elementary school system. Thus, Head Start cannot be considered in isolation; what happens *after* Head Start is just as crucial.

TELEVISION.   As we mentioned in the previous chapter, television has an enormous impact on the socialization of children. And, as used as a medium of instruction, educational TV has become an extremely important teaching tool. *Sesame Street*, a program designed to help children learn basic facts and skills, is educational TV's "star teacher." It has been shown that the more children watch the program, the more school skills they learn (Bogatz and Ball, 1971).

Sesame Street pupils show greater enthusiasm for school and readiness for the concepts being taught than do children who do not watch the program. These effects cut across socioeconomic boundaries; all children can profit from the program equally.

The potential of ETV has still not been fully tapped for its applications to the classroom nor for further programming into the home for preschool and school-age children.

When I worked with educators in Yugoslavia in 1972, I found that they were extremely interested in educational TV as a method of educating children, had been examining *Sesame Street* at great length, and at that time were planning to introduce similar programming. The use of educational TV seems to be rapidly becoming international.

Should the application of Piagetian principles stop at the level of preschool education? One proposal suggests that the entire elementary school curriculum could be based on the development of Piagetian thought structures (Furth, 1970). The curriculum would be

Elementary School Programs

THE OPEN CLASSROOM

The open classroom is a new approach to teaching that discards the traditional elementary classroom setup in which children sit at their desks, with everyone doing (or trying to do) the same thing as the teacher instructs from "center stage." Instead, in the open classroom, the room is divided into functional areas rich in learning resources; the child is free to roam about the room and use them as he wishes. A teacher and aides work with the children individually or in small groups, rarely presenting the same material to the class as a whole.

The open classroom is related to the work of Piaget. From his studies comes this concept central to the approach:

The child must be able to try things out to see what happens, manipulate objects and symbols, pose questions and seek their answers, reconcile what he finds at one time with what he finds at another, and test his findings against the perceptions of others his age. Activity essential to intellectual development includes social collaboration, group effort, and communication among children. Only after a good deal of experience is the child ready to move on to abstract conceptualizations.

The teachers begin with the assumption that the children want to learn and will learn in their fashion; learning is rooted in firsthand experience so that teaching becomes the encouragement and enhancement of each child's own thrust toward mastery and understanding. Respect for and trust in the child are perhaps the most basic principles underlying the open classroom (Gross and Gross, 1970, pp. 71–73).

(Joel Gordon)

geared to building the thought structures of the concrete operations stages by providing the child with exercises to trigger mental operations that develop and stabilize these structures. Its aim would also be to develop spontaneous thinking that would lead the child to the beginnings of formal operational thought. Operational steps and stages in development are the key elements in such a curriculum.

The reading skill, as an aspect of intellectual development, has received widespread attention in recent years. It is understood that with the ability to read a child can make long strides toward eventual full cognitive growth. In addition to its value as a source of stimulation, reading also has a psychological impact, which in turn affects cognitive development. Whether a child can read or not is a crucial factor in his self-esteem; and his ability to handle other development tasks is strongly affected by his performance in this area (Havighurst, 1952). Clearly, in a text-oriented educational system such as ours, the ability to read is a necessary condition for academic achievement.

Formerly, it was believed that instruction in reading should wait until a child was "ready." This assumption was based on the belief that reading readiness develops through maturation and cannot be modified by teaching. The work of Montessori, previously cited, did much to alter, if not dismiss, such assumptions.

While visiting Cyprus in 1972, I was particularly impressed by the early age at which children there were being taught cognitive skills. Preschool Turkish Cypriot children were being taught to read and write and did quite well at both. They were also taught advanced mathematics. Although their reading abilities may have been due in part to the highly phonetic nature of the Turkish language, the fact remains that they acquired these abilities at a very early age. It remains for future studies to determine whether this development of skills significantly affects their later school performance.

The issue of the best approach to teaching reading is still an open one, with various methods ranging from "whole word" to "phonics." Some psychologists feel the only way to resolve the question is to treat reading as a learning problem, to research the subject from the view of psychological analysis, in effect to ask: What is it that a skilled reader has learned? Only then can we devise teaching methods that provide training in the operational steps of the process (E. J. Gibson, 1965).

Questions for Thought

The inability of so many students in American educational systems to read is a problem that shocks, angers, and saddens parents, teachers, the educational establishment, and students themselves.

Many attribute this inability to inappropriate teaching techniques used by reading teachers. Still others associate the problems with ineffective language development programs. Can you locate other possible causes as well? In the school? At home?

What approaches should the teacher take toward the student who cannot read at the level considered normal for his age and grade?

SUMMARY

Language development is intrinsic to cognitive development. Whether the acquisition of language is the result of maturation, learning, or both, the language environment of a child is crucial to later achievement.

Maturational development is fundamental to stage-dependent theorists, such as Piaget, who argue that a child's ability to perform specific mental operations is directly related to his stage of development on a gradually rising continuum of cognitive growth. Specific learning tasks must therefore be matched to his maturational stage, out of which his level of cognitive development emerges, in order that the learning be assimilated and accommodated. Cognitive development proceeds, through a process of equilibration, from one plateau to another, each plateau incorporating the skills acquired in preceding ones.

Learning-environmental theorists argue that development is based not so much on maturation as on the environment through which a child comes to know and understand the world around him. He learns, thus developing cognitively, from an environment that provides a rich variety of stimuli. Such an environment has been found in so-called advantaged homes, but may be deficient in the homes of disadvantaged children. Thus, educators have implemented compensatory programs for children in the latter group. Studies of these programs indicate that environmental enrichment programs can be instituted at far earlier ages than previously thought possible, but that the benefits will be sustained only if later educational programs reinforce these early gains.

Stage-dependent and learning-environmental theories can provide the framework for educational curricula in both preschools and elementary schools. Whether a child learns because he develops or develops because he learns, the role of the educator is to design programs that efficiently and effectively capitalize on a child's unique capacities and help him toward full cognitive development. Such programs have been implemented, for example, in respect to reading, a basic skill that, like language, plays a critical role in all later learning. The importance of these programs, especially their relevance for disadvantaged children, will be discussed further on in the text.

SUGGESTED FOR   Chall, J. *Learning to read: The great debate.* New York: McGraw-Hill, 1967.
FURTHER READING   This book, based on research and classroom studies, discusses the controversy over the various methods of teaching reading. It also includes
excellent examples of the traditional (published prior to 1967) basal reading
series.

Cole, M., and Scribner, S. *Culture and thought.* New York: John Wiley, 1974.
The complex relationships and the cognitive processes are presented here.
Although this book emphasizes cross-cultural studies, it has definite im-
plications for education in America.

Furth, H. *Piaget for teachers.* Englewood Cliffs, N.J.: Prentice-Hall, 1970.
This is an easy-to-read-and-comprehend summary of Piaget's ideas, especially as they relate to school-age children.

Parker, R. *The pre-school in action.* Boston: Allyn & Bacon, 1972.
In this comprehensive survey of the major existing preschool programs,
twelve specific preschool curricula are reviewed and compared.

DEVELOPING IDENTITY AND VALUES: THE ADOLESCENT YEARS

After completing this chapter, the reader should be able to:

1 Describe and evaluate the theories of personality, identity, value, and moral development in terms of how each explains the adolescent "identity crisis."

2 Identify the leading theorists in this area, and describe the processes outlined by each that contribute to an understanding of adolescent personality.

3 Interpret the roles of parents and teachers as models, and discuss the effects these figures have on the developing adolescent.

4 Describe and give examples of teacher behaviors most suitable to the development of high self-esteem and moral behavior in students, taking into consideration the important environmental variables affecting this development.

5 Explain the sources of conflict in the life of the adolescent, and suggest methods that might be used by the classroom teacher to reduce them.

CHAPTER 3

ADOLESCENCE: THE SEARCH FOR IDENTITY AND VALUES

In the previous chapters, we have limited our discussion to the preschool and elementary school child. But does that mean that social and cognitive development cease at age 12 or 13? The answer of course is no. The period that we will now consider, *adolescence*—which begins with the spurt of physical growth at pubescence and ends with "maturity," or adulthood—is one of great change.

Society demands that the adolescent learn to deal with a world that has become for him exceedingly complex—that he accept responsibility for his actions, that he discover who he is and where he is going. Adolescence is often called a period of "storm and stress": The adolescent's body is changing; he is undergoing emotional and social upheavals that accompany these changes; and he must meet new expectations of those around him. The adolescent's foremost problem in this turbulent period is defining his own personality; that is, his *identity* and *values*.

The adolescent's search for identity—the factor in his personality that makes him unique—is an intense struggle to answer two basic questions: "Who am I?" and "Who am I not?" (Erikson, 1963, 1968). Although prepubescent children ask themselves these questions too, it is in adolescence that the individual comes to feel that if he can answer these questions, he can "make it on his own." And these basic questions lead him to ask other, more specific ones, which will have an impact on his future: "Why am I here in school?" "Why am I studying geometry or French or American history or anything?" "Why am I spending time preparing for this examination?" "What does being a man (or woman) mean for the future course of my life?"

The biological changes of adolescence are another aspect of the search for identity. "Who am I now that I inhabit a new body?" To the adolescent, these physical changes are a source of anxiety, partly because the adolescent himself must learn to accept them, and partly because society regards the physically developing adolescent in a contradictory way: It recognizes his developing physical "adulthood" but also limits his freedom by treating him as a child.

"Who am I?" also means "What do I believe?" That is, "What is my moral structure, how does my conscience tell me to act?" Morality, which constitutes yet another aspect of personality, includes the development and expression of what we think of as "conscience." This involves the internalization of values accepted by society. As our consciences develop, most of us feel a sense of obligation to behave in accordance with the norms of our society. Yet at the same time we acquire the ability to engage in critical analysis of these values and expectations and, where necessary, to reject them in favor of what our consciences tell us is right or wrong. This examina-

THE ADOLESCENT SUBCULTURE

Is there such a thing as an adolescent subculture? Many psychologists feel that one does exist and that it is characterized by distinct preferences and styles in clothing, language, political beliefs, and social values. According to J. S. Coleman (1970), adolescents create their own world because they consider the adult world a meaningless sham in which actions are often at variance with the principles that are espoused. Thus, adolescents become "aliens" in the adult world and out of their dissatisfaction create their own culture.

Another explanation for the adolescent subculture is that it is a socially distinct unit that has resulted from changing sociological patterns. Coleman suggests, for example, that the so-called hippie culture evolved to meet a pressing psychological need: the need for a sense of shared belonging in an isolating adult society that stresses competitive individualism.

tion of values and expectations involves a process of discrimination that is often a further source of anxiety for the adolescent. Consider this country's military actions in Indochina: The soul-searching about the morality of our involvement there was widespread. In particular, think of the conflicts created in draft-age young men, many of whom were adolescents: "Do I serve in the army and fight in a war my government obviously supports, even though I believe it is morally wrong?"

In his search for identity, the adolescent must determine how he is going to behave and what his attitudes toward himself and others are going to be. Imitation of adult models will strongly influence the adolescent in his decisions. And once again conflicts arise: "How am I to act," he might ask himself, "when I see my father cheat on his taxes and my teacher lie to the principal? Who, then, am I to model myself after?"

Given this overall picture of the stresses of adolescence, let us now examine the developmental processes at work. As in theories of cognitive development, two theories of personality development predominate: the stage-dependent approach and the learning-environmental approach. While we look at these, keep in mind that many psychologists believe that once a specific personality characteristic is developed in childhood, it remains stable to adulthood (Kagan and Moss, 1960; Perkins, 1958).

Questions for Thought
Think back to the "storms and stresses" of your own adolescence. What conflicts did you have? About your body? Your values? Your social behavior?

How did you resolve the question of who you are?

How might an understanding of how you "came through" help you as a parent or teacher to give guidance to adolescents experiencing these same conflicts today?

THEORIES OF IDENTITY DEVELOPMENT

Stage-Dependent Theories

In stage-dependent theories, the developmental process is seen in terms of a sequence of maturational stages that occur in a fixed and predictable order. A person must successfully complete one stage before advancing to the next. Differences within the individual from one period of childhood to another are much more important to the stage-dependent theorist than differences between children at any one period. Interest in the dynamics of identity development overrides any concern with the effects of the environment. In order to fully understand the significance of these theories for adolescence, we must briefly go back to a discussion of childhood.

FREUD.   Sigmund Freud (1938), the first psychologist to emphasize the developmental aspects of personality, believed that what happens in early childhood is critical in determining the child's future personality and ability to adjust to life. According to Freud, all children acquire their basic personalities, including their identities, by age 5, and it is considered unlikely that any major personality change will take place after this (Hall and Lindzey, 1957).

ERIKSON.   Erik Erikson (1963, 1968), a leading proponent of stage-dependent theory, has expanded on Freud's version of personality development to give further emphasis to social and cultural influences. Erikson speaks of eight stages of man, each of which centers around a different type of developmental crisis associated with a particular time of life (see Table 3-1). In his view, personality development is a life-long process, influenced by the tug between positive and negative poles.

Table 3-1
Erikson's Eight Stages of Man

Trust vs. mistrust: infancy
Autonomy vs. shame and
 doubt: first 3 years
Initiative vs. guilt:
 ages 3 to 6
Industry vs. inferiority:
 age 6 until puberty
Identity vs. role
 confusion: adolescence
Intimacy vs. isolation:
 adulthood
Integrity vs. despair:
 old age

An individual's need to engage in critical self-evaluation, to reassess who and what he is, is probably a lifelong phenomenon. Erikson sees the problem of identity as reaching a crisis during adolescence. This crisis is seen as "a necessary turning point, a critical moment, when development must move one way or another" (Erikson, 1963). In other words, even though the development of identity begins in early childhood, the struggle to see it crystallized and integrated is a developmental task for adolescence. Specifically, the task is to develop what Erikson calls a "positive ego identity." This is a reality-based conviction that (1) one is capable of deriving appropriate pleasure and prestige from mastery of the environment, and (2) one is moving forward toward a meaningful future. The

high school student who has selected a future career and is studying successfully to prepare himself for that career is said to have a
positive ego identity. The student who still questions the relevance
of everything society has to offer him succeeds in accomplishing
nothing toward reaching some control of his world, and usually
drops out. Such an individual is said to be in a state of "identity
crisis." Only when positive ego identity is finally attained are firm
ideological commitments possible, and the identity crisis of adolescence is said to be over.

Many adolescents making their way through the identity crisis
suffer the developmental hazard that Erikson calls "identity diffusion," or confusion about one's role. Part of this confusion can be
explained by taking a look at the world surrounding the adolescent:
It is almost overwhelmingly complex, disquieting, and disjointed;
members of society no longer seem to share a common body of experience or a sense of group involvement and continuity, as they
did in the past; adult models of character and identity seem vague
or disorganized; the number of available roles has vastly multiplied;
and authority figures do not seem to merit the respect they were
once accorded.

Evidence of identity diffusion can be clearly seen in the classroom. A teacher calls for analysis and evaluation of a particular issue; the student too often gives a stereotyped response, which he
has learned from those around him; the teacher's response—"Yes,
but what do *you* think?"—is met simply with baffled hostility.

The adolescent also exhibits identity diffusion in following the
behavior of his peers, for they, at least, appear to have some kind of

Imitating the behavior of one's peers is a characteristic feature of adolescence.

(Joel Gordon)

identity, in terms of a social role, that he can adopt in the absence of his own. For example, he may cut a class when they do, even though he may actually like the subject.

Often, in an attempt to come to terms with what *he* thinks, believes, or desires, the adolescent rejects all the values of the adult society. As a consequence, he may become apathetic, and refuse to attend school—or hostile, and threaten his teacher. Both behavior patterns are familiar today, and both are signs of acute distress in the adolescent. Erikson, for one, feels it is a grave mistake to pin the label "criminal" on these adolescents without regard for the underlying personality dynamics that help to explain their behavior.

Learning-Environmental Theories

Learning-environmental theorists of identity development seek to specify the learning processes that cause the developmental stages to occur. Identification is one of these learning processes, and Jerome Kagan, among other contemporary researchers, is involved in the issue of how it is learned.

Identification resembles imitation in some ways, since both involve learning by modeling. Identification, however, is more than just imitation of a model; it is also a cognitive process wherein the child adopts for himself the standards of the model by which he can judge his own behavior (Reese and Lipsitt, 1970). For example, when the teacher is called away from the classroom, a student might parade in front of the class and perform the same behaviors he has seen the teacher perform. In this situation, the student is *imitating* the teacher. But when the teacher specifically requests a student to take charge of a class in his absence, and the student behaves the way he believes the teacher would in such a situation and feels the frustration of coping with rowdiness, the student is *identifying* with the teacher. Thus, identification requires internalization; once a person learns a certain mode of behavior, whatever motivates that behavior comes from within the individual himself, not from changing conditions in the environment.

Prohibition learning and *identification with the aggressor* (Kagan, 1958) are two other types of learned behavior that occur together with the identification process. In the first, a child is taught certain "don'ts" by parents and other adult models. A child's adoption of these prohibitions is apparent to anyone who has watched a group of children playing "school." In the second type, the child identifies with the aggressor in a situation in which the aggressor's actions provoke anxiety (A. Freud, 1937). This process has also been called "defensive identification" (Mowrer, 1950). "Daddy's right, I told you not to do it," says the little boy to his brother, who is being spanked for misbehaving. Similarly, the teenager who is reprimanded by the principal for cutting school may not always be comforted by his peers; often he will be jeered at and ridiculed by those who didn't get caught, those who identified with the principal.

Why does a child identify with certain models and not with others? Such factors as the status of the model in the eyes of the child, the model's opportunities to exercise support and control, the child's view of the consequences of the model's behavior, and his view of the similarity of the model to himself will determine this (Bronfenbrenner, 1970). Through identification, the child both reduces anxiety and acquires (through his imagined participation) the same positive traits that he perceives in the model. In short, the learner reacts to events that occur to the model with whom he identifies just as if they were happening to himself (Kagan, 1958).

Questions for Thought
Since models clearly play major roles in the development of personality, what criteria should teachers apply in selecting figures—in history, in current events, in literature—to serve as models for children in their classes?
Similarly, what criteria should parents, school boards, and school administrators use to select teachers, who, as we know, are important models to children?

THEORIES OF VALUE DEVELOPMENT

As with theories of identity development, psychological explanations of the development of morality and values also fall into two general classifications: stage-dependent theories and learning-environmental theories. Jean Piaget and Laurence Kohlberg are influential stage-dependent theorists, and Albert Bandura is a leading learning-environmental theorist.

PIAGET. For Piaget (1933/1965), the development of morality and other values in children proceeds according to a system of rules and reflects specific kinds of attitudes acquired at a particular stage of development. From an investigation of children's attitudes and behavior with respect to the rules of the game of marbles and their consciousness of those rules, Piaget concluded that children go through a series of stages, which correspond to cognitive stages. When a child first learns to handle marbles, he is engaged in sensorimotor free play; he has no consciousness of the rules. Later on, he will imitate the rules he sees others use, regarding those rules as sacred and fixed, handed down by higher authority. Later still, he engages in more cooperative play, accepting the rules mutually observed by others playing the game, even though the rules may be

Stage-Dependent Theories

only vaguely understood by him. In the final stage, he understands the rules more realistically, not as something ritualistically adopted, and he gains an explicit understanding and use of those mutually acceptable rules.

Piaget also found that children undergo developmental changes in attitudes that involve morality rather than mere conformity to rules. That is, as children grow older, they crystallize their definitions of right and wrong. When Piaget presented some children under age 9 with stories in which a child did something wrong, they tended to evaluate the act solely in terms of its consequences, without any consideration of motives. In this framework, the behavior of the child who broke five cups accidentally would be judged as worse than that of the child who broke a single cup deliberately. Older children, on the other hand, tend to evaluate the apparent motives for the behavior before deciding how bad it is (Flavell, 1963).

The same tendency holds true for lying. Young children define a lie as any statement that is untrue, regardless of whether it is told unknowingly or deliberately, and they judge the severity of a lie solely in terms of its consequences. An unintentionally untrue statement that hurts somebody seems worse to them than a deliberate deception that does no appreciable damage. Older children, by contrast, seek to understand other aspects of a situation, such as intent.

Children of different ages vary in their view of justice as well

Piaget has found stage-dependent differences in the way in which children respond to discipline by authority figures.

(Bob Adelman, Magnum Photos)

(Flavell, 1963). According to Piaget, there are two kinds of what he calls *retributive justice*. In one, a child is punished (spanked, for example) for failing to do something he has been told to do, such as finishing his homework before he watches television. In the second, a child is not allowed to use the television for a specified time because he has watched television instead of finishing his homework. In the latter case, the punishment bears a logical relationship to the violation. But in both instances, the child sees the punishment as fitting the crime.

Presumably, younger children are more inclined than older ones to believe in the concept of *immanent justice*. For example, a young child who falls while running away with someone else's toy feels he has been injured *because* he has done something wrong.

Similarly, Piaget found developmental differences in *distributive justice;* that is, how rewards and punishments are handed out to the members of a group. Children under 7 tend to accept the decision of an authority figure as final; it does not matter to them whether or not everyone is treated fairly. Between the ages of 7 and 11, however, fairness becomes a major concern. And after this age, children are capable of seeing extenuating circumstances in each situation when they evaluate the distribution of justice.

In Piaget's theory of the development of moral judgment, there are two types of morality in children: a *morality of constraint*, whereby parental decisions are accepted as moral absolutes; and a *morality of cooperation*, which replaces the first by about age 11, and which grows out of the relationship among peers and is based on mutual, rather than unilateral, respect. In cooperative morality, the child makes and evaluates rules and principles on a rational basis, and his judgments take intentions into account. And, most important, at this stage of development the child feels personally responsible for the morality of his actions.

Moral development is built upon many experiences, of which parent-child interactions are very influential. One experimental study (Hoffman and Saltzstein, 1967) measured moral development among seventh grade middle-class children to determine its relationship to parental methods of discipline, based on reports by the children themselves as well as by the parents. Children who exhibited advanced moral development were found to have parents who tended not to capitalize on power and authority over the child, but rather directed the child's attention to the results of his actions on the feelings and welfare of others. Apparently, "might makes right" does not apply to the development of morality.

PARENTAL DISCIPLINE AND THE CHILD'S MORAL DEVELOPMENT

KOHLBERG.   Laurence Kohlberg's theory of moral development is also one of developmental sequences, and in many ways it adapts and further illustrates Piaget's concepts.

Kohlberg's theory (1964) of progressive stages of morality is derived from a study in which he interviewed boys 10 to 16 years of age on 10 hypothetical moral dilemmas. For instance: Joe's father promised Joe that he could go to camp if he earned the $50 for it; he then changed his mind and asked Joe to give him the money he had earned. Joe lied and said he had earned only $10 and went to camp using the rest of the money he had made. Before he went he told his younger brother Alex about lying to their father. The subjects were asked: If you were Alex, would you tell your father? From the boys' responses, Kohlberg defined six developmental types of value orientation, which he grouped into three moral levels (Table 3-2).

In the premoral level, the child determines if an act is right or wrong entirely by its consequences; his determination is an egocentric one. A child at Stage 1, for example, would respond to the hypothetical dilemma given earlier in terms of the physical consequences: "If I don't tell on my brother, and Dad finds out, he might get mad and spank me." Or: "I should keep quiet or my brother will beat me up." Later at this level, at Stage 2, the child would respond on the basis of anticipated rewards.

In Level II, the child conforms to stereotyped standards in order to gain approval; he has a very strong respect for authority and is moved by a sense of duty to behave as society dictates. Thus, most

Table 3-2
Kohlberg's Levels of Morality

Level and Stage	Illustrative Behavior
Level I. Premoral	
Stage 1. Punishment and obedience orientation	Obeys rules in order to avoid punishment
Stage 2. Naive instrumental hedonism	Conforms to obtain rewards, to have favors returned
Level II. Morality of conventional role conformity	
Stage 3. "Good-boy" morality of maintaining good relations, approval of others	Conforms to avoid disapproval, dislike by others
Stage 4. Authority maintaining morality	Conforms to avoid censure by legitimate authorities, with resultant guilt
Level III. Morality of self-accepted moral principles	
Stage 5. Morality of contract, of individual rights, and of democratically accepted law	Conforms to maintain the respect of the impartial spectator judging in terms of community welfare
Stage 6. Morality of individual principles of conscience	Conforms to avoid self-condemnation

Source: Kohlberg, L. (1963). Adapted from Hilgard, Atkinson, and Atkinson (1975, p. 80).

likely the child would think that Alex should tell his father about Joe's lie because his father "knows what's best."

In Level III, the individual's notions about right and wrong are those general principles or laws agreed upon by his society. At the same time, however, he makes judgments on the basis of a personal value system and rationally decides that to disobey may be more desirable than to obey a law blindly. The individual's conscience and self-chosen, abstract moral principles guide him. He conforms to these principles in order to integrate what is morally relevant in a given situation and to make a decision that he can live with comfortably. Children at this level would probably think that Alex should not tell his father, because, given that he had already promised, his father was wrong in not letting Joe go to camp.

In evaluating this evidence, Kohlberg (1963) points out that it is inadequate to view moral development solely as a process of socialization, or the internalization of the rules of society. Rather, changes in moral thinking result from a continual interaction between the individual and his environment.

Questions for Thought

Kohlberg's Stage 6 of moral development suggests that people conform to their individual consciences in order to avoid self-condemnation.

What would be the implications for our society if all citizens developed to this stage?

If the development of self-accepted moral principles were the goal of educators in our public schools, what conflicts might arise?

PIAGET AND KOHLBERG: A COMPARISON.　Kohlberg agrees essentially with Piaget that we can predict changes at various ages in the process of moral development. Both see the child's moral development as a progression from the simple to the more complex, or from egocentric to altruistic, as the result of encounters with the environment (his parents and teachers, for example) and growing cognitive competence (his ability to understand and solve more complex problems). *conclusion*

Both theorists believe that moral structure (like cognitive structure) must constantly be redefined in the individual. That is, when a new moral dilemma is introduced, the structure may be thrown off balance, and a new equilibrium must be established.

But Kohlberg and Piaget disagree on some points. For example, Kohlberg does not feel that older children necessarily shift from unilateral obedience to authority to mutual respect within the peer group, a point that Piaget makes. In addition, he does not consider Piaget's dimensions of morality as falling neatly into distinct unitary stages. It is possible, he maintains, for a child to be at the autonomous, or self-governing, stage in one aspect of morality, but at a lower stage in other dimensions (Kohlberg, 1964).

The reason for the young child's concern with punishment is another point about which the two theorists disagree. The behavior of a young child at home and in class is determined largely by whether his parents and teachers reward or punish him. Although Piaget and Kohlberg agree that a preschool child considers an act to be right or wrong solely in terms of its consequences, their explanations differ. According to Piaget, the child sees the adult authority as sacred, and this temporarily blocks his use of cognitive resources for independently judging the appropriateness of an act—either his own or that of another person. If this is true, it would be important to maintain a good model in the figure of a parent or teacher. According to Kohlberg, the child simply has a desire to acquire reward and to avoid punishment. ·

PIAGET AND KOHLBERG: IMPLICATIONS FOR EDUCATION.   Educators ask: How can formal education enhance moral growth? As we have seen, both Piaget and Kohlberg assume that during each stage of development toward moral maturity the individual interacts with his environment. Applying their theories to formal education would require introducing appropriately matched educational experiences that reflect real-life moral issues of direct concern to students, either as individuals or collectively, as members of society. A social science or literature course seen in this way should be designed to develop both logical and moral thought.

TEACHING FOR LIFE ADJUSTMENT

Although "life adjustment" courses are not new in American high schools, they are often dull. But there's a new one so popular that it has a waiting list ("Divorce Course," *Time,* 1974). Since 1970, Parkrose High School in Portland, Oregon, has been offering Contemporary Family Life, a 12-week course that begins with the students pretending to get married and ends with them pretending to get divorced. They search for an apartment, look for a job, prepare a budget, have a baby, buy a house, see a lawyer for a divorce—all simulations of the social, economic, and moral issues of real married adult life. Guests from the community—insurance agents, realtors, bankers, clergymen, marriage counselors, and lawyers—frequently meet with the class. Issues pertaining to the development of identity are discussed—personally and openly. Although the insights that students gain about "real life" are often disillusioning ("and they lived happily ever after" isn't always the case), one thing is certain—these students *learn*. Curriculum designs like this demonstrate the excitement of intelligently planned "reality orientation."

A teacher should never presuppose a student's level of develop-ment—that is, his capabilities for reflective or critical thinking and for problem-solving. The concepts of matching and timing enter here as in cognitive development. All too often, parents and teach-ers alternate between abstractions that the child cannot comprehend and explanations that underestimate his true grasp of a situation.

Kohlberg feels that by association with persons whose moral judgments reflect a higher stage in the developmental sequence, the child at a lower level will experience cognitive conflict, engage in introspection, and equilibrate to a more advanced stage. To provide the opportunity for this to take place, the teacher must make time for group discussion and clarify advanced levels of moral reasoning without resorting to preaching (Kohlberg, 1971). A student must be given the opportunity to "stretch" his own moral capacities, to ex-periment through interaction with others, without having imposed on him arbitrary standards that reflect the teacher's personal moral biases.

Formal character education classes in which teachers tell students how to act responsibly do not appear to have a demonstrable effect on children's moral conduct. Nevertheless, teachers should take an active interest in the moral education of their pupils, since, as we know, they are the primary adult source of moral evaluation and moral reasoning outside the home. Although some American edu-cators may reject as "moral indoctrination" the approach of the So-viet educational system, which is designed for character training (Bronfenbrenner, 1962, 1970), they must still be concerned with finding ways to help the student toward moral maturity.

Learning-Environmental Theories

The effects of learning on moral development are a primary concern of Albert Bandura, whose view is that children develop a moral sense by imitating the behavior of significant adults or peers in their environment; these serve as models for them. These imitated moral behaviors, having become those of the child, are then subject to the approval or disapproval of others in his environment, who provide the positive or negative reinforcement that influences his moral growth.

To determine how the behavior of models and social reinforce-ment combine to shape children's moral judgments, Bandura and McDonald (1963) conducted a study in which three groups of chil-dren, 5 to 11 years old, were presented with pairs of stories. One story described a person who acted with good intentions but caused damage; the other described a person who intended to hurt someone but actually did little harm. The children were asked to state "who did the naughtier thing" and why. Later, the first group observed adult models, who responded to the same stories. The models had higher levels of reasoning than the children and considered, for example, such things as intentions. When they imitated these adult responses, the children were praised by the experimenter. The second group also imitated the adult models, but they received no praise. The third group was not presented with models; however, they were praised when their responses exhibited a higher level of reasoning than would be expected for children of their age.

The judgmental responses of the children in the study were shown to be readily modifiable by the behavior of the adult models. Modeling and reinforcement combined did not have the expected effect of facilitating learning more than the presence of models alone, but Bandura suggested that this might have been due to the weak nature of the reinforcement. The use of reinforcement alone was least effective for promoting learning, since the children on their own rarely responded in a way that would lead to such reinforcement.

As expected, the older children learned from the models somewhat more readily than the younger children. However, although this would appear to be consistent with the stage-dependent explanation of morality, the results of the study do not entirely support this. The younger children were sometimes able to judge an act in terms of a person's motives (subjective aspects), whereas the older children sometimes judged an act solely in terms of its consequences (objective aspects). On the basis of the data it cannot be assumed that moral behaviors are necessarily age-specific.

Comparison of Two Approaches to Identity and Value Development

Stage-dependent psychologists, who agree that personality development occurs in a fixed and predictable sequence, do not deny the possible effects of environmental influences on a child's development. However, in their theories they give little consideration to how these influences operate on an individual basis (Snadowsky, 1973). Individual differences in development and their relation to such variables as sex, race, intelligence, social class, family, and cultural background are largely ignored.

The scope of the stage-dependent approach by itself seems narrow when set against the research on developmental differences, which has produced a large body of data attesting to the importance of environmental factors in shaping both the course and the rate of personal and social development. Johnson (1962), for example, found that moral development is related not only to age but also to sex, IQ, parents' occupations, and parental attitudes toward child rearing. Holstein (1969) found that certain patterns in family communication, such as warmth and encouragement, can facilitate moral development. Another study (Rebelsky, Allinsmith, and Grinder, 1963) indicated that there are sex differences in the development of morality; girls are more likely than boys to confess after misbehaving and tend to resist temptation more.

Clearly, then, the development of identity and values is not solely a matter of the unfolding of a sequence of stages. The role of environmental variables must be examined, too. Likewise, learning, which plays an important role in moral development, cannot be overlooked.

PLANNING FOR DEVELOPMENT OF IDENTITY AND VALUES

Home and family are critical in the development of the young child, and they continue to be important as he matures to adolescence. As the child approaches adolescence, however, the influence of the peer group on his development increases. Conflicts between parental values and peer group values erupt within the adolescent. Parents who make no attempt to understand their adolescent's peer group, or the central position that that group holds in the adolescent's life, will find that their ability to affect the personality development of their child will decrease markedly.

Child Rearing and the Family

In the years since World War II, child-rearing practices in the United States, particularly among middle-class families, have moved away from the strict, authoritarian, disciplinary techniques that were popular in the 1920s and 1930s and toward a general permissiveness.

Studies comparing the relative efficacy of different types of disciplinary measures have suggested that the love-oriented approach favored by the middle class is the most successful (Sears, Maccoby, and Levin, 1957; Miller and Swanson, 1958, 1960). Bronfenbrenner (1961) found that parents are generally more indulgent and protective with girls and more disciplinary with boys. According to the Bronfenbrenner study, teachers also tend to be more indulgent toward female students. But extremes in the direction of either affection or discipline have negative effects regardless of sex; girls are particularly affected by extremes of parental overprotection, and boys react most severely to a lack of discipline and parental support.

In addition, the sex of the parent who provides the discipline seems to affect the outcome of social and moral developments (Bronfenbrenner, 1961a). Both responsibility and leadership are fostered when the parent of the same sex has the relatively greater influence. The most dependent and least reliable adolescents are found in families in which the influence of both parents is about equal. The conclusion appears to be that children need same-sex models for guidance in social and moral development.

Changes in the structure of the American family have also contributed to changing patterns of child rearing (Toffler, 1970). The extended family of the past, in which grandparents and other relatives resided with parents and children, provided more attention, companionship, and assistance to the growing child. Continuous migration from small, close-knit rural communities to large, impersonal cities and suburbs; frequent job transfers requiring a family to move from one part of the country to another; the availability and convenience of the automobile and modern highway systems—these factors, which contribute to mobility, have contributed to making the nuclear family, rather than the extended family of the past, the dominant pattern.

Today, primarily because of the decline of the extended family structure, most parents must rear their children on their own. As economic pressures mount, more women are entering the labor force, which means that neither parent has much time to spend with the children. With the divorce rate on the rise, one-parent families have become common, which means even fewer adults to rely on for child rearing. The consequences have been that in many cases the emotional needs of children are being neglected. (Parents Without Partners is only one of many organizations helping to educate parents about the kinds of emotional problems that children face because of separation and divorce.) The question of whether the child's ever-present needs for attention and guidance are being met is an important one.

SELF-ESTEEM AND SELF-CONCEPT.   A very basic part of the influence that the family and the peer group have on the adolescent is in the formulation of his *self-esteem* (his attitude about his own *worth* as a person). One's self-esteem is intimately connected with one's *self-concept* (or *self-image*), the unified mental picture every individual has of himself. When a person experiences something new, he will either accept or reject this experience depending on whether it is compatible or in conflict with his self-image (Lecky, 1945; Rogers, 1951). One function of the self-concept is self-evaluation, by which the individual is able to measure past and present activities and predict probable success or failure in future activities. The self-concept also contains a self-enhancing aspect that urges the individual to make maximum use of his own potential. The mature individual has both an overall positive view of himself and a realistic acceptance of his limitations.

We learn both our self-concept and our self-esteem by integrating all the interactions between ourselves and our environment. In this sense, the process resembles other aspects of development. A child who is allowed to explore his environment is likely to develop a very different self-concept from the one developed by the child who

Acceptance by one's peers aids in the building of self-esteem.

(Margot Granitsas, Photo Researchers)

is fearfully overprotected by his parents. A child who senses that his parents and peers, as well as siblings and teachers, accept him for himself has a much better foundation on which to build self-esteem than a child who lacks this feeling of "fitting in."

The interaction between parent and child also contributes to the development of self-esteem. What components of family life cause a child to behave in a manner reflecting a certain level of self-esteem? In one study of self-esteem in boys (Coopersmith, 1967), the boys were categorized as low (sure they had no worth), medium (unsure), or high (thought they were good) in self-esteem on the basis of their self-evaluations, evaluations by others, and clinical evaluations. It was found that the boys' levels of self-esteem reflected those of their parents more than the actual ability of the boys themselves. For example, those who had a low level of self-esteem had mothers whose ratings in such characteristics as poise, assurance, and emotional stability were below average. On the other hand, boys who had more favorable views of themselves had parents whose self-esteem and stability ratings were also high.

The mothers of the boys with a high self-esteem level seemed to accept the responsibilities of motherhood realistically. They were neither punitive nor overly permissive; above all, they set clear and consistent standards for behavior. It was also apparent that the boys with high self-esteem tended to have closer relationships with their fathers. The mothers of boys with a low and middle level self-esteem tended to act in an inconsistent manner, being both highly punitive and permissive.

The boys with low self-esteem reported that their parents' values centered around such attributes as obedience, helpfulness, and good manners; the boys' desire to be acceptable and pleasing to others reflected these values. The boys with high self-esteem said that their parents stressed achievement; thus they were more inclined to feel that their parents valued their abilities and accomplishments.

These findings tell us that when parents are well adjusted, interested in their child (and his friends), and basically accepting (but within reasonable, clearly defined, and consistent limits), the child is more likely to want to identify with and try to emulate parentally approved behaviors. Equally important, he will have a much more positive attitude toward himself.

Social class and ethnic group (to be discussed at length in Chapter 10) and parental aspirations also have a bearing on the development of self-esteem. Adolescents are very sensitive to what their parents want them to achieve, and whereas encouraging and achievement-oriented parents can motivate the adolescent to be productive and successful, "pushy" parents can sometimes actually force their adolescents into deviant behavior. For example, when parental aspirations for academic success are unrealistically high, a higher incidence of cheating on the part of their adolescent children may occur (Pearlin, Yarrow, and Scarr, 1967). The "success at any cost" pattern of behavior is one that in the end inhibits individual growth.

Teachers should not fail to consider the family influence on the development of self-esteem in students. To do so would be to ignore an important component of the "whole" person they are seeking to educate. At the same time, they should seriously consider their own role in the development of self-esteem in their students.

Bronfenbrenner (1970) has suggested that the lack of contact between parents and children has led to an age-segregated society. Looking at the broad spectrum of family life in America, he said:

> American society emerges as one that gives decreasing prominence to the family as a socializing agent. This development does not imply any decrease in the affection or concern of parents for their children. Nor is it a change that we have planned or wanted. Rather it is the by-product of a variety of social changes, all operating to decrease the prominence and power of the family in the lives of children. . . . Our manifestations of progress have operated to decrease opportunity for contact between children and parents, or, for that matter, adults in general. (p. 99)

How are children to "see life whole," he asks, when the scope of their experiences, the values they come to see and understand, are limited to those of one age group—their peers? Adult models—not simply parents—exist in abundance, if adults will recognize and use themselves as models for the development of children. The school is obviously a primary source of these models.

The Peer Group

At what age does peer group influence, so important to adolescents, begin to assert itself? According to Bowerman and Kinch (1959), children start to shift their attention from their parents to their peers at about age 12. Hamm and Hoving (1969) indicate that children are strongly influenced by their peers as early as age 7. The tendency to lean on the peer group gradually increases toward adolescence. When tasks are clear, peer conformity decreases with age (that is, children select responses on their own), but when tasks are confusing, peer conformity increases (Hoving, Hamm, and Galvin, 1969). Thus, although peer group conformity seems to be a function of age level (Costanzo and Shaw, 1966), it is also a function of the task at hand.

The adolescent today confronts a complex social world in which he is largely segregated from adults who might guide him. Can his conformity to the social rules and norms of his peers in the face of such a confusing array of alternatives be surprising?

Several factors account for the strong influence that the peer group exerts on the adolescent. First, American parents do not spend much time with their children. This is due in part to the ado-

Sharing private information is an important part of social development.
(Robin Gibson, Alternative Curriculum)

lescent's own increased mobility and greater amount of time spent away from home. Second, every adolescent is deeply concerned with his own identity in the high school crowd, and he emulates group members who seem to be the most popular and successful. According to James Coleman (1961) in *The Adolescent Society*, American adolescents mold their aspirations and actions to follow the "in group" in their schools. Basic to communication with teenagers is an understanding of the value system of the peer group and the in-group/out-group structure that reflects it.

According to Ausubel (1954), the adolescent peer group performs several critical functions: (1) It gives or denies an individual status in his own right—that is, he is no longer identified by the status he obtains from his parents; (2) it has the potential for letting an adolescent know he is important; and (3) it provides a useful anchor and source of comfort during a difficult and troublesome period in which most adolescents share similar problems.

The relationship between peer group influence and parental influence on the adolescent is also important. Studies by Reiss (1968) and by Douvan and Adelson (1966) suggest that an adolescent tends to choose as friends those people who have the same basic attitudes and values as his parents, though perhaps in a somewhat more liberal form. When parental attitudes and those of the peer group conflict, however, the latter often win out (Reiss, 1968; Rosen, 1955). Reiss found that adolescents' attitudes about sex resembled those of their friends more than those of their parents. On the other hand, adolescents are likely to trust and be guided by their parents with regard to decisions about education and a career (McCandless, 1970). Obviously, peer group influence gradually declines as adolescents grow into young adults, leaving old friends behind and venturing out on their own into new experiences. (McCandless, 1970; Reese and Lipsitt, 1970).

The School CHARACTER TRAINING. Educators generally recognize that the schools' responsibility is more than the teaching of specific subjects; part of their job is to educate children in character and morals as well. However, because the ethical standards of our society are complex, confused, and extremely relativistic, even if a teacher presents the concepts of right and wrong unambiguously, there is no guarantee that the students' actual behavior will reflect these standards.

In a more general sense, we must ask: Does knowledge of right and wrong produce moral behavior? Hartshorne and May's (1930) character education inquiry (under the direction of E. L. Thorndike) investigated this. (Although this study was conducted many years ago, it still has relevance today.) Their goal was to measure the correlation between the child's perception of social processes (the moral consciousness he displayed) and the behavior he manifested. First, they described a situation for the child and asked what he would do if it were to occur—for example, what he would do if a fight broke out on the playground. Next, they placed the child in a test situation that would allow him to cheat, in order to see if there were a correlation between his social (moral) perceptions and the incidence of cheating. In essence, they asked: If a child has a high moral consciousness, are there still situations in which he will display immoral behavior, such as cheating? The results showed that there was no correlation between the knowledge of right and wrong and cheating, nor between either age or sex and cheating, although children from higher socioeconomic backgrounds and those with higher IQ's did tend to cheat less.

Character training in this country stresses the trait of obedience, which, in many ways, is necessary for social cohesion and functioning. Children are taught to "obey the rules," the laws of our society, be they proclaimed by parents, teachers, or government. At the same time, terrible crimes and great injustices have been committed in the name of obedience: The Nazis were "obeying orders" when they killed millions of Jews in concentration camps; how do we explain this? Is obedience always right? Or should character training provide for necessary conflicts between obedience and other values in certain situations?

In a controversial experiment designed to examine the issue of obedience (Milgram, 1963), 40 adult volunteers, all falsely assured that they were participating in a study of memory, were seated before what looked like (but was not) an electric shock generator that had switches labeled from 15 to 450 volts, with accompanying phrases ranging from "Slight Shock" to "Danger—Severe Shock." Another "volunteer"—in fact, an actor—was strapped into an "electric chair." The experimenter firmly instructed the subject to deliver to the man in the chair increasingly intense shocks each time the man gave a wrong answer to a question. None of the subjects walked out before delivering at least a 300-volt shock, despite their "victim's" obvious agony. Fourteen subjects walked out after this point, protesting the inhumanity of the experiment. But 26 subjects remained to the end, delivering the maximum shock repeatedly, despite the "victim's" continued gasps, screams, demands for release, and, finally, even fainting. The vast majority of them agonized over their actions, but they did what they knew to be wrong because they were ordered to do so by a seemingly competent authority!

The results of this experiment are grim. We cannot dismiss them, for the implications reach all of us. A teacher, for example, who is overly concerned with obedience training in itself can do great damage to a child's moral development by teaching blind obedience. Blind obedience takes away an individual's responsibility for his own actions and, by so doing, makes him less humane.

SELF-ESTEEM.   Schools influence self-esteem by providing variables that contribute to or diminish a student's feeling of self-worth. In school, each child has many opportunities to see how he measures up against others in terms of intelligence, physical skill, and popularity. This can contribute to the development of self-esteem, but the school can also hinder it if too much emphasis is placed on grades and conformity and if individual creativity is suppressed.

Teachers can help a child to develop self-esteem in several ways. They can set expectations that are appropriate for the age level and intellectual functioning of each of their students. They can stress positive activities and play down negative ones. They can also convey the feeling that they anticipate success. We saw earlier, in our discussion of the Coopersmith study, the importance of acting in a rewarding, unpunitive, and consistent manner.

When teachers are dealing with adolescents, they should make a special effort to understand the point of view of this age group (Felker, 1974). The adolescent needs opportunities to act independently but, at the same time, feel a sense of belonging. A student who misbehaves in class may be trying to act independently, even though this is not a very constructive way. The teacher should not see this as a threat to his authority and punish the student because of it. Rather, he should try to grasp the student's need by treating him as he would another adult. Teachers can also help adolescents by explaining what is happening to them—physically, socially, and emotionally—at this often confusing period in their development. Early-maturing girls and late-maturing boys need reassurance that there is nothing wrong with them. Probably most important, teachers should point out that there is nothing "wrong" with having conflicts, frustrations, and other emotional difficulties. They are not just part of adolescence; they occur throughout life. Dialogue with young people should emerge from the day-to-day encounters in the classroom, if and when the students express a need to discuss the things that are troubling them. Furthermore, such dialogue must come from a teacher's genuine interest; adolescents have an acute ability to detect phoniness.

Choosing a Vocation   In the adult world, work assumes much the same role as does school in the world of childhood. Adolescents often face a job market that is fiercely competitive and that offers somewhat limited options. In times of depressed economic conditions, such as the middle 1970s, businesses and government generally cut back on their employment offerings. This means that many adolescents must look for any job, rather than one that fits their abilities, interests, training, and ambitions.

Despite the economic slump, choosing and preparing for a vocation are an important part of developing one's identity. A person's vocation contributes to his feeling about his place in society and to his direction and purpose. In addition to its monetary aspects, work meets the basic human need to fill time with meaningful activity, to escape boredom and loneliness. And, to varying degrees, it can also provide fulfillment, challenge, and excitement. For some, work signifies autonomy, a necessary avenue to power and prestige, although for most it meets more immediate economic needs.

In the past, a woman's status often reflected her husband's occupation. But today, as more women move into the work force, they too must make early decisions about vocation and life-style.

Choosing a vocation is as basic a task to adolescence as coming to grips with the conflicts and frustrations arising from social interaction and the development of self-concepts. The vocational decisions made, with or without the guidance of others, will affect adolescents' future lives, for good or ill. Parents and teachers can—and must—help, since everyone in society has a stake in those future lives.

ADOLESCENCE: A TIME OF CONFLICT

Adolescence, as we mentioned before, includes many crises associated with developmental changes. It is a period for questioning, searching, learning, and discovery. The questions are immensely important: "Who am I?" "What can I contribute to society?" "What do I expect society to give me?" Obviously, not every adolescent in the United States deals with these questions in the same way. For many, the adolescent years pass relatively smoothly, whereas others seem to be pulled in all directions, filled with hostility, doubt, and confusion. Common to all, however, is an attempt to cope with the expectations and constraints of a society that seems perplexing and unyielding.

The adolescent whose search for answers is unsuccessful may become extremely alienated because he senses a basic dissimilarity between himself and the world. At times, this feeling of alienation leads the adolescent to a new sense of freedom and omnipotence ("I can do *anything; anything* is possible!"). To prove to himself that this freedom exists, he rejects social traditions. However, this rejection is frequently a desperate way of trying to build up a shaky self-concept. Ironically, a vicious circle often results, since discarding socially acceptable values and behavior patterns seems only to heighten the feeling of being out of step.

Adolescent conflict often takes the form of rebellion. This phenomenon is a widespread one, manifested in a variety of ways. In 1971, for example, incidents of violence occurred in the high schools of almost every major city in the United States. And for a time, huge numbers of adolescents turned to drugs as a means of rebellion. This act of rebellion cut across all social classes and reached into suburbs as well as cities.

Finding remedies to an adolescent's problems is as difficult as locating their causes. But one thing is clear: The adolescent with problems is likely to be unhappy and disruptive, if not downright destructive, and society has a responsibility to provide help and understanding.

Adolescent-Adult Conflict

Problems between adolescents and parents or teachers are frequently placed in the category "generation gap"—that war zone between adolescent and adult values where stormy conflicts break out. Arguments range from specific and seemingly trivial matters, such as dress style or dating privileges, to breakdowns in communication between adolescent and adult, a far more serious matter. The reassurance that this period of conflict is temporary, that it disappears as adolescents themselves become adults, is not very comforting to either parent or child.

Why does this phenomenon of intergenerational conflict exist? In part, it exists because the experiences, attitudes, and values of young people today are different from those of 30 years ago, and are therefore different from those of their parents. A second reason is that adolescents and adults are fundamentally different in both moral and cognitive development.

Psychoanalytic theory explains the "conflict of generations" as the reawakening of sexual impulses toward the parent of the opposite sex that was manifested during the phallic stage; one of the adolescent's problems is to resolve the conflict permanently (Freud, 1949). But the Freudian interpretation of this conflict has a serious weakness, in that it ignores social and cultural factors. Erikson, unlike Freud, recognizes the social nature of the generation conflict. According to Erikson (1968), there are two major sources of contention between adolescents and their parents: (1) the parents' failure to show recognition of adolescent achievement, and (2) the adolescent's rebellion against parental control.

Drugs, Delinquency, and Alienation

Drug abuse is an appalling reality in American society today. But it is deceptive to think that this behavior is limited to adolescents. In truth, for millions of American adults as well, alcohol, tobacco, and pills have become a way of life. The adolescent needn't look only to

**GENERATION GAP:
FACT OR FICTION?**

Turmoil and trouble are not necessarily characteristic of the relationship between parents and their adolescent offspring, but this is not to say that the relationship is always harmonious. The characteristic feature is *ambivalence*. For the adolescent, the movement toward adulthood can be exciting, but it is also anxiety provoking and somewhat saddening. The adolescent is torn between a sense of gain and a sense of loss. The parents are likewise ambivalent: On the one hand, they anticipate with pleasure the future adult status of their children; on the other, they sense that they will soon "lose" their children as they become autonomous, self-reliant individuals (Cottle, 1971).

To resolve these states of ambivalence, both adolescents and parents must make changes that will eventually lead to interpersonal accommodations. A social and value redefinition is necessary to gradually transform the concept of "family" for both parents and adolescents (Haan, 1971). The "gap" is a real one, but one that can be closed.

his peer group to find out about drug abuse; adults offer him comparable models. One sad result is that today alcoholism is no longer only an adult disease. In a nation in which 15 out of every 20 adults drink at least moderately, and 1 out of every 10 is a problem drinker, it should not surprise us that millions of American adolescents are turning to alcohol. Besides the examples set by an abundance of adult models, this trend is partly in response to warnings about the physical and legal consequences of using other drugs and partly because alcohol is relatively inexpensive.

Delinquency has also grown to frightening proportions, not only among adolescents but also among young adults and even preadolescents. Lawlessness and violence on the streets and in many classrooms are rising.

Delinquents are largely a product of the environment in which they grow up. Some commit crimes to relieve boredom and frustration, some are drug addicts who need money to support their habits, and others are trying to "get even" with their parents and society. At some point in their development most of these youngsters failed to accept the values and rules of their cultural background, and instead formed subcultures that developed their own rules and values. Delinquency, like other forms of deviant behavior, crosses all socioeconomic boundaries.

Although the home environment contributes significantly to delinquency, the overall disadvantaged environment in which some adolescents grow up influences them in this direction as well. They sense bleakness and bitterness about the future everywhere around them. And the same feelings are often aggravated by the school, where disadvantaged pupils find it hard to relate to either the curriculum or the teacher. Since many teachers subscribe to middle-class values and expectations, they may have difficulty understanding and relating to pupils whose values and standards are different from their own.

Experts who have studied delinquency largely reject the notion that the delinquent's behavior results from deep psychological problems. It is also misleading to categorize delinquency as a form of social maladjustment (Mouly, 1973). Indeed, many delinquents are very secure in their own subculture; they simply belong to a subgroup whose principles and values are incompatible with those of society as a whole.

On the other hand, society presents a somewhat deceptive image to the adolescent. The many examples today of hypocrisy and corruption in public life, along with the breakdown of traditional cultural values, family solidarity, and national pride, make it evident to the adolescent that adults do not always practice what they preach.

Schools today are meeting with little success in helping students adapt to the larger culture. The school dropout rate, for example, is high, especially in ghetto areas, where it is sometimes more than 50 percent. This is evidence of the failure of the educational system to make the values it represents seem relevant to these students. Their dissatisfaction with school is only one aspect of their basic disenchantment with themselves and society. They are all too aware of the gap that exists between aspirations and actualities.

Alienation in one of its most extreme forms occurs in the case of the adolescent runaway. Most runaways leave home only once; the causes are usually an argument with their parents, disillusionment with the school system, or discontent with other conditions in their environment. Although these individuals are no doubt troubled, their problems are basically the same in kind, if not in degree, as those that all adolescents face. There are, however, a small number of adolescents who do run away repeatedly and who often show signs of serious personal and family disintegration. They have histories of constant problems—disruptive behavior, truancy, criminal activities—and are in desperate need of professional help (Shellow, Schamp, Liebow, and Unger, 1967).

ADOLESCENTS AND SOCIETY: SUGGESTIONS FOR THE FUTURE

At the root of the sense of confusion, alienation, and futility experienced by many adolescents are the perceived ills of modern society. Thus, to explain the alienation and apathy of today's adolescents, we must take into account the gradual breakdown of basic American institutions (the family, school, neighborhood, and community), the socializing agents of our society.

If indeed our society is eroding, is there anything we can do to stop it? To this end, Bronfenbrenner (1972) has suggested that we utilize all our social institutions much more effectively so that they serve as support systems for children and their families. His specific recommendations include: (1) providing better-paying part-time employment for women who want or need to work so they can have more free time to spend with their children; (2) enhancing the traditional role of women in our society to enable them to feel real pride in their contributions; (3) reacquainting children with adults in the world of work—giving them some idea of what their parents actually do for that check that pays the bills.

Bronfenbrenner (1972) describes a program in Russia that could be applied here to implement his third point. In this program, a series of visits are arranged between groups of adults (working together in a shop, office, or factory) and groups of children, whom they "adopt." This brings the generations together: The adults have the opportunity to see the kinds of things children are doing, and the children become familiar with how and where adults make their living.

To continue Bronfenbrenner's suggestions: (4) modify adult work schedules to offer more flexibility and choice so that parents can spend more time with their children; (5) where work schedules don't allow for such flexibility, provide day-care centers that actively involve parents and that reach out into the home and community, utilizing adult models of all ages and occupations; (6) develop neighborhood and family centers that are open to everyone, where people of *all* ages can meet and establish a dialogue through which they may hear and understand viewpoints other than their own; (7) involve children in genuine responsibilities—not "make-work" tasks, but ones that have meaningful means and ends and that involve independent thinking and decision-making (how else can we expect the adolescent, for example, to understand and deal constructively with the tasks he will face); and (8) integrate the school into the broader social realities.

The experiences that children have in school should help them to develop a sense of responsibility and self-esteem. American education, with its almost exclusive emphasis on achievement in academic subject matter, seems peculiarly one-sided in comparison with other educational systems. Not only do American schools pay little attention to developing children's character, they regard the classroom as somehow sacred, as the only place where learning can take place, which virtually eliminates the opportunity for interaction among the school, home, and community. This segregation of the school from the rest of society is one of the factors contributing to the sense of alienation felt by so many adolescents.

Russian educators have found a way to integrate the school into the life of the community that might help us in this country. Besides the "group adoption" system previously described, there is another "adoption" system in the school itself, in which children in the higher grades assume some of the responsibilities for caring for the younger children. They escort them to school, play with them, teach them games, read to them, and help them learn. A similar program could be implemented here, or we could use day-care facilities as a place for older children to interact with young children. The possibilities and models exist; such a program should now be put into practice.

SUMMARY   Adolescence is a crucial stage in development, a critical period during which the search for identity and a set of values becomes paramount. Physical, emotional, and social changes occurring in the individual at this time influence the development of his personality. Psychologists are very interested in this growth, and several have constructed theories that help explain its dynamics.

Theories of personality development can be divided into two major categories: stage-dependent and learning-environmental. Stage-dependent theories view the developmental process as a clearly defined sequence of maturational stages that are both predetermined and age-specific. Differences in the individual at different stages of childhood, rather than differences between individuals at the same stage, are stressed. The differential effects of the environment and culture are largely ignored by these theorists.

Learning-environmental theories do not necessarily deny the existence of developmental stages; but the primary purpose of stages for these theorists is to specify the kinds of learning processes that take place as the individual interacts with his environment. A very important learning process in personality development is *identification*, whereby an individual patterns his own behavior after a significant model.

The problems of adolescence are the result of both the physiological and emotional upheaval within the individual teenager and the pressures and constraints imposed by society. The family, school, and peer group are all powerful influences on the development of the adolescent's personality. The contribution of the parents is at first the most significant one, but as children become older and spend more time at school and with their peers, these influences also come to play a major role in the development of identity and values. The adolescent looks to the school and to his peers as a means of building his own *self-esteem* and to provide a sense of belonging in the larger society.

Many adolescents are unable to resolve their personal identity crises and experience feelings of extreme alienation. Some become runaways or escape into the self-destructive world of drugs; others turn to violence and criminal behavior; more and more drop out of school.

Problem behavior in adolescence is often the product of a poor home environment, but not necessarily. Teachers should avoid putting the entire blame on parents as a convenient means of ignoring their own responsibility to help their students. Many educational programs in the United States are highly regimented and competitive and place most of their emphasis on the formal academic curriculum. Consequently, they tend to ignore the positive contributions that teachers can make in other areas of learning, including the development of self-esteem and character. In order to succeed in this effort, the curriculum should be relevant to the students' everyday life, and teachers should set expectations that are appropriate for their pupils' age levels and intelligence. Teachers can also help adolescents by trying to understand the kinds of problems they are facing and by providing constructive guidance for dealing with these problems realistically.

Bronfenbrenner believes that American schools need to be better integrated with other social institutions in the immediate environment. He recommends giving children opportunities to see adults at work and giving them more responsibilities at an earlier age—at home, in the classroom, and in the community. All the theories of personality development discussed in this chapter are compatible with these suggestions.

SUGGESTED FOR FURTHER READING

"An American family." A WNET—Channel 13 Production.
A series of controversial films produced for educational television that provides the viewer with an intimate view of the life of an actual family in California, whose problems in some ways typify current problems in other American families.

Coopersmith, S. *Antecedents of self-esteem.* San Francisco: Freeman, 1967.
A description of experimental findings on self-esteem that should be useful for teachers of students with problems of low self-esteem.

Erikson, E. *Identity: Youth and crisis.* New York: Norton, 1968.
Erikson describes his theory of ego identity, especially as it relates to adolescents.

Keniston, K. *Young radicals: Notes on committed youth.* New York: Harcourt Brace Jovanovich, 1968.
A comprehensive account of adolescents and youth that is not entirely negative and thus offers encouragement to teachers.

Kraemer, H. F. (Ed.). *Youth and culture: A human-development approach.* Monterey, Calif.: Brooks/Cole, 1973.
Taking a cultural perspective, this book of readings captures the tone of contemporary youth and gives some attention to explaining the problems of adolescents.

PRINCIPLES OF LEARNING AND TEACHING

The question of how people learn is of great interest both to psychologists and to educators, and a major area of inquiry and investigation.

Learning has been defined by psychologists as a relatively permanent change in behavior that results from the interaction between an individual and his environment. The conclusion that something has been learned is generally inferred from an individual's performance or overt behavior, as the definition implies. However, the two are not synonymous, because the learning process itself is not directly observable. Many psychologists think of learning as a change in the individual that intervenes between the stimulus that sets it in motion and the behavior from which the learning process is inferred.

Because learning is such a complex phenomenon, psychologists have been especially interested in developing theories of learning as a means of accounting for and bringing order to the large body of facts gathered on the subject. Ideally, any learning theory is supposed to represent a systematic interpretation of all the relevant information accumulated to date. The rationale for such a construction is to provide plausible explanations of independently observed facts and to relate these facts in terms of a conceptual framework or model. Although some learning theories may be more successful in meeting these goals than others, all learning theories can be thought of as a creative attempt to go beyond the facts and to explain *why*.

Actually, there is no one learning theory in existence today that claims to be either definitive or all-inclusive. Two different psychologists, each focusing on a different feature of the environment important to learning, might develop two very different views of the learning process. It is possible, however, to classify psychologists, both today and in the past, into groups, according to the general *types* of learning theories they have advocated. Each group of theories has relevance to education to the extent that it has suggested useful and practical ways of improving instruction.

Teachers can make use of learning theories as a basis for evaluating research on behavior and also for selecting one teaching method rather than another. Like psychologists, teachers often vary in the particular theoretical position with which they prefer to identify. Whatever this choice is, it can influence the nature of the teacher-student interactions and activities considerably.

Theories about learning, as well as those about other important aspects of human behavior, have been around for centuries. But neither the ancient Greeks, nor the scholastics of the Middle Ages, nor the eighteenth-century philosophers were able to advance beyond the level of their own speculations and untested hypotheses. These were the people we refer to today as "armchair psychologists." They did not go out into the world or even perform experiments in the laboratory to find out what the facts were—what was actually happening in a given situation under a given set of conditions. Rather, they sat back and hypothesized what seemed to them at the time to make the greatest sense. Today, psychologists have found a partial solution to the problem by identifying the variables they think are important in the behavior they are studying. They then proceed to put their hypotheses to the test by taking accurate and precise measures of the influence of those variables on the behavior in question.

Psychologists have engaged in two different types of research on learning and learned behavior. The first type is called *basic research;* the major purpose of this kind of research is to question assumptions and make our knowledge about the subject more precise and systematic. The second type is called *applied research;* its primary concern is not with obtaining maximum precision and a high level of structure, but simply with solving the pressing problems of the day. In the study of learning, much of the dispute that persists between one school of thought and another is over which aspects of the learning process are the most important in terms of explaining why man behaves as he does. Despite this disagreement, however, there are many fundamental principles and relationships on which all learning theories agree, regardless of emphasis and orientation. In the following six chapters, these specific areas of agreement and disagreement between one learning theory and another will be discussed in detail.

Since educational psychology, by definition, covers all of the areas that can be applied to teaching, many of the theories we will be discussing in this section represent applied research. On the other hand, since the question of how and why people learn and what causes learning is a very basic one, the learning theories representing basic research will be considered. We will also describe some of the major outgrowths of all these theories and discuss how they can be applied to the learning that takes place in the classroom.

Chapter 4 describes the simplest systematic attempt we know of to answer the question of why we behave as we do. The basic view is that learning is simply the result of associations between stimuli in the environment and the responses of the organism. Most associationist theorists ignore intervening variables that might be at work between the cause and the result, preferring to involve themselves exclusively with the stimulus and response aspects of learning and learned behavior.

In Chapters 5 and 6 we will discuss some dramatically different approaches to the question of why people behave as they do. Both the cognitive-field theorists and the motivation theorists feel that the associationist approach oversimplifies the real nature of the learning process. They believe that it is necessary to deal directly with the variables *mediating* between the cause and the result. Although there is some overlap in approach between the cognitive-field and motivation theories, there does tend to be a difference in emphasis. The cognitive-field theorist is primarily concerned with the relationship between learning and perception; the motivation theorist is primarily concerned with the relationship between learned behavior and the underlying goal or purpose of the individual.

Chapters 7, 8, and 9 are more applied in nature and deal directly with what goes on in the classroom. Chapter 7 deals with the different types of learning that take place in the classroom and also with the different styles of learning characteristic of the individual student. In addition, considerable attention is paid to the practical problem of preparing learning objectives in accordance with the underlying purpose of a given course or unit of instruction. A rationale for a *taxonomy of learning objectives* is presented, along with some guidelines for the actual preparation of such a taxonomy. Chapter 8 deals primarily with ways we can increase our memory, or retention, of what we have learned.

Chapter 9 applies all that we have learned in Chapters 4 through 8 to the design of classroom instruction. The various programs considered are grouped according to the chronological age of the students. Throughout this chapter we will be considering a variety of procedures, rather than concentrating on any one exclusively, in order to show the extent and scope of the practical applications emanating from the different theories of learning.

EXPLAINING BEHAVIOR: ASSOCIATIONIST THEORIES

CHAPTER 4

After completing this chapter, the reader should be able to:

1 Outline and describe the basic associationist theories of learning and give examples of the application of each in child rearing and in classroom situations.

2 Explain the use of the following in classroom learning: primary and secondary reinforcement; positive and negative reinforcement; punishment; shaping; generalization and discrimination learning; chaining; schedules of reinforcement; immediate and delayed reinforcement.

3 Identify the methods used in behavior management and give examples of management procedures that might be utilized by the classroom teacher.

4 List the advantages of programmed instruction as compared with traditional methods of instruction; outline the steps involved in designing programmed materials; design programmed materials that could be used to teach a specific concept in a classroom.

5 Outline the ethical considerations that should be taken into account in developing an education program that uses behavior management.

INTRODUCTION

Because psychology is still a young science, psychologists have had to consider several different explanations of how human beings learn. One of the most persuasive is called _associationism_—also called the stimulus-response (S-R) approach—because people naturally tend to associate their behaviors with stimuli in the environment. A person listening today to an old familiar song (a stimulus in his environment) will display happy or sad responses depending on his experiences when he first heard the song years before. By explaining the link between stimulus and response the associationists posed one explanation of why man behaves as he does.

Associationism originated in the United States several decades ago with what is known as behaviorism, the study of overt behavior. John B. Watson, the leader of what has been called the behaviorist approach to psychology, stated that psychologists should concern themselves only with what can be directly observed of the whole man. Human behavior, Watson insisted, is real, objective, and practical. To prove this, he first dispensed with consciousness as a factor in behavior; he restricted his research to only what he himself could observe, and concluded that human behavior is a matter of learned responses associated with stimuli in the environment.

Watson's first task, therefore, was to specify the laws of association between an individual's behavior (his responses) and the stimuli in the environment. He asked himself questions such as, "How do schoolchildren come to associate the ringing sound that occurs in the late afternoon with joyous excitement, and the smell and sight of a dentist's office with trepidation?"

Operating on the assumption that through the use of specific stimuli humans can be taught specific responses, Watson trained an 11-month-old child, Little Albert, to fear a white rat. Watson first showed Little Albert a white rat and established that the child showed no fear whatever of the rat. At a separate time, Watson suddenly banged two rods together behind Little Albert's head and established that the child had a spontaneous fear of loud noise by itself. His next step was to present the child with the rat and immediately bang the rods together so that the child experienced fear of a loud noise together with the sight of the rat. Watson did this many times, and soon Little Albert screamed and cried at the sight of the rat alone; in fact, as Watson soon learned, Little Albert would scream and cry at the sight of any white, furry object. Watson had demonstrated that learned fear responses can be generalized to other stimuli in the environment similar to the one that the subject was taught through association to fear—in the case of Little Albert, the white rat.

CONTIGUITY THEORY

Watson demonstrated that Little Albert could be taught to fear an initially unfrightening stimulus, the white rat, because it was shown to him immediately before a stimulus that had produced spontaneous fear.

Another psychologist, Edwin R. Guthrie, acknowledged that teaching behavior through association, as described in the case of Little Albert, was a powerful force in the learning process, but he considered it to be only a special instance of a more general principle. Guthrie proposed that a stimulus became associated with a response if they simply occurred together in time. The temporal (time) relationship between stimulus and response is called the *contiguity* factor. For Guthrie, the learning process consisted of a direct bonding of stimulus and response; learning, therefore, rested exclusively on the contiguity in time of the stimulus and response—that is, a response to a stimulus becomes established simply because it is the subject's first reaction to the stimulus. In this process, some kind of learning always occurs. As Hill (1971) put it: "If you do something in a given situation, the next time you are in that situation you will tend to do the same thing again" (pp. 41–42).

CLASSICAL (RESPONDENT) CONDITIONING

Little Albert did not have to be taught how to scream and cry when he heard the sticks banging together behind him. His crying was a *reflex* action; he cried automatically. This is an example of what associationists term an unconditioned stimulus (noise) and an unconditioned response (crying). An unconditioned stimulus is one that produces a response without learning having to take place, and an unconditioned response is one that takes place automatically.

One of the first systematical and objective accounts of these phenomena was reported by Ivan Pavlov in the early twentieth century. Pavlov's experiments involved training a subject to respond to a neutral stimulus—one that by itself would be incapable of eliciting a response—by repeatedly associating it with an unconditioned stimulus. Little Albert learned to cry when he saw the white rat only after he came to associate it with the loud noise. The white rat in this case is an example of a conditioned stimulus. Crying at the presentation of the white rat is an example of a conditioned (learned) response. This simple form of learning is called *classical conditioning*; it is also called *respondent* conditioning because the subject does not respond until after the stimulus has been presented.

Pavlov demonstrated classical conditioning in the simplest and clearest way possible by conditioning (training) dogs to salivate at the sound of a bell. A hungry dog will not naturally salivate at the sound of a bell, of course, but it will salivate at the sight and smell of food. Pavlov presented the food and rang the bell almost simultaneously a number of times so that eventually the ringing bell alone was enough to make the dogs salivate. Once this had taken place, we say that the ringing bell became a conditioned stimulus. By *pairing* conditioned and unconditioned stimuli many times, Pavlov was able to elicit the response of salivation to a conditioned stimulus (ringing bell). Salivation at the sight and smell of food at the beginning of the experiment was an unconditioned response; salivation at the sound of the bell became a conditioned response.

Pavlov discovered that the time factor in presenting the stimuli was important. The dogs salivated much more when he presented the food approximately half a second after he rang the bell. If he waited longer, the dogs salivated less.

This finding has useful implications for the classroom teacher who wants to know why children behave as they do. On the first day at school a young child may not respond in any particular way to a school bell—a stimulus to which the teacher must condition the children to respond—and may continue to talk and play after it has rung. The teacher often conditions young students to come to attention immediately after the bell has rung, using a voice that children will automatically respond to—her voice in this case is the unconditioned stimulus. The teacher will find that not many pairings of her voice and the school bell are needed before the class will come to order on hearing the school bell alone.

Using Pavlov's procedures, V. M. Bechterev (1928) conditioned dogs to raise their paws in response to a bell or a light by administering a small electric shock to their paws immediately after flashing the light or ringing the bell. The dogs raised their paws automatically when given the shock (the unconditioned stimulus) alone. By pairing the shock with light or sound (the conditioned stimuli) a number of times, Bechterev could make the dogs raise their paws in response to either the light or the bell alone. Bechterev found that the dogs raised their paws more quickly when the shock followed the light or bell by a short interval; the dogs were therefore avoiding the shock that was sure to come right after the conditioned stimulus was presented. This type of classical conditioning is called *avoidance learning.*

Bechterev's finding is also useful to the teacher. Children are afraid of people who yell in anger or scowl constantly. A teacher who cannot control his or her temper or shows a dour, unsmiling face all the time is certain to instill fear responses in children. A young student will come to associate this kind of behavior with both the teacher and the school and may choose to avoid school and stay at home.

Question for Thought

Can you make a list of classically conditioned responses typically developed during the first day of class in any school year? After you have made your list, go over it to see how many responses are associated with warmth and happiness and how many with fear.

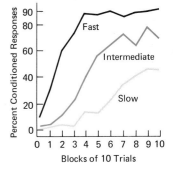

Figure 4-1. Signal learning. Gagné (1970) reports experiments in which subjects were conditioned to blink at a click sounded before a puff of air was directed at their eyes. This *anticipatory blink* occurred in response to a *signal*, and was learned at varying rates by different subjects.

(Gagné, 1970)

An important question concerning classical conditioning is whether the response to the conditioned stimulus is identical with the response to the unconditioned stimulus. Generally, researchers have found that, while similar, the conditioned response does differ from the unconditioned response. This is clearly illustrated by conditioning experiments with the human eyeblink (Gagné, 1970). The unconditioned stimulus was a small puff of air directed at the eye, and the conditioned stimulus was a clicking sound preceding the air puff by about half a second. After several pairings the subjects blinked in response to the click alone. However, the conditioned response to the click alone was found to be approximately five times slower than the unconditioned response to the air puff (see Fig. 4-1). Because of this difference between conditioned and unconditioned responses, Gagné has described classical conditioning as a type of signal learning. That is, the conditioned stimulus serves to signal the onset of the unconditioned stimulus (Gagné, 1970).

Children learn very early in life to respond to many kinds of signals around them. The sight alone of a dog may become a conditioned stimulus that signifies a possible frightening experience such as being bitten or barked at. The clap of a teacher's hands acts as a signal for the children to pay attention, and the last school bell in the afternoon is a signal for them to put their books away.

THE LAW OF EFFECT

According to Watson, Guthrie, and Pavlov, learning occurs when the stimulus and response occur close together in time. But when a stimulus is presented, and a response is given, something else happens that determines whether or not the same response will occur again. Edwin L. Thorndike (1913) proposed the law of effect to explain the association process more fully. This law states that the associative bond between stimulus and response is strengthened or weakened depending on whether a "satisfier" or an "annoyer" follows a response. If a satisfier (a reward) follows, the bond will be strengthened; if an annoyer (punishment) follows, the bond will be weakened.

Thorndike studied the behavior of chickens, cats, and dogs as they learned to escape from a specially constructed box (Thorndike, 1898). At first an animal made a series of random movements; eventually it made the required response that opened the box and revealed food—the satisfier. When the animal was placed in the box again, it took less time to make the required response and get the food. The reward itself determined how fast the animal learned to make the right response; the stimulus and response simply occurring together did not determine how rapidly the learning process occurred.

Thorndike believed that human beings learn by trial and error, or, better, by trial and success. He reasoned as follows: When confronted with a new problem, people stab in the dark, hit or miss, until they find an approach that works. When they finally do arrive at a correct solution, they stop trying alternatives; they think they have discovered the key, and will use it again when confronted with the same problem. The successful solution—the satisfier—strengthens the association between the stimulus and the response.

It would seem, then, that failure and punishment, which are annoyers, would weaken this association. But Thorndike and others discovered that they do not (Thorndike, 1932). Thorndike's studies are extremely provocative, especially to educators who believe that annoyers such as criticism, sarcasm, and corporal punishment are effective in teaching.

In a typical experiment, Thorndike presented to students who had no knowledge of Spanish a list of Spanish words and asked them to choose the English equivalent from a list of a few alternatives. The student would make a guess, and the experimenter would say whether the answer was right or wrong. Thorndike made the assumption that the correct answer was satisfying and a wrong answer was annoying and therefore a form of punishment. If right, the student, because of this association, would give the right answer again when presented with the same Spanish word. However, if the student made a wrong guess, he was likely to give the same wrong answer when presented with the same word again.

This behavior was baffling to Thorndike, and it caused him to reformulate his law of effect, and call it the *truncated law of effect*. Thorndike maintained that although satisfiers always strengthen the bond between stimulus and response, annoyers (punishment) do not necessarily weaken it; in fact, they have very little effect on it at all. Thorndike never did satisfactorily describe the role of punishment in learning, but he did establish that punishment does not automatically inhibit a response—an observation that educators have been very slow to understand. In fact, it was not until much later, after Thorndike had completed his research, that associationist theorists such as B. F. Skinner began to investigate this problem and explain the role of punishment in education.

OPERANT (INSTRUMENTAL) CONDITIONING

In classical (respondent) conditioning, learning situations involve a response occurring *after* a stimulus is presented. The experiment with Little Albert illustrates this type of conditioning; he was trained to fear a white rat by using his unconditioned fear of loud noise and pairing it with the sight of the animal. The law of effect, as theorized by Thorndike, and operant behavior, on the other hand, involve those responses that occur *before* any stimulus is presented.

B. F. Skinner is a major theorist of operant conditioning and one of the most influential contemporary psychologists in America. He is the author of many extremely important as well as controversial books dealing with learning, behavior, and the effects of both on society.

Skinner believes that most behavior, that is, the responses people make to the environment, is the product of so many stimuli that no one stimulus can be singled out and considered responsible. People *operate* in and on their environment: They walk, drive cars, make demands, blink their eyes, eat, climb stairs, yell, grab things, open their mail—in short, they emit an overwhelming number of *operants* (responses) to the overwhelming number of stimuli around them. According to Skinner, most responses (both human and animal) are emitted spontaneously at first, and any stimulus that follows a response determines whether or not that response is repeated or discarded.

People modify their behavior, therefore, depending upon what happens after they make their responses. For example, a young child is instinctively full of demands for love, attention, food, and objects. The mother, however, is free to ignore all of them until the child says "Please"; when the child does say "Please," the mother grants the request. In this way the child learns to say "Please" more often in order to get what he wants. The child's demands are really *operants;* they are attempts to create change in the environment. The mother wants to teach the child to phrase requests politely and responds only when the child utters the polite word. The mother rewards only the polite response; by learning to make the operant response of saying "Please," the child is rewarded by getting what he wants. The process of modifying behavior by rewards, or what Skinner termed *reinforcers,* is called *operant conditioning;* it is also called *instrumental* conditioning because, as in the example, the subject must select from among all the possible responses (instruments) the one that will guarantee a reward.

In order to study operant conditioning in its simplest or purest form, Skinner designed an enclosed box (subsequently called a *Skinner box*) that contained a bar or lever and a device for providing reinforcers such as food pellets, candy bars, or water. Pressing the bar would release the reinforcer. Skinner then deprived rats and

A rat pressing the bar in a Skinner box.

(B. F. Skinner. Photo by Will Rapport)

other animals of food so that they were hungry when he placed them in the box. In the box, the animals made a variety of random movements. At some point, by chance, a rat would press the bar and immediately receive a pellet of food. This reward naturally led to another bar-pressing and another pellet. In time, the rat learned to stay by the bar and press it continuously for food. The number of bar-pressings could be used to measure the strength of the operant response, which Skinner called *operant strength.*

Components of Operant Conditioning

REINFORCEMENT.   Operant conditioning is not confined to the behavior of lower animals; it occurs continually in the daily life of human beings as well, although most people are unaware of it. Humans are influenced constantly by the outcomes of their behaviors: Infants gradually come to adopt behavior that is reinforced by their parents; grades, peers, and teachers' comments influence schoolchildren; money and social approval influence adults.

Some reinforcers are physiological, and are of prime importance to the physical survival of the organism. These reinforcers are called *primary reinforcers*, for example, food and water. Other reinforcers are not necessary to the physical survival of the organism; these are called *secondary reinforcers.* At first these reinforcers are not in themselves rewarding; they come to be so when they are associated with primary reinforcers. For example, a baby learns to associate food with his mother's presence. The mother's presence alone eventually becomes a secondary reinforcer for the baby. Babies also find the presence of other humans a secondary reinforcer, and thus seek out other people because initially a primary reinforcer was always administered in the presence of a person. Many students associate parental approval with high grades; high grades alone thus become secondary reinforcers to these students. Notice that secondary reinforcers are created by the process of stimulus substitution, or conditioning.

Questions for Thought
Some psychologists have pointed out that infants whose parents smiled, cooed, and gurgled at them at the same time as feeding and touching them tend later to become children who seek approval from others. Approval in this example has become a secondary reinforcer through association with earlier satisfaction of needs. But what about infants whose parents scowled, threatened, and perhaps slapped and abused them at the same time they fed them?
What adult behaviors are likely to become secondary reinforcers for these infants as they get older?
What does this example tell us about why battered children regularly defend the very parents who have brutalized them?

NEGATIVE REINFORCEMENT AND PUNISHMENT. Reinforcers may be *positive* or *negative*. So far, we have discussed only positive reinforcers—that is, stimuli that follow operant behavior and increase its frequency. A teacher may have a problem with a disruptive student who does not pay attention in class. The teacher can begin to correct this behavior by watching the student closely and praising him immediately after he does pay attention, however briefly. If the student's moments of attention are followed by praise often and regularly, he will gradually become more and more attentive in class. Praise, in this case, is a kind of positive reinforcement.

Negative reinforcement, on the other hand, also increases the frequency of operant behavior, but this kind of operant behavior consists of escaping from the negative reinforcer. A high school girl, for example, has not been doing her homework and thinks she may fail an upcoming examination. If she fails this examination, she will probably receive a low grade for the course. This possibility frightens her, because she has had a good scholastic record so far and she is proud of it. She therefore decides to study the course material regularly every day and passes the exam with a fairly high grade. By studying regularly, that is, by increasing a certain kind of operant behavior, she escapes the threat of the failure and lowered self-esteem, both of which are negative reinforcers in this case.

Negative reinforcers thus strengthen escape responses, but they are effective only when: (1) there is an opportunity to escape them by adopting constructive behavior; and (2) that opportunity is obvious to the individual.

The teacher who is faced with a severely disruptive student is in a very difficult situation. If the teacher were to follow the procedure used most frequently in the past, he would most likely choose to punish the child, perhaps even use corporal punishment. But what exactly is punishment, and what are its effects? Thorndike was not clear in his answer to this question; Skinner is. As Skinner describes it, punishment is the administration of an aversive stimulus, that is, something undesirable, for the purpose of inhibiting the immediately preceding response (Hilgard and Bower, 1975). Its actual effects, however, are variable, depending upon the situation. In general, punishment is not effective in inhibiting specific undesirable behavior, as we have already seen demonstrated in Thorndike's studies.

Negative reinforcers, according to Skinner, differ considerably from this concept of punishment. They are employed for different purposes. Unlike punishment, negative reinforcers are designed to strengthen an escape response, not to inhibit an undesirable response. The high school girl we described earlier was generally conscientious and was reinforced for her behavior by receiving good grades (positive reinforcer). Had her teacher chosen to use the threat of poor grades as a negative reinforcer, she probably would

Figure 4-2. Flow chart showing possible responses to negative reinforcement in the classroom.

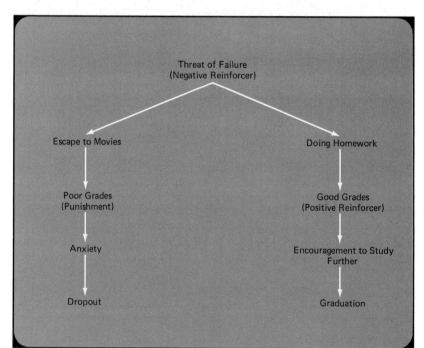

have said something like the following: "You'd better study or you might not pass the test." The girl might choose to study in order to escape this threat. She would thus be using study behavior as an escape response. But she could also choose very different escape responses—for example, dropping the course. But what would happen if she decided not to drop the course but doesn't study and as a result can't answer the questions on the test? She would be likely to receive a failing grade. According to Skinner, this bad grade is designed as punishment for her *after* she has not studied, in order to teach her to study in the future. But what escape *is* available? The lack of studying has already occurred. No escape is possible. And, as we have pointed out, punishment simply does not inhibit immediately preceding behavior! Skinner would predict, in this case, that she wouldn't learn to study.

According to Skinner, negative reinforcers follow the same learning principles as positive reinforcers—with one important distinction. The *introduction* of a positive reinforcer increases the probability that the immediately preceding response will occur again, while the *termination* of a negative reinforcer does the same thing. There is a second important difference here that the teacher ought to consider carefully: The response that is caused by a negative reinforcer is an escape response, but the escape is often not the response that the teacher intended to reinforce, and, in fact, may be just the opposite. Instead of studying as a means to escape the teacher's anger, the student might decide to cut class and, in so doing, successfully escape the negative reinforcer.

For example, let's say a child is running down a hallway. The teacher scolds the child, and tells him to go back and walk instead of run. The child then proceeds to walk in order to escape being scolded again. Notice that this procedure is effective only when an escape response is available, in this case, walking instead of running. Common forms of negative reinforcement currently in vogue in our schools are ridicule, sarcasm, criticism, and detentions. The termination of these negative reinforcers always reinforces escape responses, some of them desired by the teacher, some of them not as desirable, such as cutting class and daydreaming. Too frequently, also, the teacher does not even notice which escape response was reinforced because of the erroneous assumption that punishment alone was operating to inhibit the inappropriate behavior. Negative reinforcers used by classroom teachers increase the probability of whatever the child is doing at the time that that negative reinforcer stops!

One of the undesirable side effects of negative reinforcement is that it is very difficult to predict which escape response will be adopted. Truancy, dropping out of school, even physical counterattacks are not uncommon escape responses adopted by schoolchildren. Continuing negative reinforcement can also lead to extreme anxiety, an emotional response that makes complex problem-solving much more difficult. Each of us can recall preparing at great length for exams but doing poorly because of our fears of the outcome.

The anxiety caused by punishment or negative reinforcement often suppresses other desirable responses (Hilgard and Bower, 1975). A case in point is the child who enthusiastically raises his hand to answer a question from the teacher. The teacher calls on the child expecting, on the basis of his eagerness, a correct response. But the child has misunderstood the question, and he responds incorrectly. There is laughter, not only from the child's classmates but from the teacher as well. It is just this type of reaction that creates the high levels of anxiety found in our schools. Occasionally, a child will become so inhibited that he is too frightened to answer or to ask any questions—even to ask for permission to use the toilet!

No specific statement can be made about the effects of continued negative reinforcement on all children. As we discussed in earlier chapters, the development of children is highly individual. Each child, because of his unique past experiences, will respond differently to negative reinforcement. Each child differs not only in his reaction to negative reinforcement, but also in his reaction to the stimuli each experiences as aversive and in the methods used to avoid them. Because it is usually quite difficult for the teacher to know all of the variables necessary to predict behavior accurately,

Children who respond eagerly to a teacher's questions are positively reinforced when they give the right answer but can be negatively reinforced by classmate or teacher response when their answer is wrong.

(Eric Hartmann, Magnum Photos)

the teacher takes a greater risk in using aversive stimuli to inhibit undesirable behavior than in using positive reinforcement as a means of obtaining the desired results.

Can negative reinforcement ever be used effectively in the classroom? The answer is yes, but the circumstances under which it is effective are so rare that the preparing teacher would be wise to seek more effective methods of teaching. In one study, Hall and his colleagues (1971) found that by using very mild aversive stimuli in a classroom setting, undesirable responses could be removed. In this study, children were assigned five-minute detentions each time they left their seats without permission. The out-of-seat behavior was rapidly removed by these measures. Even five days after the detentions were discontinued, the out-of-seat behavior remained significantly below the initial rate. The authors commented that to be effective, aversive stimuli should not be physically or psychologically abusive. However, since what is abusive to one child may not be to another, depending on past experience, the teacher assumes a great responsibility in using this technique. In addition, the conditions under which it is administered should be clearly communicated to the child so that he knows the specific behavior to avoid.

EXTINCTION.   As mentioned earlier in this chapter, the rat in the Skinner box was reinforced with a food pellet, and this positive reinforcement led the rat to press the bar again in order to get another pellet—the rat was reinforced every time it pressed the bar. How long would it take the rat to stop pressing the bar if no food pellet were delivered each time? Likewise, did the high school girl mentioned earlier stop studying immediately after passing her exam because she knew she would not have to take another one for several weeks?

It has been demonstrated that behavior, if not reinforced, will gradually occur less and less frequently, and will eventually return to the rate of occurrence before conditioning was first begun. This process is called _extinction_. Extinction may take a long time, depending on how strong the response was originally; the time it takes is a good indication of operant strength.

Operant conditioning procedures, including extinction, can be put into effect without people being aware of them. A few years ago the author and two colleagues conducted an experiment with college students to demonstrate that behavior can be changed quite unconsciously (Bachrach, Candland, and Gibson, 1961). The students were first reinforced for speaking rapidly during a conversation. The experimenters used positive reinforcement such as verbal approval and head nodding to show that they agreed with everything the students said. In this situation the students increased their speaking rates dramatically (as measured by the number of words

Negative reinforcement can lead to anxiety, making it more difficult for the teacher to correct students' problem behaviors.

(Tim Eagan, Woodfin Camp & Associates)

spoken per minute). After an extinction period, during which the experimenters ignored the students' comments in conversation by not responding and apparently not even listening, the students' speaking rate slowed down considerably. During both reinforcement and extinction periods, the students were totally unaware that they had increased or decreased their rate of speech and, in fact, were shocked to learn that their behavior had been manipulated in such a manner.

Returning to the teachers who are faced with a severely disruptive student, what can we now recommend? First, we can tell them that punishment and negative reinforcement often have unwanted side effects, such as anxiety. Furthermore, we can tell them that if aversive stimuli must be used, then they ought to be used infrequently and clearly should not be severe. Teachers should also know the child and his past experiences thoroughly so as to be able to best predict the effect of a specific stimulus on a specific child. Finally, if they employ an aversive stimulus, they should clearly communicate to the child which responses he might adopt to avoid it. We might also suggest that they use extinction instead of negative reinforcement or punishment whenever possible, by simply ignoring the child's undesirable responses. This, together with positive reinforcement of the child's desirable responses, clearly will be more effective and predictable in its results (De Cecco, 1968). Further on in this chapter the use of negative reinforcement in the classroom will be fully discussed.

Operant Conditioning and Higher-Order Learning

SHAPING.   Thus far, we have learned that operant conditioning reinforces desired responses, which are at first given out spontaneously; the subject responds correctly only by chance, but when only the correct response is reinforced, he learns to modify his behavior. Learning more complex behavior, where chance is not such a large factor because there are so many possible responses, is achieved through a process called *shaping.* The disruptive student provides a good example of the shaping process. Paying attention represents only one of the many responses he can give (called his repertoire of responses), but, through chance, it probably does occur once in a while. Each time he appears to be paying attention — perhaps just by looking at the teacher — the teacher provides immediate reinforcement with a smile or good word. In the shaping procedure, the teacher begins by reinforcing all responses that are somewhat similar to, or that approximate, the desired response. Each successive reinforcement increases the probability that the student will spend more time looking at the teacher. The teacher then gradually limits reinforcement to the student's closer approaches to the desired attentive behavior, so that finally the student is reinforced only when he pays attention for extended periods of time.

Mathematics, languages, reading skills—any traditional school subject—can be taught more effectively if the teacher has a basic understanding of the technique of shaping. When the student first enters a new and difficult subject area, the teacher begins by rewarding any improvement. As the student begins to understand the basics, the teacher will reinforce only those responses that reflect an understanding of more than the basics. A simple example is teaching a child to write the alphabet. At first the teacher reinforces all attempts to draw letters, correctly or incorrectly; later the teacher withholds praise until the letters are more correctly drawn. Deciding which behaviors should be reinforced at any given time is always difficult, but shaping techniques provide a useful guide for teaching new material.

GENERALIZATION AND DISCRIMINATION. During the course of learning, an individual comes to respond in a certain way to one set of circumstances and in a different way to another set of circumstances. Psychologists call this phenomenon *discrimination*. In precise terms, discrimination occurs when two or more stimuli are responded to differentially. Discriminations are continually being made in our everyday lives, as well as in the classroom. Babies must learn to discriminate among the overwhelming number of sounds they hear. In learning to read, children must discriminate among the letters in the alphabet. College students must learn very fine distinctions among concepts in each of their courses.

The opposite of discrimination is *generalization*. There are two types of generalization, stimulus and response generalization. In *stimulus generalization*, the same response is made to two or more stimuli. Again, everyday examples are numerous. A child who is bitten by a dog might come to respond to all dogs with fear. Here the same response, fear, is generalized from one particular dog to all dogs in general. On the other hand, if a child has a rewarding experience with a dog who loves him and follows him around he might generalize his enjoyment and learn to love other animals.

Response generalization occurs when a particular stimulus evokes responses that are similar or related to the desired response. A student who is conditioned to stop talking and sit quietly when the bell rings will probably also exhibit a variety of other related responses. For example, he may pick up pencils, check to see that all books and papers are available, and look attentive.

Sometimes a generalization occurs to such an extent that it distorts reality. We call such a phenomenon *overgeneralization*. Any rigid and detailed stereotype involves an overgeneralization. The old cliché "blonds have more fun" is an overgeneralization that will be denied by brunettes and redheads alike!

CHAINING.   Thus far we have discussed how to reinforce only one desirable response in operant conditioning. It is also possible to teach a *series* of responses that must be performed in a specified order before they are reinforced. This kind of higher-order learning is called *chaining*.

Skinner taught rats and pigeons to perform very complex acts by this process. For example, he taught a rat to press a bar that released a marble; the rat then had to carry the marble to another part of the cage and drop it in a hole in order to get a pellet of food, which appeared in still another part of the cage (Hill, 1971). Of course, the rat could only approximate the first response at the beginning. The rat was then reinforced for learning the first part of the sequence. After the first part of the sequence was learned, the reinforcement was withheld until the rat learned to perform both this and the next step. This process continued until the rat learned the entire sequence. Trained in this manner, pigeons have learned to play a highly competitive form of modified Ping-Pong.

Our own lives are filled with these conditioned sequences of behavior, or chains, many of which have become ritualized. For example, a sequence of the morning ritual might run as follows: The preset alarm clock goes off; the person rises from bed and puts water on the stove to boil; he then showers or shaves; entering the kitchen again, he finds the water boiling and makes coffee, the aroma of which stimulates the appetite; he then prepares breakfast and eats it; the cat in the meantime begins to cry for food, a signal for the person to get up and feed it, and so on. As you can see, daily life often consists of sequences of stimulus-response connections that work together in a larger, overall pattern.

Superstitious behavior involves the same chaining process. Skinner (1948a) put pigeons into a box and reinforced them with grain once every minute regardless of what they did—that is, the reinforcement did not depend on any particular responses the pigeons made. Nevertheless, each pigeon developed its own sequence of movements and tended to repeat the movements it had made just before it was reinforced. One pigeon, for instance, circled to the left before going to the food box, and continued to do so, although it was not reinforced specifically for this behavior. Another pecked in a certain corner and then proceeded to the food box. The first responses in their chain were not related to reinforcement; therefore, these responses are termed *superstitious behavior*.

Superstitious responses develop in human behavior in much the same way they do in lower animals. Any chained series of responses that occurs before a reinforcement will tend to occur more frequently in the future, whether those responses actually caused the reinforcement to be administered or just happened to occur before it. I once kept a record of the clothing my students wore during examinations in one class and found that the students who received high grades in one exam tended to wear similar clothes when they came to take the next exam.

The only difference between superstitious behavior and chaining in both lower animals and humans is that in chaining the responses are connected by a causal link, and in superstitious behavior they are not.

CONTINUOUS REINFORCEMENT. The manner, or schedule, in which reinforcers are given following a subject's responses determines the strength of the responses (operant strength). The simplest schedule is called *continuous reinforcement;* in this procedure, reinforcement follows every response and produces a regular pattern of responding. Giving a gold star to a student every time he hands in a neat paper would be an example of continuous reinforcement. In everyday life, however, it is often impossible to reinforce desired responses continuously. The person responsible for the reinforcement is usually involved in other affairs, and often misses the performance of a correct response. For example, a mother who has regularly praised her daughter whenever she cleans her room may often have to go to committee meetings and is therefore not always present to give reinforcement. She may then notice that her daughter has fallen back into the habit of leaving her room messy. The withholding or absence of regular reinforcement can rapidly extinguish desired behaviors that have been established on a continuous reinforcement schedule.

INTERMITTENT REINFORCEMENT. Reinforcement given less frequently is called *intermittent reinforcement.* There are two types of intermittent reinforcement schedules, ratio and interval. On a *ratio schedule,* reinforcement is given only after the subject makes a specified number of desired responses. If a teacher rewards a child with a gold star each time the child reads three books, the teacher is using a 3:1 ratio schedule.

Reinforcement on an *interval schedule* does not depend on the number of responses a subject makes, but on the amount of time that elapses between reinforcements. In general, subjects respond differently on an interval schedule than on a ratio schedule; they learn that it is not worthwhile to give the correct response unless

Schedules of Reinforcement

GRADING: TO BE OR NOT TO BE?

(Robin Gibson, Alternative Curriculum)

The argument over grading goes on. Those opposed to grades see them as competitive, undemocratic, negative, subjective, inequitable, inaccurate, and frustrating. Furthermore, grades are considered to be punitive—they reduce or obliterate interest in a subject, and tend to reward the plodding conformer and penalize the imaginative student. Opponents have suggested and devised alternatives such as evaluations and portfolios. Those in favor of grades argue that such alternatives at least *imply* grading—especially, for instance, if a portfolio contains only a student's best work. To them, students not graded on their measures of achievement are in for a rude shock when they enter the "real" world. Thus, a nonjudgmental system such as pass/fail is, for these proponents of grades, a fraud and an illusion. One spokesman for grades suggests that the problem lies not in the system itself but in its abuse. "The failure," he says, "is with the teacher" (Moulds, 1974, p. 503). Do you agree? What suggestions would you make to improve the system? Are there yet other alternatives educators may have overlooked?

they will be reinforced. An example of this would be giving a quiz every Friday. Most students will wait until Thursday night to study for a Friday quiz.

Ratio and interval schedules can either be *fixed or variable*. On a fixed schedule, reinforcement is given according to a consistent and set pattern. A *fixed ratio schedule* provides reinforcement each time the subject gives a specified number of desirable responses. A father who gives his son a dollar for every two "A's" on his report card has placed him on a fixed ratio schedule. On the other hand, the teacher who gives quizzes each and every Friday puts the students on a *fixed interval schedule*.

A subject who cannot accurately predict which response will be followed by reinforcement is said to be on a *variable* schedule of reinforcement. On a *variable ratio schedule,* the average number of responses rather than a specified number determines the reinforcement schedule. For instance, a man may be aware that, on the average, he will get a ticket 50 percent of the time that he parks in a no-parking zone. The other 50 percent of the time he will not receive a ticket, but he cannot predict the actual instance when he will or will not be ticketed.

The time period between reinforcers on a *variable interval schedule* may be short or long; a mother may praise her children "every once in a while" just because she "happened to feel like it." However, it is important for a teacher to know that the responses established on variable reinforcement schedules, both ratio and interval, resist extinction and occur at a higher rate than those established on fixed schedules. Unannounced quizzes at irregular intervals will encourage students to study more frequently than quizzes that are always given on Fridays.

DELAYED REINFORCEMENT.   A general principle of operant conditioning is that reinforcement is most effective when it immediately follows a response. This is particularly true with young children. The traditional grading system in schools is based on the dubious assumption that children will benefit from long delays in reinforcement. Report-card grades usually are given at intervals of six to eight weeks, and papers are rarely graded immediately. More research needs to be done on the effects of these delays on children of different ages and backgrounds. Teachers should be aware of the fact that the grades they give out may have little or no effect on study habits if they are given too late.

Questions for Thought

We have described in this chapter a series of problems facing the teacher who wants to design a testing and grading system that will effectively serve as a reinforcer of proper study habits. Can you think of a system that might be more effective than the kinds of tests usually used in classrooms and the typical letter-grade system? What do you need to know about your students in order to determine how effective your new system might be?

THE SIGNIFICANCE OF ASSOCIATIONIST THEORIES IN LEARNING

Classical Conditioning

Classical (respondent) conditioning occurs continually in the classroom, although the teacher and students are usually not aware of it. As you will recall, Watson conditioned Little Albert to fear a white rat by pairing the sight of the rat with a loud noise, a stimulus that instinctively evokes a fear response in babies. The baby then generalized his fear of white rats to other white, furry objects. A parallel situation often exists in the classroom.

Teachers and parents frequently create high levels of anxiety in children by threatening them with failure (Roden and Hapkiewicz, 1973). This threat represents the unconditioned stimulus in classical conditioning. Every other activity that is accompanied by the threat becomes the conditioned stimulus by association. Sometimes a child manages to perform well in spite of the threat because the subsequent reinforcement overrides the effect of the conditioning.

Unfortunately, many children resemble Little Albert and experience great anxiety not only about wrong answers but about school in general. The simplest means at a teacher's disposal to overcome this anxiety is to discontinue threatening or punishing the students. The teacher can also try to recondition a student by creating a pleasurable situation whenever the student begins to grow anxious or frightened—for example, the teacher can encourage the anxious child to talk about hobbies or pastimes.

Operant Conditioning: The Effects of Reinforcement

POSITIVE VERSUS NEGATIVE REINFORCEMENT AND PUNISHMENT. Norma Feshbach (1972) has examined the styles of reinforcement used by mothers with their 4-year-old children. She found that working-class mothers employ negative reinforcement far more frequently than middle-class mothers. This finding is significant for two reasons. First, psychologists have shown that children tend to adopt their parents' behavior. Children whose mothers frequently use negative reinforcement are more likely to use negative reinforcement in their dealings with other children. Second, the type of reinforcement used in the home relates to learning skills. Feshbach found that poor readers tend to have parents who use a great deal of negative reinforcement, whereas better readers tend to have parents who use positive reinforcement more often.

The teacher's reinforcement style also has a strong effect on student behavior. In another study, Feshbach (1972) had children observe two 4-minute films in which a teacher gave a brief geography lesson. In one film the teachers used positive reinforcement to motivate the children, while in the other the teacher used negative reinforcement. Feshbach found that middle-class children imitated the mannerisms of the teacher who used positive reinforcement significantly more than the teacher who used negative reinforcement. This is further evidence that the negative reinforcement that is so prevalent in our public schools does not promote desired behavior.

In another classroom study, Harris and Reese (1969) evaluated several techniques used to modify undesirable behavior, and found that group pressure and positive reinforcement were the most successful, and disciplinary actions the least. These results are consistent with those of Bronfenbrenner, which were discussed in Chapter 1.

The two major drawbacks to the use of negative reinforcement and punishment in the classroom are that they raise anxiety levels in children and, in the case of negative reinforcement, may lead children to adopt undesirable escape responses. The child may also interpret the negative reinforcement as an indication of personal failure (Travers, 1967). As we shall discuss in Chapter 6, the experience of failure reduces a child's levels of performance and aspiration.

"Yes," the teacher may respond, "but some anxiety increases the child's attention span." This is true, but with important qualifications. A low level of anxiety does enable a child to sustain attention and make other conditioned responses. However, as we pointed out before, a high level of anxiety greatly interferes with complex learning processes, and once it becomes associated with them it is very difficult to extinguish. The child also generalizes the anxiety to other situations. Although negative reinforcement is sometimes effective, the possibility of its bad side effects often cancels out the benefits.

"But," the teacher may continue, "negative reinforcement allows me to control my classes more effectively." This argument is inaccurate and misleading. Under aversive stimuli children will often suppress a particular undesirable response; but in order to avoid negative reinforcement they may adopt a method of escape that is even more difficult to control. They may withdraw completely, or they may attack the teacher physically. The teacher may very well end up with less control than he had to begin with.

CORPORAL PUNISHMENT. Corporal punishment is still used in schools all over the world despite the case against it and the international calls for banning it. The following quote was observed by the author in an Athens, Greece, newspaper in 1973:

> A call to outlaw the cane in the world's schools has been issued by a convention of some 8000 teacher trade unionists here. Resolutions passed at the end of the 22nd annual assembly of the World Confederation of Organizations of the Teaching Professions (WCOTP) included one calling for a ban on corporal punishment in schools.

DISCIPLINE: MUST IT BE CORPORAL?

Anyone who ever attended a school where corporal punishment was used remembers it vividly. Few do so with pleasure; most remember the pain, anxiety, and, more often than not, resentment and open hostility toward the "grown-up" who slapped, whacked, or beat in an effort to . . . what? maintain order? get the right answer? change a negative attitude? School administrators and teachers who still resort to physical punishment have ready answers. One principal who had three paddles in his office—different sizes for children of the affluent, middle class, and slums—justified this biased treatment of children by saying, "I try to go along with parents' preferences" (Ramella, 1973, p. 26). Much of the argument for corporal punishment in the schools is based on the *in loco parentis* concept in common law. Many parents who would not physically abuse their children in their own homes allow a school free sway. Today, the National Education Association is taking a firm stand against corporal punishment as an adjunct of teaching. We don't need the "hickory stick" any more. There are better tools for education.

Most educators in the United States favor corporal punishment as a means of control. Ironically, the public is often told that corporal punishment should be used on those very students who are trying to escape still other forms of punishment.

Question for Thought

If corporal punishment is the most effective way to discipline students, why have school authorities had to design more and more effective methods of punishment?

The legal battle over the use of corporal punishment in schools continues. As recently as June, 1974, a court awarded $200 to a fourth-grade student because he was not informed that he could legally appeal a spanking he had received in school (*Pittsburgh Press*, June, 1974). In the meantime, teachers continue to employ equally harmful forms of negative reinforcement, such as criticism, sarcasm, and ridicule, with the predictable bad results.

DELAYED REINFORCEMENT. As mentioned earlier, teachers often do not reinforce their students' good performances until days and weeks later, when report cards are issued. On the other hand, they very often strengthen children's bad behavior by reinforcing it immediately. As teachers, we tend to notice the child who talks out loud and hits his neighbor, and not notice at all the child who sits quietly and does everything we expect.

BEHAVIOR MANAGEMENT IN THE CLASSROOM: WHAT THE TEACHER CAN DO

As we have seen, B. F. Skinner believes that all behavior is learned. Behavior that is reinforced will grow stronger, and behavior that is ignored will disappear. This process is a vital part of everyday life and takes many different forms. Teachers reward students with grades and praise; employers reward employees with salaries, bonuses, promotions; adults reward each other with smiles, a friendly tone of voice, compliments.

When we intentionally reward desirable behavior and ignore or punish undesirable behavior, we are engaging in what is called *behavior management* (Madsen and Madsen, 1973). Some people consider behavior management to be an insidious form of control, but they do not realize that the environment surrounding us controls all our behavior, whether or not we know and admit it. In using behavior management techniques, we are taking conscious and active control of our environment rather than letting it unthinkingly control us.

HOW DO WE HELP CHILDREN LEARN?

Michelle was a shy 4-year-old in a developmental day-care center. The teacher and aides noticed that she never completed a task. Often she seemed convinced, even before beginning, that she would fail. They were concerned about her commitment and her ability to follow through. How did they help her learn? They observed that some things drew her attention while others did not. Also, in quiet, casual conversation with Michelle, they discovered that she had specific interests. The teacher then planned tasks built around her interests and encouraged her to accomplish them. To assure success, she presented activities that were a step below the child's level of ability, then rewarded the child with praise for her performance. The result? A happy, involved, more self-assured little girl was beginning to learn about something that interested her. Note that Michelle was helped through a sequence: observation, concern for short- and long-term goals of development (commitment to a task and following it through), intervention (planning different programs), encouragement, and praise.

Select Desirable Behavior

One writer has likened teachers to architects (Bigge, 1964). Just as the architect selects the building materials that will go into a house, the teacher determines the kind of behavior he wants students to adopt in acquiring an education.

Before setting any long-term goals for students, the teacher must carefully study their current repertoires of behavior, just as a psychologist determines his subjects' current levels of response. Only by doing this can the teacher accurately assess the effects of teaching. The student's current behavior always provides the starting point for any following stage of learning. A teacher cannot reinforce behavior that does not exist in the first place. Shaping is necessary.

Teachers often describe their students as being "enthusiastic," "belligerent," "lazy," "shy," "accommodating," and so on. These words convey some information, but not enough to be useful in behavior management. They are too imprecise and must be broken down into more exact components. For instance, a teacher observes that a "lazy" child rarely turns in his homework and plays with rubber bands and sucks pencils during work periods in class. These observations are still too imprecise. The teacher must also observe how often and under what circumstances the child actually tries to work. Having gotten this information, the teacher can make the most of the stimuli that motivate the child to work and remove those that distract him.

Select Proper Reinforcers

It should be obvious by now that no single stimulus will reinforce all children equally. While teachers believe that praise, attention, and encouragement are the most effective reinforcers for schoolchildren, they find that even these stimuli are sometimes ineffective. A "problem child," for example, may stop any behavior that the teacher praises, and instead deliberately behave in a way to make the teacher lose his temper and start yelling. Teachers, therefore, have to choose the stimuli they use as reinforcers so that they suit each individual child.

Two current methods for individualizing reinforcers are the Premack principle and the token economy.

THE PREMACK PRINCIPLE. The *Premack principle,* in effect, allows the child to select his own reinforcers (Premack, 1959). The teacher must first determine how the child behaves most often during free time. A child, for example, may spend 15 minutes playing with a tape recorder, 5 minutes with a deck of cards, and 8 talking to a friend. If the child keeps to this pattern for several days, the teacher knows that the tape recorder affords the most effective positive reinforcement. The teacher can then use it as a reinforcer whenever the child behaves in a desired way.

THE TOKEN ECONOMY. The *token economy* involves a different method of allowing a child to select his own reinforcers. In this method, the teacher immediately rewards desirable behavior with a token. After the child has accumulated several tokens, he can "cash them in" for a variety of privileges or things that the child wants most. The token economy is especially effective because it can be automatically adjusted to a child's changing desires. One day it may be the tape recorder, the next day talking to a friend.

GROUP REINFORCEMENT AND COMPETITION. Group reinforcement and competition have proven to be effective reinforcers in the Soviet Union (Bronfenbrenner, 1970). In this system, a group—either a whole class or a section of it—is rewarded for what the group or section as a unit has accomplished. For example, a teacher might assign 100 arithmetic problems to each row of students in the classroom. The row that first solves all the problems might then be rewarded with a few minutes of extra recess time. One author has suggested that group reinforcement stimulates cooperation because the brighter students become motivated to help the poorer ones in order for the entire group to win.

ARE REINFORCERS BRIBES? Some educators argue that systems like the token economy are nothing more than a form of bribery. They also point out that the teacher uses the Premack principle to make students work for what the teacher used to allow them to do freely.

Furthermore, these methods sometimes make the children do things that they do not really want to do. To Skinner (1969), this argument is invalid. Reinforcers, even when they occur accidentally, determine the child's whole repertoire of behavior. Why, then, asks Skinner, is reinforcement suddenly objectionable when the teacher gives it out in a rationally controlled way? Does reinforcement become a bribe as soon as it is put into the hands of a teacher? Reinforcers of one sort or another always exist. In behavior management, a teacher does not artificially create reinforcers, he uses them.

Use Extinction

Animal studies have shown extinction to be an effective technique for decreasing a response rate to its preconditioning level. Under this procedure, the psychologists simply withheld reinforcement for a response that they had previously reinforced. To extinguish the bar-pressing response in a trained rat, the researcher would stop the food pellets from coming out whenever the rat pressed the bar.

CHILDREN AS BEHAVIORAL ENGINEERS

Behavior management has been thought of as something a teacher does in respect to his students' behavior. A California teacher (Gray et al., 1974) is changing all that. In a pilot study, he taught his students to become behavioral engineers. The subjects? Their teachers. The initial students were seven children, ages 12 to 15, who were attending special classes for so-called incorrigibles. Two were black, two white, and three Chicano. They were given instruction and practice in behavior management for one class period a day. They learned how to shape their teachers' behavior by using various reinforcers. These included smiling, making eye contact, and sitting up straight. They also practiced ways of praising a teacher—"I like to work in a room where the teacher is nice to the kids"—and ways of discouraging negative teacher behavior—"It's hard for me to do good work when you're cross with me" (p. 44). Then they were moved into regular classes for two periods a day. Many of the students had difficulty in smiling or in learning to praise the teacher with sincerity. They also had to develop the ability for small talk; after considerable training, they excelled at it. They learned to identify positive teacher behavior accurately by role playing and by studying videotapes. They also kept formal records of teacher responses in their other classes. (Trained adult aides also kept records of teacher behavior in the classes.) The results of the study showed that during the five weeks of shaping, the positive comments of the teachers increased and the negative comments decreased. Later courses with gifted students "working on" parents and peers as well as teachers were equally effective. Beyond these changes was a more important outcome for all: a more positive environment in which to live and learn.

BREAKING THE HABIT: BEHAVIOR MODIFICATION

Bad habits (like good ones) are acquired. After a time we repeat these behavior patterns without thinking; they become involuntary. And this is the problem in breaking them. Will power is often not enough, as any habitual smoker, for example, can tell you. A booklet (free for the asking) is available from the American Cancer Society (1970) describing ways to extinguish the smoking habit. Following is one method that is suggested. Can you think of others? What principles of operant conditioning are evident here? Could classical conditioning also be used? In what ways?

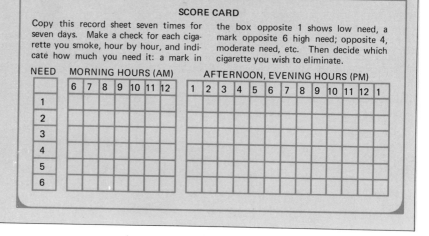

Keep a Track Record

Many smokers have found that a useful step in understanding their smoking is the keeping of a daily record on a scale like that below.

In your gradual withdrawal you may decide to eliminate those daily cigarettes that you find are rated 1, 2 or 3, i.e., ones you want least.

Or you may wish to give up first the cigarettes you like most. In any case keeping a smoking log will give you information about yourself, make you more aware of what your smoking habits are.

You may find that you are largely a social smoker, that smoking makes you feel closer to others, more welcome at a party, that you seem to have more friends.

A cigarette may play a surprisingly large part in your picture of yourself as a mature and successful person.

How do you convince yourself that people like and respect you for more important reasons than for your cigarette? Try not smoking and see.

Plus and Minus

Write down carefully, after some thought, in one column the reasons why you smoke and in another all the reasons why you should give up cigarettes.

As you turn this exercise over in your mind, new material will occur to you for one or the other columns. Thoughtful concentration on your reasons for giving up cigarettes is important in changing your behavior.

SCORE CARD

Copy this record sheet seven times for seven days. Make a check for each cigarette you smoke, hour by hour, and indicate how much you need it: a mark in the box opposite 1 shows low need, a mark opposite 6 high need; opposite 4, moderate need, etc. Then decide which cigarette you wish to eliminate.

NEED	MORNING HOURS (AM)							AFTERNOON, EVENING HOURS (PM)												
	6	7	8	9	10	11	12	1	2	3	4	5	6	7	8	9	10	11	12	1
1																				
2																				
3																				
4																				
5																				
6																				

As mentioned earlier, a teacher reinforces disruptive behavior by paying attention to it. In this case the teacher can easily identify the stimulus that is reinforcing the unwanted behavior. Sometimes, however, the teacher cannot control the responsible stimulus. (Teacher attention is certainly not the only source of reinforcement in the classroom.) The disruptive student is often reinforced by attention from other students, and this factor is hard to eliminate. Undesirable behavior can also be self-reinforcing — chewing gum is a case in point.

When the teacher cannot control the effective reinforcer, he must positively reinforce behavior that is incompatible with the unwanted behavior. If a child is daydreaming in class, the teacher can begin to reinforce attentive behavior. The child will gradually spend more time paying attention. Since the child cannot pay attention and daydream at the same time, he will eventually stop daydreaming.

Disruptive behavior will gradually disappear if the teacher ignores it, but the teacher who chooses to extinguish undesirable behavior by ignoring it should remember four important points. The first is that the child may interpret the teacher's silence as a form of approval (De Cecco, 1974). The teacher can avoid this pitfall by specifying which kind of behavior is appropriate and which is not. The second is that the child may become even more disruptive when ignored, in order to get attention and recognition. The teacher must remain steadfast in withholding anything that could be interpreted as a reward. The third point is that important reinforcement for unwanted behavior often comes from the applause of fellow students. The teacher, perhaps through the use of reinforcement, must learn to control such behavior. The last point is that the teacher must be absolutely consistent in rewarding good behavior and ignoring bad. As was pointed out before, behavior learned under an intermittent reinforcement schedule is the most difficult to extinguish — a problem the inconsistent teacher faces daily in the classroom.

Problems in Classroom Behavior Management

Behavior management can be a highly efficient teaching technique, but it is not without its problems. Skinner (1969) has identified a prime difficulty to be the improper arrangement of social reinforcers.

> Unfortunately, social contingencies are hard to arrange. To induce the members of a classroom community to behave well with respect to each other, additional reinforcers may be needed. . . . The main problem is to make these reinforcers contingent on desired behavior. They are often not available on the spur of the moment. (p. 23)

Skinner suggests that using "generalized reinforcers" such as tokens or credit points substantially alleviates this problem.

Questions for Thought
Does it serve any purpose for the teacher to ignore a rowdy student's behavior when most of the other students approve of it?
What else can the teacher do to modify the behavior of this student?

One of the primary advantages of teaching machines is that the student becomes actively engaged in the learning process.

(Rogers from Monkmeyer)

Teachers do not often realize that the physical appearance of the school and classroom can undermine the best teaching efforts. A dark and depressing school building may act as an aversive stimulus upon students, whose logical response is to stay away. While teachers cannot do much about the appearance of the building, they can make sure that their classrooms are as attractive and comfortable as possible, thereby creating a positively reinforcing atmosphere.

Just as teachers shape student behavior, students also shape the teacher's behavior (Glaser and Resnick, 1972). A teacher should realize that an attentive, serious group of students positively reinforces his own behavior and thus furnishes proof as to which techniques are effective.

PROGRAMMED INSTRUCTION

In his observations of the Boston public schools during the 1940s, Skinner discovered a number of ineffective teaching techniques. Classes were large, and the teachers taught all students the same thing at the same time without regard for individual abilities; they could provide very little immediate feedback to the students, and had to leave reinforcement primarily to chance.

Skinner designed a mechanical teaching device that instructed each student individually and provided immediate feedback. He programmed the machine to present the student with progressively more complex problems step by step. Each step (or frame) contained a question. The student would answer the question, and the machine would immediately tell him whether the answer was right or wrong. Skinner phrased the questions so that the student would most likely make correct responses, which the machine immediately reinforced, thereby increasing the probability of more correct responses. In this manner a student proceeds through a subject area from simple to complex problems and receives continual immediate feedback.

Although Skinner's teaching machines were not the first, their demonstrated success motivated educators to further develop and popularize them. Today, teaching machines are used in schools all over the United States. It is important to bear in mind, however, that these machines simply contain and present the teaching *program*. Their effectiveness depends on the arrangement of the program itself—in its stepwise presentation of progressively more difficult questions designed to shape the behavior of the student.

Programmed instruction has many advantages (Bigge, 1964). The student becomes actively engaged in the learning process; he seeks out knowledge instead of sitting passively and receiving instruction. Since each student progresses according to his own ability or temperament, no student is slowed down or left behind by his classmates. If he is absent from school, he simply takes up where he left off. Programmed instruction supplies the teacher with a record of each student's progress, thereby enabling the teacher to give supplemental instruction more precisely.

Contrary to popular opinion, programmed instruction makes the teacher's role more important, not less. The teacher no longer has to stand in front of the entire class and lecture. He can devote far more energy to students who have specific problems, which the program has isolated accurately, and to creative projects that previously would have been dropped for lack of time.

Varieties of Programming

There are two basic types of programmed instruction: linear and branching. In *linear programming*, the questions are arranged in a single line from simple to complex. Every student answers the same questions in the same order. Norman Crowder introduced branching programming in 1959 in order to suit the needs of a wider range of students. *Branching programming* routes each student individually, depending on his responses at preselected choice points. If a student answers incorrectly at one of these points, the program supplies him with more material on the subject and asks him another question. If the student answers correctly at the choice point, the program simply gives him a more difficult question (see Fig. 4-3).

Thinking and Programmed Instruction

While most educators agree that teaching machines are effective learning devices, they still have many questions about what kind of material is best suited to programming. Many wrongly assume that programmed instruction should contain only simple drills (Hilgard and Bower, 1975). Because programmed material can present a logical sequence of questions starting with the most simple and going to the more difficult, it is ideally suited to teach complex concepts, such as in mathematics, geometry, or economics, where a thorough understanding depends on the mastery of certain basic ideas.

However, some skeptical educators persist in asking if programmed instruction can really teach a student to think. A psychologist would answer that if an educator can define behaviorally what he wants a student to be able to do, he can use programmed instruction to teach anything, even poetry. All learning involves a rational process that is governed by environmental consequences. The act of writing poetry consists of responses the writer makes to very complex elements in his environment. Programmed material can successfully teach poetry appreciation and creative problem-solving (Hilgard and Bower, 1975).

Developing Teacher-Made Programs

Specially trained technicians are not necessarily the only ones who can develop programmed instruction. Any teacher can write excellent programmed material without the benefit of highly specialized instruction; a mimeograph machine is the only equipment needed. (See Chapters 9 and 10 for a description of specific teacher-made programs.)

De Cecco (1974) has listed some simple rules for the teacher who wants to develop a particular program.* The development of a program consists of three steps: preparation, actual writing, and testing and revising. You begin by selecting a topic, one that you are thoroughly familiar with. You should concentrate on only a very small portion of the subject matter (one can easily be overwhelmed with too much subject matter).

The next step is to prepare a content outline of all the material you plan to include in the program. You may have to refer to textbooks for some essential points and perhaps consult an experienced teacher who has taught the subject.

---

*This description of the development of a program should give some idea of the steps involved. However, the individuals who seriously wish to take these steps should see the suggestions for further reading at the end of this chapter.

7 Growth is directional, proceeding from head to foot. At birth the head is large in comparison to the rest of the body. As the child grows older, the rate of growth increases in the lower extremities of the body. As this occurs, the head gradually begins to look (larger/smaller) in comparison to the rest of the body.[2]

•

7 *smaller*

8 A child is able to manipulate his arms and hands before he learns to coordinate his legs. He can hold a rattle and bring it to his mouth long before he can control the movements of his legs and feet to walk.

Development, as well as growth, occurs in a h_____ to f_____ direction.

•

8 *head to foot*

9 Frequently it is difficult for a child below the age of six, whose arm may be sufficiently powerful to swing a baseball bat, to make the finer finger manipulations required for printing or drawing. When this happens we know that:

a. motor development probably has not yet developed sufficiently in his fingers. As teachers, we should be helpful rather than punitive, therefore, when he turns in sloppy printing or drawing on a paper.
b. he must have a partial paralysis of the arms.
c. he is not developing properly.
d. we should train the muscles by requiring him to create "neat" and very small but intricate drawings.

•

9 *a*

Figure 4-3. (top) A linear program from an educational psychology textbook (Gibson, 1972, p. 187). (bottom) A branching program from a textbook for dermatologists (Ramsay and Solomon, 1974, p. 124).

SECTION 10-D

IN INITIATING THERAPY, YOU WOULD BE PARTICULARLY INTERESTED TO ORDER (SELECT AS MANY AS YOU CONSIDER ESPECIALLY PERTINENT):

144	Topical paintings with nitrogen mustard (mechlorethamine)	144	[Steady and real improvement, but patient's skin becomes very reactive, and it is necessary to discontinue the medication. Eventually lesions reappear. MAKE ANOTHER CHOICE FROM THIS SECTION.]
145	Prednisone 50 mg p.o. q.d.	145	[Some improvement noted, but patient develops a gastric ulcer and it is necessary to discontinue the medication. Lesions reappear. MAKE ANOTHER CHOICE FROM THIS SECTION.]
146	Methotrexate 37.5 mg IM q. wk	146	[Improvement. MAKE NO FURTHER CHOICES FROM THIS SECTION. TURN NOW TO SECTION 10-F.]
147	Goekerman regimen	147	[No improvement.]

You must then define your objectives in behavioral terms, first by specifying the final behaviors that you want your students to perform, then breaking down these behaviors into all their major components, and finally breaking down these components still further into the individual responses that you feel your students are initially capable of making. After this has been done, you will have a chart with the most complex behavior at the top and the simplest at the bottom. Between them will be all the steps required to learn the complex behavior.

You must then construct and give two tests: one to determine whether your students can correctly answer the simplest questions at the bottom of your chart, and the second to see if they can answer the difficult ones at the top. Ideally, your students should score 100 points on the first test and 0 on the second, although this rarely occurs.

Next comes writing the program. You must first convert your chart of behavioral objectives into program frames. A frame consists of a phrase or two to set the context for the stimulus (a question or fill-in blank) that follows. The student must respond to the frame in such a way that he learns from his response. Each frame builds upon the next, until gradually more and more complex responses can be made. Following is a sample frame. The correct response is provided at the lower right-hand side.

The procedure used by experimentalists attempting to explain behavior first involves manipulating features of the environment important to behavior, and then observing the consequences.

This technique is known as the _____ method.
  a. experimental
  b. contingency

[a]

A *cue* is a hint to the student to help him make the correct response to the question in the frame. It is very important that the cueing material in your frame elicit responses that are critical to the point you are trying to make. Holland (1960) demonstrated this fact by taking an effective program and rephrasing its cueing material so as to elicit responses that were only tangentially related to the critical content. On a later test, the students who completed the altered version made more than twice as many errors as those who completed the normal form of the program.

Finally, you should test your program on a number of students. Revise where errors occur; test and revise again. Try to make your program as concise as possible. If material does not contribute to the program's effectiveness, delete it. Test again. You will know that when you are finished, your final product teaches the objectives you spelled out at the beginning.

We have not discussed other teaching techniques based on operant conditioning, such as computer-assisted instruction and individually prescribed instruction, because the teacher cannot use them without outside assistance, and they require major curriculum changes. These programs will be discussed in detail in Chapter 9.

THE SCIENCE OF BEHAVIOR: IMPLICATIONS FOR THE CLASSROOM AND EVERYDAY LIFE

Operant theory in general, and Skinner's work in particular, provides us with one highly articulate view of the nature of man. Skinner's book *Beyond Freedom and Dignity* (1971) has aroused a wide range of intense reactions. As one reviewer put it, Skinner is both "admired as a messiah and abhorred as a menace" ("Skinner's Utopia," *Time*, 1971).

In *Beyond Freedom and Dignity* Skinner argues that it is inaccurate to attribute human behavior to internal whims and desires. Consistent with his operant theory, Skinner maintains that the outside environment determines all human behavior:

The Myth of Freedom

> An experimental analysis shifts the determination of behavior from autonomous man to the environment — an environment responsible for both the evolution of the species and for the repertoire acquired by each member. (p. 205)

From this point of view, the concepts of freedom and autonomy are myths. But if man is controlled by his environment, does this mean that he cannot control his own destiny? If Skinner is right, should human beings sit back passively and wait to be shaped by the external environment? Quite the contrary, replies Skinner. With a sophisticated behavioral technology, we can take very active roles in designing our environments to best suit our own needs. This is exactly what teachers do when they use operant techniques in the classroom.

Why, then, all the controversy? According to operant theorists, the confusion lies in erroneously equating the concepts of control and punishment. For many people, the concept of control evokes the prison camps of Hitler and Stalin, examples of highly punitive control. Eliminating this kind of control, these people claim, can only make the world a better place for human beings. Of course, if the only kind of control were punitive control, Skinner would agree. The fallacy in this argument lies in the belief that by eradicating aversive control, human beings would be utterly free. However, the environment is still there, controlling all behavior as usual.

In fact, the elimination of aversive control leaves human beings much more predictably under the control of the positive reinforcers in the environment. As you recall, a teacher can effectively control students' behavior by using positive reinforcement, but when the teacher uses negative reinforcement to control their behavior, he has no way of knowing beforehand which one of a variety of escape responses they will adopt. Similarly, most governments that use punitive methods of control over their people eventually fall to those who use revolutionary activities as escape responses, and these revolutionary activities can often end up being just as punitive!

Human beings are pervasively controlled in everyday life by positive reinforcers. Society uses a multitude of them to control people's behavior. Employers reward hard work with money, promotions, bonuses, vacations. Even the elected officials in this country receive positive, and only rarely negative, reinforcers; votes and political endorsements serve as positive reinforcers to politicians, and impeachment serves as a negative reinforcer.

The average child sees 22,000 commercials a year on television, and no one can doubt that the stimuli provided by the advertising industry influence children's behavior (McFeatters, 1974). Children often ask their mothers to buy a certain brand of cereal at the store, a request based not on nutritional needs but on TV advertising. Advertising may also be responsible for the extreme emphasis on youth in our culture.

You may agree by now that a lot of our behavior is controlled, but what of it? How significant is it? Look at the world around you for the answer. Delinquency, violent crime, wars, pollution, overpopulation—all of these phenomena are an outcome of man's present behavior but at the same time control man's future behavior. Great advances in technology have given human beings a tremendous control over their environment, but unharnessed technology will do little to raise the quality of life. Sophisticated methods of birth control cannot reduce the population without man's active participation. Human beings can use nuclear energy either to make bombs or to create useful sources of power. What we need, says Skinner, is a behavioral technology that will assure man's effective and benevolent use of physical technology.

| The Use of Behavioral Technology | About 25 years ago, B. F. Skinner wrote a novel, *Walden Two*, in which he described a utopian community based on his operant theory and the behavioral technology he saw emanating from it. Although the community was made up of happy, creative individuals, the idea of it posed a grave threat to critics of behavioral control. Now, many years later, these critics point out, psychologists have advanced behavioral technology to the point where they could establish the controlled community that Skinner envisioned. |

Society has already begun to use operant theories and behavioral technology. For example, many patients seem to respond exceedingly well to token economy and behavior management systems in psychiatric wards around the country; and some types of psychotherapy have been based on behavior theory. One community reported by Holland (1974) has modified the behavior of its policemen by giving them bonuses when the crime rate decreases. Some prisons have used behavior modification techniques. In one highly publicized factory, supervisors systematically reinforced the workers through feedback checklists and social reinforcers ("New Tool," 1972). At present, behavioral technology is used most widely in our schools.

A 123-acre commune in Twin Oaks, Virginia, has patterned itself after the community of Harmony described in *Walden Two* (Kinkade, 1973). This is the first time a community has attempted to employ behavioral engineering in designing a total environment. Each member of the community shares the work equally; no one has any special privileges or titles. The community rewards good work with recognition and endorsement and ignores disruptive behavior such as hostility and jealousy.

In a review of *Beyond Freedom and Dignity,* Day and Mowrer (1972) pointed out that Skinner had failed to discuss fully the possibility that the scientists, or controllers, may abuse their power in applying behavioral techniques. These critics did not intend to diminish the importance of behavioral technology to society, but only to raise the important ethical issues of who should do the controlling, and who should control the controllers.

The Ethics of Behavior Management

Holland (1974), a University of Pittsburgh psychologist, has asked two important and sensitive questions. The first involves the decision process in which behavioral objectives are written, that is: "Who has the moral right to decide what behavior people should or should not adopt?" The second: "Who is a behavioral program *really* designed to benefit, the modifier or the modifi*ee*?" The two questions are connected; one cannot answer the first without resolving the second. Critics have pointed out that behavioral technologists have too often ignored both these questions before instituting programs. In many cases, the subjects of these programs have had no power to do anything about how they were being conditioned. For example, the spread of behavior modification units in our prisons has been the subject of much criticism and controversy over the misuse of these techniques. Prison specialists have designed programs to eliminate so-called disruptive behavior and enhance "appropriate" behavior. They have frequently used negative reinforcement on prisoners and deprived them of positive reinforcement in order to create behavior that meets only the needs of the prisons. Needless to say, abuse is by no means necessarily concomitant with behavior management techniques, although perhaps possible.

These ethical considerations also arise in the classroom. What do we mean by "desirable" and "undesirable" behavior? To answer this question, Winett and Winkler (1972) analyzed every study on classroom behavior management published in the *Journal of Applied Behavior Analysis* between 1968 and 1970.

The subtitle of their study reveals their findings: "Be Still, Be Quiet, Be Docile." Teachers consistently defined desirable behavior as keeping quiet, keeping still, and looking either at a textbook or at the teacher. They defined undesirable behavior as running around the room, talking excessively, and making too much noise. As in prison programs, the teachers wanted above all to instill submissiveness in all their students; they punished any child who was too active or too self-reliant.

Winett and Winkler (1972) went on to suggest that rather than changing the student to fit into the environment, educational planners are responsible for changing the environment itself.

> There is another role, however, for the behavior modifier that involves changing the social system that maintains the behavior, thereby creating new environments instead of patching up the results of the existing environments. In the present context, such a role involves changing the educational system. (p. 502)

Community members most concerned with the welfare of students should become involved in formulating the objectives of behavioral programs. Parents, teachers, and children themselves should jointly discuss what the objectives should be and the methods for reaching them. Certainly children would take a more active role in reinforcing each other to achieve objectives they had a voice in establishing.

Behavior management techniques have become increasingly popular in our society, and many people have become involved in their use and design. Thompson and his colleagues evaluated the effects of a one-week training course in these techniques (Thompson, Brassell, Persons, Tucker, and Rollins, 1974). The trainees were teachers who were being taught how to reinforce quiet and submissive behavior in their students. By the end of the course, the trainees were able to increase significantly the behavior they desired—one more bit of evidence to prove that we as psychologists and educators have a grave responsibility and should examine closely the questions of what behavior we should reinforce, who should make these decisions, and what our purposes are.

Skinner's theories have far-reaching implications for educators and, in fact, for all of society. Though his reflections on the role of the environment are by no means new, systematic application of them to education is:

> It is often said that a scientific view of man leads to a wounded vanity, a sense of hopelessness, and nostalgia. But no theory changes what it is

a theory about; man remains what he has always been. And a new theory may change what can be done with its subject matter. A scientific view of man offers exciting possibilities. We have not yet seen what man can make of man. (1971, pp. 205–206)

SUMMARY

In this chapter we have described associationist theories and discussed their implications. The two major branches of associationist theory are classical and operant conditioning. Through the process of classical conditioning, that is, teaching one to respond to a neutral stimulus after it has been presented, children often come to associate certain classroom stimuli, and sometimes school itself, with anxiety.

Operant conditioning involves teaching one to respond before any stimulus is presented. A response that is followed by a positive reinforcer will tend to recur. A response that is followed by a negative reinforcer (aversive stimulus) will most often result in an unpredictable escape response, which creates serious problems in the classroom for both student and teacher, and is the main argument against the use of punishment.

Two educational techniques based on operant theory are behavior management and programmed instruction. Under behavior management, a teacher immediately gives positive reinforcement for desirable behavior and ignores, and thereby extinguishes, undesirable behavior. Programmed instruction presents the student with material that is arranged in gradual steps from simple concepts to complex, and immediately reinforces the student's response to each step.

Operant theory involves many ethical problems, among them are questions of authority and desirable goals. It is a very potent system and can work toward either the greater benefit of man or his enslavement.

SUGGESTED FOR FURTHER READING

Estes, W. K. *Learning theory and mental development.* New York: Academic Press, 1970.
 An extensive treatment of learning theories and their applications; discusses many other learning theories that are based on those covered in this chapter.

Hill, W. F. *Learning: A survey of psychological interpretations.* San Francisco: Chandler, 1971.
 A review of all the major learning theories; presents current research and opinions.

Skinner, B. F. *Beyond freedom and dignity.* New York: Knopf, 1971 (also available from Bantam Books).
 Deals with the issues of control and personal freedom. A very influential book, it is unique in its importance to psychology and education.

CHAPTER 5

BUILDING UNDERSTANDING: COGNITIVE-FIELD THEORIES

After completing this chapter, the reader should be able to:

1 Describe the laws of organization described by Gestalt theorists and use these laws to explain why people behave as they do.

2 Compare and contrast the insight and productive thinking processes described by early Gestalt theorists with intuitive learning described by Bruner; discuss conditions under which each of these processes exists in the classroom.

3 Describe both pictorially and verbally the life space of any student in a classroom at any given moment; explain how all of the factors affecting this life space in turn affect student behavior.

4 Using Bruner's views on the structure of subject matter, describe how discovery methods of teaching might be applied practically with different subject matters and with students of different ages; explain the difficulties in using such an approach.

5 Select from among the differing theoretical approaches to teaching and learning a method for use with any given student at a particular stage of cognitive development; defend this method as the most useful in that situation.

How do children learn? Not all psychologists believe that learning is simply the result of a series of stimulus-response connections, the position taken in the previous chapter. Some psychologists take the position that learning can best be understood by looking at those processes that come between the stimulus and the response. The cognitive-field theorists' views on learning constitute one such departure from associationism that has profoundly influenced education.

WHAT ARE COGNITIVE-FIELD THEORIES?

Sensation, as it is given meaning through the learning experiences of the developing individual, is called *perception*. As an example of this phenomenon and its importance to living in the real world, consider a classroom of 50 students. Each student "senses" (in terms of an image on his retina) the door of the classroom as a slightly different shape. This is because each student sits in a different position in the classroom in relation to the door. However, when asked the shape of the door, each student no doubt will report that it is rectangular. He perceives it as such whatever the image on his retina because all his past experiences with doors tell him that they are rectangular. Cognitive-field theory is concerned with the many ways in which meaning is attached to sensation, or the ways in which different perceptions are developed. One of the major characteristics of this approach is what we call *relativism*. According to the cognitive-field theorists, in order for any new perception to develop—that is, for a sensation to acquire meaning for an individual—he must first relate it to, or integrate it with, other material with which he is already familiar; he must perceive it in relation to past experience (Bigge, 1964).

The physical characteristics of every stimulus provide an easily recognizable objective reality, but what a particular individual at a particular time perceives may not necessarily correspond precisely to this reality. This occurs because each person in each situation experiences a *psychological reality* as well, which is his perception of the physical sensations he receives. These perceptions may or may not accurately interpret physical reality, and even when they differ greatly from it, they still may be thought of as real by the individual. A good example of this is the optical illusion shown in Figure 5-1, which most of us are probably familiar with. In the drawing, line A *seems* to be longer than line B, but if you measure both lines, you will see that in reality they are exactly the same length.

Cognitive-field theorists use the term *field* (or, more precisely, *perceptual field*) to describe the meaning of an individual's perception at any given moment. Thus, a child who perceives a teacher as

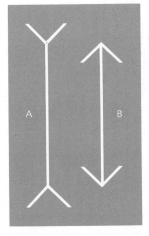

Figure 5-1. Optical illusion.

a threatening individual exists within a field very different from that of a child in the same classroom who perceives the teacher primarily as a major source of reward, and no doubt behaves in a different fashion. This field is also known by some as the *psychological world*. A person's behavior is said to occur within the total space of the field being occupied at that moment. Subsequent new experiences cause changes in the field. The field incorporates not only things that are observable at that moment, but also ideas and events of the past and future. It also includes perceptions that are abstract as well as concrete and imaginary as well as real. All of these have a potential bearing on behavior. Thus, changing perceptions of the teacher's role in terms of potential reward and punishment can change the field and psychological world of the student in the classroom and ultimately his classroom behavior.

Both maturation and experience modify our perceptions, but for the cognitive-field theorist, experience is much more important. Even a newborn infant can sense the qualities of objects and structures in his environment to a limited degree, but the ability to attach meaning to these sensations depends on experience (Travers, 1972).

Based on your past interactions with your environment you can act with dependable foresight in new situations — that is, you can behave intelligently (Bigge, 1964). Some cognitive-field theorists believe that if a person is healthy and has sensory equipment in good working order (that is, he can see, hear, feel, and smell adequately), along with a sufficient amount of time in a stimulating environment, his possibilities for perceptual experience are almost limitless, and his capacity for intelligent behavior can continue to develop for as long as he lives.

The Foundations of Cognitive-Field Theories

Cognitive-field theories are concerned with many different areas of psychology — learning and reasoning, perception, physiological and comparative psychology, and the psychology of personality; thus it is no surprise that they are usually general and all-inclusive, rather than selective and specific. Many cognitive theorists are particularly interested in the higher levels of learning (for instance, concept formation and problem-solving), but the ultimate goal is to be able to explain *all* types of learning, from the simplest trial-and-error learning and conditioning to the most complex forms of human reasoning (Marx, 1970).

Contemporary cognitive-field theory is most indebted to the contributions of the Gestalt psychologists, who laid the groundwork with their principles of perceptual organization. The term *gestalt*, first used by the German psychologist Wertheimer in 1912, means "form," "shape," or "configuration" in rough translation.

A basic principle of Gestalt psychology is that perception is a continuous process of forming and responding to relationships; the environment is thus a constantly changing whole that means more to the individual than simply the sum of its parts. For example, when a person examines the configuration in Figure 5-2 and is asked what he sees, he will usually respond with a statement such as, "two groups of dots" or "two rectangles made of dots" rather than "twelve dots"; that is, he perceives the dots as two large groups rather than individually. When a person looks at a painting, he perceives an image of what has been portrayed rather than a series of brushstrokes. Similarly, when an individual hears a familiar tune played on the piano, he probably does not recognize each of the individual notes that make up that tune, but he does perceive the overall melody, which is based on the relationship between the notes. In other words, information in the environment is meaningful because we perceive the whole by structuring and organizing its parts.

Figure 5-2

The structure we give to a perceptual field (as in Fig. 5-2) is also important in the Gestalt theory of how we learn. To the Gestalt psychologist, learning represents a basic reorganization of the perceptual field or the psychological world. This reorganization occurs every time there is a change in knowledge, skills, attitudes, values, or beliefs, although it need not necessarily be reflected in overt behavior (Bigge, 1964).

Cognitive-field theory views behavior not merely as a collection of stimulus-response associations (the associationist position), but rather as a meaningful product of perceptual changes due to interactions between the individual and his environment (Bigge, 1964; Estes, 1970).

Differences Between Cognitive-Field and Associationist Theories

Another difference between the two approaches lies in the fact that stimulus-response theories rely on observable or overt behavior exclusively, whereas cognitive-field theories utilize both objective and subjective data. Cognitive-field theorists point out that since most human beings consider their subjective experiences very important, psychologists should take those experiences into account in their efforts to understand what the learning processes mean to the individual. To the cognitive-field theorist, then, meanings and feelings are as important in learning as responses.

The cognitive-field approach should also be distinguished from that of motivation theory, which will be discussed in Chapter 6. Cognitive-field theorists are concerned primarily with the relationship between behavior and perception, whereas the basic interest of motivation theorists is the relationship between behavior and the underlying goals toward which the individual is striving. This is known as the "purposeful aspect of behavior." Some psychologists have dealt with both perception and motivation as they relate to be-havior, and in that sense could be correctly classified as either cogni-tive theorists or motivation theorists. Tolman is one such person, but because of his outspoken views on purposive behavior, his work will be discussed in Chapter 6 as part of motivation theory.

GESTALT THEORIES OF LEARNING

Gestalt psychology originated in Germany in the early part of the twentieth century, primarily as a reaction against what were consid-ered the excesses of stimulus-response behaviorism as described by Thorndike and Watson. Wertheimer is credited with having started the Gestalt movement in 1912, but there were other influential spokesmen, such as Kurt Koffka and Wolfgang Köhler.

The Laws of Organization The early Gestalt psychologists felt that a basic understanding of how individuals perceive their environment would advance knowledge of human behavior in general. When these and later theorists turned their attention to learning, they assumed that the same laws of organization they had applied to perception were also applicable to learning (Hilgard and Bower, 1975).

According to Koffka in his famous book *Principles of Gestalt Psy-chology* (1935), the guiding organizational principle for both percep-tion and learning is the *law of Prägnanz*, which includes four sepa-rate laws of organization classified within it: the laws of similarity, proximity, continuation, and closure. The law of Prägnanz states that the organization of sensory experiences tends toward simplici-ty, regularity, and completeness, rather than complexity, lack of regularity, and incompleteness (Hilgard and Bower, 1975). That is, we frequently tend to perceive objects as more simple, regular, and complete than they actually are; thus, when asked to copy drawings from memory, we are likely to overlook small details and irregulari-ties of design, and to finish incomplete drawings rather than to leave them as they are. To explain why this should take place, let us look separately at each of the laws included within the law of Prägnanz.

LAW OF SIMILARITY. The *law of similarity* states that stimuli similar in nature (for instance, in shape or color) are perceived as belonging together. This principle is demonstrated in Figure 5-3, in which the pattern that one perceives consists of vertical rows of white squares alternating with vertical rows of white circles. According to this law, the individual will probably perceive this pattern as a group of vertical rather than horizontal rows. In much the same way, a teach-er on the first day of school might group the students as boys and

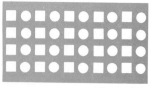

**Figure 5-3.
Law of similarity.**

girls, or blonds and brunettes, and continue to think of them according to these characteristics until he gets to know them as individuals.

LAW OF PROXIMITY. The *law of proximity* is based on the principle that stimuli occurring close to each other tend to be perceived as belonging together, as illustrated in Figure 5-4A. Because of the way the lines and dots are arranged in the figure, a person tends to perceive the stimuli as pairs of either lines or dots; it would be extremely unusual to perceive both lines and dots together in the same group. Figure 5-4B shows several parallel lines separated by spaces of varying width. The lines with narrow spaces between them are probably perceived as part of the same group more readily than the lines with wide spaces between them. Children who frequently play together in groups tend to be associated in the mind of the teacher and thought of as similar in respects other than play.

The law of proximity also applies to other senses, such as auditory perceptions. Sounds that occur close together in time are most likely associated. By using a variety of groups of sounds that represent letters and words and then spacing them with intervals of silence, the Morse code takes advantage of the law of proximity (Hill, 1971).

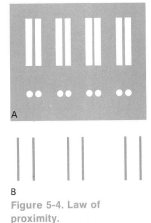
Figure 5-4. Law of proximity.

LAW OF CONTINUATION. The *law of continuation* states that the way in which the first part of a stimulus is perceived determines how a continuation of that stimulus is perceived. Look at the patterns of dots in Figure 5-5, which illustrates this principle. Because of the law of continuation, this pattern will probably be perceived as a curved line (A to D) intersecting a straight line (B to C); one's eye would not normally go from A to B or from C to D.

An example from classroom experience illustrates this law. A student who receives a higher grade on each successive test will be expected by the teacher to receive a still higher grade on the next test. This expectation is likely to affect the teacher's judgment in grading, especially when the test calls for subjective evaluation by the teacher.

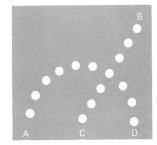
Figure 5-5. Law of continuance.

LAW OF CLOSURE. The *law of closure* is a special case of the law of continuation; it states that closed figures are more stable than unclosed figures. If students are presented with an incomplete drawing of a figure that they would normally recognize, in their minds they will automatically fill in any gaps so that they perceive it as complete. For example, show a friend the incomplete circle in Figure 5-6, allowing him to look at it for only a fraction of a second. Then ask him to reproduce it from memory. He will probably draw a complete circle.

The law of closure was illustrated in a study of forgetting by a

Figure 5-6. Law of closure.

Gestalt psychologist (Wulf, 1922/1938). As in the experiment with Figure 5-6, the subjects were shown some drawings of figures. Then they were asked to draw them from memory. The reproduced drawings were generally simpler and more regular than the originals; furthermore, they resembled familiar objects. In attempting to remember the figures as they actually appeared, the subjects "improved" upon them. A Gestalt psychologist would view such forgetting as a distortion of the original stimulus into something that provides a better gestalt—that is, into something that is simpler, clearer, and more complete (Hill, 1971). A teacher would view such forgetting as a useful phenomenon in learning something like the letters of the alphabet. Imagine how difficult learning would be if we required each handwritten letter to be perfect before we recognized it as the letter it was intended to be!

According to Gestalt theory, the perception of closure is satisfying to the individual. In fact, other psychologists feel that a sense of completion or "closure" comes about after finishing any difficult task or problem-solving activity (not necessarily a perceptual one). It is thought that any such completion acts as a positive reinforcement, so that the original stimulus, the final correct response, and the resulting reinforcement all form a pleasing gestalt for the individual (Hill, 1971).

What these four organizational principles tell us is that people tend to perceive together (and thus attach a unified meaning to) stimuli that appear to be similar, close together, and/or continuous; and that people will form the overall sensation into a logical and meaningful whole.

FIGURE-GROUND PERCEPTION. The ability to distinguish various parts of a stimulus is still another important aspect of perceptual organization recognized by Gestalt theory. Differentiating a figure from its background is the most elementary example of this kind of perception.

For example, when a student walks into a classroom on the first day of school, he encounters a vast array of things—the teacher, other students, room decorations, desk arrangement, writing on the blackboard, and so on. If he were to try to give his attention to each and every one of the aspects of this complex field at the same time, he couldn't possibly attach meaning to everything. Therefore, what he—and each of us—does is to select a particular, limited aspect of this total environment at a given moment in order to make what he sees meaningful to him. The part of the perceptual field to which he pays special attention—that is, the thing that stands out—is called the *figure*. This perceived gestalt may be the teacher, the blackboard, or any other aspect. The rest of the field—the things surrounding the figure that remain undifferentiated for him and to which he does not pay attention—is called the *background* or *ground*.

The relationship between figure and ground can change from one moment to the next. This can be seen in Figure 5-7. One can see two possible configurations: a large white vase against a blue background, or two blue profiles on either side of a white background. If one examines the picture long enough, one can eventually see both (though not simultaneously) as one's perceptions alternate between the stimulus configurations.

Figure 5-7. Figure-ground perception.

Comparable situations exist in everyday life. For example, a person might be totally absorbed in an exciting novel, but if he suddenly hears car brakes squeal outside in the street, he will get up and look out the window. Or a student might be furiously writing an exam in class, unaware that the clock on the wall says he has only three minutes remaining. Then the teacher announces that time is up. His attention shifts to the teacher and the clock.

Sometimes the background assumes a separate, important function of its own. If the material a student is trying to learn—the figure—is ambiguous, he may be able to clarify it by studying it in relation to its context—that is, its ground (Travers, 1972). For example, an instructor may use a new word, the definition of which the student does not know. However, if the student thinks of the word in the context of the sentence or paragraph in which it is being used, he might be able to grasp its meaning without consulting a dictionary.

The teacher can use these principles of organization in perception and learning when presenting new material to his students. For example, he should organize each subject in the curriculum into carefully structured units that follow one another in a logical sequence—a sequence logical both to the teacher and to the student. Clearly, what is well organized from the teacher's point of view may not be well organized from the point of view of the student. In addition, it is a good idea, if possible, to integrate material being taught in one subject area with that being taught at the same time in another subject area (for example, it would be helpful to coordinate social studies and literature in terms of common themes or concerns). Students will take a much more active interest in learning when they can see structure, relevance, and purpose in their curriculum. It is only then that meaning will be attached to the learning process.

Question for Thought:
There are many ways to describe the laws of organization in terms of visual perception. Can you think of ways to describe these same laws in terms of the other senses—for example, touch or hearing?

Insight Learning

When a person perceives a situation in a new way that results in a meaningful change in his cognitive structure, or reorganization of relationships, we say that he has achieved insight. _Insight_ is a form of discovery learning in which the end-results are finding a solution that works and developing an understanding as to _why_ it works (Ausubel, 1968; Hill, 1971). Developing insight implies "grasping" an idea; it is clear that the individual understands the concept and is not simply responding without knowing why (Bigge, 1964). Learning that involves insight is less likely to be forgotten than rote learning, that is, memorization without understanding (Bigge, 1964; Hill, 1971).

Insight involves taking in information from the environment and transforming it into some kind of new understanding. Psychologists have theorized that this process requires analyzing, synthesizing, formulating and testing hypotheses, then accepting or rejecting them, and integrating the results into a meaningful solution. However, even if a person goes through this process, it does not guarantee that he will achieve insight. He may lack the ability to make meaningful inferences from his investigations; or he may not use the correct hypotheses and still, by chance or by imitation, arrive at a solution that will work. But without understanding, the change in his cognitive structure necessary for insight learning will not take place. Older children and adults, with their greater experience in problem-solving, are more likely to achieve insights than are young-

---

FIXATION: ENEMY OF INSIGHT

We all love that moment when "the light comes on" as we're trying to solve a problem. Gestalt psychologists call this _insight_. But sometimes we feel stymied, unable to perceive the essential elements required for a solution. This condition is called _fixation_. Martin Scheerer (1963) has found that it operates in several ways. Often we cling to an incorrect assumption. For example, when asked to assemble six matches to form equilateral triangles each side of which is equal to the length of the matches, most people assume—incorrectly—that the matches must lie flat. The correct solution—building a three-dimensional pyramid—calls for a _reformulation_ or _recentering_ of one's thoughts. His studies also indicate that any type of fixation can be strengthened by too much motivation. Strong ego involvement, for example, makes for overmotivation and is detrimental to the process of finding a solution. A final factor affecting fixation is habit. We use habitual ways of responding because they're most available to us; this makes it much harder to approach a problem with a fresh perspective. Scheerer concludes: "If insight is the essential element in intelligent problem-solving, fixation is its archenemy. Fixation is overcome and insight attained by a sudden shift in the way the problem or objects are viewed . . . precisely what brings [this] about is still unknown. It remains the central problem of problem-solving" (p. 128).

er children. This shouldn't be taken to mean that the development of insight stems from maturation alone; rather, the more experienced the individual, the better able he is to differentiate and restructure a constantly expanding world and then to use this understanding as a guide for his behavior (Bigge, 1964).

The notion of insight learning as a distinct learning process was popularized by the publication in 1925 of the English translation of Köhler's *The Mentality of Apes*, which described his extensive research into problem-solving behavior. Köhler's experiments were conducted with chimpanzees. In a typical experiment, a banana was hung from the top of the animal's cage, out of reach. However, a box was placed elsewhere in the cage; if the ape moved the box and climbed on top of it, he could reach the banana. Köhler called such a solution to the problem "insight." The animal's chance exploration of its immediate environment may have given rise initially to the idea to use the box. But Köhler also observed that sometimes the ape would pause after failing to reach the banana by familiar methods and then, as if saying "Eureka!" suddenly see the solution. After seeing the ape pause in this way, Köhler came to the conclusion that insight learning had occurred. In this problem, all the stimuli necessary to solve it were clearly visible, but Gestalt psychologists have maintained that insight learning is possible even when such stimuli are not visibly present, such as when a rat searches out food in a maze, although the development of insight will be more gradual.

Insight learning can be verbal, preverbal, or nonverbal. In apes and in other lower animals, it is, of course, nonverbal; and in humans, too, it may be nonverbal. A very young child learns how to put food in his mouth, pull himself to a standing position in a playpen, and crawl across the floor; he acquires insight into solving these problems without ever putting any of the issues into words!

INSIGHT AS PRODUCT AND PROCESS.   If insight cannot always be verbalized, how can we recognize it when it occurs? In answer to this question, Gestalt theorists describe insight as both a product and a process (Ausubel, 1968). As a *product*, insight refers to the end-results of meaningful problem-solving. For example, a boy realizes that the stains on his new shirt were put there when his younger brother wore it last night. Subjectively, this means a feeling of overall satisfaction: So he borrowed it, did he! If so, he is responsible for the stain! Objectively, it includes the practical application of the newly obtained solution: He'll pay the cleaning bill!

As a *process*, insight is those steps a person takes in solving a problem. According to the cognitive-field theorist, the process of insight depends on both the structure of the problem and the past experiences of the learner. This points to a major difference be-

THE CLASSIFICATION OF PROBLEMS   Psychologists hope one day to define general principles of problem-solving. But first we need to find a satisfactory classification of problems, says Robert Travers (1967). Several psychologists, working independently, have done so (Bartlett, 1968; Guilford, 1956; Marx, 1958). They separate problems into two broad classes: those that have a fixed solution and those that are open-ended, for which many different solutions are possible. The problem of finding the correct size tire to replace a flat on your car is a fixed-solution type of problem. On the other hand, buying a car that will best suit your needs and pocketbook is an open-ended one. The latter case involves weighing the alternatives for solutions, investigating different directions, and testing hypotheses. Fixed-solution problems involve convergent thinking; that is, the thinking processes involved converge on the one and only correct solution. Open-ended problems involve divergent thinking; here the thinking processes have to move out into unexplored territory (Guilford, 1956).

tween cognitive-field theories and association theories. Association theory implies that in order to solve a problem (to give the correct response), a person needs certain prior learning experiences; he then solves the problem by associating both his behavior in the past with that in the present, and environmental stimuli he has experienced in the past with those in the present. Gestalt theorists would agree that in order to solve new problems certain learning experiences are necessary, but they believe that the structure of the learning situation is important too. Some environmental arrangements lead more easily to insight than others (Ausubel, 1968; Hilgard and Bower, 1975).

THE GRADUAL DEVELOPMENT OF INSIGHT AND THE ROLE OF CHANCE. Solutions based on insight often appear to occur suddenly and unexpectedly, but this is not actually the case. When confronted initially with a new problem, our behavior seems to be exploratory, unsure, and largely unproductive, until suddenly we discover exactly what we are looking for. And just before reaching a solution, we do not appear behaviorally to be doing anything to solve the problem. Gestalt theorists interpret this period of seeming inactivity as time used for quiet reflection, in which we restructure our perceptions so as to arrive at a solution (Hill, 1971). Insight learning involves a gradual process of progressive clarification about means-end relationships, obtained through testing hypotheses (Ausubel, 1968). We may say "Eureka!" as though surprised when we hit upon a solution, but the insight really does not come abruptly.

Chance plays a role in insight learning. Yerkes (1943) first illustrated this point in an experiment in which a chimpanzee watched the experimenter insert a banana into a tube open at both ends. The chimpanzee's task was to get the banana out, but his initial efforts were unsuccessful. There happened to be a hoe handle in the room, which the chimpanzee by chance threw in the direction of the tube. The animal stopped playing, reflected for a moment, then picked up the handle and used it to push the banana out of the tube. From a chance event came a valuable hint that led ultimately to the solution of the problem. Similar things, of course, happen in human experience all the time.

THE TEST FOR INSIGHT: TRANSPOSITION.   The only true way to determine if a person has developed insight is to present him with a situation that has the same basic characteristics as the original but that is not exactly the same in every detail, and to see if he can apply the same principles to the new situation. If he is capable of doing this, *transfer of training* or, in Gestalt terms, *transposition* has occurred. This process is important in much of human learning, including concept formation and problem-solving.

Wertheimer's *Productive Thinking* (1945/1959), published posthumously, has been a widely read and influential book on Gestalt psychology. Wertheimer was particularly interested in the thinking of schoolchildren and in the practical applications of Gestalt theory to education, and this emphasis is found throughout his writings.

Productive Thinking

In *Productive Thinking*, Wertheimer distinguished between two types of attempted solutions to a problem. Type A solutions involve originality and productive thinking. When used, they indicate that the learner understands the meaning and use of previous experience, as well as the essential structure of the problem itself. Type B solutions also use past experience, but they are *blind* solutions, really no more than trial and error. That is, solutions that were acceptable earlier but are not appropriate to solving the new problem are applied mechanically without understanding (Hilgard and Bower, 1975; Hill, 1971).

Wertheimer (1945/1959) turned to the field of geometry to compare the two approaches to problem-solving. In one study, children were first taught how to find the area of a rectangle by watching Wertheimer divide a large rectangle into many small squares. No formula memorization was involved; they were given visual evidence that the area of the rectangle was equal to the number of squares in each row multiplied by the number of rows.

The children were then presented with an unfamiliar figure—a parallelogram without right angles—and asked to find its area. Some protested that they could not solve the problem without an-

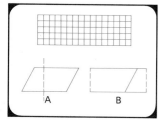

Figure 5-8. Wertheimer's parallelogram problem. (top) Rectangle divided into small squares showed the children how to find the area of the rectangle. (bottom) A and B represent the child's solution to the problem of finding the area of a parallelogram.

other demonstration of what to do; others blindly tried to follow the same procedure they had learned for finding the area of a rectangle. Of course, they obtained incorrect answers to the problem. Some children were able to get the correct answer (multiplying base times altitude) merely by trial-and-error experimentation. However, these children had no clear understanding of why the method worked. In all these cases, the children were giving Type B responses to the problem, indicating no productive reasoning on their part.

A few children did arrive at Type A solutions to the problem. One child noted that the source of difficulty was the two projecting ends, but that the part that was "no good" on one side was "right" on the other side (Wertheimer, 1945/1959). She asked for scissors, cut off the left end of the figure, and then placed it at the right end, thus converting the parallelogram into a rectangle (see Fig. 5-8). Another child, also showing conceptual understanding, converted the piece of paper into a ring, so that the two ends fit together. She then cut the ring vertically so it became a rectangle. These two subjects integrated the parallelogram problem with what they had previously learned. This reflected their ability to reorganize an unfamiliar and puzzling perception into one that was familiar and meaningful. By changing the parallelogram into a better gestalt—a rectangle—they gained an understanding of its structural relationships and discovered a logically correct and original means for achieving the goal they were seeking: finding the area of the parallelogram.

Wertheimer believed that the goal of education should be to create genuine understanding and productive thinking. Two major implications of Wertheimer's position on teaching are that rote memorization ought to be deemphasized as much as possible and that material should be presented in such a way that children would have to fill in the necessary gaps themselves rather than being led by a teacher. Only if a teacher makes it conducive for children to discover the essential nature of a problem can children respond to a problem productively instead of mechanically (Hilgard and Bower, 1975; Hill, 1971).

Question for Thought

Can you think of some ways to teach the multiplication tables in a manner that would meet Wertheimer's requirement for "genuine understanding and productive thinking"?

Topological or Vector Theory of Learning (Lewinian Field Theory)

Kurt Lewin (1935, 1936, 1951), a leading Gestalt psychologist, shared a general orientation with his colleagues but differed from them in the emphasis of his research. Whereas Wertheimer, Köhler, and Koffka were deeply involved with the technical aspects of perception, learning, and thinking, Lewin was concerned with the relationship among perception, motivation, and individual personality.

Lewin felt that a good psychological theory should be broad enough to apply to all kinds of behavior yet specific enough to describe the behavior of a given individual in a particular situation and to predict differences as well as similarities among people (Bigge, 1964).

LIFE SPACE. The major concept in Lewinian field theory is the *life space*, or psychological field, which Lewin used to predict the behavior of an individual at a particular time. A person's life space is the total psychological world in which he lives. It includes the person as a psychological entity plus all the various aspects of his environment, not necessarily as they exist in reality, but as they are perceived by him.

The study of life space and its various components always begins with an examination of the individual's total environment. Everything in the life space is to some degree interrelated or interdependent. Everything that affects behavior at a given moment is included in the field, and everything that does not is excluded. The life space incorporates events and ideas relating to the person's past or future as well as to his immediate present, as long as they influence his behavior (Bigge, 1964).

The goals of individuals, the negative consequences they attempt to avoid, the barriers that stand in the way of achieving the goals, and the actions necessary to reach the goals are all considered part of the life space. However, individuals are not necessarily aware of the influences contributing to their behavior. Sometimes we are affected by factors we do not consciously recognize; in fact, we may even deny these influences if somebody calls them to our attention. Nevertheless, consistencies in our behavior show that these influences do exist.

Consider, for example, a high school student who has a part-time job after school, and who spends an inordinate amount of her salary on expensive clothes and accessories. She would probably tell you that she is extravagant simply because she likes to look nice, or perhaps because her social life requires that she be well dressed. However, other aspects of her behavior might indicate to people who know her well that she is basically insecure and needs compliments to build her self-esteem. Her need for attention and recognition, although probably unknown to her, is as much an influence on her preoccupation with her appearance as her desire to look good.

According to Lewinian theory, the life space that represents psychological reality should be distinguished from the physical or geographical space that represents physical reality. The life space usually has some aspects in common with the physical environment, but the extent of the correspondence varies from person to person

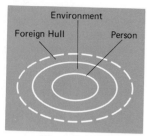

Figure 5-9. The three concentric ovals include a person, his environment, and the foreign hull of his life space, respectively. The person is part of his environment, and both are contained in the foreign hull.

because the life space is not limited to what is immediately apparent to the senses. It includes memories, expectations, abstract ideas, values, and beliefs, as well as dreams and delusions, which are formed largely from each individual's own personality and experiences. A brother and sister growing up in the same home can have very different life spaces; two students in the same class for five years of elementary school can have very different life spaces. And the life space of psychotic individuals certainly bears little resemblance to their actual physical environment (Travers, 1967). The life space is the simultaneous interaction between a person and his environment. Whether or not its content has a basis in external reality is immaterial. The only reality of importance in a life space is that one the individual perceives as real.

On the other hand, there are certain things present in a person's immediate, external environment that, for one reason or another, do not affect his behavior at all. That is, he pays no attention to these things and is seemingly unaware of their existence. They are excluded from that persons's life space and make up what is known by Lewinian theorists as the *foreign hull.* A life space may be drawn as a series of concentric ovals representing the individual, his environment, and the foreign hull (Fig. 5-9).

"MAPPING" LIFE SPACES: TOPOLOGICAL DIAGRAMS.   According to Lewin, the more we know about an individual's life space, the easier it is to accurately predict his behavior in a variety of circumstances. Because the idea of a life space is extremely complex, picturing it as a large *cognitive map* made up of many different regions separated by boundaries might be helpful in understanding it. Lewinian psychologists call such a "map" a *topological diagram* (Hill, 1971).

A topological diagram is simply a convenient way to depict visually the significant elements in a person's life space. As an example, the life space of a female teacher with professional aspirations is shown in the topological diagram in Figure 5-10. This woman, whose ultimate ambition is to become principal of her school, already is a successful teacher. The diagram shows that there are alternative paths open to her on the way to her goal. She might, for example, enroll full time in a graduate degree program in educational administration, or she might instead apply for the position of vice-principal and receive her administrative training on the job. There may be, in addition, other alternatives. Of course, she might run into barriers that she cannot pass on any one of these paths. In this case, she would have to revise her plans.

Figure 5-10 shows a life space in terms of what is most important to this teacher: professional aims. If we wanted instead to depict the life space of a youngster whose goal was to gain autonomy from his

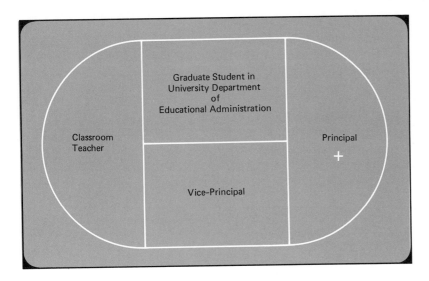

Figure 5-10. A topological diagram showing the life space of a teacher who wants to be a school administrator.

parents, the regions in the diagram would be childhood, adolescence, and adulthood, with the barriers between them.

VALENCES AND VECTORS IN LIFE SPACES.   Another important concept in Lewinian theory is *valence*. In a topological diagram, this is shown by a plus sign, as illustrated, for example, in the "principal" region in Figure 5-10. Places, objects, or situations to be avoided are said to have *negative valence*. This is shown by a minus sign in a topological diagram.

According to Lewin, the topological regions and the boundaries or barriers located between them in a person's life space determine the possible paths that a person might follow in pursuit of his goals. Since an individual cannot follow every path simultaneously, the relative strengths of the positive and negative valences of these regions are used by him to help predict which regions he is likely to approach and which he is likely to avoid—that is, valences help predict a person's behavior.

To deal with the problem of competing valences, Lewin incorporated the concept of the *vector* into his theoretical system, a term he borrowed from physics. A vector is a moving force operating in a specified direction; it is represented in a topological diagram by an arrow whose direction shows the direction of force and whose length shows the strength of force. (See Fig. 5-11.)

By comparing the direction and length of all the vectors in the diagram of a person's life space at any given moment, we should be able to determine the relative strength of all the forces acting on that person at that time. Each vector influences movement either toward

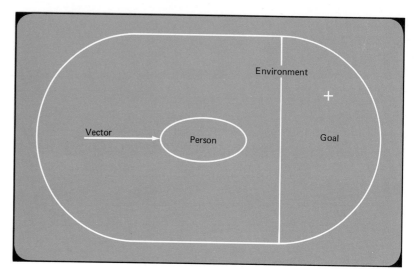

Figure 5-11. Topological diagram showing a vector.

or away from a specified goal, increasing or decreasing the possibility of change. (Bigge, 1964).

Whenever a person is forced to choose between two or more situations with valences similar in direction and strength, there is a potential for conflict. Should you do your homework and get good grades, or should you go out with your friends and have fun, but go to class unprepared? The choice between two possibilities with negative valences is a particularly difficult type of conflict (Travers, 1967). For example, a child who has stolen a dollar from the family cookie jar might feel guilty if he doesn't confess. On the other hand, if he does confess, he probably will be punished. The child may vacillate between the two unpleasant options, but eventually he must choose what to him is the least unpleasant option. In a topological diagram, the shorter of the two arrows will stand for this option.

As the individual matures, his life space grows larger, and its various regions become increasingly differentiated. This occurs because he becomes aware of different options open to him and of the valences he has assigned to them. For example, a young child may have a vague idea that he wants to be a doctor—a positive valence—but not the slightest idea of what he has to do to reach that goal. By the time he is an adolescent, his original desire may have taken on a negative valence as well, because he has learned of the long and difficult training period, or because he feels he is not intelligent enough. He will then have to differentiate the pathways to the goal of a medical career through various successive regions— college, medical school, internship, and so on. Any of these regions could conceivably evoke negative aspects as well as positive ones, such as less free time and more responsibility. If the positive aspects outweigh the negative ones or outweigh the possible competing positive valences in other areas, he is likely to plan to proceed to medical school and, finally, to a medical degree.

According to some psychologists, Lewin's vector theory—in its concern with the structure of life space and the effects on behavior of valences within that life space—neglects the influence of external physical reality on a person's choices. For example, if the ability of the individual just discussed to finance a medical education or to achieve sufficiently high grades is not considered, the theory will not accurately predict his behavior.

Actually, it is very difficult to either prove or disprove whether a person's behavior can be predicted through understanding his psychological field (Travers, 1967). In the very process of investigating what appears to be the content of a particular life space at a particular point in time, one is likely to alter it. This is possible whether one is trying to determine the content of one's own life space or that of someone else. Some psychologists and psychiatrists ask their patients many questions in order to learn what they are thinking and why they behave as they do. But simply by asking questions, and by reacting to the responses given, they become part of their patients' life spaces—thus changing them from the way they were at the outset.

IMPLICATIONS OF TOPOLOGICAL THEORY FOR EDUCATION. Some aspects of Lewin's approach can be applied by teachers. Basically, the teacher should provide pleasant, rewarding, and stimulating experiences in all situations where learning or, more specifically, cognitive restructuring is desired. Students are then more likely to seek out such a situation for their own psychological fields, and to remain there because of the positive valence associated with it (Travers, 1967). Such a suggestion, of course, would also be made by associationist theorists.

Teachers can change negative valences into positive ones by restructuring uninteresting subject matter into something meaningful, challenging, and rewarding by changing the context in which it is learned (McConnell, 1942). This position is one taken by motivation theorists, also, and will be discussed at length in Chapter 6.

The concepts of Lewin's vector theory might also benefit teachers by providing them with a new approach to understanding the thinking processes of the individual child. Teachers too often tend to view things primarily from the standpoint of their own goals and experiences rather than from the child's point of view (Travers, 1972). For a student to learn effectively, a teacher must see the relationship between his own life space and that of his students. Teachers should try to grasp not only the activities, values, and goals that are already part of a child's life space, but also the potential environmental influences not in that life space—that is, in the foreign hull. How, for example, would changes in the U.S. economy affect a child? This information would help teachers to better predict, understand, and deal with the behavior of their pupils so that they can determine what is and is not possible in the life space of a particular child.

Question for Thought

Make a list of what might appear in the life space or foreign hull of a student that might affect his classroom behavior in ways noticeably different from other students. How might you, as a teacher, use this information to individualize instruction?

 ## BRUNER'S THEORIES OF LEARNING

Jerome Bruner has been greatly influenced by the theoretical contributions of Gestalt psychology. Bruner emphasizes the Gestalt principles of organization in developing concepts of structure and insight learning, which he refers to as "intuition." According to Bruner, the primary purpose of education is the learning of skills in such a way that they can be used in other worthwhile situations (Bruner, 1966). He feels that school curricula should be organized so that once children master the early basic skills of a subject, later learning of a more advanced nature will be facilitated.

In his famous critique, *The Process of Education*, Bruner (1960) uses examples from the teaching of scientific and mathematical concepts to illustrate basic principles that are applicable to all areas of teaching and learning. Four central themes are detailed in this book, each of which assumes a major role in Bruner's theory.

The first theme is that learning involves understanding basic relationships in the *structure* of a subject, rather than merely knowing facts and techniques. According to Bruner, once a student effectively relates one aspect of knowledge to another, he will acquire a sense of direction that will add excitement to his learning process. This understanding of relationships will aid the student's retention of the material and his transfer of it to new learning situations.

Readiness for learning is Bruner's second theme. According to Bruner, the basic foundations of any discipline can be taught in a form simple enough to be meaningful even to very young children. In this respect he agrees with Piaget, who maintained that we can always teach a child if we match the subject matter to his cognitive level. Bruner disagrees with those who interpret the concept of readiness to mean that instruction in certain subjects must be postponed until the student has reached a certain level of maturity.

The desire to become a fireman, common among young boys, can be used to motivate learning.

(Leonard Freed, Magnum Photos)

As his third theme, Bruner maintains that schools should place much more emphasis on the development of *intuitive thinking*. Intuitive thinking involves the ability to arrive at reasonable but tentative formulations, prior to any actual formal analysis. It results in the "hunch" or educated guess, which may, of course, be either correct or incorrect. Bruner is not suggesting that students should rely exclusively on guessing, but he is saying that children should not be penalized for such responses. In daily life, we must often make decisions and take action on the basis of incomplete knowledge, and so Bruner feels that children should have early training in creative thinking and in recognizing the value of their guesses.

Motivation is the essence of the fourth theme. According to Bruner, a child can be motivated to learn. The teacher is essential in stimulating such a desire, and, if he is effective in this role, the student's desire to learn will carry over from the environment of the classroom to the rest of his world. Bruner feels that a teacher can best stimulate learning by creating interest in the material itself so that the student can realize that it is worth knowing. External goals such as grades, according to this approach, should be deemphasized.

Bruner is also concerned with the practical problems that occur in the implementation of his theories. Creating curriculum materials that will reflect the basic principles of a subject is the first problem. The second is designing teaching methods that will best utilize the capacities of students of different ages or grades and abilities. Piaget dealt with this problem also (see Chapter 2).

Bruner's Views on Structure

The Gestalt concept of *structure* is a key element in Bruner's learning theory. Let us, then, examine this basic concept and, in addition, consider his views on the purpose of education, in order to understand how he sees the relationship of the structure of a subject to school learning.

According to Bruner (1960), the main purpose of teaching is to "give a student as quickly as possible a sense of the fundamental ideas of a discipline—in other words, to convey the structure of a subject" (p. 3). This means the teacher must help the student to understand the subject in such a way that he can relate it to other subjects in meaningful ways. Thus, for Bruner, the structure of a subject—its fundamental ideas and the relationships among them—must be understood if the subject is to be used (Lowe, 1969). Structure presumably sets the boundaries between one subject matter and another. In addition, if understood by the student, structure provides meaning and substance to all material that is being learned (Lowe, 1969).

Structure is both a product and a process in that it includes not only the fundamental ideas of a subject but a way of perceiving the logical relationships of the ideas as well (Lowe, 1969). In this way it aids learning and memory: We *understand* more if the material is logically organized. We also *remember* more if we can see how the various ideas relate to each other.

Structure is important to memory because human memory is selective. We cannot deal with large masses of unrelated information at any one time. In fact, psychologists have shown that we can store only about seven independent ideas, or "chunks" of information, simultaneously in our memories (Miller, 1956). Obviously, by reorganizing information, we can greatly increase the total amount of material we can absorb and remember. But to be useful and productive, the human memory must do more than store information. We must be able to retrieve from our memory such information as is relevant at a particular time. Logical organization facilitates this process.

The structure and the sequence of the structured material are important topics in Bruner's learning theory. He maintains that the basic structure of any body of knowledge depends on three related aspects of learning, which he calls the mode of representation, economy, and power. These vary not only with the nature of the material but also with the age and the ability of the learner.

MODE OF REPRESENTATION.   Mode of representation refers to the basic method by which people understand and make use of their environments (Bruner, 1964, 1966). Bruner calls these modes enactive, iconic, and symbolic. Infants are capable of using only the most basic mode, the *enactive:* "a set of actions appropriate for achieving a certain result" (Bruner, 1966, p. 4). This basic mode involves processing information using only one response, such as a motor response. An infant crawling across a room to reach a doll is an example of this mode. The second mode of representation develops as the child increases in age, and is called the *iconic mode* (pictorial representation): It is "a set of summary images or graphics that stand for a concept without defining it fully" (Bruner, 1966, p. 44). A young child drawing a picture of a doll he has seen is an example of the iconic mode. The most advanced mode of representation is the *symbolic mode*, because it provides a means of going beyond what is immediately perceptible in a situation. Language plays a major role in this mode; for example, an adult describing a doll he has seen is using symbolic representation. We will discuss these three modes more fully later on in the chapter.

ECONOMY.   Economy is related to the structure of a subject and concerns the amount of information a person must learn and remember in order to understand that subject. The larger the amount, the less the economy. If, for example, we asked a child to memorize all the multiplication tables from 1 to 9 at the same time without developing a series of steps providing meaning, there would be little economy of learning. In order to learn economically, we should use initial learning, not only to acquire new information but also to get the maximum use out of it (Bruner, 1959, 1966). When a school curriculum is organized around atomistic or "episodic" units—for example, students first learn addition, then separately learn multiplication—the result is, according to Bruner, uneconomical. That is, the earlier learning (addition) is not effectively utilized to facilitate the later learning (multiplication) (Bruner, 1959). To learn multiplication, the students in a sense must begin all over again because they were not shown the relationship between the two units. A much more economical way of teaching, according to Bruner, would be to divide learning into a series of steps to explain why both parts of the curriculum—addition and multiplication—make sense. Thus what is learned as addition would be used to teach multiplication.

ECONOMY AND CONCEPT LEARNING

Does the simulation of reality help or hinder concept learning? Francis Dwyer (1972) conducted a study to find out. He compared four groups of students taking a course in the anatomy of the human heart. All groups heard the same tape-recorded lecture, but the visual aids differed. Group 1 saw no pictures, only the names of the parts of the heart flashed on a screen as they listened; Group 2 saw abstract line-drawings; Group 3 saw more detailed, shaded drawings; and Group 4 saw realistic photographs. Those who saw only simple line drawings learned the most. Those who saw the realistic photographs (the least economic) learned the least of the four groups. Evidently, reality can be uneconomical. It often introduces irrelevant and distracting details which can interfere with concept learning. "Stick to the basics" thus finds experimental support—at least in initially clarifying the critical features of a concept. Studies such as this suggest something more (as studies tend to do): that teachers need to intelligently evaluate the aids they utilize in the classroom. As a famous architect once noted, less is often more.

POWER.   The power of the material being learned is its value in terms of its applicability. Although a summary of a topic is a very economical means of presentation, it won't be as powerful as a more thorough description of the same material that teaches meaning and use. Using addition concepts to teach multiplication is a good example of this concept. Material can thus be economical in its presentation although it lacks power. However, Bruner warns us, the reverse is quite unlikely; if material is presented uneconomically, the emphasis on meaning and use will be dissipated and some of its power will be lost (Bruner, 1966).

PROPER SEQUENCING OF INFORMATION.   The sequence of the structured material is the order in which the component parts of the subjects are presented. Bruner believes that because each situation is different, there is no one sequence that will apply to all learners in all situations. Among the factors that determine which sequence will work best are the stage of development, past experiences, and individual preferences of the learner, along with the nature of the materials themselves and the criteria by which learning will be measured (Bruner, 1966).

Whatever sequence of learning materials is adopted, at some point the teacher must provide the learner with feedback about the appropriateness of his responses. In this respect, Bruner is in firm agreement with the operant theorists discussed in Chapter 4. According to Bruner, it is necessary to provide feedback when the student compares what he has done with some criterion of what he hopes to achieve. If feedback is given earlier, before the student has had a chance to respond, it might not be understood; and if it is given later, long after he has responded, it might result in forgetting and wasted effort (Bruner, 1966). Bruner shares at least one point of view with the behaviorist B.F. Skinner—namely, an emphasis on the importance of certain kinds of reinforcement in learning. Furthermore, a teacher must be specific in telling a student how he is doing. That is, the teacher must provide him with detailed information on his immediate activities as well as on his progress toward the ultimate goals he had in mind when he started his activities (Bruner, 1966). Both the timing and specificity of feedback, according to Bruner, are important to learning.

Transfer, or the application of knowledge from one area to another, is one of Bruner's major concerns. In today's complex world, vast amounts of information are available and necessary in order to cope with day-to-day interactions. It is important to provide more opportunities within the classroom for transfer of what is learned there to the outside world.

Bruner's Views on Transfer

The manner in which material is taught affects the ability of the student to use it in new ways in new situations. According to Bruner, the more organized and integrated the manner in which it is taught, the more the student can then use it as a base on which to add further information. For example, although isolated facts may become dated later on, they are still relevant to a student if he understands their basic meanings, the relationships among them, and the methods of inquiry used to acquire them (Lowe, 1969). If this approach is used in the classroom, the teacher can help the student to become a "scholar."

The important issue for Bruner is not so much what we learn, but what we can do with it or, as he puts it, how well we can cross the barrier from learning to thinking (Bruner, 1959). In order for a child to understand relationships and transfer knowledge to new situations—that is, cross the barrier—the learning that takes place in the classroom must be clearly related to everyday life (Bruner, 1965). Bruner deplores "passivity of knowledge-getting," which characterizes much of the learning that takes place in schools. In his view, the schools encourage students simply to memorize by rote, without considering the importance of understanding meaning, and to gather facts and learn formulas; the schools do not stimulate an inclination or enthusiasm to pursue knowledge. One problem with current education, according to Bruner (1959), is that:

The emphasis is upon gaining and storing information, gaining and storing it in the form in which it is presented. We carry the remainder in long division so, peaches are grown in Georgia, transportation is vital to cities, New York is our largest port, and so on. . . . There is little effort indeed which goes into the process of putting the information together, finding out what is generic about it.

So knowledge-getting becomes passive. Thinking is the reward for learning, and we may be systematically depriving our students of this reward as far as school learning is concerned. (p. 184)

Bruner is by no means alone in emphasizing the importance of transfer, and the views of other theorists concerned with its role in learning will be discussed in Chapter 8.

Bruner's Views on Cognitive Development

Bruner (1960) has proposed that "any subject can be taught effectively in some intellectually honest way to any child at any stage of development" (p. 26). On the surface this statement seems either to disregard or to nullify the years of painstaking research by Piaget and other developmental psychologists. But Bruner is not saying that the cognitive stages of development are unimportant; rather, he is stressing that the structure of most learning material is usually adaptable to different levels of cognitive functioning (Shulman, 1968). This depends, among other factors, on the method of teaching.

Although he is not denying that a child's ability to master certain

TODDLER LOGIC Bruner's proposal that children, depending on how they are taught, can learn difficult concepts before prescribed stages of cognitive development, seems to have been illustrated in a Princeton University laboratory in which 4-year-olds perform intellectual feats that theoretically only adults can do ("Toddler Logic: New Findings," *Society*, 1974). The program, designed by a specialist in cognitive psychology, Thomas Trabasso, refutes the assumption that reasoning abilities develop in discrete stages, each stage dependent on the previous one. He feels that this theory omits such factors as memory, perception, language, and personal experience. Trabasso's preschoolers were able to reason deductively—for example, Fred is bigger than John; John is bigger than George; therefore, Fred is also bigger than George. They succeeded because the experimenters made sure that the children remembered the people and their relative sizes. The previous failures of children on such tasks, asserts Trabasso, were due not to the lack of reasoning ability but to memory—the children forgot the names and sizes of Fred, John, and George. Five-year-olds were also able to group things into categories (presumably impossible before age 9) when the categories used in the problems were ones with which the children were already familiar. Thus, experience played a role in their success. Such experiments suggest that if their learning environments are arranged in certain ways, very young children are capable of solving logical problems; that they can reason deductively just as adults can.

kinds of tasks increases as he grows up, Bruner believes that even a very young child is capable of some understanding of basic ideas and concepts if he is given appropriate learning experiences. In a new situation, the child who has a foundation of appropriate learning experiences can return to the same ideas, but in a different and more advanced context.

DEVELOPMENTAL STAGES.   Bruner's approach takes into consideration Piaget's theory that the child's intellectual development occurs in three basic stages (Bruner, 1960). Piaget's theory of cognitive development, already discussed at length in Chapter 2, will not be elaborated here, but a brief restatement of the names and characteristics of the three stages would be useful in understanding Bruner's ideas. In brief, Piaget's stages are: Stage 1, *preoperational*, which occurs during the preschool years, when the child manipulates his external world through action; Stage 2, *concrete operations*, which occurs during the elementary school years, when the child can conceptualize solutions to problems in his immediate reality rather than relying exclusively on overt trial and error; Stage 3, *formal operations*, which occurs between ages 10 and 14, when the child becomes capable of formulating hypotheses and making logical deductions from them that he can later test by experimentation or observation.

Piaget's stages correspond, in order, to Bruner's three modes of representation of subject matter discussed earlier in this chapter: enactive, iconic, and symbolic. The importance of this parallel lies in Bruner's belief that teachers can combine the knowledge of both developmental stages and modes of representation to determine the language and context appropriate for teaching the structure of a discipline at different periods of childhood. Young children are thought to learn best by the enactive mode; thus, they should be introduced to ideas by having an opportunity to "act out" those ideas, since they are not yet ready for abstract thinking (preoperational stage). For example, a group of preschool children could best be introduced to some basic principles of economics by playing "store." Later, these ideas can be taught by using pictures or diagrams, as in the iconic mode of representation (concrete operations stage). Finally, the child is ready to learn and express ideas on an abstract or symbolic level (formal operations stage). This symbolic mode of representation is not only the most sophisticated way of learning something new—in this example, microeconomics—it can also be the most powerful way if the child is ready to learn in this mode (Lowe, 1969).

THE CONCEPT OF READINESS.   In setting up the elementary school curriculum, educators work under the assumption that the child who has entered first grade has completed the preoperational stage, characterized by enactive representation, and is now ready for Bruner's Stage 2—but not for Stage 3. Too often educators apply rigid rules to decide specific chronological ages at which pupils are capable of learning certain subjects. Such educators interpret the stage-dependent approach to cognitive development as meaning that a child should not be taught certain tasks until he has reached the necessary stage of cognitive development.

In Chapter 7 we will discuss the learning problems that develop when kindergarten students who have failed to pass reading-readiness tests are required to repeat kindergarten so that they might mature sufficiently before entering first grade and beginning to learn to read. Many educators have pointed out that it is a mistake to leave such children alone and simply wait for them to mature; it seems clear that with appropriate stimulation they will be ready to learn to read much earlier than if they are ignored and allowed only to repeat what they have already done.

It is the overly rigid application of the stage-dependent approach to cognitive development that Bruner disagrees with, as it does not take into account the role of teaching method; he does not disagree with the stages themselves. Bruner believes that a student should not have to wait in order to learn: Rather, the concept of readiness should be understood to take into account the subject matter as well as the child. The same subject matter, he says, could be presented

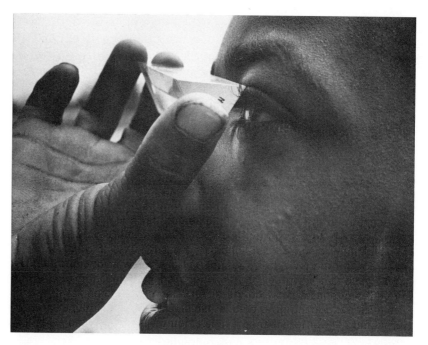

Bruner feels that a complex subject can be understood in simple terms by children at an early age; as they grow older, children can master its complexities.

(Bruce Roberts, Rapho/Photo Researchers)

first at an enactive level, next at an iconic level, and finally at a symbolic level. This logical progression from the simple to the complex in the structural representation of the subject matter is, in essence, Bruner's concept of a *spiral curriculum.*

Bruner also believes that the school curriculum, even at the elementary level, need not adhere rigidly to the general course of cognitive development. By providing the child with challenging problems a step ahead of his development, a teacher can actually lead him to higher levels of reasoning at a more rapid rate than he would ordinarily be expected to display.

Bruner's suggestions have inspired many investigators to try to determine to what extent certain aspects of cognitive development (for instance, the ability to learn the principle of conservation of volume) can indeed be speeded up effectively. The results are far from conclusive, however, and the implications for both learning and education await the outcome of further research.

Questions for Thought
Should we abolish readiness tests?
If so, what could be put in their place?
If not, what new directions might be given to teachers who use them in order to increase classroom learning?

THE ACT OF LEARNING. Bruner's concern with cognitive development is not limited to development stages and the concept of readiness; the components of learning interest him as well. According to Bruner, the process of learning a subject takes place in a series of episodes, each of which involves three integrated steps: acquisition, transformation, and evaluation (Bruner, 1960). The first step, *acquisition,* is the process of obtaining new information that can be used to either replace or refine something known previously. The second step, *transformation,* is the manipulation of information to make it fit new situations. The third step, *evaluation,* is the process of checking whether the acquired information has been manipulated appropriately. The teacher can tailor the nature of these learning episodes to the needs and capacities of the individual student. For example, the teacher can either shorten or lengthen the time spent on a particular step.

Bruner, like the Gestalt psychologists discussed earlier, stresses how *insight* contributes to learning with understanding. Although he prefers the terms "intuition" or "intuitive thinking," the basic concept is the same.

Bruner's Views on Insight

By *intuition* Bruner means "immediate apprehension or cognition" (Bruner, 1960, p. 60). *Intuitive thinking* is characterized by the development of hunches and hypotheses, by perceptions that seem to appear suddenly and dramatically. Bruner distinguishes intuitive thinking, which can precede and does not depend upon formal analysis, from the analytic approach, in which the steps taken to solve a problem are well thought out and clearly defined, and in which the learner is usually fully aware of the procedure he is following. In intuitive thinking, the learner thrashes about looking for shortcuts instead of proceeding methodically, and once having arrived at a tentative solution, he may have difficulty explaining how he reached his new understanding (Bruner, 1960).

Bruner is critical of traditional educational methods in that he feels that teachers have encouraged children to develop analytic ways of thinking at the expense of intuitive thinking (Bruner, 1960). This is not to suggest that analytic thinking is necessarily undesirable or that intuitive thinking is always preferable. Bruner's view is that the ideal learning situation is one in which analytic and intuitive thinking complement one another. By relying on intuition alone, we cannot determine the value of a new hypothesis. But by using formal analysis to test it, we can evaluate whether the intuitive solution is correct. Intuitive thinking might also lead to the formulation of new problems that could be solved by the analytic approach (Bruner, 1960).

Scholars and scientists use both intuitive and analytic reasoning advantageously. For example, a physician might first ask his patient questions, then examine him briefly, and finally make a probable diagnosis. If this preliminary diagnosis (intuitive thinking) suggests a possible serious condition, the physician would then proceed systematically by ordering tests, recommending hospitalization, or telling the patient to return for another checkup (analytic reasoning). In this way he combines the two approaches. Similarly, a scientist might make a preliminary hypothesis about the cause of an event (intuitive thinking), then follow by an experiment in which all possible causes are tested systematically and scientifically (analytic reasoning).

Bruner contends that children as well as professionals can effectively utilize both approaches to problem-solving. He is critical of the fact that, too often, geometry is not included in the curriculum of the elementary school. The axioms, theorems, and proofs of this discipline are not presented until high school, at which point, because they have not been taught the fundamentals, the student may be bewildered by these new concepts. At the same time, teachers too frequently reward these same high school students for simply memorizing without necessarily understanding the concepts being taught. To Bruner, a more productive approach would be to introduce children at a much earlier age to simple geometric configurations and fundamentals and to the intuitive strategies for dealing with them.

With a background of using intuition in geometry developed during his elementary school years, the adolescent could then presumably draw on this knowledge to go beyond mere memorization of proofs and formulas to the type of thinking in which scholars engage—discerning relationships and discovering their own proofs (Bruner, 1960).

Teachers may find it difficult to get their students to engage in intuitive thinking because the students must be willing to risk making mistakes and then learning from them. One problem is that teachers themselves often provide extrinsic rewards in the form of praise, good grades, and so on, to students who memorize the material as presented and then reproduce it in similar form on an exam. In so doing, they encourage their students to develop rote-learning abilities or, at best, analytic thinking exclusively, but at the same time they inhibit the children from developing the ability to learn through insight. Probably this is less taxing for teachers than waiting for their students to arrive at what Bruner terms the "magic moment" of insight. Whatever the cause, American schools do emphasize extrinsic rewards as opposed to the intrinsic rewards of discovery, and it is this practice that Bruner finds so unfortunate (Bruner, 1960).

Interestingly, Bruner's position on intuitive thinking is itself intuitive. Although he recommends studying the usefulness of intuitive learning in different academic disciplines, he himself has not engaged in such research, nor has it been carried out on a systematic basis (Bruner, 1960). Moreover, Bruner is quite vague as to what, exactly, the term *intuition* incorporates. As Lowe (1969) views this issue:

> The deductive formal testing stage for the notion of intuition has not yet been achieved by psychologists, as Bruner knows. He admits that it is even impossible at the present time to behaviorally and precisely define intuition. Still, the appeal is there. What teacher can fail to be attracted to a position that encourages individuality, freedom, and creativity and discourages dreary formalism? Think of a school in which students are motivated to discover principles and relationships among ideas with the same drive that mature scholars have. Think of a school in which teachers themselves act on intuitive hunches and are thrilled by working with ideas. Think of a school in which the intrinsic rewards of discovering structure are all the motivation that a student needs. Imagine the sheer delight of having students engaged together in first intuitive and then analytical thinking. Of course, the idea has appeal. But is it an inspired fantasy? (pp. 146–147)

Questions for Thought

What is the relationship between what Bruner calls "insight" and what educators and others call "creativity"?

What does this tell us about how we might teach for creativity?

BACK TO BASICS "Students can't carry through an idea in writing; they have no idea what a paragraph is; they are unable to string details together in a logical sequence" ("Bonehead English," *Time,* 1974, p. 106). Thus a director of Freshman English describes incoming college students. The blame for this state of affairs most often is placed on the curriculum in secondary schools. Too often today, says one educator, we state our immediate educational objectives in terms of "desired behavior, general abilities, or adjustment," when we should be thinking in terms of "achieved knowledge or specific abilities" (Ebel, 1973, p. 69). The primary purpose of American education is to develop in students the ability to think—so states the Educational Policies Commission. Others ask: What good is it if students can't effectively communicate what they think? There has been a considerable drop in verbal scores on the Scholastic Aptitude Tests and College Boards over the past ten years (Shiels, 1974). Parents are calling for a return to curricula that teach the basic structures of a subject. Their concerns are reflected in the comment of Kenneth Clark, head of the Metropolitan Applied Research Center in New York City: "I don't believe a child can play any constructive role in this society if he is unable to spell or to read, or if he does not have an elementary sense of grammatical structure" Shiels, 1974). Education today obviously faces a challenge: to make the attainment of specific skills compatible with larger objectives.

Bruner's Views on the Problems of Teaching

Bruner's theories suggest that the schools must drastically alter their curricula in order to truly contribute to the intellectual development of the child, and that teachers are capable of implementing these changes.

He contends that the traditional practice of teaching specific facts or skills, without imparting the underlying principles that give structure to the subject, makes long-term retention and transfer extremely difficult. Furthermore, the practice offers little intellectual excitement to the learner (Bruner, 1960). Instead, schools should stress the general principles that make up a subject. Teachers must make a subject seem interesting and worthwhile; without this, learners are apt to quickly forget the material, and much of their learning will have become wasted effort. This belief has led Bruner to formulate his ideas on discovery teaching, which are discussed in a later section.

Although Bruner appears to be more optimistic than many other psychologists in the degree to which he feels his recommendations can be implemented in the schools with the intended results, he also recognizes that educators and psychologists must deal with difficult problems if his proposals are to succeed. In Bruner's own words (1960):

Designing curricula in a way that reflects the most basic structure of a field of knowledge requires the most fundamental understanding of that field. It is a task that cannot be carried out without the active participation of the ablest scholars and scientists . . . Much more effort in the actual preparation of curriculum materials, in teacher training, and in supporting research will be necessary if improvements in our educational practices are to be of an order that will meet the challenges of the scientific and social revolution through which we are now living. (p. 32)

APPLICATIONS OF COGNITIVE-FIELD THEORY TO THE CLASSROOM

The theories of perception and learning originating in early Gestalt psychology and developed later in cognitive-field theory have affected classroom procedures in a variety of ways. Two of the most important applications of these theories are in the teaching of perceptual skills and the discovery method of teaching.

Teaching Perceptual Skills

The teaching of perceptual skills—as involved in learning to read, for example—is the core of the elementary school curriculum. E. J. Gibson (1969) describes her approach to perceptual learning as both a specificity theory and a differentiation theory.

By *specificity* in perceptual learning, Gibson means that through practice a person increases his ability to derive information from the environment. In the process of learning to read, for example, a child learns through experience with letters to identify specific aspects of them critical to meaning. He or she also learns to modify his perceptions so as to *differentiate* among the many letters of the alphabet. Perceptual learning, to Gibson, is an active process of filtering and abstracting information.

Gibson maintains that it is the unchanging properties of the environment that the individual learns to extract and identify. For example, each musical instrument has unique tonal properties, and for this reason a person with a trained ear can differentiate among them when an orchestra plays a symphony. The properties remain constant, and the trained individual can identify each instrument under any circumstances. In daily life, of course, the objects are much more complex, and we must differentiate among their distinctive features on the basis of a combination of properties. For example, when a person picks up a book to read, he extracts many different and complex properties to determine if it is a novel or a textbook.

DEVELOPMENTAL DIFFERENCES IN PERCEPTION. In the course of learning and development, many perceptions become less generalized and more precise, as a person learns to discriminate the subtle differences among stimuli. This might explain why older children are less variable in their perceptual judgments and have shorter reaction times in discrimination tasks than do younger children (E. J. Gibson, 1969). In other instances, though, our perceptions may be more generalized, as we detect additional structural relationships and commonalities (for example, hearing two symphonies new to you but recognizing by many similar qualities that they are both by Mozart).

Considerable evidence suggests that the effectiveness with which the four Gestalt principles of perceptual organization are utilized is both age-related and intelligence-related (Honkavaara, 1958; House, 1966; Rush, 1937; Spitz, 1964).

Do young children initially display a global perception of the world, and then, as they grow older, progressively differentiate the details? Or do they begin by noticing only isolated details and gradually, in the course of learning, combine them into an integrated whole? Actually, at any age, both an object's distinctive features and its overall structure are important considerations in one's ability to distinguish it from many other objects. Organizing available information into bigger chunks so that a larger total amount can be understood, and narrowing down the set of distinctive features to those that are most important, are equally significant aspects of perceptual learning (E. J. Gibson, 1969).

Gibson (1969) explains developmental differences in perception as the result of the fact that young children are simply less experienced, and therefore less adept, at extracting the constant elements from stimuli presented to them. She feels that perceptual skills can best be taught by providing young students with less complex material, since too much information will confuse them in their process of selection. Actually, children begin to appreciate stimulus material with few but essential details at a very early age. An example is their fondness for cartoons and comic books. Many teachers have found that cartoons and comic books are useful teaching devices.

REDUCTION OF UNCERTAINTY AS REINFORCER. According to Gibson, the most potent reinforcer in perceptual learning is intrinsic to the structure of the material to be learned. This reinforcer is the *reduction of uncertainty*. Only by discovering the distinctive features, constant properties, and overall structure can the student reduce uncertainty and transform what would otherwise be mere clutter and confusion into meaning (E. J. Gibson, 1970). Gibson, like Bruner, feels that reinforcement should be inherent in the learning process itself. In the process of learning to read, reinforcement should come with the excitement of comprehension.

Many teachers have found that cartoons and comic books are useful teaching devices.

(Richard Frieman, Photo Researchers)

DEVELOPMENTAL DIFFERENCES AND SPIRAL CURRICULA. Bruner is the major proponent of what today is known as *discovery teaching*, a teaching method requiring the rearrangement of subject matter structure so that the learner is able to go beyond the evidence presented to new insights (Bruner, 1962). The so-called spiral curriculum mentioned earlier in the chapter is, to Bruner, the ideal teaching program for accomplishing this goal. This curriculum is designed to teach specific agreed-upon and fundamental ideas and principles. It is constructed so that students of different ages and

The Discovery Method of Teaching

developmental statuses can approach it at varying levels of complexity (Bruner, 1960). In the spiral curriculum, early learning, which requires a simple level of understanding, serves as preparation for later learning with deeper understanding (Bruner, 1966). The same basic notion would apply to a technical subject such as science or mathematics as well as to a discipline such as literature or art. For example, in the spiral curriculum, children in elementary school probably would not be required to read Shakespeare's original works, but they might be prepared to pursue this activity later by first being introduced by their teacher to the significance of human tragedy and the various ways it has been depicted in literature.

DISCOVERY TEACHING AND REINFORCEMENT. Discovery teaching is not incompatible with the well-documented notion that reinforcement is important to learning. Although Bruner and his colleagues concede that students do need regular feedback concerning the appropriateness of their responses, at the same time they fear student dependence on the teacher's corrections. The learner needs to develop self-sufficiency so that when a teacher is not available, he can take over the task of correcting himself (Bruner, 1966).

Tackling a problem independently, correcting oneself as one goes along, and, most important, deriving satisfaction from the resulting discoveries are behaviors characteristic of scientists and scholars. And it is not coincidental that Bruner suggests that teachers develop the same abilities in their pupils. A major purpose of discovery teaching is to bridge the gap between the world of the scholar and the classroom world of the student, a point Bruner (1960) makes in *The Process of Education:*

> Intellectual activity anywhere is the same, whether at the frontier of knowledge or in a third grade classroom. What a student does at his desk or in his laboratory, what a literary critic does in reading a poem, are of the same order as what anybody does when he is engaged in like activities—if he is to achieve understanding. The difference is in degree, not in kind. (p. 14)

PLANNING THE CURRICULUM. The teacher alone should not develop a curriculum; the task requires close collaboration among teacher, subject-matter specialist, and psychologist. Moreover, any basic changes must be tested by careful observational and experimental methods. The criterion of success is not simply increased achievement, but whether the children are making sense of the material and organizing it into a meaningful whole (Bruner, 1966).

In addition, curriculum planners must pay more attention to individual differences in students. Children vary considerably not only in general ability but also in specific skills, subject-matter preferences, approaches to solving problems, and need for external reinforcement. The implications of these individual differences for a curriculum are given by Bruner (1966):

> If a curriculum is to be effective in the classroom it must contain different ways of activating children, different ways of presenting sequences, different opportunities for some children to "skip" parts while others work their way through, different ways of putting things. A curriculum, in short, must contain many tracks leading to the same general goal. (p. 71)

Bruner feels that discovery teaching would be a vast improvement over present teaching methods. Not only would children learn and remember more from their classroom activities, but they would derive more pleasure from the experience. Testing hypotheses and solving problems would become an exciting adventure for them. Their reward would be their increased understanding of the structure of the subject—along with the realization that understanding was obtained in large measure through their own discoveries.

However, a major problem that has arisen in implementing the discovery method in today's schools, where traditional teaching methods are used, is that much of the children's time and effort that could presumably go into this discovery learning is instead spent trying to figure out exactly what the teacher wants.

PRACTICAL IMPLEMENTATION OF DISCOVERY TEACHING.   Researchers have provided a variety of practical ways in which Bruner's ideas on discovery teaching might be implemented in an actual classroom. Two suggestions that clearly illustrate the nature of the discovery approach will be considered here.

Bigge (1964) has proposed an application of insight teaching to a multiplication lesson. In a fourth-grade class about to learn how to multiply by 9, the teacher first asks the pupils to review the multiplication tables they have already learned—2s, 3s, 5s, 10s—and makes sure that they understand the basic relationships. As the teacher begins to write the new table on the blackboard, he asks the class to supply the answers based on the knowledge they already have of the other multiplication tables. Thus, for example, since they have already learned in the multiplication table for 3s that $3 \times 9 = 27$, they can be led into the discovery that 9×3 equals the same amount.

The discovery method might also be applied to a history unit, a collection of poetry, or any other aspect of the curriculum. Bruner himself offered an illustration pertaining to an actual sixth-grade geography lesson (Bruner, 1960). In this lesson each student in the class was given a map of the central states that showed only bodies of water, agricultural products, and natural resources. Based on that information alone, the students were asked to locate Chicago. One child reasoned that a large city required lots of water, and so placed

Chicago at the junction of three lakes. Another child reasoned that a major city, because of its large population, would need to have a good food supply, and thus placed Chicago in what would be Iowa. Other children had different hypotheses, and a lively discussion ensued as to where Chicago belonged on the map. The fact that no one in the class produced the correct response was not as important, Bruner felt, as the excitement and reward of learning by discovery.

AN EVALUATION OF THE APPROACH.   Bruner sees several important advantages to the discovery method of teaching:

1. It leads the student to a better understanding of the basic ideas and concepts of a subject—its structure.
2. It aids the student in applying both memory and transfer to new learning situations, as well as in original learning.
3. It encourages the student to think and work on his own, without having to rely on directions and feedback from another person.
4. It encourages the student to think intuitively and to formulate and test his own hypotheses. Thus, he can deal more effectively with unstructured situations, not only in school but in everyday life.
5. It provides the student with a sense of inner satisfaction, independent of extrinsic rewards.
6. It makes learning intellectually stimulating to the student, who will approach difficult subject matter and time-consuming problem activities with interest and enthusiasm.

Bruner's enthusiasm for discovery teaching is not shared by all psychologists. Some feel that many of his claims are exaggerated and that the arguments made to support the method are based more on intuitive conviction than on well-established empirical evidence from properly controlled studies (Ausubel, 1968; Smedslund, 1964; Travers, 1972).

Ausubel (1963, 1967, 1968), for example, has been highly critical of Bruner, primarily for conveying the impression that discovery teaching is the *only* way that classroom learning should take place. Ausubel does acknowledge that discovery learning may be useful to concept formation during the child's early years of schooling, but he feels that meaningful learning can occur in many situations without it (Ausubel and Sullivan, 1970).

Ausubel and Robinson (1969) distinguish between discovery learning, in which the student himself discovers and gives structure to the subject matter, and what they call *reception learning*, in which the material to be learned is presented in "more or less final form" to the student. The multiplication tables are usually learned by reception learning; reading an eyewitness account of an historical event is another example of this form of learning. Ausubel maintains that although reception learning is not characterized by the independent search that Bruner considers so important, it can still be an important, meaningful, and active learning experience. The process of reception learning could involve any or all of these active steps:

1. The student relates new material to relevant ideas already established in his cognitive structure.
2. The student seeks to understand similarities and differences between new material and related concepts and propositions.
3. The student translates what he has learned into a frame of reference that reflects his own experience and vocabulary.
4. The student reorganizes his existing knowledge so that he can formulate new ideas.

In addition to asserting the active nature of reception learning, Ausubel contends that it is not all necessarily rote, and that discovery learning is not all necessarily meaningful. The conditions under which learning takes place will determine whether it is rote or meaningful.

A second major critic of Bruner's discovery learning is Skinner, who feels that the shaping of behavior, which involves continual direction and feedback, is necessary to learning. There is an extensive discussion of Skinner's methods of shaping behavior in Chapter 4.

Gagné, whose view of the objectives of education is totally dif-

Discovering what you can build yourself with your own hands, according to Bruner, is preferable to being told what you can do.

(Robin Gibson, Alternative Curriculum)

ferent from that of Bruner, is a third major critic of Bruner. For Gagné, these objectives consist of capabilities, which are defined in terms of the precise behaviors the teacher wants a student to master. In other words, his emphasis is entirely on the *products* of education, whereas Bruner's concern is with education as a *process* (Gagné, 1970; Shulman, 1968). For Gagné, the goal of learning is the *end;* the means used to reach it (discovery learning, guided teaching, rote memorization, or some other approach) can be evaluated only in terms of this end.

Gagné and Ausubel share the belief that most instruction should follow a carefully guided, step-by-step program. The child should solve a problem actively, yet he should do so in the systematic sequence and manner established by the program. This contrasts with Bruner's program, in which learning is an active but unsystematic process.

Because Gagné and Bruner differ fundamentally on the purpose of education, attempts to weigh the relative merits of particular aspects of the two approaches have not been very productive. However, Gagné has been an influential contributor to learning theory, and his work will be discussed in detail in Chapter 7.

In summary, a teacher has no golden rule to follow, since valid arguments can be made for both the discovery and the guided instruction methods. Empirical evidence generally suggests that guided learning does tend to increase immediate learning and retention. The evidence of long-term retention is not nearly as clear, however. The discovery approach, on the other hand, does appear to facilitate the transfer of basic principles to new situations, but at present we have no evidence from which to conclude that the techniques and strategies associated with discovery learning are subject to similar transfer, although Bruner has said that original learning by discovery leads to the ability to learn more by discovery.

SUMMARY Cognitive-field theory has had a strong influence on educational psychology. Its basic concern is with the interaction between the individual and the environment he perceives, which is called his psychological world or perceptual field. The meaning that each individual gives to his perceptual field is called his cognitive structure. It is believed that the individual's cognitive structure goes through a continual process of change and reorganization that is basic to learning.

Contemporary cognitive-field theory, currently dominated by the ideas of Bruner, received its impetus from the Gestalt movement. The Gestalt psychologists were interested primarily in perception, but much of their research has been applied to learning processes as well. They emphasized the fundamental importance of simplicity, structure, and regularity—the good gestalt—in all perceptual learning.

Insight is another aspect of learning that the Gestalt psychologists considered to be highly important. Insight is a form of discovery learning equivalent to a hunch or hypothesis and is considered a necessary skill for solving problems. The great influence of the Gestalt psychologists on Bruner is clearly reflected in his ideas about discovery teaching and his frequent use of the terms *structure* and *intuition.*

Learning by discovery differs markedly from the more traditional method of classroom instruction known as *reception learning.* In discovery learning, the task is deliberately made open-ended, so that students may be free to develop and pursue their own hypotheses.

The relative merits of different methods of classroom instruction, including Bruner's discovery method, are an issue to which educators and psychologists devote much attention. Bruner's own prolific writings on the subject have inspired many reactions from the psychological community, both pro and con. As a result of this debate, a variety of new methods of instruction have been developed; these will be discussed in Chapter 9.

SUGGESTED FOR FURTHER READING

Bigge, M. L. *Learning theories for teachers.* New York: Harper & Row, 1964.
This book contains good summaries of the major learning theories, with especially fine accounts of Gestalt theory and Lewin's cognitive-field theory. The later chapters will interest teachers who want to apply learning theories to the classroom.

Bruner, J. S. *Toward a theory of instruction.* Cambridge, Mass.: Harvard University Press, 1966.
In this text, Bruner discusses his theory of instruction with specific applications for the classroom. This book is especially relevant for teachers or future teachers of social studies, English, arithmetic, and elementary school subjects in general, as Bruner uses examples of instruction in these disciplines.

Hilgard, E. R. (Ed.). *Theories of learning and instruction,* Sixty-third Yearbook of the National Society for Study of Education. Chicago: University of Chicago Press, 1964.
An excellent book of readings that contains scholarly accounts of applications of learning theory to the classroom. Other issues, such as motivation, theories of instruction in specific areas, and educational technology are also included.

Hunt, D. E., and Sullivan, E. V. *Between psychology and education.* Hinsdale, Ill.: Dryden Press, 1974.
This book applies directly to education Lewin's formula that behavior results from both the person and the environment.

Shulman, L. S., and Keislar, E. R. (Eds.). *Learning by discovery.* Chicago: Rand McNally, 1966.
A collection of papers about discovery learning that should be helpful to anyone trying to determine whether or not he wishes to use this method in his classroom.

CHAPTER 6

MOTIVATING THE STUDENT IN THE CLASSROOM

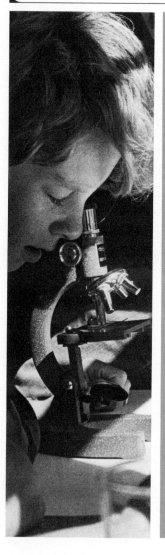

After completing this chapter, the reader should be able to:

1 Explain the position of motivation theory in describing learning; relate this position to other theories of learning.

2 Describe the variables inferred by the motivation theorist to describe what goes on within the individual when learning takes place, and explain how each of these variables affects the learning process.

3 Describe the separate basic theories of motivation as well as the specific needs, drives, and motives operative in learning situations; relate each to classroom learning situations in particular.

4 Plan specific teacher behaviors as well as broad curriculum designs that will increase achievement motivation, level of aspiration, and creativity of students.

WHAT IS MOTIVATION THEORY?

Associationists (discussed in Chapter 4) used as the basis for their research two things: stimuli in the environment and responses made by the individual. What another group of psychologists calls learning, however, is actually what takes place *between* the stimulus and the response. It is that which intervenes between the two that interests both the cognitive-field theorist (discussed in Chapter 5) and the motivation theorist. The cognitive-field theorist concerns himself with the individual's *perceptions* of the world around him; the motivation theorist with his *goals*, *needs*, and *drives.*

Perhaps the clearest link between these three perspectives (associationism, cognitive-field theory, and motivation theory) can be found in the purposive behaviorism of Edward Tolman (1932/1951). Tolman considered all living organisms to be goal-seeking creatures, and, further, that behavior cannot be properly understood without considering the purposes behind it. Most behavior of living organisms is engaged in for some purpose. For example, rats have been known to crawl through mazes for hours in order to get small amounts of food or drink, elephants are said to journey for several days in order to die in a specific location, and students study for exams in order to pass courses.

Although Tolman differed from the classical behaviorists in that he looked beyond the simple relationship between stimulus and response, he preferred to consider himself a behaviorist. He shared with the associationists the strong belief that the study of psychology should be made more objective by focusing on measurable behaviors rather than on subjective experiences. He differed, however, from such men as Watson in the procedures he used to analyze behavioral acts.

Tolman felt that more fruitful analysis would result if behavior were examined in common-sense units, which he termed *molar behaviors*, rather than subdivided into very small units, or *molecular bits.* For example, the behavior involved in cooking a meal or going to a doctor's office could ostensibly be broken up into an endless number of molecular bits, but Tolman felt that this extensive subdivision would result in losing the meaning, or gestalt, of the behavior. One clearly understands the behavior described as preparing a meal, for example. The many specific motions involved in lighting a stove or peeling a carrot, however, are meaningless unless they are described in terms of the larger activity. Driving a car, as another example, is composed of numerous types of movement (molecular bits), but if the observer examined each movement individually without looking at the whole behavior he would lose sight of the reason for driving in the first place. Only by focusing on molar behaviors can we relate any behavior to its underlying purpose.

Tolman shared views with cognitive-field theorists as well in his concern for cognition, a variable intervening between stimuli in the outside world and responses made by the individual. Cognition, according to Tolman, is the sum total of a person's understanding of how the environment is structured and how it operates. This process enables people to use their environment effectively in achieving their goals. For example, a man knows that a car can get him from one place to another; he therefore uses it for that purpose. A student studies for an exam because he knows that this will help him to receive a higher grade.

Finally, Tolman's interest in human needs suggests that we also should consider him a motivation, or drive-reduction, theorist. The relation between a person's needs and his behavior, however, has been outlined in more detail by other psychologists interested in motivation theory.

According to the motivation theorist, what goes on inside the individual—his internal state, how he "feels"—determines to a large extent both the energy he expends and how he behaves. This internal state—or "feeling" of the person—cannot be seen or measured directly. We must simply infer its presence. Two concepts that Tolman introduced into his theories, needs and cognitions, are examples of such inferred internal states. Other motivation theorists have postulated other inferred variables to account for behavior.

Needs, Drives, and Motivations

A *need* is a requirement that must be met by an organism for optimal adjustment to the environment. A basic assumption in motivation theory is that an organism behaves in order to reduce its needs. From a biological perspective, certain needs, such as those for food and water, must be met for the organism simply to survive. Because of their essential nature, they are termed *primary needs.* Most learning experiments conducted with animals have made use of these primary needs by first depriving the animals of food or water and then using the safisfaction of these needs as reinforcers.

Of course, explaining human behavior solely in terms of these primary needs would be inadequate. Most needs of civilized people in affluent societies such as ours are not necessary for survival, but rather for adjustment to a complex social structure. For example, we commonly refer to our need for achievement or for companionship. Students in college may be there because of a need to achieve or because of a need to understand our complex world. Needs such as these, the fulfillment of which optimize a person's adjustment to his social as well as physical environment, yet which are not essential to physical survival, are known as *secondary needs.* Psychologists explain the development of secondary needs in terms of their association with primary needs. We will consider some of them shortly.

According to the motivation theorist, when an individual has a need, whether primary or secondary, he is compelled to act so as to reduce this need state. This compulsion—the internal state within the individual that generates activity—is called a *drive*. Like all variables intervening between stimulation by the environment and the individual's response, drive is inferred from measurable circumstances. Drive strength is usually inferred by the motivation theorist from the degree of need (as measured by amount of deprivation) or from the level of activity demonstrated in response to the need.

Let's take the example of a newborn baby who cries and squirms when it is hungry. One could assess the strength of the baby's drive in terms of either the number of hours since its last feeding (degree of need) or the vigor of its crying and squirming (activity level). As can be seen from this example, these two measures of drive strength are usually closely related.

This example also illustrates the functional role of drives. Drives are represented by undifferentiated, undirected behavior. A newborn baby's crying and squirming, though energetic, is, at the outset, simply undifferentiated behavior; in other words, it does not directly enable the baby to obtain its food. Furthermore, at this point the baby does not "know" that it wants food. Since it has never experienced feeding through its mouth, we cannot assume that it "knows" it wants to eat in that fashion. It simply has an unmet need that compels it to some activity. Drive strength, in and of itself, does not provide the means by which a person can learn how to reach a particular goal. Rather, its principal function is to *energize* behavior. It is only through a continual pairing of needs with specific behaviors that the baby will learn what behaviors it should exhibit in order to satisfy its needs and thus reduce its hunger drive.

Motivation, unlike drive, includes both *energy* and *direction* (Marx and Tombaugh, 1967). Most people have strong motives to act; that is, not only do they tend to act energetically, they will also direct their energies toward specific goals. This directional property of motivation involves a past history of learning: A person must learn what behaviors will enable him to reduce his drive strength. Motivation requires previous repeated pairings of the appropriate behavior with states of drive reduction. The baby just described learns gradually through repeated feedings by its mother that a bottle of milk reduces the feelings that accompany hunger drive. The same baby, once motivated to cry in order to obtain the specific goal of milk, later will learn to reject a bottle of water presented to him when he is hungry. Motivation, in the true sense of energized behavior directed toward a particular goal, develops gradually.

Although drive strength does appear to make learning more efficient, we should not readily conclude that children will perform best under conditions in which their drive strength is highest. Children who are intensely driven are often so determined to achieve their goals that they lose patience with the work required to achieve them (Travers, 1967).

The effectiveness of drive strength in children's learning must also be considered in light of the complexity of the task at hand (Marx and Tombaugh, 1967). Children who are highly aroused usually perform better on simple rather than complex assignments. High levels of arousal or drive strength usually cannot be maintained for the length of time required to accomplish a very complex task. High levels of anxiety also interfere with complex problem-solving. These points are not meant to confuse the prospective teacher, but simply to point out that the relationship between drive strength and learning is a complex one, which should be carefully appraised in light of a number of factors.

To complete our brief summary of motivation or drive-reduction theory, one more concept must be introduced: homeostasis. Actually, homeostasis is a sophisticated way of saying what we have already described—that is, people tend to act to reduce their needs, whether primary or secondary; and people act to reduce needs in order to maintain equilibrium, a steady or balanced internal state of being; we call this state *homeostasis*.

The purest example of homeostasis can be seen in the physiological functioning of our bodies; for example, in the action of our white blood cells in destroying alien germs. The germs create a disturbance in the body that is resisted by the white blood cells; when the white blood cells have destroyed the germs, proper balance is restored.

Examples of homeostasis in psychological functioning are not quite as clear-cut as this physiological one. The principal problem in psychological functioning is that the so-called state of balance has never been precisely defined by motivation theorists. If human beings do indeed seek a psychologically balanced state of being, this homeostatic level varies from individual to individual, and for any single individual at different times. For example, some adventurous people always seem to be seeking great amounts of excitement and stimulation, whereas others always prefer less stimulation. Children in a classroom differ enormously in terms of the kinds of environments in which they feel most comfortable—that is, those environments that best meet their needs.

Questions for Thought

If motivation occurs only after repeated pairings of appropriate behavior with drive reduction, do you think the student who always receives the lowest class grade will ever be motivated to work for grades in school? Why?

THEORIES OF NEED SYSTEMS AND MOTIVATION

Maslow's Hierarchy of Needs

One of the most original attempts to deal with the complexity of human motivation can be found in the work of Abraham Maslow (1943, 1954, 1968). Maslow theorized that all human motivation can be portrayed in terms of satisfying a hierarchy of needs. This hierarchy, as Maslow described it, is composed of a number of different types of need* arranged in such a manner that each need becomes dominant when prior, or lower, needs have been gratified. Maslow's hierarchy is shown in Figure 6-1.

Physiological needs, in Maslow's framework, are the most basic of all; they must be gratified before any higher needs can fully emerge. If a person's physiological requirements are not met, he will be preoccupied with these deficiencies. The thoughts and fantasies of a starving man, for instance, will be dominated by images of food. Even his dreams, more often than not, will center on food-oriented themes. Educators certainly are aware of the fact that hungry children are less able to pay attention in school than those who have been given enough to eat.

Although Maslow characterized physiological needs as the most basic in his entire hierarchy, his writings do not emphasize the significance of these needs in modern life. Unfortunately, today we know that often these needs are not being fulfilled in our society; hunger is a worldwide problem that exists in the United States as well as elsewhere (Anderson, 1974). Large numbers of schoolchildren arrive in class each morning in this country without having eaten breakfast. In Chapter 10 we will discuss the poor academic results, as predicted by Maslow, of not meeting this basic need.

Next in the hierarchy are *safety needs,* which on occasion dominate the lives of adults. (Alexander Solzhenitsyn describes in *The Gulag Archipelago* how very suddenly this type of need takes dominance in the case of arrest and imprisonment in a totalitarian regime.) It is in the daily lives of infants and children, however, that safety needs are most clearly expressed under normal circumstances in our society. During these initial years of life, human beings usually are most helpless and most in need of stable and orderly environments. When a child's world is disrupted, no matter what his age, his safety needs come to dominate growth and development. An illustration of this is Maslow's (1968) example of a toddler who, in his mother's company, slowly and cautiously explored a strange room. While his mother was present he gradually became more energetic in his explorations, but when his mother suddenly left, the

---

*In this chapter, we will discuss five basic needs as Maslow defined them. In some of Maslow's popular writings a seven-level presentation of these same needs is given; for our purposes now, however, we will discuss the five most basic needs.

Self-
Actualization

Esteem
Needs

Love and
Belonging Needs

Safety Needs

Physiological Needs

Figure 6-1. Maslow's hierarchy of needs. (Maslow, 1954)

toddler immediately ceased his exploratory activity and looked frantically for her. To quote Maslow (1968):

> Growth forward customarily takes place in little steps, and each step forward is made possible by the feeling of being safe, or operating out into the unknown from a safe home port, of daring because retreat is possible. (p.45)

Third in Maslow's hierarchy of needs is *love and belonging.* Once an individual feels safe in his environment he will turn toward others in order to achieve fulfillment. Friendships, love relationships, and group acceptance emerge as the dominant concerns at this point. According to Maslow (1943), when a person is thwarted in satisfying this need, maladjustment and even severe psychopathology may ensue.

Educators and child psychologists alike are keenly aware of the importance of this need in the lives of school-age children (Travers, 1967). If a child experiences difficulty in getting along with his classmates and teachers, it is highly unlikely that while in school he will be able to reach his learning potential. For a young child, school is the first real testing ground for establishing his place among other children. If he fails in this endeavor, school can become a hostile environment associated with much fear and anxiety.

Next in Maslow's hierarchy are *esteem needs.* In this category he includes both the need for self-respect and the need for respect from others. From self-respect comes confidence, independence, and freedom; and from the respect a person receives from others comes

The need for love and belonging is third in Maslow's hierarchy.
(Leonard Freed, Magnum)

a sense of prestige and appreciation. If these needs are not satisfied, a sense of inferiority will emerge. The individual will constantly be concerned with his own inadequacies and, at the same time, will fear the condemnation of others.

The last, and perhaps most far-reaching, need is the need for what Maslow termed *self-actualization* (see p. 192), which can be considered a prime goal of an educational system designed to educate "the whole child." Maslow (1943) defines this need as

> the desire for self-fulfillment, namely, . . . the tendency for him (the individual) to become actualized in what he is potentially. This tendency might be phrased as the desire to become more and more what one is, to become everything that one is capable of becoming. (p.382)

According to this definition, each person must find for himself his own path toward actualization.

With this hierarchy of basic needs at hand, some of the more frequent misconceptions about Maslow's theory should now be clarified. First, Maslow did not believe that each need must be absolutely and fully gratified in order for the next higher need on the pyramid to be operative. Rather, he believed that each basic need gradually emerges as its predecessor is relatively, but not completely, fulfilled. As Maslow (1943) explained: "A more realistic description of the hierarchy would be in terms of decreasing percentages of satisfaction as we go up the hierarchy" (p.338). In other words, the average adult has a greater percentage of his lower needs satisfied and a lesser percentage of his higher needs satisfied. None of his needs may be completely gratified at any given time.

Second, no behavior can be described exclusively in terms of a single need. Behavior in Maslow's framework can be multimotivated. To use one of Maslow's own examples, making love may be partially motivated by each of the basic needs in the hierarchy.

Third, psychologists point out that not all behavior can be analyzed in terms of motivational factors alone. Some behavior, such as the smile of a happy person or the brisk gait of a person taking a morning walk, can be more adequately described as expressive than as motivated behavior. Incidental or accidental learning (such as your knowledge of the color of your next-door neighbor's front door) cannot be explained in terms of motivational factors either. And rote habits or mannerisms—such as the way a student carries his books or the particular door (if there are two) that he habitually uses to enter the classroom—often cannot be sufficiently explained simply in terms of ungratified needs.

Finally, there is evidence that Maslow's sequence in which the needs become dominant is sometimes reversed. We all know that throughout history the severest physiological deprivations have

COMMON CHARACTERISTICS OF MASLOW'S SELF-ACTUALIZED INDIVIDUAL

Maslow (1954) described 15 common characteristics of what he calls the "self-actualized individual." He conceived of these characteristics as providing a composite picture of a well-adjusted individual that could serve as a goal toward which all people might strive.

1. *Efficient perception of reality and comfortable relations with it.* Excellent judges of character, self-actualized individuals can distinguish sincerity from falseness better than most. In addition, they do not have a pressing need to mold reality into neat categories but rather accept it with all its complexities.

2. *Acceptance of self and of others.* They are not defensive about themselves or their beliefs. They have nothing to hide and nothing to protect and are therefore open to and accepting of others.

3. *Spontaneity.* They are not concerned with impressing others; they feel free to think and act spontaneously. They are, however, careful not to intentionally distress other people.

4. *Problem centering.* These individuals approach problems with no personal biases. Self-interest does not sway them from a clear-sighted perception of the facts.

5. *Detachment; the need for privacy.* Their lack of rigid attachment to any set of particular ideas allows these individuals to be relatively objective in their judgments. Although they are not antisocial, they do value the time they spend alone.

6. *Autonomy; independence of culture and environment.* They are not rigidly tied down to the culture in which they reside.

7. *Continued freshness of appreciation.* They have a real sense of joy in experiencing all aspects of life.

8. *Mystic experience or the "oceanic" feeling.* Self-actualized individuals have "feelings of limitless horizons opening up to the vision, the feeling of being simultaneously more powerful and also more helpless than one ever was before, the feeling of great ecstasy and wonder and awe, the loss of placement in time and space, with, finally, the conviction that something extremely important and valuable had happened" (p. 216).

9. *Social interest.* The self-actualized person has a strong sense of the unity and brotherhood among all human beings.

10. *Interpersonal relations.* They usually have a small number of very deep and rich relationships with both men and women.

11. *Democratic character structure.* They are relatively free from prejudice and jealousy.

12. *Discrimination between means and ends.* They are, for the most part, patient people. They often enjoy the work involved in achieving a goal as much as the achievement of the goal itself.

13. *Sense of humor.* Their humor is constructive rather than destructive; it is not aimed at hurting or putting people down.

14. *Creativeness.* In their everyday lives they tend to be original and inventive.

15. *Resistance to enculturation.* They can appreciate views very different from their own.

been tolerated in a very few individuals who are able to martyr themselves and maintain higher-level ideals. This behavior is sufficiently uncommon that we refer to such individuals as "heroes" or "heroines," or perhaps even "saints."

Question for Thought

The United States has a long history of giving aid to underdeveloped nations. Citizens of these nations frequently have responded by accepting this aid to help provide for some of their basic needs, but then opting for some form of totalitarian government. Americans often have expressed amazement at this behavior, and have wondered why people seem to give up so easily what we have called the "basic need" for freedom. How might Maslow's hierarchy of needs be used to explain this phenomenon?

David McClelland and his associates postulated, and experimentally investigated, the motive to achieve what in our culture we feel to be "success" (McClelland, Atkinson, Clark, and Lowell, 1953). Varying in strength from individual to individual, *achievement motivation* can be defined as a persistent attempt to achieve what is thought to be success. This is, of course, what the educator depends upon in teaching; clearly, increasing achievement motivation in students would aid the learning process considerably. Certainly, without achievement motivation, all of the stimuli we use as reinforcers — praise, high grades, approval — would be useless.

Achievement Motivation

VARIABLES AFFECTING ACHIEVEMENT MOTIVATION.   McClelland and his associates described a number of techniques designed to heighten achievement motivation, based on two programs they had conducted: (1) an attempt to train businessmen in India to adopt a more productive attitude toward achievement (McClelland, 1965), and (2) work with school-age children in the United States (McClelland, 1972). These techniques are particularly relevant to educational practices. Firstly and most basically, a person must be taught that he can and will develop the ability to achieve. Desire alone will get a person nowhere if he feels that the goals he sets for himself are not within his power to achieve.

Secondly, McClelland suggested that a person is more likely to increase his achievement motivation if he is given a clear idea of what he must do in order to achieve his goal. Suggestions about the concrete actions involved are always helpful; abstract ideas offer little assistance to a person if he cannot translate them into specific actions. To help a person gain a clearer perspective of his progress toward achieving his goal, McClelland also recommended that the individual keep an actual record of the concrete tasks in which he

DOODLEY HIGH OR DOODLEY LOW? Everything we do has some significance for psychologists—even doodling. One psychologist has used it as a nonverbal means of measuring achievement motivation (Aronson, 1958). He asserts: "Since graphic expression lends itself both to quantification and to careful and leisurely scrutinization, it appeared a desirable mode of expressive behavior for investigation" (p. 250). The results of Aronson's study indicate that:

1. High achievers' doodles contain more single, unattached, discrete lines, while those of low achievers are more overlaid, fuzzier.
2. "Highs" tend to leave a smaller margin at the bottom of a page than do "lows."
3. "Highs" draw more diagonal configurations.
4. "Highs" draw more S-shaped (two-directional, nonrepetitive) lines and fewer multiwave lines (lines consisting of two or more crests in the same direction) than "lows."

Sounds preposterous? Consider the meaning of these graphic expressions in respect to high achievers. They tend to:

1. Economize activity, be new-motion-oriented, unrestrained.
2. Expand activities to broad areas.
3. Be unafraid to "lean forward," "fall," be "off-balance."
4. Resist wasting time in unnecessary, repetitive motions.

One doodle may well be worth a thousand words!

has engaged. In this way, frustrations are kept to a minimum, because he has a written record of his actual accomplishments.

Finally, McClelland felt that it is important for an individual to be shown how to link his goals to his everyday life. By everyday life he meant not only a person's daily activities but also his general feelings about himself and his status within his group. According to McClelland, a person should be made to see that a heightened motivation to achieve will bring with it a heightened sense of self-satisfaction as the goal is reached. It is also likely to bring greater respect from friends and from associates at work. Overall, an individual must be able to perceive the numerous benefits to be had by increasing his achievement motivation.

John Atkinson suggested three critical postulates particularly important to the teacher (Maehr and Sjogren, 1971). The first is that the concept of achievement motivation is relevant only in those situations in which an individual both perceives himself as responsible for the end-result and understands that his achievement will be evaluated against a given standard of excellence. The concept does not pertain to chance events or nonevaluative tasks. Thus, the teacher wanting to increase achievement motivation ought to specify student roles clearly and spell out in detail what is wanted.

The second postulate is that there are two conflicting motivations involved in achievement goals: One is motivation toward achieving success; the other, toward avoiding failure. In other words, some individuals are more concerned about how successful they will be, as, for example, the student who studies in order to graduate magna cum laude. Such an individual is called by Atkinson "achievement-oriented." Other individuals are more concerned about their possible failures, as, for example, the student whose prime concern in studying for an examination is that he will get a passing grade and will not have to repeat the course. Such an individual is called "failure-oriented." Atkinson considers these two goal orientations to be personality characteristics that tend to endure despite specific happenings in the lives of the individuals concerned. To the motivation theorist, understanding these orientations is necessary in order to establish goals and to formulate meaningful learning sequences to reach these goals for each individual student.

Being successful at what one does can be a strong motivating force for achievement.

(Inger McAbe, Rapho/Photo Researchers)

Third, Atkinson postulates that a person's motivation to perform a task will be influenced by his perception of its difficulty. Evidence suggests that achievement-oriented individuals consistently prefer tasks that they consider to be moderately difficult (Maehr and Sjogren, 1971). Tasks perceived as too difficult or too easy are less preferred. This tendency can be generalized even to a preference for jobs and school curricula that present moderately difficult challenges.

Not only do achievement-oriented subjects prefer tasks they consider moderately difficult, they also tend to persist longer at these tasks than at others. In a study in which subjects experienced failure in a task they were told was easy, achievement-oriented subjects persisted significantly longer than failure-oriented subjects (Feather, 1963). When they succeeded at a task they were told was very difficult, the achievement-oriented subjects tried harder than the failure-oriented subjects.

Implications of all of these findings for the teacher are obvious. Once again, evidence shows the importance of individualizing tasks and task difficulty to meet the perceived needs of individual students.

The data regarding the role of perceived task difficulty are not as clear-cut for failure-oriented subjects as they are for achievement-oriented subjects. Failure-oriented individuals also show some very slight preference for what they consider to be moderately difficult tasks, although this preference is not nearly so marked as in the case of those who are achievement-oriented.

According to Atkinson's theory, a student's personality is a primary determinant of which tasks will be most effective in motivating him. Specifically, we would predict from this theory that tasks perceived as moderately difficult would be most highly motivating for achievement-oriented students, whereas an easier task may be perceived by the failure-oriented students as moderately difficult and thus a more appropriate motivator. If this is true, one way to motivate all students at an optimal level might be to allow them to set their own goals and then grade them accordingly. A study conducted by Alschuler (1968) provides empirical support that this suggestion will work. In his study, students were presented with a learning task in the form of a self-competition game. The students set their own goals, then were evaluated according to the terms they set for themselves. This procedure was found to increase significantly their levels of achievement in the task.

Questions for Thought

If we allowed all students to set their own goals and then graded them accordingly, how would we, as teachers, determine final grades?

How would we determine the meaning of graduation from elementary or high school?

Can you outline a procedure that would be fair to all?

LEVEL OF ASPIRATION.   Among the variables affecting achievement motivation and achievement itself is *level of aspiration*—that is, the individual's *expectation* of his own future success or failure. In its purest form, level of aspiration is based upon an individual's rational evaluation of his past performances and his desire to perform better in the future. But the way in which an individual makes this evaluation is, of course, affected by his unique personality. The following generalizations concerning level of aspiration should be of particular interest to educators (Gardner, 1940).

Individuals whose levels of aspiration might be considered too high, based on their past performances, usually have a strong need to achieve; that is, they are achievement-oriented. They tend to be dissatisfied with their current levels of performance, no matter what these performance levels are at the time. Those whose levels of aspiration might be considered too low are, for the most part, insecure individuals who tend to have histories of failure and who are concerned primarily with the threat of failure; that is, they are failure-oriented. Finally, persons with what might be considered optimal (or moderately positive) levels of aspiration seem to set realistic goals and are generally successful achievers.

Clearly, level of aspiration has many implications for the teacher. We will return later to this topic and discuss both the variables that appear to affect it as well as its effect on achievement motivation.

CULTURE AND MOTIVATIONAL INDOCTRINATION

In a conversation with another psychologist (Harris, 1971), David McClelland speaks of three kinds of motivation—achievement, power, and affiliation. An examination of a culture's reading material for children, he says, will reveal the value it places on a particular motivation and wishes to instill in its children at any given time. He and his associates collected standard second- through fourth-grade readers from all over the world and selected a random sample of 21 stories from each.

They found that in similar stories—for example, those about children building a boat—cultures differed in the element they emphasized. In one culture the story would emphasize the construction of the boat, how it is made so it stays afloat—achievement motivation. In another culture the story would focus on the fun the children had working together—affiliation. A third culture would center the story around a "hero," a boy who led the other children, telling them what to do—power.

This stress on a particular kind of motivation in a culture amounts to a motivational indoctrination of the young that reflects the values of the establishment or ruling class of that country. This indoctrination can also be effective on groups within a country. For many years black children learned through their reading that their roles in a white society were subordinate; thus (by implication) there was no need for achievement or power orientation. But today, says McClelland, "The psychologist has the tools for finding out what a generation wants, better than it knows itself. . . . With such knowledge man has a fair chance to shape his own behavior and, for the first time, to decide his own destiny" (p. 75).

Competence Motivation

Related to McClelland's and Atkinson's concepts of achievement motivation is Robert White's (1959) concept of *competence motivation*. In reviewing other theories of motivation, White pointed out that a whole range of human and animal behaviors had been consistently ignored by theorists. Walking, exploring, perceiving, thinking, and even playing behavior had not, for the most part, even been considered, or, if they had, were given only cursory attention by motivation theorists. White argued that each of these behaviors is derived from an intrinsic need to deal effectively with the environment, and thus should be considered as motivated behavior. They are selective, persistent, and directed behaviors, which result in a general "feeling of competence or efficacy." By "feeling of competence or efficacy" White did not mean that the individual necessarily engages in these kinds of behavior in order to master the environment. Rather, he meant that the goal of these behaviors is simply getting to know what the environment is all about, "discovering the effects he—the individual—has on the environment and the effects the environment has on him." According to White, it is this *process of discovery* that is satisfying, not the subsequent knowledge or mastery that might follow. He considered these behaviors to be intrinsically rewarding in and of themselves.

White argued further that the long-term consequences of these behaviors are biologically significant. As a result of these behaviors, the individual eventually learns to interact effectively with the environment. Human beings, as compared with lower animals, must learn many more behaviors to adjust to their environments. It is only very gradually, by continual exploration and experimentation, that human beings develop enough responses to adjust to the environment. Opportunity to explore and to experiment within the school environment provides one means of satisfying this need of the developing child.

Stimulation and Exploration as Needs and Motivations

Just as McClelland and his associates hypothesized an independent motivation to achieve, Harry Harlow and his associates attempted to demonstrate the existence of an independent *manipulation drive* (Harlow, Harlow, and Meyer, 1950). Specifically, they noted that rhesus monkeys actively and persistently took apart and manipulated puzzles when no external reward was provided. Further, they found no evidence to indicate that the monkeys had learned to associate this manipulatory behavior with any primary drive. They concluded that manipulation is not a secondary drive, such as described by the motivation theorists discussed earlier; rather, it is, in a sense, an independent but nonphysiological drive.

Along these same lines, and related to White's description of competence motivation, Berlyne (1957) has suggested the existence of an *exploratory drive* in humans. In one experiment, he had each subject sit alone in a dark room. By pressing a key, the individual could project a picture onto a screen for about a quarter of a second. In this way, the subject was able to view a number of different slides, although he was permitted to repeat any particular slide as often as he wished.

In reviewing his data, Berlyne noticed that the subjects consistently preferred those pictures that were most novel or incongruous. In one series of pictures, for example, a depiction of an elephant's head attached to a dog's body was repeated more often than other more conventional pictures. Berlyne concluded that human beings have an intrinsic need to explore that which is novel or unfamiliar.

A further inquiry in this area was conducted by Davis and Buchwald (1957). In their experiment, they established the obvious—namely, that the sensory stimulation provided by pictures of nude females is pleasant to males. In this study, male college students revealed heightened excitation, as measured by perspiration of the palm of the hand, when shown pictures of nude females.

In each case, the findings suggest that human beings often seek stimulation rather than avoid it: Berlyne's subjects chose the novel, Davis and Buchwald's subjects continued to look at the pictures even after arousal, without drive reduction taking place. Results such as these complicate matters for traditional motivation theorists, who attempt to describe all motivation by drive reduction or reduction of arousal alone.

To add to the controversy, some psychologists have objected to the trend of proposing a new drive each time a new behavior that appears autonomous is revealed. They feel that proposing such drives as curiosity, exploration, manipulation, and even a stimulus-seeking drive explains nothing. Naming, they suggest, is not equivalent to explanation. In addition, they are opposed to generating long lists of drives because it violates the law of parsimony, which states that the best explanation is the simplest.

The Need for Identity

Erik Erikson's concept of *identity* was discussed in Chapter 3 in the context of developmental theory. Because we have already discussed this concept in detail, we will reexamine it only briefly—this time as a motivational construct. In terms of motivation theory, identity can be viewed as a psychosocial need that the adolescent must satisfy.

As you may recall from Chapter 3, Erikson defines identity as a subjective feeling of selfness. The individual's identity is attained by answering the questions: "Who was I?" "Who am I?" "Who am I not?" According to Erikson, although one's identity is formed throughout childhood, it is not until adolescence that it becomes the individual's primary psychological concern. The adolescent's identity is not established in one dramatic moment; instead, the answer to "Who am I?" develops gradually. How does this process work? In part, the adolescent learns to adapt to a changing body and to the increased social demands that accompany this period of rapid change. During this time, preparation is made to enter the adult world, with all its many responsibilities. The adolescent does a great deal of thinking during this period in which past achievements and crises are integrated with present interests, desires, and expectations.

Ideally, the adolescent achieves identity through interactions with others—peers, teachers, family. In many cases, however, this process does not go smoothly. The adolescent may become confused or overwhelmed, perhaps as a result of an inability to come up to the ideals expressed by parents or friends, or to settle on a satisfying vocation; possibly there has been a traumatic relationship with another person. Despite such setbacks, the adolescent's need to establish an identity remains. According to Erikson, this need is not unlike a primary need, which leads in turn to a drive state and ultimately, for the successfully adjusted individual, to drive reduction and eventual homeostasis.

In some instances, the adolescent assumes what Erikson terms a "negative identity." The adolescent usually reveals this so-called negative identity by rigidly assuming a role that is inconsistent with the roles he was taught were highly acceptable. As Erikson (1959) describes it:

> Many a late adolescent, if faced with continuing diffusion, would rather be nobody or somebody bad, or indeed, dead—and this totally, and by free choice—than be not-quite somebody. (p.132)

Homeostasis is thus reached, even if the outcome is an undesirable one.

Question for Thought

Could this explanation of a negative identity be used to explain why, in many cases, children of prominent parents, who have not themselves accomplished major goals, suddenly perform acts that are considered socially unacceptable in the societies in which they have grown up?

The Need for Equilibrium

Piaget's work, already discussed in detail in the context of cognitive development (see Chapter 2), can also be viewed correctly as a statement about the nature of human motivation and will be described here briefly. Actually, Piaget's concept of motivation can be considered a direct extension of drive-reduction theory. The following excerpt from Piaget (1967) makes this point quite clear:

> A need is always a manifestation of disequilibrium: there is a need when something either outside ourselves or within us (physically or mentally) is changed and behavior has to be adjusted as a function of this change. For example, hunger or fatigue will provoke a search for nourishment or rest; encountering an external object will lead to a need to play, which in turn has practical ends, or it leads to a question or a theoretical problem. A casual word will excite the need to imitate, to sympathize, or will engender reserve or opposition if it conflicts with some interest of our own. Conversely, action terminates when a need is satisfied, that is to say, when equilibrium is re-established between the new factor that has provoked the need and the mental organization that existed prior to the introduction of this factor. Eating or sleeping, playing or reaching a goal, replying to a question or resolving a problem, imitating successfully, establishing an affective tie, or maintaining one's point of view are all satisfactions that, in the preceding examples, will put an end to the particular behavior aroused by the need. (p.516)

The key words in this passage are "equilibrium" and "disequilibrium." For Piaget, maximal equilibrium in a cognitive sense means the ability to think in a logical and rational manner. This characteristic of thought is fully attained in the adult only with the completion of the formal operations function. Disequilibrium, then, is a characteristic of thought that continues until this final level of understanding—this equilibrium—is achieved. While this is true in terms of maximal equilibrium, it is important to remember that Piaget considers the process of cognitive development to be a gradual process of construction.

Every stage in a child's cognitive development is, for Piaget, an advance over the previous stage. As each new stage is reached, the developing child achieves new modes of adaptation and the ability to assimilate new concepts in the environment, placing him once again in a new state of disequilibrium. It is only through playing, imitating, exploring, and questioning that a child gradually comes to distinguish the possible from the impossible, the logical from the illogical. Thus, to Piaget, the progress toward this end-point is as inherent a property of cognitive life as are eating, drinking, and breathing in the biological sphere. Piaget (1967) states: "It should be noted first that equilibrium is not an extrinsic or added characteristic but rather an intrinsic and constitutive property of organic and mental life" (p. 102).

Anxiety, according to the motivation theorist, is an internal fear response that has generalized from the original single feared stimulus to many stimuli (Gibson, 1972). It does not lead to a particular goal. Rather, it is an intervening variable that is inferred from such physiological indices as increased pulse and heart rate. Anxious people also tend to exhibit many noticeable indicators of their anxiety, such as increased perspiration and nervous tics. People generally feel better when their anxieties are reduced. Thus, in the context of drive-reduction theory, anxiety can be considered as a drive.

Fear and Anxiety as Drives

The evidence indicating that the anxiety response is generalized to many stimuli comes from a variety of sources. For example, Watson, as you may recall from Chapter 4, conditioned 11-month-old Albert to fear a white rat (Watson and Rayner, 1920). His fear response soon generalized to fear of other white furry objects as well.

Neil Miller (1948) later demonstrated in a now classic study that rats will persistently avoid a situation that in the past was associated with a fear response. Miller trained rats to avoid being shocked in a white compartment by going through a curtain into a black compartment. He then discontinued the shocks completely, employing what could be termed, in operant conditioning theory, extinction. However, the rats did not extinguish the response of entering the black compartment, no matter how long Miller continued the trials without shock. Further, they continued to stay out of the white compartment and showed signs of distress when placed there.

What happened? According to Miller, fear of shock in the white compartment had generalized to anxiety felt whenever they were placed in that compartment. Just as entrance into the black compartment had at first stopped the shock, later it reduced the generated anxiety. Then, even though shock was no longer present, each escape to the black compartment resulted in drive reduction.

The effects of anxiety manifest themselves in important ways in human beings. The "job-jumper" is an individual who finds he cannot remain at any one job for any length of time. Such a person frequently quits suddenly, without being able to give a reasonable explanation to himself, his family, or his employer. The prognosis for a job-jumper is usually poor: Frequently, the rate at which he quits jobs increases with each subsequent job. Motivation theory explains the actions of the job-jumper when we realize that this person is highly anxious in each new job situation. With each successive job, more anxiety is produced; he knows that quitting reduces the anxiety drive, and the probability is thereby increased that he will quit the next job—if it comes along!

Behavior similar to this occurs with the student who cuts school steadily. Unfortunately, a great many teachers in the United States still believe that fear and anxiety are effective tools to curb undesirable behavior. They reason that if a child is punished or at least threatened with punishment each time he misbehaves, his fear of punishment will soon cause him to cease such behavior. What these teachers don't realize is that a child treated in this way may then generalize his fear response to *other* school-related activities.

One way that students may alleviate school-related anxiety is to cut classes, thus avoiding the anxiety-producing situation. Just as the job-jumper experienced drive reduction together with quitting, so will such a student experience it when he cuts classes. Furthermore, a student with such fears will find learning very difficult and often impossible. Although fear and anxiety may be highly effective sources of motivation, their effects are far from desirable.

D. O. Hebb (1946) suggests that fear and anxiety will be produced when an individual encounters a new situation in which there are both familiar and unfamiliar components. According to Hebb's theory, fear results when the individual's expectations of what should occur in any given new situation are not met. This explains extreme fear of corpses or mutilated human bodies—particularly in our society, where death often is a taboo topic. One expects a body to move and is frightened when it doesn't. Following logically from Hebb's theory, those persons with the greatest experience in a variety of situations are least likely to experience unfamiliar components and develop fear in new situations. This principle was verified by a study by Levine, Chevalier, and Korchin (1956) which showed that rats subjected to electroshock in experimental situations in infancy were less anxious in new situations than rats who were left alone with their mothers and without being shocked.

Hebb's theory also helps to provide a rationale for the practice of rearing children with multiple mothers. With more than a single mother in attendance, infants and children usually are exposed to a much wider range of experience, especially in terms of interpersonal relations. Children reared in such a manner are generally less anxious in new situations than children reared by one busy mother alone. This fact has been validated to a great extent by investigations of children reared with multiple-mothering (Bettelheim, 1969; Mead, 1962; Yarrow, 1964).

The relationship between anxiety and learning is complex. It was believed for many years that high levels of anxiety always inhibit learning. It is true that many of the physiological components associated with anxiety are not particularly helpful in a learning situation. Taylor (1951), however, found that persons with a high level of anxiety could be more quickly classically conditioned to blink their eyes than persons having a low degree of anxiety. At least in a simple task such as eyelid-blinking conditioning, higher levels of anxiety seem to be helpful. Similarly, Montague (1953) found that high-anxiety individuals performed better than low-anxiety individuals on a simple rote-learning task. These results, however, were reversed when more difficult rote-learning tasks were introduced (Castaneda, Palermo, and McCandless, 1956; Montague, 1953). High anxiety, in other words, appears to be beneficial when a task is extremely simple, and a hindrance when a task is difficult.

The teaching method employed in the classroom seems to influence the relationship between anxiety and learning. In one study, it was found that high-anxiety children taught in a formal and structured manner encountered no more difficulty in learning to read than low-anxiety children. If, however, the material was presented in an informal and unstructured manner, the low-anxiety children outperformed their high-anxiety counterparts (Grimes and Allinsmith, 1961).

MOTIVATING STUDENTS: WHAT THE TEACHER CAN DO

The implications of motivation theory for education should by now be apparent. But what specific actions can teachers take to increase motivation and learning in the classroom?

The Hierarchy of Needs and Classroom Learning

Maslow has proposed that human motivation is best conceived of as a hierarchy of five basic needs to be satisfied. According to his theory, if lower, more "primitive" needs are not met, individuals will not attempt to meet needs more advanced in the hierarchy. Thus, it is foolish to attempt to teach children who are hungry—that is, who have not satisfied their need for food. They simply will not be interested in higher-level needs. Yet there are large numbers of such children in the United States who come to school hungry every morning.

As a child's nutritional needs are satisfied, safety needs, according to Maslow, then become dominant. The teacher must keep in mind that children, especially young children, can easily be frightened by a strange and hostile environment. If a child is reprimanded persistently for each mistake he makes, and if he feels that such reprimands threaten his safety, he will soon withdraw or perhaps become very defensive in order to protect himself. Only when he is accepted for what he is can a child feel safe. And only when he is safe can he grow and develop. Love and belonging needs are next on Maslow's hierarchy. It is important, in this regard, that a teacher perceive school not only as a place where children learn facts and skills, but also as a place where a child develops numerous interpersonal relationships. The teacher should encourage children to work and play together, especially during their free-time activities. Projects in which the cooperative activities of several students are required strengthen the child-to-child network.

Teachers should encourage children to work and play together.
(Lynn McLaren, Rapho/Photo Researchers)

One of the most important roles a teacher plays is to serve as a model for students to follow. If a teacher relates to each student honestly and respectfully, students will in turn tend to adopt this same attitude among themselves. And if a teacher experiences and displays enjoyment in getting to know each of his students, so too will students begin to see that everyone has something special to offer.

Next in the hierarchy are the esteem needs. Not only must the teacher convey respect toward each student, he must also provide opportunities in which the child develops self-respect. This is a most difficult task. While acknowledging that there are individual differences between students, the teacher should try to convey the idea that respect is due not only for achievement but for the struggle to achieve as well.

Offering false praise to a child for his work is undoubtedly one of the worst things a teacher can do. Children are amazingly adept in perceiving this sort of insincerity and tend to resent it deeply (Travers, 1967). Children more often prefer honest feedback, even if it is negative. A child will be more motivated to try to do his best when he knows that a teacher can differentiate between his halfhearted attempts and his utmost efforts.

Finally, we arrive at Maslow's highest need—the need for self-actualization. Many educators believe that the qualities Maslow incorporates into the concept of self-actualization can serve as useful ideals toward which education ultimately should be aimed. Self-actualization is a concept that is not easily put into words, much less translated into specific educational practices. It is, as Maslow points out, qualitatively different from any of the other needs in the hierarchy, and represents a continual striving to grow and develop. In short, it is a struggle simply to be.

Maslow (1971) writes:

> If we want to be . . . teachers . . . what we must do is to accept the person and help him learn what kind of person he is already. What is his style, what are his aptitudes, what is he good for, not good for, what can we build upon, what are his good raw materials, his good potentialities? We would be nonthreatening and would supply an atmosphere of acceptance of the child's nature which reduces fear, anxiety, and defense to the minimum possible. Above all, we would care for the child, that is, enjoy him and his growth and self-actualization. (p.189)

Teachers frequently complain that many schoolchildren simply are not motivated to learn. Earlier in this chapter we described several techniques that McClelland adopted to raise achievement motiva-

Develop Achievement Motivation

tion.* In 1965, McClelland began to explore ways to implement achievement motivation training programs to help schoolchildren in the United States. McClelland (1972) described two studies (one in St. Louis, one in Boston) that he and another researcher, Richard de Charms, conducted, aimed at raising the achievement motivation of junior high school and high school students. The programs developed used many of the same techniques described earlier to teach children directly how to think, talk, and act like people with high achievement motivation, and then to help them examine carefully the extent to which they wanted to plan their immediate futures according to this model. Emphasis was on setting goals, building morale, and self-study. The two studies, however, differed in two respects. In the St. Louis project, the teachers themselves were trained to administer the achievement motivation training programs to their own students. The program continued throughout the year. In the Boston project, the children had brief, intensive courses that were conducted over a period of, at most, four weeks. These were distinct from the students' other classes, and were conducted by a specially trained staff that was unaffiliated with the school system.

The programs differed clearly in their results. The Boston program yielded only insignificant gains in boys' gradepoint averages and scores on standardized tests and no gains for the girls. Study of the effects of the project on nonschool activities, however, showed that students tended to spend their time in more achievement-related ways, as, for example, planning for future careers.

The St. Louis project produced different results. The children's scores on standardized tests of basic skills rose considerably from one grade to the next as compared with control subjects who had had no achievement motivation training.

Further, students in this project from ghetto schools were able to bring their scores on standardized achievement tests up to grade level, and sometimes above. The achievement test scores of other ghetto children who have not had the opportunity to participate in the achievement motivation training usually fall farther and farther below grade level as they progress through school.

Clearly, then, achievement motivation training is helpful in increasing student motivation. The important questions still unanswered, though, are: "What sort of classroom climate is best suited to increase achievement motivation? How should the teacher behave toward his students?" To answer these questions, Richard de Charms used questionnaires designed to measure the St. Louis stu-

---

*Although McClelland referred specifically to the need for achievement (nACH), in keeping with the definitions we gave earlier in the chapter we will refer to achievement *motivation*, for it was the direction and energy used to reduce the need for achievement that McClelland was discussing.

dents' perceptions of their teachers' behavior in the classroom. He examined both students who had had achievement motivation training and those who had not. He focused on the extent to which all these students felt that they or their teachers controlled activity in the classroom and were the originators of classroom actions. The responses were significant: Those students who demonstrated gains in school learning tended to perceive themselves, not their teachers, as originators of their own actions and controllers of their own activities. This was true both for students who had participated in the achievement motivation training program and for students who had not had this opportunity! Apparently, even though the training programs themselves were important to the development of achievement motivation, the general classroom climate established by the teacher was also of major importance. Further, it seemed, teachers who had been trained in achievement motivation tended to have classrooms with climates that fostered motivation, whether or not they actually gave their students formal training in motivation.

Apparently, then, teacher behavior is exceedingly important in determining whether or not students are motivated. How can the teacher create a classroom climate in which students see themselves as originators of their own actions and controllers of their own activities? It is by developing this feeling in students that positive gains in school performances will be obtained. McClelland suggested that the answer can be found in Jacob Kounin's work on classroom management techniques.

Kounin (1970) found that several approaches are involved in promoting a classroom climate that will increase student involvement and allow students to control, design, and participate in classroom activities. First, the teacher must provide a sufficient challenge to his students through a variety of approaches in order to interest and excite them. Second, the teacher must insure participation and require student responsibility for activities. And third, the teacher must, through letting the students know that "he knows what's going on regarding the children's behavior," make each student feel accountable for what he accomplishes in the classroom.

McClelland (1972) attempted to relate these three approaches to those procedures employed by teachers trained to promote achievement motivation.

[Motivation training] involves both for the teachers and for the pupils . . . an improved technique for insuring that these processes are heightened in the average classroom. The motivation training materials and methods are novel and varied, so that they insure *attention.* They are tailored to individuals and require *participation* by everyone in the classroom in playing a game of filling out a form, and they give very precise *feedback* on an individual basis as to whether the person has done the

LET *ME* DO IT: ACHIEVEMENT MOTIVATION

Evaluation of students' performance is traditionally part of a teacher's duties. But a study (Klein and Schuler, 1974) reveals that through use of student self-evaluation teachers not only can effectively reduce the time they spend on this task but also increase and improve academic performance. Students *want* the opportunity to evaluate themselves. The subjects of the study were students in two third-grade math classes in an inner-city public school in Pittsburgh, Pennsylvania. The students were using the Individually Prescribed Instruction (IPI) Math Program, under which they complete workbook pages and take a test that measures skill performance per unit of work. Ordinarily, the teacher evaluated their workbook performance. However, the students were told that if they passed the first test in their present skill they would earn the right to evaluate all workbook pages for their next skill. The children were also free to proceed at their own pace and to attempt to master their next skill test at any time they chose. Failure on a test meant loss of the self-evaluation privilege. The results of the study show that the students improved test-passing behavior when it depended on self-evaluation. Both the percentage of tests passed and test scores were higher. The study suggests that the opportunity to be more autonomous, as demonstrated in self-evaluation rather than teacher-evaluation, is a strong motivating factor in academic performance.

exercise well or not. . . . In using the materials the teacher is automatically applying many of the techniques which Kounin found to be associated with better work involvement in the classroom. [The teacher] is also doing things which ought to make pupils feel more like originators in the sense that they are making decisions in connection with the various exercises as to what they want to do next. (p. 144)

Quite clearly, motivation training techniques foster classroom climates that are conducive to increased learning.

INCREASING LEVELS OF ASPIRATION. A student's level of aspiration—his expectation of future success or failure based upon his past performances and his desire to improve—will exert a strong influence on his choice of tasks and on his feelings about which tasks are too difficult for him. Because of this link it is worthwhile to consider the factors that tend to raise and lower a student's level of aspiration and to look at relevant studies that have been done in this area.

In an early study, Child and Whiting (1949) explored the relationship between an individual's past history of successes and failures and his level of aspiration. Their results closely matched those of many other studies. Three basic conclusions came out of this research and are important for the teacher to consider in interpreting student behavior. The first is that success generally leads a person to raise his level of aspiration and, conversely, that failure generally leads him to lower his level of aspiration.

Consider, for example, a child who consistently does poorly in arithmetic. Imagine further that his textbook is so arranged that each problem is coded according to its level of difficulty, with level 1 problems being the simplest and level 3 problems the most difficult. Working on the assumption that a past history of failure tends to lead to a lowering of the level of aspiration, we would expect him to avoid level 2 and level 3 problems and to concentrate exclusively on level 1 problems. Furthermore, if he continued to experience failure in math, he eventually would come to expect failure even in the simplest of problems. His level of aspiration would be severely diminished.

But now look at the child who has done well in schoolwork. We would expect, according to Child and Whiting's conclusions, that this child would tend to have very high expectations of success when he approaches new situations. Indeed, it is just this type of child, whose level of aspiration is high, who would probably meet new challenges with zeal.

Child and Whiting's second conclusion is that the effects of success and failure on a child's level of aspiration become more pronounced as his successes or failures become more pervasive. That is, the more he encounters failure, the less likely he is to raise his level of aspiration; and the more he encounters success, the more likely he is to raise his level of aspiration.

Therefore, the teacher should aim to raise the aspiration levels of his students so that the children approach new problems enthusiastically and realistically. To accomplish this, the teacher must structure his classroom activities in such a way that every student has a chance to succeed in most of what he does. At the same time, the teacher should not eliminate failure altogether in classroom experience. A child who experiences no failures in school will develop a distorted image of his own abilities, which will be a poor preparation for the real world, where, as we all know, failure is as much a part of life as success. Remember also what we pointed out earlier in the chapter—that tasks perceived as moderately difficult are preferred more than tasks that are too easy (Maehr and Sjogren, 1971). A student who always completes tasks and never experiences failure is very likely to be bored and unstimulated.

Child and Whiting's third conclusion concerns the teacher: Teacher expectation also affects aspiration levels. That is, a teacher's expectation of how well each student will perform in school may in itself influence students' aspiration levels. If a teacher expects a student to perform well in the classroom, his behavior toward that student will probably be consistent with that expectation. The teacher's behavior, in turn, may influence the student's self-evaluation and perhaps affect his behavior as well. Such a chain of events has been termed the *self-fulfilling prophecy* or the *Pygmalion effect*.

This phenomenon as it exists in the classroom has been investigated by Rosenthal and Jacobson, who published their findings in a controversial book, *Pygmalion in the Classroom* (1968).

In their research, Rosenthal and Jacobson first administered non-verbal intelligence tests to a large group of children in grades 1 through 6. The teachers were told that the purpose of the test was to discover which students would be most likely to show substantial academic progress in the coming year. Each teacher was given a list of students who, based on the test results, were the most likely candidates to exhibit such academic growth. Actually, the students on this list were chosen totally at random and made up 20 percent of the entire school population. Rosenthal and Jacobson "tricked" the teachers in order to prove the theory that the students singled out as possible intellectual bloomers would show significantly greater gains than other students. At the end of the school year, Rosenthal and Jacobson once again administered intelligence tests to the children. According to the researchers, the expected bloomers, especially in the first and second grades, did in fact show greater gains on the test than their "nonbloomer" classmates.

Rosenthal and Jacobson reported that these results showed that teacher expectation affected not only self-evaluation but also performance. A number of replications of this study as well as similar studies have been performed with similar results. (See, for example, Barber et al., 1969; Barber and Silver, 1968; Claiborn, 1969; Fleming and Anttonen, 1971; José and Cody, 1971; Leacock, 1969; Rothbart, Dalfen, and Barrett, 1971; and Shore, 1969.) However, some researchers have reported a series of problems related to this study. Unfortunately, for example, Rosenthal and Jacobson did not examine how the teachers conveyed their expectations to the students. Also, many theorists have criticized the Rosenthal and Jacobson study on technical grounds. Thorndike (1968), for example, questioned the validity of the tests used and the IQ scores obtained. Clearly, further research is needed on the phenomenon of the self-fulfilling prophecy.

SEX DIFFERENCES AND ACHIEVEMENT MOTIVATION. We noted in passing that the girls involved in the Boston achievement motivation training did not show any improvement. Many researchers have studied the effects of sex differences on achievement motivation. Studies using tasks that are perceived by the subject to reflect individual intelligence or leadership ability have shown significant differences in achievement motivation between men and women.

For men, such tasks were found consistently to arouse and heighten their achievement motivation (McClelland, Atkinson, Clark, and Lowell, 1953). Women, on the other hand, failed to exhibit this expected increase in their achievement motivation (Fontana, 1971). Consistent with this pattern is the finding that women themselves tended to project greater achievement strivings to men than to women (Veroff, Wilcox, and Atkinson, 1953).

It has been pointed out in some studies that women feel that achievement strivings are more appropriate in males than in females in our culture, and thus they tend to repress these strivings in themselves (Blumberg, 1974a). A study conducted by Houts and Entwisle (1968) supports this idea. These investigators found a significant relationship between good grades and achievement motivation only for those women who openly expressed their competitive feelings in the classroom, that is, women who appeared to accept achievement strivings as appropriate to the female sex role. This relationship did not hold in the case of seemingly more tradition-minded women, who tended to inhibit their competitive strivings in public.

Matina Horner (1972) has probed this phenomenon in her research. She found that the women she studied felt that academic success would threaten their femininity and possibly lead to social rejection. Two thirds of her subjects expressed feelings of anxiety and guilt in response to a story about a woman who was at the top of her class in medical school. They experienced, in Horner's words, a "fear of success."

This fear of success was strongest in highly intelligent women reared in an atmosphere in which achievement was valued. Interestingly and sadly, these same women who experienced fears regarding success were also found to have a high need for achievement. Horner suggested that this resulted from two contradictory pressures. On the one hand these women were encouraged to do their best in school, while at the same time they were expected to get married before they graduated from college. This was difficult to accomplish, since they felt that academic success would make them appear less feminine and consequently less likely candidates for marriage.

Child-rearing practices are often examined in an attempt to explain these sex differences in achievement motivation. Dyk and Witkin (1965), for example, found that mothers generally discouraged any signs of assertiveness in their daughters but valued it in their sons. This finding is especially relevant in conjunction with reports indicating that independence or mastery training is important in fostering a high need to achieve (Atkinson, 1958; Rosen and D'Andrade, 1959; Winterbottom, 1958). Males apparently develop a stronger need to achieve than females because they are taught to value independence and self-reliance early in their childhood. This was not the case for women, at least not in the 1950s and 1960s, at the time these studies were conducted.

Today, in the 1970s, with the increase in strength and popularity of the women's liberation movement, achievement strivings in women have grown. Especially important is the fact that women themselves are beginning to feel that achievement strivings are just as appropriate in women as they are in men (Alper, 1974). And, not unexpectedly, more and more research findings seem to be showing a decrease in sex differences in achievement motivation.

Questions for Thought

What changes do you think we can expect to find in achievement motivation, in student grades, and in courses of study selected by female students in the next ten years?
How do you think these changes will affect our society?

Group Reinforcement and Competition as Sources of Classroom Motivation

In Chapter 1, in describing the Soviet system of preschool education, we pointed out that the primary emphasis in their system is upon sharing and group cooperation. Soviet children are taught from very early ages to be self-reliant group members and to always value the interests of the group above those of the individual. This orientation is, of course, continued throughout a child's entire education.

In Soviet schools, all activities, including work as well as play, are carried out in groups of various sizes. Whereas in the United States *individual* students are often given special privileges for good behavior or academic excellence, in the Soviet Union the *group* that has performed best will be specially rewarded. Competition occurs between groups of children rather than between individuals. Each student is evaluated weekly by his peers, with his status determined primarily by how much and how well he has contributed to his own group. The bright child is motivated to help the poorer student, who is in turn motivated to improve his performance so that he too can better serve his group.

In the United States, this kind of group support is usually secondary to individual competition. However, one experimental attempt to use group reinforcement proved quite successful (Cohen and Filipczak, 1971). The National Training School for Boys is a residential treatment center for male adolescents who have had extended histories of failure both at home and at school. Its directors feel that a child continues to fail because he has experienced so few successes, and because he has received so little support from those around him. Consequently, they decided to set up schedules of reinforcement that were individually tailored to each boy, whatever his level of proficiency, so that he could achieve numerous successes. To keep individual competition at a minimum in the classrooms, programmed texts and teaching machines were used.

But the key to the program's success can probably be found in its use of group reinforcement. Everyone in the school supported the progress made by each boy. If a boy showed marked improvement in his studies, the teacher pointed this out to his classmates, who then gave their congratulations. Even the correctional officers—in effect taken out of their traditional role as punishers and put into the role of encouragers—provided support to the adolescents. They were also encouraged to give the boys special bonuses for good behavior. According to Cohen and Filipczak, both the boys and the officers enjoyed this setup. Eventually, the boys came to realize that their fellow students, as well as the entire staff, were always behind them.

If cooperative activity and group support are beneficial, one might ask if and when competition has any redeeming qualities. Competition varies in its effects from situation to situation and from individual to individual. For example, competition as a teach-

Competition can be a strong motivator.

(Bruce Roberts, Rapho/Photo Researchers)

ing device has been shown to be more beneficial in simple or mechanical tasks than in more complex problem-solving tasks (Ahlstrom, 1957; Clifford, Cleary, and Walster, 1972; Shaw, 1958). The effects of competition in this case must be evaluated in terms of the complexity of the task at hand. A teacher would be wise to rely on competition in the classroom as an effective source of motivation only when dealing with fairly straightforward learning tasks.

Competition appears to be a more effective source of motivation when the competitors have a chance to succeed and when they are fairly evenly matched (Strong, 1963; Vaughn, 1936). The implication of this finding for teaching is that competition is most beneficial to just those children who need it least—the ones who are already doing well. They will be the ones who will tend to succeed in competitive situations and get the best grades. Going back to the drive-reduction model discussed at the beginning of this chapter, you will recall that motivation occurs *after* drive reduction has taken place and does not occur in the absence of drive reduction. Since only winners experience drive reduction, it will be the winners who become most highly motivated to achieve.

Creativity: A Major Goal of the Teacher

Creativity, the ability to solve new and different problems in new and innovative ways, is a stated goal of most classroom teachers. Creative thinking plays an important role in acquiring knowledge. Certainly, if a person is flexible and original in his thinking, he can approach new material from a wider number of perspectives and interpretations. Creativity also seems to be an important factor in achieving vocational success. Creativity is probably the most distinguishing feature of people who are at the top in their fields. For all of these reasons, it has been suggested that it is highly important to identify creative children in the classroom and to promote creative thinking in all classroom activities.

E. Paul Torrance (1960) has developed a number of innovative methods to identify creativity in the classroom. One such method involves presenting a child with a group of toys, which he is free to play with. He is then asked to think of ideas for improving each toy so that it would be more fun to play with. The subject's responses to this suggestion provide a basis for evaluating his inventiveness, flexibility, and constructiveness.

Another method is Torrance's "Ask-and-Guess Test." Here the subject is presented with a picture and asked to think of as many questions as he can that would help him to better understand the action or event presented in the picture. The subject's ability to formulate hypotheses is then assessed by examining his responses to two questions posed by the investigators. In the first, he is asked to make as many guesses as he can as to the possible cause of the event shown in the picture, and in the second, he is asked to guess the possible consequences of the event.

Identifying creativity is, of course, only the first step. If creativity is to flourish, it must be promoted. And this second step is more difficult than the first. Unfortunately, even though it is stated as a major goal, creativity is not encouraged in most American schools. In fact, the highly creative student too often becomes alienated from both his teachers and his peer group. If we are to remedy this situation, we must first examine why it happens.

One contributing factor is that teachers are often threatened and intimidated by the numerous questions that the creative student asks. Teachers who are not creative themselves are made extremely uncomfortable by original and novel questions for which they have no prepared answer (Marx and Tombaugh, 1967).

Teachers generally find the highly intelligent student more desirable than the highly creative student. (Interestingly, creativity clearly differs from intelligence.) If given the choice between a student who is both highly intelligent and highly creative and a student who is highly intelligent but not quite as creative, teachers (particularly those teaching in rigid, traditional classrooms) will more often than not choose to teach the less creative student.

A second factor contributing to the alienation of the creative student is that the kinds of test usually given by teachers emphasize recall of facts and discourage creative thinking. The creative student is particularly penalized when he takes standardized tests, for on these tests he is asked to provide one, and only one, appropriate answer. Original and novel answers are considered inappropriate and thus given less or no credit. This is a problem that is compounded by the fact that colleges and universities use standardized achievement tests to assess prospective students. Thus, the intelligent but less creative child receives reinforcers throughout his school career for his more limited, although highly successful, test-taking achievement.

A final factor is the popular stereotype of the creative student as being either an artist, writer, or musician. As a result of this stereotype, many students who show creativity in the natural and social sciences are given little recognition (Marx and Tombaugh, 1967). However, the art student does not benefit from this attitude, either. On the contrary, although the artist may be lavished with attention, he is often expected to produce too much too quickly, and thus feels as stifled as the creative science student.

It is to be hoped that teachers will become more aware of the contribution that their creative students can make. They should learn to recognize and reward creativity when it appears in their classrooms, for, when all is said and done, whether creativity will blossom or fade depends on whether teachers decide to reward or punish it.

LET'S PRETEND: INCREASING CHILDREN'S FANTASIES AND CREATIVITY

(Jan Lukas, Rapho/Photo Researchers)

"Parents and teachers can encourage and increase children's fantasies. The benefits in attention span, self-control, concentration, and learning make all the horsing around worth it," says Joan Freyberg (1975, p. 63). In short, imaginative play fosters intellectual development, creativity, and emotional growth. The preschool years are particularly significant ones, because youngsters tend to show their imaginativeness in observable play; in later years imaginative activities are less observable and less subject to change.

The most important catalyst in increasing children's fantasies is the attitude of adult models in the child's environment. Parents and teachers who encourage pretending, who demonstrate and teach it, help a child develop this important skill. Dr. Freyberg offers these suggestions for encouraging imaginative ability: enact stories in which adult and child add both sound effects and voice changes, stories to which a child can make up his own ending; synchronize activites and pretending (for example, suggest going on a boat voyage at bath time); give a child free-form items from which he can make "pretend" objects; encourage a child's role playing. Freyberg suggests that make-believe play involves sustained and complex sequences of behavior. The imagination it calls forth enhances creative thought and helps a child achieve an integration of his experiences.

Reduce Anxiety and Its Effects

Earlier in this chapter we pointed out that anxiety—an internal fear response generalized to many situations—is best conceived of as a drive that the individual seeks to reduce. The most common way to reduce anxiety is to avoid the situation with which fear is originally associated. And, because anxiety is generalized fear, people tend to avoid whole situations as well as the specific aspects that initially caused the fear. This point was illustrated earlier in the examples of the job-jumper and the student who cuts school, each of whom avoided an entire situation because of anxiety associated with one part of it.

That most anxiety is unpleasant is widely accepted. Widespread anxiety often accompanies neurotic and psychotic disorders, and is frequently the symptom that motivates people to seek the help of a therapist (Travers, 1967). On the other hand, some minimal level of anxiety does appear to be experienced as pleasant and desirable. And in some cases, individuals prefer quite substantial levels of fear—for example, the Evel Knievel type of thrill-seeker. Most frequently, however, individuals prefer mild levels of anxiety. The tremendous popularity of amusement park rides, in which people pay money to experience mild fear and anxiety in controlled situations, reflects this preference.

In the classroom the reduction of extremely high levels of student anxiety is a very important and difficult task for a teacher to accomplish. Although we can advise a teacher to refrain from using punishment as a source of motivation on the basis of what we have studied of learning theory, it is not as easy to provide a teacher with a list of do's and don'ts concerning anxiety in other aspects of a classroom situation.

Let us take the case of the anxiety generated by the test-taking situation. This anxiety interferes with a student's ability to think rapidly and clearly, whether the student is one who has a record of past failures or one who usually does well in school. In an experiment with college students, Goldberg (1973) studied only those students who had maintained at least B averages. He found that test anxiety is particularly detrimental to those students whose self-images rest heavily upon school performance. They tended to fear school in general; that is, their anxiety reactions to testing spread to a wide variety of school-related activities. Furthermore, they tended to have relatively low opinions of themselves as measured in tests of self-esteem.

In an attempt to reduce the amount of anxiety experienced by college students, colleges have offered the pass-fail grading option to their students. It is thought that this grading method will relieve the constant pressure to maintain or better one's grade-point average. Some faculty and students feel that with this pressure relieved, students ought to feel freer to explore a subject without fear.

To examine the effects of the pass-fail system on the behavior and attitudes of college students, a team of researchers administered several hundred questionnaires to students at a large midwestern university who had selected this option (Hales, Bain, and Rand, 1973). The results of this study were somewhat conflicting. On the one hand, a great majority of students reported less anxiety in their pass-fail courses than in their regularly graded courses. But this was counterbalanced by student reports that they were less motivated to learn and to work in their pass-fail courses than in their regular courses, in which grade reinforcements were given. Although the pass-fail system seems to reduce anxiety, it also seems to lower the motivation to learn and work for students who are used to being reinforced by grades.

Another technique that has been proposed for reducing anxiety is put to work in the context of competency-based education (Young and Van Mondfrans, 1972). Competency-based education is discussed in detail later in this chapter. The main principle here is to provide the student with specific information about what he must do to complete his education. In some forms of competency-based education not only is the student informed of precisely what behaviors he must exhibit both in projects and in examinations, he is also allowed to examine the test before he actually takes it. Competency-based education makes the assumption that students and faculty agree on what constitutes competency in any given subject matter. All students agree to meet a certain level of competency, although each student may take different amounts of time to meet his goal. This procedure does not appear to have the pitfall of reduced motivation to learn and work that sometimes accompanies the pass-fail option. Providing the student with the information of exactly what he needs to know appears to have two benefits: It reduces his anxiety while at the same time motivating him to learn and to work.

Different Kinds of Classroom Motivation

A number of researchers have rejected the idea that external rewards of some kind must be present in order for a subject to be motivated (Berlyne, 1966). Harlow, for example, whose work we discussed earlier, found that his monkeys would actively manipulate puzzles, although they received no material rewards for this behavior (Harlow et al., 1950). Rather, the reward seemed to be intrinsic to the behavior itself. Harlow called this *intrinsic motivation*.

INTRINSIC MOTIVATION. As we mentioned earlier, humans have an exploratory drive. Certain properties in stimuli, among them complexity, novelty, change, incongruity, and surprise, seem to produce intrinsic motivation. This kind of stimulus (for example, a jigsaw puzzle or something much more intricate) apparently causes a discrepancy or conflict between what is expected or known and what is presented. Some writers have suggested that the person is motivated to solve the problem by a need to reduce tension (Bigge, 1964). However, whatever the mechanisms involved in this process, it does seem to be a pervasive source of motivation. Students generally are not stimulated by the extremely familiar and the known. Rather, it is new material that interests them, because it raises questions instead of resolving them. It is the type of material, in other words, that sets up a sort of symbolic conflict in their minds, most often resulting in what we would call intrinsically motivated behavior.

Similarly, intrinsic motivation can be the source of a student's preoccupation with certain kinds of problems for hours on end, when no external reinforcements are provided. It is also this same phenomenon of intrinsic motivation that serves as a basis for Bruner's discovery method of teaching, discussed in Chapter 5.

Problems that raise questions seem to be reinforcing to students. Let us look at some suggestions made by Berlyne (1966) for ways in which intrinsic motivation can be effectively created through "conceptual conflict" and used in the classroom. In natural science, for example, the teacher can use experiments to contradict student expectations. Many experiments have been devised that result in particularly surprising outcomes. Students not only enjoy such demonstrations but, just as importantly, tend to remember the explanations or principles behind them.

Another possibility is for a teacher to produce intentionally a state of doubt in students by presenting them with a general proposition that may or may not be true. The students may try to resolve their doubts by investigating the evidence for and against the proposition. Once again, according to the advocates of intrinsic motivation, the student is primarily motivated by the problem itself, rather than by a desire to obtain an external reward of some kind.

In a similar manner, the teacher can create a state of uncertainty in his students by presenting them with a problem that has a number of possible solutions. Berlyne (1966) refers to a geography lesson in which students had to "guess the locations of cities on a map showing only the natural features of the territory." In order to resolve their uncertainty, the students had to gradually eliminate possibilities until the correct solution became apparent.

Another technique a teacher can use to motivate students is to ask them to imagine themselves in a very difficult practical situation. For example, if a lesson concerns adaptation to the environment, have the students describe what they would do if they were lost in the middle of a deep forest with only enough water to get them through one day. Of course, in order for them to visualize themselves in this situation and to come up with any solution, they would need sufficient information about the nature of the forest to work with.

The possibilities for classroom activities such as these are limitless. Every teacher should keep in mind that the main goal in designing such activities is to maximize intrinsically motivated behavior, behavior that is engaged in for its own sake rather than to obtain an external reward.

Questions for Thought

Do you think that *all* learning by students in our school systems can be motivated through intrinsic reinforcement? That is, can *all* required learning be made enjoyable?
What would the teacher have to do to meet this goal?

Over the past several years, Moore and his colleagues have designed educational environments to bring out children's natural tendencies to explore (Moore and Anderson, 1969). Among the basic principles guiding Moore's work is the idea that a learning environment should be responsive to the individual, providing him with feedback. He has used modern technology, such as the talking typewriter, which instantly provides the student who is learning to read with knowledge of results. Another principle is that the learner should have a good deal of freedom within the learning environment to explore a variety of alternatives to whatever he is doing. Still another principle behind Moore's work states that the child should not be pressured into participating in any activities. Moore means this quite literally. Children should be free to come and go as they please. Moore believes that if the learning environment is effective, children will come to appreciate and take advantage of the opportunities to learn and create. It is in this last principle in particular that Moore reveals his complete faith in the power of intrinsic motivation.

EXTRINSIC MOTIVATION. So far in this section we have focused on behavior motivated by intrinsic rewards and not on behavior motivated by the desire for an external, or extrinsic, reward. For example, if a child studies for a test solely for the purpose of obtaining a good grade, we would say that he is extrinsically motivated.

Although some theorists report that material learned through extrinsic motivation is not as effectively mastered or retained as material learned through intrinsic motivation, there are numerous exceptions. For example, experimental evidence from one study indicates that children from environments of low socioeconomic status respond more favorably to extrinsic than to intrinsic sources of motivation (Terrell, Durkin, and Wiesley, 1959). In this same study, middle-class children responded better to intrinsic than to extrinsic sources of motivation. The topic of social differences will be discussed more fully in Chapter 10, but this finding should be noted here in connection with motivation — namely, that teachers should seek the motivation device that is most effective for each individual student. Individualization of instruction seems most appropriate in teaching, no matter which learning approach — intrinsic or extrinsic motivation — is used.

Plan the Curriculum for Motivation

Among the many different curricula designed to boost student motivation is *competency-based education* (Young and Van Mondfrans, 1972). This curriculum enables each student to take an active role in determining his own educational goals through an individualized partnership with his teacher.

In one such competency-based instructional program, at the beginning of the school year each student meets with his teacher to discuss goals for the coming year (Young and Van Mondfrans, 1972). With the teacher's help, the student decides on very specific goals that they both feel are appropriate for his current level of achievement. The student himself then can determine the particular strategy to use to achieve these goals. In such a competency-based program, the role of the teacher is to help and guide the student in reaching the goals he has set for himself.

One of the primary advantages of this type of approach is that it benefits the slow student as well as the advanced student. Since each student's goals remain confidential, the student competes with no one but himself. Even if his goals are actually below what is considered standard for his particular grade level, the student can still derive great satisfaction from meeting them.

A related curriculum program uses *individualized student-teacher contracts*. It differs from competency-based education in its more specific reliance on operant principles. The contracts themselves specify in detail what behaviors will be rewarded, when they will be rewarded, and how they will be rewarded. Brian Frieder (1970) has suggested several guidelines for making the most effective use of these student-teacher contracts. The contract, first of all, should be very specific and clear. The child must always know exactly what and how much he must do in order to receive a specified reward. Second, the contract must be fair. That is, the reward itself must be appropriate to the action required to obtain it. The exact details of what is fair must, of course, be negotiated between the student and teacher. Third, the contract should always be stated in positive terms, so that the child is made aware of what he can do in order to get a reward, rather than what will happen if he doesn't live up to the contract. In other words, the contract should be based exclusively on positive reinforcement. Finally, a teacher should agree only to those terms that he himself can realistically and systematically fulfill. The teacher should consider this point very carefully, for if he breaks the contract, the trust that hopefully has been established with the student will be seriously damaged.

SUMMARY

The motivation theorist is interested primarily in the variables intervening between stimulus and response that influence a subject's choice of goals. This orientation contrasts with that of the associationists, who limit their analysis solely to the relationship between stimuli and responses, and with that of the cognitive-field theorists, who focus on the way in which a person's perceptions of the world are organized.

There are many classroom applications of the various motivation theories.

Motivation theorists are concerned with the energy and direction used to reduce our needs and drives, that is, the way in which we direct our energy toward specific goals. Humans have a natural tendency to strive toward a steady or balanced state of being, a state we call homeostasis.

Maslow discussed a hierarchy of needs in which physiological needs must be satisfied before any other needs emerge. Also important to motivation theorists is achievement motivation and the variables that affect it, such as personality and level of aspiration.

Berlyne and White theorized that there is a human need to understand and explore the environment and to seek stimulation from it. The importance of fear and anxiety as drives is also stressed by motivation theorists. We avoid situations that we associate with fear. It has been shown, however, that those people who have experienced fear in a variety of situations are least likely to fear new situations.

Researchers have demonstrated that students are best motivated when they encounter frequent successes in their endeavors. This applies to their academic work as well as to their interpersonal lives. Classrooms should thus be structured so as to optimize the successes of the students. However, falsely praising a student does more harm than good; a student can become overconfident if he encounters no failures at all, and occasional failure, when combined with appropriate and immediate feedback, can be beneficial.

Group competition, cooperation, and support are better sources of motivation than competition between individuals. This is especially true for the slow student, who usually encounters failure in individual competition. One way to alleviate this situation is to have the student set his own personal goals and thus only compete with himself. In doing this the slow student can derive great satisfaction in achieving his own goals, even if these goals leave the student somewhat below the standards established for his grade level.

Anxiety has been shown to inhibit motivation and interfere with complex problem-solving. One way to reduce anxiety in general, and test-taking anxiety in particular, is to introduce a pass-fail system of grading. Test-taking anxiety is also reduced when a student has a clear idea of what is expected from him, as in competency-based education.

Finally, several techniques for optimizing intrinsic motivation have been suggested. Basically, this means taking advantage of the student's inherent curiosity and desire to explore the world. It was mentioned in this context that extrinsic sources of motivation are occasionally more effective than intrinsic sources.

SUGGESTED FOR FURTHER READING

Cofer, C. N. *Motivation and emotion.* Glenview, Ill.: Scott, Foresman, 1972. This book, a classic in the field of motivation, is very comprehensive, covering both the theoretical and experimental literature in the field, and as such is an excellent resource book on the topic of motivation.

Holt, J. *How children learn.* New York: Pitman, 1967. Holt describes in a lively way how children can grow to enjoy learning if given the appropriate opportunities. Included here are many examples of intrinsic motivation in action.

Maslow, A. H. *Toward a psychology of being* (2nd ed.). New York: Van Nostrand Reinhold, 1968. In this book, one of the best accounts of his theory of motivation, Maslow discusses at length his concept of self-actualization.

SPECIFIC TYPES, OUTCOMES, AND STYLES OF LEARNING

CHAPTER 7

After completing this chapter, the reader should be able to:

1 Identify five major types of learning that occur in school, and explain the relationship of each type of learning to the skills that are taught in school.

2 Describe teaching methods that can be used to increase skill in all of the five major types of learning.

3 Prepare a list of learning objectives for a given area of instruction and describe them in behavioral terms. Classify each of these objectives according to Bloom's taxonomy of cognitive learning objectives, and revise prepared objectives to meet all the categories of his taxonomy.

4 Identify the different learning styles that can be anticipated in a class of students. Outline methods by which teachers can assist student learning by making use of each student's independent learning style.

Chapter 7 examines, in much greater detail than in previous chapters, the specific *types* of learning that take place in the classroom and the different *styles* of learning that students use. Whereas in previous chapters we dealt with *general* theories describing the ways that people learn, in this chapter we will deal with the *specific* types of learning that take place in the classroom; for example, perceptual learning, language learning, and motor learning. (In other words, in the earlier chapters we used what Tolman described as the molar approach, compared to the molecular approach we will use in this chapter.) A second difference between this chapter and the preceding ones is the focus on the *outcomes* of learning and the ways they can be measured, rather than simply on the learning process. A last focus of attention in this chapter is on the *individual differences* among learners that ultimately affect the *styles* in which they learn — a third factor to which teachers should pay special attention for optimal classroom learning.

TYPES OF LEARNING

Perceptual and language learning are both basic to the structure of formal education. Perceptual learning was studied in detail by Gestalt psychologists, as described earlier in Chapter 5. Both language and perceptual capabilities are necessary for the development and mastery of reading and writing skills, which are necessary, in turn, to all later learning.

Motor learning tends to receive much less attention in school, but it is also critical to the learning of many skills, particularly at early grade levels. For example, learning how to print the alphabet is considered essential if the child is to profit from further education.

Conceptual learning and problem-solving, first popularized by the Gestalt psychologists in the early part of this century, are considered essential skills by cognitive learning theorists, such as Bruner, as well as by educators in most fields.

The last type of learning that will be discussed here is attitude learning. The development of socially desirable attitudes — such as respect for oneself and for others, responsibility and cooperativeness, and a positive attitude toward learning and education — is one of the principal functions of public schools today.

Perceptual Learning   Perceptual processes are important in many different kinds of learning situations, ranging from simple sensory discrimination tasks to complex acts with many component parts, such as reading. In fact, the widespread problem of disabilities in reading and other academic areas has often been attributed to defects in visual and auditory perception (Glaser and Resnick, 1972). The inability of students to read satisfactorily is one of the major educational problems of our time. In fact, it is cited as the single highest cause for teenagers dropping out of school before graduation (J. T. Gibson, 1972). The essential role of perceptual skills in learning to read thus deserves the special attention of any teacher.

Many educators believe that attempting to teach children to read is pointless until they demonstrate by their performance that they have reached an appropriate level of maturity. In a way, this does make sense, because the evidence shows that children who fail initial reading-readiness tests will be unable to keep up. However, it may be just as detrimental to these children's progress simply to wait for them to "mature" before giving them any reading instruction at all. Time alone cannot turn a nonreader into a reader if a sufficient amount of environmental stimulation and experience is lacking (J. T. Gibson, 1972).

Eleanor Gibson (1965, 1968) has analyzed the task of learning to read in terms of a hierarchy involving four stages:

1. Learning to speak.
2. Learning to discriminate printed letters.
3. Learning to decode letters to sound (a very difficult process in the English language, since there is no one-to-one spelling-sound correspondence).
4. Learning to perceive higher-order units (which is what distinguishes good readers from poor readers).

Eleanor Gibson's research on discrimination in learning to read (stage 2) has been concerned largely with identifying the distinctive features (horizontal lines, vertical lines, and so on) of each of the 26 letters. According to Gibson, letters vary in the degree to which their identifying features are the same as or different from other letters. Using a list of 12 possible distinguishing features, she constructed a chart, showing for each letter in the alphabet which features are present and which are absent. A sample of 4-year-old children then "read" the chart; Gibson showed that the number of features shared by one letter and another was directly related to the number of errors due to confusion (Gibson, 1965, 1968). The data suggests that perceptual learning is indeed a major factor in being able to discriminate one printed letter from another, and, ultimately, in learning to read.

Gibson, Pick, Osser, and Hammond (1962) have also investigated the perceptual processes involved in learning to convert letters to sounds. Nonsense words were projected one at a time on a screen to a group of college students, who were directed to write down each word as it appeared. Half of the words were pronounceable, having a high spelling-to-sound correlation (for instance, "glurk"), and the other half were unpronounceable, having a low spelling-to-sound correlation (for example, "ckurgl"). As expected, the pronounceable words were correctly perceived much more often than the unpronounceable words. Good readers especially perceived those pseudowords that fit spelling-syntactical rules better than those pseudowords that did not. According to Gibson (1965), similar word structure generalizations should apply to the learning of real words.

One characteristic that distinguishes good readers from poor readers is the ability to learn higher-order units. Evidence shows that good readers do not read each letter; they read the whole word at once. Moreover, when words are arranged in a sentence or paragraph, good readers don't read just one word at a time but a group of words (Gibson, 1968).

What implications do these findings have for teaching reading in the classroom? Chall (1967) has pointed out that children of low to average intelligence and disadvantaged backgrounds probably benefit most from a code emphasis in early reading learning, as opposed to a meaning emphasis. Using a code (phonic) emphasis, children are taught to "sound out" what they are reading; on the other hand, with a meaning emphasis, they are taught to look at a word or part of a word as a whole unit and attach meaning to it. In practice, though, coding and meaning aspects of reading are closely related. Attention to both coding and meaning, with an understanding of the perceptual processes involved, is ultimately important for optimal learning for all children.

Motor Learning

The importance of the development of motor skills to all school learning is often underestimated by teachers in the United States. In some foreign countries, such as the Soviet Union and China, "physical culture" is a major component of every school curriculum — not just an additional course.

Motor learning covers much more than the skills commonly taught as part of a physical education program. Motor activities enter into every sphere of our lives — work, play, eating, washing, dressing, and performing chores around the house. Motor skills are needed to accomplish many tasks, but they also open up new doors to hobbies and leisure-time pursuits.

For people engaged in mechanical and construction trades, motor skills are, of course, of prime importance; the exacting and often hazardous nature of their work demands that these skills be highly developed. Nurses, doctors, teachers, office workers, salespeople, and so on are also engaged in activities that call for some display of their motor ability.

Without the development of motor skills, children would never be able to learn to walk, run, jump, hop, or skip. Even the basic activities of reading, writing, and speaking would be impossible, because these also depend on motor skills. But because these more advanced activities are usually thought of by educators in terms of their association with verbal and perceptual skills, we tend to overlook the important motor component that is involved as well.

A TAXONOMY OF MOTOR LEARNING BASED ON SUBJECT MATTER.   Because motor learning encompasses such a variety of behaviors, Merrill (1972) found it useful to construct a taxonomy (classification scheme) of motor skills based on subject matter taught in school. The five different areas of motor skills he identified include physical education, communication, fine arts, language, and vocational skills. Each of these five categories is in turn broken down into smaller categories. The five major categories and their subdivisions are listed in Figure 7-1.

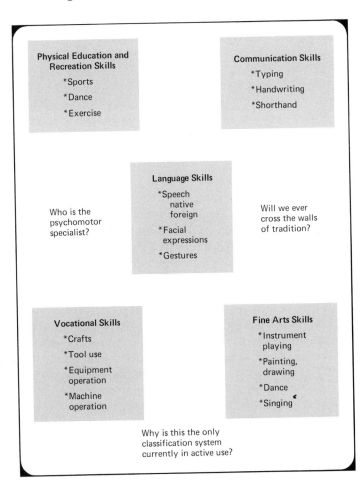

Figure 7-1. Five areas in which motor skills are important.

(Redrawn from Merrill, 1972, p. 388)

All five of the categories of motor learning included in this taxonomy are taught in the schools. For the vast majority of students, *physical education* is a required part of the curriculum from elementary school through college. The skills taught by physical education teachers include activities such as swimming, tennis, volleyball, and calisthenics. At the same time, other teachers are contributing to the development of *communication* and *language* skills. Penmanship is, of course, given heavy emphasis in the early grades, and in junior high and high school, special courses may be offered in typing and shorthand. Speech is also an important part of the curriculum, and all students know the experience of participating in class discussions and presenting oral reports. In addition, schools provide extensive instruction in foreign languages, and an important part of any good foreign language course is practice in conversation.

Similarly, the teaching of *vocational* and *fine arts* skills is found in many segments of the school curriculum. Students in junior high or high school commonly take at least one shop course, in which special skills, such as cooking, sewing, woodworking, and electrical wiring are taught. A growing number of teenagers also take driver education courses. Moreover, many adolescents and young adults who do not plan to attend college go instead to vocational or trade schools, where they receive special training for a vocational occupation. Finally, many schools provide specialized instruction in such areas as music, art, drama, and dance. For students with interest and talent, extracurricular activities such as the glee club, orchestra, theater club, and art club are available as well.

BASIC PRINCIPLES OF MOTOR LEARNING.   The basic principles of motor learning are in many instances the same ones that apply to other kinds of learning. Among them are the usefulness of verbal descriptions and demonstrations, emphasis on selective attention, discrimination of relevant distinguishing features such as those described by Eleanor Gibson in her alphabet chart, and the importance of reinforcement—including feedback about the quality of performance, that is, knowledge of results (Merrill, 1971b).

Thus, for example, a person wishing to learn to play tennis would be helped by first observing other people as they practice the various kinds of strokes and play a competitive game. The newcomer to the sport would also be helped by learning the rules of the game and how to keep score. Later, when he is ready to play against an opponent, he needs to become proficient in anticipating and responding to his opponent's moves. Feedback about performance ought to be immediate and obvious—that is, whether or not the player can hit the ball and get it over the net. But if the new participant hopes to improve his skill in the game to any appreciable extent, he will probably require some additional guidance and suggestions from an expert, not to mention a great deal of practice.

"Every spring in the Sports Palace in Tokyo, up to 5,000 very small and very beautiful Japanese children give a fantastic mass violin concert—without rehearsal or even a fixed program. The music is such that one very old gentleman was moved to tears on hearing it. His name was Pablo Casals" (Pronko, 1969, p. 52). Such accomplishments are the work of Sinichi Suzuki, founder of the Talent Education Institute that bears his name. About 30 years ago, Suzuki, violinist and teacher, first refused and then accepted a 4-year-old as his student. "Too young," was his initial reaction. But he noticed that the child understood and spoke the Japanese language very well. If this was so, reasoned Suzuki, then the child most assuredly could master the violin. After all, no one learns his native language from a printed text; he begins by babbling, then going on to genuine speech which is constantly shaped and refined. This led Suzuki to a listen-and-play method of teaching the violin.

Students may start violin lessons at any time from two and a half years of age on. Their motivation comes from a background rich in fine music. Parents must have an appreciation of music, and music must be an intrinsic part of the home environment. Lessons are private and flexible; a lesson may terminate at the first yawn. There are no music stands or practice books. No coaxing, forcing, or threatening is used. Suzuki also rejects all extrinsic rewards. There is no rivalry for prizes, no city or state contests. The child grows musically, depending on his developing skill for reinforcement (much the same process as in language development). His early study models are concert violinists he hears on records or tapes; later, as he refines his bowing, fingering, and other techniques, the transition to note reading is made in gradual stages. A child comes to read notes because they logically constitute the visual pattern of his musical mother tongue.

Through these analogues of language development, Suzuki's institute has taught some 15,000 children to play the violin over the past 30 years. And the starter of it all, the young 4-year-old? He was Toshiyo Eto, later a master violinist at the Curtis Institute of Music in Philadelphia and an international concert performer.

LISTENING AND LEARNING: THE LANGUAGE OF MUSIC

(UPI)

The old saying that "practice makes perfect" is not necessarily true, but in the development of complex motor skills, practice with knowledge of results (feedback) is the only way that high levels of proficiency can be attained (Merrill, 1971b).

MOTOR LEARNING AND MOVEMENT THEORY.   In many respects, motor learning is similar to other kinds of learning. At the same time, however, motor learning has certain distinctive characteristics. *Movement theory* is based on the distinctive characteristics of motor learning (Hunter, 1972).

The basic principle of movement theory is that most learned behavior involves movement of one kind or another. For example, the child learns through movement to differentiate between "me" and "not me," and this distinction is essential to the ability to integrate and assign meaning to form. Furthermore, motor behavior is the major channel through which cognitive and emotional behavior become apparent to others; it is observable behavior which indicates to others that learning has taken place (Hunter, 1972).

Movement theory is based on the premise that readiness does not simply develop; it is the result of appropriate experience in movement. The learner needs instruction in the kinds of movement and other skills that are conducive to readiness. Once the condition of readiness has been established, movement theory can be used to analyze the complex skill according to its component elements. Catching a ball, for instance, first requires a certain maturation of the muscles; the individual must physically be capable of the movements involved. Later, accomplishing the task involves both appropriate positioning of the body in space and time, and opening and closing one's hands at the precise moment that the ball can be caught. Only when *all* these steps have been accomplished can we say that the individual has learned to catch a ball.

Movement theory can be very helpful to the teacher in planning a curriculum. However, as Gentile (1972) has pointed out, placing the major emphasis of instruction on movement may result in confusion. The student must be taught not only how to execute the required movements but also how to recognize and process the relevant information about the environmental conditions that control those movements. Otherwise, there is no guarantee that the actual motor behavior engaged in is appropriate for the situation. For example, a child may be taught how to catch a ball quite accurately when it is thrown to him. However, if he is not also taught how to judge the timing of the ball's arrival in his mitt by the speed with which it is thrown together with the strength of the pitcher, this ability will not help him on the ball field.

THE ROLE OF THE TEACHER.   The teaching of complex motor skills, whether in physical education, typing, shop, driver education, or

In most schools, physical education is a part of the curriculum from the elementary years on.

(Joel Gordon)

any other part of the curriculum, is a difficult and demanding responsibility. Teachers who take on such assignments should be experts in the performance of the same skills themselves (J. Travers, 1972). Often this is not the case, however—particularly in elementary school, where the regular classroom teacher may be expected to provide instruction not only in the traditional academic disciplines, but also in such activities as physical education, music theory, sewing, and shop. With only minimal (if any) formal training in teaching these very different subjects, a teacher cannot possibly create optimal learning conditions for the students.

According to Gentile (1972), teachers can aid the learning of motor skills by dividing the learning process into two broad stages. Stage 1 involves getting the idea of the movement—learning what has to be done. Stage 2 is called the "fixation/diversification" stage. As the learner fixates or concentrates on those aspects that must be learned, he diversifies his movements, that is, he increases the number and kinds of responses he makes.

During Stage 1, the major function of the teacher is to help students develop an understanding of the goal of the activity so as to motivate them to persevere. Learning and refinement of most complex skills, including motor skills, require thinking about the task. It is best if this cognitive aspect of the learning activity is introduced at the beginning in order to avoid unnecessary goal confusion on the part of newcomers to the task.

During this stage, the teacher is also responsible for appropriately structuring the learning environment and helping the student identify and selectively attend to the features of the environment important to a particular task. Only when it appears that the learner genuinely understands the basic purpose of the task and the crucial relationships involved should he be shown how to perform it. Pictures, diagrams, movies, and models are all helpful in displaying appropriate form. To maximize understanding, however, verbal instruction is always important (Gentile, 1972).

Once the learner has performed the required movement, he needs to have his performance evaluated. Sometimes he receives this feedback from the act itself. Sometimes what he learns through his actions may need to be supplemented by additional feedback from the teacher. In general, the learner provides the cues as to whether this additional information is needed; teachers often show a tendency to give a student unnecessary assistance too quickly.

Stage 2 in the learning of motor skills involves a combination of fixation and diversification. During this phase of learning, the student successively concentrates or fixates on different aspects of the total task; and, in so doing, his repertoire of responses becomes much more diversified. He increases the number of responses he makes and, at the same time, learns to vary them according to environmental conditions. A major role of the teacher in this stage is to arrange for sufficient practice (Gentile, 1972).

A characteristic feature of Stage 2 of learning motor skills is that certain components of a motor task can be eliminated from practice and other more sophisticated elements added. Once the student finds that it is no longer necessary to concentrate on the crude or general kinds of movement that characterized his early learning, he is ready to refine his skills and focus on the secondary tasks that contribute to a smoother and more polished performance (Gentile, 1972). Learning to drive a car reflects this progression of skills. Most people learning to drive are extremely cautious their first few times at the wheel, and drive very slowly for fear of an accident. However, with increased practice the clumsiness is diminished, and the driver gradually becomes expert in all the required manipulations. Skilled and experienced drivers usually have enough confidence in their ability to handle their vehicle to willingly engage in other activities simultaneously, such as listening to the radio and carrying on a conversation.

In learning to drive, Stage 1 can often be covered in a few days; Stage 2 may take weeks, months, or even years. It usually takes a lot of time and practice to progress from the slow, hesitant, awkward movements that characterize initial learning to the rapid, precise, and seemingly involuntary movements that characterize the skilled performer (Gentile, 1972). In a typing class, it may take most of the students a whole semester from the time they first start to learn the location of the keys and which finger to use, to the time they can "touch type" rapidly and accurately. With some complex skills—for example, playing the flute—the skill to be learned is so complex that years of intensive training may be required to reach desired levels of proficiency. This is certainly true for those who wish to become professional athletes or accomplished musicians (Fitts, 1962).

THE NEED FOR PRACTICE.   Throughout our discussion of motor skills, we have emphasized the importance of practice. Researchers and teachers differ, however, in their opinions about the amount of practice necessary and the way it should be organized. The relationship between practice and retention will be discussed at length in the next chapter, but the topic is briefly considered here as it relates to the development and retention of motor skills. Practice can occur mentally as well as physically. In one study (Johnston, 1971), for example, female subjects gained expertise at the motor skills involved in volleyball when *mental* practice was used.

A number of experts believe that overpractice, rather than just practice to the point of a specified achievement level, is the best way to learn a motor skill. According to some authorities, training in complex motor skills, regardless of the amount of practice, should always be programmed to provide extensive practice in the various component parts separately, rather than in the whole task all at once (Fitts, 1962). In a swimming class, for example, the students might concentrate on kicking in one session, arm movements in another, and breathing in a third—before attempting to coordinate all three of these skills. This kind of instruction is sometimes called the "progressive part method," because the various component movements are developed separately and sequentially. However, unless an effort is made to integrate these parts into a "psychological whole," performance is likely to become mechanical (J. Travers, 1972).

In order for practice to be effective, it must be meaningful. That is, the conditions provided for learning should resemble, as much as possible, the conditions under which performance actually takes place once the skill is developed (J. Travers, 1972). At the same time, the frequency and duration of practice should be adapted to individual levels of proficiency, as well as to the difficulty of the task itself. This concept of meaningfulness is discussed in greater depth in Chapter 8.

The published research in this area quite clearly prefers practice distributed over a period of time rather than massed practice. Other research findings suggest that early in learning, practice periods should be brief and carefully spaced to minimize frustration and fatigue. Later, as the learner's skill and confidence increase, the practice periods can be longer and more frequent, until such time as a satisfactory level of proficiency has been displayed. Then, in order to maintain that level of proficiency, engaging in a small amount of practice occasionally would be most helpful (J. Travers, 1972). The amount of practice required varies, of course, with the degree of complexity of the skill. How different this suggested schedule is from the ways in which most students cram just before a testing session! Ironically, we usually cram in order to save study time—the result is noticeably wasteful!

INDIVIDUAL DIFFERENCES.   Even when all the basic guidelines for teaching motor skills are followed, a difficult problem remains: What should the teacher do about individual differences in abilities? Many physical education teachers insist that everyone in the class engage in the same activity despite obvious differences in personality and motivation and the fact that some pupils far outshine others in strength, motor coordination, and agility (Fitts, 1962).

Age differences are important in motor learning (Sloan, 1955). Most preschool children, for example, have not yet shown sufficient muscular development to be able to write; 7-year-olds tend to have a much easier time (J. Travers, 1972). Age differences are also significant in the development of athletic skills; for example, older children can generally run faster and jump and throw farther than younger children. Three-year-olds, in comparison with 2-year-olds, tend to be fairly adept at walking, running, and jumping, but they are still unable to hop and skip or throw and catch a ball. Most 6-year-olds can do all of these things.

In addition to age differences in motor development, one often

THE GREAT DEBATE   Can—and should—girls compete with boys in interscholastic athletics? The debate on the issue goes on. Those who answer "they can" cite evidence such as the 10-year-old girl from Honolulu who almost made the National Football League Hall of Fame in 1974, punting, passing, and kicking with the boys in a special competition for youngsters (Levenson, 1975). Those who answer "they should" are the courts. The Commonwealth Court of Pennsylvania, for example, has declared that interscholastic competition must be opened "to girls in all sports—including football and wrestling" (Langdon, 1975, p. 1). In a majority opinion written by the only woman on the Commonwealth Court bench, Judge Genevieve Blatt, the court stated that "the notion that girls as a whole are weaker and thus more injury prone, if they compete with boys, especially in contact sports, cannot justify (their exclusion) . . . in the light of the Equal Rights Act" (p. 1). Judge Blatt's decision, however, amounted to a policy statement; it noted that the state sought no change in the practice of discrimination against female athletes who wish to participate in football and wrestling. Accommodations to the law will mean changes in many traditional American social attitudes. Perhaps, again, it is the children who will lead us.

finds sex differences. In many, but certainly not all sports, endurance tests, and mechanical tasks, boys typically surpass girls as they grow older. With the advent of the feminist movement in the classroom, and with physical activities once provided only for boys now added to girls' curricula, it is quite possible that these differences in ability will vanish.

Anyone providing instruction in motor skills—and almost no teacher is excluded from this category—needs to have both a demonstrable expertise in the special skills being taught and some familiarity with developmental psychology. Only then can a teacher determine whether or not a given individual in the class has the physical, mental, and emotional readiness to undertake a particular kind of learning.

THE PURPOSE OF LANGUAGE.   Human beings are not the only species who have a system of communication (dolphins and bees do also, for example), but human language differs from language of lower animals in several important respects. According to Susan Ervin-Tripp (1964), human language has three unique characteristics: (1) the many possible combinations of a limited number of elements; (2) the existence of arbitrary but conventional meanings for these combinations; and (3) the ability to refer to distant objects and events and intangible concepts. It is these three characteristics that make human language so expandable and flexible (De Cecco, 1974). Because of them, we can create new sounds and sound combinations and new ways of structuring these sounds into words and sentences. Increased age, education, and experience enable us to add to our vocabulary and find many different ways of expressing our thoughts. In addition, changes taking place in society often demand that special new words be incorporated into our language, and other words, although popular in the past, inevitably become obsolete. Think of all the additional words in our vocabulary created by the computer, space technology, advertising, and today's political scene!

The meanings of words can be either representational, associational, or both. The *representational meaning* of a word involves the intervention of a response to that word other than, and in addition to, the verbal response. For example, upon seeing the word "pain," a person could conceivably conjure up a picture or representation of himself experiencing pain. In this example, the word "pain" has also represented the actual feeling of pain. *Associational meaning* involves the ideas or thoughts that readily come to mind upon seeing or hearing the stimulus word (R. M. Travers, 1967). For example, the person just described, upon seeing the word "pain," might associate this word with the experiences he had when he broke a leg, fell down a flight of stairs, or burned himself on a hot

Language Learning

stove. Here, the person made associations between the word and his experiences.

Another important point about human language is the comparability across cultures (De Cecco, 1974). Although we all know that different languages are spoken and read in different parts of the world, and that there are many terms specific to given cultures, many basic concepts—dealing with government, family patterns and relationships, or nature, for example—are known and understood in most cultures, although the words themselves are different. Moreover, because human language is so adaptable, we can talk about any point in time (what we did in the past, or what we plan to do tomorrow); we are not limited to immediately observable events or objects. Whatever the subject, human language can range from highly concrete to highly abstract.

Language is an important aid in discrimination learning (Gagné, 1970). Children at early ages learn to distinguish features of their environment—shapes, sizes, colors, numbers, and so on. Older children and adults, of course, are continually required to make not only these relatively simple discriminations, but also ones that are much more complex. Without the availability of language for symbolic representation, our capacity for discrimination learning would be extremely limited.

Language clearly is a basic skill in communication which affects an individual's ability to adapt to all aspects of the environment. It is the vehicle by which all other skills are acquired and mastered — including the abilities to speak, read, write, and perform all other derivative skills.

LANGUAGE AS A PRODUCTIVE SYSTEM.   Human language is by definition a productive system, a creative act of the individual. In the course of just a single day, for instance, one reads, hears or constructs hundreds of sentences, no two of which are alike. Moreover, once a sentence has been constructed, it is rarely repeated in identical form. The exceptions to this rule are expressions such as "How are you?" and other salutations, which are repeated over and over again out of habit. They do not refute the basic notion, however, that under most conditions we usually create new sentences instead of repeating the ones we have used previously (Shenker, 1971).

The capacity to generate an infinite number of sentences using a finite number of words is based on the assumption that a person has mastered the basic principles of the language, or the manner in which words are effectively and meaningfully combined. However, we all know that many combinations of words heard in everyday conversation, which are intended to be sentences, are far from perfect grammatically. In many cases they are, in addition, not very meaningful. Many people use a kind of verbal shorthand, especially

Henry Higgins, the illustrious phonetician of G. B. Shaw's *Pygmalion*, could pinpoint a person's geographical background merely by listening to his speech. Dr. Clyde Rousey, a Menninger Foundation speech pathologist, can detect psychological flaws by similar means (Cromie, 1975). Speak up and he'll tell you if you're shy or aggressive, prone to heart attack, suicide, or alcoholism. Rousey has devised a test wherein a person "speaks about 50 words into a tape recorder, swallows, sings the scale, and describes the way he or she hears certain words and sounds" (Cromie, 1975, p. 16). He bases his test on the fact that people go through successive stages in their psychological development. Each stage has conflicts that must be resolved; at the same time, it also has speech sounds that must be mastered. For example, the first six months of life involve the expression of basic drives, such as hunger and thirst. In parallel, in the first six months of life a child attempts to master vowels. In the next six months ego functions and relations with parents begin to emerge; at the same time, the child copes with consonants. If there have been problems in satisfactorily resolving the conflicts, claims Rousey, the use of vowels and consonants will be incorrect. Difficulty with the "th" sound as in "both," for example, indicates problems rooted in the early father-child relationship; a distortion of the "L" sound (as if swallowing it), suggests problems with the mother-child relationship. Rousey has found that most speech distortions center on consonants, indicating that many emotional problems begin between 6 months and 1 year of age. He cites evidence for the link between speech problems and emotional illness in the fact that "80 to 90 percent of all psychiatric patients have speech and voice disorders" (Cromie, 1975, p. 16). By listening to a person's speech, says Rousey, we can more accurately diagnose the root of his psychological problem.

YOUR SPEECH: A MIRROR OF EMOTIONAL DEVELOPMENT?

with friends, colleagues, and family. From time to time, all of us make slips of the tongue, jump from one topic to another, or start a sentence but never finish it because we forgot what we wanted to say. These mistakes do not necessarily mean that a person has an inadequate knowledge of the principles of sentence structure. Instead, these mistakes might be caused by fatigue or some distraction.

In other words, there is a distinction between linguistic competence, or knowledge of principles, and linguistic performance, or translation of this knowledge into action (Dale, 1972; Slobin, 1971). This distinction leads us to a discussion of the interests and concerns of experts on language—linguists and psycholinguists.

LINGUISTS AND PSYCHOLINGUISTS. *Linguistics* is a branch of science dealing with the fundamental structural principles of languages.

These principles are believed to enable someone who "knows" a language to use it in a meaningful, productive, and innovative way (Shenker, 1971).

People who specialize in this area of study are called *linguists,* and those among them who are concerned with the psychological aspects of language structure are called *psycholinguists.* Both the linguist and the psycholinguist are interested in determining the roots of a person's knowledge of language (linguistic competence), but the psycholinguist is also interested in the *performance* aspects of language. Pure linguists are not particularly concerned with the everyday use of language, but rather with the underlying abilities that determine language competence. Psycholinguists, on the other hand, do consider the everyday use of language, because they are attempting to understand psychological factors that can account for discrepancies between knowledge and performance (Slobin, 1971).

Both of these specialists are concerned with grammar and sentence structure. Traditionally, the major interest of American linguists and psycholinguists has been in constructing a so-called generative grammar, a system of rules and principles governing the relationships between sound and meaning, for the English language. A newer and more controversial approach is based on the theory that there is a universal grammar applicable to all languages (Shenker, 1971).

The contemporary approach to linguistics was first developed in 1957 by Noam Chomsky, one of the most influential figures of our time in the field of linguistics; it is based on the idea of *transformational grammar.* Sentences are constructed and related to one another by means of underlying rules of syntax called *transformations.* Because we are familiar with the language that we speak, we tend to use it without explicitly identifying all of these rules. We seem to have an intuitive mastery of them, because we consistently apply them in a prescribed manner (De Cecco, 1974). One common example of a transformation is the change in the meaning of a word from positive to negative by the addition of a contraction, such as the suffix "n't." ("Would" becomes "wouldn't," "could" becomes "couldn't," "is" becomes "isn't," and so on.)

The primary purpose of studying transformational grammar is to identify and explain the basic principles affecting the production and understanding of meaningful sentences; that is, to explain how we distinguish between sentences and nonsentences, to relate sentence structure to both meaning and sound, and to account for any possible sentence that might be constructed (Slobin, 1971).

Noam Chomsky has taken the position that there is a universal grammar, which theoretically is as much a part of French, German, Swahili, or any other language as it is of English. According to Chomsky, this grammar includes abstract constructs and principles.

He believes that the mind of the child is not molded as a result only of stimulus and response in the environment, as the behaviorists claim, but has intrinsic properties that facilitate the learning process. From birth, says Chomsky, individuals have an intuitive understanding of language principles. The intuitive knowledge of these principles makes specific language learning possible later on in the life of the individual.

Chomsky rejects the approach to learning taken by the behaviorist or associationist psychologists. For Chomsky, the primary area of concern is not immediate observable events but the underlying thought processes of the human mind which makes these observable events meaningful. He considers language simply one means by which the nature of the human mind may be studied and understood (Chomsky, 1968; Shenker, 1971; Slobin, 1971).

LANGUAGE LEARNING IN CHILDREN.   Evidence from various studies suggests that mastery of language structure and various transformational principles occurs in the preschool years. According to De Cecco (1974), the child's knowledge at this stage is intuitive; the rules that are being learned can seldom be stated explicitly.

For example, Berko (1958) reported a study showing that preschool and first-grade children appear to have a basic knowledge of the rules for forming plurals, possessives, and other transformations. In this study, children were shown stimulus cards, each containing an unfamiliar nonsense word, a picture, and a question (in the form of an incomplete sentence) designed to test the child's knowledge of a certain grammatical principle. (See Figure 7-2 for a sample card using the nonsense word "wug" to test the child's knowledge of the rule for forming plurals.) The children's verbal responses to these cards, according to Berko, showed that knowledge of English grammar is not a matter of simple memorization. If it were, the subjects would have refused to take the test on the grounds that they didn't know the answers, having never heard of these words. Instead, they used relevant grammatical principles with these nonsense words.

According to Carol Chomsky (1969), a complete knowledge and understanding of grammar rules does not take place until sometime between the ages of 5 and 10. In general, the results of a multitude of studies suggest a gradual consolidation of language structure from kindergarten to adolescence but also indicate abrupt shifts in performance between kindergarten and first grade and between the fifth and seventh grades (Palermo and Molfese, 1972).

We spent some time earlier in this text (in Chapter 2) discussing the relationship of linguistic development to cognitive development. When young children reveal deficiencies in certain areas of language, either their cognitive development has not yet reached

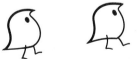

This is a wug.

Now there is another one.
There are two of them.
There are two_____.

Figure 7-2. One of Berko's tests for the formation of plurals. (Brown and Fraser, 1964, p. 46)

the level where the linguistic forms in question have become meaningful, or they have not yet discovered the appropriate ways to express their knowledge verbally (McNeill, 1970). At the same time, though, modeling and reinforcement also play an important role in language learning. Bandura and Harris (1966) found that both procedures are as basic to verbal learning as they are to social learning. Modeling and reinforcement are discussed extensively in Chapter 1.

Questions for Thought

If it is true, as Carol Chomsky says, that grammar rules of adults are acquired by children between age 5 and age 10, what happens to the child who apparently learns a different set of rules at home than is normally used in the larger society?

Can a child be taught successfully at school *not* to use the rules he has already developed? Or should he be taught instead that there are two different sets of rules he must learn, one to use at school and later at work, and the other to use at home among his family and peers?

What evidence do you have for your answer?

THE ROLE OF THE TEACHER.   Linguistics has important implications for classroom instruction, particulary in teaching children to read. To give an example, the correspondence of *phonemes* (the smallest

Modeling and reinforcement play an important part in language learning.

(Hanna Schreiber, Rapho/Photo Researchers)

distinguishable units of sound) to printed symbols in the alphabet (*graphemes*) makes word recognition much easier (Bloomfield, 1933; Fries, 1963). Many words in our language, particularly the "easy" words that make up the basic part of first- and second-grade textbooks, can be classified according to a characteristic phoneme—grapheme pattern—for example, book, look, cook; cake, make, take; bell, sell, tell. By presenting basic patterns like these to their pupils, teachers can help beginning readers acquire a feeling for important sound-to-spelling relationships, which will, in turn, assist them in reading independently (Dale, 1972). Teachers then must provide instruction in combining words into sentences that are meaningful as well as grammatically correct.

The lack of perfect correspondence between phonemes and graphemes in the English language, however, has been a source of frustration to teachers. Consequently, some educators have taken the radical approach of temporarily abandoning the use of our traditional writing system—that is, in initial reading instruction (the first grade)—using instead a system developed by Sir James Pitman (Pitman and St. John, 1969) called the Initial Teaching Alphabet (ITA). The ITA is much closer to a perfectly alphabetic system—because of its one-to-one phoneme—grapheme relationship—than our traditional alphabet (see Table 7-1).

A study by Warburton and Southgate (1969) showed that children learn to read faster by using the ITA method than by using our standard English alphabet. However, they may have difficulty later switching from the ITA to the conventional alphabet. Furthermore, whether the early advantages associated with the ITA approach are maintained on any long-term or permanent basis is not clear (Dale, 1972).

Since the practicality and long-term usefulness of the ITA method are still undetermined, most reading teachers, with the exception of those involved in experimental programs, are hesitant to use it. As long as teachers continue to use our current alphabet system, a critical problem in reading instruction is determining which unit is most basic for perception of written language. The oldest approach was that the letters of the alphabet were the basic perceptual units; instruction in reading began with the ABC's. Subsequently, with the emergence of the Gestalt movement (discussed in Chapter 5), the emphasis shifted to the "whole word" method of instruction. The difficulty with the first approach is that a single letter is not always pronounced in the same way. The difficulty with the second approach is that it is uneconomical; every new graphic combination must be learned independently. One possible solution to the problem might be to teach what are called the "higher-order invariants." These one-syllable units are generally longer than single letters but shorter than entire words; their basic characteristic is

Table 7–1

Examples of the Initial Teaching Alphabet

Character	Example	
ʧh	ʧhurʧh	church
ŋ	siŋ	sing
ʃh	ʃhaft	shaft
ţh	ţhaut	thought
ɉh	ɉhis	this

a one-to-one correlation between grapheme and phoneme or spelling and sound. Examples of the "higher-order invariants" are the sounds produced by such letter combinations as "ph" and "oo." Learning these combinations should automatically lead to recognition and correct pronunciation of countless words.

Linguistics also has implications for spelling instruction (Dale, 1972). Teachers should point out whenever possible that the spelling of many words is not purely arbitrary, but understandable in terms of the spelling of a related word. For example, a child would be more likely to spell the word "medicine" with a "c" instead of an "s" after being shown the relation of this word to the word "medical."

Minority group students who speak a dialect other than the standard white middle-class dialect frequently have problems in both spelling and reading. Communication difficulties between student and teacher or student and textbook because of discrepancies in both speech patterns and environmental experience can easily lead to problems. A variety of special orientation programs such as Head Start and the Bereiter-Englemann reading program have been created to help prepare disadvantaged preschool children to make a better adjustment to the regular public education system. A dramatically different approach to the teaching of minority group children has been taken by Nancy Johnson. In the Johnson program, children are taught how to read with materials prepared from stories that they tell themselves in their own vocabularies. The high level of interest and motivation that results from this procedure seems to produce dramatic improvement in reading skills (J. T. Gibson, 1972). This and other programs designed for the socially disadvantaged child will be discussed in detail in Chapter 10.

Concept Learning and Problem-Solving

WHAT IS A CONCEPT?   A concept is an abstraction or idea that permits the learner to classify a variety of related phenomena into a convenient, meaningful category. Concepts enable the consolidation and systematization of huge quantities of data and allow communication and discussion of complex issues between individuals. They also provide order and stability in an uncertain and ever-changing world (Bernard, 1973; Glaser, 1968; R. M. Travers, 1967). According to Gagné (1965c), concept learning produces a certain fundamental change in human performance that is independent of subject or content.

Concepts can be divided into two broad categories: concrete and abstract (Gagné, 1970). *Concrete concepts* are ideas that can be linked to a class of observable objects (for example, house, book, furniture) or object qualities (for example, color, size, shape). As children acquire concepts of this sort, they realize that they are grouping to-

This girl is learning the concept of equal volume.

(Bob S. Smith, Rapho/Photo Researchers)

gether various objects or object qualities that are very different in appearance. But they are also responding to these stimuli in terms of some property they all have in common; this makes classification possible. *Abstract concepts* cannot be directly linked to observable objects or object qualities in this manner; they are definitional. The physical concepts of force and work; the language concepts of noun, verb, adjective, and adverb; and the mathematical concepts of fractions, decimals, and percentages are several of the important abstract concepts taught in school.

The formation of concepts is a continual process, which probably can never be considered complete. Of course, simple concepts such as addition and subtraction of color versus no color usually are mastered at an early age. But there are also advanced abstract concepts in such areas as physics, economics, and psychology that require years to develop. With increased learning and experience, concept formation changes to accommodate our ever-increasing store of knowledge.

It is important to distinguish between concepts and principles (Gagné, 1965c). Although related and interdependent, these terms represent two different kinds of capacity, calling for different methods of instruction. Basically, learning a concept means being able to give a common name or response to a class of stimuli varying in appearance. It also involves recognizing which dimensions of a stimulus are relevant in determining if it belongs in a particular conceptual category and which are incidental (Glaser, 1968; Markle and Tiemann, 1970). For instance, when an American child learns that there is a common bond between a fire engine and an apple, and that this bond is the color red, he has learned the concept of color. Learning a principle, on the other hand, means being able to combine related concepts into rules that say something about those concepts (De Cecco, 1974; Gagné, 1965c). Clearly, the latter process is more complex.

FOUNDATIONS OF CONCEPT AND PRINCIPLE LEARNING.   Concept and principle learning are closely related to language learning. On the one hand, theorists point out, one does not necessarily have to use words in order to learn a concept. Lower animals, human infants, and aphasics (people who lack the ability to use language because of brain damage) are all capable of some degree of concept learning (Carroll, 1964; Harlow, 1949; R. M. Travers, 1967). On the other hand, as a means of progressing from the simple and concrete to the complex and abstract, appropriate descriptive language is a distinct and obvious advantage.

The availability of language facilitates the task of concept learning considerably, because language serves as an economical and convenient way of ordering and classifying many different sets of observations. Language also contributes to greater uniformity in the use of concepts by different people. In addition, children are constantly encountering new words that serve as cues to the existence of concepts they don't yet know about, but perhaps should. Their natural inquisitiveness leads them not only to learn the meaning of the word, but also to place that word in a conceptual category. Finally, language enables the learner to grasp the relationships among different concepts and to express these relationships in a meaningful, precise, and understandable way (R. M. Travers, 1967).

Once the learner becomes involved in this discovery and expression of relationships among a set of concepts, his attention shifts from concept learning to principle learning. Principle learning, in turn, has an important bearing on the act of problem-solving, a complex form of behavior which was discussed extensively in Chapter 5. When a student solves a complex problem correctly, it is possible to infer that he has learned a higher-order principle. The inference can be confirmed by asking the student to solve a similar problem. Changes in behavior associated with successful problem-solving tend, as a rule, to be long-lasting and readily applicable to new situations (De Cecco, 1974).

How do children actually acquire concepts, principles, and problem-solving abilities, and what, if anything, can the schools do to help? On this issue, as on many others in psychology, there are two opposing theories. The first is the stage-dependent view held by Piaget, Kohlberg, and others (discussed in Chapter 3), which states that concept development progresses through a series of stages that occur in a fixed and determined order. The second theory is the learning-environmental approach, exemplified by the work of Bandura (also discussed in Chapter 3), which maintains that concepts are primarily products of experience and that the order of development is not necessarily invariant or fixed according to a determined time scale, since different children have different experiences at different times in their lives, depending on both individual learning situations and on cultural experiences (Bernard, 1973).

THE ROLE OF THE TEACHER. The opposition between these two viewpoints is difficult to resolve. Rather than attempt at this time to choose one theory over the other, we should concentrate on what teachers can do to make concept learning easier and more meaningful.

Concept learning in school may be taught by inductive or deductive methods. The *inductive method* consists of presenting a series of positive and negative instances of a concept, allowing the learner to infer the concept from the invariant properties that are constant in all these instances. In contrast, the *deductive method* involves presenting concepts by verbal definition and description. In the classroom, heavy emphasis on the inductive method is given in what Bruner calls the "discovery" approach. Discovery learning, according to Bruner, leads to greater retention and greater transfer to new situations (see Chapter 5 for details). On the other hand, this method is considered by some to be inefficient and time-consuming. However, teaching by purely deductive methods, for example by lecturing, might not be sufficient for a child to identify all the critical aspects needed to understand a concept in its totality, according to critics (Carroll, 1964; R. M. Travers, 1967). Perhaps the best approach to the teaching of concepts is to use a combination of both methods.

The purpose of teaching concepts in school is, in part, to provide the child with definitive meanings for various terms, but this should not be considered the only purpose. Teachers should also provide practical experience in using concepts and in discovering the higher-order relationships or principles that give a set of concepts their underlying structure. In addition, teachers ought to transmit the ability both to modify concepts as necessary and to organize one's experience so that it makes sense in terms of one's existing concepts (Glaser, 1968).

Teachers can facilitate concept learning by presenting material in a lucid but interesting manner and by using books, films, and other instructional aids, which make the subject seem interesting and relevant. For the most effective results, however, an organized plan of approach is advisable. The following procedures and guidelines were designed for this purpose.

1. A general rule for teaching any new concept is that several illustrations, differing in appearance, should always be presented. Otherwise the concept that actually emerges from the instruction is apt to be incomplete and the learning process is closer to mere rote memory (Gagné, 1965c, 1970).

2. After the lesson has been completed, the teacher needs to determine whether or not the designated learning has taken place. The acquisition of a concept is best demonstrated by seeing if the student can apply it to a new situation not directly encountered during the learning phase. If the student can only give an exact replica of what the teacher said in the lesson, the goals of the instruction have not been accomplished (Gagné, 1965c; Markle and Tiemann, 1970).

In addition to these two general points, the following are some specific guidelines for the teaching of concepts suggested by R. M. Travers (1967).

1. Reduce the number of irrelevant dimensions in the presentation, so that the relevant ones will stand out more clearly.

2. Be as precise and explicit as possible in presenting the relevant attributes. Use concrete examples and simplified representations. Avoid presenting concepts in such abstract terms that they lose their meaning.

3. Give the learner additional time to view the material *after* giving feedback as well as before. This procedure enables students to review the information presented according to its appropriate interpretation and thus to generate hypotheses.

4. Help the student to code the new information verbally.

5. Present the concepts in an order that is consistent with their structure. General concepts, which are closely tied to observables and have a relatively low level of abstraction, should be taught first. (For example, a child should have a general concept of direction before being asked to find different places on a map, and he should have the ability to read a map before being taught about latitude and longitude.)

6. Illustrate both positive and negative instances of the concept in question. (For example, in teaching the meaning of the physical concept "work"—which is different from the everyday usage of this term—illustrations should be given not only of activities that do constitute "work" for the physicist, but also of those that do not.)

Travers' last point is particularly important and is often over-looked by teachers. Satisfactory demonstration that a new concept has really been learned includes not only correct generalization to situations showing similar instances but also correct discrimination of noninstances. Teachers should keep this point in mind when they are preparing examinations to test understanding of concepts. Any test items they use, however, which are intended as nonin-stances of a concept, should bear at least some ostensible resem-blance to test items that do illustrate the concept, or the task becomes too easy (Markle and Tiemann, 1970). (Thus, for example, on a mul-tiple-choice question relating to the concept of "treaty," names of other kinds of historical documents would be far better noninstances than names of people or places.)

In addition to all the guidelines just listed, we must add one more—the need to consider individual differences, in both ability and learning style, and to adapt methods of instruction accordingly. Simple and straightforward methods of teaching concepts may very well be the only ones suitable for children of limited ability; but children capable of independent reasoning and high levels of ab-straction should be able to benefit from greater emphasis on inquiry and discussion and less emphasis on drills and definitions (Ber-nard, 1973; R. M. Travers, 1967). Another useful approach might be to call on the more able learners to help explain and demonstrate a difficult concept to the rest of the class (McCullough, 1960).

Attitude Learning

The development of values and attitudes was discussed extensively in Chapter 3, from both theoretical and practical standpoints. The emphasis was on the contribution of these processes to the per-sonality development of the individual, particularly during the ado-lescent years. A number of important variables influencing attitudi-nal development were examined separately—including the family and home environment, the school, and the peer group. Negative influences and their effects on adolescent behavior were discussed as well.

The present section on attitudes is intended to take a closer look at attitudes as a type of learning and, specifically, at the importance of school-related variables in shaping and changing attitudes in the student.

Attitudes are not directly observable in themselves; they are re-flected in and by observable behavior. For example, if a student has a good attendance record, does his homework regularly, participates in class discussions, and volunteers for special projects, it might be reasonable to infer that he has a favorable attitude toward school. On the other hand, a student who is frequently absent or late, does not do his homework regularly or pay attention in class, and never volunteers for extra assignments would be said to have a poor or indifferent attitude toward school. Behavior, then, serves as a convenient indicator of attitude.

Many studies have been conducted to determine to what extent the schools can influence attitude change. Unfortunately, however, most classroom studies have limited value, because they provide little information about the specific mechanisms involved and do not identify the aspects of the curriculum that are or are not responsible for producing such changes.

One approach to the study of attitude formation was to determine whether or not providing verbal reinforcement for a statement with which subjects initially did not agree would result in attitude change. Scott (1957) explored this possibility by having students engage in debates, requiring them to take positions that were opposed to their existing beliefs. Presentation was followed by verbal reinforcement, which was meant to indicate that one of the speakers had won the debate. The results of post-tests indicated that those students who had "won" the debate, as compared with those who had "lost," showed a significant change in their attitudes toward the original statement.

In another study demonstrating a similar phenomenon, Festinger and Carlsmith (1959) exposed students to a boring set of tasks and then paid them to tell other subjects that the tasks were interesting and enjoyable. On a subsequent test of their enjoyment of the tasks, the original subjects, who earlier displayed a negative (noninterested) attitude, appeared to have shifted to what the researchers termed a positive (interested) attitude.

Other investigators, also using a reinforcement model, have indicated parallels between the learning of attitudes and the learning of concepts. According to Rhine and Silun (1958), for instance, many of the concepts we learn tend to have definite positive or negative values associated with them; the values can be strengthened as a result of reinforcement from others for both the desired behavior and one's attitude toward it. Prejudice, thrift, and laziness are a few examples that readily come to mind.

All of these studies, and many others, suggest that attitudes are learned and that teachers, parents, or peers can either establish or modify them under conditions of appropriate reinforcement. On the other hand, not all of the published data seems to be consistent with the notion that extrinsic reinforcement is a necessary condition. For example, Rosenberg (1960) suggested to subjects under hypnosis that they take more liberal views on various controversial issues and succeeded in modifying their behavior without providing them with extrinsic reinforcement. The explanation that is usually given for data of this sort is that most human beings do not like to perceive inconsistencies in themselves and will therefore try to change in a direction that will reduce these inconsistencies (R. M. Travers, 1967).

There are, of course, many other factors affecting attitude learning—age, race, and sex, for instance (Flanders, Morrison, and Brode, 1968). The extent of praise and encouragement given by the teacher also appears to be important to some children, as indicated in a study by Morrison (1966) with sixth- grade pupils. Assessments of the teachers' behavior obtained by trained outside observers were correlated with students' shifts in attitudes toward school as determined by attitude inventories given to the pupils. The results indicated that children whose teachers rarely used praise and encouragement tended to shift their attitudes in a negative direction much more so than children whose teachers often used praise and encouragement.

Questions for Thought

With the exception of some open classroom advocates, teachers generally do not list attitude learning as one of the major goals of their teaching programs. In our society, whose responsibility is it, if not that of the teacher, to instill attitudes?

Further, whose responsibility is it to ensure that the attitudes instilled are, indeed, those of the greatest value to our society?

OUTCOMES OF LEARNING

The earlier sections of this chapter deal with the different types of learning that take place in the classroom. In this section we are more concerned with the various *outcomes of learning* or, in other words, the *objectives of learning*. The degree to which the students themselves are capable of fulfilling these objectives varies, of course, with the age, intelligence, sophistication, and motivation of the individual learner. The teacher's responsibility for initiating and promoting learning, however, is apparent with all students at all levels of ability and readiness.

Every program of instruction has one or more learning objectives, even though these objectives are not always stated explicitly and in behavioral terms. In fact, the majority of teachers probably do not outline their objectives at all. Recently, however, largely due to the research efforts of educational technologists and the impact of such innovations as the teaching machine and computer-assisted instruction, a growing number of teachers are beginning to realize the importance of outlining learning objectives for effective teaching on their part and effective learning on their students' parts. The vari-

A Rationale for a Taxonomy of Learning Objectives

ous ways in which instructional planning can help teacher and student alike have been summarized by Gagné and Briggs (1974). Many of the points they made are included in the following pages.

One important reason for considering learning objectives and specifying them in behavioral terms is simply that teachers need to know the nature of the behavior they are hoping to ultimately establish; this is called the *terminal behavior* (Bernard, 1973; De Cecco, 1974; Feldhusen and Treffinger, 1971; Gagné, 1965a). In other words, what should the student enrolled in a particular class be able to do after leaving the class that he could not do previously? What should he be able to do as a result of a particular unit or lesson covered in the class that he might not have been able to do previously? Knowing the answers to these questions makes it easier to plan lessons sensibly and effectively.

Most instruction should be capable of modifying several aspects of behavior simultaneously. This fact makes the behavioral specification of objectives all the more necessary. It is important to distinguish between the different classes of behavior changes being sought, because different techniques of instruction probably will be necessary to successfully produce learning in all of these areas (Gagné, 1965a).

Another important reason for specifying learning objectives is that they are the only means of properly evaluating the effectiveness of what the teacher is doing in the classroom. Otherwise, a test or other measure of the student's achievement, although it says something about the student, cannot say anything about the effect of the instruction on the student's performance. Moreover, assuming that instruction is at least partially responsible for increased learning, there are no other means of identifying which aspects of the instruction are contributors and which are irrelevant (De Cecco, 1974; Gagné, 1965a; Merrill, 1971a). All of these factors must be known by the teacher if he is to improve instruction.

Gagné (1965a) also suggests that behavioral specifications of learning objectives can be used to make the students and the teacher aware of the purpose of the instruction, and of what should be derived from it. According to motivation theorists, as we learned in Chapter 6, this information heightens student motivation and gives students incentive to participate actively in the learning process. It also provides important feedback, since it tells the students whether or not they are making progress and learning, understanding, and responding appropriately.

In order for a learning objective to be of value, it must have two characteristics: *clarity* and *importance* (Vargas, 1972). The clarity can be achieved by stating objectives in terms of observable behaviors. But an objective, no matter how well stated, is not worthwhile unless it also makes some contribution to the overall goals of education.

Therefore, the task of specifying learning objectives should not be approached as if each learning experience demands some unique form of behavior not found in any other learning experience. Such an approach would tend to lead to the learning of petty details and trivia. A much more effective approach is to determine the general classes or categories of behavior that are desired in a given situation or, in other words, to plan on the basis of a *taxonomy of objectives* (Merrill, 1971b, 1972). This is the approach taken by such research- ers as Gagné, Bloom, and Merrill and is emphasized throughout this chapter.

A taxonomy of learning objectives tells the teacher at a glance the fullest possible range of objectives that are available in a learning situation. Obviously, it is neither feasible nor appropriate to try to achieve all of them for every topic and for each lesson. But the teacher does have a helpful reminder of the possibilities and can use the taxonomy systematically to check off, for any given topic, the kinds of objectives that would be most appropriate and impor- tant to emphasize (Krathwohl, 1964).

BLOOM'S TAXONOMY OF OBJECTIVES FOR COGNITIVE LEARNING.   Ben- jamin Bloom and his associates (Krathwohl, Bloom, and Masia, 1956) have developed a taxonomy of learning objectives. The first part of the taxonomy applies to cognition, or the ability to think and understand, and includes six main categories: knowledge, compre- hension, application, analysis, synthesis, and evaluation. The first four of these categories of objectives apply to skills involving *under- standing and concept formation;* the last two apply to skills involving *creativity.* The various classes of behavior are arranged in hierar- chical order from simple to complex and from concrete to abstract. An outline of Bloom's taxonomy of cognitive learning objectives follows (Bloom et al., 1956, pp. 201–207):

1. *Knowledge* includes what is usually referred to as rote memory. The student reproduces, with little or no change, the material presented during the instruction phase. Some common examples include memorizing definitions, reciting a poem, and stating specific facts and rules. Knowledge should not be confused with comprehension, since it is quite possible to learn and repeat something by rote, without having any idea of its meaning.

2. *Comprehension* means being able to restate or identify restate- ments of written or pictorial information in a form that is *not* an exact replica of the original. Examples include such activities as paraphrasing, summarizing, answering direct questions based on material in a paragraph, and translating from one language to another.

   Comprehension can still reflect a very low level of understand- ing, since it does not require the ability to grasp the full implications of the material presented or the ability to relate old material to new material.

3. *Application* means being able to solve problems that are similar in principle or method but different in form from ones seen previously. Thus, for example, a student might be asked to apply the rules of English grammar to the construction of sentences with nonsense words. In order for a learning objective to qualify as an application objective, there must be some application of principles or conceptual relations. If all that is involved is the application of simple concepts, the task, strictly speaking, is comprehension, not application.

4. *Analysis* involves being able to break down an entity into its component parts. Examples include such activities as interpreting a poem by stanza and comparing one food with another in terms of their component nutrients. As in the application objective, the examples given by the student (on a test, for instance) should not be identical to those used in teaching. Otherwise the learning task is reduced to mere rote memory, and the skill being displayed is knowledge rather than analysis.

5. *Synthesis* means being able to combine knowledge, skills, ideas, and experiences to create a new and original product. Examples include such diverse activities as writing an essay, drawing a picture to depict the four seasons of the year, constructing an exhibit for the school science fair, and designing a dress.

   Unlike most instances of the preceding learning objectives, synthesis does not involve a correct or best possible solution. Any product that meets acceptable standards of workmanship in combination with the student's expression of creativity meets this objective.

6. *Evaluation* involves the ability to judge whether or not a person's work meets the specified criterion, or the ability to compare it against someone else's work. What distinguishes this activity from both comprehension and application is that expression of an individual viewpoint is required. As with synthesis, there is not any one "right answer," but the person involved in evaluation should be able to give some rationale as to why he thinks as he does.

   One example of evaluation is giving a critical opinion of a book, along with one's reasons for holding such an opinion. Another example is comparing the advantages and disadvantages and the overall serviceability of two different learning theories (stimulus-response behaviorism versus the Gestalt approach, for instance)—again with the ability to state the underlying reasons for one's opinion.

By classifying the objectives for a given area of instruction according to these different levels, it is possible to see what kinds of learning outcomes are likely to result from the instruction as planned, and whether or not these are all the outcomes that are desired. Teachers may find, for example, that the original lesson plan places very heavy emphasis on the acquisition of knowledge and the technique of analysis, and very little on other important learning outcomes such as application and synthesis. In such instances, the teacher might want to modify the plan somewhat to incorporate a wider range of objectives.

It is particularly easy to think of "knowledge" objectives and, consequently, to design and teach a unit or even an entire course requiring little more than the rote memorization of facts (Vargas, 1972). These objectives alone rarely capture all that is useful and important to know in a subject. Therefore, whenever possible, objectives should be carefully designed so as to incorporate all the relevant skills.

For example, in teaching the concept of hypothesis testing as related to the scientific method, it is not sensible to confine the class merely to memorization of the terms and steps in the process if one wishes to teach higher-level objectives. Students can be encouraged to describe the procedure in their own words and to give examples of both positive and negative instances. Afterward, each of them can be asked to design an original experiment, utilizing what they have learned in a creative and innovative way. The class as a whole can then discuss these experiments and take turns evaluating each other's work.

Questions for Thought

Looking back at Bloom's taxonomy of learning objectives, why might a wider range of objectives than simply acquiring knowledge and comprehending it be of value to a student?

Can you give some examples both in and out of school situations?

PLANNING OBJECTIVES FOR ATTITUDE LEARNING.   Attitude learning, in marked contrast to cognitive learning, tends to be greatly neglected by teachers or, at least, not discussed as openly and freely. Ideally, cognitive and attitude learning should be complementary, but in practice, political and social forces dictate that our schools be very cautious about the role they should play (if any) in disseminating attitudes. Many educators feel that this position is self-defeating; it is fine to impart knowledge, but unless that knowledge is related to the learner's attitude toward everything he does, there is little likelihood that it will have a long-term effect on behavior. In summary, according to these educators, the purpose of education should not be simply to increase children's knowledge and other cognitive skills, but also to foster positive attitudes toward learning, both in and out of the classroom. Therefore, much of the same rationale that has been offered for planning instruction on the basis of a taxonomy of learning objectives for cognitive skills should also be applied to attitude learning. The teacher can help the student learn positive attitudes toward school by designing classroom activities that are both realistic in terms of their level of difficulty and enjoyable for the learner. In other words, as both association theorists and motivation theorists remind us, students tend to have positive attitudes toward courses and subject matter that are at the appropriate level for them and toward courses that provide rewarding experiences instead of frustrating ones.

CRITICISM OF LEARNING OBJECTIVES. Not all educators, however, agree that it is important or even appropriate to define learning objectives in behavioral terms. These critics of behavioral learning objectives feel that the teacher should be concerned not only with those behavior changes that might occur at the end of the school year, but also with the permanent changes that might be expected at some unspecified time in the future (De Cecco, 1974; Ebel, 1963, 1970). In response, Gagné (1965b) claims he is not opposed to formulating hypotheses about behavior in the distant future if desired, but that some indication of more immediate learning is necessary for a demonstrable change in the future. Furthermore, he contends, the only way of knowing that learning has occurred at any point in time is by changes in a person's behavior.

The critics of learning objectives say that there appears to be something mechanistic, dehumanizing, and dictatorial about the entire approach. Learning objectives result in putting the teacher, rather than the student, in control of the kinds of learning that take place in school. The taxonomists answer first, that teachers have a responsibility, because of their role in the socialization process, to transmit the ideals and values of the larger society; second, that teaching is not necessarily mechanical simply because objectives are planned—many different techniques are possible in both teaching and testing (Popham, 1968; Wight, 1972).

Still another point of opposition to the use of learning objectives stated in behavioral terms is the feeling that the kinds of learning outcomes that can be readily put to use involve only trivial aspects of behavior, not the really important outcomes of education. This argument holds some weight, particularly when the task of preparing objectives is sloppily or hastily done; it is not easy to write a set of good and useful learning objectives. Many people new or unskilled at this kind of project do indeed specify outcomes that are petty and insignificant (Popham, 1968; Wight, 1972). The taxonomists' reply, however, is that well-written, explicitly stated objectives actually make the discovery of important instructional outcomes easier. Because they are so explicit, the teacher can study them carefully, and identify and eliminate any objective that seems irrelevant or unimportant (Popham, 1968).

A related argument is that expecting teachers to specify learning objectives in terms of measurable behaviors is unrealistic simply because very few teachers do this (Miles and Robinson, 1971; Popham, 1968). The reply is simple:

> There is obviously a difference between identifying the status quo and applauding it. Most of us would readily concede that few teachers specify their instructional aims in terms of measurable learned behaviors; *but they ought to.* What we have to do is to mount a widespread campaign to modify this aspect of teacher behavior. . . . The way teaching really is at the moment just isn't good enough. (Popham, 1968, p. 517)

Question for Thought

Considering all of the objections cited earlier in this section to the use of learning objectives that are specified in behavioral terms, can you suggest any other way a teacher can clearly determine that he has accomplished whatever it was that he decided to do in the classroom? Give reasons for your answer and examples if you can.

Preparing Learning Objectives

Instructional planning is frequently done for entire courses, with several different topics that are in turn divided into subtopics and lessons. The rules that apply to planning the objectives of a course should also be followed in preparing an outline. That is, the broader, more inclusive areas are broken down into their logical subdivisions. In addition, the plan for some courses, such as history, probably should be arranged according to the order in which the subject matter evolved (Gagné, 1974).

Most courses, topics, and even subtopics are designed with more than one learning outcome in mind. To assure that all of the learning outcomes are accomplished, careful planning is necessary at the beginning. Otherwise, the instruction may overemphasize one learning outcome at the expense of another which is inadvertently excluded. Gagné (1965b, 1974) and Tyler (1964), among others, have pointed out that an important part of this planning should be the consideration of *prerequisites.* It is important that the students have all the learning capabilities necessary for new instruction to be meaningful. The following is a list, arranged in order of increasing complexity, of the six classes of behavior Gagné considers important to education.

1. A simple *connection:* learning to connect the word "mama" with one's mother.

2. A *chain* or *sequence:* learning to count from one to ten.

3. *Identification:* learning to distinguish a maple leaf from an oak leaf.

4. A *concept:* learning classes of objects or events; e.g., in chemistry, the concept "gas."

5. A *principle:* learning a chain of concepts; e.g., that birds fly south in the winter.

6. A *higher order principle* or *general principle:* learning to apply a principle to a new situation; e.g., the use of metaphor in an English composition (Gagné, 1965b).

Learning goals as stated by many teachers who are unskilled in the design of these objectives are often vague. The following example for a high school geometry course is typical:

> The purpose of instruction is to have the students know the basic principles of Euclidian geometry.

That might indeed be the main goal of the course, but it does not provide any information about how a given teacher will achieve that goal. Nor does the statement communicate what the student will learn. Learning objectives expressed in behavioral terms, on the other hand, tell the teacher—in observable and measurable terms—exactly what skills a student should have as a result of instruction.

According to Mager (1962), a well-stated learning objective has the following three characteristics:

1. It describes in behavioral terms what the student will be able to do when instruction has been completed.

2. It describes the conditions or circumstances under which the learned behavior will occur.

3. It describes the extent to which the specified behavior can be expected. In other words, it suggests an acceptable criterion level for performance.

Learning objectives are, in one sense, similar to the classroom activities leading up to them—they both are specified in behavioral terms. The difference between them is that the learning objectives are considered the ends of instruction, the skills the teacher wants the class to develop, and classroom activities are the means that are used to achieve these ends. Objectives therefore should not be tied to any one reference book or exercise; they should be stated in terms that permit the use of a variety of procedures (Esbensen, 1967; Vargas, 1972). A given text or exercise can be used as an example, though, to clarify the kinds of behavior the objective entails. Of the following four statements of indices of learning that a teacher might elicit, only the last one meets all the foregoing criteria for learning objectives.

The following are six behaviorally stated learning objectives taken from Vargas (1972, pp. 119,121,123,130). Try to match each of them with one of the levels in Bloom's taxonomy. Then check your answers.

MATCHING LEARNING OBJECTIVES TO BLOOM'S TAXONOMY

1. Tell in one sentence the meaning of the poem "The Oak Tree."
2. Design and construct a poster to communicate at least two of your views on school rules concerning dress.
3. Criticize a research study on the appropriateness of statistical methods for the problem selected, using the text as a reference.
4. Spell correctly at least 80 percent of the words in the sixth-grade speller.
5. Pronounce unfamiliar words or nonsense syllables that follow the silent "e" rule.
6. Trace the main theme and secondary theme of a play such as one by Shakespeare, citing the characters involved, the conflicts and allegiances, and the ways in which the themes are developed.

Answers
1. Comprehension
2. Synthesis
3. Evaluation
4. Knowledge
5. Application
6. Analysis

1. Read the play Othello and pay special attention to Shakespeare's use of character.
   (This is an activity, not an objective.)
2. Understand the concept of "tragic hero" as used by Shakespeare.
   (This could be an objective of learning, but it is not expressed in behavioral terms.)
3. Be able to explain the reasons for Othello's downfall.
   (This objective is expressed in behavioral terms, but it is specifically tied to one task only.)
4. Demonstrate an understanding of the Shakespearean concept of "tragic hero" by describing, in essay form, three different factors that lead to the downfall of a figure such as Othello.

The following is another example of an explicitly stated learning objective. It was suggested by Esbensen (1967) for an area of instruction much simpler than a Shakespearean play. It is included here to demonstrate the point that explicitly stated learning objectives can be written for both complex and simple tasks.

Shown the letters of the alphabet in random order (in both upper and lower case form), the student is able to say the name of each letter with 100 percent accuracy. (Esbensen, 1967, p. 247)

This objective is clear and precise, and is stated in behavioral terms. We know exactly what the student should be able to do as a result of instruction, under what conditions, and according to what criterion of performance. We know the technique of measurement the teacher is planning to use to determine if the desired learning has taken place. At the same time, the behavioral specification is sufficiently all-inclusive so as not to be limited to one question exclusively.

Studying test items is one of several techniques that might help a teacher prepare meaningful and appropriate learning objectives. For example, the following arithmetic items all seem to be testing the same kind of skill:

$$
\begin{array}{ccc}
43 & 55 & 72 \\
+27 & +65 & +19
\end{array}
$$

The skill they are testing is the ability to add a two-digit number by means of the carrying principle. This is the learning objective for which the test items were designed.

Studying test items will also help a teacher identify the format in which the class should be able to apply their learning. Choosing from a set of alternatives on a multiple-choice test, for example, is easier than the less-structured free recall. It does not measure the same ability. Indicating whether or not a new example is correctly applied to a given concept is easier than thinking of a new example on one's own; which is one reason why many students prefer multiple-choice tests. However, they should remember that in real life, when their skills are subjected to the ultimate test, they will more likely be responsible for recall than for recognition of learned material (Vargas, 1972).

Another good source of information for writing learning objectives is the textbook the teacher will be using. The book you are now reading, like many others, lists objectives at the beginning of each chapter, and while they do tend to be quite general, they can help both the teacher and the student think of additional objectives. Questions for thought provided within each chapter, or exercises of the sort describing learning objectives, provide useful additional information.

Objectives (or information suggesting objectives) that are obtained from a textbook need to be critically evaluated by both teacher and learner. The objectives should contribute to the broad goals of both teacher and student, and no important objectives should be omitted. The use of a taxonomy of learning objectives, such as the one by Bloom described earlier in this chapter, should make this task easier by indicating the kinds of objectives that are being emphasized, as compared to the kinds that are not being emphasized. Then, if a given taxonomic category that seems important is underrepresented, the set of objectives and consequent activities need to be revised (Vargas, 1972).

Many students find that it is easier to learn something if they use special memory (mnemonic) devices. Jack Crawford (1969) has edited an entertaining and easy-to-read manual (CORD) with guidelines for instructional planning using these mnemonic devices to good advantage. The writers of the manual have broken down the important components of any learning objective into ABCDs—*audience, behavior, condition,* and *degree.* In other words, a properly written learning objective, according to this manual, should answer each of the following questions as clearly and precisely as possible.

LEARNING YOUR ABCDs CAN BE FUN!

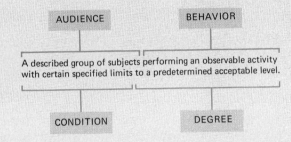

A. For what *audience* of people is the specified instructional outcome intended?
Examples: Third-grade students with average reading ability; eleventh-grade students in an American history class.

B. What observable and measurable change in *behavior* will be used to demonstrate that the desired learning has taken place?
Example: Third-grade students with average reading ability will be able to read aloud any designated paragraph in their textbook.

C. Under what *conditions* should the desired behavior change be expected? (If possible, the conditions should be generalized to real life.)
Example: Third-grade students with average reading ability will be able to read aloud any designated paragraph in their textbook which their teacher has assigned for homework.

D. What *degree* or performance criterion signifies an acceptable level of performance?
Example: Third-grade students with average reading ability will be able to read aloud any designated paragraph in their textbook which their teacher has assigned for homework with 100 percent accuracy.

STYLES OF LEARNING

In the earlier parts of this chapter we discussed types of learning, methods of instruction, and outcomes or objectives of learning, with the major focus on the overall relationship between the teacher and the students. It is important to keep in mind, however, that there are major differences in learning styles from one student to another, and that these differences can have a noticeable effect on classroom learning.

Learning styles (also referred to as *cognitive styles*) are the different ways in which people process information in the course of learning. They include individual preferences in both perceptual organization and conceptual categorization—that is, perceiving, thinking, remembering, and solving problems (Ausubel, 1968; De Cecco, 1974; Kagan, Moss, and Siegel, 1963; Messick, 1969). In addition, some investigators, such as Ausubel (1968), believe that learning styles are also a reflection of individual differences in personality and motivation.

The importance of paying attention to individual differences in learning has been emphasized ever since the advent of "progressive education." However, more often than not, recognition of individual differences has simply meant providing for different amounts of time to do the required work, depending on the person's ability. The result is that teachers have learned how to adapt their methods of instruction to differences in pace, but not to differences in style (Bernard, 1973).

Reissman (1966) was one of the first educators to emphasize the importance of learning styles. He pointed out that each individual has a distinct style of learning, in much the same way that each individual has a distinct personality. The three basic types of learning style he identified are visual (reading), aural (listening), and physical (doing). According to Reissman, most people show a distinct preference for one of these methods as compared with the others. Many socially disadvantaged children have learning styles that are characterized by hyperactivity, distractibility, and difficulty in settling down. Often these children have more difficulty performing tasks that require "reading" or "listening" than performing tasks that require "doing."

In addition to the learning styles identified by Reissman, other aspects of behavior that might also be classified as learning styles are the mode of response and the thinking pattern (Nations, 1967). *Response mode* in this sense refers to the manner in which an individual prefers to work, alone or in a group. *Thinking pattern* refers to the tendency of some individuals to gather details first and organize them later, as compared with the tendency of others to look for the overall picture first and to obtain supporting information afterward.

Reissman's (1966) position with regard to learning styles is that they are developed early in life as a result of a combination of predisposition and environmental experience, and are not later subject to fundamental change. Consequently, teachers should help each individual student discover the learning style that is most effective for him and use this information in formulating learning plans. Thus, for example, the child who likes to learn by actively doing, but dislikes reading, might begin to take more of an interest in reading activities if they were combined with role-playing activities.

Variables Affecting
Learning Style

In the beginning of this chapter we pointed out that children vary not only in their ability to learn and their level of achievement, but also in how they learn. Each child evolves a personal way of processing information and learning concepts—that is, each child perceives, thinks, remembers, and solves problems according to his or her own unique style. In studying the ways in which children learn, psychologists have identified many factors related to personality and temperament that influence a child's performance in the classroom (Messick, 1970).

First of all, children vary greatly in their level and *span of attention*. Some can pay attention for long periods of time, while others are easily distracted or frequently daydream; still others pay attention only to what interests them. By observing the attentive behavior of students, a teacher can determine which children need to be monitored during class instruction, and which children can handle long assignments (Shumsky, 1968). There are important individual differences in depth and scope of attention that determine how vividly a child experiences what he is learning (Messick, 1970). Children also differ in their ability to select relevant environmental cues and ignore extraneous ones (Hagen and Hale, 1972).

The *capacity for independent work* also varies greatly from child to child. Some can work with very little supervision; some need a little help at the beginning of an assignment and none thereafter; some need help sporadically; and some need it constantly. A teacher who is aware of these differences can separate the independent pupils from those who need more direction so as not to slow the progress of the entire class. Many children have to be taught how to manage the time they spend on a project.

A child's *rate* of learning is not necessarily the same as his capacity to learn—some pupils work slowly but still manage to learn a great deal. A child who works slowly may be overcautious or sluggish but still have high ability. A child who works quickly may be very intelligent and able to comprehend a great deal, but he can also be impulsive, impatient, and disorganized. Many children work at various rates depending on the assignment, and the teacher should take this into account when assigning homework. There is a danger in forcing a child to learn at a rate incompatible with his natural rhythm and abilities (Shumsky, 1968).

As was discussed in Chapter 5, a child's readiness to learn and his expectations of what the learning situation will be have a powerful effect on what he actually does learn. His typical style of *perceiving* also largely determines what and how he learns. Shortly after World War II, Asch and Witkin and their associates at Brooklyn College first identified important differences in children's modes of perceiving. They found that some children have the ability to make fine discriminations and isolate items from a surrounding context; they called this kind of active analysis *field independence.* Other children tended to be overwhelmed by the complex organization of a field or object and could not discriminate between figure and ground; the researchers called this kind of passive, unanalytic acceptance of a problem *field dependence* (Messick, 1970; Witkin, Dyk, Paterson, Goodenough, and Karp, 1962; Witkin, Goodenough, and Karp, 1967).

Children's *memories* also work in different ways: Some children tend to confuse and blur present objects and events with similar ones in the past; other children can't see any similarities between present and past events, even when the events are almost identical (Holzman and Klein, 1954; Messick, 1970).

Researchers have also found a wide variation in children's *willingness to accept new perceptions, experiences, and surroundings* (Klein, Gardner, and Schlesinger, 1962; Messick, 1970; Sperry, 1972). This is particularly noticeable in children's reactions to the first day at school and to new and unfamiliar activities. Some children accept new experiences as a challenge, and seem relaxed and receptive almost immediately; others are so apprehensive that they develop headaches and stomachaches, or they panic when the teacher introduces new subject matter (Shumsky, 1968).

Children have many different styles of forming concepts, solving problems, and thinking. In studying the ways in which children select hypotheses and process information, researchers have isolated tendencies toward impulsiveness *(impulsivity)* and reflectiveness *(reflectivity).* Because of a desire for quick success, impulsive children make immediate, often wrong, responses; they blurt out the first answer that occurs to them without stopping to think through a problem and consider alternatives. Reflective children have more anxiety over a wrong answer and tend to think about a problem first; they consider various possibilities before deciding upon an answer and take their time in responding (Kagan, 1966; Messick, 1970). Children with average intelligence often do poorly in school because of their impulsivity and distractibility (Hallahan, Kauffman, and Ball, 1973).

There are also great differences in children's views of the world and of other people's behavior; some children see others in a rather elementary, one-dimensional way, while other children are capable of seeing the world in a discriminating and multidimensional way (Messick, 1970). Researchers have also studied children's *tendencies to use either broad or narrow classifications* (Messick, 1970; Pettigrew, 1958), and have attempted to determine whether these classifications are based on concepts that have been thought through in an orderly, discriminating manner.

Because children show such vast differences in learning styles, it has been frequently suggested by educators that all should not be taught by the same method and thus homogeneous grouping is desirable. Actually, there are arguments both for and against the homogeneous grouping of students (this will be discussed in Chapter 11).

Planning for Different Learning Styles

There is also evidence that class size may be related to student achievement. Templeton (1972) reports one study in which 224 high school students were randomly assigned to average-size classes (24–27 students) and large classes (45–52 students) in business and government courses. The results showed better scores on teacher-made tests for the smaller-size class in the government course but not in the two business courses. Also, class size did not make a difference in the students' attitudes toward school.

A report by Woodson, on the other hand, suggests that sometimes class size does make a difference but that additional factors need to be considered. For example, the class size seems to affect low-ability students more than high-ability students and students in the lower grades more than those in the upper grades. Class size also appears to be more relevant to tests of general achievement than to tests in a specific subject area (Templeton, 1972).

Another approach, which has been taken by a few investigators (Olson, 1971; Vincent, 1968), is to consider the relationship between class size and various characteristics of instructional quality—for example, individuality of instruction (the extent to which the instructor meets the needs of individual students), interpersonal regard, creativity, and amount of group activity allowed. The results show a definite negative relationship between the number of pupils in a class and ratings on the various indicators of quality. Apparently teachers are able to use more variety in instructional methods, and to better adapt these methods to individual needs, capabilities, and learning styles in smaller classes. Reducing class size usually allows for increased interaction between teacher and student.

Questions for Thought

What are the problems encountered by a teacher of a large lecture class in planning for different learning styles of students?
Without changing the size of the class, can you list some possible methods of solving these problems?

How do all these considerations affect the decision as to whether or not, and under what conditions, teachers should group their students into small units for learning purposes? Interestingly enough, even though there is heavy emphasis in the literature on finding methods of grouping students to create increased learning, the data suggest that grouping alone does not necessarily accomplish the intended results. Clearly, much more research is necessary on the relationship between the method and the outcomes of teaching, taking into consideration the vast individual differences in students' learning styles.

SUMMARY   Chapter 7 describes in detail the thinking of various psychologists on types of learning, outcomes of learning, and styles of learning. The nature of the learning process varies, not only with the content of the material but also with the purpose of the instruction and with the ages, abilities, and learning styles of the students. In some instances, teachers need to realize how different types of learning can take place in the same subject. In other instances, teachers need to realize how the same methods of instruction can sometimes be applied to different subjects.

There are at least five major categories of capabilities that account for human learning. Each of these capabilities makes possible a particular learning outcome or educational goal. The complex task of curriculum planning can be greatly facilitated by consideration of these different types of learning.

Perceptual learning was discussed in relation to the task of learning to read. The widespread problem of disabilities in reading among schoolchildren can often be traced to deficits in skills involving perception. Eleanor Gibson has conducted some promising research in which she has attempted to isolate and analyze the various perceptual processes that appear necessary for reading.

Motor learning is one type of learning that is often overlooked by teachers, but it, too, affects much of our behavior, both in and out of the classroom. Motor learning is essential to such basic activities as reading, writing, and speaking, as well as to tasks of a much more complex nature requiring extensive training and practice. Teachers can facilitate the acquisition of motor skills by dividing the learning process into two broad stages: (1) getting the idea of the movement, and (2) fixation/diversification. Age and sex differences in motor skills, and individual differences in strength, motor coordination, agility, personality, and motivation all need to be taken into consideration.

Language learning is basic to all forms of communication, to the acquisition and mastery of almost every skill, and to our very survival as social beings. The people who study the structure and use of language are known as linguists and psycholinguists. Their extensive research into the degree of correspondence between phonemes and graphemes, or sound and spelling, has provided new insights into the various kinds of linguistic skills that must be acquired for a child to learn to read. Many special programs designed to help children with reading and spelling difficulties have evolved as a result.

Concept learning and *problem-solving* are closely related to language development, but in a complex way. Language is not absolutely essential for learning a concept or solving a problem, but it facilitates the task considerably, particularly in dealing with concepts that are abstract and complex, and with relationships among different concepts, which are called principles. Concepts are usually taught by deductive methods, with heavy emphasis on guided learning and verbal definitions and descriptions. Other ways of teaching concepts include the inductive or "discovery" method or a combination of both approaches.

Attitude learning is another controversial and often neglected area of the school curriculum. Many, but not all, of the published studies in this area suggest that modeling with reinforcement plays a major role. One study showed that the extent of praise and encouragement offered by the teacher appears to be significantly associated with changes in attitude in a positive or negative direction over the course of the school year.

Many psychologists (Gagné, Bloom, and Merrill, for example) have maintained that instruction should be planned on the basis of a *taxonomy of learning objectives* specified in behavioral terms. A widely used taxonomy applicable to cognitive learning was described, which illustrates the hierarchical progression of six different learning objectives. The six outcomes, in order of complexity, are knowledge, comprehension, application, analysis, synthesis, and evaluation. Although it is neither feasible nor appropriate to always try to accomplish all of these outcomes in one course or topic, careful consideration of them is helpful in producing those kinds of learning that are consistent with both the specific objectives of the course and the long-range goals of education. Planning instruction on the basis of a taxonomy of learning objectives also facilitates the task of testing and measurement, which are designed to determine to what extent the students have actually learned to do what the instruction was supposed to teach them. Also, the students are more likely to be aware of the purpose of the instruction and what they are expected to get out of it. In addition to preparing learning objectives that are applicable to a class as a whole, teachers should be aware of the tremendous differences that can be observed between one student and another, in terms of both ability and learning style. Since these individual differences can have strong effects on classroom learning, they have important implications for the differential design of the curriculum.

SUGGESTED FOR FURTHER READING

Bloom, B. S., Krathwohl, D. R., et al. *A taxonomy of educational objectives.* Handbook 1, "The cognitive domain," 1956. Handbook 2, "The affective domain," 1964 (one-volume edition, 1969). New York: McKay.

These two texts are the classic books on classification of education into specific areas. They should be considered as excellent reference material for developing educational objectives.

Dale, P. S. *Language development: structure and function.* Hinsdale, Ill.: Dryden Press, 1972.

Dale's book is a fairly easy-to-read summary of psycholinguistics and the development of language in children. The chapters on reading, early education, and black English should be of special interest to teachers.

Gagné, R. M., and Gephart, W. J. (Ed.). *Learning research and school subjects.* Itasco, Ill.: F. E. Peacock, 1968.

This book is a summary of a symposium relating to the topics of cognitive and perceptual learning. The emphasis is upon direct applications to instruction. Following the presentation of the papers, the book summarizes the other participants' discussion.

Gibson, E. J. *Principles of perceptual learning and development.* New York: Appleton-Century-Crofts, 1969.

Describes the views of a major theorist on perception and perceptual learning theory. It is also an excellent resource book for perceptual learning and development in general.

Mager, R. F. *Preparing instructional objectives.* Belmont, Calif.: Fearson Publishers, 1962.

This delightfully written programmed text is the best known and most widely used source for teachers who want to develop educational objectives for their courses. Mager's approach makes the task seem easier.

Sperry, L. (Ed.). *Learning performance and individual differences.* Glenview, Ill.: Scott, Foresman, 1972.

This is an excellent collection of readings relating to individual differences in the learning situation. Teacher expectations, learning and cognitive styles, and instructional styles are the major topics covered.

Vargas, J. S. *Writing worthwhile behavioral objectives.* New York: Harper & Row, 1972.

Vargas has developed extremely clear examples of how a teacher can build behavioral objectives. This self-instructional book should prove to be an excellent aid in developing worthwhile objectives in the cognitive domain. It is an invaluable aid for the teacher.

REMEMBERING, FORGETTING, AND TRANSFERRING LEARNING

After completing this chapter, the reader should be able to:

1 Describe the different types of memory that have been studied in human beings, and explain the importance of each in the classroom.

2 Explain why we both remember and forget according to several basic approaches to learning discussed in this text.

3 Use each of the approaches discussed to explain what the teacher can do to increase remembering and to decrease forgetting, and what the student can do to reach this same end.

4 Select methods for measuring classroom learning that are most appropriate to the goals of instruction and to the particular subject matter being studied.

5 Explain why transfer takes place from classroom learning to other situations, and why this transfer is critical to good learning.

6 Outline the conditions under which both positive and negative transfer occur, and describe procedures that can be used to increase positive transfer and decrease negative transfer.

CHAPTER 8

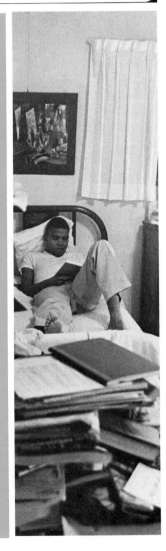

INTRODUCTION

The process of learning has occupied our attention for the past several chapters. To explain learning in its totality, however, we must now examine two aspects of learning, remembering and forgetting, and the related phenomenon of transferring learning to new situations. A good way to gain appreciation of the role of remembering in human functioning is to imagine a world in which human beings did not possess the ability to retain information. If we forgot everything we were taught, language and communication would be impossible, and learning would cease—teachers would be out of jobs!

What teachers must recognize is that for their role to be effective, not only must children acquire skills and information, they must be able to retain these things and apply them to new situations as well. For example, in order for a student to learn how to do the operations of long division, he must remember what he has learned previously about how to add, subtract, and multiply. The importance of retention cannot be overestimated.

Learning and remembering are complementary aspects of a continuous process (Ellis, 1972), and this should be kept in mind at all times by the teacher. But learning and remembering are not synonymous. We distinguish between them by saying that remembering refers to the retention of information *after* learning has taken place (Hulse, Deese, and Egeth, 1975). In other words, learning can be seen as a kind of information input, and remembering as the availability of this information to you at a later time. Think of this as a "storage" process: Through learning, you acquire the material to be stored; through remembering, you store it (*retain* it) until you need it, at which time you take it out of storage (*retrieve* it) and use it. This is an oversimplified picture; in the course of this chapter, we will describe in detail how this process works.

In addition to remembering what we learn, we also *transfer* this learning; that is, we use what we have already learned to do or learn something new in a different situation. In Chapter 5, you will recall, we spent a great deal of time dealing with Bruner's consideration of the importance of transfer. This phenomenon must be well understood by the teacher; if students were unable to use what they had learned in one context to facilitate learning in another, teachers would have to begin from the beginning each time they taught something new. For example, to learn a foreign language—French, let us say—students must transfer to French the general concepts that they have already learned about the English language—sentence structure, spelling, verb tense, and so on. In the new situation, they may acquire the information that "maison" means "house"; but to learn enough French to be able to converse in it, they must transfer the learning that in French, as in English, this word is a noun, that it can be pluralized, that it can be modified by an adjective, that it can be the subject of a sentence, and so on.

Transfer of learning in the classroom also means transferring what is learned in the school to real-life situations. For example, in school, a child learns to add a column of figures; when he plays baseball, he should be able to use this information to add up the runs, hits, and errors. When he grows up, he will use this same information to balance a checkbook. These examples, although simple, point to the significance of transfer of learning: What we learn and remember is valuable to us only when we are able to use this material in a new situation.

Remembering and forgetting have long interested psychologists. Hermann Ebbinghaus (1913) was a pioneer in this field. His studies concerned how much we forget during various time intervals after the termination of learning. Using himself as a subject, Ebbinghaus learned a list of nonsense syllables (combinations of letters totally without meaning). He waited set periods of time—minutes, hours, days—and then relearned the nonsense syllables. By varying the intervals between the original learning of the lists and the relearning, and by comparing the amounts retained, Ebbinghaus found that he forgot the largest amount during the first few hours after learning, and that after about 24 hours he hadn't forgotten much more. Numerous studies since that time by other experimenters have confirmed this finding (Kintsch, 1970) that the greatest amount of forgetting occurs immediately after learning.

Of course, the length of time after learning is not the only factor affecting how much we retain. Another factor is the meaningfulness of the material. Meaningful material is remembered better than meaningless material, such as the nonsense syllables that Ebbinghaus learned (Underwood, 1964). The manner in which the material is originally learned also affects retention. Learning in which trials are spaced over time is more likely to be retained than learning massed into a single session (Ciccone, 1973). Indeed, experience tells us all that we remember more material for an examination if we space our studying over several days than if we cram it into one all-night session right before the examination . . . a fact we forget all too often!

Three Types of Memory

Thus far we have been looking at memory and forgetting as a whole process; however, it is generally acknowledged by psychologists that there are at least three distinct types of memory: sensory information storage, short-term memory, and long-term memory (Lindsay and Norman, 1972).

SENSORY INFORMATION STORAGE.   Sensory information storage refers to our perception of the world through our senses—that is,
what we see, hear, feel, smell, and taste. This type of memory is extremely short-lived; several experiments have shown that we retain
an accurate sensory image for at most one second (Simon, 1972). For
example, tap your fingers against your arm several times. You will
find that the feeling of the taps—the sensory image—lasts for a split
second. Or listen to these taps; the image of the sound will fade
quickly (Lindsay and Norman, 1972). You might also open and close
your fist and see how long you retain the resulting sensory image
on your skin.

The important distinguishing feature in sensory information storage is that although you retain the knowledge that you tapped your
fingers, or heard the tapping, or smelled a daffodil on a rainy day,
you do not retain the *sensation* of feeling or hearing or smelling. For
this reason, cognitive memory does not fall into the category of sensory information storage.

SHORT-TERM MEMORY.   In short-term memory, we store material as
an immediate and direct *interpretation* of sensory stimuli. That is,
we remember an interpretation of an event, not the event itself. For
example, when the telephone operator gives you the number you
wish to dial, you do not retain an image of the specific sounds he
has made when he spoke, but rather a grouping of numbers that
you wish to use at the moment. Short-term memory is direct, re-
tains only a small amount of information, and is short-lived unless
rehearsed, that is, mentally reviewed. Unless you make an effort to
remember that phone number, you will quickly forget it.

LONG-TERM MEMORY.   Of the three memory types, long-term memory is perhaps the most important and complex. To remember
thoughts, ideas, or information for a long time, you must make a
concerted effort. Examples of long-term memory are remembering
the meanings of words, procedures involved in complex problem-
solving, and events long past. For instance, you might remember a
book that you read and enjoyed as a child—its title, who gave it to
you, something of the plot, how you felt about it at the time. The
capacity of long-term memory for storing information is thought to
be huge, much greater than most of us normally make use of.

A COMPARISON.   Let us review and compare the three types of
memory. Sensory information storage is of brief duration, and the
items in it cannot be rehearsed or stored for more than a split second. In short-term memory, we remember small bits of information
for short periods of time, although this can be prolonged by re-

"I'll never forget you." How often high school graduates mark that promise in one another's yearbooks. In recent research on long-term memory, several psychologists have found that the promise is, indeed, kept (Bahrick, Bahrick, and Wittlinger, 1974). We remember names and faces of our classmates for years, even decades, though we may move both physically and psychologically away. With names and pictures out of the past, the experimenters jogged the memory of 392 high school graduates who ranged in age from 17 to 74. The subjects were divided into nine groups based upon the amount of time since they graduated. On a preliminary free-recall test, recent graduates recalled more names than those who had been out of school longer. Recall performance was found to steadily decline with age, the amount of decline diminishing gradually per year. Friends, unsurprisingly, were most easily recalled. The recall of names was much better when the subjects were prompted by pictures to which they matched names. With these visual cues, even those subjects in their 50s and 60s could identify three-fourths of their classmates. The psychologists suggest the reason for this long-term memory: High school students generally have four years in which to acquire and store information about their classmates. They learn only small amounts at a time and then use the information over and over again. Thus, as the study suggests, there's far more than nostalgia behind those unforgettable high school days.

LONG-TERM MEMORY: THOSE UNFORGETTABLE HIGH SCHOOL DAYS

hearsal. Long-term memory requires work and involves more complex types of information, but it is long-lasting.

If a teacher informs a class that a certain piece of information is interesting but not crucial to remember (for example, the current population of New York City) and that another piece of information is important to remember (for example, how urban-suburban population patterns have shifted in the past 25 years), the students will store the first item in their short-term memory and make an effort to store the second in their long-term memory. They will remember the first quickly and easily for a brief time afterward, but to remember the second at a much later time they will have to work at it. It is important for teachers to keep this in mind if they want their students to engage in effective learning. Increasing long-term memory will be discussed in detail later in this chapter.

WHY WE REMEMBER AND FORGET

Associationist Theories

As we mentioned in detail in our discussion of associationist theory in Chapter 4, we learn because we make associations between stimuli and responses, and we build upon these associations for later learning. From this perspective, "a memory is nothing more than a response produced by a stimulus" (Osgood, 1953, p. 550), and forgetting is a weakening of a stimulus-response association.

Psychologists adopting this approach seek to determine which factors influence this weakening of associations after learning (conditioning) has occurred. Their research involves specifying why forgetting occurs and the degree to which it occurs, and determining the circumstances that affect the amount of forgetting.

FADING.   One of the simplest explanations of why forgetting occurs is known as the fading theory. This theory proposes that learning creates actual changes in the brain. These structural changes in the nervous system associated with learning are called *memory traces*. It is assumed that these traces, the representations of items in the memory (Lindsay and Norman, 1972), can be retrieved at a later time. With time, however, these traces are said to gradually fade, and forgetting occurs. In this explanation, time would appear to be the variable accounting for forgetting.

The work of Ebbinghaus, mentioned earlier, has been explained by this approach, and his data have been found to be consistent with it in that the degree of forgetting increased with and was directly related to time elapsed since original learning. Clearly, however, this relationship between time and forgetting is not linear; that is, the memory traces did not fade gradually. Instead, the forgetting was rapid at first and then slowed significantly. Ebbinghaus relearned the list of nonsense syllables in less time than it took him to learn it originally. This would seem to support the claim that memory traces are induced by learning and revived in the process of relearning. This claim supposes some sort of neurological change within the brain itself that fades with time, but can, under such circumstances, be renewed.

Despite the claims of its proponents and some evidence that learning may indeed bring about neurological changes, the fading theory of forgetting by itself leaves many unanswered questions. Adequate neurological evidence still needs to be forthcoming in order to back up the claim that (1) learning creates actual changes in the brain, and (2) time is the cause of the fading of these memory traces. There is also a lack of information about the other factors that may cause forgetting in combination with the passage of time (Hilgard and Bower, 1975).

INTERFERENCE.   A second associationist theory of forgetting explains it in terms of the phenomenon of interference. This theory proposes that new and old learning compete; that is, one interferes with the other, and so the ability to remember both is limited.

The classic study first documenting interference in the memory process was conducted by Jenkins and Dallenbach (1924), who found that subjects remembered more when learning was followed by sleep than when it was followed by activity. In their study, subjects learned lists of nonsense syllables and were tested for retention after time. One group of subjects learned the nonsense syllables prior to regular working activities; the second prior to sleep. At the end of a specified period of time, both groups were tested. The subjects who slept after learning retained more. Jenkins and Dallenbach reasoned that since more learning obviously goes on during wakefulness than during sleep, this inability to remember after wakeful activity was due to the interference of new learning.

The more similar two things to be learned are, the more interference. The term applied to interference in which subsequent learning interferes with earlier learning is known as *retroactive inhibition.* For example, you might have difficulty in remembering an algebraic concept you had just learned if you followed it immediately by learning a geometric concept; this difficulty would be due to retroactive inhibition.

A second type of interference has been proposed as well. In this case, prior learning interferes with the ability to remember new learning. This is called *proactive inhibition.* Proactive inhibition can occur simultaneously with retroactive inhibition. Suppose that a child studies a chemistry lesson immediately prior to studying a physics assignment. If he later confuses the chemistry concepts with physics concepts, we would say that proactive inhibition has occured. That is, earlier chemistry studying interfered with the ability to learn and retain the physics concepts. Of course, retroactive inhibition may take place simultaneously, and the student will find that his physics studying interferes as well with his chemistry learning.

These two principles of interference have significance for teachers in the way in which they present material to students. The extent of interference between two tasks is a function of the similarities and differences of the subject matter presented to the learner together with the responses he must make in the learning situation. If the subject matters of two tasks are similar, the amount of interference increases with the difference between the required responses in the two situations. If the responses required of the student are different, however, there will not be as much interference.

An example ought to clarify the situation. Suppose that a French teacher gives an assignment to a student in which the student's task is to translate a list of words into French. An hour later, in Spanish class, the same student is asked by his Spanish teacher to translate an almost identical list of words into Spanish. We could expect in this situation a great deal of interference; the student no doubt will make a large number of errors mixing French and Spanish words. The subject matter is almost identical in each task, while the required responses, French translation and Spanish translation, are different. It clearly would be beneficial for this student if the two language teachers were to arrange assignments so that the student did not have to translate the same words in the two classes.

A teacher can even more effectively limit the effects of such interference by sequencing material so that dissimilar subjects follow one another; for example, follow an English lesson with an art lesson.

Questions for Thought
If you were in charge of arranging a class schedule for a high school student taking the courses listed below, and if all the courses were offered at all times of the school day, how would you arrange his classes to cause the least interference? Why?

chemistry
English
French
Italian
physics

If it is absolutely necessary to teach two languages one immediately following the other, how might the teachers plan together to cause the least interference between the two languages?
How would you arrange the schedule of a typical elementary school child in the second grade?

EXTINCTION.   As a final note to this discussion of associationist theories, it should be pointed out that forgetting, as we have been discussing it, clearly differs from another associationist concept often confused with it, the concept of extinction. Extinction was discussed at some length in Chapter 4, and is the result of the removal of reinforcement from a learning situation. Extinction does not cause a general fading of responses, nor does it occur as the result of interfering activities such as those described here. Furthermore, extinguished behavior frequently reappears spontaneously as one of an individual's responses—clearly not "forgotten" by the individual at all.

Motivation Theories   Motivation theories of forgetting focus upon the individual's motivation to learn and remember material. As you will recall, motivation was discussed at length in Chapter 6. According to this approach, a person will remember one piece of material better than another because it is more meaningful to him; it is this meaningfulness that motivates him to remember it. Why can a young boy remember all the starting lineups of the baseball teams in the American League on a certain day, but not the multiplication tables? The answer may be motivation.

RECONSTRUCTING MEMORY: THE POWER OF SUGGESTION OF WORDS

Eyewitness testimony rests on the ability to reconstruct the memory of an event. And many factors can affect the way a witness "remembers" what he saw. The questions asked about an event can alter his memory; in fact, changing even one word in a single question can systematically alter an eyewitness account (Loftus, 1974). An experiment was recently conducted to examine the influence of an interrogator's language. The subjects were students who were shown films of automobile accidents they had to remember and report. After viewing a film, each subject filled out a 22-item questionnaire containing 16 irrelevant and 6 critical questions. Three of these 6 questions asked about items that had been present in the film, while 3 others asked about items that had not actually been present. For half the subjects, the critical questions began with "Did you see *a*," as in "Did you see a broken headlight?" For the rest, the critical question began with the words "Did you see *the*," as in "Did you see the broken headlight?" Thus the sentences differed only in the form of the article *a* or *the*. Results showed that those witnesses who received questions with *the* were much more likely to report having seen something that had not appeared in the film. Those who received questions with *a* were more likely to respond "don't know," both when the object had been present and when it had not. Following another film, the experimenters conducted a test on judgments of speed resulting in an accident. The subjects indicated higher rates of speed when the questions used words such as "smashed," "collided," and "bumped" rather than "hit" and "contacted." A week later, the subjects of this test, without viewing the film again, were asked whether they had seen any broken glass, although, in fact, there had been none in the film. More than twice as many subjects who had answered questions containing the word "smashed" reported seeing the nonexistent glass as those queried with "hit." The experiment reminds us again of the power of suggestion that words carry. "I saw it with my own eyes" is no guarantee of accuracy.

Motivation theory has also been used to explain the finding that a person is able to recall an uncompleted task more readily than a completed one. This phenomenon, known as the *Zeigarnik effect*, has been explained by motivation theorists' assumption that the person is less motivated to remember a completed task for the very reason that it is finished. If, however, one has to go back to a task that has not been completed, he needs to remember the task in order to finish it.

In terms of motivation theory, the most far-reaching explanation of forgetting is the psychological mechanism of repression. According to Freud, we push painful experiences out of our conscious mind and into our unconscious mind as a way of preserving status of what he called the ego; that is, we repress them. Similarly, learning that is associated with painful experiences is repressed.

According to this approach, a student who has a great deal of fear and anxiety in the classroom would probably remember little of what was taught there—he would repress the memory of experience *and* the learning. Teachers can counteract forgetting through repression by making the classroom a less fearful place, and thus making learning more pleasant.

Gestalt Theories

The basis of Gestalt theories of memory and forgetting is the *laws of organization* (see Chapter 5). According to Gestalt psychologists, the main determinant of remembering is good organization (for example, clear contrast between figure and ground) rather than time. That is, material that is poorly organized when learned will fade more quickly than material that is well organized. Actually, if the material presented was originally poorly organized, the memory can become transformed to a more organized entity. This occurs, for example, in the case where a subject recalls that a picture is a complete circle, when in actuality it is incomplete. This, as you will remember, is an example of the law of closure.

Cybernetic Theory or Information-Processing Approach

The most recent approach to the study of remembering and forgetting compares the functioning of the mind with similar processes in a computer. This is termed the *cybernetic theory* or *information-processing* approach. Encompassing a large number of particular theories, the general feature of this approach is its central focus on how information flows from its initial input into memory storage to its final output as retrieved memory. In attempting to describe how this process of information flow occurs, a theoretical model is hypothesized by these theorists to account for what happens when we remember and forget. The model can then be used in helping to identify and understand the possible mechanisms involved in memory.

In generating a theoretical model, cybernetic engineers put computers to work to examine the general requirements a computer must meet in order to be able to solve certain types of problems. For instance, a computer must have some sort of analyzer that initially examines incoming information before it can be processed by another part of the computer. This is the kind of general feature of a computer that is incorporated into the theoretical model of human memory.

This model of information processing is put to use answering two questions: (1) How is information placed into storage? (2) How is this information retrieved at a later time? In the first question, interest centers on which perceptual attributes of an item are extracted for storage in memory. For example, when you are looking for a new car, you store a great deal of information about the cars that you see: the color, number of doors, engine size, manufacturer, and so on. Each fact is a variable which you must use in deciding which car to buy. Each "car" is then stored under each of these categories. This process has been described as analogous to a cross-referencing system in a library, in which a book may be found catalogued under a variety of categories (Travers, 1967).

Encoding is an interesting phenomenon that occurs during storage (Tulving, 1972). This process enables us to reduce or abbreviate the amount of information stored for a particular item. For example, when we see a cat, we note that it has four legs, whiskers, two eyes, and so on. But we do not have to store each of these bits of information separately. Rather, we form an image of the cat that includes all this information in a *chunk*, and we store this chunk instead (Bower, 1967).

Organization is another aspect of storage. In this process, bits of stored information are related to one another (Tulving, 1972). It is possible, however, that through organization, interference (as described previously) will result: One piece of information might disrupt another piece of information while it is being stored.

Cybernetic engineers distinguish between storage and retrieval of information. The storage process, as we mentioned, is concerned with input, whereas the retrieval process is a search for information activated by a memory task. Retrieval, however, is not simply a matter of searching through all the items in the memory storage until the appropriate one is found. The manner in which the searching proceeds is a function of the cues that guide the search (Wood, 1972).

Let us assume for a moment that a subject is asked to remember a list of eight items, but he can recall only five of them. If we provide him with a category for the forgotten items (a cue), he will be more likely to remember them. If the cue is "fruit," he might now be able to remember that the three missing items are "apple," "pear," and "banana." The items had been stored, but to retrieve them his search had to be initiated by a cue. The help provided by cues is one reason why many students find multiple-choice questions easier than essay questions on a test.

HOW TO INCREASE LONG-TERM MEMORY

Earlier we noted the three types of memory—sensory information storage, short-term memory, and long-term memory—and mentioned briefly the importance of the third in education.

Often the goal of long-term memory is not achieved. For example, cramming for an exam the night before may possibly place enough information in your short-term memory for you to pass the exam, and maybe even get a good grade. However, this material will not be retained for any length of time, and so, though you may have "passed," you have not really "learned." As we mentioned earlier, spacing study sessions is preferable to massing study in one session.

Question for Thought

Even though we all can give numerous reasons, both theoretical and practical, for not cramming for exams, most of us continue to do so. Can you explain this behavior in terms of any specific learning theories such as associationism and operant conditioning?

What the Classroom Teacher Can Do

What can the classroom teacher do to enhance long-term memory? Several suggestions will be described which have been shown to help achieve this goal.

MAKE LEARNING MATERIAL MEANINGFUL.   When we discussed motivation theories, we suggested that the more meaningful that material is to a person, the more motivated he will be to remember it. Long-term retention is greater with meaningful learning than with rote learning (Ellis, 1972).

How do we define "meaningfulness"? One measure of meaningfulness is _association_ — that is, which responses are elicited by a particular piece of learning. The more associations an idea brings about, the more meaning that idea is said to have for a person. In this sense, the concept of "weather" might be meaningful to a fourth-grader, since he has many associations with it, but the concept of "nuclear physics" will not.

Another measure of meaningfulness is _familiarity_. In a study in which subjects were asked to remember different kinds of sentences, it was found that the closer a sentence was to the natural language order — that is, the way an individual usually speaks — the better it was remembered (Miller, 1973).

The fact that more frequently occurring words and common word order are more familiar, more meaningful — and thus better retained — has important implications for teachers. In presenting material to students, teachers should be aware that the children's lack of familiarity with the language used in the material may hinder their learning and retention. For example, taking most young children to see Shakespeare's _Romeo and Juliet_ in the original version would not help their learning — the language used would be totally unfamiliar to them — whereas taking them to a play that is produced specifically for youngsters and that uses the language level they have mastered would be effective. It is particularly important for teachers to understand this when working with socially disadvan-

The rapt expressions on the faces of the audience of a children's play illustrate the importance of making learning material meaningful to children.

(Margot Granitsas, Photo Researchers)

taged children. What some teachers think are deficiencies in learning that such children exhibit may stem simply from unfamiliarity with middle-class language used in the schools, not from any deficiency in cognitive ability. Presenting materials chosen specifically for their level of language ability and in their own dialects would provide them with something familiar and thus something that will be better retained.

A third measure of meaningfulness is the degree to which facts in the material presented are *related* by virtue of an overall rule or principle (Bigge, 1964). This should bring to mind the Gestalt theories of memory, which are built upon the laws of organization. To aid retention, a teacher should present an understandable principle before giving students the factual information explained by that principle. Within such a framework, the facts will be better remembered. For example, in beginning a unit on transportation in the early primary grades, a teacher could provide a framing question such as "How do people get from one place to another?" before proceeding to the specifics—boats, cars, planes, and so forth.

PROPERLY STRUCTURE THE CURRICULUM.   As we have seen, organization and structure enhance long-term retention. The spiral curriculum discussed by Bruner and described in Chapter 5 is one example of a curriculum specifically structured to increase memory and transfer. Other structural designs have also been developed to reach these same goals.

Curriculum structure often reflects the organization found in textbooks. How then should text material be structured to aid long-term retention? It is generally acknowledged that questions placed in a body of text material facilitate learning; but the *location* of the questions in the body of the material is the important variable. Locating questions before a text section has been found to be helpful, although the effect of the questions on retention appears to be limited to the specific information called for by the questions. Locating questions after a text section has been found to facilitate retention of both specific and general text material (Glaser and Resnick, 1972). This is the reason that *Questions for Thought* have been placed throughout this text at ends of sections or paragraphs dealing with provocative subject matters.

In addition to the location of questions in a body of material, their *frequency* effects long-term retention. It has been found that too frequent questions presented before the introduction of a new subject decrease retention because they seem to disrupt the continuity of the prose materials, and that frequent questions presented after the material increase retention. The *type* of question preceding the material also seemed to affect recall. Specific questions were found to aid retention more than general questions (Glaser and Resnick, 1972).

Factors related to the organization of the text material itself affect retention as well. For example, it has been found that structuring material by object names rather than by attributes seems to facilitate retention (Glaser and Resnick, 1972). Retention probably would be increased if the material in a transportation unit were organized by object names (boats, cars, planes) rather than by the attributes that these objects share (motor, speed, passenger, capacity, and so on). Text material organized around introductory topic sentences has been found to be retained better than text material that is well integrated throughout but lacks topic sentences (Gagné, 1969). (Note, for example, the first sentence of this paragraph; it is the topic sentence around which the paragraph is organized.)

The *arrangement of tasks* for increased retention is a topic to which teachers should pay attention. In the past, research in this area has focused on the effects of presenting the parts of a task separately versus presenting the task in its entirety. Although the research has not always provided definitive answers as to which method is most effective, some suggestions can be made on how to best subdivide and arrange learning material into parts. Keep in mind that such subdivision should adhere to the laws of organization expressed by the Gestalt theorists.

First, the individual parts should not exceed the memory span of the students (Cook, Morrison, and Stacy, 1935). The length of the segments should be appropriate for the student's cognitive level. In order to determine optimal length of each part, the teacher clearly must be familiar with the cognitive level of the child, as we described in Chapter 2.

Second, the parts should reflect the logical structure of the material as a whole. Thus, if the student's task is to learn the major cities in the United States, the cities might be organized into groups or parts according to geographical location, thus reflecting the overall geography of the country—for example, all the cities on the East Coast. If for some reason the parts in a particular learning situation do not reflect the whole, they should in any case contain an organization of their own that makes sense to the student.

Third, the *type* of material should determine the way in which it is divided into parts. Some material can be organized into a hierarchy of skills or information; that is, easier skills or pieces of information can be grouped together and presented before more difficult skills are introduced (Gagné, 1970). Sometimes, it is useful to present the task in its entirety first so that students can get an overall picture of what is involved in the task. This introduction can be limited to a brief presentation followed by detailed presentations of the component parts.

REDUCE THE EFFECTS OF INTERFERENCE.   Earlier we alluded to the significance to the teacher of the principle of interference and provided an example of how the effects of interference can be reduced somewhat. In general, the teacher should avoid situations in which learning materials that are similar in substance but different in the required responses follow one another. To increase retention, the teacher should not, for example, follow a lesson on English grammar with one on French grammar. It would be preferable by far to follow the English grammar lesson with art, or perhaps chemistry, leaving the French lesson for another day or part of that day.

PROVIDE FOR OVERLEARNING.   Overlearning is learning that continues after material *appears* to be learned and remembered; such review has been found to reduce forgetting, especially of factual material. Overlearning should be distinguished from drill or rote learning; indeed, it does not have to take these forms, although sometimes it may. For example, practicing addition learned in school by checking a supermarket receipt is overlearning; doing dozens of addition problems of exactly the same type as those done in class is drill.

Each time you read a book or magazine you are engaging in overlearning how to read, although obviously that is not your purpose in reading. Similarly, when you practice a skill such as swimming or skating, you are overlearning that skill. People say that once you have learned how to swim, you never forget; that is because every time you swim you are overlearning.

A teacher can guide a child in overlearning in the classroom by teaching him how to practice, although the burden of practice is the child's own responsibility. The teacher can provide contexts in

PIANO LESSONS: STRIKING A NEW CHORD

Anyone who ever took piano lessons as a child remembers the rule "Practice makes perfect." And practice meant many long and lonely hours sitting at the keyboard. Not so any more. Dr. Robert Pace, professor of music education at Teachers College, Columbia University, and education director of the National Piano Foundation, uses a method of group instruction that is so successful it is being adopted all over the world (Brooks, 1974). "A pair of youngsters get a private lesson together once a week, plus a weekly group lesson—with several others pairs of students—in the fundamentals of music—harmony chords, improvisation, writing music, and ear training. In these groups one child may play notes on the piano while another listens and evaluates his work, and still another writes on the blackboard the notes he hears the first child play. This audio/visual/tactile approach helps each child to actually feel the notes while he's seeing and hearing them" (p. 48). The system works because it allows children to benefit from one another's strengths; a child strong on rhythm, for example, can help a child who is weak in this area. Knowledge is thus shared, and reliance on one another motivates the children to practice. Happily, for today's piano students, isolation and competition are no longer "necessary" components of music education.

which the child can use skills and abilities learned earlier; each time the child engages in these activities—that is, engages in overlearning—he increases the probability of long-term retention. A teacher can, for instance, upon completion of a reading unit on children in other countries, have his students select library books on similar themes to read at home.

The teacher should keep in mind that the amount of overlearning a student achieves is related to the number of trials it takes him to learn the material initially. A student who learns quickly may be bored by too many practice homework assignments. On the other hand, a student who learns slowly may grasp the material only at the end of a series of homework assignments, and so will need more opportunities to practice and thus to overlearn. What this means for teachers is that they should take individual differences in learning rates into consideration when they provide opportunities for overlearning.

Questions for Thought

It has often been suggested that, to teach most effectively, individual differences among students must be taken into consideration. Suggest as many ways as you can in which a teacher might measure individual differences that are important to learning, and then use these measures to provide optimal overlearning for each student. In short, when is enough practice enough?

What are the ways a teacher can tell that it is time to stop practicing and go on to other matters?

PROVIDE IMMEDIATE FEEDBACK.   The necessity of immediate feedback for optimal learning and retention is stressed by association
theorists because it serves as a reinforcer for most students. A reinforcer, as we discussed in Chapter 4, is any stimulus that affects
the probability of a response being emitted. Positive reinforcers
—those that increase the probability of the immediately preceding
response being emitted again—are generally considered more effective than negative reinforcers, which encourage escape responses.

Feedback is most effective when it is immediate, because then
there is less possibility for chance and/or erroneous associations.
If feedback is delayed, a child may associate the feedback not with
the correct response, but perhaps with an irrelevant or incorrect
response.

What can teachers do to provide immediate feedback? One thing
they can do is to give diagnostic tests that pinpoint problems that
students might encounter in a particular area; following their analysis of the students' tests, they can let the students know immediately what they have done correctly and what they still have to work
on. Teachers can respond promptly to student performance on exams, and they can help students to evaluate their own performances
on exams (Kryspin and Feldhusen, 1974b).

PROVIDE FOR STUDENT ORAL RECITATION.   Educators generally agree
that oral recitation aids students in remembering subject matter.

**Oral recitation helps
students remember subject
matter.**

(Fred Lyon, Rapho/Photo
Researchers)

This view is consistent with the position of the associationists, who emphasize that active response by students should be encouraged so that reinforcement can be offered (see Chapter 4).

The success of oral recitation as a classroom technique to increase long-term retention depends on several factors: the degree of abruptness in introducing new material, the rate at which students are paced, the type of subject matter, and the ability and temperament of the students. Through experimentation, the teacher will have to discover for himself the optimal amount of oral recitation to use in the classroom. For instance, oral recitation may prove to be effective in teaching the conjugation of verbs in a foreign language in an elementary school classroom, but it may be ineffective in teaching formulas in a college chemistry class.

What the Student Can Do

As we mentioned in connection with the teacher's role in overlearning, the ultimate responsibility for increasing long-term retention rests with the student himself. The way in which a student goes about studying, whether he is a fast or a slow learner, will determine in large measure his achievement in school. Hints on methods to improve study habits abound, but the student alone must decide if he will adopt them. No teacher or parent can force a student to study properly; the role of these adults is limited to guidance and encouragement. The rest is up to the student.

DEVELOP PROPER STUDY HABITS. Ellis (1972) has outlined five interrelated techniques to improve study habits. First, survey the material to get a "preliminary organization" of it so that you will have an overall idea of the author's direction. For example, in this book you might read the behavioral objectives, the section headings, and the chapter summaries.

In the second technique, you "focus your attention on your task and eliminate irrelevant stimuli" (Ellis, 1972, p. 131). If you are studying this chapter while watching television, turn the set off.

The third technique is a matter of providing yourself with rewards after you have achieved certain subgoals determined by you in advance. This is called "self-management of contingencies" (Ellis, 1972, p. 132), and it operates to reinforce your achievement in studying. For instance, you might schedule a five-minute coffee break after you have finished the material on "What the Student Can Do," keeping in mind that you have achieved one subgoal and must return to study the next section or subgoal.

The fourth technique involves further organization of the material. Even if a text is well organized, you must be able to impose your own structure on the material, whether by taking notes or writing an outline or by some other method that suits you.

As the fifth technique, Ellis suggests that you practice what you have learned, or the items in your memory storage will fade. Do not simply measure how much you have studied, but concern yourself with putting the material to use. For instance, although you may complete this chapter in record time, your studying has not been effective in facilitating long-term retention unless you can retrieve the information discussed here and put it to use—in this case, as a teacher.

SPACE AND TIME STUDY SESSIONS.   As we mentioned earlier, massed studying is less effective in promoting long-term retention than is studying distributed over a number of sessions. There are several reasons for this. First, one long cramming session will lead to boredom and mental and physical fatigue, which will interfere with your ability to learn and remember material. (By the end of an all-nighter with no breaks, how much were you able to absorb and remember?)

Similarly, in massed studying, you have a greater buildup of frustration. Your frustration at not being able to master a complex topic may grow in any studying situation, but if you get away from the topic entirely and return later, you will be fresher and better able to conquer it. On the other hand, if you attempt to study a difficult concept in one unbroken effort, you are overdoing it. Without any pauses, your frustration will grow even more. Bigge (1964) cites the

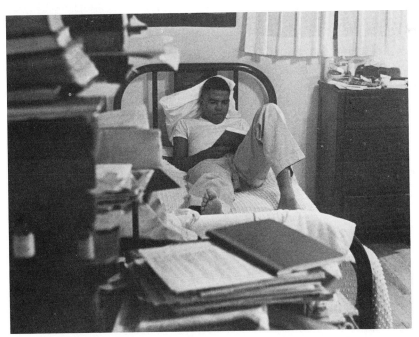

Massed studying is less effective for long-term retention than studying distributed over a number of sessions.

(Cornell Capa, Magnum)

case of a man in his 40s who, after years of watching others, one summer finally attempted to learn to swim. Throughout that summer he encountered a great deal of frustration and remained a very poor swimmer. But after a winter's break, he was able to catch on and learned to swim with ease the following summer. Without some sort of break, however, the man's attempt to learn to swim would probably have ended in dismal failure because of his continual frustration.

The low efficiency of massed studying for long-term retention is also due to the fact that it does not allow for much feedback. In an educational psychology course, for example, you might read a chapter on motivation and compare it with your class notes on the topic. In class the next day, you will have an opportunity to ask your instructor any questions that might have arisen on this topic. When you return to the chapter and your notes, any problems you might have had with the material will have been resolved. Similarly, when a teacher gives a homework assignment to a class and then reviews it and returns it, the students are provided with feedback, so at their next study session they know what is correct or incorrect in what they have done. If, however, you failed to study until the night before an exam, or did not hand in any homework assignments, you would have missed out on this feedback.

Spaced studying, through the processes of repeated review and feedback, also provides a way to overlearn, which, as you now know, is probably the best method for enhancing long-term retention.

The effectiveness of spaced studying varies with the type of material to be learned. Spacing seems to facilitate the retention of meaningless material to a greater extent than meaningful material (Travers, 1967). Nevertheless, both types of material are always retained significantly better if the studying is spaced rather than massed.

PROVIDE FOR OVERLEARNING.   As we mentioned earlier, overlearning requires effort and diligence. Without practice, even the most basic skills can be forgotten. An extreme example of this occurred during World War II, when it was revealed that many illiterate armed forces inductees had previously learned to read (Travers, 1967). It is apparent that they had not practiced their reading skills after leaving school.

UTILIZE ORAL RECITATION.   There are many ways in which you, as students, can use oral recitation as an aid to remembering. For instance, you can participate actively in class discussion, which will enhance your retention of the material as well as give you feedback on the correctness of your responses. Secondly, you can talk about your classwork at home to a friend or relative. This will enable you to get a better idea of what you know and to retain the information for a longer time.

Without practice, basic skills can be forgotten. The oral practice that takes place in a language lab is an aid to retention.

(Robert de Gast, Rapho/Photo Researchers)

PRACTICE MNEMONICS. Psychologists have recently become interested in special strategies for memorization known as mnemonics (Coltheart, 1972), which can be of great use to students who need to memorize large amounts of information. One procedure for memorizing lists of nouns, for example, has been described by Miller, Galanter, and Pribram (1960). It requires the subject to memorize a list by associating each noun with part of another already known list. As an example, let us look at the following word-number pairs: one/bun, two/shoe, three/tree, four/door, five/hive, six/sticks, seven/heaven, eight/gate, nine/line, and ten/hen. Once each of the numbers in this list is paired with a rhyming noun and studied together, the task of remembering any list of ten nouns becomes much easier. All that one has to do is associate each of the nouns in the noun-number pairs with the new noun to be remembered. For instance, if the new word is house, you might visualize a house squashed inside a bun. You might try this technique yourself to see how really effective it can be.

A similar strategy known as the loci method was developed long ago by the Greeks and analyzed in some detail by Bower (1970). In this method, one does not have to remember any initial list of basic words. All one has to do is take a particular geographical location and visualize each word to be remembered on or in a particular place in the location you have chosen. You might choose, for instance, the block on which your home is located and place items in spots going from one end of the block to the other. Say one item is "banana." You might then visualize the tree at one corner of your block as a banana tree, and continue on from there.

While these techniques have been shown to be useful for memorizing word lists, their relevance to learning and retaining concepts taught in school has not been fully demonstrated. Perhaps it is best to rely on such strategies only when it is necessary to remember material in rote fashion, that is, material that does not require conceptual understanding.

In the classroom, the teacher will want to have some way of assessing how much of what has been learned is retained by the students. What follows are several methods for measuring remembering and a discussion of what the teacher might expect to find when he uses them. (Keep in mind that we can measure only what is retained; what is forgotten is defined as that which can no longer be measured.) These methods will be discussed in more detail in Chapter 14.

Methods for Measuring Remembering in the Classroom

RECALL. The recall method is the most familiar measure of remembering. It requires the student to remember as much information as he can with only a minimum number of *cues*—that is, suggestions as to the correct answers—provided to him.

This method is implicitly used by foreign language teachers when they ask students to translate words from the foreign language into English, or, conversely, when they ask students to recall the foreign language equivalent of an English word.

Recall can be tested through the use of various types of questions. One type is the essay question: "Explain the interference theory of forgetting and tell how interference can be prevented in the classroom." Another type is the fill-in question: "_____ inhibition is the type of interference in which earlier learning interferes with new learning." A third type is the identification question: "Identify three types of recall questions that a teacher may use in the classroom."

The recall method is generally considered to be the *least sensitive* measure of remembering. That is, it is least capable of the common testing methods of measuring very small amounts of information retained. It is less likely than other methods to detect a difference between students who know nothing and those who have difficulty remembering. The recall method may be inappropriate when examining students on complex and detailed material; in such cases, the recognition method provides a better index of what the student has remembered.

RECOGNITION.   In assessing recognition, the teacher provides the student with many cues. The multiple-choice question is the most frequently used type of recognition question. You have all had multiple-choice questions in which you receive a list of responses, including the correct one as well as incorrect ones, and were required to recognize the correct one. Here is an example of a recognition question of the multiple-choice type:

> A student who cannot remember some French pronunciations because a lesson on them was followed immediately by one on English pronunciation is said to have experienced
>   a. retroactive inhibition
>   b. proactive inhibition
>   c. overlearning
>   d. transfer of learning

Because of the number of cues provided, recognition is considered to be a more sensitive measure of remembering than the recall method, in which the answer has to be constructed totally from memory. However, when the items on which memory is to be tested are familiar to the student, either the recall or the recognition method will be effective (Davis, Sutherland, and Judd, 1961), since the additional cues provided in recognition are not necessary for remembering. Furthermore, age is a variable affecting the success of these two methods. It seems that the additional cues provided in recognition tests are more necessary for children than for adults (Hall and Pressley, 1973).

Questions for Thought
When you take tests in educational psychology, what is the format you prefer most?
Is the reason for your choice based primarily on your ease of studying or on your goal in taking this course? Explain.

RELEARNING.   Relearning, which you will recall from the discussion of Ebbinghaus's work, is the most sensitive measure of remembering. Ebbinghaus (1913) compared the number of trials needed to learn a list of nonsense syllables with the number of trials needed to relearn it at a later time. If a student takes 80 trials to learn the multiplication tables originally, and only 20 trials to relearn them later, we would say that there was a *savings* of 75 percent over the trials necessary to originally learn the tables.

Relearning clearly is a more effective method than either recall or recognition in measuring material that seems to be forgotten. Although a student may not be able to recall or recognize a series of facts, he may nevertheless be able to relearn the material in fewer trials than he needed the first time he was exposed to the material. We can explain this only by assuming that he has retained, at a minimum level to be sure, some of what he had learned. A teacher could put the relearning method to work when giving students dialogue in a play to learn; he could time how long it took the students to learn the dialogue and then how long it took them to relearn what they had forgotten.

Questions for Thought
Considering the types of test questions discussed in the previous section, which would be the most appropriate for testing the concepts in this chapter? Why?

TRANSFER OF LEARNING

What Is Transfer?

Transfer of learning is the process "that occurs whenever the existence of a previously established habit has an influence upon the acquisition, performance, or relearning of a second habit" (McGeogh and Irion, 1956, p. 299). This concept, which is important in understanding learning, is a significant one for teachers. Our purpose in examining this phenomenon here is to pinpoint the conditions under which classroom teaching influences other situations. We want to know how learning simple skills influences later learning of more complex subject matters. And we want to know how what is taught in the classroom influences the child in his real-life experiences.

POSITIVE AND NEGATIVE TRANSFER.   There are two forms of learning transfer: positive and negative. *Positive transfer* occurs when learning in one activity facilitates learning in a new or similar activity (Ellis, 1972). The conditions under which positive transfer will take place will be one of the following:

1. The two activities have identical elements in them.
2. The two activities have similar required responses.
3. The two activities have similar required techniques.
4. The two activities have similar principles of action.

Classroom applications of the principles of positive transfer abound. For instance, when a student learns arithmetic, then uses the elements of this subject matter when he takes up accounting at a later time, positive transfer occurs. Reading-readiness programs offer a good example of positive transfer in practice. These programs provide young children with exercises that develop the basic skills needed in learning how to read—for instance, discriminating among letters that look alike. If the programs are successful, these identical skills are transferred to learning to read.

BRINGING THE MOUNTAIN TO MOHAMMED

Every teacher knows that textbook information is more easily learned when a student can relate it to real life; when he can see concrete evidence, theories become clearer. This is the rationale behind students' field trips to museums, business establishments, zoos, and farms. But present-day educational costs have frequently forced cutbacks in such trips. One enterprising teacher of a science class at Bellevue Junior High School has found a way to circumvent the loss of her students' field trips to a farm or zoo to observe live animals ("Animals Go to Northgate School," *Pittsburgh Press*, 1975). She's bringing animals to school. One such guest of honor was Gretchen, a goat, and her newborn kid, Heidi Ho Ho. The visit was timed so that it fit into the students' current study of the life cycle of mammals. Said Suzanne Glencer, the teacher: "I kept the umbilical cord of Heidi to show the youngsters an example of the relationship between mother and child before birth" (p. 9). During the visit some of the students also got a chance to milk Gretchen. When the class reaches the point where they're studying the biology of egg-laying animals, Suzanne plans to bring in three different types of chickens. If you can't bring Mohammed to the mountain . . .

In terms of subject matter itself, the teacher has many opportunities to aid positive transfer in his students. English lessons are one obvious instance; students will have to speak and write every day of their lives, and they should learn how responses required in English composition and oral recitation tasks resemble those that they will perform later on in life. Greek mythology, with its emphasis on pride and its tragic consequences, has much to offer students about human relationships. The teacher should point out the similar elements in all people (and in Greek gods, who, after all, have human qualities)—elements that students need to understand if they are going to be successful in their dealings with other people.

The teacher's basic task, then, in facilitating positive transfer, is to provide elements in the classroom that exist in real life, whether they be cognitive skills that exercise the mind and allow it to grow or subject matter and experiences that will occur in later life.

Negative transfer is said to take place when learning in one area interferes with or impedes learning in another area. Negative transfer is another term for retroactive and proactive inhibition discussed earlier. Ellis (1967) points out an example on the motor level of functioning: An American usually has difficulty adjusting to driving on English roads because the English drive on the left side of the road and he has learned to drive on the right. Here the tasks are similar (driving), which provides the setting for transfer; however, the responses are different (different sides of the road), which increases the chances of negative transfer.

Examples of negative transfer in the classroom are numerous. We point them out for the very reason that the teacher should avoid such situations. A teacher may be presenting a certain type of poetry in class—for example, the sonnet—noting its unique length and rhyme scheme. For homework, he assigns several poems and asks the class to find the rhyme scheme in them; these poems, however, are *not* of the sonnet type—they may contain fourteen lines, but do not have the sonnet rhyme scheme. Consequently, because they use the same responses on their homework as they used in class, the students may well be unsuccessful, and we would say that negative transfer has taken place.

The earliest formulation of transfer was embodied in the *doctrine of mental discipline*. According to this doctrine, the mind is composed of faculties such as memory, will, attention, reasoning power, and judgment, which are analogous to muscles in that they need *exercise* to function adequately and become strengthened. Though acknowledged today as theoretically and empirically unsound, this doctrine had a profound effect on American education from its inception to the end of the nineteenth century.

Early Development of the Concept of Transfer

Bigge (1964) cites a statement written in 1865 by a state superintendent of public instruction in Pennsylvania to illustrate how influential these ideas were in the United States:

> The intellectual faculties can receive culture only by judicious exercise. . . . No means are known whereby the faculties of the mind can be developed but by exercising them. By the potent spell of the magic word Exercise, is evoked all human power. (p. 249)

Let's see what sort of exercise these educators recommended.

The exercise came through the study of difficult, and usually classical, subject matter. Latin, Greek, and mathematics were considered ideal subjects for the training of the mind. The intrinsic worth of the subject matter itself was considered to be unimportant, for long after the subject was forgotten, the effects of the training were thought to remain. They believed that the mind was generally strengthened so that it could function better in any subject toward which it was applied.

In fact, it was thought that the more boring and burdensome the subject matter, the more discipline it would require (Bigge, 1964). Thus the more unpleasant and difficult the subject matter, the better. We should all be thankful that our educational training took place after this era of mental discipline!

The first psychologist to seriously question the doctrine of mental discipline was William James in his classic work *Principles of Psychology*, published in 1890. James himself first memorized over 100 lines of Victor Hugo's poem *Satyr*. Then he extensively "exercised" his faculty of memory by memorizing Book I of Milton's *Paradise Lost*. Finally, he tested the theory by once again trying to commit to memory the same number of lines in a different passage from *Satyr*. He found it took longer the second time than it did on his first attempt. Exercise had apparently not strengthened his mind at all. (This is not to say, however, that through experience one cannot learn to memorize more. One learns this because one discovers different devices that help in memorizing, not because one has "strengthened" the mind by memorizing.)

Following James' work, more scientific experiments were undertaken, which led eventually to the demise of the mental discipline doctrine. Thorndike's monumental study of high school was particularly important in this area. This study (Thorndike, 1924) involved a comparison of scores of high school students on a test of reasoning before and after a year's study of the regular high school curriculum. Thorndike reasoned that if classical studies improved the mind, then those students who had taken classics during the previous year would perform better on the test than students who had taken courses in other subjects, such as drama or home economics.

The former group performed only slightly better on the reasoning test than did the latter group. Thorndike accounted for this very slight difference by the initial differences in IQ scores between the two groups, not by any difference in subject matter studied. Thus, he suggested that studies of particular subject matters designed for the purpose of improving the mind did not, in fact, increase mental ability. His findings dealt a fatal blow to the traditional belief that classical subjects enhance a student's general reasoning power.

We now know that transfer takes place, but *how* exactly does it take place? There are two broad theories of transfer—identical elements and generalized principles—that attempt to specify exactly what is transferred from one activity to another.

Theories of Transfer

THEORY OF IDENTICAL ELEMENTS.   As we noted, Edward Thorndike (1924) presented evidence to refute the mental discipline doctrine. But what did Thorndike suggest as a replacement for this theory?

Thorndike believed, on the basis of numerous experiments, that transfer occurs only within a very restricted range of conditions. This range was defined in his now-famous theory of identical elements. Thorndike felt that each individual activity is composed of many precise movements and connections. Transfer occurs to the extent that two activities share in common these composite elements.

Unfortunately, Thorndike was never very precise in specifying exactly what he meant by identical elements. As R. M. Travers (1967) has commented:

> Thorndike [1923] is actually vague concerning what he means by identical elements. In one sentence he speaks of identical elements as "mental processes which have the same cell action in the brain as their physical correlates" (p. 359). However, he does add, "it is of course often not possible to tell just what features of two mental abilities are thus identical." [pp. 239–240]

But even though Thorndike's theory was never completely developed, it contains some basic educational implications.

In general we would say that the amount of transfer from one learning situation to another would depend on the degree to which they both involve responses using the same concepts, operations, and/or symbols. For instance, more positive transfer will take place if one studies mathematics rather than French literature in preparation for a career in accounting. Along the same lines, this theory provides a good starting point for constructing sequences of courses. Of course, it is obvious why one teaches algebra before introducing calculus. Not only is algebra less complex, but it contains many of the symbols and symbolic relational content found in calculus. It should be noted that the organization of the curriculum is considered important by other theorists interested in transfer of learning. We read earlier in Chapter 5, for example, of Bruner's concern for curriculum structure and transfer.

Notice how Thorndike's rationale for adopting teaching material differs from the rationale in the doctrine of mental discipline. Latin, for example, becomes not a course for the exercise of the mind, but rather a means to facilitate learning in other subject areas. Latin might be introduced because its grammatical constructions and vocabulary enable students to gain better insights into the English language as well as other languages they might study.

The theory of identical elements also provides a rationale for bringing more courses into the curriculum that deal with real-life situations. Such topics as community problems, family and personal living, and so on can help to bridge the gap between the classroom and the everyday world. In general, Thorndike's theory suggests that teachers should not assume that transfer is a magical process that occurs frequently and readily from one subject area to another. Instead it suggests that teachers ought to gear their instruction to very specific topics. The direction of teaching is best, according to this framework, when it goes from specific to general and not the other way around.

Question for Thought

Classical Greek and Latin are still taught as part of the curriculum to many students today, but usually not for the purpose of exercising the mind. These subjects are now taught for their applicability in solving certain problems related to linguistics, to name just one purpose. Can you give some examples in which learning of classical Greek or Latin may be transferred to situations other than those already cited in this text?

THEORY OF GENERALIZED PRINCIPLES. Charles Judd (1908) proposed a theory of transfer that contrasts in many ways with Thorndike's theory of identical elements. Judd suggested that the process of transfer is based upon an understanding of the principle or generalization underlying the responses made in two or more activities. If a general principle is understood, Judd claimed, all the instances of the principle will be put into perspective and readily understood. Judd (1939) defined this kind of general principle as "a kind of summary of many experiences. It makes possible the proper interrelating and interpreting of a whole body of varied experiences" (p. 496).

Judd's classic dart-throwing experiment (1908) illustrates the power of his theory. Two groups of 11-year-old boys were first given training in trying to hit a target placed approximately 12 inches under water. Their training differed in one respect. The principle of refraction, that is, the distortion of light under water, was explained to one group and not to the other. Both groups, however, were allowed to master the task to an equal proficiency.

Two new tasks were then presented to the boys in both groups. These tasks simply involved a change in the depth at which the object was placed under water, first to 4 inches and then to 8 inches. The results clearly supported Judd's theory. The group that was instructed in the principle of refraction performed significantly better in both of these instances. In other words, transfer was exhibited only when the subjects understood the principle underlying the tasks they engaged in.

These results represent a serious challenge to Thorndike's theory of identical elements. All three dart-throwing tasks have a good deal in common by whatever standards one adopts. Accordingly, Thorndike would have predicted that transfer should have been manifested by both groups. At least in this context Judd's theory provides a much better explanation of the data than does Thorndike's theory.

Further support for Judd's theory comes from a study comparing different methods of teaching Latin (Hamblen, 1925). The measure of transfer in this experiment was the degree to which the study of Latin facilitated the ability of a student to understand English derivatives. Three teaching conditions were employed. In the first one, no effort at all was directed toward promoting transfer; in the second, many examples of derivations were introduced; and in the third, these examples were related to the principles of derivation. The degree of transfer was found to be significantly greater under the third condition. Again we see that identical elements were not sufficient to induce transfer, although an understanding of the principles involved was.

Numerous classroom examples can be generated to fit Judd's model. The main criterion, of course, is for the student to recognize two situations as related by and organized under the same principle (Thornburg, 1973). The principle of division as illustrated in the context of short division should thus transfer to the learning of long division. Similarly, if this text teaches principles of educational psychology properly, you should be able to apply the principles you learn to a variety of situations you will encounter in your student teaching and later in your regular classrooms.

Actually, the teacher can make use of Thorndike's and Judd's theories at the same time. For example, in some cases it may not even be necessary for two tasks to share any common elements, as long as they are related through some common principles. Learning how to drive a car, for example, may facilitate learning how to operate a motorboat. Here both the mechanics and instrumentation differ in the two tasks, yet because of some shared principles, there is a possibility for at least some transfer to occur. Perhaps this is what the cognitive-field theorists referred to as the "gestalt" of the task, which tended to allow for greater transfer.

The problem of specifying more precisely when transfer will occur even if two tasks share a principle in common still needs to be elaborated. One significant step in this direction was made in the context of an experiment conducted by Haslerud and Meyers (1958). Simply stated, they found that a principle was more likely to effect transfer if a student himself derived the principle as opposed to merely having the principle recited to him by the teacher. We are then left with a further recommendation of the discovery method of teaching (you might review Chapter 5 to refresh your memory on this approach).

In general, the educational implications derived from Judd's theory are quite different from, and even contrary to, those derived from Thorndike's theory. Instead of proceeding from the particular to the general, Judd recommended that teaching ought to proceed from the general to the specific. It is, for Judd, the generalized principles that enable a student to relate a wide diversity of facts and concepts. Rather than studying a large number of fractions to understand how they operate, one would simply use a few illustrative examples to explain the theory behind the operation of fractions (Bigge, 1964). In economics, the notion that single-crop economies can lead to disaster enables the student to put into perspective numerous historical and present-day examples (Travers, 1972). Judd, as should be obvious by now, considered transfer a most pervasive phenomenon.

In conclusion, the similarity between Judd's position and the Gestalt position should be noted. The Gestalt psychologists, of course, stressed that the organization of an entity was more basic than its individual components. Thus both the Gestalt psychologists and Judd differ from Thorndike in emphasizing the importance of higher-order principles over particulars. In fact, the only source of meaning for particulars is found in organization and higher-order principles.

HOW TO INCREASE POSITIVE TRANSFER IN CLASSROOM LEARNING

Once again, regardless of the theory espoused, the necessity for positive transfer in the classroom cannot be overemphasized. The goals of education cannot be realized unless what is learned in the classroom is related or transferred to situations outside the classroom. Within the classroom, positive transfer reduces the sheer amount of material that must be learned by providing a means to facilitate learning from one situation to another. In these concluding sections suggestions for increasing positive transfer will be elucidated so that they can be readily adopted by the experienced teacher as well as by the teacher-in-training.

MAKE CLASSROOM TASKS SIMILAR IN SOME RESPECT. The fact that there are a number of ways in which similarity of tasks can and has been defined does not reduce its influence as a factor in the process of transfer (Ellis, 1967). In general, one would be safe in assuming that positive transfer will be increased to the extent that two activities are similar or, more precisely, that they have similar stimuli or responses.

One way in which similarity has been defined is in terms of a known physical scale such as size or brightness. Let's say we changed the traffic rules so that cars would be required to stop at an orange light instead of a red light (Ellis, 1972). Drivers would probably have little difficulty obeying the new signal. In other words, there would be a high degree of positive transfer between the two conditions. The similarity between the two stimuli—their color resemblance—would be the condition that would facilitate positive transfer between the two situations.

Similarity has also been viewed in terms of the judgments of subjects (Ellis, 1967). Two or more stimuli are presented to each subject who then rates the stimuli according to their perceived similarity. The variety of dimensions that can be employed is almost unlimited.

Notice that these two methods of assessing similarity parallel the difference between Thorndike's theory and Judd's theory. Thorndike's theory of identical elements would be more compatible with a definition of similarity in terms of objective, externally established criteria, whereas Judd's theory of generalized principles would be more compatible with a subjective determination of similarity. Subjective similarity, in Judd's theoretical framework, would reflect the degree to which a subject related stimuli through a given principle.

Whichever criteria one adopts, the teacher should try to arrange the curriculum so that the concepts and information introduced are similar in nature. This strategy will, of course, optimize the degree of positive transfer that takes place. On the other hand, the teacher should definitely try to avoid situations where different responses to very similar stimuli are learned.

On the elementary school level, a teacher might, for instance, teach a unit on energy production. The subject matter could be introduced with a general account of how energy makes things work. Then several examples could be shown: a water wheel and a windmill, each running a simple engine of some sort. The general principle of energy making things work would bring about positive transfer in Judd's sense from the first example to the second. In teaching an elementary school unit on drawing skills, a teacher might first ask the students to produce their own drawings. As a homework assignment, they could be required to make up a list of examples of art they see around them in their daily lives. In class, they could be asked to relate their lists—posters, graffiti, pictures on the walls at home, and so on—to their own work. Positive transfer will occur through their perception of similarities, and hopefully they will come to see something of what goes into making a drawing, whether their own or someone else's.

On the high school level, an English teacher could present two different works of literature—for example, a poem and a play—that illustrate similar themes. He could also present two works of literature by the same author—for example, *A Tale of Two Cities* and *Great Expectations* by Charles Dickens—and point out that although the plots and themes of the two differ, similar elements deriving from the author's unique style and point of view tie the two together. Thus, positive transfer would occur, and the students would understand the richness of the literature provided by Dickens.

POINT OUT SIMILARITIES BETWEEN CLASSROOM TASKS AND TASKS IN OUTSIDE SITUATIONS. The process of transfer from classroom to applications outside school has been stressed throughout this chapter. Needless to say, the teacher should not assume that such transfer will occur automatically. Only when students have the *expectation that transfer will occur* will it take place. In fact, merely pointing to the possibility of transfer can significantly enhance its occurrence.

In an experiment conducted 45 years ago (Dorsey and Hopkins, 1930), two groups of subjects received comparable training in a specific area. Then they were all given a test on which they could show the benefit of that training. One group had been given explicit instructions on how to apply the previously learned material to the test material; the second had not been given such instructions. The result was that the group receiving transfer instructions performed significantly better on the test.

By pointing out how concepts discussed in class can actually be applied in outside situations, the teacher can help to increase students' positive transfer to these later situations (Andrews and Cronbach, 1950). In teaching addition and subtraction, an elementary school teacher could have students make up sample checkbooks. The very obvious application of classroom arithmetic to real-life circumstances would be seen by the class. At a higher level, a high school economics teacher, in presenting a unit on the stock market, could have his students "invest" in a sample portfolio of stocks and bonds and have them follow in the daily newspaper the fluctuations in the market value of their holdings. At both the elementary and high school levels, teachers could develop economics concepts by using examples of the inflation-recession cycle as they affect the students' daily lives: Has the high unemployment rate made it difficult for you to get a summer job? Why? Has your mother told you that you'd have to wait for next year until you can get a new bicycle? Why?

The opportunities to relate classwork to real life are endless. It is up to the teacher to be aware of them and use them as frequently as he can.

TEACH FOR GENERAL (NONSPECIFIC) TRANSFER: LEARNING HOW TO LEARN.   Thus far we have tried to pinpoint the specific dimensions of similarity that facilitate positive transfer. Transfer, however, can also occur between two situations that share general (nonspecific) factors (Ellis, 1972). Through practice on related tasks, students become progressively more capable of solving new tasks, although the new tasks may be more difficult (Ellis, 1972). They have learned general techniques of problem-solving or modes of attack, regardless of the specific content of past situations. In effect, through general transfer, they are *learning how to learn.*

The existence of this phenomenon has been documented by Harry Harlow (1949). In his work with monkeys, Harlow investigated a discrimination-learning problem. A monkey had to discriminate between two objects. If it picked the one arbitrarily chosen as "correct," it received a reward. Eight monkeys engaged in 344 different discrimination tasks, each of which was run for a predetermined number of trials. The critical finding was that the monkeys gradually performed better on each new task, despite the fact that the tasks differed in terms of the attribute rewarded. For instance, a red ball and not a yellow ball might be correct in one task, the attribute being "redness"; and in the next task, a red triangle and not a red ball might be correct, the attribute being "triangular shape." The monkeys improved in their ability to solve the general problem. In other words, they learned how to learn.

Teachers can find many ways to put this principle into action. In general, practice in problem-solving can enable a student to better solve problems in the future, although the teacher should always be aware that practice for its own sake is of no value. Specifically, let us say a teacher has his class learn how to figure out percentages. He can then present them with instances in which the problem is to find a percentage—for example, interest on a bank account, sales tax, a tip on a restaurant check, and so on. In this way, they will transfer the general problem-solving ability to new tasks, without rote practice.

As Judd demonstrated long ago, the outcome of practice depends on the context in which it occurs. More recently, an experiment extended this idea and determined that even the manner in which a principle is introduced affects the extent of transfer (Overing and Travers, 1966). The results of the experiment indicated that transfer is best facilitated when the introduction of a principle is preceded by a practice problem. This "warm-up" practice problem enables the individual to better comprehend the principle than if it were introduced "cold."

PROVIDE SUFFICIENT PRACTICE.   Overlearning works to ensure transfer in the same way that it works to increase long-term retention. That is, once having mastered a task, the student is more likely to transfer his skills to another task. For instance, a biology student who masters through practice the techniques involved in dissecting a frog will be better able to move on to a more complicated specimen, a fetal pig, let us say.

In some cases, however, initial practice on one task may increase the probability of negative transfer to another task. If the two tasks require different responses to similar stimuli, then negative transfer will occur. However, if the first task is sufficiently well learned, positive transfer will occur, even in these cases. In the dissection example, not *all* techniques are alike for dissecting a frog and a fetal pig, and some negative transfer may take place. But if a student has learned the general techniques of dissection, he will be able to transfer his skills without being inhibited by the differences in responses required in the two tasks.

A biology student who masters the techniques of dissecting a frog will be better able to move on to dissecting a more complicated specimen.

(Bruce Roberts, Rapho/Photo Researchers)

In addition to practice, positive transfer is more likely to increase if there is a wide variety in training tasks; that is, the more variety the student encounters as he engages in overlearning a given task, the better are the chances that there will be positive transfer to other tasks. For this reason, we emphasize once again that repeated drills on the same material have little value. By presenting problems to his students from a number of perspectives, a teacher can facilitate positive transfer. For instance, in teaching students to use punctuation correctly in compound sentences, he can present different types of sentences on which students can practice — declarative sentences, questions, and commands. This will serve to stabilize learning and thus make it more transferable.

DEVELOP MEANINGFUL GENERALIZATIONS.   Although we have stressed how important it is to learn principles, such learning is not a goal in and of itself. If students have learned a principle, yet can apply it only in a restricted number of contexts, the principle is not meaningful. Teachers should be aware of this, and to avoid it should present the principle to their students in several ways and in several contexts, so that it is generalized. As Andrews and Cronbach (1950) comment: "One may memorize Caesar's biography, or may observe in it the consequences of concentrated power" (p. 304).

To avoid too great an emphasis on the particulars of subject matter at the expense of the meaningful implications of the material, teachers have many options. For instance, they can present several tragedies by Shakespeare — *Macbeth*, *King Lear*, *Hamlet*, and *Othello*, for example — to point out the general nature of the tragic hero. Although the particular qualities of each man should be discussed, the outcome of the study of this subject matter should be an understanding of the general concept of the tragic hero. Similarly, a discussion of American foreign policy should not deal solely with the United States' relations with one nation — for example, the Soviet Union — but rather how our philosophy of foreign relations is manifested in our dealings with a number of nations — for example, the Soviet Union, France, Spain, and so on.

DECREASE NEGATIVE TRANSFER (INTERFERENCE).   Negative transfer is more likely to occur when different responses are associated with the same or very similar stimuli in two learning situations. Negative transfer does not occur when the stimuli in two tasks are very different; rather, it occurs when the stimuli in the two tasks are only slightly different. For instance, we would not expect negative transfer to occur between algebra and English literature, but we would expect it to occur between algebra and geometry.

The meaningfulness of the material appears to affect the degree of negative transfer. Ausubel (1968), for one, has suggested that negative transfer is minimal when material is meaningful. Thornburg

(1973), on the other hand, has summarized several studies that reveal that negative transfer has occurred with meaningful material. Underwood (1957) tried to clarify these data by considering other variables, such as time of learning, emotional and motivational factors, distribution of practice, and so on.

In general, though, negative transfer is reduced by making material more meaningful. In fact, this reduction of negative transfer might clearly have been what Bruner was advocating in his discussion of discovery learning. Discovery learning, you will remember from Chapter 5, requires that subject matter be organized in such a way that it will be meaningful to the student.

Negative transfer is related to the storage and retrieval processes. Greeno, James, and DaPolito (1971) have proposed a model for such a relationship. They suggest that negative transfer involves two processes. The first is concerned with interference in storage; it is their hypothesis that it is difficult to store a stimulus-response association if the stimulus has been stored previously in association with a different response. For instance, if "Benjamin Franklin" has been stored as the discoverer of electricity in lightning, interference will occur when trying to store him as a United States ambassador to France unless special attempts are made on the part of the learner.

The second process in negative transfer is concerned with the retrieval process. The hypothesis is that negative transfer will occur when a stimulus has been used as a retrieval cue at a former time; in other words, when the same item acts as a cue in two different retrieval systems. For example, if "Benjamin Franklin" is a retrieval cue for "Famous American Scientists" and for "Famous American Diplomats," there might be interference.

RECOGNIZE INDIVIDUAL DIFFERENCES IN POSITIVE TRANSFER ABILITY. Individual differences do tend to affect the facilitation of positive transfer. Certain variables are correlated with this differential ability, although it should be noted that this does not mean that individual characteristics cause positive transfer. These characteristics include the following:

1. Age—in general, the older the child, the more capable he is of positive transfer (Gladis, 1960).
2. IQ—the higher the child's IQ, the more capable he is of positive transfer (Craig, 1953).
3. Motivation—anxiety, for example, tends to hinder positive transfer (Spence, 1964).

The phenomena of remembering, forgetting, and transferring learning are considered as complementary aspects of a continuous learning process. In this chapter, theories and practical classroom applications of these phenomena are presented. The long-term memory of skills learned in school and the transfer of learning are the goals toward which the teacher should aim.

SUMMARY

There are three types of memory: sensory information storage, short-term memory, and long-term memory. The last is obviously the most important in education.

Theories of memory fall into several general categories, and they are related to theories discussed in earlier chapters. Associationist theories (Chapter 4) view memory as a "response produced by a stimulus"; this approach includes fading theory, which explains forgetting as the fading of the neurological memory trace, and interference theory, which proposes the processes of retroactive and proactive inhibition. Motivation theories (Chapter 6) invoke the psychological mechanism of repression to explain forgetting. Gestalt theories (Chapter 5) rely on the laws of organization to explain the fading of the memory trace. Cybernetic theories postulate a model of information flow to explain the memory process.

The goal of increasing long-term memory can be achieved in many ways. The teacher can help the student to reach this goal by making the curriculum meaningful, structuring the curriculum appropriately, reducing the effects of interference, providing immediate feedback, and providing opportunities for student oral recitation. The student himself can develop proper study habits, can space and time study sessions, can provide for overlearning, and can practice mnemonics to increase his long-term retention.

The degree of remembering can be measured in several ways: recall method, recognition method, and degree of relearning.

Transfer of learning is explained by two different theories: Thorndike's theory of identical elements, which postulates that transfer occurs to the extent that two activities share a common element, and which disproved the mental discipline doctrine; and Judd's theory of generalized principles, which maintains that transfer occurs from one act to another if they are related by a common principle. The methods that a teacher can use in the classroom to increase positive transfer are: making classroom tasks similar to those outside school, pointing out similarities between classroom tasks and tasks in outside situations, teaching for general (nonspecific) transfer (learning how to learn), providing sufficient practice, and developing meaningful generalizations. Most of the techniques that enhance long-term memory also facilitate positive transfer.

SUGGESTED FOR FURTHER READING

Duncan, C. P., Sechrest, L., and Melton, A. W. (Eds.). *Human memory: Festschrift for Benton J. Underwood.* New York: Appleton-Century-Crofts, 1972.

This book contains the papers presented at a conference of psychologists on human memory in 1971. All aspects of memory and forgetting, including theoretical models and research evidence, are discussed.

Ellis, H. C. *The transfer of learning.* New York: Macmillan, 1967.

Ellis does a good job of covering all aspects of transfer of learning. The final section contains reprints of original articles by well-known theorists such as Underwood and Harlow.

Halacy, D. S. *Man and memory.* New York: Harper & Row, 1970.

This is an easy-to-read book on difficult memory theories covered in this chapter. Halacy also reports on ways to improve long-term memory, as well as on physiological and computer memory models.

Journal of Verbal Learning and Verbal Behavior and *Memory and Cognition.* These two monthly journals contain articles devoted to the topics discussed in this chapter. Current theoretical models and experimental research are reported here.

Norman, D. A. (Ed.). *Models of human memory.* New York: Academic Press, 1970.

This collection of readings contains detailed descriptions of memory and forgetting prepared by theorists covered in this chapter. Other models are also discussed.

ALTERNATIVE INSTRUCTIONAL DESIGNS FOR THE CLASSROOM

CHAPTER 9

After completing this chapter, the reader should be able to:

1 Select innovative instructional designs or design new instructional techniques through reorganization of existing school staffs in order to individualize instruction and increase classroom learning.

2 Justify selection of these techniques on the basis of learning and developmental principles discussed earlier in this text.

3 Select available instructional equipment and other educational materials most suitable for these instructional techniques.

4 Justify choices of instructional techniques in terms of their effectiveness in increasing learning at different chronological age levels and for different individuals.

5 Assess the value of each technique on the basis of needs of particular students, faculty, and communities.

INTRODUCTION

We are concerned in this chapter with the application of theory to classroom instruction. The instructional designs we will consider require major changes in the curriculum and a great deal of planning and effort on the part of many people. The preceding chapters in Part 2 emphasized classroom applications and innovations that teachers can implement themselves. Before proceeding further, let us review these classroom applications.

Chapter 4 covered the basic principles of relatively simple kinds of learning (for example, conditioning) and their application to behavior management in the classroom. Classical conditioning was considered in relation to the development of fear and anxiety in the school environment. Operant conditioning was discussed in terms of the beneficial effects of positive reinforcement on student learning (particularly attention and praise from the teacher) and the detrimental effects of continued negative reinforcement. The interest that the behavior management approach to teaching has generated was also discussed.

Chapter 5 was devoted to cognitive learning theories — from the basic laws of organization introduced by the Gestalt psychologists in the early twentieth century to the views of prominent contemporary learning theorists such as Jerome Bruner. The cognitive approach to teaching is geared toward building understanding. The teacher helps the student appreciate the structure of a subject, and encourages the use of intuition and insight. Bruner and his followers emphasize an approach called "discovery teaching," in which students learn primarily through questioning and exploration.

Chapter 6 was concerned with learning as a form of purposeful behavior. Theorists of this approach believe that classroom learning is motivated by and can be applied to a wide variety of human needs, including achievement, identity, equilibrium, curiosity, and exploration. We also described Maslow's hierarchy of needs, which proposes that if a child's basic needs such as hunger have not been met, he will not be motivated to satisfy what Maslow considers more advanced needs such as self-actualization. This problem is often seen in socially disadvantaged youngsters as a result of poverty.

In Chapter 7, three related aspects of learning that are of particular importance to teachers were discussed: types of learning, outcomes of learning, and individual learning styles. We described five different types of learning — perceptual learning, motor learning, language learning, concept learning and problem-solving, and attitude learning — and their application to the classroom. We examined the differences in students' learning styles, and indicated how teachers could use this information to aid learning.

Chapter 8 considered various theories of retention and forgetting. Two basic goals of educators with regard to memory are to increase long-term retention and to facilitate transfer of information to new learning situations.

As we mentioned, the applications discussed in these earlier chapters require for their implementation only the innovativeness of the individual teacher. Chapter 9, on the other hand, examines instructional designs that require either a major reorganization of the school or the adoption of elaborate equipment intended to provide feedback. Both of these innovations require the joint efforts of an entire school staff (and, in some cases, the community) for their implementation. The goals of these programs are similar to those mentioned in previous chapters: to allow for greater individualization of instruction.

Certain curricular innovations presented in this chapter require hardware (such as the computer-assisted instruction programs); others do not (for example, the open classroom method). Teachers can now make use of a wide variety of communication media and modes of instruction. Many traditional methods are still used, including tutoring sessions, lectures, student recitation, class discussion, laboratory work, and homework assignments (Gagné, 1970). In addition, teachers can experiment with techniques such as demonstrations, motion pictures and television, programmed instruction, and assessment exercises. Thus, the teacher can blend the most effective elements of traditional education with a variety of technological innovations.

ALTERNATIVE INSTRUCTIONAL DESIGNS FOR PRESCHOOL EDUCATION

Many innovative and important instructional designs for preschool education were discussed at some length in Part 1. In this chapter, we will examine two additional innovations—Montessori teaching and educational television. Although they are not new, Montessori schools have, in recent years, become more and more popular in the United States. Modern Montessori schools are providing stimulating sensory environments where young children learn to speak, read, and write with unprecedented ease.

A newer approach to early education, educational television, has gained international acclaim through its ability to entertain and educate youngsters at the same time. An example of educational TV programming is the now famous *Sesame Street*, which will be discussed in detail.

The Montessori method of teaching is one of the oldest and one of the most successful methods of increasing cognitive development in preschool children. This approach has recently become popular

Montessori Programming

Children at work on a prereading exercise in a Montessori classroom.

(Nancy Hays from Monkmeyer)

in the United States, but the Montessori movement has been active in European education for decades.

Maria Montessori, an Italian doctor, developed her theories of education through extensive work with slum children in Italy. After observing the turbulence and chaos of the children's home conditions, Montessori determined that they could be successfully educated only in a carefully manipulated, orderly environment. Through her efforts to structure such classrooms and her work in creating materials that build sensory and cognitive skills, Montessori developed a theory of teaching and learning. Her ideas became the basis for a network of schools which spread across the European continent during the early 1900s, and which are today renowned throughout the world.

A key notion in Montessori teaching is the "planned environment." The cleanliness, neatness, and stability of the classroom are of prime importance. Everything in the classroom, from the dimensions of the furniture to its arrangement, is carefully designed with the youngsters in mind. Ideally, the program allows for freedom of movement within the room, but the children must be orderly and must use materials properly. The teacher carefully demonstrates how to handle the materials in order to prevent random, disruptive, or destructive use of them by the children (Banta, 1972).

Montessori education emphasizes motor and sensory training, as well as overall cognitive and social skills. Montessori saw all of these areas of education as interconnected; she believed that the child must master sensory and motor tasks in order to succeed in intellectual areas, such as reading and writing. Montessori created letters and shapes cut out of brightly colored sandpaper, with which she taught cognitive skills to 4-year-olds. The children were given a letter, told its name, and encouraged to repeat the name while rubbing their fingers over the letter and tracing its pattern. Through the use of such materials and methods, 4-year-olds have learned to read and write in a month and a half.

Montessori believed that preschool children have an almost insatiable thirst for new words and an almost inexhaustible capacity for learning them. She demonstrated that young children could learn and retain difficult scientific and technical terms. Montessori believed that the word-learning process could be stimulated even further by presenting words that related most directly to the objects and experiences in the child's home environment (Montessori, 1967).

Montessori also felt that preschool children should not be segregated by age for the purpose of learning. Thus, a typical Montessori classroom includes children of ages 3 to 6 (Montessori, 1967). Montessori believed that the learning atmosphere is more interesting if children of different ages are in the classroom together. Younger children will often ask for and receive assistance from older ones. This is satisfying to the older children and at the same time allows the younger children to learn by observing other children.

In Montessori schools, separate classrooms are normally maintained for the 3- to 6-year-old group and for the 7- to 9-year-old group. But even in this arrangement, the children pass freely from one classroom to another. They observe each other's behavior and learning, work on certain common projects, and learn to relate to children of different ages. Sometimes, the younger children are surprised to discover that they can understand the material being taught to the older children (Montessori, 1967).

Montessori (1967) summarized all of these points in the following description of the classroom atmosphere in her schools:

> The child's progress does not depend only on his age, but also on being free to look about him . . . . Our schools are alive. To understand what the older ones are doing fills the little ones with enthusiasm. The older ones are happy to be able to teach what they know. There are no inferiority complexes, but everyone achieves a healthy normality through the mutual exchange of spiritual energy. (p. 228)

Private Montessori schools, usually serving middle- and upper-income children, have recently been established in many cities in the United States. In one sense, this development is ironic, since the Montessori method was originally designed to meet the needs of low-income slum children in Italy. However, many urban school systems have developed preschool programs for socially disadvan-taged children that rely heavily on the Montessori method.

Question for Thought

Montessori used many of the basic learning principles discussed in earlier chapters in her approach to teaching. Can you suggest particular theorists who would be likely to advocate her approach?

Public Educational Television for the Preschool Audience

One of the limitations of many preschool educational programs in the United States such as the Montessori program is that a young child typically attends school for only three hours a day. Yet the same child may spend an equal or greater number of hours at home watching television. For this reason, the development of public educational television programs for preschool children can, if properly designed, fill the void that now exists in the education of young Americans.

As a method of instruction for the preschool children, educational television (or ETV) is a popular and welcome medium combining sight, sound, motion, and instantaneous transmission.

"ETV" and "instructional television (ITV)" are often used inter-changeably, but the terms do not mean the same thing. The ETV designation is generally reserved for programs on noncommercial channels that the Federal Communications Commission has specifi-cally allocated for educational purposes (Steinberg, 1974). ITV, on the other hand, refers to special broadcasts that provide formal course instruction in a logical sequence. Whereas ETV programs are usually transmitted in open circuit systems available to the public at large, most ITV programs are transmitted via cable in a closed cir-cuit system, thus restricting their availability. Many college cam-puses and some school districts receive ITV.

Of all ETV programs, best known by far is *Sesame Street*. *Sesame Street* has become famous throughout America and around the world. The material on *Sesame Street* is carefully planned and exten-sively researched. The staff considers such factors as how preschool children learn, how their environment is structured, and the range of experiences they normally have. *Sesame Street* presentations rely on *modeling* as an important variable in shaping young children's be-havior. The model on *Sesame Street* may clap his hands, snap his fingers, say a letter of the alphabet, or do any number of other things that, when the children imitate them, can produce changes in both their simple motor skills and their verbal aptitude.

A special effort is made to use models that socially disadvantaged children can identify with, such as members of various minority groups. These models speak in the language or dialect most familiar to minority children, as well as in standard English. The use of minority group models certainly accounts in part for the enormous appeal of *Sesame Street* among socially disadvantaged children.

A critical problem for the staff of the program is how to maintain the attention of the preschool child. *Sesame Street* uses a variety of techniques to keep children entertained and therefore attentive. Material is made familiar through repetition. In addition, a group of characters (animated figures, puppets, cutouts, as well as real people) are featured regularly, each with a distinct personality. Thus,

COMMERCIAL TELEVISION SHOWS: NEW LEARNING RESOURCE

The E. Washington Rhodes Middle School in North Philadelphia has a new course that is attracting national attention (Waters, 1974). The Language Arts TV Program is an experimental project devised by two Philadelphia teachers, Bernard Solomon and Michael McAndrew, who were concerned about the reading problems that underlie most academic failure. Most inner-city children, they found, are not interested in the reading texts prescribed for them. They provide neither motivation nor relevance, with the result that "three out of four students in most major urban schools read below grade level" (Waters, 1974, p. 7). What *are* children interested in? Television. Solomon and McAndrew decided to incorporate the unlimited resource of commercial television shows into a teaching program.

The course features one class per week with television sets and three follow-up classes per week without them. In the TV-reading classroom, children sit before a small videotape recorder and two television monitors. The *Lucy* show, for example, progresses by starts and stops; the children glance up at the screen to take in a visual joke, then attend to the scripts on their desks. The teacher switches off the TV to introduce a new fact, make an observation, or ask questions that prompt class discussion. The children often read and "act" parts in a script; in fact, during the course of a year, each student works his way through six 35- to 80-page scripts (provided by the shows' producers).

With the emphasis still on reading, the program includes other subjects (which utilize various teaching materials in conjunction with the TV shows). A segment of *Sanford and Son* might lead to a discussion of racial attitudes; *Kojak* and *Police Woman* might lead to a study of courts, law enforcement, the judicial system; and *The Waltons* might serve as the text for a class on history, psychology, philosophy, economics, or religion. The possibilities, says McAndrew, are limitless for the inventive teacher.

The program has turned on both students and teachers. Absentee rates for both groups have dropped. In class, teachers are more imaginative and students more eager to learn. Reading scores have risen. The success of the Language Arts TV Program has prompted queries and visits from educators at all levels, from grade school to university. Even the Children's Television Workshop (*Sesame Street*) has come to Solomon and McAndrew for lessons.

the children become acquainted with (and attached to) such figures as the Cookie Monster, Big Bird, and Kermit the Frog. *Sesame Street* also employs many special audiovisual effects. For example, the alphabet is taught with a device called a "speech balloon," which spouts from the mouth of one of the characters.

The *Sesame Street* staff believes that children deserve respect — that they are important people in their own right. Characters on the program speak at a vocabulary level that children can understand and identify with. They avoid preaching or telling children exactly what to do in each situation. Instead, they assume that children are intelligent, and are capable of reasoning and learning.

Sesame Street is constantly being evaluated by both educators and parents, and tests have been conducted to determine its effects on children's learning skills. The results show that the program not only improves cognitive skills but also builds positive attitudes such as cooperation.

Another prominent and successful children's educational television program is *The Electric Company*, created in 1971. This program is designed primarily to teach children to read. Like *Sesame Street*, it uses special effects such as animation and music to hold the viewer's attention. However, *The Electric Company* is for a somewhat older audience than *Sesame Street*; it is geared to children in the first four grades of elementary school (Cazden, 1972; Steinberg, 1974).

Questions for Thought
On the basis of all of the hours spent by the American child in front of the TV set at home, and the clear-cut evidence that TV can serve as a potent educational tool, we are faced with the necessity of asking ourselves a very important question: Who ought to determine what goes into educational TV programs? Educators together with TV production staffs? Private enterprise (in the case of commercial TV)? Officials appointed by the TV station? Parents?
What decisions ought the public to have in monitoring such programs?
If you think monitoring should occur, can you think of a viable method of implementing it?

ALTERNATIVE INSTRUCTIONAL DESIGNS FOR TRADITIONAL PUBLIC ELEMENTARY AND HIGH SCHOOL PROGRAMS

Montessori teaching and educational television have made important contributions to the education of preschool children. Yet the remarkable progress that a child can make during these years becomes meaningless unless subsequent school experiences are equally rewarding. For this reason, many curricular innovations have been developed to stimulate and assist the learning of public school students of all ages. These include the open classroom method of learning; various programs emphasizing individualized instruction; methods that rely on technological aids to help in classroom education; and teaching methods that depart from traditional student and teacher roles. All of these innovative programs will be discussed in detail in this section.

During the last 20 years, classroom procedures based on rigid, authoritarian disciplinary measures have been widely challenged, both in the United States and abroad. One alternative, developed over the past 50 years by the British Central Advisory Council for Education, advocates a more informal style of teaching and is commonly known as the *open classroom.*

The Open Classroom

Actually, such terms as the open classroom, open education, and informal teaching refer to an underlying attitude toward education, rather than to a particular method of instruction (Gibson, 1972). These terms describe the key recommendations of the 1967 Plowden Report, a comprehensive analysis of modern British primary school practices conducted by the British Central Advisory Council for Education.

The Plowden Report was concerned with the quality of instruction in the British "infant schools," schools for children from age 5 to age 7 or 8. One of the critical findings was that the most successful schools tended to be "open" in their approach to teaching. Administrators allowed a considerable amount of freedom both in daily classroom activities and in curricular planning. Children in such schools showed increased interest in schoolwork and excellent rapport with teachers (British Central Advisory Council for Education, 1967).

The open classroom method had its roots in the motivation and cognitive-field theories of learning and in the theoretical work of such researchers as Piaget and Montessori (Gibson, 1972; Gross and Gross, 1970). Piaget determined that the ways and rates at which children learn depend on their particular stage of development. Montessori's method is also based on the premise that children learn at different rates and that the classroom environment must be sufficiently flexible to accommodate children with a variety of interests and abilities.

Open classrooms, therefore, contain many different kinds of learning materials for children at varying stages of development, in order to stimulate curiosity and interest. The major responsibility for choosing materials rests with the teacher, who continually talks with students about their interests and preferences (Allender, 1972; Featherstone, 1971; Gibson, 1972).

Resnick (1971) has suggested that the open classroom teacher, by

A UNIQUE EDUCATIONAL RESOURCE

Instead of a book, children in Walnut Creek, California, can check out a bunny—or possibly a rat, guinea pig, or chinchilla—at the community's Pet Library Club, a bustling part of the Alexander Lindsay, Jr., Museum (Clifford, 1975). These are among the 250 animals youngsters can take home for a week. A prime (but not exclusive) purpose of the library is to give children the opportunity to learn the responsibility needed in taking care of a pet. The library provides a cage and food. The only requirements to join the pet-lending program are that a child be 6 years old and that the parents sign a consent form. With parents and children participating, instances of mistreatment are a rarity. Says the museum director, Sam Smoker, "We probably have the most extensive checkout program of its kind in the country. Mostly we try to have animals that are native to our area. It's only through getting to know and understand the wild creatures that people can learn to appreciate and protect them" (Clifford, 1975, p. E-1). Not that the children can take out wild animals. But by taking home the tame, domesticated varieties, they learn the value of nature's creatures and a sense of responsibility toward them. And there is yet another aspect to the program. The director notes: "People have fears regarding certain animals and by getting to know them these fears can be overcome." Thus, through the adult volunteers who work with local schools, Claire, the resident boa constrictor, is taken on tours to classrooms where the children can pet her. Black vultures are also other visitors, staff members insisting that "to know a vulture is to love a vulture." Whether that is true or not is debatable. One thing is not. The Pet Library Club, judging from the children's response, is dealing in best sellers.

questioning the students and giving them individual attention, serves as a powerful model for building a positive attitude toward free inquiry and environmental exploration.

THE OPEN CLASSROOM IN ENGLAND.   The open educational system in England is often described as the "integrated day program," because there are very few fixed time periods for which a specific activity is compulsory (Rathbone, 1972). Instead, individual teachers and students organize the school day as they wish. Each child is generally free to perform the particular activity that interests him or her at any given time. The children can either explore a certain part of the room or remain in a familiar work area. They can work alone or in a group. Teachers will normally move around the room, working for a certain period of time with one child or a group of children, then moving on to another area. Within any given day, one child may work on a variety of different projects, sometimes alone, sometimes with various friends, and perhaps also with the teacher

(Featherstone, 1971; Fisher, 1972; Gross and Gross, 1970; Hassett and Weisberg, 1972).

The British open classroom teacher has much greater freedom from external demands and expectations than does a traditional American teacher. He is given more responsibility for what happens in the classroom; fewer curricular decisions are made by the British headmaster than the American principal. Curricular changes the teacher wishes to incorporate in the program are usually allowed, as long as they are financially possible (Fisher, 1972). Much of this freedom is explained by the fact that the British educational system is decentralized. There is no predetermined course of study, and no district or city-wide testing program. Instead, the teacher works with individual children or with small groups and develops a curriculum that specifically suits the needs of each child. He rarely presents material to the class as a whole (Fisher, 1972; Gibson, 1973b; Gross and Gross, 1970; Hassett and Weisberg, 1972).

This is not to suggest that the role of an open classroom teacher is an easy one. In fact, the open classroom teacher has enormous responsibilities. He or she must be sensitive to the needs of a large number of children and must be able to develop individualized instructional tasks for each of them. Rather than formulating one lesson plan for 30 children, the open classroom teacher may need to develop 30 separate lesson plans every week.

Thus, we see that the "open" attitude toward elementary education is a flexible one. Learning objectives, methods of instruction, and organization of time are adapted to the needs, capabilities, and interests of the individual student. In addition, the classroom itself is arranged in a flexible manner. Children may not even have desks; instead, they work on benches, tables, countertops, and easels, as well as on the floor. The room is divided into many separate work areas, so that different activities can take place at the same time. The class also may make use of space outside of the classroom, including hallways, other rooms in the building, and outdoor areas (Fisher, 1972; Gross and Gross, 1970; Rathbone, 1972).

Observers unfamiliar with the characteristics and rationale for the open classroom sometimes find the atmosphere noisy and chaotic. Many are accustomed to seeing students seated at their desks, quietly doing their work. It can be startling, at first, to see students constantly moving about the room on their own initiative (Featherstone, 1971; Fisher, 1972). The relaxed approach to discipline can sometimes create problems. But, as Fisher (1972) suggests, when the curriculum is geared to the children's interests, when they have a say in selecting their own materials, and when the teacher has an accepting attitude, the discipline problem should be minimal.

THE OPEN CLASSROOM IN THE UNITED STATES.   The trend toward informal education has spread from England to the United States

(Fisher, 1972; Gibson, 1973b). Both urban and rural school systems have instituted a variety of open classroom methods and techniques. In addition, a number of university-based teacher-training programs have shifted toward this approach. As a result, a growing number of American teachers are running "open" classrooms (Gibson, 1972; Gross and Gross, 1970).

A major advocate of informal education in the United States is Professor Lillian Weber of the City College of New York. After studying the British infant school system, Weber introduced in the New York City public schools the *open corridor method* of teaching, in which hallways are used as supplemental areas for learning, thus helping to eliminate overcrowding. Children are free to walk through the corridors, study material displayed on the walls, and engage in activities of their own choosing (Gibson, 1972).

However, American children may have more difficulty than British youngsters in adjusting to the open classroom atmosphere. Perhaps as a result of the long history of centralized schools in the United States, American youths seem more accustomed to authoritarian methods both at home and in school; the same seems to be true of American teachers. It is clear that not all teachers feel comfortable with the informality and lack of structure of the open classroom. Thus, many advocates of informal education do not recommend its use by teachers who are more comfortable with an authoritarian style (Hassett and Weisberg, 1972; Kohl, 1969).

An open classroom.
(Monkmeyer)

Kohl (1969) offers practical suggestions for teachers who wish to make their classrooms more informal, but are having difficulty getting started. He recommends that at least ten minutes per day be set aside as a kind of "free" period. During this time, children may choose from a variety of activities, or do nothing at all if they so desire. The teacher should step out of the way while the "free" period is under way, but should be alert and ready to assist or talk with students.

AN EVALUATION OF THE OPEN CLASSROOM.   One of the major questions about open education involves the role of the teacher. Madden (1972) has emphasized that one of the teacher's responsibilities in an open classroom, is to exercise control and to provide systematic positive reinforcement. He recommends helping students to develop responsible freedom of choice and self-direction in small, sequential, reinforced steps. When this procedure is followed, "the result can and should be the development of a humane classroom culture in which each child can learn not only to be free and independent but how to reconcile the demands of social learning upon freedom" (Madden, 1972, p. 106 – 107).

In practice, then, the open classroom is not designed simply to be "permissive." A good open classroom teacher does not ignore a defiant or uncooperative child. Instead, the teacher attempts to learn why the misbehavior occurred and how it can be avoided in the future. The use of arbitrary punishment as a means of suppressing disobedience is discouraged in open education. For the open classroom to be successful, the relationship between teachers and students must be one of mutual trust and respect (Kohl, 1969).

Advocates of open education deemphasize testing as a means of evaluating students' progress. They maintain that the success of open education cannot be measured by routine paper-and-pencil achievement tests. In fact, there is some evidence to suggest that children in traditional schools, at least in Britain, perform somewhat better on such tests than do children from more informal classes (Featherstone, 1971; Gibson, 1972). However, Featherstone (1971) feels that the difference is not a true one. He contends that it reflects the greater exposure to test-taking that children receive in traditional schools.

More recent investigations of inner-city children in American open classrooms indicate that these children score higher on standardized achievement tests than do their peers in traditional classes (Israel, 1969; Pines, 1967; Schneir and Schneir, 1971). Children from informal classrooms also seem superior in other dimensions of achievement, such as creative writing skills. In addition, many open classroom teachers have reported improved attendance, less tension, and fewer tantrums and angry confrontations (Gores, 1970).

Apparently, children enjoy learning in an informal educational environment. However, the long-term effects of open classrooms are uncertain at this time.

Questions for Thought

In Chapter 4, we spent a great deal of time discussing "behavior modification" and the "control of behavior." At least one behavioral psychologist has described the successful teacher of the open classroom as an "insidious behavior modifier"—that is, a behavior modifier who is extremely successful at modifying children's behavior at the same time that children think that they are making all the decisions for themselves. Do you agree with this description of the successful open classroom teacher? Why?

Instruction Individually Prescribed for the Student

Montessori teaching and other forms of informal education such as the open classroom are designed to meet the needs of individual students. Yet there are many other ways of designing a curriculum so that each student can learn at his or her own pace. One of these methods, individualized instruction, is actually an application of programmed instruction techniques.

As noted in Chapter 4, programmed instruction has its roots in

A teacher goes over a programmed instructional package with a student.
(Mitchell Mandell, Alternative Curriculum)

operant theory. Immediate feedback about the correctness of one's response is a central part of programmed instruction. In addition, students are given an important role in shaping their own learning. They receive encouragement to ask questions, think independently, make decisions and commitments, and develop special interests (Wolfson, 1968).

Traditionally, American schools have provided more or less fixed curricula. Little attention has been given to the needs of individual students. In recent years, however, this emphasis has shifted. Many psychologists and educators have asserted that all students can fulfill normal classroom objectives if necessary learning materials are provided on an individual basis. For this method to be successful, each student must receive proper stimulation and must be allowed to proceed at a comfortable and individually determined pace (Cronbach, 1967; Klaus, 1971).

Individualized instruction, as the name implies, offers special individualized plans of study based on each student's needs, interests, and abilities. Teachers make frequent evaluations of students in order to diagnose strengths and weaknesses and to prescribe appropriate lesson plans (Gibson, 1972).

Actually, individualized instruction is a difficult term to define, since it includes a wide variety of teaching practices (Gagné and Briggs, 1974; Wolfson, 1968). The present discussion will focus specifically on the methods of programmed learning, one way to individualize instruction.

MODULAR INSTRUCTION.   Individualized instruction is not a haphazard process in which the teacher tells children to simply "do your own thing." Materials are carefully planned and are presented in a highly organized, systematic manner. Some individualized instruction programs are structured around separate sequential units of study, known as *modules.*

There are many different methods of organizing modular programs. Common techniques include clear performance objectives for each unit; specified materials and learning activities; a means of self-evaluation; and a means of verifying that designated objectives have been met.

Project PLAN, begun in 1967, is a prime example of an educational program organized around modules and teaching-learning units (Gagné and Briggs, 1971; Klaus, 1971). Each grade (first through twelfth) has its own set of instructional objectives for language arts, social studies, science, and mathematics. A module consists of about five or six objectives, or about 10 to 15 hours of study. Each student is tested to determine his abilities, interests, and general knowledge before he begins modular instruction. The results of these tests are evaluated, and the student, his teacher, and sometimes his parents then begin to plan his individual course of instruction (Klaus, 1971). The student progresses sequentially from one module to the next in accordance with his own capability and interest. Students can also redesign their programs to suit their own abilities and aspirations (Klaus, 1971).

All record keeping in Project PLAN is computerized. Each participating school has its own special computer which receives and stores complete records for each student (Gagné and Briggs, 1974). We will discuss this aspect of Project PLAN more fully in the section on computer-assisted instruction.

EVALUATION OF INDIVIDUALIZED INSTRUCTION. Individualized instruction programs challenge both the teacher and the student. The children must assume a significant amount of responsibility for their own education, while the teacher must act as diagnostician and counselor. Thus, not only must the teacher "know the materials," he must help students to develop the necessary self-management techniques (Leinhardt, 1973; Lindvall and Bolvin, 1970).

Gagné and Briggs (1974) see individualized instruction as responsive to the needs and capabilities of the individual learner. They find this method effective because it allows the student to work at a rate appropriate to his or her talents, and because it provides immediate and helpful feedback.

Individualized instruction also attempts to build closer relationships between students and teachers. Advocates of the method report that the students feel that they are learning worthwhile information, and they gain a sense of self-importance in the process of managing their own learning. They say that students also realize that the teacher is concerned about them as individuals, because he or she listens to their problems and focuses on their own specific needs (Gagné and Briggs, 1974; Jackson, 1968). According to Gagné and Briggs (1974), teachers who have learned the necessary management techniques often prefer individualized instruction to conventional teaching methods.

Obviously, individualized instruction involves a large amount of planning and record keeping. Yet this time and energy are viewed by many as a solid investment; individualized programs can be exciting not only for students but also for teachers.

The Use of Technology in Classroom Instruction

Many educational reforms of the twentieth century—including some already discussed in this chapter—rely on changes in curriculum, methods of instruction, or classroom management. Yet, in the past decade, a whole new frontier of educational innovation has been opened. A wide variety of technological devices now exist to help the classroom teacher—and more are appearing each year. These include educational television (discussed earlier in this chapter), audiovisual devices, teaching machines, and computers.

Classroom audiovisual aids, unlike radio and television, have the special advantage of local control. They can be selected by individual students or groups when they wish. A student can use such aids at his own pace, instead of following a set schedule (Klaus, 1971).

The various classroom audiovisual aids can be divided into still visuals (charts, maps, slides, etc.), motion visuals (films), and audio recordings (cassettes, records, and tapes) (Klaus, 1971). Most of these aids can be enjoyed individually, as well as by the class as a whole.

TEACHING MACHINES.   Teaching machines were discussed briefly in Chapter 4. We refer to them again because they illustrate the impact of technology on American education.

Not all instructional devices that students control themselves can be properly called teaching machines. A teaching machine must reward the learner for the appropriateness of his response. These machines have many of the qualities of a game, and make learning an enjoyable experience.

Most teaching machines present material in small units or frames, one at a time. These units are followed by questions that require overt responses from students. The machine then provides feedback as to the correctness of the response.

The success of teaching machines depends primarily on the content and design of the instructional program. Various studies suggest that there can be as much as a 50 percent saving in learning time compared with a more traditional program (Skinner, 1972). Actually, this statistic should not surprise us. Teaching machines offer students self-pacing, logical and orderly progression of material, and frequent and immediate feedback. None of these advantages can be found to the same extent in traditional instruction.

THE USE OF THE COMPUTER IN INSTRUCTION.   Computers are a relatively recent addition to the educational scene. Yet they have been used and tested at all educational levels, from kindergarten through graduate school.

The computer has a remarkable capacity for collecting, processing, storing, and retrieving large amounts of information. This is its key asset in an educational program. Individualized instruction methods have particular need for computer assistance. The computer can provide background data for each student and can store test results. It can provide a complete listing of the materials used by each student during each class. The computer evaluates and scores student responses with remarkable speed. It develops special plans of study geared to the individual learner (Cooley and Glaser, 1969; Hall, 1971). Finally, the computer can suggest how close a student is to his individually prescribed level of achievement.

There are almost no limits to the potential uses of computers in education. Currently, computers are being used as laboratory computing devices. Many schools also use computers for information storage and retrieval. Teachers and administrators can record and process important data regarding students and curriculum. For example, computers can determine scheduling of classes, perhaps even taking into account the effects of interference as discussed in Chapter 8.

There are other applications of computer science to education. Goodland, O'Toole, and Tyler (1966) have demonstrated the value of computers in locating references and audiovisual aids for teachers. A recent and less publicized development has been the grading of essay tests and compositions by computer. Research with one such computer has been done at the University of Connecticut. This computer analyzes a whole essay for ideas, organization, style, mechanics, and creativity. It makes comments similar to those of a teacher and assigns a grade—all within a total time of 30 seconds! Of course, only the teacher can determine the variables that the computer measures in analyzing the essay.

Often the primary function of the computer in individualized instruction is to assist teachers and students in planning and record keeping. The instruction itself is not generally automated; this type of instruction is called *computer-managed instruction* (CMI). In some instances, though, the computer itself prescribes learning materials on an individual basis; this type is called *computer-assisted instruction* (CAI) (Cooley and Glaser, 1969).

Most CAI systems in use today are equipped with a small television screen, which serves as the display apparatus, and with a typewriter keyboard, which students use to respond to test items (Hall, 1971). CAI involves continual interaction between the student and the program. The computer functions as a teaching machine; it presents information, asks questions, and records and evaluates responses.

Some CAI programs suggests appropriate topics and materials for students, but the actual decision is made by the teacher. In other programs (such as tutorial systems), the computer determines the nature and sequencing of material. This requires elaborate and extensive equipment, and thus school systems have rarely been able to afford such computer programs (Hall, 1971; Jerman, 1970; Klaus, 1971).

One of the most sophisticated CAI programs is Project PLAN, which was mentioned earlier in the chapter. Each school involved

**THE ROBOT
WHO TEACHES
IN THE BRONX**

"I know Leachim likes me; he gave me an extra question," said the child in Mrs. Freeman's fourth-grade class at P.S. 106 in the Bronx (Radolf, 1974). Mrs. Freeman smiled, delighted that Leachim has such a devoted admirer. Just who is Leachim? No ordinary collection of nuts and bolts, but a bona fide, programmed robot. Lights flashing on top of his head, he speaks in a metallic voice to each individual student. He "knows" them by matching the sound of their voices to their voiceprints coded in his memory bank. He's an advanced piece of computerized machinery, his "glass belly" bulging with an intricate maze of switches, buttons, tapes, and wires. He was "born" in Yonkers on the kitchen table of Mrs. Freeman and her husband, Michael.

Leachim, Michael Freeman decided, could provide individualized and specialized instruction in his wife's class. The robot has seven reference books, including a dictionary, processed into his data bank, and he can recall whatever pages are necessary for aiding a student. He can evaluate a student's performance and then reprogram his tapes to fit the student's new learning needs. He has infinite patience, and he often compliments the children with little jokes. "Today Leachim said he saw smoke comin' out of my ears cause I was thinkin' so hard," one boy proudly declared (Radolf, 1974, p. 29). Leachim doesn't hesitate to tell the students when they're doing badly either. Either way, the children love him. With him, a child is spared the psychological trauma of failing before a teacher and his peers; a headset permits a student to work with Leachim without disturbing the rest of the class. And a child's success with the robot builds confidence for his later efforts in the classroom.

Leachim's programming is designed to last six months; then his taped, programmed curricula are changed by Mr. Freeman. And he has another advantage over other computers. Mrs. Freeman knows that the only way to abuse him is to rely too heavily on him. He is, for her, a teacher's aid, a supplemental tool, and as such he has his greatest value and potential. As she points out, Leachim allows her "to devote more time to the human side of teaching" (Radolf, 1974, p. 29).

in the project has its own computer terminal. Every student receives a complete computerized record of activities, test scores, and overall progress (Gagné and Briggs, 1974). Teachers receive daily printouts indicating students' previous accomplishments. There is a heavy emphasis on testing; test results give teachers accurate, up-to-date information about each student's progress.

The last example of CAI that we will consider is the Edison Responsive Environment, or "Talking Typewriter," developed by O. K. Moore. This program, aimed at teaching language skills to young children, consists of an electric typewriter keyboard and several integrated display mechanisms, all linked to a computer. Initially, the child simply presses various typewriter keys at random and a recorded voice identifies the letters being typed. Later, alternate modes of instruction (for example, displaying letters, words, and even sentences) are presented on the screen above the console. The child locates and presses the corresponding keys.

The "Talking Typewriter" has not been widely used because of its cost. But it has taught reading and writing to preschool and older children with impressive speed (Klaus, 1971). The "Talking Typewriter" is an example of *autotelic* activity, that is, according to its designer, the only reward it offers is the activity itself. It is called a *responsive environment* because the learner, working at his or her own pace, is free to explore the apparatus and can receive immediate feedback (O. K. Moore, 1966; O. K. Moore and A. R. Anderson, 1968, 1969).

Clearly, computer technology is already an important part of American education. Yet some experts believe that computers have even greater potential for assisting instruction. Klaus (1971) sees electronic data processing equipment being used increasingly to assist school administrations and to manage individualized instruction programs.

There are also criticisms of the use of computers in education. Controversy has resulted from the inordinate amount of time, energy, and money necessary for computer systems. CAI programs, in particular, require a great deal of equipment and high installation costs. The use of computers has also been attacked for contributing

"You mene I've bin spending this whol term with a defektiv reeding machin?"
(Sidney Harris, Saturday Review/World)

to social problems in the schools. A study by Brod (1972) found that junior high school students (mostly from low-income, Mexican-American families) in a CAI program had a reduced perception of the teacher's authority. Such attitudes are traditionally considered "undesirable" by school administrators. A further concern is that machines and computers cannot understand or show concern for the learner in a human sense. Children are well aware that even the most humanlike instrument is still a machine (Jackson, 1968).

It is difficult to speculate about CAI's future. If cost and maintenance problems can be minimized, improved technology may reshape education dramatically. The critical question is how to adapt instructional techniques to individual needs. Computer systems can accumulate information over time that will help to solve this problem. Thus, as our knowledge about learning processes expands, we may witness extraordinary new developments in computerized instruction.

Questions for Thought
In these days of increasing costs, what do you think will be the position of teacher's unions on the development of devices that can replace teachers in the classroom? Check your answer to this question with union leaders in your community. Do you agree or disagree with them? Why?

Some types of instruction radically redefine traditional student and teacher roles. Among these are team teaching, modular instruction, the nongraded class, and precision teaching. Each of these methods shifts the responsibilities for education in a variety of ways.

Programs That Reorganize Traditional Student and Teacher Roles

TEAM TEACHING. Team teaching is a relatively new approach to education which is presently being practiced in hundreds of elementary schools, high schools, and colleges. No single teacher is the "full-time boss" in the classroom; instead, a number of teachers share responsibility. There are several different varieties of team teaching:

1. *Hierarchical teaching.* Team members and their assignments are arranged in hierarchical order. At the top of the hierarchy is the team leader, an experienced teacher with extensive academic preparation. The leader has a light teaching load and handles many administrative duties. Other members of the teaching hierarchy include senior teachers (experienced teachers who receive extra pay), regular teachers (with little or no previous experience), and part-time teaching assistants and clerical workers.

2. *Coordinate or co-teaching.* Several teachers work together with a large group of pupils (e.g., 3 teachers and a group of 90 students).

The teachers function as equals and plan the classroom program together. One teacher may assume responsibility for a particular lesson. On other occasions, the class may be divided into smaller units, with each teacher taking one section.

3. *Team teaching across departmental lines.* The curriculum is arranged to cover two or three related subjects (e.g., American history and American literature). Usually, two different teachers will run the class, each presiding in the subject area that he or she knows best. Both teachers may be present at the same time, especially when beginning a new unit. The two teachers also meet regularly outside of class to plan the course of study.

4. *Trading groups.* Teachers agree to take on different aspects of each other's work. For example, one teacher might agree to teach music for another, if the second teacher runs a science class for the first. This "trading" is frequent in elementary schools. It occurs to a lesser extent in high schools.

Teachers often feel they can pursue their individual interests and talents through the team approach. Since large numbers of students are involved, material is not repeated separately to many different sections of a class. Thus, the total staff time required for teaching activities may be reduced. In addition, special staff and helpers relieve teachers of administrative burdens. Technical personnel assist in the use of audiovisual aids.

Team teaching has distinct advantages for students. They are exposed to differing points of view, and rarely receive instruction from a teacher who knows little about a particular subject. Most important, the students are given many opportunities to take responsibility for their own education.

Offsetting these advantages are a few significant problems. Individual student-teacher interactions are minimized under team teaching, as a large number of students and teachers are involved in the program. Students are constantly shifted from one teacher to another, and many experienced teachers end up handling only lecture classes. The possibilities for individualized instruction are quite limited. Thus the special needs of particular students may be neglected in a team teaching system.

Educators must weight the advantages and disadvantages of team teaching. They must also determine if the benefits of the approach justify increased additional costs. The issue is a controversial one, and further research seems necessary.

MODULAR INDIVIDUALIZED INSTRUCTION. Modular individualized instruction was discussed earlier in reference to Project PLAN. Like other forms of individualized instruction, it encourages students to play an active role in their own learning. Once the student is told about a particular module, he or she is free to pursue learning independently. In this way, modular instruction differs markedly from traditional classroom instruction. The teacher does not lecture; the student does not sit and take notes.

Modular individualized instruction is also flexible enough to meet the varied needs of individual students, in terms of both content and form. Modules can be used with students of all ages and with any subject matter.

Opportunities for self-testing occur frequently, and immediate feedback is provided. As a result, students are less anxious about tests than their peers in traditional classes. The emphasis is on mastery of material, rather than on competitive grading. Thus, even the slower students gain satisfaction from completing a module. When grades are given, many students in modular programs achieve the highest grades possible (Ferster and Perrott, 1968; Russell, 1974).

Yet modular education also has certain drawbacks. The process tends to be time-consuming, because of the need for continual evaluation. Modular materials are arranged and employed in much smaller chunks than are conventional learning materials. Each set must be stored separately so that all necessary references are kept together. In addition, an adequate supply of all modules must be kept on hand so that a number of students can work on the same materials simultaneously (Gagné and Briggs, 1974). All of these factors place great responsibility on the teacher. He must constantly work on organization, counseling, evaluation, monitoring, and diagnosis.

NONGRADED CLASSROOMS.   The Montessori preschool system discussed earlier in the chapter is a prime example of the nongraded classroom, that is, a classroom that integrates children of varying ages. Young children ages 3 to 6 may learn at their own rates within the same Montessori class. In this section, we will focus on the application of this principle for elementary and secondary education.

The basic principle behind nongraded education is that not all children of the same age are capable of learning the same things (as described in Chapter 2). Therefore, age segregation is not necessarily conducive to maximum learning (Clark, 1967). For example, in a typical class of 6-year-olds, a few children may be able to read materials designed for 8- or 9-year-olds. Others may not yet know how to read, and still others may be able to read introductory materials. If all of these children are required to complete similar tasks, the slower children can become overwhelmed, while the brighter children become bored. By contrast, in a nongraded classroom, different levels of reading matter are available for each group of children (Clark, 1967).

There are no rigid criteria for nongraded education. Each child works at his or her own pace, according to his or her own capabilities. Failure is minimized, since students are not forced to attempt overly difficult tasks. Instead, they are presented material that is within their ability range. At the same time, teachers do not bore children with work that is too easy for them.

Nongraded classes fulfill both educational and social objectives. The teacher in such a class recognizes that "people learn from differences as well as similarities and . . . from meeting and living with different kinds of people" (Clark, 1967, p. 260). The mixture of ages helps create a diverse and lively atmosphere, which can be as educational for children as any set of materials. Of course, the nongraded classroom has disadvantages for the slower student in perpetually having more rapid students pass him by. On the other hand, pressure to go more rapidly than is possible for the slow student is removed by this method of teaching.

But managing and teaching a nongraded class is a difficult job. Teachers must place children in appropriate instructional groups and must assume a large degree of responsibility for what each child learns. Unlike the traditional teacher, the teacher in a nongraded class cannot rely on a particular textbook or syllabus to find the "normal" curriculum. The specific needs of each student must be determined, and materials that will meet the student's needs must be prepared.

PRECISION TEACHING. Precision teaching, like the nongraded classroom, is primarily geared toward the needs of the individual child. The method was first conceived and developed by Ogden R. Lindsley, professor of education at the University of Kansas. Precision teaching emphasizes *monitoring* of the child's performance, rather than simply aiming for proficiency. Performance is measured by determining the frequency (per unit of time) at which a particular desired response occurs. Improvement, the variable considered most important, is measured in terms of acceleration (increase in the frequency of desired responses) and deceleration (decrease in the frequency of undesired responses). For the precision teacher, improvement is synonymous with learning (E.C. Johnson, 1971; N.J. Johnson, 1973).

Research on reinforcement originally suggested that teachers can change students' behavior by manipulating consequences. It is from such research that the precision teaching method was developed. The cumulative record created by reinforcement theorists served as the prototype for the *Standard Daily Behavior Chart*, the tool precision teachers use to measure students' performance and progress (E.C. Johnson, 1971). Thus, precision teaching can be seen as a form of behavior management.

Originally, the teacher was expected to do the recording and charting that are essential to precision teaching. However, the preferred method today is to have students do this work themselves. Each student keeps a daily record of the frequency of correct and incorrect responses for each pinpointed movement. At the end of the day, the information is transferred to the Standard Daily Behavior Chart. (The chart is standard since its format and structure are uniform for each child.) Such charts give both student and teacher immediate daily feedback on behavior changes.

When a pupil fails to improve over an extended period of time, the teacher may change something in the learning environment in order to motivate the child. For example, easier learning materials could be substituted. On the other hand, if a student has made no errors at all, more demanding material can be introduced. Under precision teaching there is no stigma to making a mistake. An error is viewed as a learning opportunity; it tells student and teacher where improvement is needed (N.J. Johnson, 1973).

According to N.J. Johnson, children should be given a voice in determining consequences. This increases the probability that each consequence will be personally reinforcing to the individual. A consequence of extra recess time, although it seems universally appealing, will not stimulate learning if a particular child hates recess.

Little research exists on the long-range effectiveness of precision teaching. However, the method does provide inexpensive and useful information on each student's strengths and weaknesses. The teacher can quickly realize which materials help each child most. Precision teaching is also helpful in planning individualized programs and in differentiating between significant and insignificant behavior changes—a most important bit of information for teachers.

The precision teaching method was employed in Operation Upgrade, a Model Cities project run by Dr. N.J. Johnson in Kansas City. This program will be discussed in detail in Chapter 10.

GROUP REINFORCEMENT, PARAPROFESSIONAL TEACHING, AND PEER TEACHING.   Many of the methods discussed in this chapter involve shifting of responsibilities away from the teacher. In some cases, paraprofessional aides can use reinforcement techniques with students. In addition, students themselves (called peer teachers) can assume much of this burden.

Soviet schools provide an example of peer teaching. The Soviet Union relies heavily on group reinforcement in every setting where children congregate (as was pointed out in Chapter 1). Group reinforcement comes not only from the teacher but also from the peer group. Young children frequently criticize and correct each other's behavior—with or without the presence of the teacher or other adults.

Despite the success of peer teaching in Soviet schools, it is rarely used in American schools. But it has been effective in both experimental situations and community programs. For example, self-help groups such as Alcoholics Anonymous and Recovery, Inc., are based on the principle that people with similar problems can help one another. In Mobilization for Youth, high school students tutor peers and younger students. And in Flint, Michigan, sixth-graders with reading difficulties tutored fourth-graders with similar problems. Both groups showed substantial improvement as a result of the tutoring program (Riessman, 1965).

The helper role is a valuable one for the child. It contributes to his or her feelings of self-esteem and to eventual leadership potential. The child realizes that others think highly of him or her, and this leads to higher self-expectations. Thus, peer teaching may be a useful means of strengthening the confidence of students with learning difficulties.

Questions for Thought

Considering the economic problems facing schools today, which is most likely to be employed in your classroom tomorrow—computerized instruction or reorganization of staff to provide for the needs of students?

Do you think that each of these approaches is equally useful to the classroom teacher? Justify your answer.

ALTERNATIVE INSTRUCTIONAL DESIGNS FOR UNTRADITIONAL ELEMENTARY AND HIGH SCHOOL PROGRAMS

We have examined a variety of educational reforms, many of which have been utilized in public classrooms. While the results of these programs are impressive, many students, teachers, and parents still find it impossible to work within the structures of traditional public schools (or private schools). Instead, "alternative" or so-called free schools have been established across the United States. These schools generally offer students a great deal more freedom than is allowed in traditional institutions.

The Free School Movement

The "free school" movement in the United States began in the 1960s and has gained momentum. In the period from 1967 to 1972, for example, the total number of free schools jumped from about 25 to approximately 600 (Graubard, 1972). This increase undoubtedly reflects a widespread dissatisfaction with traditional forms of education.

Students in the 1960s were greatly influenced by the writings of outspoken critics of existing schools such as John Holt, Herbert Kohl, George Dennison, and Paul Goodman. These writers denounced the rigid authoritarian nature of classroom instruction and the emphasis on grades, discipline, and conformity.

Concerned observers came to see traditional schools as little more than a custodial atmosphere for American youth. Parents, teachers, and students themselves began to question whether any solution was possible within the public school system. This led to a search for an alternative type of schooling (Graubard, 1972; McCauley, Cornbush, and Scott, 1972).

A 1971 survey by the New Schools Director Project involved collecting data on existing free schools in the United States. A total of 346 schools were included in the study, none of which had any affiliation with the public school system. Thirty-nine states were found to have at least one free school, with the heaviest representation in New York, California, Massachusetts, and Illinois. Many free schools were found in the large urban centers of these four states. Presumably, such regions include many persons who share the free school philosophy and have the resources to create educational alternatives (Graubard, 1972).

Most free schools are staffed by regular full-time teachers and by part-time community volunteers. Enrollment is generally small (perhaps 30–40 students), and the staff-to-student ratio tends to be high (often one full-time teacher for every seven students). Within such a small school community, staff and students are well acquainted. There is none of the impersonality or alienation of a large urban high school. The "school" itself may be located in a storefront, an old barn, an abandoned building, or the teacher's home. Some free schools have no home base at all (Graubard, 1972).

Many of these schools survive by charging tuition—usually on a sliding scale based on family income. However, some of the free schools surveyed did not charge any fees. These include community schools and street academies supported by foundation grants.

There are many different types of free school. Nevertheless, it is possible to group such schools into a variety of categories, depending on predominant characteristics of each institution (Graubard, 1972):

1. *Classical free schools.* These are small communities (such as the Summerhill Ranch School in Mendocino, California) which cater almost exclusively to the white middle class. These schools tend to be quite expensive. They stress emotional and expressive development rather than formal academic learning. The atmosphere is generally apolitical.

2. *Parent-teacher cooperative elementary schools.* These schools are often created by young, white, middle-class parents with a liber-

al attitude toward education. Parent boards control the schools, and some parents also serve on the faculties. Tuition is paid on a sliding scale, but few children from poor families are found in these cooperatives.

3. *Community elementary schools.* These schools tend to be larger and more organized than the average free school. Cultural consciousness and pride in relation to racial or ethnic status are emphasized. Parent and community groups are instrumental in determining policy.

4. *Free high school*

   (a) *Alternative academic high schools:* These schools are designed to attract students disenchanted with the traditional school system, but who are likely at some point in their lives to go on to academic programs. Their role is to prepare students for this return.

   (b) *Alternative vocational high schools:* These schools consist mainly of disillusioned dropouts and potential dropouts whose prime interests are vocational rather than academic. The focus of the educational program is on remedial work and vocational guidance.

   (c) *Street academies for poor minority youth:* These schools are a far cry from classical free schools. The atmosphere is often relatively disciplined; the instructional methods may be conventional. The main emphasis is on college preparation. In that

Teacher and students in an alternative elementary school program in Pittsburgh.
(Robin Gibson, Alternative Curriculum)

sense, the orientation is quite different from the dominant white free school culture. Harlem Prep, with over 600 students in 1975, is the best-known street academy.

Alternative schools thus run the gamut from politically active "liberation schools" in the inner city to rural utopian experiments. Despite this diversity, all free schools share a dissatisfaction with traditional education and a desire for a more humane learning environment (McCauley, et al., 1972).

SUMMERHILL.   Summerhill, one of the first free schools and perhaps the most famous and controversial alternative school, was founded by A. S. Neill in 1921 on the principle that the school should be made to "fit the child" (Neill, 1960). It is a residential school located in an English village about 100 miles from London.

In his writings Neill stated that children have the innate capacity to learn and grow without adult intervention. He said that schools should not impose major restrictions on a child's activities. Thus, at Summerhill, all classes are optional. Students attend or miss classes as they please, with no fear of punishment. In addition, they are encouraged to express feelings and emotions—including sexual feelings—in a free, uninhibited manner.

Neill consistently asserted that his students learn a great deal, despite the absence of required classes, formal examinations, and grading. He described Summerhill as "possibly the happiest school in the world," as a school with "no truants and seldom a case of homesickness" (Neill, 1960, p. 196). In his view, children need to know that authority figures respect them and approve of their actions. At Summerhill, this need is satisfied.

Critics have insisted that Summerhill is not as democratic as it purports to be. All students come from well-to-do families, and are thus a rather atypical group of children. Furthermore, the beneficial effects of a Summerhill education have been questioned by educational authorities. According to the Ministry of Education, Summerhill graduates show unusual interest and determination, yet their actual achievements are not impressive (Rafferty, 1970). In a way, this might prove the success of the program, for Neill didn't care if his students "achieved" in the normal sense of the word. What was most important to Neill was their emotional well-being.

DESCHOOLING.   Another radical approach to education is *deschooling* (also known as the "inverse of schools"). This approach was pioneered by Ivan Illich. As the name implies, it is an educational program that eliminates the need for schools. Learning takes place through the individual's interaction with community resources.

According to Illich (1971), learning can become self-motivated (rather than teacher-motivated) if the learner is provided with new links (or channels) for the dissemination of education. These channels would replace schools as the supplier of knowledge. Presumably, they would contain all necessary resources for learning. Any learner, regardless of age or formal credentials, would be granted full access to these channels.

The first network proposed by Illich consists of *reference services to educational objects.* These include any institution open to the public that contains materials useful for learning. At present, libraries and museums perform this service; Illich points out that laboratories, factories, airports, and farms could also function as reference services.

The second network Illich proposes is *peer matching.* This service would match interested students with peers with similar goals. Students would simply submit their names, addresses, and interests. They would then be sent back names and addresses of peers with comparable objectives.

The third proposed network includes *skill exchanges.* This service is, in reality, a kind of catalogue. Experts in a field ("skill models") would list their skills, their addresses, and the conditions under which they would demonstrate these skills. Potential learners could contact the skill models and arrange appointments. Formal qualifications would not be needed to become a skill model. The only requirements would be knowledge of a skill and willingness to share it with others.

The fourth and final network proposed is really a subcategory of skill exchanges and consists of *reference services to professional educators.* A directory would list the names, addresses, and self-descriptions of those persons willing and able to provide leadership in difficult areas of study. These educators might guide students in their use of the other networks. The only criteria would be knowledge of the subject and a responsible attitude. Specific training and experience in areas such as public relations, curriculum planning, and record keeping—all of which are essential in the public schools—would be irrelevant under Illich's system.

Thus, according to Illich (1971), "the alternative to social control through the schools is the voluntary participation in society through networks which provide access to all its resources for learning" (p. 101). This statement is highly controversial; many observers question the need to create entirely new institutions to replace the school. Could not—and should not—the schools be the major vehicle for social change?

THE PARKWAY SCHOOL. The Parkway School (Resnik, 1971) is a remarkable "free school" funded by the Philadelphia Board of Education. It has operated since 1967 under the direction of John Bre-

How does a teacher help a 17-year-old functional illiterate to read? **TESTAMENT**
Here is a testament to one teacher from her pupil ("From a Student, **FROM A STUDENT**
1971):

You see, this is how I learned to read. For the first quarter [at the Parkway Program in Philadelphia], I thought I was hopeless. For 17 years I hadn't learned to read, and it's hard. So my teacher, Wendy, she's kind of out of the ordinary. She took most of her time, I couldn't understand, writing a book for me. She made cards for me with pictures on them. I'd have to go home and study the cards, write the words. Sometimes I miss them, sometimes I don't. On Wendy's lunch time she'd take me to Sansom Village. She'd make me read all the records and little signs. She'd help me with the words I didn't know. Boy, I'd feel down cause there's lots I didn't know, and she'd write them down. One time she brought in some jelly beans to class. She shocked me, too, cause I'm not a kid. I like jelly beans. She laid the jelly beans on the table. She had pages from a book she wrote for me, and for every word I got right, I got a jelly bean. Boy, I worked. Hard pages were worth more jelly beans than easy pages. . . .(p. 189)

Wendy, she brought in newspaper ads and if you take your girl to the movies you have to look up the time. That was really successful, looking at papers and reading the ads. That was real nice. We were talking about dating and girls and what's happening. And she'd go home and write it up. She'd say those are your words so why don't you read them. So we'd go over it. And that same day I'd know the words on that paper. I don't know how you learn to read, but sure, this is a big step. How many 17-year-old boys who can't read, learn about 50 words in one day. See, it amazes me, when she brings in something you said the next day; when you go over it, you can read some words. If you study those words, when you see them again, you will know them. . . .(p.190)

. . . when a school lives up to the word *educate*, I think I should look at that system closely because Parkway is trying to be a great big family. We are concerned about misfortuned kids. All I can say now is that Parkway really helped me and my misfortune. And now I have come to a big step, and I hope to make something out of that big step."
(p. 191)

mer. Actually, it is a "school without walls" with no permanent building of its own. The "classroom" is the surrounding community of Philadelphia—the museums, hospitals, businesses, libraries, and colleges.

In February, 1970, there were seven students in the graduating class of the Parkway School. All were college bound. By 1971, the school had more than 500 students, along with 30 full-time teachers and 30 university interns. The school community is organized into separate "units," each of which includes approximately 130 students and 10 faculty (half of whom are interns.) Everyone in a unit belongs to a tutorial which offers academic assistance and plans parties, picnics, and other social activities. Weekly town meetings are held in which students discuss general problems and organize activities and projects.

The curriculum is highly individualized. Each student decides (within very broad limits) what he or she wants to learn at a given time. Although many students prepare for college, they feel this is a more humane way than the rigid approach in traditional schools.

There are no examinations or competitive grades. Performance is evaluated on a pass-fail basis; in addition, a student receives a written report from the instructor. Even the school admissions procedure is random, determined by public lottery.

The Parkway program offers a practical solution to the over-crowding in Philadelphia's high schools. It is a clear example of a traditional public school with an exciting, diverse curriculum. While cognitive skills are by no means neglected, there is interest as well in developing affective skills.

On the negative side, many Parkway students feel overwhelmed by the range and quantity of course offerings. Students complain that many tutorials, town meetings, and lectures are boring. They frequently cut classes. In addition, Parkway students have caused property damage in local institutions, and there have been instances of racial tension. These problems point to a serious and difficult question: Can the Parkway program continue to service and flourish within a competitive and alienating society? Or, to pose another dilemma, how experimental can a school be when it must depend on public support and funding in order to exist?

HARLEM PREP.   Harlem Prep, which began as an independent non-sectarian college preparatory school and eventually became part of the New York City School System, opened in October, 1967, with 49 students (Carpenter and Rogers, 1971). In June, 1968, 35 students graduated, and all went on to college. In 1975, approximately 600 students were enrolled in Harlem Prep. A large percentage continue their education in leading colleges and universities throughout the United States.

Harlem Prep was designed as an alternative program for Harlem teenagers who were disillusioned with public schools. The original site was the auditorium of an armory in central Harlem. In 1968 the school moved to its present location, a remodeled supermarket. The spacious room has no partitions; adjacent clusters of chairs define the various classes. This structure allows students to move freely from one class to another. They are required, however, to make up any work missed in their regular class.

The students and faculty of Harlem Prep represent a wide variety of racial, religious, ethnic, and political backgrounds. This setting promotes tolerance, harmony, and understanding. Students become less prejudiced and obtain a better sense of themselves and of others.

The curriculum covers a broad sample of subjects, including traditional college preparatory material. Special attention is given to contemporary social problems. The Harlem Prep program, unlike many such efforts, does not exist to help teenagers get out of the ghetto. The goal is to interest students in community service work.

Harlem Prep is nationally known as a huge success, not only in helping students get into colleges, but in fostering positive attitudes toward learning. More than 150 colleges and universities actively recruit candidates from Harlem Prep—a radical switch from the days when no one would even consider ghetto youths with past academic difficulties.

THE PITTSBURGH FREE LEARNING ENVIRONMENT (FRELEA). The Pittsburgh Free Learning Environment is an alternative program for middle-school children (fourth to sixth grade) offered by the Children's FRELEA School at the Washington Education Center. The small number of children in the program come from diverse socioeconomic backgrounds. The main goal is to provide an open, humanistic climate in which students take an active role in their learning. Spontaneous inquiry and independent thought are encouraged.

Students have access to a wide range of learning materials in FRELEA. The teacher's role is to help students pursue individual learning. In addition, many interested observers—in-service and pre-service teachers in training, parents, tutors, aides, and custodians—are available to work with students. Peer teaching is stressed; many students learn as much from one another as they do from the teacher (Pankopf, 1974).

The program stresses basic skills, but students select their own learning materials and proceed at their own rate. Cognitive skills are not the only focus; there is also emphasis on creative and social skills. Teachers aim for an integrated curriculum which oversteps traditional boundaries between various disciplines (Pankopf, 1974).

FRELEA conducts in-service workshops which familiarize principals, superintendents, teachers, and other staff members with the goals and methods of the program. There are similar workshops for parents and interested adults.

In summary, the Pittsburgh Free Learning Environment is in some ways similar to and in some ways different from other alternative schools. Unlike most free schools, FRELEA insists that all students master basic skills. Yet the children have an important voice in determining what and how they learn.

EVALUATION OF THE FREE SCHOOL MOVEMENT. As we have indicated, the goals of the free school movement include greater freedom

**EDUCATION
BY CHOICE**

Quincy, Illinois, has become an educational mecca, the site of conferences on educational alternatives. What brings school administrators to this small (population 45,288) town is Quincy's Senior High School II, where juniors and seniors can choose any one of "seven separate subschools, each with different courses and styles of teaching" ("Choice in Quincy," 1975). The alternatives among which students choose are:

The Traditional School. As the name suggests, this is the conventional school most students know, with regular assignments, lectures, grades, row seating, and required courses.

The Flexible School. This is similar to the Traditional School, but students can leave classes after a lecture to pursue independent studies—with the teacher's permission.

The Project to Individualize Education (PIE). "Students select their own courses and determine how often they will attend classes." They may select independent studies or encounter groups.

The Career School. This one is for students who are not college-bound, who plan to find full-time jobs after graduation. "They attend regular classes half the day and work part time."

The Work-Study School. This alternative is structured for those "who are on the verge of dropping out and need extra help in their academic subjects." Their program is divided into eight brief periods after which the students work part time each day.

The Special Education School. This is for slow learners, with the curricular emphasis on vocational training. Students may take such varied courses as cooking, carpentry, auto mechanics, gardening, and child care.

The Fine Arts School. In this school "the students make their own schedules, work at their own pace," and select from "more than 50 courses, 28 of them arts-oriented." Some students have written a blues-rock musical; "others tour the city in an old school bus giving free performances as a 'School of the Street.'"

Education by choice is no sudden innovation in Quincy, which may, in part, be why it has such enthusiastic community support. With options running from classes highly structured to almost totally free, it has something to offer each and every student, thus proving that alternative education can be made available within the system.

for students and a more humane learning environment. Many free schools have successfully established an informal and unstructured climate. Yet prominent educators question the ultimate viability of the free school movement. They claim that the popularity of alternative education will decline as its inherent problems become more obvious.

Students are often sent to free schools because they get into trouble in regular classes. The principal decides that the best way to deal with these students is to send them elsewhere. Thus, free schools find themselves with students whose enrollment is somewhat involuntary—a serious contradiction to the "free choice" principle of the schools.

Other serious problems facing alternative schools include inadequate advance planning; insufficient funding due to low tuition; inadequately trained and poorly paid staff members (who tend to be young and inexperienced); and high staff turnover (Graubard, 1972; Zarembka, 1974).

It is difficult to predict whether these problems can be surmounted. Ultimately, free schools may collapse or like Harlem Prep be absorbed by the more affluent and powerful public school system. Further, many free schools are dependent upon grants or private contributions. In times of economic trouble, which have occurred during the 1970s in the United States, these kinds of projects may suffer a great deal.

ALTERNATIVE INSTRUCTIONAL DESIGNS FOR HIGHER EDUCATION

All of the programs discussed thus far in the chapter have been geared to young children or teenagers. In this section, we will examine alternative programs that service college-age adults and older Americans. These programs are designed to motivate their students to take a renewed interest in education.

The examples to be described are familiar to me because they were developed at the University of Pittsburgh. However, many other schools have instituted similar programs to attract new students and to encourage adults to further their education.

THE ALTERNATIVE CURRICULUM AT THE UNIVERSITY OF PITTSBURGH. The Alternative Curriculum (AC) at the University of Pittsburgh is a special program for college freshmen consisting of discussions and workshops. There are no traditional classes or assignments. The purpose of the program is to help students become more independent and autonomous. The students plan their own learning activities and organize their study time. They do not rely on staff members, and do not conform to teacher-defined goals (B. Moore, 1974; Townsend, 1974).

AC students choose the activities that they wish to pursue at a particular time—independent reading, workshops, group discussions, or cooperative projects with other students. The students take responsibility for scheduling their work so that it is completed by the end of the semester. Teachers provide few specific guidelines as to what and how to study.

At the same time, students are encouraged to discuss their interests, goals, and learning strategies with teachers, other staff members, and fellow students. Each student is expected to consult with a staff member at least three or four times during the semester. These consultations ensure that at least one teacher is aware of each student's activities. AC students are also encouraged to contact special resource people outside of the program staff. These "experts" help students with a particular area of interest (Townsend, 1974).

All AC students have the opportunity to cultivate and pursue new areas of knowledge. They read books on any subject that interests them, and talk with people who are directly involved in a field of study.

In addition, students in AC become involved in projects that often cross many disciplines. The theory involved in this approach is that educators too often narrow the range of student activities and interests by restricting them to a very specific discipline. For example, when a student taking a psychology course in a traditional college program becomes interested in a question related to biophysics or biochemistry, which came out of his study of psychology, he cannot go to the psychology instructor and ask to change the program in order to answer his question in depth. He must wait until he takes a biology course — if he ever does — and if he remembers the question.

The way the project system works in the AC program at the University of Pittsburgh can be best illustrated by one of the projects undertaken by the 1974–1975 AC freshman class, which involved the development of this textbook. AC students, studying alternative instructional design, did studies of school programs in the city of Pittsburgh, provided much of the information presented in this chapter, and photographed and developed in their darkrooms examples of these programs that best described what was most important to them about each of the programs. Some of the Alternative Curriculum students' pictures are in this as well as other chapters in the text.

THE UNIVERSITY OF PITTSBURGH EXTERNAL STUDIES PROGRAM ("THE UNCOLLEGE"). The University of Pittsburgh External Studies Program (UESP) involves adults who are unable to travel, or do not wish to travel to the university to attend classes. These students work at home with individually programmed courses. Learning proceeds according to self-management and individualized instruction techniques. All tests are self-graded. Written papers are sent to an instructor who provides immediate feedback.

UESP students can design an individualized course of study that meets all degree requirements. They receive free personal and career counseling at the counseling center. In addition, they attend three workshops per term, in which they meet with faculty members, ask questions, and attend discussion groups. UESP students are encouraged to form study groups and to contact instructors by phone or mail if problems develop.

I teach one course in the External Studies Program in principles of instruction and find that these students constitute one of my most excited and enthusiastic classes.

Questions for Thought

In this chapter, we have examined alternative curriculum designs developed for students from preschool age through adulthood. What are the basic differences between the approaches that seem to be most effective at different ages?

Can you explain these differences on the basis of what was discussed earlier of the development of the individual in Part 2 of this text?

Or do the same techniques work effectively at all ages because they employ the same meaningful learning principles?

Chapter 9 examines instructional designs that necessitate major changes in school curricula. All of these innovations represent applications of theoretical material presented in earlier chapters. The programs all stress more individualized instruction. Examples were presented at various age levels, from preschool to adult. **SUMMARY**

The Montessori approach to preschool teaching has demonstrated that very young children can master skills such as reading and writing. Montessori emphasized the need to respect each child as an individual. She based her program on the assumption that children have a natural inclination for learning. When the environment was carefully manipulated, her students made remarkable strides in developing their cognitive, sensory, and motor skills.

Educational television is another important innovation that has affected American youth. Its major limitation is that it is a one-way communication system.

The open classroom is a curricular innovation in public elementary and high school programs. A flexible learning environment is established which easily adapts to the interests of the children. Fixed time periods for specific activities are eliminated under open education. The teacher permits each child to pursue his or her own choices.

Another approach to elementary and high school education designed to meet students' needs is individualized instruction. This approach applies programmed instruction techniques. Teachers set common objectives for all students, but they prepare individualized plans of study. Frequent testing, immediate feedback about students' responses, and continual evaluation of students' progress help account for the success of individualized programs.

Some individualized instruction programs have been computerized. The computer is ideally suited for this task because of its vast capacity for collecting, processing, storing, and retrieving important information about each student. Usually, its primary function is to assist instructional planning and record keeping. In some programs, however, the computer itself serves as a means of instruction. The first type of instruction is called computer-managed instruction; the second type is known as computer-assisted instruction.

Other types of instructional design which radically redefine traditional student-teacher roles include team teaching, modular instruction, and nongrading. These methods promote individualized learning, but entail a great deal of planning and organization.

Precision teaching is a relatively new approach to elementary and high school instruction. It is similar in some respects to behavior modification, although precision teaching relies primarily on reinforcing carefully measured behavior changes to shape behavior. Students keep cumulative records of daily behavior changes. These charts provide a reliable index of learning and improvement.

Group reinforcement and peer teaching are approaches to education that are practiced extensively in the Soviet Union but are seldom found in American schools.

Various alternative programs exist for students who find traditional instruction inadequate and limiting. These programs range from comparatively "free" environments such as Summerhill (in which a small number of well-to-do students learn in an unrestricted environment) to highly structured programs such as Harlem Prep (where disadvantaged youths receive college preparatory training). Ivan Illich has advocated the elimination of schools entirely ("deschooling"). He proposes a series of educational networks that would allow students to learn from the resources in their own communities.

There are also various alternative designs for adult education. Two examples from the University of Pittsburgh were described: the Alternative Curriculum and the External Studies Program.

All of the instructional designs discussed in the chapter reflect a widespread dissatisfaction with traditional modes of instruction. This feeling prevails both within public education circles and the free school movement. As the needs of our society change rapidly, the educational forms of earlier decades have proven inadequate. Students throughout the United States, at all age levels, seem to learn more effectively from a more individualized educational framework. The innovations presented here all share this goal, and differ primarily in structure and technique of implementation.

SUGGESTED FOR FURTHER READING

Drumheller, S. J. *Handbook of curriculum design for individualized instruction.* Englewood Cliffs, N.J.: Educational Technology Publications, 1971. This is an easy to follow "how to" book on developing curriculum material from behavioral objectives. Specific guidelines and exercises are included to aid the teacher or the curriculum developer in individualizing instruction.

Gross, R., and Osterman, P. (Eds.) *High school.* New York: Simon and Schuster, 1971.

High School should be required reading for all prospective teachers if they want to know the pupils they will be teaching. Actual diaries of students and teachers are included. The entire last section of the book is devoted to alternative approaches to education.

Klaus, D. J. *Instructional innovation and individualization.* Pittsburgh: American Institutes for Research, 1971.

This book elaborates numerous topics relating to alternative curricula. Uses of technology as applied to education are discussed. Klaus also evaluates other instructional methods as he discusses them.

Kohl, H. R. *The open classroom.* New York: Vintage Books, 1969.

This is an excellent handbook for teachers who want to try open classroom techniques. Kohl recounts his own personal experiences along with those of his students and other teachers, gives advice where needed, and provides reinforcement for the novice teacher.

Postman, N. and Weingartner, C. *Teaching as a subversive activity.* New York: Delacorte, 1969.

Postman and Weingartner have designed an instructional system that they claim makes the student unaware that he is learning. This book is especially good for teachers of so-called unmotivated high school students; yet everyone should be able to get some practical knowledge from reading it.

3

DIFFERENCES AMONG INDIVIDUALS: EFFECTS ON LEARNING AND TEACHING

Throughout this book we have emphasized that teachers will be most successful when they approach and understand their students as individuals, since each one has distinct needs, problems, abilities, interests, and past histories of reinforcement. Successful teachers are aware of different styles of development and learning and of the effects of individual maturational rates and environments on behavior. To deal with these differences successful teachers must be flexible. They must take into account many factors such as the age, intelligence, physical and emotional health, general adjustment and attitude, and past achievement of each of their students when designing instruction.

All major theories of development and learning take individual differences into consideration, although some theories emphasize this point much more than others. We have seen, for example, how family, peer group, school, mass media, social class, sex, and race each serves as an important transmitter and interpreter of culture. Since the combined influence of all these variables is never precisely the same for any two people, each growing child develops into a unique cultural product.

Learning-environmental and stage-dependent theories were discussed earlier in this text to point out the effects of environmental stimulation and maturation on behavior, and the resulting differences among individuals. Actually, both types of theories recognize the considerable importance of interaction between the individual and the environment, but they do so in different ways. Learning-environmentalists, such as Bruner, Bijou, and Baer are most directly concerned with the effects of the external environment on individual differences between one child and another.

Operant conditioning theorists, such as Skinner, point out that conditioning will not be successful unless appropriate reinforcers are selected. This can be done most effectively when the subject's past history and distinct personality are taken into consideration. Cognitive-field theorists have also been very much aware of the effect of individual differences on learning and behavior. The Gestaltists, for example, discovered important individual differences in the way we perceive the stimuli in our environment. Individual differences are an important area of study for the motivation theorist as well, since needs, drives, and goals vary considerably from person to person. Even Piaget's stage-dependent theory of cognitive development allows room for the idea that no two children are the same. Through the use of two basic concepts, assimilation and accommodation, Piaget shows how the continuous interaction between the environment and the learner might affect each child in a highly individual way.

Individual differences among learners continue to play an important role in the chapters that follow. Part 3, "Differences among Individuals: Effects on Learning and Teaching," focuses on such individual differences, and specific methods of designing instruction to meet the needs of these individuals are discussed in detail.

Chapter 10 concerns socially disadvantaged children who come from a background of poverty and social isolation. The socially disadvantaged are defined by Havighurst as those in the bottom 15 percent of the population in terms of income and educational achievement. Obviously, children with such a background have many problems: poor health, malnutrition, poor self-concepts, defeatist attitudes toward education and society, and very low levels of aspiration. We point out that traditional educational programs have not been very successful in dealing with these students and describe special intervention and compensatory programs that are now being developed to help them.

Chapter 11 concerns those students whose behavior, on one or more dimensions, represents a significant departure—either positive or negative—from the behavior of the average population. At one end of the scale is the handicapped student. Students in this category display some type of serious problem or disabling condition (mental, physical, sensory, or emotional) that makes learning under usual classroom conditions much more difficult for them than for other children. At the opposite end of the scale we find the gifted student, who is much more capable of succeeding than the average student. The emphasis in the chapter is on how to provide, through the network of the public schools, and, most currently, through the new mainstreaming programs, the kinds of programs and services that respond to the individual needs and differences of all these children.

Chapter 12 deals exclusively with problem behaviors. The problem behaviors discussed in the chapter are those most common in the classroom: anxiety, withdrawal, hyperactivity, and aggressiveness. Problem behaviors specifically related to the stress of adolescence are discussed as well. The chapter points out some of the things the teacher can do to help these students to understand and accept themselves as individuals and make a healthier adjustment to their environment.

Chapters 10, 11, and 12 all focus on the effects of differences among students in classroom learning; Chapter 13 turns the emphasis around from the student to the teacher. Reference has been made throughout the text to the importance of the teacher in effective classroom learning, but this is the first chapter in which teacher behavior is the major subject of discussion. In Chapter 13, the teacher is studied in terms of the special role this person is expected to play in the public school system—as a human being and also as a leader—and the effects of this role on classroom learning. We also discuss some important current issues affecting each teacher's attitude and outlook, such as school desegregation and busing, censorship of materials and subject matter, and the degree of personal freedom allotted to both teachers and students. The question of teachers' accountability—to the world and to themselves—is examined in depth.

TEACHING THE SOCIALLY DISADVANTAGED

CHAPTER 10

After completing this chapter, the reader should be able to:

1 Outline the characteristics of the population described by Havighurst as "socially disadvantaged" in terms of cultural background, health, expected behavior, attitudes, and self-concepts.

2 Explain why these characteristics make it more difficult for children from socially disadvantaged backgrounds to learn in school.

3 Describe the behaviors of teachers that are most effective in helping socially disadvantaged children to learn in school and, conversely, those behaviors that clearly serve to decrease learning in socially disadvantaged children.

4 Evaluate in terms of their short- and long-term effectiveness in increasing learning and improving self-concepts the solutions educators have attempted both within the public schools and in special programs designed for the disadvantaged.

5 Design "ideal" educational solutions to the problem of the socially disadvantaged, given the knowledge we now have both of programs that have been successful and of those that have failed in their attempts to increase learning in the socially disadvantaged.

Backgrounds of the Socially Disadvantaged

WHO ARE THE SOCIALLY DISADVANTAGED?

Robert Havighurst (1969) first used the term *socially disadvantaged* in an address to an American Psychological Association audience to describe the bottom 15 to 20 percent of the population in terms of income and educational achievement. In that address he pictured a sizable subculture of low-income Americans all characterized by an absence of steady employment, a low level of educational and technical skills, a dependence on government assistance programs, and, most importantly, an isolation from the remainder of society. According to Department of Labor Statistics, the income difference between rich and poor is growing (Bronfenbrenner, 1975).

With this growing difference, we can expect even greater isolation. The category of "socially disadvantaged" does not include any one single racial or ethnic group, although disproportionate numbers of some ethnic groups fall into the category. For example, although many black Americans fit such a description, the growing black middle class does not. The same is true for other ethnic groups. Many people might guess that America's socially disadvantaged are primarily nonwhite. Actually, almost two thirds of this disadvantaged group are English-speaking whites. At the time of Havighurst's address, some 20 million disadvantaged whites were located at the bottom of America's socioeconomic structure, along with 8 million blacks, 700,000 Puerto Ricans, 2 million other Spanish-Americans, and 500,000 American Indians.

The socially disadvantaged live in what Oscar Lewis (1966) first labeled a "culture of poverty" within a wealthy society. This culture (or total pattern of behavior or living patterns relating to what they eat, how they earn their livings, what interactions they have with other subcultures, and so on), according to Lewis, is quite distinctive. For example, the poor live at or near subsistence levels throughout their lives. They tend to be dropouts from school and thus are limited to unskilled, low-paying jobs. By their late twenties they have already passed their peak earning years. The disadvantaged tend to have difficulty focusing on long-term aspirations; day-to-day existence is a hard struggle. They cannot hold out for jobs that promise security and advancement.

The stark lives of the urban poor are in marked contrast to popular images of our "affluent society":

> Peter sleeps with his brother in one bedroom. The three girls sleep in the living room, which is a bedroom. . . . There is not very much furniture about. The kitchen has a table with four chairs, only two of which are sturdy. The girls sleep in one big bed. Peter shares his bed with his brother. The mother sleeps on a couch. . . . The apartment has no books, no records. There is a television set in the living room, and I have never seen it off. (Coles, 1968, p. 1320)

Almost two-thirds of America's socially disadvantaged are English-speaking whites.
(Morath, Magnum)

Rural poverty may be different in certain respects from urban poverty, but it is hardly better. Eight-year-old Sally comes from a migrant-worker family.

> [Her home] stands on four cement blocks. The cabin lacks curtains but does possess that old stove. . . . Near the stove there are three beds with mattresses but nothing else. Ten human beings use the mattresses: Sally's grandmother, her parents, and the seven children.
> These are people to whom a toothbrush is a strange instrument. Who have been to a doctor once or twice in their lives, and never to a hospital. Whose children must take turns going to school because they share the available clothing. (Van Brunt, 1972, p. 71)

Within such bleak environments, socially disadvantaged children receive little guidance or supervision. It is not easy for them to develop the verbal and intellectual skills necessary for success in the educational world. Their parents are often uninterested in formal learning, and they may unknowingly pass along to their children a fear of failure and a negative self-image.

It is important to distinguish between what we have termed "socially disadvantaged" and what earlier writers sometimes referred to as "culturally deprived." The latter term has often been employed in the past to explain the educational problems of low-income and minority group children. However, the term "cultural deprivation" has come under fire for its alleged white, middle-class biases (Tulkin, 1972). At best, the expression can only be considered a misnomer.

The deprivation of the poor is related to income and achievement, not to culture. It is impossible, certainly, to deprive an individual of his own living pattern; thus the expression has no meaning. Social scientists who have judged some minority subcultures to be culturally deprived are actually referring to the deprivation of middle-class living patterns. The concept of cultural deprivation thus appears to assume an inherent superiority of one set of cultural values above another. One example of this concept has been the deficit approach to education. This approach assumes that children who are taught their own native dialects in their homes rather than standard English are being deprived of proper language training (J. T. Gibson, 1972). It follows, according to proponents of this approach, that the proper role of the school is to make up for the ensuing deficit, that is, to change the child to make him "fit" into what is assumed to be an ideal system.

The term "socially disadvantaged" contains no such assumptions, and more easily allows for differences among cultures. Futhermore, unlike the cultural deprivation theory, the concept of social disadvantage lends itself to a more objective analysis, in which the responsibility for the plight of the poor is placed on and can be remedied by the larger society that controls the educational system as well as the economic system.

Questions for Thought

Think of the meaning of the following two statements: (1) The child must be changed to meet the needs of the system in which he is to be educated. (2) The system must be changed to meet the needs of the child.

Which do you think we do in our school systems?

Which is the more ideal solution to the problems of the socially disadvantaged? The more realistic?

Health of the Socially Disadvantaged

America's socially disadvantaged tend to suffer from severe health problems, many of which can be directly linked to hunger and malnutrition. Today, with increased news coverage of malnutrition and hunger in wide areas of the world, we tend to ignore these same problems in our own country. However, the Citizens' Board of Inquiry into Hunger and Malnutrition in the United States reported (*Hunger USA*, 1968):

> Hunger and malnutrition take their toll in this country in the form of infant deaths, organic brain damage, retarded growth and learning rates, increased vulnerability to disease, withdrawal, apathy, alienation, frustration, and violence. (p. 10)

Hunger and malnutrition are widespread conditions in America as well as elsewhere in the world. In fact, the Office of Economic Opportunity estimated as long ago as 1969 that some 14 to 15 million Americans were unable to afford a minimally adequate diet. The Select Senate Committee on Nutrition and Human Needs suggested that there are 10 million hungry Americans. The federal food stamp program, in which American poor are provided with a way to purchase food at a lower cost, was one attempt to solve this problem. Still, the world hunger crisis described in the media shows that the number of malnourished people, both abroad and in this country, is increasing dramatically each day.

Low-income people, of course, suffer the most from poor diet and malnutrition. Surveys have shown that satisfactory diet, that is, diet that provides sufficient nutrients for adequate growth and development, can be directly linked to income level.

The results of this widespread malnutrition are disastrous. Infant mortality rates among families with incomes under $3,000 are about one and a half times the rates for families with incomes of $10,000 and more. In addition, infant mortality rates for nonwhites are almost double the rates for whites (HEW, 1970).

Malnutrition also leads to a wide variety of physical problems and diseases. One study found that low-income infants were 6 months to 3 years behind their peers in physical development (Kotz, 1969). A Seattle doctor estimated that between 50 percent and 75 percent of all poverty children in this age bracket suffer from nutritional deficiency anemia, as compared with only 5 percent of children seen in private practice (*Hunger USA*, 1968).

The socially disadvantaged also run the risk of many diseases associated simply with poor living conditions. One example of this is lead poisoning. The children of the urban poor often pick up and eat the lead-based paint flakes that fall off decaying walls. The Department of Health, Education, and Welfare believes that, as late as 1974, 2.5 million of these children ran the risk of contracting lead poisoning. Of these, 125,000 may already have the disease, which can lead to retardation, permanent brain damage, and even death.

The health problems of socially disadvantaged children raise serious questions for educators. As we discussed in Chapter 6, physiological needs are primary in Maslow's hierarchy of needs. A hungry or sick child will not pursue his needs for love and belonging, esteem, or self-actualization as easily as a well-fed or healthy child. As the Citizens' Board of Inquiry into Hunger and Malnutrition pointed out as long ago as 1968, "Hunger for food overrides hunger for knowledge" (*Hunger USA*, 1968).

A child comes to school with no breakfast—except perhaps for a cup of coffee. He has no lunch and no money for a school lunch. He may carry some candy to nibble on to appease his appetite. Teachers and principals have repeatedly told the Board the obstacle which hunger places in their way—in the form of listlessness, fights over food, inattentiveness, acute hunger pangs, withdrawal, a sense of failure. (p. 19)

The Board concludes that "the ultimate costs are to be found in patterns of social unrest, distrust, alienation, withdrawal, and frustration."

Behavior and Attitudes of the Socially Disadvantaged

A third approach to describing socially disadvantaged children is in terms of behavioral and attitudinal patterns. Especially significant are the negative self-images that tend to be instilled in these children. Many qualities and customs of the disadvantaged are considered strange, inappropriate, or simply "wrong" according to middle-class norms, and, frequently, according to middle-class teachers. The disadvantaged child is besieged with these judgments and learns to feel incompetent, inadequate, and out of place in middle-class institutions (Karnes, Zehrbach, and Jones, 1971).

The problem of self-concept is most serious for black and other minority group children; the racism of white middle-class society begins to affect their own images of what they are and what value judgment to place on their self-worth at an early age. For example, Kenneth Clark reported in 1965 that, as early as 3 years of age, black children reject dark-skinned dolls as "dirty" or "bad" and prefer white dolls.

As we shall see later in this chapter, these particular behaviors representing lowered self-esteem seem to be on the decline, particularly with the advent of black studies programs designed to increase self-esteem. The underlying problem, however, still remains to be dealt with.

Various behavior patterns follow directly from poor self-concepts. Disadvantaged youth are prone to passivity in school, and find it difficult to adapt to delayed rewards (Karnes et al., 1971). They frequently violate middle-class social mores—by being either excessively boisterous or overly withdrawn; by speaking without permission; by refusing to defer to authority figures; by using "street" language that is considered improper in school; by solving problems through combat and violence; and by reacting in a hostile manner to constructive criticism from the teacher. All of these behavior problems are learned through and are socially acceptable within the "culture of poverty" from which disadvantaged youths come. Yet the values and social codes of the disadvantaged are not accepted as appropriate—and often not even understood—by middle-class teachers.

Given the norms of the school, these behavior patterns program the disadvantaged child for failure. The child enters school with a

DEVELOPING SELF-CONCEPTS THROUGH COMMUNITY ACTION

East Los Angeles is a community of 110,000 people, virtually a separate city within Los Angeles' borders. It used to be drab, dangerous, and deserted at night, with more than its share of vandalism, burglaries, and car thefts. Yet there has been a remarkable change in the barrio ("The Mural Message," *Time,* 1975). Today, there is "an increase in community pride, a new awareness of self-worth." What has brought about the difference? Approximately 200 huge murals on the sides of once-drab buildings, murals which vividly depict the Chicano heritage. The idea of wall paintings was the idea of John and Joe Gonzales, who felt that community art might give the residents more of a sense of belonging to the neighborhood. Local artists were persuaded to provide the inspiration; they have designed bright abstracts, realistic scenes of barrio life, mannered portraits of saints, Aztec warriors, and campesino heroes. Says one resident, "It's fabulous to come out and see what beautiful paintings we have. People used to get depressed or angry and take it out on their homes. Now they take better care of them." In the Maravilla district of town, members of a street gang worked with artist David Lopez on a Virgin of Guadalupe mural. A psychologist working with them found that "once they work on a mural, they verbalize a problem instead of lashing out blindly at society." Vandalism in the area has dropped sharply. Today, elementary school classes are brought to "East Los" to study the murals as part of their history lessons. The message that now comes through is the citizens' pride in their heritage. The murals have worked such wonders that the Bicentennial Committee has commissioned 1,530 new murals throughout the entire city of Los Angeles.

shaky self-concept and quickly learns that his identity, culture, and life-style are seen as offensive by his middle-class teacher. Alienation and withdrawal are bound to follow.

Poverty: A Vicious Cycle

We have seen how the malnutrition, negative self-concepts, and behavior patterns of socially disadvantaged children contribute to their failures in the schools. Ultimately, this failure leads to a vicious cycle, as pictured in Figure 10-1.

The "culture of poverty" in which disadvantaged children grow up, described by Oscar Lewis, directly affects their failures in the schools. Because of these failures, disadvantaged children often drop out early, cannot find steady employment, and end up as disadvantaged adults stuck in the same pattern of poverty. Their children must then be reared under the same difficult conditions, and they find themselves in danger of failing in the schools. And the cycle goes on and on.

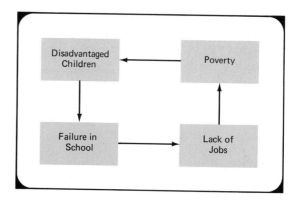

Figure 10-1.
Poverty: a vicious cycle.
(Donegan, 1973)

Questions for Thought

As Figure 10-1 shows, the cycle of poverty seems to present an endless cycle of problems for disadvantaged children. Given this cycle, how might the teacher help to stop the bad effects?

How would a federally funded breakfast program assist the teacher?

Understanding the causes of the often very different behavior of socially disadvantaged children, how should the teacher respond?

WHY ARE WE FAILING?

What Are the Issues?

The chart presented in the previous section outlines a vicious cycle of continuing poverty. It is important to understand how difficult it is for a socially disadvantaged child to break out of this pattern. Success in the school system and later in society is an almost impossible task for the socially disadvantaged.

Yet, while much discussion correctly focuses on the vast majority of disadvantaged children who fail to learn in our schools, it is nevertheless true that a small minority of disadvantaged children, despite all the roadblocks described earlier, are successful in learning in school, learning later to earn a living, and thus in escaping the poverty cycle.

ADAPTABILITY. The successful child of a socially disadvantaged background—that is, the disadvantaged child who, despite all odds, is able to learn in school—must be unusually *adaptable*. He must make the difficult transition from the behaviors accepted by the "culture of poverty" at home to the behaviors accepted by the alien, usually middle-class, environment of the school (Bernard, 1973). In order to succeed in the educational system, the disadvantaged child must learn to communicate with other students and teachers, and must find ways to gain approval within the new guidelines of the classroom.

LANGUAGE DIFFICULTIES.   There are many reasons why these goals are extremely difficult to attain. One of the most basic problems involves language. Linguists and psychologists have stressed the relationship between preschool language development and success in school (Ruddell and Graves, 1968). The child who begins the educational process with well-developed oral language skills of standard English starts off with a tremendous advantage. As studies have consistently demonstrated, this child usually comes from a middle-class or upper-class background.

Socially disadvantaged children encounter language difficulties as soon as they begin formal education. For children from Spanish-speaking homes, for example, the language problem is obvious. School may be their first exposure to written or spoken English, and there are hardly enough bilingual programs for the large number of Spanish-speaking children in the United States.

For black children, the problem is more complex. In recent years, linguists have shown that such children are often taught a dialect of "black English," which has marked differences from the formal, middle-class "standard English" of the schools. Some teachers have disapproving and somewhat contemptuous attitudes toward black English:

> One result of this attitude is poor mental health on the part of the pupils. A child is quick to grasp the feeling that while school speech is "good" his own speech is "bad," and that by extension he himself is somehow inadequate and without value. (Seymour, 1971, p. 175)

It is easy to see how these language difficulties compound the self-image problems of black children.

A classroom in New York City where instruction is in both English and Spanish for the benefit of students of Puerto Rican background.

(Van Bucher, Photo Researchers)

There is now evidence that poor black children as well as Spanish-speaking children in the United States should be thought of as bilingual. Studies by Baratz (1969), Marwit, Marwit, and Boswell (1972), and Genshaft and Hirt (1974) all suggest that these black children are learning a well-ordered dialect that is different from standard English but not deficient. The Genshaft and Hirt study showed that when black and white children were matched for social class and nonverbal intelligence, both groups performed equally well on verbal tasks involving standard English. Further, on tasks involving black English, the white children performed significantly worse. This confirms the theory that disadvantaged black children are learning two languages: black dialect for use at home, standard English for use in school.

These studies all point toward a need for increased bilingual education in this country. There are a number of highly successful pilot projects in bilingualism. Particularly important are the experiments in Montreal—the St. Lambert project (Brock, Lambert, and Tucher, 1973; Lambert, 1972)—and in Culver City, California (Cohen, 1974). In each of these, English-speaking children were instructed in many subject matters in a second language foreign to that spoken in their homes (French for English-speaking students in Canada; Spanish for English-speaking students in California). The children became competent in the new language, remained proficient in the native language, and performed well in nonlanguage subjects using the same curriculum as children who were not bilingual. This procedure is not new; bilingual education has been carried out extensively in the Soviet Union as well as many other countries, where children frequently successfully learn many subjects in other than their native tongues.

Since the 1968 passage of the Bilingual Education Act, which calls for teaching of subject matters in both English and native language for children unfamiliar with standard English, experimental bilingual programs have expanded in urban America. Yet bilingual education for disadvantaged children is still a highly controversial issue in the United States, especially in the case of black English. It seems clear that if disadvantaged children speak a different dialect from their teachers, either the children must learn standard English, or the teacher must learn to communicate in the children's dialect, or, as many educators have come to realize, both must happen at once.

Some educators believe that there must be "total acceptance of the child's nonstandard dialect spoken at home" if any language program is to succeed (Strickland, 1973). Others insist that consideration of such dialects by teachers will make the teaching of reading much more difficult (Vail, 1970). Professor Toni Cade of Rutgers, a noted black writer, poses the basic dilemma for socially disadvantaged minorities. She opposes tampering with ghetto accents, but at the same time advocates the learning of standard English, because "if you want to get ahead in this country, you must master the language of the ruling class" (Seymour, 1971).

THE EFFECT OF REWARDS AND PUNISHMENTS. The work of Robert J. Havighurst (1969) provides a useful theoretical model for understanding what we have accomplished so far in reducing the learning problems of socially disadvantaged children. Havighurst argues that teachers have lacked a systematic theory of the effects of rewards and punishments on poor children. He cites the findings of Davis (1965) to back up his contention that tangible, material rewards are important in stimulating disadvantaged children in school:

**What Have We
Accomplished So Far?**

> Davis . . . noted that his wife, then working as a substitute teacher in the Chicago public schools, made a discovery about the way that disadvantaged children may learn arithmetic. In a second grade in a ghetto school she found several children, including one 9-year-old boy, who could not count beyond two or three. The following day was Valentine's Day, and she brought some candy hearts to school. She told the children that they could have as many candy hearts as they could count. *The 9-year-old boy thereupon counted 14 candy hearts.* (Havighurst, 1970, p. 315)

The secret apparently lay simply in finding the appropriate stimulus with which to reward the child.

Havighurst also demonstrated that different socially disadvantaged groups have different kinds of reward systems that appear to be most effective. As an example, he cites a study by Wax (1969) of Cherokee and Sioux children. These children form a close-knit group that opposes individual excellence at the expense of peers.

> In oral reading, the whole class tends to read together in audible whispers, so that the child supposed to be reciting can simply wait when he comes to a difficult word until he hears it said by his classmates. Generally, pupils like to work together and help each other. Consequently, the weak students are carried along by the stronger ones, and the stronger ones do not exert themselves to excel the weaker ones. (Havighurst, 1970, p. 315)

Reward in this group apparently is provided through feedback that is meted out primarily by peers. Havighurst contrasts these children with Appalachian disadvantaged children, who get rewards mainly from the family circle rather than peers, and with poor black children, who, interestingly, depend more on approval or disapproval from the teacher. This may be because they are less likely than Indian and Appalachian children to have both parents in the home, and, according to Havighurst, they probably also receive less parental approval-disapproval.

TEACHER EXPECTATION AND THE SELF-FULFILLING PROPHECY.　Despite these differences in cultural background, socially disadvantaged children face many similar problems in the educational system. One of the most serious is teacher expectation. As was discussed in Chapter 6, Rosenthal and Jacobson (1968) have pointed to a "self-fulfilling prophecy" or "Pygmalion effect," whereby the negative expectations of middle-class teachers about disadvantaged children may contribute strongly to failure in the schools.

Although the Rosenthal and Jacobson study was criticized by many educational theorists on technical grounds, the "self-fulfilling prophecy" hypothesis itself has been supported by data from a Hunter College study of 14 new teachers in inner-city schools (Fuchs, 1972). The diary of one of the young teachers is especially revealing. Her own words make the pattern of teacher socialization clear. At first, she is warm, friendly, and respectful toward her students. But after a talk with a more experienced teacher, she begins to assimilate the prevailing values of the school. She blames the children's family backgrounds for their failure, rather than questioning the workings of the educational system. Soon she is "tracking" her class—choosing a select few "good" students for special attention, and labeling others as "slow" and thus, in her eyes, not deserving as much attention. In merely using one term, "slow," she manages to write off most of her class as being hopeless.

PROMOTING POSITIVE SELF-IMAGES.　The problem of teacher expectation cannot be separated from the negative self-images of disadvantaged children. When these children enter an alien school system, they often will be fearful and uncertain. This is particularly true of those who come from minority groups. If they enter with self-doubts, and if they are immediately faced with a teacher who reinforces their negative self-concepts, failure is almost a certainty. And it is easy for a teacher to make disadvantaged children feel inferior and out of place—whether by overt actions or by subtle, even unconscious, facial expressions and tone of voice.

In an earlier section of this chapter, we spoke of the special self-concept problems of black children, particularly as exhibited by their preference for white dolls. In more recent years, there has been evidence to suggest that with more and more people becoming aware of the particular problems of socially disadvantaged children and accepting their "different" behavior, black pride and self-esteem are on the rise. One study of doll preferences among black children (Hraba and Grant, 1970), for example, duplicated a similar study conducted 30 years before. The differences in the findings

The socially disadvantaged youngster faces a formidable opponent in the development of self-esteem—the prevailing apathy and sense of decay that characterize ghetto living. Often, broad-scale social welfare programs, however well designed or funded, fail because they do not provide opportunities for leadership and strong community involvement—a sense of vested interest that builds a feeling of attainment and community pride. Today there is growing recognition that the upgrading of ghetto life must come from within the community itself. This is the foundation on which self-help programs are developed.

A prime example of community-initiated self-help is the Ozanam Cultural Center of Pittsburgh, Pennsylvania. It is a community center sponsored by the Catholic diocese, located in one of the city's most neglected and deprived areas, the Hill District. Through its continuing development of recreational, educational, and cultural activities, Ozanam involves hundreds of youngsters and adults in personally productive endeavors. Programs include organized sports leagues in baseball, basketball, volleyball, and midget football; educational courses in developmental reading and math for college preparatory work; instruction in personal hygiene and grooming as well as free medical care services at nearby hospitals; and arts and crafts geared to develop creative energies. A particular source of pride for the community is the Ozanam Strings, a group of 60 black violinists from kindergarten through the eleventh grade who perform throughout the city.

The success of the programs at the Ozanam Cultural Center, which is staffed by paid professionals and community volunteers, signals new orientations for those it serves. By providing constructive activities that develop the human resources of the community, the center is breaking the traditional patterns of apathy, frustration, defeatism, and loss of self-esteem.

THE OZANAM CULTURAL CENTER: DEVELOPING HUMAN RESOURCES IN THE GHETTO

were striking. In 1939, 67 percent of the black children preferred to play with white dolls, and only 32 percent chose black dolls. In 1969, 70 percent of the black children chose black dolls and only 30 percent chose white dolls.

Another interesting finding related to self-concept developed from a study of racial integration (Busk, Ford, and Schulman, 1973). It was learned that both black and white students in integrated schools showed higher self-images in terms of both academic and social achievements than did their counterparts in segregated schools. The researchers concluded that "the more influential factor affecting the student's self-concept is not ethnic membership but the racial composition of the school he attends" (p. 60).

It is not entirely clear which factors are most important in promoting positive self-concepts among disadvantaged children. Teacher initiative, integrated education, and ethnic pride movements may all contribute. It is clear, however, that socially disadvantaged children will not succeed in our educational system without self-confidence (developed through support and encouragement both from family and teachers) and a sense of their own capacities and potential. Instead of increasing the children's self-doubts, the schools must join with society as a whole to build their self-esteem. In this next section we will give some suggestions as to what the school can do.

 ## SOME SOLUTIONS AND PROGRAMS

Changing Our Traditional Programs

It is evident from our discussion that socially disadvantaged children come from backgrounds and face problems that vary greatly from those of their middle-class counterparts. Some teachers, however, simply ignore the differences between disadvantaged and privileged children and treat every child in the same (often middle-class) way. Other teachers recognize that disadvantaged children are, in fact, "different," but they make the children feel defensive and even ashamed about their values, their life-styles, and their ethnic identities.

These two approaches are, of course, equally destructive to the disadvantaged child. The schools can instead *capitalize* on cultural differences. They can recognize that socially disadvantaged children come from cultures with distinctive patterns and values, and can use this knowledge to teach adaptability and skills necessary to live productive lives.

For example, disadvantaged children demonstrate play patterns that are unlike those of the middle class. According to many authors, behaviors such as running, pushing, and shoving are characteristic of the play of disadvantaged children (Mosby, 1971). One way to prepare such children for constructive play experiences rather than wasteful exercise is to provide interesting teaching materials in the classroom which seem familiar and are clearly relevant to children's lives. The truly successful teacher chooses materials carefully, selecting whatever will meet the needs of an individual child at a certain moment (Dennison, 1969).

Studies have shown that the behavior of teachers in the classroom can have a marked effect on student performance (Ryans, 1961). A teacher who is excited about learning may help excite students; a teacher who is pessimistic and cynical will only feed the students' dislike of the school system.

It is crucial that the teacher of the disadvantaged respect the children and their cultures. The teacher often is the key factor in the performance of children in school. Next to parents, he may be the

A volunteer teaching assistant in the District of Columbia public schools was assigned to a class of fifth-grade children who were reading at second-grade level. They sat stiffly in their seats, trying to cope with "see Spot run" primers. But reading can and should be fun, thought the teacher. Why should there be this air of defeatism? So the next day she brought one 11-year-old a rousing Jules Verne novel from her home library. The child was so entranced by Verne's adventure story that he begged her for the book. She wrote his name on the flyleaf and gave it to him. And a great idea was born (Starnes, 1975).

What followed was a deluge of 25 million paperback books selected by children as their own in a program aptly called Reading Is FUNdamental (RIF). Launched as a pilot program in the District of Columbia schools in 1966, RIF in 1975 had 350 chapters in 48 states, and hoped to double that number in a year or two. Financial support has come from foundations, fraternal and service organizations, corporations, and the government.

The response to the program was instantaneous. Children in the pilot program who were reading three and four years behind their grade levels became avid readers almost overnight. Parents also became enthusiastic partners in the plan. Surveys taken since indicate that more than 90 percent of the parents say the program has increased their children's reading skills. Sixty percent say their children have encouraged them to buy other books. Children are learning that reading is fun.

EVERYBODY DOESN'T "KNOW" THAT JOHNNY CAN'T READ

most significant adult in a child's life (Banks, 1972). If the teacher begins with a negative attitude toward the racial or ethnic background of students, the classroom environment will hardly be a friendly atmosphere for learning.

Building a model for appropriate student behavior is not simple. As Henry (1972) points out:

> Poor children often come to school unfed, after wretched nights torn by screaming, fighting, bed-wetting; often they cannot sleep because of cold and rats. They come to class hungry, sleepy and emotionally upset. To start routine schoolwork effectively at once is impossible. (p. 106)

As just one beginning to solving this problem, Henry proposes government-supported school breakfast programs, in which teachers and students eat breakfast together. He sees this as a way of not only feeding hungry children but also bringing together students and teachers in an informal atmosphere.

In general, student behavior will be linked directly to the presence of motivating materials in the classroom and to appropriate teacher behavior. In a warm, respectful, exciting, and nonthreatening classroom environment, disadvantaged children may overcome their hesitations and indulge their boundless curiosity for knowledge. If a classroom is lacking in these qualities—if a teacher cannot communicate to children that they are important and worthwhile members of society—nothing else that he may do will encourage disadvantaged children to improve their educational skills.

Early Childhood Intervention Programs

America's socially disadvantaged are in dire need of quality preschool programs. As Mary Keyserling (1972) states, the absence of such programs causes serious problems for socially disadvantaged children and parents.

Keyserling reports that in 1972 some 4.5 million women with children under the age of 6 were job holders, mostly out of economic necessity. Approximately 2 million of their children were left in homes that were not their own. Of these, only 700,000 spent the day in licensed day-care centers. Furthermore, many of the children stayed in substandard facilities supervised by untrained persons. Some apartments that were licensed as proprietary day-care centers for 6 children were caring for as many as 47.

Children of the socially disadvantaged need more than day care. They need early childhood education programs that will stimulate their cognitive development as well as their emotional and social well-being. Such programs could be helpful for infants and toddlers as well as older children (Dale, 1972). "The sooner the better" is not a bad rule in this situation, for once the disadvantaged children have fallen behind their more affluent peers, their educational success is in jeopardy.

PARENT-CHILD INTERVENTION PROGRAMS.　One approach to remedying the learning difficulties of disadvantaged children has centered on intervention programs involving parents.

Karnes, Teska, Hodgins, and Badger (1970) report on a program in Champaign-Urbana, Illinois, in which mothers were the primary agents of intervention. Twenty mothers were recruited from inner-city neighborhoods for the pilot project. Each agreed to attend a two-hour weekly meeting during which she would be instructed in teaching techniques to use with infants (varying in age from 12 to 24 months). In addition, a portion of each meeting was reserved for discussion time, in order to build a supportive atmosphere for the mothers and foster their sense of dignity and efficacy. The aim was to stimulate the cognitive and verbal development of the children using, the natural mother in place of an elaborate outside program at as low a cost as possible.

After completion of the program by 15 mothers, IQ testing of the children revealed substantial improvement in learning skills. The results compare favorably with other studies that have relied on college graduates or professional tutors to do the same work.

Jason, Clarfield, and Cowen (1973) studied an intervention program involving 10 inner-city toddlers in Rochester, New York. These children met frequently with college undergraduate "helpers" over a five-month period. In addition, home sessions were conducted at which parents were present. The program stressed cognitive and verbal development and social behavior.

Jason and his colleagues found that "a saturated infant stimulation program with parent involvement helped significantly, at least in the short run" (p. 57). There were significant improvements in the cognitive skills and social behavior of the children. In addition, mothers became progressively more interested in the program and more actively involved in stressing similar goals in the home.

Nimnicht and Brown (1972) developed a training course for parents in connection with their toy library at the Far West Laboratory for Educational Research and Development. Parents were instructed in the use of certain educational toys and in the basic concepts and facts of child development. Particular emphasis was placed on the children's needs for healthy self-concepts and on positive reinforcement for the children.

One of the key findings of the program was that parents' attitudes toward their children improved noticeably. In their descriptions of their children, the parents used words that showed that they were more respectful toward their children and more confident of the children's abilities. Nimnicht and Brown argue that increased parental praise and approval will inevitably encourage healthier self-concepts in children. These researchers also learned that the children showed significant improvement in nine intellectual areas: color naming, color identification, shape naming, shape identification, numerical concepts, relational concepts, problem-solving, verbal communication, and verbal comprehension. This success seems attributable both to the quality of the educational toys used and to the interest and enthusiasm of the parents. In fact, several parents mentioned that the discussion sessions with other parents were the most helpful part of the course.

Schaefer (1972), after evaluating various parent intervention programs, concluded that "working with mothers is an effective method for producing gains in intellectual functioning." However, he also points to the major drawbacks of such programs. They cannot in themselves be a total educational answer for the problems of disadvantaged children. And there must be sufficient *follow-through* if the gains of these programs are to be preserved. Schaefer points to the need for "early and continuing support for parents in their roles as educators of their own children and as students of the theory and practice of education in the home."

EARLY CHILDHOOD SCHOOL PROGRAMS. As we discussed in Part 1, in the past decade many important preschool education programs have been instituted around the country. Often such programs have been focused on the educational needs of socially disadvantaged children.

One of the most interesting is Caldwell's children's center in Syracuse, New York (Caldwell, 1968). This center was created to test the hypothesis that the first three years of a child's life constitute the optimal time for educational enrichment programs. It was designed to serve about 25 children between the ages of 6 months and 3 years, who generally attended the center from six to nine hours daily, five days a week. Almost all of the children were from disadvantaged backgrounds.

The content of the Caldwell program placed heavy stress on spoken language skills. In addition, there were attempts to promote social and emotional development and perceptual, motor, and cognitive skills. Behind all of these efforts was a belief that the child must feel secure and masterful in order to develop a positive self-image and succeed in the educational world.

Caldwell and her staff tested these ideas by evaluating the progress of all children who had been using the center for more than three months. Caldwell noted that these children showed IQ *gains* just at the age that disadvantaged children often register *declining* test scores. Caldwell's data suggested further that the children from the most disadvantaged families gained the most from the center's program, and that those children who had benefited most from the enrichment program had spent the longest time in it.

Another finding of importance was that the children showed gains in terms of social competence and no increase in symptoms of emotional problems. There had been concern by some that, due to the young age of the children, increased physical illnesses or emotional problems might result from the enrichment program. In fact, these fears seem to be unfounded, and the success of the Caldwell center seems clearly established.

Probably the best-known preschool intervention program is Project Head Start, originally sponsored by the federal government's Office of Economic Opportunity. Head Start came into existence in the summer of 1964 at 13,400 educational centers across the nation, serving 560,000 disadvantaged children. Initially, it was planned as an eight-week introductory program for disadvantaged preschool children, designed to prepare them for public school education. Head Start was enthusiastically praised by parents, teachers, and pupils, and by the end of the 1960s had expanded into a broad, nationwide preschool program for inner-city children.

But Head Start's growth and popularity must be reevaluated in the light of critical research on the educational value of the program. A study by the Westinghouse Learning Corporation and Ohio Uni-

The Head Start program provides cultural enrichment to preschool children in preparation for public school education.

(Uzzle, Magnum)

versity concluded that Head Start apparently did not significantly increase the intellectual capabilities of inner-city children (Cicirelli et al., 1969). *It is extremely important to note that the researchers indicated that the problem was not to be found within Head Start itself, but rather with the absence of satisfactory follow-through programs.* It makes little sense to spend large sums of money to enrich the learning experiences of disadvantaged children before they enter the public schools, only to cut them adrift at that point.

Questions for Thought

If it is true that Head Start children *do* increase their skills significantly during their program, but lose this advantage when subjected to the standard programming of the public schools, what do you think would be the best solution to the problem? Close down Head Start? Develop other preschool programs that would be more effective? Or change the public school programming?

How often do you think political considerations, rather than consideration of children, influence the answer to these questions?

THE BEREITER-ENGELMANN PROGRAM.   Perhaps the most highly structured current educational program for disadvantaged children is one designed by Bereiter and Engelmann. The critical assumption of this program

. . . was that disadvantaged children differed from others only in what they had and had not learned previously, so that an effective compensatory education program could be designed simply by starting at a lower level of presumed initial knowledge and moving more rapidly and efficiently, thus enabling the children to catch up to others whose initial levels of knowledge were higher. (Bereiter and Engelmann, 1968)

Bereiter and Engelmann's program has been heavily criticized by some educators because of the strict adherence to structure, and by others because of the assumption implicit in Bereiter and Engelmann's educational theories—that, indeed, the disadvantaged are *deficient* in skills, not that their skills are *different*. Nevertheless, as we shall see, the program has produced some startling results.

An experimental group of 15 children was recruited from a predominantly black, poor community in Champaign-Urbana, Illinois. These children attended special classes for two hours a day, five days a week. A fairly rigid schedule was established. The class was divided into three work groups of five children each. After a 10-minute free-play period to begin the session, each work group went off for a 20-minute class in language, arithmetic, or reading.

After the initial class period, the whole group would reunite for a 30-minute break in which they could sing, snack, and use the rest rooms. This break period was followed by another 20-minute subject class. Next came another 20-minute period in which all 15 children got together for reading and discussion of stories. A final 20-minute subject class concluded the day's schedule.

The general instructional strategy involved pattern drills conducted at a rapid pace. At first a verbal formula was learned by rote: "This *apple* is *red*," "This is a *cup*," "This *cup* is *full*." Gradually, more complicated variations were presented to the students.

The language program focused on developing "the minimum essentials of language competence."

Arithmetic was viewed and taught primarily as a "science of counting." As in the language program, pattern drills were heavily stressed. Rather than formally presenting explicit rules of arithmetic, the teacher encouraged the children to learn these rules implicitly through constant repetition of various example patterns.

The reading program centered on an explicit rule system that was tied to a restricted vocabulary. Initially, the children were exposed only to three-letter (consonant-vowel-consonant) patterns. In addition, a few of the more difficult consonants were excluded, and only lowercase letters were included.

This program has resulted in dramatic increases in Stanford-Binet scores. (Stanford-Binet is a highly respected test of intelligence. It will be discussed in detail in Chapter 15.) As Table 10-1 indicates, 4-year-olds in the Bereiter-Engelmann program showed consistent and significant improvement after one year. This improvement was generally greater than that of the control group, which was not part of the program. Furthermore, the 1964 and 1965 experimental groups

Year entering	Pretest score	Score after 1 yr.	Score after 2 yr.
1964	97.6	104.2	106.8
1965	97.0	111.5	120.4
1966	91.1	102.9	—
1965 control	94.5	102.6	99.6

Table 10-1

Stanford-Binet Test Results for 4-year-old Children in the Bereiter-Engelmann Program

After Osborn (1968, p. 47)

both increased their scores a second time after two years, whereas the control group's scores fell in the second year.

Bereiter and Engelmann (1968), in analyzing the results of various testing procedures, conclude:

> [By] devoting twenty minutes a day to instruction in each area, disadvantaged preschool children can acquire in two year's time: (1) enough language learning to take them from a year or more below average up to an average level of performance; (2) two and one-half years' worth of arithmetic learning, by primary school standards; (3) slightly over one and one-half years' worth of learning in reading and spelling, by primary school standards.

EFFECTS OF EDUCATIONAL TELEVISION. The popular educational television series for children, *Sesame Street*, was described in detail in Chapter 9. Educational studies have demonstrated that *Sesame Street* has effectively communicated basic skills, facts, and concepts to preschool children (Bogartz and Ball, 1971). Teachers claim that frequent viewers are better prepared for school than are children who only watch occasionally. Research tends to bear out this view.

The television show has had particularly important implications for disadvantaged children. Among frequent viewers, disadvantaged children seem to benefit as much as the more affluent viewers, and black disadvantaged children benefit as much as the white disadvantaged. While it can be said that young children of all backgrounds have gained from *Sesame Street*, its particular impact on socially disadvantaged children cannot be ignored.

OPERATION UPGRADE. In July, 1968, a community-based reading project known as Operation Upgrade was begun in a low-income neighborhood in Kansas City, Missouri. The educational theories of Dr. Nancy Johnson (1973) formed the central focus of this program. Its goal was:

Programs for School-Age Children

> . . . to provide an educational and motivational intervention program for inner-city children who face frustration and failure in their everyday school experience because of poor reading ability.

Operation Upgrade has produced remarkable results with the use of a system of precision teaching. Students in the program in Kansas City are pictured here.

(Dr. Nancy Johnson)

Operation Upgrade took place in seven tutoring locations in the target area. At each center (usually rooms provided by the community), high-school-aged tutors instructed the children. The tutors were supervised by adult program directors, and all tutors and directors were community residents.*

Each tutor was responsible for five children. The tutor met individually with each child for 45 minutes per day, five days a week, generally after the regular school day had ended. The sessions continued until the child had reached grade level.

Johnson's system of precision teaching provided the educational method for the tutoring process. As we mentioned in Chapter 9, the goal of precision teaching is to monitor the improvement of students. In simple terms, improvement takes place when a child's correct responses (words read correctly) go up (acceleration) or when a child's incorrect responses (words read incorrectly) go down (deceleration). Such improvement, in terms of reading more words correctly and at the same time making fewer errors, is the measure of learning under precision teaching.

The teacher or tutor (or peer teacher) must follow four basic steps under the precision-teaching system. The first is to pinpoint. The teacher carefully observes the child and *pinpoints* (or precisely identifies) his problem areas in reading.

The teacher must pinpoint *movements*—or specific behaviors of the pupil—in order to clarify which responses the pupil must accelerate and which responses he must decelerate.

The next step is to *record* and *chart* significant movements. This is essential if the teacher is to understand the pupil's progress (or lack of progress.) Teachers record the daily *frequency* of certain movements by dividing the *number of movements completed* by the *number of minutes allotted.*

According to Johnson, without record sheets and charts it would be impossible to remember, in the detail that is necessary for optimal learning, even one pupil's performance from day to day. By keeping careful written records, the teachers and tutors can quickly learn if a child is improving in key movements. Often the children are encouraged to involve themselves in these record-keeping tasks (and thus participate in evaluating their own improvement).

The next (and crucial) step is to *indicate change.* By examining a student's charts, the teacher can sense improvement or lack of improvement. If the student seems to be in a rut—that is, if he does not increase the number of words per minute that he can read or if he does not increase his ability to comprehend—the teacher must determine what can be changed in order to help the student perform better. A child may fail to show improvement if the work is

*If the classroom teacher wishes to utilize this technique he may use peer teaching instead, in which older students serve as tutors or paraprofessionals.

too easy, if the work is too difficult, or if he has become bored or lost interest.

But what about the child who suddenly shows an unexpected decline—a deceleration in the frequency of correct responses and an acceleration in the frequency of wrong responses? This child may, of course, be ill or emotionally preoccupied. If not, the child may have become bored with the work, and may need what is known as a consequence, that is, a reinforcer. Possible consequences might include gold stars, extra time in the game or library areas of the room, positions as line reader or blackboard eraser, or rewards in terms of a medium of exchange like poker chips, play money, or, in the case of Operation Upgrade, points. But the consequence must be determined for each child as an individual.

The final step in precision teaching is an old adage: "If at first you don't succeed, try, try again." The teacher must never lose confidence in his ability or in the ability of the pupil. One strategy for change may fail; one consequence may prove to be useless in motivating the student. It is then proper to experiment with another strategy. The successful precision teacher keeps trying, and it rarely takes more than a second attempt to bring results.

These techniques of precision teaching formed the basis for the tutoring sessions in Operation Upgrade. A typical session may have included (Johnson, 1973):

1. Oral reading from graded reader—2 minutes
2. Graded reader comprehension check—5 minutes
3. Oral reading from newspaper—2 minutes
4. Work in reading skills workbook—10 minutes
5. Oral reading from peer stories—2 minutes
6. Peer stories comprehension check—5 minutes
7. Basic sight vocabulary drill—2 minutes
8. Write own story (twice a week)—10 minutes
9. Oral reading—own story (twice a week)—2 minutes

After these exercises, the tutor reviews mistakes and new words, goes over missed comprehension questions with the pupil, and records the pupil's frequency in movements such as "reads words correctly," "reads words wrongly," "writes words correctly," and "writes words wrongly."

A crucial element in Operation Upgrade was teaching children to read by using stories that they themselves had written, as well as stories written by their peers. These stories were extremely popular with the students. Examples of some of the stories written by the children and used for reading lesson material are given in the accompanying box.

The Operation Upgrade staff experimented with various methods of using the children's stories before settling on a workable compromise. Presentation of uncorrected stories led students to absorb the mistakes in them. On the other hand, using adult-corrected stories caused the students to lose interest. It is important to understand this issue from the viewpoint of the student who, from seeing his own work in print, is learning for the first time how important and worthwhile he really is. As one student angrily declared after examining her corrected story, "That ain't none of mine." If teachers fail to understand the importance of the student's work to the student as an issue of self-worth, they can easily "turn off" the socially disadvantaged child.

Eventually, as a compromise, a "story game" system was designed (Johnson, 1973):

My Self

I like myself. I like to talk to myself. When I go to bed I look funny. My aun think I look fat. I don't look fat. My sister think I am small. I don't think I look small.

Story Game (Thinks That)

1. He *thinks that* he's smart.
2. My mother *thinks that* I should rest.
3. My brother *thinks that* it is going to rain.
4. My aunt _____ _____ I look fat.
5. My sister _____ _____ I am small.

The "story game" method allows teachers to preserve the children's original writing in its natural form, while at the same time errors can be pointed out in a helpful and supportive way. In preparing a "story game," the teacher will not concentrate on all of the errors in a child's story, but rather on those that are most important and most relevant to the child's current level of ability.

The results of Operation Upgrade were striking. Of 476 pupils in the period from November 1, 1971 to May 31, 1972, only 138 pupils dropped out and 4 percent (20 pupils) moved out of the area. Of the remaining 318 pupils, 62 showed such improvement that they reached grade levels and were phased out of the program. The 256 pupils who remained in the program throughout the whole period *all* showed significant improvement. And this success was achieved at a cost of only $2.89 per tutoring session!

As Johnson (1973) concluded:

Operation Upgrade clearly demonstrates the significant role that inner-city high school youth can play in helping to rescue their younger counterparts from continued school failure. All that is needed is leadership

Once upon a time there was a boy name the great John. He was so great he had a lion for a pet. One day the great John saw a man in the river so I swooped down and got the man out of the river. And so the same day I saw a plane falling so I flet up to catch the plane and I took the plan to the airport. And when the great John put down the plane he fixed it with his laser gun. And that same night the great John hear a rattling noise in bed so he looked out the window and saw some thives. And so the great John got on his suit and flew out the window and got the thieves and took them to jail. And the great John went back home. So that morning the captain of the air-force called the John and said he seen some flying sacers and he wanted me to fly up and see what was the matter the next episode tomorrow. (Johnson, 1973)

Money Money

There was this man he always thought of money he would always play pitch. I know how to play it 2 to 5 people can play every one gets a penny and throw it to the line whose ever penny gets to the line closer. Wins the rest of the people's money. He was a grambler. His mother name him money, because very time he say some money he would always take it. Until people start asking for money. He wanted to change his life. Buthe couldn't so he started to gramble. And gave almost all his money away. (Johnson, 1973)

On my way home I seen a man run out in the street and he all most got hit by the driver of the car and the man start to kus the driver got out and the driver jump out of the car and they start to fight and the police can came and put them in the car and drove away on the a red light and went down town. (Johnson, 1973)

springing from the community or the schools (preferably both) to organize and mobilize their skills. Just as clearly, it demonstrates the value of precision teaching to such a project.

Compensatory Programs for Older Students

Most enrichment programs for the disadvantaged are focused on preschool or elementary school children. It is often believed that if a disadvantaged boy or girl has not shown academic potential by adolescence, it is "too late" to do anything. This line of reasoning is circular, because although most educators and psychologists agree that the optimal age to help disadvantaged children is in the first several years of life, the absence of special assistance once children have become older will only serve to ensure continued failure, and thus provide "proof" that such youths were doomed from the start.

Surveys at a variety of universities support the contention that the disadvantaged *can* be helped to succeed in the schools and continue on to achievement at the college level (Green, 1969). Many disadvantaged youths who have entered college as "high-risk" students have compiled acceptable academic records when supported with tutorial and counseling assistance.

One support program, providing extensive tutorial and counseling services at Southern Illinois University in 1966, exceeded even its own predictions. The university's Counseling and Testing Office had projected that out of a group of 100 high-risk students beginning their programs, the average grade would be 2.2 (equivalent to a low D). It was predicted that 24 students of the 100 would fail to make a 2.0 (D) average, and that only 1 student would score as high as 3.0 (C). In actuality, the results were quite different. Of the 74 students who remained in the program, 65 bettered their predicted grade-point levels. Thirty of the 74 were at or above 3.0 (C), while only 5 were below 2.0 (D). Similar successes with high-risk students through tutorial and counseling programs have been reported at the University of California campuses at Berkeley and Los Angeles.

Experiments at the high school level have been more frequent than college-level programs. One of the best known has been the nationwide program Upward Bound, which has functioned as a special tutorial aid for inner-city high school students preparing for college.

One Upward Bound program particularly worthy of discussion is the innovative curriculum project at St. Louis University (Hyram, 1972). The 120 Upward Bound students were divided into six heterogeneous groups. Each was led in learning activities by a team consisting of teachers specializing in different fields.

For each week of the program, there was a specific inquiry core, consisting of a set of basic questions relevant to the students' lives. For example, the questions for the fifth week included:

> What's my greatest holdback?
> Is it really my race or religion?
> Is it the economic level in which I was born and raised?
> Is it really within me, my personality, my values, my speech, my attitudes, and my ways of acting toward people?
> Am I as limited in my opportunities as I think? (Hyram, 1972, p. 320)

Activities in the various subject areas for the week were structured around these core questions. Thus, the curriculum was intended as a unified search for knowledge that would be directly tied to the lives of the disadvantaged students, rather than a series of fragmented academic and vocational subjects.

Some compensatory programs at this age level have been more successful than others. But it seems clearly established that socially disadvantaged adolescents should not be "written off." In an effective program, a large number of these youths can make dramatic progress.

SUMMARY

More than 30 million Americans can be labeled "socially disadvantaged." These white, black, Puerto Rican, Mexican-American, and American Indian citizens compose the bottom 15 to 20 percent of the population in terms of income and educational achievement.

The socially disadvantaged are trapped within what has been called a "culture of poverty" in a relatively affluent society. They suffer from underemployment and unemployment, dilapidated and overcrowded housing, hunger and malnutrition. In addition to these very pressing physical and material problems, the poor are hampered by negative self-concepts. Often these feelings of inadequacy and self-doubt contribute to the widespread difficulties of poor children in our school system.

When these children fail in school, a vicious cycle of poverty is perpetuated. The disadvantaged youths drop out, have difficulty finding a job and making a living, and are soon living in poverty just as their parents were. Eventually, their children will enter the schools just as they did—hungry, malnourished, intimidated, hesitant, and programmed for failure.

A great variety of educational remedies has been advocated (and instituted) to address the educational problems of socially disadvantaged children. These programs can be distinguished in two important ways. In terms of age level, some efforts (Project Head Start, the Caldwell program, *Sesame Street*) have been directed at very young children, while others (including Upward Bound and university "high-risk" support programs) have focused on adolescents.

Educational programs for disadvantaged children also differ in terms of basic philosophy and approach. Operation Upgrade teaches reading by using stories written by the children themselves. The Bereiter-Engelmann program stresses rote learning and drill practice. The Caldwell project emphasizes the disadvantaged child's need for a positive self-image. The St. Louis Upward Bound program utilizes discussion periods focused on the fears, conflicts, and problems of disadvantaged adolescents.

These differences do not necessarily imply contradictions. It is apparent that the schools must drastically change their educational philosophies—and their concepts of reward and punishment—if they are to solve the problems of disadvantaged children. Programs are needed at all age levels to provide enrichment, tutoring, and counseling support. These programs must help disadvantaged children improve in language, reading, arithmetic, and other skills. The programs must also help the children to develop more favorable self-concepts. There is no "either-or" that is applicable here; a massive effort is needed in all of these areas if disadvantaged children are to have a real chance to escape the "culture of poverty."

SUGGESTED FOR FURTHER READING

Coleman, J. *Equality of educational opportunity* (the Coleman Report). Washington, D.C.: Department of Health, Education, and Welfare, Government Printing Office, 1966.
This report is certainly the most definitive work of the twentieth century on the topic of the "socially disadvantaged." It is useful reading for those who want to consider it in light of the controversy it has precipitated.

Gibson, J. T. *Experiencing the inner city.* New York: Harper & Row, 1973.
This is a workbook designed for teachers who want to find out what their students' life in the inner city is like. The book contains a series of experiences, each looking at a different aspect of the city, such as food services and health services. The perceptions of the inner-city child in his day-to-day life become more clear as the experiences are followed.

Harvard Educational Review. *Challenging the myths: The schools, the blacks, and the poor* (Reprint Series No. 5). Cambridge, Mass.: Harvard University Press, 1971.
This book is a collection of reprints from the *Harvard Educational Review* most frequently requested by teachers. Learning patterns of the disadvantaged, teacher expectations, and methods of teaching are among the issues discussed.

Havighurst, R. J. "Minority subcultures and the law of effect." *American Psychologist*, 1969, 25, 313–322.
This article serves as the theoretical framework for this chapter. It is taken from a major address given by Dr. Havighurst before the American Psychological Association in 1969. The viewpoint is a fresh and very worthwhile approach to studying the disadvantaged.

Karnes, M. B., Zehrbach, R. R., and Jones, G. R. *The culturally disadvantaged student and guidance* (Guidance Monograph Series). Boston: Houghton Mifflin, 1971.
Although part of a series marketed for counselors, this book is definitely applicable for teachers. The disadvantaged child is discussed in terms of demographic, cultural, and psychological characteristics. The section on ways of responding to disadvantaged children is especially helpful for teachers.

Kohl, H. *36 Children.* New York: Norton, 1968.
Kohl describes his experiences as a teacher of disadvantaged children. Actual writings by his students are included as evidence of how teachers can motivate their students to learn. This novel-like book is enjoyable as well as informative for anyone who will be working with disadvantaged children.

Lesser, G. *Children and television: Lessons from Sesame Street.* New York: Vantage Books, 1974.
A useful reference for teachers who wish to find ways of making use of *Sesame Street* to greater advantage in their classroom teaching.

IDENTIFYING AND TEACHING STUDENTS WITH SPECIAL NEEDS

CHAPTER 11

After completing this chapter, the reader should be able to:

1 Describe the various characteristics that make up the broad category of children whom we describe as having special needs; describe these needs in terms of special instructional procedures as well as in terms of special teacher skills.

2 Describe procedures available to teachers through school systems for the diagnosing of special needs; use the results of these procedures in ways most advantageous to this special group of students as well as to other students in the classroom.

3 Compare and contrast the use of special education classes with current concepts of mainstreaming in terms of their differential effects on students with special needs, students with average needs, and teachers.

4 Describe and evaluate specific instructional procedures for children with special needs in terms of their worth to these students as well as to other students; discuss specific problems that each procedure poses in terms of the teacher's role in the classroom.

5 Assess the value of each of the special services provided by school systems for children with special needs in terms of the importance of each service in helping provide adequate instruction for those needs.

WHO ARE THE STUDENTS WITH SPECIAL NEEDS?

Johnny, a frail boy in the first grade, takes very little interest in classroom activities. He has not begun to read like the other children in the class. He refuses to talk or play with them, and he seems lost in a world of his own. The school psychologist administers an IQ test and discovers that his functional IQ is 68. Is Johnny mentally retarded, or is he suffering from a severe emotional disturbance that interferes with his achievement? Additional tests, observation, and perhaps a medical examination are necessary to determine the nature and extent of his problem as well as the best way to deal with it.

Alice, now in the fifth grade, used to be an "A" student. Now, her work has begun to deteriorate, and the teacher is unable to determine the cause. However, she notices peculiarities in Alice's posture and observes that Alice runs and plays awkwardly during recess. The teacher requests a diagnostic evaluation by the school psychologist. Tests suggest the possibility of organic brain damage. The school psychologist then advises Alice's mother that her daughter should have a thorough medical examination.

A child with special needs is one who stands apart from the rest of the class because of some characteristic, either desirable or undesirable, that makes special instructional procedures necessary if that child is to develop to his fullest capacity. These children may be handicapped in terms of eyesight, speech, hearing, intelligence, or motor coordination. Or, they may have far above average intelligence and creativity.

We do not ordinarily think of the gifted child as a problem. However, he can be a problem if not sufficiently encouraged and instead left to stagnate in a large impersonal classroom geared to the "average" student. The teacher has a serious obligation to identify all children with special needs and help them in the best way possible.

This is not to say that children with special needs should be treated differently in all situations. They do require special attention and consideration, but aside from their special needs, these children are the same as all other children. They have the same requirements for development—reinforcement, discipline, love, attention, and so on.

Johnny has been classified by tests as mentally retarded. We have already pointed out that this means that we must determine ways to make it easier for Johnny to cope with his disability. But what does it mean in terms of comparing Johnny with other children of average intelligence? How does Johnny differ from these children? One way to answer this question is to consider the normal curve.

Special Needs and the Normal Curve

All human traits—for example, intelligence, height, weight, aptitudes, and personality characteristics—when measured in sufficiently large populations of people, spread themselves in a bell-shaped curve known to statisticians as the *normal curve*. The normal curve is used in Chapter 14 to describe the ways we can expect achievement scores to spread themselves over large groups of people representing the population as a whole. Attributes of the normal curve and its relationship to what is known as average are outlined in further detail in Appendix 2.

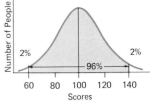

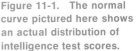

Figure 11-1. The normal curve pictured here shows an actual distribution of intelligence test scores.

To explain the use of the normal curve in relation to the child with special needs, that is, the child who is extremely different in some ways from the average, let us take Johnny's special trait, low intelligence, and compare it to intelligence in an extremely large population of people. We would arrive at a curve that looks like Figure 11-1. It shows IQ scores along the baseline (the axis) with percentages of the population falling at each point along the curve. These are described on the body of the curve. The shape of the curve would appear approximately the same, no matter what trait we selected for our example.

The IQ score obtained by the single largest number of people falls at the midpoint of the distribution of scores and is considered average. Thus, an IQ score of 100 is considered average. When we consider IQ scores above 130 on this distribution, we are considering scores high above average—that population we refer to as "gifted." Similarly, when we consider scores below 70 on the same distribution, we are considering scores well below average—in this case, the group to which Johnny belongs and which we refer to as mentally retarded. As Figure 11-1 shows, these two populations taken together comprise approximately 4 percent of the total population—a group we consider special in terms of mental ability (Glass and Stanley, 1970; Ullmann and Krasner, 1969). Statistically, this percentage of exceptional cases, either high or low, may seem small. When applied to the total population of the United States, however, this figure translates into 8 million people!

Question for Thought
In looking at the normal curve, we see one way to describe the child with special needs—the statistical way. Another way we can describe these children is in terms of their needs. Can you think of any other ways?

Johnny and Alice are two among a small percentage of the children and adolescents in the United States who fall at one tail of the normal curve and who are classified as handicapped in some way. These include visual, aural, physical, mental, or emotional handicaps. Some children are handicapped in more than one way.

Thirty years ago, the most severely handicapped were often regarded as different kinds of people who presented a heavy burden

The Handicapped Student

to society. They were frequently placed in custodial institutions where they remained untrained, uneducated, and unprepared to lead fulfilling lives. More recently, it was still felt that these children had no place in traditional classrooms with other children. As a result, crippled, retarded, and disturbed children often have been grouped together in a "special education" class and taught by one teacher. Only very recently have laws been passed to give these children the same rights as average children to education in a regular classroom. We will discuss this later in the chapter.

VISUAL HANDICAPS

Mary is a poor reader and has difficulty keeping up with classroom activities, but tests indicate that she does not have low intelligence. In fact, she merely has a sight problem. Her difficulty in school is due to having trouble seeing the blackboard and her textbook.

Often, all that is needed to correct a problem such as Mary's is evaluation by an ophthalmologist, and a pair of eyeglasses. Other students, however, are not so fortunate, and have bad eyesight even after correction. We call this group the *visually handicapped.*

SPEECH, LANGUAGE, AND HEARING HANDICAPS

Scott sits in the last row of his third-grade class and spends most of his time daydreaming. As a result, he is falling behind the rest of the class. His teacher is annoyed with him until one day she realizes that he cannot hear what she is saying.

If the teacher had not realized Scott's handicap, she might have misdiagnosed him as mentally retarded or emotionally disturbed, simply because of his poor performance.

Teachers must be alert to the symptoms that hard-of-hearing children generally display. These are: inattention, failure to respond, very slow or faulty speech, and educational retardation not explainable by low intelligence. However, none of these symptoms by itself is indicative of a hearing defect. Accurate diagnosis can be made only after the child is given a hearing test, in which the degree of hearing impairment is determined. Approximately 5 percent of school-age children have some degree of hearing loss.

Children with very severe hearing impairments need special instruction outside the regular classroom. However, those with slight to moderate impairment can remain in regular classes with the help of hearing aids or built-in amplification systems in the classroom.

Hard-of-hearing children often display faulty speech. The American Speech and Hearing Association has estimated that 5 percent of all schoolchildren have speech defects serious enough to demand therapy (Karagianis and Merricks, 1973). Some children

A teacher in a class for children with speech impairments demonstrates to a student the muscle movements needed to make a sound.

(Fried, Magnum)

Technological innovation is proving a boon to visually handicapped children in the Madison Elementary School in Santa Monica, California ("Closed-Circuit Sight," *Human Behavior*, 1975). The nearby RAND Corporation has developed an individualized, closed-circuit TV system, called Randsight, which the Madison School is using. The experimental model can be used by a teacher and three students. Each has his own closed-circuit TV screen, camera, and a lighted, movable platform. An additional camera, suspended from the ceiling, can pick up images from any location in the room. Essentially, the system works like a giant magnifying glass, producing a bright, high-contrast image of whatever the cameras focus on—the teacher, the blackboard, or a book or paper on the student's desk. The images picked up by the cameras can be used full-screen, split-screen, or superimposed with a flick of the master controls, operated by the teacher. Depending on how the cameras are manipulated, the teacher can give individual attention or encourage group interaction.

With the help of this machine, the visually handicapped are learning to read and write like their normal peers. Many are able for the first time to share the visual experience of their classmates, and they now can take an active part in class discussions. As their teacher notes, "It makes them feel really good about themselves" (p. 30). Says the system's designer, Samuel Genensky, an engineer who is himself legally blind: "Kids who might have had to use braille all their lives can now enter the mainstream of sighted society" (p. 30). The project has sparked international interest, and researchers at RAND are presently contemplating an eight-station model that would be cheaper to build as well as more practical for larger classes.

JOINING THE MAINSTREAM THROUGH TECHNOLOGICAL INNOVATION

(UPI)

have the multiple handicaps of impaired speech and mental retardation, hearing loss, or physical deformity. Most defective speech is due to social disadvantages.

Most speech defects involve problems of articulation—omissions, substitutions, distortions, and additions of sounds. Impaired hearing is often responsible for these. Voice and pitch defects are the second most prevalent problems. The voice may be too high, too low, or monotonous; or it may have an unpleasant nasal quality or hoarseness. There are also rhythmic defects such as stuttering and stammering. Finally, and least prevalent, is delayed speech—a marked retardation of the ability to speak. This disability can be due to mental retardation, severe emotional disturbance, lack of environmental stimulation, neurological impairment, or loss of hearing (Karagianis and Merricks, 1973).

Because children with speech and hearing handicaps have difficulty communicating, their problems are often complicated by the ridicule of children insensitive to these handicaps. It is crucial that the teacher recognize and deal with this possibility before deep emotional scars become a part of the child's personality.

PHYSICAL AND NEUROLOGICAL HANDICAPS.   As you will recall, Alice's teacher was afraid that she might have organic brain damage. Virtually every classroom contains one or two children like Alice who have some neurological or orthopedic handicap such as a physical deformity, paralysis or epilepsy, or who suffer from a disabling disease such as cerebral palsy or muscular dystrophy. Some of these children may use crutches or wear braces, or they may even be confined to wheelchairs. Other children suffer from chronic debilitating diseases such as arthritis, diabetes, heart trouble, hemophilia (a serious blood defect), cystic fibrosis, severe allergies requiring heavy medication, and asthma (Karagianis and Merricks, 1973).

Epilepsy is a noncontagious neurological disorder characterized by seizures. It is important for teachers to understand seizures so that they themselves are not frightened by them and so that they can help the epileptic child reduce his own anxiety. There are two types of epileptic seizures, classified medically as grand mal and petit mal. During the *grand mal* seizure, the child loses consciousness, twitches convulsively, and may lapse into a coma. *Petit mal* seizures are less severe. These cause the child to lose motor control and stare blindly for a few seconds. Epileptic attacks can usually be controlled by drugs. When they cannot, teachers and students should be prepared to deal with them. The child's parents, doctor, or school nurse should give the teacher directions for helping the child should an attack occur in school.

MENTAL RETARDATION.   Because Scott was falling behind the other children in his class, his teacher might have thought that he was mentally retarded. He was not, but, as we stated before, approximately 2 percent of the child population when classified by IQ are significantly deficient in both thinking capacity and social behavioral adaptation. The four classifications of retardation are: the profoundly, severely, trainable, and educable retarded.

Very few retarded children are *profoundly retarded.* In addition to very low intelligence, they often have multiple handicaps, such as blindness and deafness. They usually cannot speak, and their motor development is extremely limited. The profoundly retarded cannot learn to take care of themselves and must be constantly supervised. Most of them require lifelong care in institutions, and many die in childhood

Severely retarded children also tend to be multiply handicapped and generally require constant supervision and medical care, and for this reason, often are placed in institutions. Some severely retarded children can learn to help themselves after intensive and prolonged training, and, as adults, perform simple tasks in closely supervised situations. Speech is often absent or very limited.

Trainable children are only moderately retarded and are less likely to have multiple handicaps and obvious physical defects. They can speak, and their motor development may approach normalcy. While they are not capable of reading or doing complex arithmetic, they can learn to take care of themselves and to become more socially aware. Such children are considered trainable, and may eventually become partially self-supporting at jobs in sheltered workshops.

Although they require special programs and classes, most (85 percent) of all mentally retarded children are *educable*. Their physical appearance and motor development are relatively normal, and their handicaps are often not detected until they begin school, when their poor ability becomes obvious. These mildly retarded children are sometimes difficult to manage in the classroom because they require a lot of individual attention and often become discipline problems. They can learn basic elementary skills in childhood, and crafts, graphic arts, and physical education in adolescence. As adults, they are capable of performing simple jobs in the community.

LEARNING DISABILITIES.   Learning-disabled children are often categorized by their teachers as "slow learners," but unlike the mentally retarded, they may have average, or even above average, IQ scores. They have many different kinds of problems that involve reading ability, memory, concentration, motor ability, and disruptive behavior. It is difficult to detect and diagnose learning disabilities, because there are no clear-cut symptoms common to all cases. Many children stand out, however, because they have a history of delayed speech and difficulty in motor coordination and memory (Bradbury, 1972).

The most noticeable learning-disabled children tend to have severe behavior problems. They are often impulsive, aggressive, have infantile tantrums, and are poorly socialized (Berryman and Perry, 1974; Bradbury, 1972). These are also the symptoms of a condition known as *hyperactivity*. Many hyperactive children have responded to drug therapy. Amphetamines such as Ritalin and Dexedrine have helped reduce hyperactivity and improve self-control (Bradbury, 1972). However, the use of these drugs has caused enormous controversy because teachers and others who are incompetent to recommend them have in some cases administered them routinely to any disruptive child. Clearly, any drugs given to a child should be administered by professionals with the doctor's and parents' consent, and not by an unknowledgeable teacher. Even then, drugs tend to be greatly misused and are not the only solution. It is crucial that public knowledge and understanding of the administration of these drugs be increased. (See Chapter 12 for a further discussion of ways to control hyperactivity.)

The largest group of learning-disabled children consists of those who have language difficulties, particularly in reading. At least 10 percent of all children with average or above intelligence suffer from the little-understood learning disorder called *dyslexia* (Bernard, 1973; Ellingson and Cass, 1966).

Dyslexic children show a wide variety of symptoms. These symptoms are quite common in preschool-age children, even those who later become good readers. For example, both very young children and dyslexics may confuse spatial relationships such as left and right. They thus reverse the order of letters, syllables, and words. (They read "b" instead of "d," "tap" instead of "pat"). They also may confuse up and down and invert pairs of letters such as "m" and "w" or "d" and "p" (Bernard, 1973; Ellingson and Cass, 1966). These symptoms become significant if they persist after the child is in school.

There is no known cause for the cluster of problems called dyslexia or for other learning disabilities. Neurological and genetic theories have been advanced, but there is no definite proof of genetic or physiological causes. The dyslexic or otherwise learning disabled child behaves in ways that defy the development pattern of the so-called normal child, and none of the specific techniques that work with normal children seem to help the learning-disabled. Because learning-disabled children may be of normal intelligence, they do not elicit the patience and sympathy that adults give the mentally retarded and other handicapped children.

SOCIAL-EMOTIONAL HANDICAPS.   Children with problem behaviors will be discussed in Chapter 12—they require a full chapter in themselves. Let us say for now that it is crucial for the teacher to understand that there is a close and important relationship between a child's emotional adjustment and his readiness to learn. Children with school phobias or severe anxiety of a more general type may be too self-preoccupied to be receptive and responsive to what the school has to offer. This statement also applies to children with other problems, who show the same lack of response and receptiveness. Children with a low self-concept are convinced they are going to fail before they even try. Other children show an extreme and basic mistrust of the educational environment and of the teacher as an authority figure. Youngsters from socially disadvantaged backgrounds frequently display this behavior. Because mistrust lowers both motivation and achievement, the child is likely to experience difficulties in cognitive and social development.

Questions for Thought

We have been discussing many categories of special needs. Often children with special health or mental problems have social-emotional handicaps as well. Why do you think this is so? What might the teacher do to help?

A summer workshop for students gifted in music.

(Armstrong, Rapho/Photo Researchers)

The Gifted Student

Gifted children, those who are much more capable than the average at succeeding, are the "happiest" of children with special needs. As mentioned earlier in the chapter, they comprise approximately 2 percent of the school population when classified according to IQ. A child who shows outstanding general intelligence or special aptitudes in the visual and performing arts, writing, mechanics, and leadership belongs in the gifted category. There are many different ways in which giftedness can be expressed. Some ways are primarily manifestations of intelligence, and others are demonstrations of creativity. Of course, many children who have a special talent or aptitude, on which basis they might be considered creative, also happen to excel in the area of general intelligence.

IDENTIFYING STUDENTS WITH SPECIAL NEEDS

Identifying the Handicapped

The importance of early identification of children like Johnny, Alice, Mary, and Scott, children with special needs, was pointed out in the preceding section. In most extreme cases—for example, the severely retarded or those with major physical handicaps—the problems are identified well before the child enters school. Much more frequently, however, the child's needs do not really become apparent until he enters school and tries to adapt to the competitive classroom situation so common in our society. Even then, far too many children who need special help go unnoticed for too long.

Although the teacher can often spot a child with special needs, he should also rely on the screening services of medical and educational specialists to determine the nature of the problem and what to do about it. Every state now offers services for children with special needs through the public school system, but the regulations vary drastically from state to state. The following are some general principles for identifying children with particular problems.

HEARING IMPAIRMENTS.   Hearing impairments can be identified by regular audiometric screening tests. Children who fail a test should be retested, and if they fail again, they should be referred to an audiologist.

PHYSICAL HANDICAPS.   Children with physical handicaps should be referred to medical specialists for complete physical examinations as well as educational and psychological evaluations.

MENTAL RETARDATION.   By far the greatest number of children who need special help are the trainable and educable mentally retarded General intelligence and adaptive behavior are the criteria for determining what kind of special help the child needs. In order to be officially considered educable, a retarded child must achieve a score between 51 and 75 on a standardized IQ test such as the Wechsler or Stanford-Binet; to be considered trainable, the child must score between 25 and 50 (Florida State Department of Education, 1974).

LEARNING DISABILITIES.   Children with learning disabilities are often mistakenly believed to have low general intelligence and are sometimes put into classes for slow learners and into nonacademic high school programs (Robinson, 1973). Their symptoms are also thought to be signs of immaturity and emotional disturbance. In either case, educators often overlook the possibility that the trouble is due to a specific learning disability. If tests given to these children do not disclose poor intellectual ability, other diagnostic tests are required, such as medical, optometric, and audiometric examinations. Above all, they require examinations that test for specific learning disabilities.

School psychologists have a wide variety of diagnostic tests for learning disabilities available. A child can be given just one or two or an extensive battery of them. Marianne Frostig, founder of the Frostig Center of Educational Therapy in Los Angeles, advocates testing sensorimotor abilities, language, perception, thought processes, and social and emotional behavior to diagnose the disability and form a composite picture (R. P. Anderson, 1970; Frostig and Maslow, 1973). A standard IQ test such as the Wechsler test can reveal wide discrepancies between verbal and performance IQs. Others such as the Bender-Gestalt and the Frostig Developmental Test of

Through studies now being conducted, indications show that chemicals will be developed in the near future "that can raise or lower IQ and memory, strengthen clusters of special abilities such as verbal skills or mathematical reasoning, and provide help not only for slow learners and underachievers but for all children in all schools" (Bard, 1974, p. 49).

James V. McConnell, a professor of psychology at the University of Michigan, has proven that a chemical called ribonucleic acid (RNA)—a substance that triggers protein production in the brain—can migrate from one being to another. It is RNA, he concludes, that is responsible for memory. McConnell trained flatworms, through electric shock, to contract when a light was flashed. Then he fed these flatworms to a second set that did not have this training. The second group learned to contract on cue twice as fast as the now-digested first group. Why? Because they consumed the memory proteins of their predecessors. They in effect "swallowed memory." McConnell foresees the day when chemicals responsible for memory will be understood well enough to be synthesized in the laboratory.

James McGaugh of the University of California has been able to radically alter the learning ability of mice by injecting them with metrazol (a chemical stimulant to the central nervous system). Notoriously stupid mice became stars, outperforming their hereditarily superior companions. On the other hand, Roger Davis and Bernard Agranoff of the University of Michigan injected goldfish with puromycin (an antibiotic that blocks protein formation), only to find that trained fish promptly forgot what they had been taught. Obviously, some chemicals can erase learning.

As fantastic as all this may seem now, the potential of chemically aided learning—particularly for children with learning disabilities—is great. Will it become a reality? Only time will tell.

Visual Perception can detect minimal brain dysfunction. Psycholinguistic tests such as the Illinois Test of Psycholinguistic Abilities can isolate visual and auditory problems. Standardized achievement tests in reading, spelling, and arithmetic can also yield useful diagnostic information.

Golick (1970) has classified and described 10 broad categories of children's learning disabilities for teachers and parents. None of these categories is exclusive, however, and many children experience difficulty in several categories at the same time. They are:

1. *Poor body awareness.* Confusion over the location of different parts of the body (as revealed by children's drawings showing arms extending from heads, and so on); difficulty assessing size and telling right from left; lack of fine motor coordination; in-

ability to participate in ball games, jump rope, or put together jigsaw puzzles; difficulty in learning to print and write.

2. *Poor ability to combine movement and vision.* Poor eye–hand coordination; clumsiness; inability to follow a moving target or
judge distance; inability to throw or catch a ball.

3. *Visual inefficiency.* Inability to notice particular features in the
environment, even with perfect vision; inability to give selective
attention or screen out competing stimuli; bad distance vision
for both distant and near objects.

4. *Poor listening ability.* Cannot process information to keep up
with the speaker; easily distracted by other noises; inability to
distinguish word sounds.

5. *Integrating information from several sensory channels.* Difficulty
associating letters of the alphabet and their sounds, though capable of handling tasks that are primarily visual or auditory.

6. *Poor grasp of sequence.* Difficulty remembering things in order
such as days of the week, letters of a word, or word order in a
compound word or sentence.

7. *Poor sense of rhythm.* Difficulty reciting a poem, singing a song,
bouncing a ball, or jumping rope.

8. *Problems with concepts.* Difficulty in forming categories and recognizing differences and similarities between objects. Poorly
developed concepts of time, number, and space.

9. *Problems in style of learning.* Difficulty learning and remembering names, telephone numbers, multiplication tables. Possible
good performances in analytic and intuitive tasks that do not
involve memory.

10. *Gaps in general knowledge.* Inability to learn basic general information such as parents' first names, what parents do for a living, names of cities, etc.

SOCIAL-EMOTIONAL HANDICAPS. Emotionally disturbed children
may be extremely shy and withdrawn, distracted, hyperactive,
and/or overly sensitive. Their learning problems are not due to low
intelligence or poor health. Generally, they have trouble getting
along with classmates. Their emotions and feelings are sometimes
inappropriate to the situation, and they are often depressed. They
develop physical symptoms in reaction to problems at home and in
school. The screening of these children requires the cooperative efforts of teachers, psychiatrists, pediatricians, and social workers
(Florida State Department of Education, 1974).

Identifying the Gifted   The prospective teacher might think that, through superior academic achievement, the gifted student will identify himself. However,
these children, after demonstrating superior ability early, frequently

become bored with unchallenging class work, and their work gradually slides toward mediocrity. An IQ test often can provide evidence to show that these students' low achievement is due to something other than lack of ability.

PROGRAMMING FOR STUDENTS WITH SPECIAL NEEDS

Although the public schools today absorb a great many children with special needs, they do not provide equally competent specialized instruction for all needs (Borinsky, 1973). Handicaps such as speech impairments, retardation, learning disabilities, and problem behaviors are the most common in the school-age population. The public schools have in the past separated these children from children of average physical and mental ability and put them in special education classes.

This policy began when IQ tests were first used to screen children with low intelligence and isolate them in special classes. Crippled, emotionally disturbed, and learning-disabled children were included in these classes as well. Special education classes initially were designed for the purpose of meeting the needs of these children through homogeneous grouping and special instruction. Frequently, however, special education teachers have found themselves with too many different kinds of problems all in one class — and without enough resources to provide for the individual needs of the students.

Furthermore, children in special education classes may be labeled as inferior and stupid by their peers. Teachers tend to think of them as "impaired," "disabled," "hopeless," or "disadvantaged." Once so labeled, these children find it difficult to regain self-respect in the eyes of their classmates and teachers and, later, their employers. As we have emphasized before in this text, children commonly derive their sense of self-worth from the evaluations of others. Therefore it is not surprising that children with special needs often apply these derogatory labels to themselves. Because they have been taught to think poorly of themselves, they perform poorly in class (Jones, 1972).

Some educators have suggested that homogeneous groupings have not improved the academic performance or social development of children with special needs. Teachers of special classes for handicapped pupils find it impossible to adapt the curriculum to each child's level when children are segregated according to physical handicap instead of mental ability and social maturity (Karagianis and Merricks, 1973). It has also been shown that educable retarded children do not necessarily benefit from being placed in special classes (Pedrini and Pedrini, 1973). In the great majority of cases, the

Mainstreaming: A Rationale

special physical and medical needs of crippled children can be met in the regular classroom (Karagianis and Merricks, 1973). Black and Latin-American children with special needs suffer the double penalty of being separated because of their ethnic status as well as because of their special needs, and then are denied the specialized instruction that was the original rationale for the segregation (Jones, 1972).

Recently, parents of children with special needs have brought court suits against school boards that advocate what they consider uncritical homogeneous grouping, claiming that their children have the same rights as average children to education in a regular classroom. The courts have responded by mandating the integration of these students into regular classes whenever such placement does not interfere with the education of others. This has given rise to the procedure known as *mainstreaming*—that is, bringing students with special needs of all kinds into the mainstream of American education (Pedrini and Pedrini, 1973; Stearns and Swenson, 1973). (The implications of mainstreaming will be discussed later in the chapter.)

There are valid arguments for and against keeping children with problem behaviors in regular classes. Many such children improve considerably by remaining in ordinary classrooms where they are exposed daily to the positive influence of other children who are better adjusted. However, very aggressive children not only are able to drain the teacher but, without proper supervision, may disrupt the entire class. A compromise has been to place these children in a special class two or three times a week temporarily until they show by their behavior that they can participate in the regular program (Central Advisory Council for Education, 1967; Karagianis and Merricks, 1973).

Research in British schools suggests that mainstreaming is beneficial and that many handicapped children are able to make a satisfactory academic adjustment in ordinary classes (E. M. Anderson, 1973). Most British educators feel that segregating the handicapped does not serve anyone's best interests. It may actually make it more difficult for them to accept and live with their disabilities (Central Advisory Council for Education, 1967).

Mainstreaming: Services to Students with Special Needs in Heterogeneous Classes

In spite of the obvious benefits to children with special needs, their integration into the regular classroom introduces another set of tasks for the teacher. Mainstreaming does not do away with the need for specialized services—it makes them more urgently needed than before. Although many of the special needs of these students can be met in the regular classroom, they will have to be given careful attention to determine the best curriculum for each. Teachers with various special skills will have to coordinate their efforts to deal with all the unusual problems that will arise. First, school personnel—regular and special education teachers, resource specialists, administrators, psychologists, social workers—and parents will have to act as a team. Regular classroom teachers will have to train themselves for a much wider variety of student interaction and group dynamics in order to promote the acceptance of children with exceptional needs in regular classes. Additional personnel—paraprofessionals, case managers, tutors, and specialists in child development, instruction, resource learning, and diagnosis—will have to be introduced to give children with special needs the individualized instruction they require (Bruininks and Rynders, 1972). If it is to be a success, mainstreaming will require innovations in curriculum, instructional methods and even school architecture (Birch, 1971).

Questions for Thought

Considering all of the characteristics of children who might be in your class in a regular heterogeneous classroom, what additional skills would you as a teacher like to have? What additional resources would you like to have available?

EDUCATION SUPPORTIVE SERVICE TEAMS. Supportive services are designed to allow mildly handicapped children to remain in ordinary classes. They can also be extended to the more severely handicapped who must receive part of their instruction in special classes (Michigan State Department of Education, 1973). Some, but not all, of these services are found in most school districts, and they vary tremendously from state to state.

1. *Psychological services:* The role of the school psychologist typically involves assessment, intervention, and evaluation of severe student problems, as well as consultation and administrative work (Bernauer and Jackson, 1974; Fairchild, 1974; Reilly, 1974). The psychologist integrates information from his own analysis with that of teachers, parents, and community agencies to form a composite picture of the child. Having made a diagnosis, the psychologist recommends a course of action to help the child make a better adjustment. He then determines whether his intervention has been effective by evaluating feedback from teachers and parents.

2. *Counseling services:* Unlike the psychologist, the counselor helps all students and not just those with serious problems. Although he often works closely with the school psychologist, the counselor focuses mostly on important educational decisions, and not on therapy (Michigan State Department of Education, 1973; Tyler, 1969).

3. *School social workers:* The school social worker arranges meetings with the child, the parents, and teachers in an effort to cooperatively help the child adjust to school. In severe or pathological cases, the social worker, together with the psychologist, might decide to place the child in a special school or residential institution. He must then help the parents to accept this decision, and, later, show them how to help their child when he returns to the community (Breyer, Lapp, Calchera, and McCarthy, 1974; Michigan State Department of Education, 1971, 1973).

4. *Physical therapists:* The physical therapist helps children with bone, muscular, or joint defects by providing individual exercise and treatment programs on the recommendation of a medical specialist (Michigan State Department of Education, 1971, 1973).

5. *Occupational therapist:* Handicapped children also may require an occupational therapist to help them develop their sensorimotor abilities, and later during adolescence, help them fit these abilities with available employment or careers. Occupational therapists help students form good work habits and develop a sense of personal responsibility, particularly in self-care skills. Even severely handicapped children should learn to dress and bathe themselves, attend to personal and health needs, and learn basic social and safety principles (Hart, 1972; Michigan State Department of Education, 1974).

6. *Speech correctionists and audiologists:* The speech correctionist helps children with articulation problems, stuttering, and defective speech due to cleft palates and hearing impairments. The latter may also require the service of an audiologist.

7. *Physicians:* No diagnosis of a handicapped child is complete without a medical examination by a qualified physician. Some children will also require the services of an ophthamologist, or neurologist. Schools that do not have these medical services should make the necessary referrals.

8. *Director of special services:* All special programs for children with special needs should be under the close supervision of a special education director. The director should have previous teaching experience in both regular and special classrooms and be able to help with curriculum planning, learning materials, and testing methods. He should also be able to help teachers manage classrooms, write behavior objectives, and prescribe and evaluate individual instruction programs (Michigan State Department of Education, 1973).

The success of the integrated classroom depends not only on the teacher's ability to handle the vast differences between children, but also on *regular communication between the school and the parents.* Schools cannot provide adequate services to children with special

A teacher in a school for the deaf uses a mirror to help her students learn to pronounce words.
(UPI)

needs without involving the parents. Parents have many important roles to play. They should consult with the teachers and provide important information concerning the child's activities and development, work with the social worker and school psychologist, submit written reports, and participate in family therapy sessions when necessary. They can join parent-awareness groups to discuss common problems and attend lectures and films presented by special education teams (Bernauer and Jackson, 1974).

Parents of handicapped children should have access to a school advisory or counseling service that provides support and encouragement and helps them decide upon a workable solution for the education of their child.

ADDITIONAL SPECIAL PROGRAMS FOR THE HANDICAPPED. There are many kinds of remedial classes in the public schools. These classes are attended at special times so that students spend the rest of their time in regular classrooms. Two examples of remedial classes are reading and speech correction. Speech therapy classes are designed to correct problems in articulation, voice, and rhythm, and often use behavior modification techniques (see Chapter 4).

Reading difficulties have been studied to the point that schools of education now offer graduate training leading to the Ph. D. degree in reading. Despite these developments, only a minority of children with reading difficulties receive remedial instruction.

Remedial reading programs should include a thorough, initial diagnosis of each pupil's disabilities. Classes should be limited to four or five students so that the teacher can give the necessary individual attention. Instruction should be carefully organized into realistic short-term goals, and the teacher should motivate the children by giving them concrete evidence of their progress. Basic reading skills should be developed first, then comprehension and reading rate. (Woestehoff, 1970).

Research shows that remedial reading classes are more effective if they meet frequently. One study (Silberberg and Silberberg, 1965) indicates that in one project children given two hours of remedial reading instruction every day for five weeks showed a five-month reading gain. Short courses have not proven effective with children having severe reading difficulties such as dyslexia, which was described in detail earlier in this chapter.

Because reading disability cripples a child in all subjects, the school has a serious responsibility to provide reading matter of an appropriate level of difficulty for each child. Teachers in integrated classrooms will have to assign work according to individual ability.

ADDITIONAL SPECIAL PROGRAMS FOR THE GIFTED.   Gifted students are more capable than the average in their ability to organize material, express shades of meaning, use imagery and analogies, and analyze. However, bright children also need guidance. The highly gifted are not necessarily gifted in every subject, and the teacher should consider their strong and weak areas. Some are socially mature; others cannot get along with anybody (Central Advisory Council for Education, 1967). Considering these factors, should gifted children be segregated in classes by themselves, or can their needs be met in the regular classroom?

1. *Ability grouping: pro and con.* Ability grouping is generally done by dividing students at a particular grade level into homogeneous classes usually based on IQ scores or, in some cases, IQ scores in combination with reading achievement scores.

Many educators have assumed that ability grouping facilitates teaching as well as learning because it reduces the range of differences between students. Both rapid and slow learners are supposed to benefit because instruction is geared to the capabilities of each group. Theoretically, it motivates the high-ability students to apply themselves and gives the slow learners more opportunity for success (Bayuk, 1972; Heathers, 1969).

However, many critics have shown that ability grouping increases discipline problems and creates elitist, undemocratic attitudes among students and teachers. According to Urevick (1965), this kind of "artificial stratification" gives students in advanced classes a false sense of superiority and students in slower classes feelings of inferiority and a defeatist attitude toward education. Moreover, students in slow classes too often receive inferior instruction. They then score badly on tests, which reinforces the belief by them and their teachers that they are indeed slow learners. Students in advanced classes, on the other hand, sometimes suffer from an overemphasis on competition and grades instead of learning for its own sake.

Findley and Bryan (1970) reported that besides reinforcing unfavorable self-concepts and stigmatizing slow learners, ability grouping also reinforces the social class system. A disproportionate number of children from minority and disadvantaged groups get segregated into slow classes, thereby depriving them of the stimulation they could be receiving from high-achievers in an integrated class.

Those who argue for the heterogeneous class say that it provides every child with valuable insights about others and enables students to learn from each other as well as from the teacher. Brighter students can help the slower ones academically and socially, and slower students can help the brighter ones develop compassion and understanding (Heathers, 1969; Urevick, 1965).

Question for Thought

Some educators have pointed out that even ability grouping in special lessons (such as reading) in otherwise heterogeneously grouped classes may affect self-concept. In a first-grade class in which good students are in one reading group and average students are in another reading group, what do you think happens to the self-concept of the student who finds himself in the "slow" group and who knows that he is reading slower than the others?

2. *Acceleration.* Acceleration allows a gifted student to progress more rapidly through school by skipping one or more grades. Klausmeier and Ripple (1962) studied the effects of acceleration on bright second-grade pupils in Racine, Wisconsin and reported that accelerated students performed as well or better than an equally bright unaccelerated control group. One negative effect of acceleration was that the accelerated pupils were not readily accepted socially by older students in the higher grade.

Occasionally, there is a student so exceptionally intelligent that he can skip several grades with no harmful effects. One extremely gifted boy skipped four years of high school, entered college at age 13, and at age 18 was at work on his Ph.D. degree (Stanley, 1973). In 1973, researchers at Johns Hopkins University studied the effects of "radical acceleration" on extremely bright students (those who score in the top .5 percent of their age group on the Scholastic Aptitude Tests). These students took college courses for credit while in high school, which enabled them to skip several grades and enter college early. This study showed that these students made satisfactory personal adjustments and had no major academic problems (Stanley, 1973).

Acceleration does not always produce favorable results, however. Husen (1967) studied students in 12 countries and found that disadvantaged children who entered school earlier than other children of the same backgrounds were more likely to develop negative attitudes toward school. In addition, many educators and psychologists are concerned about social difficulties that might be encountered by bright children who are accelerated and spend all of their school time with children much older than themselves.

3. *Enrichment programs.* Enrichment programs have been developed to try to counteract some of the bad effects of ability grouping and acceleration by allowing gifted students to remain in regular classrooms. They do this by providing individually prescribed instruction, special classes, seminars, and other activities geared to

COLLEGE FOR KIDS

College courses for 5-year-olds? That's what's happening in Marin County, California (Blakeslee, 1975). Gifted children from kindergarten to ninth grade may take a variety of college-level courses such as electronics, computers, marine biology, and so forth. The courses are specifically designed for them and taught by college professors. The purpose of College for Kids is to supplement the students' education in their regular schools. It is designed to fill a void of special education for the gifted that existed in more than one-third of the local public schools when the program began. Dr. Jared Sharon, director of community and college development at College of Marin, parent school of College for Kids, explains, "Our program is not intended to advance a student beyond the grade to which he normally is assigned but rather to enrich his background. Our central purpose is to make available unique learning experiences that any single school district could not provide by itself" (p. 39). College for Kids makes full use of resources that the public schools don't have—the science computer center, the marine biology laboratory, audio-visual equipment, speed reading machines, binocular microscopes, etc.

The professors at College for Kids are all enthusiastic about the program. Vic Seegar, who teaches physics to third, fourth, and fifth graders, explains the rewards of the program both to him and to the students:

"One day I was explaining nuclear energy to them, and I told them how the sun is just a great big nuclear reactor up there in the sky. One child then raised his hand and asked, 'If we already have that great big nuclear reactor up in the sky, why do we need any more down here?'" "What could I say?" Mr. Seegar said, smiling broadly. (p. 39) their needs. Under Project CLUE in Memphis, for example, gifted students in the fourth through sixth grades attended two optional half-day seminars each week and spent the rest of their time in the regular classroom. The seminars provided an informal, relaxed atmosphere and flexible seating arrangements. The teachers gave no grades but continuously evaluated student performance in critical thinking and creativity (Memphis City School System, 1974).

THERAPEUTIC APPROACHES FOR CLASSROOM TEACHING: WHAT THE TEACHER CAN DO.   The court-mandated process of integrating children with special needs into traditional, heterogeneous classrooms puts heavy demands on the teacher. Handicapped, learning-disabled, retarded, and gifted children, as well as children with problem behaviors, enter these regular classes knowing that they have special needs and are different in some way. Because of this, the teacher must have a special set of capabilities in order to build an effective and therapeutic learning environment.

Handicapped children are likely to have poor self-concepts and other feelings of inadequacy. These show up in a variety of ways, such as lack of consideration for the rights of others, and other problem behaviors. These children may have reached widely varying levels of cognitive development, and their classroom performance varies accordingly. The teacher, therefore, not only must develop a set of behaviors that will reduce fear and tension in these children, but also must be familiar with child psychology principles and appropriate methods of teaching in order to assess each child's learning problems (Rappaport and McNary, 1973).

1. *Teacher characteristics.* According to Rabinow (1964), successful teachers must have characteristics that allow them to "work productively, without dogmatism or disorganization" in promoting a child's growth. Other characteristics include: skill in working with individual students and small groups; openness to new ideas and methods; acceptance of individual learning differences; ease in a structured classroom; and a combination of warmth, patience, and firmness (Cruickshank, Junkala, and Paul, 1968). The teacher must know how to help children overcome their problem behavior by using classroom activities to improve self-concepts and build academic skills. This calls for constant self-control, honest and constructive expression of feelings, and a helping attitude that is not too approving or permissive (Dubois, 1974).

2. *Teacher education and training.* If mainstreaming is going to succeed, the regular classroom teacher must be competent to deal with a child who has a variety of disabilities. For example, a child with reading disabilities is also likely to have emotional and communication problems. "Resource teachers," who are able to deal with

many disabilities and who can assist the regular teacher in meeting all of the special needs of these children, are necessary to help the regular teacher (Association for Education of the Visually Handicapped, Philadelphia, 1970).

3. *Individualized instruction programs.* Because of the uniqueness of the needs of these students, teachers should be prepared to use a variety of teaching methods as, for example, individualized instruction methods. Computer-assisted instruction may also be very useful for children with learning difficulties (see Chapters 9 and 10). As you will recall, precision teaching is based on operant conditioning and behavior modification principles. It uses the following techniques: (a) pinpointing specific behavior areas for improvement; (b) recording the frequency of these behaviors; (c) modifying teaching techniques; and (d) rewarding appropriate behavior with powerful reinforcers.

Charts and audio and video tape recordings of classroom behavior can be precise records of changes in student performance (Galloway, 1972; McDonald, 1971; Phillips, 1972; Starlin, 1971). By furnishing an accurate record of how a child is actually performing in a particular situation, the method also enables the teacher to evaluate his own influence and plan more effective programs (Cohen and Martin, 1971). Precision teaching methods have been shown to be very successful with the educable mentally retarded and blind

---

TEACHER RESPONSIBILITIES WITH INDIVIDUALIZED INSTRUCTION

1. *They like children in spite of their faults.* They realize that children who are singled out for special help have already experienced more than their share of failure, and need a teacher who will be warm, accepting, and understanding.

2. *They base remediation on diagnosis of each child's problems and needs.* They carefully consider individual strengths and weaknesses, likes and dislikes.

3. *They start their instructional program at the child's present level of functioning.* They build the child's self-confidence because the initial task leads to success.

4. *They break down the learning task into small, manageable steps* and encourage success with various kinds of reinforcement (tangible and intangible), especially praise.

5. They are *flexible* in adapting a variety of remedial techniques to the needs of different children.

6. They realize that diagnosis and remediation are complex tasks that require the *cooperation* of a physician, psychologist, social worker, other teachers, and parents.

(From Narang, 1973, pp. 49–51)

institutionalized children with behavior problems (Phillips, 1972). They are also effective with learning-disabled and gifted children (Starlin, 1971).

As mentioned earlier in the chapter, mainstreaming is a highly desirable procedure because it allows students to learn from and about one another and encourages beneficial social adjustments in the child with special needs. Segregated classes for students with special needs are often based on extremely arbitrary classifications. In addition, they tend to promote poor self-concepts, destructive labeling, and other psychological damage. Integrating these students into regular classrooms is the ultimate satisfactory solution. However, this process will entail a drastic reorganization of the present school system, the reeducation of teachers, and the introduction of many new kinds of personnel to provide special services.

Special Education: Services to Students with Special Needs in Homogeneous Classes

THE HANDICAPPED.   In spite of the move for mainstreaming, it is realized that the behavior of some children still calls for special classes or separate facilities of some kind. As mentioned earlier, one aggressive, hyperactive, attention-seeking child in some cases can keep an entire class from learning. In such a situation, the special needs of one child must be weighed against the need to provide a suitable learning environment for all children. For some children with problem behaviors special, segregated classes that they attend all day have been the only solution.

Some educators, however, advocate the use of "resource rooms" for these children. Under this arrangement, they may still attend regular classes with their peers part of the time and learn the regular curriculum as much as possible, but they also have frequent access to the resource room for special equipment, services, and instruction not available in the regular classroom (Pedrini and Pedrini, 1973).

Under the court mandates, it is highly probable that large numbers of homogeneously grouped special all-day classes will be abolished over the next few years. Some will have to be maintained for the severely handicapped, who otherwise would not be able to attend school at all. Others will be partially integrated into regular classes to provide short-term intensive remediation. This will prepare certain handicapped children for eventual full participation (Karagianis and Merricks, 1973). Under a partially integrated program, a child attends special classes for academic subjects and regular classes for music, art, and physical education.

THE GIFTED.   Special classes for gifted students through ability grouping have sometimes resulted in detrimental effects to both

CLASSROOMS FOR THE AUTISTIC

Autistic children in regular public schools? Impossible, their parents have always been told; their needs are too complex. Yet today, under growing demands for constitutional rights to equal education, the doors of public elementary schools are opening to these children (Sage, 1975). In California, for example, there is a program that is educating autistic children aged 2 to 9 at three elementary schools. Says Florence Needels, the project director, "I knew that if I could put together an expert in language and an expert in behavior modification, I'd have something fantastic" (p. 39). She also needed community support. Backlash from the parents of normal children drove the program from one school while it was still in the planning stage.

Behavior modification is basic to the success of the program. Isolation rather than corporal punishment is used to bring behavior under control. Once this is accomplished, the major goal is the development of useful language. Progress towards this goal is often painstakingly slow. Children must be taught to recognize objects and the names of the objects, to understand commands such as "give me" in relation to these objects, and to articulate these words through constant repetition. Then they must learn to use this newly acquired language in meaningful ways. Whatever works, from token economies to sign language to verbal praise and demonstrated affection, is the method used with each child.

Generally they are kept completely separate from the regular school children, but occasionally a normal child is brought in to play with the more advanced autistic children, to serve as a model and perhaps take him to lunch in the school cafeteria or to other school activities. Once a week, the school holds a workshop in behavior modification so that parents can learn what will help them extend their children's education into the home. With programs such as these in California, home life for the family of the autistic child is at last beginning to normalize. Certainly, the program has shown that autistic children can benefit from education. Two autistic girls are now working their way through standard reading and arithmetic manuals used in special education courses; one 3-year-old boy is already reading! With results such as these, "probably other programs like the one in California can no longer be denied" (p. 42).

high- and low-ability students. Undoubtedly, however, there will be continued demand for homogeneous grouping of the gifted, particularly from parents of these children. In order to decide what is most effective for each child, it will clearly be necessary for teachers, psychologists, and parents to carefully weigh the pros and cons in light of each individual child's development. Some exceptionally intelligent children have been accelerated one grade or several in order to provide the necessary challenges and stimulation. Enrichment programs can instruct gifted students individually or provide special seminars in creative topics while they attend regular classes.

Some children, such as the severely and profoundly retarded and those with severe physical, emotional and sensory handicaps, require more special care than regular schools can provide. The special schools listed below limit their enrollment to these handicapped children and use intensive techniques to develop their abilities.

Programs and Services for Students with Special Needs Outside the School

VISUAL AND AUDITORY HANDICAPS.   Special schools for the deaf and blind still exist because it is thought that these children require careful, methodical, and patient instruction. Precision teaching has worked successfully with the blind and deaf, both in institutions (Phillips, 1972) and at home using the children's parents as teachers (Young, 1972). Many educators, such as B. J. Young (1972) believe, however, that children with some hearing or vision and sufficient mobility should be integrated into regular schools. This is beginning to take place in many school districts.

MENTAL RETARDATION.   Raising and caring for a seriously retarded child at home is a difficult and demanding responsibility that not all families can accept. However, institutions do not always provide the best opportunities for growth and development. The current trend is to develop community resources that can relieve the families of retarded children of some of the burden. In fact, 96 percent of all mentally retarded people in the U. S. are cared for outside of institutions (Karagianis and Merricks, 1973). What this statistic doesn't reveal, however, is whether the care these people are receiving outside of institutions is better than it would be in an institution.

The Eastern Nebraska Community Office of Retardation (ENCOR) provides a comprehensive plan for education and caring for the retarded in the Omaha area. The profoundly retarded receive close medical supervision in an institution; others attend developmental centers for educational and vocational training. School staff members work closely with parents, and the child is kept with his natural family whenever possible and in the community (Galloway, 1972).

LEARNING DISABILITIES.   There are many special schools for children with severe learning disabilities. These schools use innovative techniques such as individualized instruction and intensive tutoring. In many cases, physicians and psychiatrists are on the school staff.

SOCIAL-EMOTIONAL HANDICAPS.   Schools for children with social-emotional problem behaviors use much the same procedures as those for learning disabilities. They also provide a full range of psychiatric and psychological services. These schools are designed for children who cannot possibly function in a regular classroom. Methods for dealing with autism, which is characterized in part by the absence of communication skills, have been developed at the Neuropsychiatric Institute School at UCLA with operant conditioning techniques (Hewett, 1965).

PHYSICAL HANDICAPS. Special programs have been developed for the physically handicapped, both through association with hospitals and through private organizations. Decisions to place children in such programs depend on need and on the medical assistance available. More and more frequently, physically disabled children who do not need constant medical assistance and who are sufficiently mobile to get to regular classes are being mainstreamed into the regular public school programs. Ramps are being built for wheelchairs, and facilities for dealing with other disabilities are also being provided.

SUMMARY   A small proportion of children in the average classroom display either exceptionally high or low learning abilities, or have disabling conditions that are serious enough to warrant special training. Disabled and low-ability pupils include the mentally retarded, the learning-disabled such as dyslexics, the physically handicapped, those with social-emotional problem behaviors, those with neurological disorders, and those with severe visual, hearing, or speech impairment. The high-ability student, that is, the gifted, also has special needs.

The teacher usually cannot make a precise diagnosis on the basis of observation alone. Therefore, specialists such as school psychologists, counselors, social workers, doctors, and physical and occupational therapists should examine children with special needs, diagnose the situation, and prescribe the remedial action.

Gifted children constitute the "happiest" category of children with special needs. They excel in general intelligence, creativity, or leadership. Early identification and encouragement of their special abilities is very important, and many schools provide special services such as ability grouping, acceleration, and enrichment programs.

Mainstreaming is the process of integrating children with special needs into a regular classroom. Some researchers have found no clear or consistent advantage in segregating these students in special classes. Instead, special classes have encouraged labeling and have reinforced poor self-concepts among disabled children. Mainstreaming exposes children with special needs to many different types of people and provides greater opportunities for learning and for healthy personality development. The special needs of these children can be met by special supportive services and remedial programs.

The regular classroom teacher must be competent to deal with children having a variety of disabilities, work closely with special education teachers and parents, and be open to new methods such as individualized instruction and precision teaching.

Some students will always need special services beyond what is available in the regular classroom. Some of these students are placed in homogeneous classes within the public school system, while others must be sent to special schools or treatment centers.

Golick, M. *A parents' guide to learning problems*. Montreal, Quebec: Association for Children with Learning Disabilities, 1970.

SUGGESTED FOR FURTHER READING

This book has many specific and helpful tips for teachers of students who have learning problems. Since it is intended for parents, all of the advice is quite easy to understand as well as practical. The materials for the various suggested activities described in the book are readily available and inexpensive.

Golick, M. *She thought I was dumb but I told her I had a learning disability*. Montreal, Quebec: Association for Children with Learning Disabilities, 1970.

This book offers many practical tips for helping these children — both for teachers and parents. It discusses the early identification of children with learning disabilities. Golick points out that such children may have to be taught things that ordinary children pick up on their own.

Karagianis, L. D., and Merricks, D. L. (Eds.). *Where the action is: Teaching exceptional children*. St. John's, Newfoundland: Memorial University, 1973. (ERIC Document Reproduction Service No. ED 084 764)

An excellent collection of readings relating to all topics covered in this chapter. In addition to identifying the problems of children with special needs, specific programs and methods of teaching such children are discussed.

Stone, S. C., and Shertzer, B. (Eds.). *Guidance and the exceptional student*. Guidance Monograph Series (Series V). Boston: Houghton Mifflin, 1970.

Although the books in this series are intended for counselors, there is much relevant information for teachers of children with reading disabilities, learning disabilities, sensory handicaps, the mentally retarded, and the gifted.

CHAPTER 12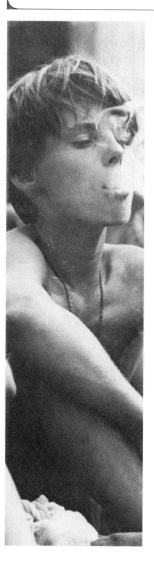

IDENTIFYING AND TEACHING STUDENTS WITH PROBLEM BEHAVIORS

After completing this chapter, the reader should be able to:

1 Describe the characteristics of the child with problem behavior and evaluate the importance to the child and to society of different types of problem behavior; compare and contrast the behavior of this child to the child we refer to as "well-adjusted" or "average."

2 Describe the variables associated with problem behaviors of schoolchildren that stem from: home environment, the child's relationship with his teacher, the child's perception of the school as a learning environment, and society as a whole.

3 Suggest procedures for the teacher to follow in order to deal with problem behaviors; suggest behaviors that will aid the child as well as other students in the class.

4 List skills of particular help to the classroom teacher in mainstreaming children with problem behaviors, and suggest specialized personnel available through the school system who can assist the teacher.

5 Distinguish between the child who is especially creative and who should be rewarded for this behavior and channeled in socially acceptable directions, and the child who is exhibiting problem behaviors destructive both to himself and to society.

WHAT ARE PROBLEM BEHAVIORS?

In Chapter 11, we discussed children with special needs. As we pointed out, children can have special needs of many kinds. The visually handicapped child, for example, has very special needs that are quite different from those of the average child. In this chapter we will deal with children with another kind of very special need— children who have difficulty adjusting personally and socially to their environments. We often call these children emotionally disturbed. What they really are are children with problem behaviors— behaviors that are problems for themselves and for those around them.

In Chapter 3, we dealt with the development of the critical components of personality—identity and values. Each individual's unique way of behaving is determined by these. Children with problem behaviors often are said to have personality problems. Before we begin discussing these children, we will discuss how the well-adjusted personality and "average" behavior differ from that of the child with poorly adjusted personality and problem behavior.

In Chapter 11, a statistical and graphic model of the normal curve was presented as one way of describing the difference between the average child and the child with special needs. For example, the mentally retarded child falls at the lowest end of the normal distribution in intelligence. In the same way, the child who has a low ability (in comparison with his peers) to cope socially and emotionally with his environment falls into a similar position on the normal curve. According to this description, the child with "average" ability to cope in these ways, what we usually describe as the well-adjusted personality, falls at the center of the curve. The extremely mature child with "above-average" ability to cope falls at the very opposite end of the normal distribution from the child with very low coping ability. Such an "above-average" child might represent Maslow's description of the self-actualized person, described in detail in Chapter 6. (See Chapter 11 for the description of exceptionality and the normal curve; see Appendix 2 for a detailed description of this curve as well as statistical definitions of average.)

Average and Problem Behavior: A Statistical Model

A view of the well-adjusted personality, other than the statistical one, is presented by Havighurst (1953). He describes it in terms of the ability to perform certain "developmental tasks of life" that an individual must learn in order to achieve what he terms "healthy growth." These tasks vary from society to society; what is acceptable in one society may not be acceptable in another. In our society,

Well-Adjusted and Poorly Adjusted Personalities: A Clinical Model

for instance, the developmental tasks of the middle years of childhood include learning the physical skills needed for games, getting along with peers, and developing competence in reading, writing, and arithmetic. In adolescence, the tasks include establishing mature relationships with peers of both sexes, achieving emotional independence from parents and other adults, and preparing for economic independence later in life. Successful achievement of the developmental tasks of a particular stage usually leads a person to success in future tasks, and, presumably, a well-adjusted personality. Failure in the tasks leads to difficulty with future tasks, societal disapproval, unhappiness, and, ultimately, problem behaviors.

There are many other theories about what constitutes the well-adjusted personality. Some of these define personality in terms of what is sometimes called "mental health." Bernard (1973) states that mental health "refers to the processes of living a full, happy, harmonious and effective existence" (p. 242). To Journard (1971), an individual with a healthy personality will receive personal satisfaction from playing his role (which he does well) and will continually grow emotionally. Coleman and Broen (1972) propose the goal of "comprehensive mental health," that is, the total health and well-being not only of the individual but of the family, community, and society as well.

In this book, we avoid the term "mental health" because we feel that it brings to mind a false analogy with physical health and therefore is an inappropriate and oversimplified concept. For the same reason, we do not use the term "mental illness." Physical problems have largely organic bases. In the view of most psychologists, on the other hand, problem behaviors more often are related to past learning experiences and, in many cases, can be treated with educational and therapeutic techniques.

Questions for Thought

Can you think of some developmental tasks that exist in our society that do not exist in primitive societies?

What kinds of skills do we require of our children that these primitive societies do not?

If there are different kinds of skills required of children in different societies, does it follow that a child exhibiting certain behaviors may be well-adjusted in one society and poorly adjusted in another?

Problem Behaviors   According to the National Institute of Mental Health, approximately 10 to 12 percent of the 50 million elementary school children in the United States have some sort of problem behavior that requires therapy. Furthermore, among the 15 million children being raised in a poverty environment, one out of three falls in this category. These figures tell us that problem behavior is currently a serious issue in the United States, and one that needs immediate attention. With the advent of mainstreaming, as described in Chapter 11, more and more of these children will be in the regular classroom.

Sociologists and social psychologists study behavior from the perspective of societal values and concepts of reward and punishment. Societal standards or norms are considered the model for well-adjusted behavior. Those who follow the norms are rewarded by society. Deviation from the norm is considered problem behavior. However, social values, attitudes, and norms vary from period to period and from one society to another. What is considered exceptional or problem behavior in the United States in 1975 may be considered "normal" in 1980; it may also be considered "normal" in China in 1975. In this sense, problem behaviors can be viewed as behaviors that do not satisfactorily meet the requirements of the developmental tasks outlined by Havighurst. In our society, a 10-year-old who is withdrawn and does not play as well with his peers as he is expected to, or an adolescent who exhibits extreme emotional dependence on his parents at a time when adolescents are supposed to be developing independent behavior would be thought of as showing problem behavior. In a society where withdrawal is acceptable for 10-year-olds or where adolescent dependence is acceptable, this behavior would not be considered a problem.

The category "problem behavior" includes many different types of behavior. Among the most significant in our society are: hyperactivity, the withdrawal reaction, overanxiousness, the runaway reaction, and unsocialized aggressive attitudes (Bernard, 1973). Each of these will be examined in detail later in this chapter.

Above all, when we study problem behaviors, no matter how we

The withdrawal reaction is one of the most significant types of problem behavior in our society.

(Malloch, Magnum)

define them, it is important to keep in mind that there are millions of children with these problems who must be helped. Witness the unhappiness of this 11-year-old:

> I don't like to be around many people. I dislike some of people in my class. . . . I'm always doing the wrong things. I wish people didn't ask about my family. I don't like to talk about me. People always calling me names. I don't like the people on the street I live on. I'm always getting in fight. . . . People always comparing me with my sister. . . . I sometimes have nightmare [sic, entire paragraph]. (Long, Morse, and Newman, 1971, pp. 111–112)

FACTORS RELATED TO PROBLEM BEHAVIORS IN SCHOOLCHILDREN

Family-Related Factors

As we mentioned in Chapter 1, probably the most important element in the socialization process is child-rearing in the home. The child's personality, which is the end product of this process, is affected by the way he has been reared. An unsupportive, troubled, and unhappy home will have a very bad effect on the development of a child's personality.

As we discussed in Chapter 1, the family-related factors that can influence the development of problem behaviors include the mother-child relationship, the father-child relationship, divorce, and the overall home environment.

A mother can influence her child's behavior by providing reward and punishment, by instructing the child clearly and consistently, and by acting as a model (Kagan, 1971).

A father can influence his child's behavior in similar ways. Perhaps more important are the negative effects caused by a father's *absence* from the home. For example, the child may have difficulty establishing normal sex-role identification (Bernard, 1973). Another factor is divorce, which often tends to make the child insecure and unhappy because of the frequent unhappiness and family tension preceding it. It also tends to decrease the strength of the emotional tie between the father and the child in families in which the father leaves and the mother rears the children independently (Landis, 1960). Finally, a child reared in a home in which constant battles occur, whether between parents or between parents and children, may feel that his world is threatened. He may, at times, believe that he is responsible for this bad situation, especially if they're fighting about him. At any rate, such an atmosphere may cause anxiety (Bernard, 1973).

Although family-related factors have a great influence on the child's personality development, sometimes a damaging one, problem behaviors are rarely the result of these factors alone. Other factors must be considered in drawing a complete picture of the causes of problem behaviors.

Questions for Thought
How do you think changing family styles and the divorce rate in the United States have affected behavior—particularly classroom behavior?
Can you give some examples?

A child "lives" in school much in the same way that he "lives" at home. He spends a large portion of his time in school during his early years, particularly if he attends preschool. School experience can have a profound effect on the development of the child's personality. The teacher should keep in mind that the way the school shapes the child's behavior is similar to the way the family shapes it. In fact, although we have spoken of the home as the primary influence on personality development, one theorist (Zimiles, 1967) argues that, in at least one respect, the school environment may be even more influential than the home environment. Family life follows a fairly fixed pattern to which the child can easily adapt, but school life confronts him with constant changes—new teachers, classmates, intellectual tasks, social demands—that require him to become sensitive and flexible enough to adapt.

School-Related Factors

THE CHILD'S PERCEPTION OF SCHOOL.   How, then, does the child perceive his "life" at school? To the very young child, school can be a great adventure or an intimidating trial (Sarason, 1972). In this country, the experience of being separated from his mother for the first time may be a traumatic one for the youngster entering preschool or kindergarten. In addition, he must confront the highly structured school environment for the first time. In this complex new environment, he meets a new authority figure: his teacher. It is difficult for the child to determine how to relate to this stranger, since he may have had no previous experiences with such a person. Although this unfamiliar adult shares certain features with his parents and other relatives, the teacher may seem to have far greater power than the nonrelated adults he has known before.

In addition to a new adult figure and a new social organization, the elementary school child also confronts new social pressures. In the classroom and on the playground, he meets and interacts with other children. Through these interactions, he learns new lessons about what to say and what *not* to say; what to say to whom; how to act and how *not* to act; and how to obtain friendship, respect, and affection from other children and from the teacher. In elementary school, the child is presented with an array of subject matter and skills to master. The various new ways of relating to others and the intellectual activity may at times cause the child to feel that school is a bewildering place.

THE ADOLESCENT'S PERCEPTION OF SCHOOL. To the adolescent, school is a place to which he *must* go (Gross and Osterman, 1971). Indeed, school attendance is a legal requirement. Whereas truancy from school is illegal, staying home from work in an office or factory is not. Thus, adolescents are controlled in a way in which other groups in society are not, and perhaps resent school for this very reason.

The school itself also regulates and restricts adolescent behavior. High school dress codes offer a basic example of such restrictions. Thousands of students in high schools across the country have been suspended in the past decade for the way they dress or the length of their hair. Because appearance is so important to adolescents, repressive dress codes may lead to anger and alienation.

Repressiveness in high schools has other, more serious elements. In a report made by a group of high school students in Montgomery County, Maryland (Montgomery County Student Alliance, 1971) several stifling effects of the schools on children and adolescents were mentioned. Among them were fear (of bad grades, punishment, failure, and so on); dishonesty; destruction of eagerness to learn; alienation as a result of dishonesty and the premium put on conformity; blind obedience to authority, stifling of self-expression and honest reaction; narrowing scope of ideas; and prejudice.

> Perhaps most tragic is what the school system does to the emotional and mental attitudes and subconscious of its students. The system . . . is willing to and does label students as "failures" at age eight, twelve, or seventeen. . . . Further, tension has been shown to be an integral part of the school experience, with very damaging effects. (p. 111)

The feelings expressed by these students may seem radical, harsh, and unsupportable; on the other hand, they may be entirely justifiable. Certainly, they reflect the intense feelings of distrust, alienation, and even hatred that many adolescents have for school. These feelings, which cross race, sex, and class lines, are shared by many teenagers across the nation. These views indicate that the school, perceived as a repressive institution, can cause what may sometimes be considered "deviant" or problem behavior patterns among adolescents.

Questions for Thought

Looking back at *your own perceptions* of your high school days, are the student sentiments listed above harsh and exaggerated or real and justified? Are schools in fact repressive?

TEACHER PERCEPTIONS OF STUDENTS. Having discussed student perceptions of schools and teachers, we should turn to teacher perceptions of students, which is a key factor in school achievement and in problem behaviors. As you will note in the report by adolescents in Maryland, problem behaviors among students may actually be a result of the way teachers and school systems perceive and treat their student populations.

A teacher sensitive to student needs can recognize a troubled child and be an important resource for helping him (Cowen, Gardner, and Zax, 1967). The teacher need not be trained in therapy in order to offer assistance. Many times, simply being warm, supportive, and willing to listen will be of help. When a more serious problem arises, a sensitive teacher can direct the student to counseling services.

On the other hand, in a 1928 study of classroom teachers, Wickman cast serious doubt on the ability of teachers to diagnose student problem behaviors. He showed that there was an extremely small relationship between ratings of problem behaviors by teachers and ratings of the same problems by clinicians. For example, teachers tend to ignore highly withdrawn children, focusing instead on aggressive and highly aggressive youngsters. Clinicians, on the other hand, consider withdrawal a warning of more serious problems in the future, and therefore a symptom that should be watched. Teachers and clinicians rated the seriousness of problem behaviors very differently. For teachers, the most serious problem behaviors involved immorality and action against authority (heterosexual activity, stealing, masturbation, obscene notes, impertinence, destruction of school materials, disobedience, profanity, and impudence.) Clinicians were much less concerned about such behaviors and saw only one of these problems, stealing, as "making for considerable difficulty."

In a 1959 review of follow-up studies on teachers' and clinicians' attitudes toward problem behaviors, Beilen found considerable evidence to support Wickman's conclusions. Beilen noted that teacher attitudes had shifted in the 30 years since the Wickman study was done. This shift narrowed the difference between the attitudes of the two groups. However, Beilen reasserted that "the teacher's role remains principally task-oriented; the clinician's, more adjustment-oriented" (p. 185). He suggested that these role differences contribute to the varying perceptions each group has about child behavior.

In a later follow-up study, Tolor and his colleagues (1967) found that teachers still remain particularly critical of aggressive and emotionally expressive behavior. Elementary school teachers seem most prone to categorize such behavior as pathological. Experience also proved to be a significant variable. More experienced teachers react to aggressive behavior more like psychologists, whereas less experienced teachers tend to label a wider range of behavior as abnormal.

The majority of recent studies, in contradiction to Wickman's findings of almost 40 years ago, suggest that teachers are good predictors of the future achievements and difficulties of their students. Keogh and her colleagues (1974) interviewed 58 kindergarten and primary grade teachers in order to find out which behaviors teachers felt would lead to future problems. They found a consensus among teachers as to what constituted high-risk symptoms. The researchers argued that since the teacher is generally the first professional to see a child interacting with peers, he probably is the best person to screen a child for clinical examination.

A study by Gullotta (1974) also notes the teacher's potential importance in aiding the student with problem behaviors. Gullotta described teacher attitudes and expectations in treating a student with moderate problems. He found that the majority of teachers were willing to keep such a child in their classes as long as they were assisted by supportive services, and that they rejected the solution of institutional treatment for the moderately disturbed child. These results suggest that teachers are willing to perform a counseling as well as a teaching role, as long as children with problem behaviors also receive more expert attention. This is an extremely important finding in light of current planning for mainstreaming in the United States, which was discussed in Chapter 11.

On the other hand, teacher perceptions of student problem behaviors can become self-fulfilling. Teachers may treat talented students with respect and support and "write off" children with learning disabilities or problem behaviors. Teachers sometimes assume that these students cannot be helped and thus turn their attention elsewhere. As discussed in Chapter 10, teacher biases and expectations can become a self-fulfilling prophecy that contributes to the low self-esteem of many schoolchildren, especially those from socially disadvantaged groups. This is serious, since low self-esteem increases feelings of anxiety and can lead to a variety of problem behaviors.

Coopersmith (1968) compared children with high and low self-esteem and found that youngsters with high self-esteem are active, expressive, eager to voice their opinions, and relatively free of anxiety. They trust their own perceptions and expect to be treated well by others. They are confident and optimistic about their lives and rarely develop psychosomatic conditions such as insomnia or headaches.

By contrast, children with low self-esteem are discouraged and depressed. They feel isolated, unloved, and unable to solve their problems. Many are shy, hesitant, and afraid of antagonizing others. They remain in the background of their peer groups. They tend to be self-conscious and preoccupied. They dwell on their own difficulties, which only adds to their isolation from their peers.

Although serious problem behaviors are often difficult to deal with, sometimes help for a child may be as simple as the click of a camera. A case in point: Three education professors concerned with ego development felt that there may well be a relationship between the way we look through the "I" of a camera and the way we see ourselves ("Instamatic Therapy," *Human Behavior*, 1973). Reality, they reasoned, often lies in the eye of the beholder. In a pilot program at Eastplain School in Massapequa, New York, they employed what they called "instamatic therapy" to help certain youngsters develop self-confidence. The participants were 25 children regarded as "uncommunicative" by their mothers. Each child was given an instamatic camera, but film for only 12 pictures. Quickly realizing the limitations of their equipment, the youngsters snapped only those scenes that were important to them. They became quite firm about what they did and didn't want, and more and more painstaking about arranging people and things to their satisfaction. Forced to focus and concentrate, they imposed order on the world around them. The photos then became a tangible surrogate reality and means of starting conversation. More self-confident, these formerly withdrawn youngsters became eager to discuss their new photographic careers. As they developed new friendships, they became real parts of the new world discovered through the camera's "I."

Coopersmith's findings are relevant to our discussion of the classroom teacher's perception of problem behaviors. The teacher who expects a child to be slow or disturbed may well intensify that child's feelings of low self-esteem. Such false expectations may result in an increased incidence of withdrawal or antisocial conduct on the part of the child. The way in which the family and school affect problem behaviors is intimately related to society at large.

Society-Related Factors

Family-related and school-related factors affecting problem behaviors should be understood within the perspective of society at large, since they are, in a sense, society-related factors as well. Among the many social factors contributing to the development of problem behaviors are such conditions as poverty, unemployment, racial prejudice and discrimination, violence, and alienation. These, in turn, affect family and school factors.

SOCIAL STRESS AND "FUTURE SHOCK". In his book *Future Shock*, Alvin Toffler (1970) suggests that the rapidly accelerating change in present-day American society places great social stress on everyone. This rapidly accelerating change "is a concrete force that reaches deep into our personal lives, compels us to act out new roles, and confronts us with the danger of a new and powerfully upsetting psychological disease. This new disease can be called 'future shock' " (p. 10). Toffler explains that future shock is "culture shock in one's own society" (p. 11). As he says,

> We are simultaneously experiencing a youth revolution, a sexual revolution, a racial revolution, a colonial revolution, an economic revolution, and the most rapid and deep-going technological revolution in history. We are living through the general crisis of industrialism. In a word, we are in the midst of the super-industrial revolution. (p. 186)

All of this has attacked our traditional bases of stability — the nuclear family, the neighborhood, the church, the school, and so on. It has brought vast and devastating changes. Various behaviors "reflect the everyday experience of masses of ordinary people who find they can no longer cope rationally with change" (p. 365).

If Toffler's analysis is correct, future shock is probably one of the most significant social factors currently producing problem behaviors. Faced with constant change and turmoil on the one hand and the collapse of traditional sources of stability on the other, we are under extreme psychological pressure. Withdrawal, alienation, anxiety attacks, or aggressive reactions could easily result from this. It cannot be established here whether society is responsible for our behaviors or whether it is the other way around. But it is known that these behaviors occur more frequently in troubled urban areas, where changes in social patterns and general social disintegration have been most severe.

SOCIOECONOMIC STATUS AND PREJUDICE.   As we discussed in Chapter 10, many social factors, such as the interrelated problems of poverty, unemployment, and low socioeconomic status, can have a serious impact on a child's self-esteem and personality and can thus lead to the development of problem behaviors.

Studies have shown a high incidence of problem behavior among persons with low socioeconomic status (Sarason, 1972). Such maladaptive behavior is a predictable response to the vicious cycle of poverty (outlined in Chapter 10). Children raised in low-income homes often live in an atmosphere of fear, apathy, and normlessness. In school, such children lack a sense of hope, self-confidence, and the intellectual background necessary for success. This leads to a profound sense of alienation and to social behavior that seems rebellious in relation to middle-class standards.

Problem behaviors appear to be particularly severe among victims of racial prejudice and discrimination. Black Americans, for example, seem especially susceptible to what is called paranoia, that is, extreme suspicion of others. William Grier and Price Cobbs (1968) have said that certain forms of paranoia, depression, and antisocial behavior represent normal, healthy adaptations that black people must make in order to survive within a hostile and racist white society. Although this "black norm" may conflict with white psychological formulations, it is "a body of characteristics essential to life for black men in America, and woe be unto that therapist who does not recognize it" (p. 179). If Grier and Cobbs are correct, the fact that black Americans develop problem behaviors (by white American standards) is not only *predictable*, it may be *essential* for black survival in a prejudiced society.

ANOMIE. Anomie (personal disorientation, anxiety, and social isolation) is a condition that often arises when a social structure is disintegrating and traditional norms are eroding. Anomie leads to feelings of rootlessness, and this generally results in alienated behavior. Such alienated behavior may include racial and religious prejudice, passivity and withdrawal, or participation in extreme political or religious movements. We see the effects of anomie in adolescents, whose feelings of alienation may lead them to join "gangs" inclined to criminal conduct or to experiment with hardcore drugs or utopian youth movements.

COMMON PROBLEM BEHAVIORS IN THE CLASSROOM

In this section, we will discuss common problem behaviors that the teacher should be able to recognize.

Withdrawal

The extremely withdrawn child is shy, fearful, secretive, and apathetic. He feels unable to cope with everyday problems, and has trouble forming close friendships. Rather than facing the unpleasant and frightening realities of life, he turns to daydreaming and fantasy as a means of escape. This isolates the child even more, cutting him off from interaction with and feedback from peers. As a result, the child's already fragile sense of reality can become even more shaky (Bernard, 1973).

Let us take the case of Cathy, a 6-year-old girl from a middle-class family. Cathy is a withdrawn child. She is timid and apprehensive and seems afraid of her teacher and classmates. She remains in the background during recess, musical activities, dancing, and other group activities. Although most of the children seem to like her, she has few close friends and spends most of her free time alone. She enjoys and excels in individual activities such as painting, but is reluctant to show her work to others or to work with classmates on joint projects. She often appears to be talking to herself or day-dreaming.

As the Wickman, Beilen, and Tolor studies demonstrated, teachers often ignore shy and withdrawn children like Cathy and focus instead on antisocial, aggressive children who disrupt classroom routines. Clinicians, on the other hand, recognize and are concerned with behaviors associated with the withdrawn child. It is easy to understand how a teacher confronted with 35 students may concentrate on those who continually interfere with the normal functioning of the class. But the withdrawn student, who causes no trouble and whose worst offense is daydreaming, may need just as much assistance and counseling (and perhaps more) as the aggressive, antisocial student.

The withdrawn child who lives in an oppressive family atmosphere, and who is offered no supportive services in school, may become a runaway. In a sense, running away is a physical form of withdrawal reaction, since a psychological "flight from reality" often characterizes the withdrawn child. The timid, fearful child escapes into fantasies and daydreams into an unthreatening, self-constructed universe. The runaway escapes in a more physical sense, hoping to find a more satisfying (or less repressive) living situation elsewhere. Yet both children obviously have not found

THE SHY AMERICAN Heart pounding, pulse racing, blushing, perspiring—and more—the average shy American struggles to cope with the social demands of his world. The consequences of his shyness, according to a recent study at Stanford, may be temporary self-consciousness and excessive preoccupation with his own reactions, or it may be an enduring isolation that forces him into a life of excruciating loneliness (Zimbardo, Pilkonis, and Norwood, 1975). Rarely is the shy individual given attention, for the chaos within is often hidden by his outward appearance of calm. He often seems to be merely modest, discreet, and introspective—certainly no problem to others. In fact, his public behavior often amounts to what can be characterized as nonbehavior. Unable to assert himself, his poor self-projection allows others to overlook his real assets. By the same token, his nonbehavior may mask a lack of self-confidence and inadequate social skills—indeed, in extreme cases, even deep pathological problems. This confusion for others, the researchers suggest, may be a contributing factor in further imprisoning him in his shyness.

What can be done to free the shy individual? The researchers suggest various kinds of guidance, modeling, practice in social skills—even Dale Carnegie courses—but, they conclude, primarily we must "understand and change cultural values, . . . for shyness is not essentially a personal problem. It is really a social problem" (p. 70).

"ideal" solutions to their problems; the runaway cannot control his surroundings in the same way that the withdrawn daydreamer can. Adolescent runaways often encounter poverty, drugs, prostitution, and crime in their new environment.

The unsocialized, aggressive child is generally hostile, disobedient, destructive, and volatile (Kleinmuntz, 1974). He frequently disrupts the class. He has a violent temper and may verbally attack teachers and other authority figures. In certain situations, he may physically threaten or attack the teacher. The aggressive child may engage in other antisocial and criminal behaviors as well, including stealing, vandalism, fighting (sometimes with deadly weapons), and arson. If such behaviors occur in the context of group activity, especially during adolescent years, the aggressive child is referred to as a "group delinquent."

Violence and Other Forms of Aggression

In American society, family-related factors seem particularly critical in causing aggressive behavior in children. In one study (McCord, McCord, and Howard, 1961), several factors that led boys to become aggressive were brought out. Generally, the parents of excessively aggressive boys were found to be rejecting, unaffectionate, and punishment-oriented. Although they frequently threatened their sons, they did not supervise them closely and were inconsistent in their use and methods of discipline. They made few demands on the boys, perhaps reflecting a low level of parental expectation. The parents themselves were often socially deviant, and in many cases the relationship between the parents was filled with conflict and dissatisfaction.

The family environment of nonaggressive boys was quite different from this. Their parents were warm and affectionate with them. Their manner was rarely threatening or punishing, although they did firmly supervise their children and disciplined them in a consistent way. High demands were placed on the boys, which may suggest a high level of parental expectation. The parents of nonaggressive boys tended to be socially conforming rather than deviant. The relationship between the parents was affectionate and characterized by mutual respect and a low degree of conflict.

One implication of such studies of aggressive behavior is that punishment does not stop further aggression. Rather, punishment causes children to intensify such conduct (Bernard, 1973). This is relevant to the issue of the use of punishment in the schools. As discussed in Chapter 4, many teachers believe that only through the threat of punishment can discipline and obedience be maintained. Such teachers employ various types of punishment to keep students in line, including detention, extra assignments, public criticism and humiliation, and corporal punishment. However, as noted, the effects of punishment may be the exact opposite of what is intended—increasing, rather than reducing, the students' inclination toward antisocial conduct.

The findings of the McCord study on aggression are also related to Coopersmith's work on self-esteem discussed earlier. Aggressive children tend to come from families in which rejecting, punishing parents have low expectations for their children. Such children, in turn, usually develop a low sense of self-esteem. It may well be that there is a direct relationship between low self-esteem and aggression. By contrast, nonaggressive children tend to come from families in which parents have high expectations for their children. These youngsters usually develop solid and positive self-concepts.

Hyperactivity   Although hyperactivity is properly categorized as a neurological impairment, it is discussed here because of its high visibility in the classroom. Like the unsocialized, aggressive child, the hyperactive child is very noticeable to the teacher. This child is generally overactive, restless, excitable, and impulsive. He is in constant motion and can never seem to sit still. In school, the hyperactive child rarely completes a work assignment and tends to play the clown or talk out of turn. He also displays many types of antisocial conduct, including fighting, lying, stealing, vandalism, and cruelty to animals (Stewart, 1970).

Hyperactive children have particular learning difficulties in school (Campbell, Douglas, and Morgenstern, 1971). When faced with a task in which they must choose from a number of responses, they tend to react impulsively and select quickly without thinking. If a confusing series of alternatives is presented, they will choose the most obvious answer, even if it is not the best.

Hyperactive children are not, however, characterized by inferior mental ability. They may have high intellectual potential, but their impulsiveness and restlessness prevent them from achieving this potential. As a result, their homework is likely to be sloppy and disorganized, and they make careless mistakes in reading.

Some psychologists suggest that the tendency to hyperactivity may be inborn, although many other explanations are possible. Many parents of hyperactive children have noticed that their hyperactive child behaved differently from their other children, even before age two (Stewart, 1970). Hyperactive children also tend to have many health problems in their first year, and many show poor coordination and delayed speech development.

Evidence of the biological basis of hyperactivity comes from the effects of drug treatment on hyperactive children (Stewart, 1970). Certain drugs, which act as stimulants for most people (particularly amphetamine and methylphenidate), help instead to tranquilize the hyperactive child, who then becomes better able to concentrate, relate to peers, and perform school tasks.

As we discussed in Chapter 11, drug therapy for hyperactive children has become a controversial issue in school systems. Support for the administration of drugs comes from a number of studies that have described the positive effects of stimulating drugs on the behavior and performance of hyperactive children. Yet criticism of the widespread use of drugs in the treatment of hyperactive school children is growing. Many parents, teachers, and psychologists have questioned the safety of this drug use as well as the implications of controlling what may be considered socially undesirable behavior. Stimulating drugs have only a temporary effect; when the drug wears off, the child reverts to his typical behavior. In addition, there is the serious danger that hyperactive children may become addicted to the drugs after they have been treated over a long period of time. This possibility frightens many parents of hyperactive children. A further criticism has been the administration of these drugs by people unqualified to do so.

Other methods of treatment have been proposed to deal with the problem behaviors of hyperactive children. Hopefully, through the use of these techniques, hyperactive children can be helped without the use of drugs.

A study by Dr. Benjamin F. Feingold indicated that elimination of certain food additives from the diets of hyperactive children improved their behavior (Feingold, 1973). Feingold reported that 16 out of 25 hyperactive children who ate foods without certain artificial colorings or flavorings became significantly less aggressive. Of these 16, the four who followed the prescribed diet most closely improved most dramatically. Feingold's results were perhaps due to food allergies rather than pure hyperactivity. However, the Feingold study has prompted a full-scale revision of school menus in California.

Another method of treatment involves training hyperactive children for improved self-control. Simpson and Nelson (1974) used breathing techniques and other body controls to help hyperactive children control various motor behaviors and maintain concentration. The research findings suggested that such training can help hyperactive children develop better self-discipline and control their own actions.

Question for Thought

In some classrooms, teachers have discovered that giving children coffee serves to decrease hyperactivity. As the parent of a hyperactive child, what would be your response if you found that a teacher was giving your child midmorning coffee breaks?

Severe Anxiety   The child with *severe anxiety* symptoms is often overactive, restless, and unable to concentrate on schoolwork. Because he behaves this way, the child may be misdiagnosed as suffering from hyperactivity (Doyal and Friedman, 1974), and stimulants that are effective in treating hyperactive children may be mistakenly applied. When placed on such medication, the child with excessive anxiety shows even more severe symptoms.

There are three common types of anxiety reaction (Cameron, 1963). In the *chronic* anxiety condition, the child appears tense and fearful over a long period of time. He is under continual strain and is usually fatigued, but the cause of this anxiety is unclear to the casual observer. If such strain becomes acute, the child may suffer from an *anxiety attack,* in which he becomes extremely agitated for a short period of time. An extreme anxiety attack may lead to a *panic reaction,* the most serious type of anxiety reaction.

Anxiety levels differ, and it should be noted that when we speak of anxiety as a problem behavior we mean a high level of anxiety. A low level of anxiety is not necessarily bad; it often has good side effects, such as keying yourself up to study for an exam.

Doyal and Friedman (1974) report that the child with anxiety symptoms often feels rejected by his parents. Take the case of Jim, a fourth-grader whose negative classroom attitude seemed related to hostility to his parents. When asked which member of his family he had the most fun with, Jim replied, "Sometimes I think it's the cat." Jim seemed angry about his father's lack of concern and commented, "I can't disturb him when he is reading, and when he is not reading, he is gone" (p. 163).

Anxiety can be a basic cause of a child's failure in school. As discussed earlier in the chapter, school is a strange and even frightening world for the young child, filled with unfamiliar academic tasks and new social roles. The demands of this new situation produce mild anxiety symptoms in many, if not all, children. But for that small number of children who bring prior fears and uncertainties to school with them, the added stresses of this new situation can lead to more severe anxiety symptoms.

SCHOOL PHOBIA.   *School phobia,* one of the most common symptoms of school-related anxiety, refers to a child's reluctance (or refusal) to go to school. It is usually caused by extreme fear of some aspect of the school situation (Waldfogel, Coolidge, and Hahn, 1957). The child may be afraid of the teacher, a particular classmate, the recess period, the school staircases, or any number of details of the school environment. Physical symptoms, such as stomachaches, headaches, or various pains, often accompany the anxiety, and the child will make these symptoms his reason for staying home.

The case study of B. provides insight into some possible causes and treatments of school phobia (Weinberger, Leventhal, and Beckman, 1973). B. had a background of poor school attendance dating back to the sixth grade. Throughout eighth grade, she had failed to attend school and had been characterized by a local clinic as "schizoid and extremely narcissistic." Like many children who are afraid of school, she was good at playing upon her parents' own child-rearing anxieties and guilt feelings in order to avoid going to school.

B. was 15 years old and in the tenth grade by the time the school psychologist was consulted. The school psychologist (after consulting a clinical psychologist) eventually took a direct approach. In a meeting with B., he gave her three rather unpleasant choices: (1) she could go to school voluntarily; (2) her parents (or the police) could forcibly bring her to school; or (3) the school could refer her to the juvenile court as a delinquent, which might lead to confinement in a state home for girls. B. smiled hostilely and replied, "I am obviously being boxed in by you and have no choice" (p. 85).

However, the problem was not yet solved. As we discussed in Chapter 4, a noxious stimulus does not by itself inhibit the immediately preceding response. After attending school for five days, B. was absent on the sixth day. Her mother called the school to say that B. had an infected foot and could not leave the house. B's doctor explained to the psychologist that the abrasion which led to the infection could have been self-inflicted.

The final step in helping B. to attend school came the following week, when her father told the psychologist that he was "fed up" with B.'s behavior. The psychologist then asked the father to help in another direct approach to B.: He was to inform B. that she had 15 minutes to get dressed and ready for school, and that after that time had passed, he would take her to school, dressed or undressed. After various attempts to stall, B. eventually complied. The decisive stand taken by her father seemed to be the crucial element. Three months later, B. was only infrequently absent from school and her grades were good.

What is the psychological explanation for the outcome of B.'s case? According to psychologists, B.'s school phobia derived from her earlier ability to manipulate her parents' anxiety and from her insecurity as to their strength. Apparently, her father's strength in the last instance proved to be a reassuring experience for her.

We do not mean to use this case study as a model of treatment for all school phobias. Rather, we present it because it is useful in understanding some of the causes and manifestations of school phobia. Not only was B. calculating and manipulative, she was also extremely successful in playing on her parents' anxieties in order to stay out of school. School phobia is more common in very young children than in adolescents (Waldfogel et al., 1957), but even young children seem skillful at playing on their parents' anxieties in order to stay out of school.

DEPRESSION. *Depression* is another problem related to anxiety. Symptoms of depression include motor retardation, appearances of sadness, despair, and suicidal ideas or threats (Friedman and Doyal, 1974). Drastic mood swings that prevent normal functioning or grief reactions that continue for months at a time can also be symptoms of depression.

Alan, 10 years old, an only child, is a case of a depressed child (Friedman and Doyal, 1974). Alan was often sad, performed poorly in school, and suffered from headaches, stomachaches, and sleeping difficulties. His depression seemed to begin at the time of the break-up of his parents' marriage; his father had left the house when Alan was 5 years old.

At his first session with a psychologist, Alan was obviously depressed and somewhat hostile. As the sessions continued, his desire to talk increased, and he often cried when discussing his father. His suffering over the separation led to periods of aggressive acting-out, but generally these periods were followed by longer ones of guilt, sadness, and withdrawal.

Freud and many of his followers view depression as anger against a loved one that has been turned inward against oneself. According to this approach, rather than express anger, the child keeps all the hostility inside and lapses into grief, sadness, or physical symptoms.

Adolescent Problem Behaviors

As we discussed in Chapter 3, adolescence is a period of particular stress and crisis. One undergoes important physical, emotional, and social changes during adolescence, including a growing awareness of one's own sexuality. At the same time, the adolescent must make the difficult transition from childhood, and dependence on parents and family, to adulthood, and independence from parents and family.

The peer group comes to represent an alternative social system for the adolescent. The distinct values, pressures, and rewards of the peer group compete with the norms of the family and the school. Peer group acceptance supports the adolescent in periods of unsureness about himself, especially during conflicts with parents or school authorities.

Adolescence tends for many to be a time of unrest, confusion, tension, conflict, and an almost desperate search for identity, individuality, and meaning. Adolescents often become alienated or depressed, especially when the conflicting pressures of family, school, and peer group mount. The teacher should understand the problems that occur at this age.

By early adolescence the peer group has become a distinct social system with norms that compete with those of parents and school.

(Suris, Rapho/Photo Researchers)

ALCOHOL AND DRUG ABUSE. Alcohol and drug abuse are serious problems among adolescents, although not limited to this age group. The reasons adolescents turn to alcohol or drugs were discussed in Chapter 3. Many adolescents receive little or no valid health information about dangerous drugs. When informing adolescents about drugs, parents, educators, and law enforcement officials too often use scare tactics (Clark, 1967). Adolescents quickly learn that many of these warnings are unrealistic. If the same authority then gives them valid information—for example, that heroin is addictive—they may not accept it.

THE RUNAWAY PHENOMENON. The runaway phenomenon is another manifestation of adolescent problems. As discussed earlier, the runaway is in a sense acting out an extreme form of withdrawal. There is also another view of the runaway. In one study (Shellow, Schamp, Liebow, and Unger, 1967), runaways were separated into two distinct groups: frequent runaways, a relatively small group; and teenagers who run away occasionally or only once. The frequent runaways were characterized by a pattern of family disorganization, failure in school, and, in some cases, criminal behavior. The members of the larger group of occasional or one-time runaways were also troubled but had less need for custodial care and individual therapy. For them, running away "may be any one of a number of things ranging from a cry of despair to a victory yell." These youths seem to have much in common with their peers who did not run away: "A plain, forthright expression of dissatisfaction with home or school" (Shellow et al., 1967, p. 29).

SEXUALITY.   Sexuality is an important concern for the adolescent. During adolescence one must come to terms with one's sexual identity. Today this task is even more complex, for our society has recently been in the midst of a "sexual revolution." Sexual freedom is increasing among both adolescents and adults, and traditional norms of sexuality and relationships between men and women are breaking down.

Women in particular have responded to these changes. A survey by Brody (1967) indicates that today's female college student, compared with her predecessors, is much more likely to enjoy her first sexual experience and much less likely to feel guilty or worried about it. The development of a serious and outspoken women's liberation movement has changed the climate of traditional heterosexual relationships. Women are increasingly demanding more satisfying lives, whether in terms of sexuality, careers, or family responsibilities. At present, adolescent females (and males) are maturing during a period in which traditional notions of femininity and masculinity are being challenged.

Our ideas about homosexual relationships are changing too. Most clinicians used to assume that homosexuality was in itself a sickness. This idea is now being reevaluated, and, as Hoffman (1970a) points out, many aspects of homosexual life become understandable when homosexuals are perceived as an oppressed minority group victimized by a hostile and biased majority culture.

WHAT CAN BE DONE

Mainstreaming: The Teacher's Role in the Regular Classroom

As we explained in Chapter 11, *mainstreaming* (keeping children with special needs in regular classrooms) seems to be the best way to treat problem behaviors. Mainstreaming is a two-way process: children with problem behaviors learn from "healthy" children; and "healthy" children learn by interacting with the more troubled children, especially in terms of how, when, and why they must control their own desires and impulses, tolerance for individual differences, and the value of helping peers with problems (Clark, 1967).

Many educators, who feel that children with problem behaviors will be too difficult for the teacher and for other students, oppose mainstreaming. Evidence exists, however, that mainstreaming programs can help children with problem behaviors. One example of an effective program that prepares children with problem behaviors to be mixed with "average" children is Project RE-ED (Zax and Cowen, 1972). The idea behind this project is that effective education is the best form of therapy. The program uses a 24-hour-a-day treatment approach over a six-month period. During the week the children live in two residential centers; on weekends they go home to their families.

Project RE-ED aims at short-term, concrete educational goals, rather than at therapeutic goals. The school day is focused on instruction in basic academic skills such as reading, arithmetic, and language (Lewis, 1967). Most teaching is individualized. In addition, the children are helped to develop simple socially useful skills such as roller skating, swimming, or bicycle riding. A specific goal of the program is to assist children with problem behaviors in learning such skills so that they can more easily interact with their peers. The overall goal is to prepare the child for functioning in a normal school and home environment.

TEACHER ATTITUDE TOWARD PROBLEM BEHAVIORS. We have stressed thus far how advantageous mainstreaming can be for the child with problem behaviors. At the same time it must be admitted that the child with problem behaviors presents particular difficulties for the teacher in the regular classroom. First, of course, is the problem of the child who "acts out" in the classroom and keeps the teacher from doing his job in educating the other children in the class. When this occurs, and when it becomes clearly impossible to continue teaching, even the strongest advocates of mainstreaming would suggest the removal of such a child—for the benefit of the rest of the class and for more intensive help than the teacher can provide.

The second difficulty is helping the child with problems to learn most effectively. Although education can be a useful tool in resolving problem behaviors (Rhodes, 1963), several assumptions must first be made. The first assumption the teacher begins with is the specific attitude that students with problem behaviors are just like other children in that they can be motivated to learn, grow, explore, and discover. If a child is consistently treated with an effective blend of warmth, sensitivity, firmness, and direction, he may realize his potential.

The second assumption is that the teacher must design teaching strategies and curriculum with the needs of troubled children in mind. Rhodes (1963) believes that through the use of such a curriculum, education in the schools can contribute greatly to increasing the probability of success in the lives of children with problem behaviors.

The child with problem behaviors needs a full education in the schools. In addition to academic training, he must also learn new concepts of self and methods of interacting with others. Again, the teacher must believe that the child has within him the desire to enjoy life and school, to have friends, and to develop satisfying ways of interacting. The teacher's concern is how to foster such growth within a classroom environment.

King and Frignac (1973) have developed a series of educational and behavioral goals for teachers and parents who work with children who exhibit problem behaviors. Among the behavioral and educational goals are the following:

Human Relations. Goal: To develop ability to socialize with other people. Objectives: The student will:
  (a) Display socially acceptable manners.
  (b) Respect other people's property.
  (c) Understand the concept of sharing.
  (d) Work cooperatively.
Home and Family. Goal: To recognize the importance of being a responsible and contributing member of home and family. Objectives: The student will:
  (a) Recognize and understand relationships among family members.
  (b) Gain an awareness of own and others' roles.
  (c) Appreciate the individual rights of family members.
            Participation in Family Activities
  (d) Recognize and respect adults in authority.
  (e) Recognize that every family has its own living pattern and style.
Social Initiative. Educational Goal: The student will experience opportunities to build self-confidence through social participation. Objectives: The student will:
  (a) Be given opportunities to perform as a leader.
  (b) Accept reasonable rules of the group.
  (c) Be given opportunities to succeed socially. (pp. 2–3)

BEHAVIOR MODIFICATION.   One method to implement these behavioral goals is behavior modification. (The basic principles of behavior modification theory were discussed in Chapter 4. More elaborate forms of behavior modification, including those that require reorganization of curriculum, were discussed in Chapter 9.)

Thus far in the text, behavior modification has been described as a technique for changing simple, undesirable problem behaviors. In fact, this technique may have a wider and more significant application. As we have seen in Chapter 10, a child's self-concept is crucial to his success or failure in school. A study by Parker (1974), although limited in value because of methodological problems, indicates that a behavior modification program can improve students' self-concepts. This supports the position of social learning theorists who say that one's self-concept results from a set of learning experiences and can be modified like any other behavior.

A solid behavior modification program might aim at a variety of educational and behavioral goals. As Rhodes (1963) writes:

AN OREGON PROGRAM FOR HYPERACTIVE CHILDREN

Says Hill Walker, director of the Center at Oregon for Research in the Behavioral Education of the Handicapped:

At six or seven years old, acting-out children (also described as hyperactive, hyperaggressive, or even emotionally disturbed) already tend to be outsiders. These children are very difficult to manage. They are accustomed to peer rejection and teacher dislike. Usually, it doesn't faze them. What's more, principally because of their acting-out behaviors, they're often below grade level in academic skills" (Hackett, 1975, p. 11).

In an effort to help these youngsters, the Center at Oregon developed Contingencies for Learning Academic and Social Skills (CLASS), a program designed to change disruptive children's negative behaviors.

The CLASS program is one of behavior modification through standard reinforcement techniques; the children earn "points" and praise for proper behavior. The procedures involve the cooperative efforts of a CLASS consultant, the classroom teacher, principal, parents, and child.

During the first five days of the program, the consultant assumes the major responsibility. The important thing is to get the help of the child's classmates — by working on their own assignments and not disturbing the student while he is working. The goal is to make the child behave appropriately 80 percent of the time (a normal average) — not only in class, but also, in time, during lunch and play periods as well. When this goal is reached, the child is given his point card to take home to his parents, who then reinforce him further with *their* praise and reward. Inappropriate behavior means being sent from the classroom. Since good behavior earns extra privileges for the entire class, and thus results in class approval never experienced before, the child learns to suppress behaviors that result in exclusion.

The program works because the key elements are there — the necessary understanding of goals and techniques, full participation and cooperation by everyone involved, and an earnest desire on the part of those who help to change their own often negative attitudes and patterns of response toward the hyperactive child.

Education can add an important dimension to the existing approaches to emotionally and socially maladjusted children. Its basic human concerns and major human goals differ quite radically from those of the clinically oriented professions. It is not concerned with cure or eradication of pathology or disease. It has no pills, no chemicals, no tranquilizers to be administered to sick organisms. Its methods all address themselves to positive drives — drives toward knowing, learning, discovering, exploring. . . . (p. 155)

A well-planned behavior modification program, based in a supportive educational environment, can significantly alter the behavior problems of children.

IDENTIFYING PROBLEMS FOR THE SPECIALIST. The teacher's role in helping children with problem behaviors begins with his conducting an accurate screening of such children. He is in a decisive position to identify a child's problems and to recommend a form of counseling. If he fails to notice a troubled child (as mentioned earlier, teachers often ignore the child who is withdrawn), the child's problem behaviors may continue for years without treatment.

According to Bower and Lambert (1961), the teacher must carefully observe learning difficulties, unsatisfactory interpersonal relationships, inappropriate behavior, unhappiness, and repetitive symptoms of stress. Significantly, they caution the teacher to engage in screening rather than diagnosis. But the teacher must be aware of his limitations in this area. Careful observation of student behaviors is desirable, but at the same time the teacher must not hesitate to seek professional help when a problem seems serious.

SEPARATING CREATIVE BEHAVIOR FROM PROBLEM BEHAVIOR. In many cases, it becomes difficult for a teacher to distinguish between creativity and problem behaviors. As Wickman and later researchers indicated, teachers tend to respond negatively to aggressive and hyperactive children, whose behavior interferes with the teacher's role and with the normal classroom routine. In some instances, this negative response carries over to the creative child, who also questions (or rejects) classroom norms and procedures. Although the teacher should seek to maintain the effective functioning of the classroom as a unit, he should not stifle the creativity or individuality of any student in the process. Conformity does not necessarily mean "good adjustment," nor does creativity necessarily imply the presence of a problem behavior.

Calling in the Specialist

Schools today are assuming an increasingly prominent role in treating problem behaviors (Snapp, McNeil, and Haug, 1973). Because of this added responsibility, the schools must often seek skilled health professionals from the community.

"Outside" professional help may not always mean help from outside the school itself. Snapp and his colleagues (1973) offer a model for the development of in-school services for children with emotional problems. They argue that the school psychologist should assist school personnel in mobilizing other available resources and in developing a plan of action to deal with a child's problems when the psychologist is unable to solve them on his own. Part of the Snapp model involves having the school psychologist develop programs whereby resource people, called "helping teachers," would be placed in each school to work with children and consult with teachers. These "helping teachers" would have training in psychology as well as in education. Their primary goal would be to help maintain children difficult to teach in regular classrooms (mainstreaming) and to insure that these children have a productive experience in these classrooms. The "helping teacher" would have a classroom in which individuals or groups of children with problem behaviors could be isolated—hopefully, briefly and temporarily—for more focused treatment.

Nugent (1973) argues that the functions of the school psychologist, the social worker, and the counselor should be differentiated. He recommends that school psychologists handle involuntary referrals involving classroom difficulties between student and teacher; that the social worker handle involuntary referrals in which the critical issue seems to be family interactions or school-family tensions; and that counselors handle voluntary cases.

As Rhodes (1970) reports, many intervention measures have been developed to help deal with children with problem behaviors. Two relatively new types deserve mention. In *crisis intervention*, a specialist enters a situation at the moment of intensive upset and disruption. He tries to calm both the student and the school officials, and in so doing demonstrates to school personnel the way to handle an extremely agitated child. In *community liaison*, a school specialist acts as a go-between for the child and the school. He may act as an advocate for the child in court or with mental health agencies, as a coordinator of various community agencies working with the child, or as an intervening agent in the child's home or classroom.

Intervention measures include a variety of therapeutic techniques. We will now consider three principal types of therapy: individual counseling, individual behavior therapy, and group-centered approaches.

INDIVIDUAL COUNSELING.   Individual counseling may follow the *nondirective* approach, in which the therapist assumes that the patient is able to solve his own problems, with the support and assistance (but not the *direction*) of the therapist. Nondirective therapy is *client-centered* in that the client (patient) himself is responsible for much of the process of change.

The *directive* approach maintains that a trained professional's direction of the therapeutic process is crucial to the patient's progress. Directive counselors believe that constant nondirectiveness on the part of the therapist is inappropriate and harmful, and they criticize nondirective therapy for basing strategies for change on the patient's sick and neurotic feelings.

INDIVIDUAL BEHAVIOR THERAPY.   Individual behavior therapy is based on the following view:

Behavior that is harmful to the individual or departs widely from accepted social and ethical norms should be viewed not as some kind of disease but as a way—which the person has learned—of coping with environmental demands. Treatment then becomes a problem in "social learning." (Bandura, 1967, p. 388)

In a case study of Lisa, a 6-year-old, we can see how individual behavior therapy is used (Cooper, 1973). Lisa showed symptoms of school phobia. During kindergarten, she cried daily, claimed that she was sick, and asked if she could go home. The same pattern continued for the first six weeks of first grade. Eventually, the case was reported to the school psychologist. A conference with the mother revealed that Lisa had been an unwanted pregnancy. Lisa had been severely ill on three occasions by the time she was 4 years old. During Lisa's illnesses, her mother always gave her a great deal of attention, possibly because she saw her child's illness as some kind of punishment for her being an unfit mother. The school psychologist explained to the mother that by giving Lisa special attention when she claimed to be sick at school, she was unintentionally rewarding Lisa's undesirable behavior. They agreed to a strategy whereby the mother would attempt to reverse this process: Instead of giving Lisa special attention when she said she was ill, the mother would reward her for positive comments about school. The mother was also instructed to ignore Lisa's complaints about illness. After following through on this program for three weeks, the mother was impressed with Lisa's changed behavior, and the psychologist transferred responsibility back to the teacher. Eight months later, both the mother and the teacher reported that Lisa was happy in school and was no longer complaining of illness.

This case study presents an instance of successful intervention using a form of behavior therapy. However, it should be remembered that most behavior modification programs will depend on the teacher's active involvement and enthusiasm as well (Fine, Nesbitt, and Tyler, 1974). If the teacher is not cooperative, well-organized, and systematic in his application of the techniques, the therapy will not succeed.

GROUP-CENTERED APPROACHES.   Many therapeutic approaches can be categorized as "group centered" (Harper, 1974). Most are based on the theory that in a group an individual can receive acceptance and encouragement from many members, whereas in individual therapy such acceptance comes only from the therapist. A group offers the patient the opportunity to work out personality changes within an interpersonal context. A therapist is always present in the group, and he can clarify matters or intervene when necessary.

One development in group-centered approaches in the 1970s is the sensitivity training/encounter group/T group movement. As Back (1972) observed, "The catchword for the sensitivity training movement is 'here and now'"(p. 277). The National Training Lab-

A group offers the individual an opportunity to work out personality changes within an interdependent context.

(Sepp Seitz, Magnum)

oratories (N.T.L.) described sensitivity training as a way to teach people to become more aware of their own feelings and motives as well as those of others.

Although the techniques and procedures of such groups vary, group members generally attempt to speak frankly about their personal feelings, including self-doubts and hostilities (Havemann, 1969). In the course of such revelations, angry clashes, moments of deep warmth and affection, laughter, weeping, and bold confessions may occur.

Although there is value in such groups, if they are not run by trained and competent professional leaders, the highly volatile encounters that take place may result in severe psychological damage to some of the participants. In one study (Yalom and Lieberman, 1971), it was reported that encounter groups had a rather high "casualty rate," that is, a significant number of individuals surveyed (almost 10 percent) suffered "considerable and persistent psychological distress" as a result of the group experience.

Another group-centered approach is *family therapy* (Harper, 1974), in which the therapist treats the entire family, rather than the individual. The theory underlying this approach is that balancing and opposing types of pathology tend to exist within a family. These pathologies can best be addressed by treating the family unit as a whole rather than treating each family member (or one of them) separately.

SUMMARY

Problem behaviors can be understood as deviations from statistically average behavior patterns in which the behaviors exhibited lead to difficulties in learning and in interaction with others.

Millions of American children enrolled in public schools manifest various problem behaviors. Among the most significant are withdrawal and runaway reactions, unsocialized aggressive attitudes, hyperactivity, and anxiety reactions. These disorders are all affected by a variety of family-related, school-related, and society-related factors.

Certain problems are particularly associated with adolescence. The teenager undergoes important physical, emotional, and social changes, including a growing awareness of sexuality. Adolescence is a time of stress and crisis for youth. Drug abuse, sexual problems, and runaway reactions are often associated with this stage of life.

The teacher of children with problem behaviors can play an important role in educational and behavioral development. Behavior modification techniques may be especially useful in changing specific behaviors, and even in improving the self-concepts of disturbed children. The teacher must work in conjunction with trained health professionals, and must not be afraid to ask for assistance when he feels uncertain or uncomfortable.

A vast array of psychological theories and methods are available to the specialist working with children with learning and behavior problems. These include individual counseling (either directive or nondirective), individual behavior therapy, and various group-centered approaches (including sensitivity and encounter techniques and family therapy).

SUGGESTED FOR FURTHER READING

Axline, V. *Dibs: In search of self.* Boston: Houghton-Mifflin, 1964.
This is a case history of a small boy, and a description of the psychotherapeutic approach that helped him.

Golick, M. *A parents' guide to hyperactivity.* Montreal: Quebec Association for Children with Behavior Disorders.
Golick describes hyperactivity, including identification and treatment of hyperactive children. The advice she gives is equally appropriate for teachers as for parents.

Long, N. J., Morse, W. C., and Newman, R. G. *Conflict in the classroom: The education of emotionally disturbed children*, 2nd ed. Belmont, Calif.: Wadsworth, 1971.
This book is an excellent collection of readings on children with emotional problems. The first section illustrates common emotional problems with passages from literature. The remainder deals with identifying, treating, and teaching children with these problems.

Psychology in the Schools.
A monthly journal devoted to all aspects of educational psychology, including current theory and research on student personality and adjustment.

Quay, H. C. (Ed.) *Children's behavior disorders: Selected readings.* Princeton, N.J.: Van Nostrand, 1968.
This book of readings covers all of the issues dealt with in this chapter as well as other clinical topics.

TEACHER BEHAVIOR AND CLASSROOM ACHIEVEMENT

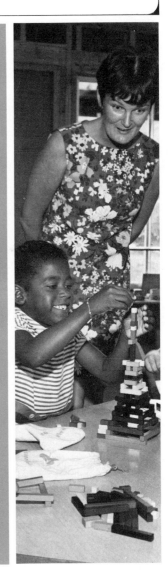

CHAPTER 13

After completing this chapter, the reader should be able to:

1 Describe the ways in which teacher behavior can affect student learning and student self-esteem.

2 Describe those teacher behaviors most and least effective for good classroom leadership.

3 Select a personally acceptable view of the appropriate role of the classroom teacher, based on understanding of what that role implies for both the teacher and the student; describe this role in terms of its function either in preserving or in improving the culture; detail the effects of community pressure and rapid social change on both the role of the teacher and the daily decisions he must make.

4 Evaluate the pros and cons of teacher accountability in light of the needs of the student as well as community pressure for accountability; select a personally acceptable view of accountability compatible with personal views of the goals of teaching.

THE ROLE AND IMPORTANCE OF THE TEACHER IN THE PUBLIC SCHOOL SYSTEM

Throughout this book we have stressed the importance of the teacher in shaping student behavior and encouraging student achievement. But what exactly is the role of the teacher? How do the teacher's personal characteristics, such as attitudes, interests, and expectations, affect the learning of students in the classroom? What are the variables that affect teacher behavior? And how does this behavior affect the students? The answers to these questions are crucial for the prospective teacher.

Conflicting Roles of the Teacher

Because teachers in our society are subject to many contradictory demands and constraints from the schools, the community, and society in general, it is difficult to state specifically what they are expected to do and what model of behavior they should present to their students. According to Bigge (1964), the confusion lies in whether teachers should *preserve* current cultural standards by reinforcing and transmitting them to the young, or whether they should try to *improve* these standards, which may involve breaking down traditional ideas and attitudes.

Over the past century, much of the responsibility for culture transmission, that is, socialization, formerly assumed by the church and the family, has been shifted to the school. In the nineteenth century, the adults in villages and small towns taught children moral, social, and political values; today, with most people living in impersonal, industrialized cities, the schools have had to assume this responsibility (Bigge, 1964).

THE TEACHER'S ROLE AS IMPROVER OF CULTURE.   Some teachers find certain attitudes and values in our society objectionable and would rather not pass them on to the young. They are disillusioned with things as they are and would like to help create a better society through educational reform. However, because of the emphasis on individual rights in this country, the teacher who sees himself as the improver of culture is frequently criticized for overstepping his role, because he often imposes middle-class values on children from non-middle-class subcultures (Katz, 1971). The real problems are: (1) how to teach basic learning skills to both privileged and disadvantaged students so that all have an equal chance to learn; and (2) how to decide which are the important areas of learning for children in a school setting in which it is agreed that parents should have a strong say in what is taught to their children. Interestingly enough, these problems of giving optimal education to all and still meeting the needs of parents seem to be peculiar to our society and its democratic value system. In contrast, for example, the issue of violating individual civil liberties by deciding what its children will be taught does not arise in such societies as, for example, the People's Republic of China and the Soviet Union, which use national government-controlled curricula to reform and politically indoctrinate the masses (Fraser and Hawkins, 1972).

THE TEACHER'S ROLE AS PRESERVER OF CULTURE.   A contrasting position is taken by many people who feel that the role of the teacher is not to change our society but to transmit and preserve its prevailing traditional attitudes and values. Teachers with this attitude tend to be more conservative than the "improvers" (Prince, 1957). They recognize that our culture is changing rapidly, but they do not feel it appropriate for them to promote change, and are bothered by unconventional attitudes and behavior. These teachers feel that the teacher has only a limited right to judge and try to change the attitudes of society. But they too are caught in a conflict because our culture is full of contradictions, and this makes it difficult for them to identify what the prevailing attitudes are.

Questions for Thought
Do you see yourself as a "preserver" or "improver" of the culture? Why?

OTHER SOURCES OF ROLE CONFLICT IN TEACHERS.   Young, married teachers, those who teach in communities different from those in which they grew up, and those who do not have many friends or are dissatisfied with their school administration are more troubled by role conflicts than others. All teachers, however, must deal with some incompatible demands from various segments of the community and the school administration (Getzels, 1963):

1. *Conflict between cultural values and institutional expectations.* Parents expect schools to teach children to be studious, hard working, and independent; however, our culture expects them to be sociable, popular, well-rounded, and considerate.

2. *Conflict between role expectation and personality.* An authoritarian teacher may find himself in a school where the principal promotes permissiveness, and vice versa. A teacher who sacrifices his own preferences in order to conform to others' expectations will resent this situation; one who tries to fulfill his own needs and ignores the community's and administration's wishes will be looked on as inefficient and ineffective.

3. *Disagreement on role expectations among different reference groups.* The school principal expects the teacher to cover the prescribed curriculum in the time allowed; the parents expect him to appre-

ciate the uniqueness of each child and give individualized instruction.

4. *Conflict caused by inconsistent role expectations.* A teacher may have his professional judgment challenged and have to submit to the decisions of people who do not have comparable training or experience. Teachers are expected to be good citizens, yet they are not allowed to be outspoken about their political activities or participation in controversial social movements.

WHAT SHOULD THE TEACHER DO?   There is no simple answer to this question. A teacher may choose the role of either "preserver" or "improver," or both. Whatever role he chooses, however, the successful teacher will be concerned with what students at a particular age should be learning, how it should be taught, and how it should be tested. According to Carl Rogers (1971), teachers can help students learn by showing a concern for what subjects interest students and by creating a psychological climate in the classroom in which learning is enjoyable. "Preserver" or "improver"? The right approach might lie in striking a balance. A teacher should have some control over what subject matter is taught, but he has an equal responsibility to make learning stimulating and exciting for the learner. He must consider the needs and values of students in his class, but at the same time give weight to those of the school administration and the community.

The Importance of the Teacher in Affecting Classroom Achievement

As we have pointed out several times in this book, teachers strongly influence not only their students' academic achievement but their self-concepts as well. A student can easily tell how a teacher regards him when he compares the way the teacher behaves toward him with the way the teacher behaves toward his classmates. Researchers have suggested that the teacher's expectations of a student have a considerable impact on academic performance. You will recall Rosenthal and Jacobson's study (1966), in which the teachers' higher expectations of a randomly selected group of students were communicated to the pupils and resulted in those pupils scoring higher on ability tests, even though they were of average intelligence. As we pointed out in Chapter 6, although the experiment was widely criticized on technical grounds, similar results have been obtained in other experiments under more controlled conditions.

It is clear that a teacher's predisposition will ultimately affect the way in which he reacts to his students. This, in turn, will affect student achievement. A pupil who senses that his teacher has low expectations for him is more likely to perform poorly in class than another pupil who senses that his teacher has high expectations for him. We have referred to this as the self-fulfilling prophecy. Palardy (1969) demonstrated the effect of self-fulfilling prophecies in a study of reading achievement differences between first-grade boys and girls. Many teachers have the expectation that first-grade girls will be more successful at learning how to read than first-grade boys. Palardy demonstrated, however, that boys whose teachers believed they could do as well as girls performed better than those whose teachers did not expect them to read as well as girls. Hanari and McDavid (1973) also showed that teacher expectations are not always logical and can be based on stereotypes and emotions. In their experiment, they found that teachers were influenced in their grading of students by the names of the students. Those students with more common names actually received higher grades than those with unusual names!

The teacher's style of instruction also has a great influence on student performance. For example, Domino (1971) found that college students who were taught by professors with teaching styles consistent with the students' achievement orientation—"conformity" (preservation) or "independence" (improvement)—learned significantly more and were more satisfied with the curriculum. It is crucial, then, that we understand how teachers develop their predispositions.

THE TEACHER AS A HUMAN BEING

Because the teacher plays a critical role in shaping children's intellects and personalities, it is important to examine the personal position of the teacher and the ways outside conditions affect his life. What are the major problems, concerns, and conflicts facing teachers today, and what can the teacher do about them so that they will not reduce his effectiveness in the classroom?

More than most citizens in this country, teachers come face to face with contemporary social issues such as sex and race biases, censorship, personal freedom, and so on. They must take stands on controversial issues that directly involve the school, such as busing and textbook censorship. Teachers who fight restrictions on personal freedom and student rights often come into conflict with school authorities and community leaders.

The Teacher's Participation as a Citizen and a Community Member

SCHOOL DESEGREGATION AND BUSING. The subject of school desegregation and busing has been a major political issue in the 1970s that directly affects teachers and students. In 1972, at a public expense of $1.5 billion a year, approximately 20 million pupils (43 per-

Despite the proven educational advantages of racially integrated schools, the busing of students outside their neighborhoods has persisted as a political and social issue, sometimes requiring police protection for the children involved.

(UPI)

cent of the total public school enrollment) were being bused to school in order to facilitate racial desegregation (Pettigrew, 1973). The primary purpose of busing is to counteract the educational inequalities in overcrowded inner-city schools (Spence, 1972). Experimental busing programs in several large cities have shown that minority group children who are bused to an integrated school make significant academic gains, while white middle-class children who are bused to an integrated school perform as well as, or better than, those who remain in a segregated white school (Green, Smith, and Schweitzer, 1972). Furthermore, research has shown that people who have attended integrated schools as children have far more positive racial attitudes than those who grew up racially isolated (Green, Smith, and Schweitzer, 1972).

Despite these advantages, a strong antibusing movement arose in the early 1970s due to deeply rooted racial prejudice and persistent doubts about maintaining educational quality. As of 1972, 69 percent of a sample of adult Americans were opposed to busing (Pettigrew, 1973). In fact, the issue has become so controversial that the Supreme Court (in *Swann v. Charlotte–Mecklenberg Board of Education*) had to uphold federal court rulings and declare busing constitutional for the purpose of dismantling dual school systems (Harvey and Holmes, 1972).

However, the Supreme Court's *Swann* decision has not provided clear guidelines for desegregating schools in the cities and the suburbs. Suburbs generally have their own school districts, and busing regulations that apply to city schools do not apply there. The result is that inner-city schools continue to be predominantly black and those in the suburbs almost all white (Harvey and Holmes, 1972).

It has been much more difficult to desegregate schools in the North than in the South. The dual school systems in the South were the result of specific state laws (de jure segregation) that are now unconstitutional; the dual systems in the North were the result of segregated residential patterns (de facto segregation). As a result, the courts have been able to force integration while limiting the need for busing student population in the South much more than in the North (Sinowitz, 1973a). Desegregation orders have not been easy to enforce in Northern cities. In fact, the Supreme Court has had to intervene to force many communities to cooperate.

School boards in Northern cities have attempted a variety of solutions to the problem. For example, in one urban area, white children were bused to predominantly black schools, while at the same time black children were bused to predominantly white schools—using both state and local financial support for the program. Children were bused only to schools whose facilities and instruction were considered at least as good as (and preferably superior to) those of the neighborhood schools they would have attended without busing. Even programs like this are not always accepted favorably, however; an example is the tension over the introduction of busing in Boston in the mid-1970s.

Attitudes toward busing vary widely, depending on the community. Teachers get caught up in the controversy, but are relatively powerless to do very much about the ensuing ill effects on students without taking strong stands as "improvers" of society.

CENSORSHIP OF TEACHING MATERIALS AND SUBJECT MATTER. Two examples of censorship and community action illustrate how a teacher's activities can be limited. The first involved a massive protest in 1974 by families in an isolated coal-mining section of Kanawha Valley, West Virginia. They insisted that $400,000 worth of English textbooks be removed from the local school on the grounds that the books were un-American, anti-Christian, and obscene. Hundreds of students boycotted classes and many people were arrested during the controversy. The Board of Education finally restored the books with the provision that any student who found them objectionable would not be required to read them; however, boycotting and violence continued (Franklin, 1974; "Those Books are Restored in West Virginia," *New York Times*, Nov. 10, 1974).

The second case involved a new ninth-grade textbook on Mississippi history that the State Textbook Purchasing Board rejected, allegedly because of the amount of attention it gave to the black experience. The book was intended to replace an earlier segregationist textbook that ignored the civil rights movement and black contributions in Mississippi. School districts were eventually permitted to use the new book only if they used their own funds to purchase copies, not those of the state ("Bias Charged in Book Rejection," *New York Times*, Nov. 10, 1974). A revised version of the old book, with mention of only 13 blacks as compared with 365 whites, was readopted.

Decisions by school boards such as those in West Virginia and Mississippi ultimately affect what teachers and students do in the classroom. It is clear from these descriptions that the teacher, acting in his role as citizen, must take some stand. But the way he acts in his role as teacher will depend on whether he considers himself a "preserver" or "improver."

Questions for Thought

If you were in either of the two communities described above and were employed as a teacher, your job would involve teaching certain specific skills. Do you see any problems that might prevent you from achieving your goal?

What might you do to reach your goal in spite of the kinds of external pressures described?

SEX BIAS IN THE SCHOOLS.   The issue of sex bias has affected many areas of American life, including education. Just as the requirement to eliminate racial segregation in education is rooted in law, so is the requirement to remove sex bias. Both Title IX of the Education Amendment of 1972 and the proposed Equal Rights Amendment begin by providing specific guidelines for eliminating sex bias in schools (Fields, 1974b; Levy, 1972).

Feminists and child-development specialists have called attention to the many ways in which schools perpetuate different sex-role expectations for boys and girls. Many studies have shown that teachers pay more attention—both positive and negative—to boys than to girls and are more concerned with boys' social adjustment (Levy, 1972). Although most schools are gradually changing their curricula to include both males and females in all classes, some schools still have sex-segregated classes and activities such as physical education, home economics, shop, and so on. Even when together in the same classes, teachers expect boys to excel in math and science and girls in English.

A special task force of the National Organization for Women (NOW) conducted a two-year study of sex stereotyping in children's textbooks and discovered that males were in 69 percent of the illustrations and females in only 31 percent. Boy-centered stories outnumbered girl-centered stories by a ratio of 5:2; adult male characters outnumbered adult females by a ratio of 3:1. The illustrations frequently depicted boys as strong, brave, and competitive and girls as small, fearful, and helpless. The stories in these textbooks gave a much greater range of activities to boys than to girls, who were invariably portrayed as passive observers (Jacobs and Eaton, 1972). Although texts are expected to change with pressures placed on publishers to decrease sex-stereotyping, this change is expected to come slowly.

The importance of the results of these studies is twofold. First, as we discussed earlier, the student is strongly affected by teacher expectations. Sex bias influences that expectation. Second, the female teacher is often herself a victim of sex bias, sometimes without realizing it. In education, as in other occupations, women may hold fewer administrative jobs than men and earn less pay for an equal amount of work—85 percent of elementary school teachers are women, 79 percent of elementary school principals are men (Levy, 1972). Since teachers serve as models for students, a female teacher's situation becomes contradictory ("Sex Bias," 1974). Female teachers must teach students the importance of equality, yet they themselves often are proof that equality is not always a reality.

For years union activity and federal legislation have been involved in equalizing women's pay and reducing sex discrimination. The Equal Pay Act of 1963 (an amendment to the Fair Labor Standards Act) requires "equal pay for equal work" ("Sex Bias," 1974). The Civil Rights Act of 1964 (amended in 1972 to include teachers) under Title VII has enabled teachers to sue school districts and institutions for sexual discrimination in hiring. Title IX of the Higher Education Act of 1972 prohibits educational institutions from engaging in sexual discrimination in educational programs and activities (Dushane Emergency Fund, 1974).

Nevertheless, in spite of the gradual advances, female teachers are still faced with sex bias in the behavior of their colleagues and quite often in their own attitudes. The school counselors who adopt the role of "preserver" still steer girl students into homemaking or traditionally feminine occupations. A recent study of secondary school teachers in New York City showed that most teachers want to see male students become dominant, independent, and assertive, and

---

ASSIGNMENT: ASSERTION

Perhaps what more females need today are courses such as the one given by psychologist Roland Tanck at George Washington University's division of continuing education for women ("Assignment: Assertion," *Time*, 1975). It is one of hundreds of "assertiveness" courses that have sprung up around the country at universities and counseling centers. Their proliferation attests the chronic need for this kind of training. As one teacher explains, "Traditionally, women have been unassertive. They have played the roles men and society have given them rather than seeking their own" (p. 65). Often they are the victims of the "compassion trap—the need to serve others and provide tenderness and compassion at all times." So they are "put upon." Their wishes in a situation are frequently the last to be considered, or are simply ignored: Mom wants to go to the movies, but daughter needs to have a dress ironed, so Mom stays home and complies. Junior has been home sick all day wearing Mom to a frazzle, but Dad calls to say he is bringing clients home for dinner. "Oh dear," says Mom—and prepares a feast. What else can she do?

Plenty. As the classes point out, assertiveness is an art to be developed like any other. Through hypothetical conflicts, students learn such techniques as the "broken record," a simple, repeated no; and "fogging," saying no while generously agreeing with one's adversary. ("I agree with you absolutely that the dress needs to be ironed. But I'm not going to do it.")

A good deal of course effort is expended on "home/work" assignments. And the results can be traumatic. Some marriages have broken under the strain. Nevertheless, the vast majority of women are enjoying their new selves. Continuing education, for them, is moving in *new* directions.

female students become submissive, emotional, and concerned with their appearance, even though the teachers themselves insisted that they treated all students equally (Levy, 1972).

Clearly, then, teachers must be made aware of and attempt to remove their own biased attitudes before sexism can be reduced in the schools. Prospective teachers can enroll in women's studies courses, join consciousness-raising discussion groups with their colleagues, and participate in workshops and in-service training programs (Dorros and Browne, 1973; Howe, 1973; Levy, 1972).

The National Education Association (NEA) has recommended that all instructional material should provide a positive self-image for every student, regardless of sex or race, and should avoid suggesting that one group is inferior or superior to another (Dorros and Browne, 1973; Wise, 1974). But perhaps of equal importance is the removal of bias toward female teachers, for as long as it exists it will ultimately affect teacher behavior.

THE TEACHER'S PERSONAL FREEDOMS. Compared to American teachers, British teachers are allowed considerably more freedom in their classroom activities. They are expected to formulate their own curriculum objectives, lesson plans, and teaching methods, and there are no uniform minimum standards from school to school. Many American teachers who accept assignments in British schools have difficulty in adjusting to this, and feel that they are left too much on their own (Fisher, 1972).

Part of the reason for this lies in the fact that American teachers generally have never had the same personal freedom as other professionals in their political activities, organization membership, sex lives, marital status, and so on. Furthermore, many school boards prefer that teachers play the role of "preserver" only, thereby forcing them to conform to community values and standards (Sinowitz, 1973b).

The Supreme Court has held that school boards who fire nonconformist teachers often violate the due process clause of the Fourteenth Amendment and the First Amendment rights of freedom of association and privacy, especially if the teacher's conduct does not interfere with his ability in the classroom.

The case of *Pickering v. Board of Education* provides an interesting test of whether or not a teacher's atypical behavior interferes with school operations or classroom performance. Mr. Pickering was dismissed by the community school board for writing a long, sarcastic letter to the local newspaper criticizing the way the board raised and allocated funds. The board claimed that not only were Pickering's accusations false, but "detrimental to the efficient operation and administration of the schools of the district" (Schimmel, 1972, p. 258).

The Supreme Court ruled in Pickering's favor. The court maintained that his criticism was not meant as a personal vendetta, but was simply a matter of a difference of opinion that had no effect on Pickering's ability as a teacher. The court concluded that "a teacher's exercise of his right to speak on issues of public importance may not furnish the basis for his dismissal . . ." (Schimmel, 1972, p. 259).

The American Federation of Teachers (AFT) holds that teachers as professionals have unconditional freedom of speech in the classroom and unrestricted rights to associate, organize, and strike. The AFT takes the position that teachers as citizens have the same constitutional rights and freedoms as any other American citizen ("Academic Freedom and the Rights of Faculty," AFT).

THE STUDENT'S PERSONAL FREEDOMS. Students are also beginning to gain personal freedoms that they did not have before. A recent federal law gives parents of elementary and high school students, as well as college students themselves, full access to their school records (Fields, 1974a). This law was partially based on the premise that students have the right to know what kinds of information are on file about them, since school authorities use this information to make important decisions about them throughout their school careers and afterwards. But the fact that this right has now been made law will undoubtedly affect teacher behavior. Now the task of stating confidential information very carefully so that it does not imply something other than the truth is defined by law. This important task is made even more difficult because, to guard against misuse of records, teachers must carefully explain the information to persons who may be less competent to interpret test scores, medical diagnoses, and psychiatric evaluations.

Students also have gained the right to practice their religion anywhere they wish, including school, but the school does not have the right to force religion on any student. The Supreme Court ruled in 1962 that all laws requiring religious practices in the schools were unconstitutional because they violated the First Amendment provision that the government must maintain strict separation between church and state (Panoch, 1974). As in every other matter affecting the teacher's attitude, the teacher must caution himself not to let a student's religious persuasion affect his attitude toward the student.

Some of the Major Dissatisfactions with Teaching

According to an NEA research specialist, teachers most frequently list bad working conditions as their primary dissatisfaction with teaching. The most common complaint is overcrowded classes ("Finding Out," 1972). Overcrowded classrooms, with all the attendant management problems, reduce teaching efficiency and op-

SCHOOL RECORD KEEPING: PROBLEMS AND GUIDELINES

From birth to death, the pattern of life is duly recorded. A good deal of that pattern today comes from school records. Increasingly, the reasons for and implications of keeping school records are being questioned. So is what is being recorded.

A study conducted by sociologists David A. Goslin and Nancy Bordier in the late 1960s on the record-keeping practices of 54 representative school districts found that "almost all kept anecdotal records made by teachers, special health data, notes on interviews with parents and students, correspondence from home, records of referrals, delinquency reports and other 'high security' data" (Divorky, 1974, p. 38). Hard or soft data—it made no difference—all wound up in official permanent files. Furthermore, the researchers discovered that "the records were consistently little used by teachers and school staff despite the rationale that the dossiers were needed to guide teachers in their relations with individual students." Who did use them? Social service agencies, police—even government agents! Following this study, a group of prominent educators, lawyers, and social scientists gathered to consider the ethical and legal implications of its findings. Their report suggested guidelines for record keeping based on these principles:

1. No information should be collected about students without the informed consent of the parents and, in some cases, the child.
2. Information should be classified so that only the basic minimum of data appears on the permanent record card, while the rest is periodically reviewed and, if appropriate, destroyed.
3. Schools should establish procedures to verify the accuracy of all data maintained in their students' records.
4. Parents should have full access to their child's records, including the right to challenge the accuracy of the information found there.
5. No agency or persons other than school personnel, who deal directly with the child, should have access to student data without parental or student permission (except in the case of a subpoena).

timum learning; an uncrowded classroom provides a relaxed environment, increases attentiveness and participation, allows more individual instruction, and reduces discipline problems.

Overcrowded classrooms are due in large part to the spiraling costs of education. Shortages of funds have produced layoffs, cut out special programs and services, and canceled proposed innovations and improvements. These economic measures have compromised the quality of education and have also reduced teachers' salaries and fringe benefits. Although the unionization movement has helped to combat salary reductions, teachers often still have grounds to complain about salaries.

Maternity leave policies have aroused as much concern as salaries. Many school districts have traditionally forced expectant teachers to take a leave of absence or resign from the school system upon reaching a certain stage in pregnancy. However, the Courts declared forced maternity leave unconstitutional in 1971, having decided that it was arbitrary and discriminatory and violated the Fourteenth Amendment. Title VII of the Civil Rights Act of 1964 also protects pregnant teachers and grants them the same benefits, including sick leave pay, that apply to any other "temporary disability" (Dushane Emergency Fund, 1972). A teacher can now continue working as close to the end of her pregnancy as she chooses, providing she can fulfill her duties in the classroom.

According to nationwide surveys conducted by the NEA in 1968 and 1972, many teachers feel left out of school policy-making. In the 1972 survey, 52 percent of the respondents wanted more say in the selection of school principals; between 40 and 50 percent wanted more influence in teacher evaluation procedures, salaries, fringe benefits, curriculum and school calendar planning, textbook selection, and student discipline.

Another very common complaint involves the accountability of teachers, who, while being held accountable to themselves and their students, are at the same time under continual pressure to conform to community standards and expectations. These dual demands of accountability reflect the conflicting roles of the teacher that we discussed earlier in this chapter. Certainly, the teacher should be entitled to freedom of expression, but, as the Supreme Court pointed out, this freedom must not interfere with the teacher's ability to perform in the classroom. Certainly, teachers must be accountable for what students learn. If they are not, who should be? Accountability is an important and controversial issue for teachers today. The pros and cons as well as the substantial issues will be discussed in detail at the end of this chapter.

In 1974 the NEA conducted a survey among teachers to determine which problems they felt kept them from teaching more effectively. The following is a list of the problems they felt had considerable or some impact (Bartholomew, 1974, p. 79):

Considerable
Parents apathetic about their children's education*
Too many students indifferent to school*
Physical facilities limiting the kinds of student programs*
The wide range of student achievement
Working with too many students each day
Too many noninstructional duties
The values and attitudes of the current generation

*Problems that appear to affect secondary teachers more than elementary teachers.

Some
Diagnosing student learning problems
The lack of instructional materials
The quality of instructional materials
Disruption of classes by students
Little help with instruction-related problems from school
   administrators
The psychological climate of the school*

Not only are teachers dissatisfied with many things that affect their work adversely, but they are quite articulate about how these problems can be solved. Clearly, teachers all over the United States are concerned with their working conditions, their personal freedom, and their salaries; and they are insisting more and more frequently that their grievances be discussed at the bargaining table.

Questions for Thought
Very frequently teachers complain that what was taught to them in teacher preparation courses did not describe the problems that exist in the real teaching world. From the examples just given, do you think it simple or difficult to use the tools provided in teacher preparation to teach basic skills to your students?
Will learning any specific method of teaching work effectively in all situations? Why?
What other problems might you expect to encounter?

The Impact of Unionization

While there has been considerable controversy over the role of teacher unions, unionization is now a well-established part of our educational system. It affects not only elementary and secondary schools but community colleges and universities as well.

One large and powerful national teacher's union is the American Federation of Teachers (AFT), an affiliate of the AFL-CIO; its members include preschool, elementary, secondary, and college teachers from all parts of the United States. The union does not accept administrators, superintendents, principals, or anyone else who has the power to hire, fire, or discipline a teacher.

The aim of AFT is to improve the status and welfare of teachers and to provide better educational opportunities for students. Some of its specific goals include:

1. A salary schedule that provides adequate pay differentials based on training and experience. (However, the AFT is opposed to merit pay, as will be discussed later in the chapter.)

2. Adequate state tenure laws that protect teachers from being dis-

---

*Problems that appear to affect secondary teachers more than elementary teachers.

charged without demonstrable cause after a reasonable probationary period.

3. Improved pension plans, sick leave pay, and other benefits.

4. Programs to reduce class size.

COLLECTIVE BARGAINING.   The impetus behind unionization was the belief held by many that unions such as the AFT can accomplish much more than an individual acting alone because they are able to use collective bargaining. *Collective bargaining* is a process by which any organized group of employees, acting through union representatives, jointly determines with their employer their wages, hours, and conditions of employment. Representatives of both sides meet together at the bargaining table to present their respective proposals and to discuss and negotiate terms. Meetings continue until they are able to draw up a mutually agreeable contract ("How Collective Bargaining Works," AFT).

When an impasse occurs, with either or both parties refusing to compromise, it can be handled by mediation, fact-finding, arbitration, and—as a last resort—a strike. However, collective bargaining does not prevent teachers, or any unionized workers, from taking up their grievances with their employers directly.

Union contracts, made possible by collective bargaining, now are responsible for teachers' salaries and are a means of voicing their grievances and receiving recognition. Many teachers attribute reduced class loads, more adequate staffing, and a larger say for teachers in determining school policy to collective bargaining (Hottleman, 1972).

Collective bargaining operates at the state and local level as well as at the national level; it is legally sanctioned for teachers in most states but is used more often in large cities (Hottleman, 1972).

STRIKES.   The controversy over the legality of strikes by public employees, including teachers, is still raging. But strikes are becoming a major economic force in the United States. Ultimately they affect the teacher's ability to teach and, therefore, the learning of the student. The major issue in teachers' strikes is usually salary. Other issues have included class size and teacher involvement in school policy decisions.

Whether or not to strike poses a new dilemma for the teacher. He must weigh the positive effects that may result from a strike against the immediate effects it will have on the students. Sometimes strikes can persist for weeks or even months. Although a strike may result in long-term benefits for both the teacher and his students, a long strike may interfere with student learning time and, ultimately, student achievement. There is no easy answer for the teacher on this issue.

It has been only recently that teachers have overcome their traditional reluctance to organize and strike.

(Wide World)

Questions for Thought
Should public employees strike?
What happens to classroom learning during a teachers' strike?
Examine newspaper descriptions of strikes during the past few years. What was accomplished? Could means other than strikes have been used to accomplish teacher goals? Would these means have been as effective in changing working conditions?
If there were a teachers' strike in your school district, would you play the role of "preserver" or "improver" of the culture? What would you do?

THE TEACHER AS A LEADER

Effective leadership—that is, knowing how to guide and help students to acquire the skills, knowledge, attitudes, and values necessary for appropriate adjustment to society—is not easy to develop. We will first discuss some factors that contribute to effective leadership in teachers, then some serious problems that prevent the teacher from acting in the best interests of the students, and finally some solutions to these problems.

Factors in Effective Leadership

Some teachers have an attractive, pleasant, friendly manner that students cannot help but like; others are overly strict, efficient, and brisk—they command respect, although students are less likely to appreciate them.

Teachers' classroom behavior also varies according to their views on how students learn (McDonald, 1965). Some teachers believe in the use of positive reinforcement, and they are generous in praise. Other teachers believe that a quiet, orderly classroom and respect for authority promote learning; they tend to be strict and demanding, and some use negative reinforcement to maintain discipline.

These views on learning determine the kinds of decision teachers make in conducting their classes. For example, whenever a student asks a question, the teacher must decide whether it is important enough to stop and answer. A teacher who repeatedly dismisses students' questions is likely to inhibit their curiosity. On the other hand, students may regard a teacher who stops to answer every question as disorganized and inefficient.

Clearly, then, the teachers' behavior will determine pupil behavior. According to one study, a teacher who is understanding, friendly, organized, businesslike, stimulating, and original will have alert, active, confident, responsible, self-controlled students (Ryans, 1961). Cultural variables from the community, combined with the teacher's predispositions, may influence student behavior in particular situations. For instance, the effectiveness of a teacher's style will

Teachers who are stimulating and original have been found to have alert and confident students.

(Sean Eager, Magnum)

sometimes depend on whether the school is located in a small, medium-sized, or large town. Mattsson (1974) found that introverted and reserved teachers were most successful in small towns whereas extroverted and outgoing teachers were most successful in large towns.

CHARACTERISTICS OF TEACHERS WHO ARE EFFECTIVE LEADERS. According to Pearl (1972), the teacher who is a true leader shows the following characteristics:

1. *Appreciation for diversity.* A teacher should always be willing to hear new ideas and should therefore encourage full and open debate in the classroom.
2. *Willingness to be energetically accountable.* A teacher should be prepared to defend his or her beliefs when challenged.
3. *Willingness to negotiate honestly.* Conflicts are necessary in any educational system, but they can be resolved beneficially if the teacher is willing to negotiate.
4. *Recognition that some conflicts are irreconcilable.* A teacher should be able to handle conflict intelligently and know how to prevent violence. When a conflict cannot be resolved, the teacher should not push for a pseudo-agreement, but should instead use common sense. If there is a serious conflict between student and teacher, the teacher might request to have the student transferred; if the conflict is between two students, the teacher should separate them.
5. *Ability to view rules in the context of ends.* Instead of being slaves to rules, teachers should be concerned with what is just and fair.

TOO LITTLE UNDERSTANDING OF THE STUDENT. A teacher must be sensitive to the needs and feelings of the students. All children—the bright and the not-so-bright, the well-behaved and the unruly— need regular support and encouragement. Criticism is important,

Problems Stemming from Poorly Used Leadership

but if it is overdone it becomes destructive. Children are notorious for their cruelty to one another: They tattle, insult, ridicule, and are capable of giving precise, malicious criticisms of each other. They can also be quite sensitive to one another, and the degree to which they are depends largely on the model set by teachers and the image they project.

REINFORCEMENT OF COMPETITION. Although we are a competitive society, the teacher must guard against reinforcing competition that may be destructive. The teacher must be aware that each child seeks approval and attention from the teacher at the expense of other children. The following example shows how the teacher can serve as an agent in reinforcing competition:

> Boris had trouble reducing 12/16 to its lowest terms, and could get only as far as 6/8. Much excitement. Teacher asked him quietly if that was as far as he could reduce it . . . . Much heaving up and down from the other children, all frantic to correct him. Boris pretty unhappy. Teacher, patient, quiet, ignoring others, and concentrating with look and voice on Boris. She says, "Is there a bigger number than 2 you can divide into the two parts of the fraction? . . . No response from Boris. She then turns to the class and says, "Well, who can tell Boris what the number is?" Forest of hands. (Henry, 1957, p. 123)

In this example, the teacher is reinforcing classroom competition at Boris' expense. It is crucial that the teacher realize the negative effects that classroom competition can have, especially on children like Boris.

REINFORCEMENT OF DOCILITY. Many children quickly learn not to reveal their true emotions and therefore put on an act—the name of the game is to please the teacher by telling him what he wants to hear. Children easily find out what the teacher wants to hear by paying close attention to the kinds of answers the teacher has reinforced in the past. A highly competitive classroom atmosphere generates considerable anxiety, which the students can make more tolerable by trying to obtain the approval of the teacher through docile, compliant behavior. Some teachers, moreover, encourage this puppetlike behavior because it bolsters their own self-esteem, power, and importance.

TOO LITTLE LEADERSHIP AND TOO LITTLE CONTROL. Teachers often use positive reinforcement as a means of establishing their leadership in the classroom. The effectiveness of this procedure becomes diluted at times, however, particularly in a poorly established and designed open classroom. Unwanted student behavior is often the result of this uncertain social context, in which the teacher sometimes expects too much self-discipline of students and at other times ignores inappropriate behavior. Instead of specifying learning objectives, the teacher has a mistaken faith in the ability of students to totally direct their own learning (Allender, 1974).

It is very important to realize that the comparatively free atmosphere of the open classroom, in which the student is allowed to select the learning materials and specific behaviors through which he will learn specified skills, does not have to be incompatible with the teacher's ability to maintain control. A teacher in any kind of classroom can and must provide some structure to the learning situation. Teachers should help students plan and evaluate their work and schedule their activities so that there is a realistic balance between self-direction and teacher guidance.

AUTHORITARIAN LEADERSHIP. "Authoritarian leadership" is a vague term that encompasses a wide range of behavior, not all of it harsh, brutal, or ineffective.

Many researchers have studied the contrasting effects of authoritarian and democratic leadership on students. A classic study by Lewin (1953) found less conflict and aggression and higher morale in groups with democratic leaders, but greater productivity in groups with authoritarian leaders. However, this increased productivity lasted only when the teacher was present to oversee the work. Other researchers have not been able to find any clear-cut evidence that either style of teaching consistently produces high productivity or superior learning (Anderson, 1959). Some investigators suggest that authoritarian leadership is most effective for simple, concrete tasks, while democratic leadership is most effective for complex ones (Anderson, 1959).

There are many problems with the research in this area, the most serious being that many investigators have grossly oversimplified the two types of leadership. Neither extreme indicates how ordinary teachers behave in an everyday classroom. Authoritarian leadership does tend to be harmful when a teacher fails to consider the class as a group and the interactions between students. Students build up an inner resistance and show only a superficial compliance toward this kind of teacher. The group loses its cohesiveness, and the teacher becomes ineffective as a leader (Flanders and Havumaki, 1960).

PUNITIVE LEADERSHIP. As we pointed out in Chapter 4, the use of negative reinforcement and punishment, especially corporal punishment, is not effective in teaching. In fact, it is often detrimental. Child psychologists and educators are concerned over the continued use of negative reinforcement and punishment in the schools despite the mounting evidence against it. They feel that it produces long-term psychological damage.

Continual punishment in school leads children to associate anxiety and hostility with the learning situation (Hechinger and Hechinger, 1974). Although it may subdue a child temporarily, it does not produce any lasting positive change (Redl and Wattenberg, 1959). Children may bury their aggressive and antisocial tendencies for a while, but they are likely to erupt later in more serious forms. Punishment also teaches the child that abusive behavior, such as nagging, criticizing, even the use of physical force, is a socially accepted way of solving problems. For these reasons the NEA Task Force has urged all teachers to end the practice of "inflicting pain on students, except for purposes of restraint, or protection of self or other students" (Hechinger and Hechinger, 1974, p. 84).

A study by Kounin and Gump (1961) showed that children with punitive teachers tend to be preoccupied with aggression and are more inclined to misbehave. Children with nonpunitive teachers have greater trust and faith in the "rightness" of what their teacher tells them and are more concerned with the effects of misbehavior on learning and achievement.

The fact remains that punishment is still widespread in American schools. Only three states (New Jersey, Massachusetts, and Maryland) and a few cities (New York, Boston, Chicago, and San Francisco, for example) explicitly ban corporal punishment. Elsewhere in the country, hitting children is not only tolerated, it may be expected (Hechinger and Hechinger, 1974). The NEA Task Force reported that students and teachers have changed their attitudes toward corporal punishment very little over the last decade.

It has been reported that teachers and school administrators sometimes inflict punishment to an outrageous extent. The following is a child's statement of his own experience in the Dallas public schools:

> Oh, we get lots of licks. In one class, for every minute you're late, you get a lick. And in another class, a teacher took me down to the assistant principal to get some licks because I'd been chewing on my pen and there was ink on my mouth. The assistant principal, he used three paddles on me, and he broke two of them. (Hentoff, 1973, p. 20)

Some Solutions for the Teacher

The teacher can avoid many of the problems discussed in the previous section if he can get to know each of the students' individual interests, concerns, and problems (Kahl, 1973). One method is to have each student evaluate himself and discuss his problems openly. Whenever possible, the teacher should get to know something about a child's background and family through conferences with parents, or with parents and child together.

We have repeatedly emphasized the importance of using positive reinforcement whenever possible instead of punishment and negative reinforcement to shape student behavior. Although teachers are aware of the value of tangible and intangible positive reinforcers in promoting desired behavior, they tend not to use them, particularly in situations in which they themselves are harried and pressured. A study by Byalick and Bersoff (1974) revealed that only 32 percent of the teachers in their sample actually used the forms of positive reinforcement they said they preferred. An earlier study by deGroat and Thompson (1949) revealed that most teachers direct their approval and disapproval toward just a few students and give little feedback of any kind to the majority. As one might expect, teachers gave most of their approval to bright, hard-working students and expressed disapproval to the low achievers.

Teachers also need to be alert to the kinds of interactions that occur between themselves and their students. In most classrooms, the teacher initiates more interactions than the students (Bellack et al., 1963), and most of these interactions consist of the teacher lecturing, instructing, and criticizing (Flanders, 1966). According to one study, a "superior" teacher talks and directs less and, instead, encourages the students to participate more (Amidon and Giammatteo, 1965). One effective way of communicating with younger children and engaging their participation is to touch them (Dunaway, 1974). Warmth, kind words, friendliness, and helpfulness promote more active participation in older children (Cogan, 1958; Ryans, 1960).

The Flanders system of interaction analysis can help teachers assess the patterns of interaction in their classes (Campbell and Barnes, 1969; Flanders, 1963; Kryspin and Feldhusen, 1974). Flanders identified several categories of verbal communication in the classroom. Of these he distinguished between "indirect teacher talk" and "direct teacher talk" and found that indirect talk gave students a much wider range of responses and encouraged participation to a greater degree than direct talk.

Flanders' categories of indirect teacher talk are:

1. *Accepting Feeling:* Acknowledging and accepting a student's expression of emotion without making judgments about it.
   Examples: "I understand how you feel."
                      "We all feel that way sometimes."

2. *Praise and Encouragement:* Praise consists of statements like "That's right," "Fine," "Terrific." Encouragement, "Go on," "You've got the idea," "Tell me more."

3. *Accepting and Using Ideas:* Clarifying or elaborating an idea provided by a student.
   Examples: "I see your point."
                      "I think what Mary is trying to say is the following."

4. *Asking Questions:* A range of specific and broad, open-ended

EXCERPTS FROM "A LOVE LETTER TO A DEAD TEACHER"

Dear Mr. Stock:

You probably wouldn't remember me, even if you were alive. I sat in the third row back in your English 512 class in South Side High School in Newark, New Jersey. You gave me an A minus for being unprepared.

You had asked us to write a composition in class about one of Hardy's heroines, but I had neglected to read the book assigned. Caught off guard, writing frantically against the clock, I described a young woman, the room she sat in, the beam of light from the high window, her hands in her lap, the thoughts in her head. I anticipated failure, disgrace, worst of all—your disappointment. Instead, you gave me a minus for being unprepared and an A for something uniquely mine. Your scrawled comment in red ink on my paper read, "This isn't Hardy's character, but you've made yours very real."

Startled into gratitude, I became aware of my own possibilities. You *recognized* me. . . .

I don't think you knew what you did for me, Mr. Stock. We teachers seldom know whom we influence or even why. It was not my defects you emphasized, but my worth.

Other teachers dealt differently with us, demanding discipline or wooing us with false camaraderie.

You assumed one simple fact: If the lesson was interesting, we would be attentive. We were more than attentive. We hated to see the period end, for you knew when to ask the provocative, unexpected "Why?" which tumbled upside down our whole cluttered cart of preconceptions and set us thinking long after the dismissal bell. You did not try to charm or to beguile us. You never pretended to be a pal. You were a *teacher*. Your dignity was unassailable. Because you respected yourself and us, we were able to respect ourselves. . . .

When one of us returned after an absence, you would say, "We missed you." When one was unprepared, you would shake your head: "Too bad; we were hoping to know what *you* think." You treated us as adults, your equals, and so—in your class—we were . . . .

And you shared with us your loves. "Listen to this!" you would say, eagerly opening a book, unashamed to be moved by a poem, unafraid to use words like "magnificent." . . .

Are teachers like you really dead? I think not—as long as there are people who can still say: "I had a teacher once . . . who made that difference!" Perhaps at this very moment someone, someplace, is saying this about one of us. That is our immortality.

Your former pupil, Bel Kaufman.

Bel Kaufman, "A Love Letter to a Dead Teacher," condensed from *Today's Education* (March-April, 1975), 20-23.

questions such as "What is photosynthesis?" and "What is the relationship between force and work?" will promote greater student interaction (Flanders, 1963, p. 255).

Direct teacher talk restricts the range of student responses and consists mostly of explaining and informing, giving directions and comments, scolding and reprimanding, and defending authority. Many teachers use direct techniques more often than indirect, but the superiority of indirect techniques is clear. Students exposed to these positive behaviors do better scholastically and develop better attitudes toward learning (Amidon and Flanders, 1967; Flanders, 1967; Flanders and Simon, 1969; Kryspin and Feldhusen, 1974a; Morrison, 1966; Samph, 1967). Analysis of the kinds of talk taking place in the classroom can provide the teacher with valuable clues about his own intention and actual behavior and the means to reduce the discrepancies between them (Amidon and Flanders, 1967; Amidon and Hough, 1967; Flanders, 1963, 1965, 1970).

However, self-evaluation does not necessarily make the teacher a better instructor (Doyle and Redwine, 1974). No matter how much we talk about the teacher as a leader, we should also remember that the teacher as a human being is constantly being influenced by all the students in the class.

TEACHER ACCOUNTABILITY

School communities across the United States have begun to accept the idea of teacher accountability: that the teacher, not the student, is ultimately responsible for what and how much a student learns. In this section, we will examine the meaning of this trend, its problems and issues, and its effects on teacher behavior and student achievement.

Increasingly, the public is holding teachers (as well as principals and superintendents) accountable for what children learn in school. Some school districts must justify their expenses by showing how much the students actually accomplish (Barro, 1970; Lessinger, 1970; Rosenshine and McGaw, 1972).

What Is Teacher Accountability? What Does It Really Mean for the Teacher?

Several factors are responsible for this recent change in thinking. There is a growing body of knowledge that demonstrates exactly how much we can change children's behavior through exciting and stimulating learning environments. The many programs discussed in Chapter 9 support this view. In Chapter 14, we will discuss competency-based education, which is derived from the premise that all children have the ability to learn. This premise is partially responsible for bringing teacher accountability to the forefront. If all children have the ability to learn, then it is the teacher, not the student, who is responsible for what the student learns.

The "taxpayers' revolt" has also given impetus to the accountability movement—the public has become increasingly concerned with what our local, state, and federal governments are doing with education funds. During the last 10 years, the push to improve the quality of instruction has resulted in huge expenditures for educational "inputs," such as books, instructional techniques, in-service training programs, and other resources. With costs higher than ever before, the public is demanding proof that the "outputs"—objective results of improved learning based on such factors as standardized test scores and the number of students graduating from high school—are worth the expense (Elam, 1971; Gall and Ward, 1973; NEA Instruction and Professional Development Staff, 1972).

Effects of Accountability: Implications for Education

The accountability movement is causing many changes in the schools. Instead of judging a school's quality by its classrooms and equipment, the public now may judge it by its output in student achievement (Lessinger, 1970). Not only must schools be committed to providing equal educational opportunity for all children; now they must be committed to the idea that every student must learn something and be willing to experiment with many different programs to insure better student performance (Glass, 1972; Lessinger, 1970; Mecklenburger and Wilson, 1971). Teachers are beginning to use learning objectives in their instruction and to test students frequently to determine whether they have attained those objectives.

Accountability has become a very controversial issue, and there are many compelling arguments for and against it. Both need to be considered.

ARGUMENTS FOR ACCOUNTABILITY.   Those in favor of accountability claim advantages such as the following:

1. Teacher responsibility to see that all students learn to the best of their abilities will be helpful to disadvantaged and minority-group students, who would have been allowed to fail under the traditional system (Gall and Ward, 1974).
2. Students will be highly motivated to learn because now they will be less likely to blame their difficulties on their lack of ability (Gall and Ward, 1974).
3. The emphasis on results will motivate teachers and students to keep trying new approaches until they find one that works (Lessinger, 1970).
4. School facilities will become more open, flexible, and oriented toward the individual instead of the group (Lessinger, 1970).

5. Testing will become more objective and rely more on proven ways to increase learning. Staff, facilities, and equipment will be used more efficiently (Gall and Ward, 1974; Lessinger, 1970; Mecklenburger and Wilson, 1971.)

6. Accountability will inform the public on what is happening in the schools to a greater degree and create closer ties between school and community (Gall and Ward, 1974; Lessinger, 1970).

ARGUMENTS AGAINST ACCOUNTABILITY.   Those against accountability claim the following:

1. The idea of accountability is too simplistic. Parents and students themselves should be held accountable. Teachers have no control over what a student does outside school (Farrell, 1972; Gall and Ward, 1974; NEA Instruction and Professional Development Staff, 1972).

2. Accountability overemphasizes test scores. Teachers may simply "teach to test" and ignore other important aspects of a subject. Students may become so involved in getting good scores that they will ignore learning for its own sake (Farrell, 1972; Gall and Ward, 1974).

3. Accountability reduces education to a series of inputs and outputs instead of treating it as a complex dynamic process that involves individual needs and feelings; the new curriculum considers only the student's rate of learning and ignores individual differences in interest and ability (Farrell, 1972; Gall and Ward, 1974; NEA Instruction and Professional Development Staff, 1972).

4. Accountability prevents teachers from using their professional judgment in carrying out instruction programs by setting arbitrary, "inhumane" performance requirements (NEA Instruction and Professional Development Staff, 1972).

5. Learning objectives set too narrow a limit on instruction (Gall and Ward, 1974).

6. Accountability is just an excuse to coerce teachers and slash education budgets (NEA Instruction and Professional Development Staff, 1972).

The idea of accountability and the radical changes it implies have raised difficult questions for which there are no clear answers (Howsam, 1972). Who should be accountable to whom and under what conditions? To what extent should teachers be involved in curriculum planning and decision-making? To what extent should students be involved? Who should assess teacher competency and how should it be done? Who should receive the results of an evaluation? What effect should these results have on salary and tenure?

Special Problems and Issues in Accountability

Also, who is to blame if a student fails a test because he hasn't done his homework? Who is to blame if a highly recommended textbook fails to live up to expectations? According to a 1972 Gallup poll, many parents and educators feel that the teacher is *not* primarily to blame for educational failures. They feel that the cause is the child's home life.

If we grant, however, that teachers are at the very least partially accountable for what students learn, we must then decide which evaluating and rating procedures to use for a fair and accurate assessment. Table 13-1 provides a revealing comparison between teacher evaluations as they are and as they ought to be. We can see that evaluations fail to account for working conditions, parents' aspirations, and children's readiness to learn. Teachers with large classes or learning-disabled children might receive poorer ratings than they deserve, if the evaluator ignores these considerations. Teachers frequently have no control over curriculum and teaching strategies, and therefore are not necessarily accountable for performance results.

If we leave aside the question of which learning objectives to measure, we are still faced with the question of *how* to measure them. How does one measure desirable behavior such as independence, self-confidence, and good citizenship? (McKenna, 1973; Rosenshine and McGaw, 1972). Moreover, many people feel that even with testable behavior, the testing instruments themselves are imprecise, unreliable, and misleading (Rosenshine and McGaw, 1972).

Who should evaluate a teacher's performance is another difficult

Table 13-1

A Comparison Between Teacher Evaluations as They Usually Are and as They Should Be

Teacher Evaluation	
The Way It Usually Is	The Way It Ought To Be
Evaluation is threatening to teachers.	Evaluation should be something that teachers anticipate and want because it gives them insight into their own performance.
They see it as something that is done to them by someone else.	It should be something in which teachers have a part along with students, parents, and administrators.
It is used mostly for determining teacher status relative to dismissal, tenure, and promotion, even though instructional improvement is often advertised as its major purpose.	Evaluation should be used to diagnose teachers' performance so they can strengthen their weaknesses through in-service education.
Teachers often are unaware of the criteria used to judge them.	Teachers should take part in developing or selecting evaluation instruments so that they know the criteria against which they are judged.

From McKenna (1973, p. 55).

question. In practice, many people—students, parents, other teachers, supervisors—informally evaluate a teacher on the basis of their own observations or hearsay, and they do this from a unique point of view that severely limits their ability to accurately assess a teacher's competence (Tolor, 1973; Wicks, 1973).

Some feel that students are the best judges of a teacher's effectiveness because they are in daily contact with teachers' abilities. Although students can readily say whether they find a teacher stimulating or boring, they cannot necessarily judge which teachers actually help them learn. Students are not in the best position to identify a teacher's weak areas or to suggest improvements in instructional methods. They are also biased by their own attitudes and by grades (Rosenshine and McGaw, 1972; Wicks, 1973).

Wicks (1973) suggests voluntary self-appraisal and mutual self-appraisal with colleagues and supervisors, then having another person compare the two. The teacher should have some say about who this independent evaluator will be and about which instruments and criteria the evaluator will use. The teacher has a right to be fully informed of the evaluator's recommendations and to discuss and challenge them if necessary (McKenna, 1973; Wicks, 1973).

TENURE AND MERIT PAY. If evaluation results show that some teachers are clearly more effective than others, should they be paid more? Furthermore, should tenure laws be modified so that inadequate teachers can be dismissed?

State tenure laws now provide job security to most teachers by protecting them from arbitrary demotion and dismissal. School boards must abide by due process procedures and show sufficient cause before they can discharge a teacher. Many people consider these policies a breakthrough for education and teachers' rights. Others would like to see them abandoned, especially school administrators who resent the loss of power and taxpayers who resent paying salaries to teachers they consider inadequate. The AFT and the NEA, of course, would like to see tenure provisions extended (Sinowitz, 1973c).

Those against the tenure system would like to substitute merit pay in place of it. They argue that merit pay will attract better teachers and weed out the unqualified, and that since other professions and businesses give our merit increases, why shouldn't the schools? (Wilson, 1962).

The NEA and AFT are opposed to merit pay for several reasons. One is that ratings are a matter of personal judgment and bias on the part of the rater. Teaching involves so many different capabilities that it has been impossible for supervisors to agree on a precise dollar value for any one of them. Moreover, every teacher has both good and bad qualities (Fondy, 1973; Wilson, 1962). Furthermore, incompetent teachers are supposed to be screened out during their probation periods on the job, if they haven't already been during their formal training and student teaching (Wilson, 1962). Merit pay might also produce competitiveness, suspicion, distrust, and resentment in an environment that should be based on mutual trust and cooperation. It might also ruin the relationship between teachers and supervisors by putting too much power in the hands of administrators.

Accountability to Oneself   Teachers may be accountable to principals, school boards, communities, and students, but most of all they are accountable to themselves. A teacher cannot do a good job unless he enjoys what he is doing. Teachers who are dissatisfied with their role should analyze the causes to see if they can do something about them. If they cannot avoid certain problems, they must determine whether or not they can live with them. Teaching, like any other job, can be frustrating and unpleasant. A teacher who finds the job unpleasant nearly all the time should not be in the classroom.

Kuhlen (1963) has shown that when teachers believe that teaching satisfies their inner needs, they will always find it rewarding; if teaching does not, they are bound to find it unpleasant. Clearly, teachers who are personally satisfied with their work will be far more effective with their students than those who are not. Successful teaching and high-quality education, therefore, depend as much on self-accountability as on any other factor discussed in this chapter.

SUMMARY   There are no universally agreed-upon expectations in this country of the role a teacher should play in educating children. Much of the burden of teaching attitudes and values has come to rest on the schools. Therefore, teachers are often caught between the need to transmit traditional, conservative values (to preserve the culture), or to transform old values through innovation and reform (to improve the culture). Whatever role they choose, teachers strongly influence their students' academic achievement, attitudes toward school, and self-concepts.

Teachers find themselves in the center of some very serious social controversies such as desegregation and busing, textbook censorship, classroom sex bias, and restrictions on their own rights and personal freedom. These issues must ultimately affect their classroom behavior.

Teachers in recent years have become very outspoken on their dissatisfactions and professional problems. Their complaints center on working conditions, class size, discipline problems, inadequate supplies, school board and community infringements of personal rights, salaries, and fringe benefits such as maternity leave. Collective bargaining and recent legislation have attempted to alleviate some of these problems and to protect teachers' rights as citizens.

Teachers must be leaders in the classroom. However, their leadership ability is often compromised by too little understanding of students, excessive reinforcement of competition and docility, too little or too much control, and excessive use of punishment. Teachers can avoid these excesses by combining warmth and understanding with assertiveness and self-control. They should get to know their students as individuals and provide them with as much positive reinforcement as possible. They should establish a relaxed learning environment and interact with students continually through indirect means such as praising, encouraging, questioning, and accepting instead of explaining, lecturing, informing, directing, and reprimanding.

The public now holds teachers, not just students, accountable for what and how much students learn in school. This has resulted in a demand for objective proofs of learning by means of standardized test scores. Other educators claim that accountability is too simple an idea, that parents and outside activities strongly influence a student's school performance. Accountability also raises many complex questions about teacher evaluation—what kinds of behavior should be evaluated and who should evaluate it. However, no matter how much teachers are accountable to others, those who take their work seriously are ultimately accountable to themselves.

SUGGESTED FOR FURTHER READING

Gage, N. L. (Ed.) *Handbook of research on teaching.* Chicago: Rand McNally, 1963.
Gage has compiled an outstanding collection of research on teaching. Topics such as how to do teacher observations, experimental design and analysis, and personality characteristics are included. The final section is devoted to teaching specific disciplines such as social studies or English.

Rubin, D. *The rights of teachers.* Washington, D.C.: The American Civil Liberties Union, 1972.
This book outlines the legal rights of teachers. It also tells how teachers can investigate to determine whether any of their rights have been denied to them, and what they can do about it.

Sperry, L. (Ed.) *Learning performance and individual differences.* Glenview, Ill.: Scott, Foresman, 1972.
This book of readings focuses on learner-environment interactions in the classroom. The influence of the individual teacher and student is stressed through readings on expectations, learning, and instructional style.

Today's Education.
The National Education Association publishes this journal ten times a year. This journal, more than any other single source, covers all current topics on teacher behavior. All sides of controversial educational issues are expressed by teachers, administrators, and government law makers.

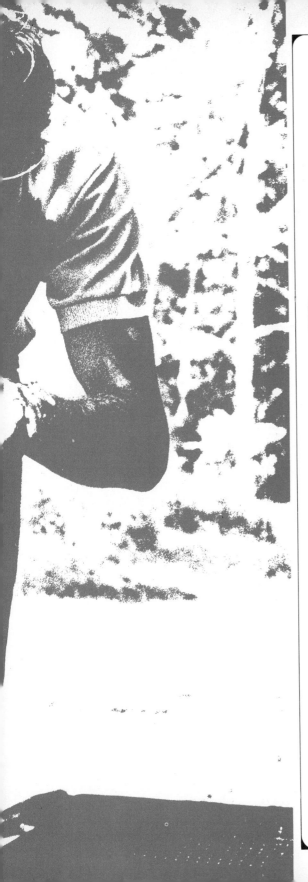

4

USES AND
METHODS OF
EVALUATION

The fundamental objective of any type of instruction is to cause learning, that is, to cause desirable changes in behavior. Evaluation—through tests and other devices—determines whether these changes have in fact been made.

There seems to be a great deal of disagreement among teachers and students over the value of testing and other methods of evaluation used in our schools. The real problem, however, is not *if* we should evaluate behavior, but *how* this should be done. Evaluation is indispensable to our system of education. Without testing of achievement, neither the teacher nor the student would know where he stood. Testing can be used not only to evaluate a student's progress, but also to evaluate a teacher's success at achieving his learning objectives. Tests can also be used to predict a student's success in a particular subject, and to diagnose areas in which he may need help. Perhaps most important is the use of test results by the teacher to assess student learning while it is taking place. Standardized tests of ability and achievement can be used to compare students from across the country.

The controversy clearly is not whether or not we should evaluate. Rather, it is really about what we should do with these evaluations.

Chapter 14 deals with teacher-made tests for the classroom. It discusses the purposes of classroom testing—how tests may be used to evaluate students, to form a part of instruction itself, and to help individualize instruction. The different types of test items and how they should be written, how teachers can construct tests, and how tests should be graded are all discussed in detail. The advantages and disadvantages of objective testing and essay testing are examined.

Special note is taken of the implications of competency-based instruction: its effect on classroom testing and, ultimately, on grading procedures.

The purposes of grading and types of grading systems and management of school grades and records are considered.

Chapter 15 deals with standardized tests, which are designed by professionals for a national market. Standardized testing has become commonplace in the United States. Recently countries that have never before employed standardized testing are trying their best to adopt our system. By so doing, they are adopting both our strengths and our weaknesses.

Standardized testing is used to measure achievement and ability. Chapter 15 discusses the meaning of these tests as well as the manner in which their scores are interpreted.

This chapter briefly relates the history of standardized intelligence testing and touches on major theories of intelligence. The nature of the IQ and the question of its stability are further topics. The inherent bias and problems of many standardized tests are evaluated, and suggestions as to ways they can be improved are discussed.

EVALUATING CLASSROOM LEARNING

 CHAPTER 14

After completing this chapter, the reader should be able to:

1 Describe both norm-referenced and criterion-referenced testing in terms of their roles in the teaching-learning process.

2 Identify and describe the uses and abuses of classroom testing, in terms of the validity and reliability of the testing instruments themselves and the effects of the type of testing selected on both student and teacher behavior.

3 Select and evaluate different types of testing instruments and test items in terms of their usefulness in measuring classroom learning.

4 Evaluate alternative forms of testing used in competency-based and other instructional models in terms of their abilities to measure learning objectives.

5 Select a grading system compatible with goals of teacher and students given a specified teacher, student group, and set of learning objectives; justify this selection in terms of its meaningfulness and utility to both teacher and student.

TESTING: A MEANS OF EVALUATION

Testing and other methods used to evaluate behavior have been increasingly under attack by professionals as well as the general public. The evaluations themselves (as grades or in other forms) and the uses to which they have been put have also been criticized. In both public schools and colleges, students have rebelled against rigid systems, teachers have been deeply concerned, and a variety of experimental solutions have been developed.

At some universities, for example, experimental courses have attempted to do away with evaluation of individual differences in behavior entirely by giving all students identical letter grades for their efforts. In some cities public schools have stopped measuring ability to learn by means of standardized tests (this type of test will be discussed in Chapter 15). In other cities teachers and psychologists, seeing the faults of ability-testing programs, have begun to press for substitutes.

In the confusion resulting from these conflicts, a fundamental issue has become confused: The question is *not*—as some apparently believe—whether we should evaluate behavior. Without evaluating our behavior in some way we cannot know whether we have reached our goals. The real question is this: What are the most meaningful ways to evaluate?

Purposes of Classroom Testing

Evaluation when used correctly is an integral part of the teaching-learning process. In some new programs testing is used even before teaching has begun in order to diagnose a student's strengths and weaknesses and then to select learning activities appropriate to these strengths and weaknesses. Testing can also be used by the teacher at the end of the course as a means of evaluating what effects the course had on the class and which areas of the course need to be improved (Cronbach, 1963). Perhaps most important, however, is assessing student progress while learning is actually taking place. The results of such testing can be used in ways that will help the teacher in instructional planning and help the student in the actual learning process.

The process of testing itself can be a major part of the teaching-learning process. Pressey (1932) and his colleagues at Ohio State University (Little, 1934) were the first to dramatize this by showing that frequently administered tests can be highly effective teaching instruments when they are used as a source of constant feedback. Pressey initially developed an elaborate device that he called a "multiple-choice teaching-testing apparatus." This device provided immediate knowledge of one's results. Later, the punchboard was developed, a small board in which holes were provided correspond-

DIAGNOSTIC TEACHING

''Martha, let me see you pirouette again,'' says her ballet teacher. Outside on the baseball diamond, Mark's coach tells him to ''hit me another grounder.'' Each instructor is giving an impromptu ''test'' to determine the learner's level of proficiency. They will not give grades; rather, their observations will provide the basis for corrections and appropriate guidance in developing higher levels of proficiency. Their students may not even be aware that they are being tested, that tests are an important part of their learning. What Martha and Mark's teachers are engaging in is formative evaluation. In terms of the learning process, they have clearly in mind the behaviors (in this case physical activities) their students should be demonstrating. By attending to what their students do wrong, they can prescribe alterations in their students' learning procedures.

This kind of testing for the purposes of diagnosis and remediation of student errors is familiar. We've all experienced it, but more often in terms of physical activities rather than intellectual ones. It seems easy to develop behavioral objectives that describe physical activities. With practice, it is just as easy to develop behavioral objectives that describe mental activities. For ''diagnostic teaching,'' clear objectives are a necessity.

This kind of teaching also requires practice in developing other important skills, as a recent exploratory study indicates (Dodd, Jones, and Lamb, 1975). Elementary math student teachers significantly improved their competency in developing suitable remedial procedures by practice in describing and illustrating students' errors in single- and double-digit multiplication.

As one educator notes, ''If we wish to change the purpose of [testing] . . . the individual teacher must use some competencies he or she does not now possess'' (Hartman, 1975, p. 274). Clear objectives serve diagnosis, while description and illustration of errors serve remediation. All are necessary components of those competencies. And all are part of diagnostic teaching.

ing to each answer. Correct choices could be punched through the board, giving knowledge that a correct answer was chosen. Incorrect answers could not be punched through. The punchboard gave results similar to the initial teaching-testing apparatus, showing again that feedback provided by tests can increase student learning (Angell and Troyer, 1948).

Knowledge of student progress is crucial for the teacher in planning instruction. The teacher can use tests to discover which teaching methods are most effective in changing student behavior. Test scores can also be used by the teacher to evaluate whether or not students have mastered learning objectives in a certain unit of instruction; that is, whether or not they have met a certain criterion of learning. Such testing is called *criterion-referenced testing*. These tests show which pupils have mastered the learning objectives and which need more help. They also show what each individual student can and cannot do. Such knowledge is necessary for the teacher in assigning the correct plan of instruction. This is especially important for methods of individualized instruction, as explained in Chapter 9.

A *norm-referenced test* is used as a means of comparing scores within a group. Traditionally, American schools have been concerned primarily with norm-referenced testing. In other words, schools have compared students with each other and ranked them in order of their comparative excellence in academic achievement.

An illustration of this is a testing system in which students are assigned grades on the basis of a comparison with other students in the class. Norm-referenced testing has sometimes been used improperly in the classroom by what teachers refer to as "marking on the curve." This usually means arranging raw test scores (original number of questions answered correctly by the student) in order from high to low and assigning different grades to predetermined proportions of each rank. For example, the top 10 percent of the scores may be given an A (the highest rank), the next 20 percent a B, and so on. Usually the largest proportion get the middle mark, a C.

Teachers who mark on the curve base their grades on the assumption that in every classroom, raw test scores are distributed in the same manner as those scores obtained by a statistical hypothetical sample, the normal distribution. The normal distribution, as you will remember from Chapters 11 and 12, describes an infinitely large population.

Suppose that we were to select randomly such an infinitely large number of people and measure differences in their performances on a specified examination of 1000 questions. The horizontal axis of the graph in Figure 14-1 would show the number of correct answers out of 1000. The vertical axis would show the number of people who answered the questions correctly. With an infinitely large number of people, the curve of scores would look like the curve in Figure 14-1. The smoothness and regularity of this curve is due to the fact that the behavior of such a large number of people is being measured. Appendix 2 describes in detail the attributes and the basis of the normal curve. When we know the basis of the curve itself, we realize immediately that the validity of the assumption of normality is directly related to the *size* of the population. That is, the more people there are taking an examination, the more likely it is that their grades will be normally distributed. When teachers "grade on the curve," they are making the assumption that their own small

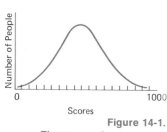

Figure 14-1.
The curve of scores on a test with an infinitely large population.

classes of 20 or 30 students will have scores that match the shape of the normal curve. The problem is, however, that teachers sometimes try to "grade on a curve" that does not exist naturally in their small classrooms (as it would if the population were infinitely large), and thus are often forcing students into molds in which they do not belong. Let's take an extreme example. Suppose a teacher gave a test to a very bright class of students. The lowest grade was 90 and the highest grade was 100. The largest proportion of students received 95. If the teacher were marking on a curve and assigning letter grades, a 95 would be a C. This means that the student did average work in relation to the rest of the class. Unfortunately, it does not show that in this case "average" means 95 percent correct. The problem with norm-referenced testing is that the only evaluation made is where each student ranks *in relation to* the other students in his class. No attempt is made to evaluate whether or not each individual student has met the learning objectives.

Questions for Thought

Assume that you are a teacher of a class of gifted high school students and that a prospective student comes to you and asks your grading procedures. He points out that if he remains in the regular class he will probably fall at the "top of the curve" and have higher grades to present to colleges for admission. What would you, as a teacher, advise him to do? Enter the standard class or gifted class? What type of evaluation procedure would be most likely to meet the needs of a student such as this one?

Social Implications of Testing

What are the social implications of norm-referenced testing? Certainly this kind of testing fosters competition rather than cooperation among classmates. The bright students in the class described earlier must battle each other for a few points on a test. Nevertheless, some educators report that norm-referenced testing does provide the incentive for those who are good at academic subjects to work hard for success, and in a sense that kind of incentive supports the ideals of academic achievement.

Does norm-referenced testing have the effect of encouraging students to work only for marks and not for knowledge? Terwilliger (1971) says no, that such an outcome could only come either from a failure on the teacher's part to define the goals of instruction or else from careless procedures of evaluation. The incentive for some students, however, even bright ones with high motivations to achieve, will sometimes be to cheat rather than to study. (See Chapter 6 for a discussion of achievement motivation.) Furthermore, students who receive average grades without effort may not be motivated to learn more than what is required to get by. Perhaps the negative effects of

**CHEATING:
A WAY OF LIFE?**

Steve Jantzen, an editor for a weekly educational publication, regularly visits schools. On his return from one, he wrote the following to a friend, a high school principal:

I wonder if the high school I visited recently is typical of high schools elsewhere in the U.S. . . . If it is, then teachers and administrators had better take notice: THE EDUCATIONAL SYSTEM IN THEIR CHARGE MAY BE IN SERIOUS TROUBLE.

The students I spoke with said that everyone in school makes a practice of cheating on tests. Not just many or most—so they claim—but EVERYONE. Could this be true? (Senior Scholastic, May 8, 1972, p. 4)

Cheating is one of those subjects that occasionally rises to claim local or even national attention—Regents exams are stolen in New York, service academy classmen defy the honor code, students in one or another university openly buy term papers and theses—and a public outcry goes up. And down. Nobody applauds cheating, but its prevalence has become commonplace. And, all too often, accepted—at least by the students.

Many educators echo Jantzen's question. They cannot close their eyes to the answer. Cheating, as two educators have pointed out, has become a part of the school experience, of "the stress on grades, on passing, on good results at all costs" (Georgiady and Romano, 1971, p. 272). And behind this emphasis on grades, they claim, stands that most American of concepts—competition. To win has become the name of the game—any game. Our society today, they observe, is competitive, unreasonable, and demanding. If you're not counted among the winners, you're not counted. Individual uniqueness, as a result, has been demeaned.

But, the authors have noted, cheating has another cause—and "justification"—a conflict of value systems. Children are taught what is "right," but often they don't see it practiced. Said one university senior, shrugging off the ethical implications of buying a term paper, "It's a lot like the business world. School is becoming a business, and buying a paper is just one more phase of that business. I don't feel there's anything morally wrong" ("Enterprise: Cheating, Inc.," *Newsweek*, March 20, 1972, p. 89).

Even on the high school level, such justifications are evident. Jantzen noted that when students discussed cheating with him,

. . . they declared that cheating was (1) universal, (2) necessary, and (3) very easy. After I'd finished questioning them, their teacher asked them one more question:

"When do you cheat?"

"When you don't know the answer," one student readily responded.

That line broke up everyone. . . . In this school—if the students are telling the truth—grades seem to be a farce and cheating a joke. . . .

norm-referenced testing, particularly when grading on the curve, are most severe for the slow student—the one who is always at the bottom of the curve. As we discussed in Chapter 6, a person's level of aspiration is based on his history of success and failure. It is likely, then, that the student who is always at the bottom of the curve will become convinced that he will always fail.

Thus, although norm-referenced testing may serve some purposes for some students, the teacher must be aware of its drawbacks. Many educators feel that a more humane approach, and one more in line with the basic aims of education, is to give every student a chance to succeed in his own way and at his own pace and so move on to his own top level of achievement. Norm-referenced testing often does not permit this.

Criteria of Good Tests and Their Evaluation

In Chapter 15, we will discuss the purpose and nature of standardized tests developed by professionals specifically trained in testing. Here we are concerned with the teacher-made test. Whether norm-referenced or criterion-referenced tests are used, all the purposes of classroom testing cannot be fulfilled unless the tests have certain desirable characteristics. The two most important characteristics are reliability and validity.

RELIABILITY.   A test is *reliable* if it gives the same scores on repeated testing. Reliability is the extent to which everyone gets the same raw score (number of correct answers) when the test is repeated. Or, in the case of norm-referenced tests, it may mean that if the raw scores of a group are arranged in order from high to low, on repeated testing everyone will keep the same rank in the group. In other words, a test is reliable if it measures *consistently*. Reliable tests require a large amount of care and thought in development.

Many influences affect reliability. Some are related to the specific type of test used and will be discussed in a later section. But others involve the pupils themselves or the immediate testing situation. Assuming that a student's knowledge of a subject has not changed, a different score on a retest (or, what is usually more practical, a second test on the same subject but in a different form) may be caused by differences in the student himself. He may be in good health one day, but not feeling well another day. He may concentrate well on one occasion, but be distracted by emotional problems or by exciting events he is looking forward to on the next occasion. In addition, the classroom may be quiet during the first testing, and noisy during the second, which might distract him. Some of these influences, such as varying health, will affect some members of the class and not others. Other influences, such as variations in noise, will affect all students in the class, but not all to the same degree. The general tendency will be changes in scores. There will probably be changes in the raw scores of individuals, and there may also be changes in an individual's place in relation to others in the group, so that the top student of the first testing may no longer be on top the second time. To the extent that these influences affect test scores, the test measures less consistently—in other words, less reliably.

VALIDITY.   A test may measure reliably but this does not mean that it is valid. A test has *validity* if it measures what it is supposed to measure. No one would give students a set of arithmetic examples to measure their knowledge of geography. An arithmetic test is not a *valid* measure of knowledge of geography because it does not measure what it is supposed to measure. But even something that seems to be testing geography may not be doing its job as well as it should. A teacher-made achievement test in geography that includes questions from only about half of the topics covered in class is not a very valid test of what was taught in that class. An achievement test is valid if its questions representatively cover the area of knowledge that the test is intended to measure. This kind of validity is called *content validity;* other kinds of validity will be discussed in the next chapter.

The teacher should try to create tests that are both reliable and valid; they should measure consistently, and they should measure what they are intended to measure. The example of using an arithmetic test to measure knowledge of geography shows that a reliable test may not be valid for the purpose chosen. The most reliable arithmetic test in the world will not measure knowledge of geography. On the other hand, a valid test by definition must also be reliable; it will always measure consistently.

It is the teacher's responsibility to remain as detached and fair as possible in evaluating test results. If tests are not evaluated fairly, then they become invalid indicators of what a student has learned. Chapter 13 showed the many influences on the teacher that might affect his judgment, which in turn affects the students. The teacher should guard against this as much as possible. In addition, the teacher should avoid what is called "the halo effect." A student who is neat and well behaved is not necessarily learning more than one who is sloppy and rude. A student who is good in one subject is not necessarily good in another. A student who has worked hard in the past may be lazy now. The teacher who fails to recognize these truths, and thus imagines that the neat polite child is automatically clever and studies hard, is limited by his own belief in the halo effect.

Questions for Thought
Can a test be absolutely reliable without being valid?
If a test is valid will it always be reliable? Why?

DEVELOPING CLASSROOM TESTS

Construction of a valid classroom test requires preparation and planning. The test will be used to measure achievement in some area of a school subject. The teacher must first break this area down into smaller content areas, or subtopics, and decide how important each subtopic is. The more important subtopics should have more questions devoted to them.

If the teacher has been conscientious in developing learning objectives at the outset of the unit, the goals of the test will be clear, because the test will be used as a means of evaluating whether or not these objectives have been achieved. The learning objectives will affect the types of question chosen and how each question is phrased. The teacher should know whether he wants the students to show merely memory of facts or whether he wants to test for an understanding of facts and the ability to apply them. He could also test to see if students can organize facts and ideas or develop an argument. Whatever the goals of the lesson, questions should be designed to measure that goal. Here, too, the more important behaviors should have more of a certain type of question devoted to them.

But to do this, the teacher must understand the kinds of questions that test each kind of behavior.

ESSAY TESTS. Various types of test questions are available for the classroom. Most likely you are familiar with essay tests. In answer to an essay question the student is expected to write some connected prose ranging in length from a few paragraphs to several pages. The essay test can be used to test memory of facts, understanding of them, and the ability to apply them. This kind of test, however, is at its best when used to do what no other test can do—test the ability to organize material or to develop an argument. Here is an example:

Types of Tests

> State your position for or against the tax bill recently proposed in the state legislature. Support your position by developing an argument from the relevant facts.

Essay questions help the student sharpen his reading and writing abilities. A major disadvantage of the essay test, however, is that only a few questions can be answered during the usual testing period, with the result that the test cannot provide a representative sampling of content. Furthermore, the grading of essay tests is often subjective and unreliable. Two different teachers grading the same set of essay papers may not assign the same grades to them, nor may

THE TEST AS A TEACHING AND LEARNING TOOL

Most examinations rely on knowledge, the lowest level of a student's cognitive development. Although this is probably the easiest type of examination to construct, the educational growth of a student is not dependent on knowledge alone but rather on the comprehension and ability of a student to apply, interpret, and analyze. This is especially true in science education. In testing only knowledge, we fail to make the examination an integral part of the total learning experience of the individual. If an examination is based on all cognitive levels, the grade takes on meaning. If we further analyze each question on the examination, we can even diagnose failure and prescribe appropriate remedies, making the test a powerful teaching and learning tool. (Cusimano, 1975, p. 181)

The author of this statement is a teacher of biology at a high school in New York. His name is Vincent Cusimano. And he has for a long time thought on the question: What does a grade on an examination really mean? His answers have led him to formulate an examination which has meaning in terms of all the levels of Bloom's taxonomy. First, he divides the material for an examination into major concept areas. Within each group, he then lists the facts that the student should know to properly understand the concept. Fact questions comprise that part of the examination calling for knowledge. The next part of the exam tests comprehension. Here, each question tests the student's ability to interpret and form concepts from his knowledge. A third part of the examination includes a number of questions that test application of knowledge. "By application," he reminds us, "a student will be able to use these concepts in a new situation that may differ from previous experiences to a greater or lesser extent" (p. 176). He finishes the examination, usually, with a summary question that requires the student to either analyze, synthesize, or evaluate those concepts he is testing.

This type of examination, Cusimano admits, is "extremely time-consuming." And the results must be carefully analyzed. He takes four steps in analyzing them: "(1) tallying each question, (2) converting the tally to percentages for difficulty and discrimination value, (3) analyzing the problem questions, and (4) diagnosis" (p. 177). The results, assuredly, are worth these efforts. Cusimano's final statement is well worth repeating and remembering:

An examination is not a marking tool, separate and distinct from a student's learning experience. With proper application of these construction and analysis techniques, we can truly test ability and understanding. A grade on an examination will become a meaningful measure of both teaching and learning, and, in the end, a means for improving both. (p. 181) the same teacher grading the papers twice assign the same marks both times. Also, as we mentioned before, teachers may be prejudiced against students whose handwriting is illegible, whose paper is untidy, or whose grammar or spelling is faulty. Such a prejudice may be reliable (that is, consistent), but it is not valid — unless the test is designed to measure tidiness, grammar, or spelling. A test that is supposed to measure competence in history should not be measuring competence in grammar or handwriting.

There are techniques, however, for increasing the reliability of essay test grading. Most of these will be considered in a later section; but there is one such technique that should be considered here. The problem of representative sampling of content can be solved by using a series of short-essay questions. In taking this type of test the student writes only one or two sentences in answer to each question. A typical example follows:

> Describe the basic characteristics of a valid test of achievement. List in order their importance from most to least important.

In this kind of test a great deal more content can be sampled than by the essay question method, and the grading will be more reliable. However, testing for the ability to develop an argument or organize a large body of material may not be possible using this method.

OBJECTIVE TESTS. The *multiple-choice question* is known to most American students. If properly written, this kind of question can be used to test not only memory of facts but different mental processes as well, such as reasoning ability, etc. For example, selecting the correct answer to the question that follows would require an application of knowledge rather than just memory of a fact, provided, of course, that the actual example used in the question had not been discussed in course work.

> A baby begins to whimper. The mother rushes to bring its bottle in order to keep the baby from crying. The baby learns from then on that when it wants a bottle, it should whimper. The behavior of the mother is an example of:
>
> A. operant conditioning   C. avoidance conditioning
> B. retroactive inhibition   D. generalization

The great advantages of the multiple-choice test are its flexibility, the wide sampling of content possible on a single test, and the ease and objectivity of scoring. The disadvantage is that multiple-choice items are difficult to write so that the correct responses required of the student are good measures of the goals of the teachers, and that the alternative incorrect choices or distractors are equally valid indicators of inappropriate learning.

There are other objective tests useful for special purposes. The following is an example of a *true-false item*.

Achievement evaluation should be designed to determine if, and to what extent, learning objectives have been met.   T   F

True-false items have some merit—a very large number of items can be answered in one testing period, and the scoring is easy and reliable. However, it is difficult to use true-false tests to measure anything but memory of facts, often minor facts, and it is difficult to write true-false items well. Furthermore, with the multiple-choice question with four choices the student has only a 25 percent chance of guessing the correct answer. With the true-false item, with only two choices, this probability increases to 50 percent.

The *matching item* can also be used to provide variety in tests.

Each of the authors listed on the left wrote one of the books listed on the right. Match the letter of the book with the name of its author.

_____ Jane Austen	A. Wuthering Heights
_____ Emily Bronte	B. David Copperfield
_____ Henry James	C. Pride and Prejudice
_____ Ernest Hemingway	D. Look Homeward Angel
_____ Thomas Wolfe	E. Vanity Fair
	F. Mrs. Dalloway
	G. A Farewell to Arms
	H. The Ambassadors

A *short-answer question* (not the same as a short-essay question) asks the student to fill in a blank after a direct question.

What is the process through which children learn what is socially acceptable? _____

If the blank is part of a sentence, the item is called a *completion item*.

Children learn what is socially acceptable through what is called

_____.

Scoring both short-answer questions and completion questions is easy and reliable if the questions are clear. Both types are quite limited in what they can test for, however; they usually test only for memory of facts.

Not all tests, of course, have to be written. With young children for whom reading might be a problem, it is an excellent idea for the teacher to read the test questions aloud, and have the pupils write down the answers. Oral tests are particularly useful for the teacher with students who are poor readers. Often the reason why students perform poorly on tests is because they can't read the questions!

Oral tests are also useful because answers can be challenged and discussed. Often doctoral exams are oral for this very reason. The oral exam allows considerable flexibility.

Questions for Thought

Many college students prefer certain types of test and suggest that they study in a different way for each type of test. Do you have a preference for a certain type of test?

If so, can you give a reason for this preference?

How does this reason fit in with the overall objectives of your college experience?

When evaluating skills and knowledge, a teacher can use tests, papers, reports, participation in class, homework, and so on. Very often, testing is the most important of these, and it is part of a teacher's job to do the best testing possible.

Evaluating and Improving Classroom Tests

WRITING OBJECTIVE TESTS.   Writing good objective test items (multiple-choice, true-false, matching, short-answer, and completion) is extremely difficult, but can be learned through practice. Thought and care in the construction of questions will be well repaid in the increased validity of the test. Some hints for improving the construction of test items follow,* with multiple-choice items considered first.

1.   State each item in as few words as possible. Here is an example of a wordy item:

Among the many great plays written by William Shakespeare are several famous and beautiful tragedies. An example of one of the tragedies that he wrote is

A. Macbeth   C. A Winter's Tale
B. Dr Faustus   D. Measure for Measure

A student's time would be saved if he had to read only this:

Shakespeare wrote the tragedy

A. Macbeth   C. A Winter's Tale
B. Dr Faustus   D. Measure for Measure

2.   The reading level of the items should not be too difficult for

---

*The hints outlined here apply to both norm-referenced and criterion-referenced tests. However, specific recommendations on constructing the latter are discussed later in this chapter.

any member of the class, unless reading ability is what is being tested. Obviously, no one would write an item for children like the following one, but even many older students would find it difficult to understand.

> An explanation of the observable preference of many persons for wearing light-colored apparel during the summer months is to be sought in the phenomenon of heat transference known as
> A. conduction   C. radiation
> B. convection   D. none of these

A test in science should not turn into a test of reading comprehension. Written more simply, the item looks like this:

> Many people wear light-colored clothing in the summer because light-colored clothing takes up less heat through
> A. conduction   C. radiation
> B. convection   D. none of these

3. As much as possible of the item should be contained in the lead-in to the choices. This lead-in is called the *stem*. Besides helping to make the wording economical and the reading easier, this rule guides the teacher in defining the question to be answered at the outset. The following shows what happens when this is *not* done:

> A nerve has been
> A. defined as a bundle of axons, dendrites, and cell bodies
> B. defined as a bundle of axons
> C. defined as a bundle of dendrites
> D. defined as a bundle of synapses

The item has been improved in this version:

> A nerve has been defined as a bundle of
> A. axons, dendrites, and cell bodies   C. dendrites
> B. axons   D. synapses

4. The wording of an item must be clear. The answer to the next question depends on exact knowledge of what is meant by "origin" and by "printing."

> The origin of printing is to be found in
> A. an adaptation of the wine press
> B. Gutenberg's invention of movable type
> C. the Chinese invention of movable type
> D. the need to reproduce documents and books easily

Actually, any of the choices might be considered the right answer, because the stem does not state the question clearly.

5. All the choices should seem at least possible and should attract some responses. Otherwise, the number of effective choices is reduced, and the probability of getting the right answer by chance is increased.

> A child is putting coins in a machine in order to obtain candy bars. At first he obtains a few bars, but then the machine, having been emptied, keeps returning the coins. After several unsuccessful attempts, the child walks away in disgust. This situation best illustrates
>
> A. projection   C. instrumental conditioning
> B. avoidance conditioning   D. extinction

All the choices here are terms from learning theory except the first, which comes from psychoanalysis. Because choice A is from a different field, it will be eliminated more readily than the others, and should be replaced by another term from learning theory—for example, "negative reinforcement."

6. Be careful to omit clues that unintentionally give the answer away.

> HCl is the formula for an
>
> A. base   C. polymer
> B. free radical D. acid

The word "an" in the stem reveals the answer. The same item would be better written this way, although this might seem to contradict hint 3:

> HCl is the formula for
>
> A. a base   C. a polymer
> B. a free radical D. an acid

7. Avoid using the word "not" or any other negative if you can; negatives often confuse unnecessarily. If you must use "not" in either the stem or the options, underline it so that students will not make a mistake in reading.

> Homeostasis does *not* occur when someone
>
> A. suffers from diabetes
> B. drinks a lot of water after exercise on a hot day
> C. shivers on a cold day
> D. manufactures ribonucleic acid

8. Make sure the items are independent of one another. It is not fair to have the answer to one item depend on the answer to anoth-

er. It would be unfair to use both of the following questions in the same test:

The Would-Be Gentleman was written by
A. Corneille   C. Molière
B. Racine   D. Marivaux

The author of *The Would-Be Gentleman* also wrote
A. *The Cid*   C. *The Miser*
B. *Phaedra*   D. *The Game of Love and Chance*

A student might know that Corneille wrote *The Cid*, that Racine wrote *Phaedra*, that Molière wrote *The Miser*, and that Marivaux wrote *The Game of Love and Chance*, but if he did not also know that Molière wrote *The Would-Be Gentleman*, he might well answer both questions incorrectly.

9. Even well-written multiple-choice items sometimes have more than one correct or true answer; this is why the test directions should tell the student to choose the single *best* answer. Make sure that each question does indeed have a single best answer.

The most impressive theme of *The Remembrance of Things Past* is
A. time   C. love
B. memory   D. social change

The meaning of "most impressive" is sufficiently clear, but what impresses one reader may not impress another; thus the question has no single best answer.

Some of these hints for multiple-choice items apply to true-false items as well. In fact, in writing any sort of test the teacher should try to be brief, to make the reading level easy for all members of the class, and to make the questions unambiguous. There are other points to remember in making up true-false tests:

1. Do not be unclear; each statement must be either true or false.

Sigmund Freud originated our idea of the unconscious mind.   T F

The idea of the unconscious mind was not really original with Freud; on the other hand, his work shaped our ideas on the subject to such an extent that it could be argued that the statement is true.

2. Do not give away the true statements by making them noticeably long. The following is not a good statement for a true-false test:

Although *a cappella* originally had a narrower meaning, drawn from reference to the style of singing in the large chapels of Europe, today the phrase is usually used to refer to any choral music that is unaccompanied.   T F

3.   Put only one idea in each statement.

Michelangelo did not admire Titian's genius, and regretted that Titian
did not paint in Michelangelo's style.   T   F

Of the two ideas expressed here, the first is false and the second is
true; this is a confusing, deceptive item.

A few more observations are in order about other types of short-
answer test. A matching item should not involve a very long list of
choices. If the list is long, the student will spend too much time
reading and checking one list against the other. The choices should
be all of one kind. In the matching example given earlier, the
choices are all authors who wrote in English. Note that the authors
are presented in chronological order so that the item has a basic
framework, and that there are more works listed than authors so
that guessing will not be too easy for the student. Other matching
items will suggest their own way of ordering the choices. It is all
right to have an answer used more than once in a matching item if
this possibility is made clear to the student in the test directions.

In short-answer or completion items, the blanks should all be the
same length, otherwise the length of the blank can be a clue to the
answer. It is especially important to make completion items clear.

The first U.S. president was _____.

could be filled in correctly with "George Washington," "a Virgini-
an," or "a man of British descent."

After a short-answer test has been given and scored, the information obtained from the scores can help the teacher improve future
testing. Each item has to be examined separately to discover its
characteristics. How difficult was the item? (That is, what percentage of students answered it correctly?) How well did the item discriminate between those who had learned and those who hadn't?
(That is, when the students who received a high score on the total
test are compared with those who received a low score on the total
test, did more of the high scorers get the item right?) If the item is
multiple-choice, did all the choices attract responses?

The difficulty of an item can be determined by calculating the
percentage of students who got it right. If 90 percent of the students
got the item right, it was easy—if 15 percent got it right, it was
hard. In constructing a test designed to positively reinforce the students, a teacher might want all the items to be easy, but this would
not be so on a norm-referenced test, which compares students with
one another. If everyone gets all the items right, it is impossible to
compare them. But neither must the items all be very difficult; if no
one gets more than a few items right, again there will be no basis for
comparison. A blend of easy, difficult, and in-between items, with

TESTING: A LEARNING EXPERIENCE

Arthur Adkins (1975), Associate Professor of Secondary Education at the University of Maryland, notes that "in the minds of many, testing and grades are inseparable, but they need not be" (p. 271). Tests, he thinks, rather than grades, offer more systematic feedback and provide a more meaningful source of motivation for students. To put the emphasis where it belongs, he makes this suggestion:

Tests are ordinarily made by teachers (I am not speaking of standardized tests at the moment). What if students made them? Mine do. They write test items, both essay and multiple choice. . . . My students write these items on assigned areas of the course they are taking, . . . on facts or concepts within that area which they consider important. They do this because I think that formulating a test question on an important fact or idea is a learning experience. They also do it because, frankly, I believe that a teacher should do nothing which he or she can get students to do, whether it is to ask a question or to answer it. (p. 271)

Adkins gives his high school students models to use in developing test questions. Then, working in groups of three or four, they mutually decide on item content and phrasing, offering criticism and suggestions for revision. Writing multiple-choice items is fairly easy for them, he has found, since students often know better than the teacher what alternative answers would attract those who may not know the correct or best response. Writing essay questions is somewhat harder; while selection of content and clarity of phrasing is important here, formulation of a scoring guide is essential. "Often," he says, students discover that "what seems like a good question for an essay exam turns out to be unanswerable, or unscorable in any reasonably objective manner" (p. 272). Such questions are then used for discussion or study.

Once the various groups' test items are selected and refined, they are assembled into a test, duplicated, and administered to the class as a whole. Just taking the test supplies a further learning experience— and scoring it, even more so. Multiple-choice tests are easy to score, because the method of scoring is objective. (It is this, rather than content, he reminds us, that is necessarily objective.) He groups students for scoring the essay test much the same as for writing the items and the scoring guides. Often, he asks them to score responses using someone else's guide. Analyzing and evaluating the test, he says, is indispensable: "Why should item analysis be an exercise reserved for teachers or computers or experts in measurement? It is a chore, but it is the one best way to improve tests and test items. It can be done in class, it can be done by students, it can be fun" (p. 273). And most importantly, he concludes, it is a valuable learning experience at any level.

most of them in-between, will produce the spread of scores desired on a norm-referenced test.

If the low scorers on the test tended to get the item right and the high scorers tended to get it wrong, something is wrong, either with the item or with the way the subject was taught. Such an item is said to discriminate in the wrong direction. Items discriminate in the right direction when questions are answered correctly by more high scorers than low scorers. The *degree* of discrimination (in either direction) is measured by a statistic called an index of discrimination. A simple way to prepare the index of discrimination is explained by *Short-Cut Statistics for Teacher-Made Tests* (Evaluation & Advisory Service, 1964). A simple formula for computing this index, also called the validity index, will be found in Appendix 5.

Once the teacher has obtained this kind of statistical information, he can learn still more by discussing with the class those items that are in question. He may discover ways to revise items to make them better—to make them easier or harder, to cause them to discriminate in the right direction, to replace easy or misleading choices with better ones. In this way he can reword and thus rescue ineffective items for a future file of test questions. He should continue to make counts of responses and to calculate indices in the future, since a single class is a small sample of students, and, in any case, the index may change as teaching changes. Sometimes what needs revision is not the item itself but the way the content matter was taught.

WRITING ESSAY TESTS. Essay tests are sometimes called "subjective tests" because grading is often unreliable or even unfair. Marshall (1967) found that minor errors in English accounted for lower grades on an American history test, although the grading supposedly measured only the content of the answers. In a similar study by Marshall and Powers (1969), it was found that neatly written answers were graded higher on the average than those which were only fairly neat. Similarly, papers without errors in spelling and grammar were graded higher on the average than those with such errors. According to a study by Huck and Bounds (1972), neatness made a difference in the grades assigned to essay tests by graders who were themselves neat, but that graders who were themselves untidy were not biased against untidy papers. Follman, Lowe, and Miller (1971) found no difference, however, in the grades assigned to typed themes and those assigned to written themes. They did find, however, that themes graded last received higher grades than those graded first! Such a finding might suggest that graders tend to become more sympathetic as they become fatigued.

Teachers can make essay tests more objective by taking certain precautions, some of them in the grading itself, and some in writing the test questions. In constructing an essay test it is necessary to define clearly the question the student is supposed to answer. Such a question as

> Tell what you know about attempts to raise silkworms as a commercial venture in the United States.

is too vague. The same question is more sharply phrased in this manner:

> Explain why raising silkworms has never been a commercial success in the United States.

Also, do not ask too many essay questions for the testing time allowed.

When it comes to grading, read all the papers through at one sitting. In addition, read all the answers to one question first, then go back and read all the answers to the second question, and so on. Perhaps most important of all, prepare in advance a set of model answers to all the questions so that there is a fixed standard to judge the students' answers by. Ahmann and Glock (1971) recommend an analytical system of scoring in which each model answer is broken down into component parts and a number of points assigned to each part. Irrelevant material is corrected but not scored, regardless of whether it is right or wrong.

Various authorities recommend grading papers without looking at the students' names.

ALTERNATIVE APPROACHES TO CLASSROOM TESTING

Criterion-Referenced Testing and Competency-Based Instruction

Instruction with the aim of having an entire class achieve competence and based on the assumption that everyone has the capacity for learning has been discussed before in this text. The reader will remember that teachers were given suggestions in Chapter 4 on developing their own programs for this purpose and that Chapter 7 dealt with clarifying specific learning objectives for the classroom; the matter was also discussed in relation to teacher accountability in Chapter 13. Criterion-referenced testing is, as has been shown earlier in this chapter, the basis of competency-based instruction — instruction that is geared toward achieving specific learning objectives.

USES OF CRITERION-REFERENCED TESTING AND COMPETENCY-BASED INSTRUCTION. An important problem in criterion-referenced testing is determining the tasks that should be selected for mastery. In other words, how do you choose the learning objectives for each student?

What tasks must be mastered before further learning takes place? for safe performance in a laboratory or when driving a car? for job proficiency? What does a student need to know for everyday life? Are the skills being called for appropriate to the students' developmental level? The objectives selected should not be arbitrary choices, Gronlund (1973) advises.

If possible, Gronlund continues, the teachers in a school should cooperate in deciding what kinds of learning are to be mastered. The teachers should strive toward arranging learning objectives in sequence and identifying the minimal skills needed at each stage before going to the next. In addition to working with each other, teachers should consult authorities in subject matter and curriculum for assistance. Airasian (1971) found that groups of teachers working together on the measurement of competency-based learning could quickly define the order of objectives, construct test items, and develop corrective exercises.

As we mentioned earlier in this chapter, teachers used to expect that one third of a class would be superior in performance, one third would be passable, and one third would fail. But this assumption is changing. We now state more objectively that almost everyone can learn—if the teacher can teach. This is the assumption behind competency-based instruction.

People, of course, do differ in many ways. Many ask, "Isn't it true that not everyone has the aptitudes needed for learning?" Perhaps an aptitude is merely an ability to learn quickly—perhaps everyone can learn if everyone is given enough time.

Criterion-referenced testing can, as we've mentioned, be used to

Criterion-referenced testing helps to avoid the stress on competition that sometimes results in a norm-referenced testing situation in which students are compared with each other.

(Bruce Roberts, Rapho/Photo Researchers)

diagnose individual difficulties so that the teacher may modify instruction for a particular student. This kind of ongoing evaluation is called *formative evaluation*. Norm-referenced testing is less sensitive. It usually does not specify just where a student goes wrong and so is less suited to diagnosis (Popham, 1974). A final evaluation, *summative evaluation*, is done at the end of the term, either to measure a student's success or to measure the success of the program of instruction, in order to decide whether or not it should be repeated, and, if so, how it can be improved. Criterion-referenced teaching lends itself to summative evaluation.

However, not all educators agree that criterion-referenced testing performs these functions. Ebel (1971), for example, believes that, despite the seeming paradox of it, this kind of testing does not really tell us what students can do. Norm-referenced tests are better at the job, he thinks, for "Excellence or deficiency are necessarily relative concepts" (p. 283). The learning objectives required in advance by criterion-referenced testing actually suppress good teaching, he feels, because, although establishing learning objectives beforehand is a very good thing to do, the learning objectives required by criterion-referenced testing are too narrow and inflexible. Although such objectives are sometimes practical, ". . . knowledge and understanding consist of a complex fabric which owes its strength and beauty to an infinity of tiny fibers of relationship. Knowledge does not come in discrete chunks that can be defined and identified separately" (p. 285). Criterion-referenced testing is suited to measuring basic skills, Ebel concludes, but basic skills make up only a small portion of what we teach. (Some of these limitations were discussed in the section on teacher accountability in Chapter 13.)

DESIGN OF LEARNING OBJECTIVES AND CRITERION-REFERENCED TESTS IN COMPETENCY-BASED INSTRUCTION. Glaser (1962) presents a model of teaching in which learning objectives are designed according to the behavior exhibited by the students before instruction begins. Often, however, the classroom teacher will not be able to take entering behavior into account when designing learning objectives. In this case, the learning objectives together with entering behavior of students are used to design appropriate methods of instruction.

Popham's (1973) model is very similar. Learning objectives lead to preassessment (criterion-referenced testing); instruction follows; and then evaluation (more criterion-referenced testing) provides feedback and leads to new decisions about curriculum and methods of instruction.

Gronlund (1973) makes a number of recommendations for constructing criterion-referenced tests. The unit of study to be covered by a test should be brief, so that the test will not be too long. This will lead to frequent testing. Frequent testing may result in more immediate feedback and more frequent diagnosis of problems and assignment of remedial work.

The desired behavior must first be determined, and component tasks that will be used to evaluate whether or not it has been exhibited must be identified. It will usually not be possible to include every task of interest in the test, but the sampling can be representative. It will be easier to make it so if the test covers only a brief unit of study, and if the learning objectives have been clearly defined.

Each task included in the test must coincide with a particular performance specified under the heading of a general learning objective. For the sake of reliability, several examples of each type of task should be included.

Exactly which tasks the students are to perform must be clearly and precisely stated in planning the test. Are the students to spell words of a certain degree of difficulty? Add three-digit numbers with carrying?

The standard of performance that is to be met must also be stated exactly; that is, how much the student must know before you are satisfied that the learning objective has been achieved. Is the student to solve correctly 90 percent of the arithmetic problems? 80 percent? In determining this percentage, the teacher must decide what level of mastery is needed for the next stage of instruction or for safe performance of an activity such as driving. The teacher can then adjust the percentages up or down when experience indicates the necessity.

Discrimination of the items is usually not of any interest on a criterion-referenced test, since the test was not designed to compare the students who take it. Ideally, there would be a very small spread of scores on a criterion-referenced test. If the teacher's goals have been met, students taking the test will have mastered the responses required.

There are many methods of teaching, but some are better suited to a particular teacher than others, just as some are better suited to a particular student than others. Overcoming learning disabilities may mean choosing the right method for the student and the teacher.

Positive attitudes toward the self are fostered in a student when he can learn—through a system in which *everyone* can learn. In such a system the purpose of evaluation is *not* to rank students in order to give them grades, but to let them know what stage of learning they have reached, and how they should continue from there in order to develop to their fullest capacity.

We have only begun to realize these ideals fully. But experimental programs such as those discussed in Chapter 9 demonstrate that these ideals can indeed be met.

Cooperative Planning

Some educators argue that the contributions a student makes to his own education—that is, the ideas he creates for himself from the content of the course or the thinking of the teacher—are most important. The student himself is a source of his own learning.

If this is so, then it is appropriate for students to cooperate in selecting the methods of their own instruction and testing. Jensen (1973) describes how undergraduates at the University of Nebraska have successfully cooperated in selecting the method of instruction in a large class in introductory psychology. No lectures are given in the course; instead, mimeographed material is handed out regularly. Films are presented regularly; each film is shown many times during one week, and students are free to choose when to attend it. Either the instructor or a graduate assistant is always in attendance in a discussion room, and students can ask questions or discuss the course at any time. Students also choose when they will take tests. A computer produces from a pool of test items a few thousand equivalents of each weekly test; if a student does badly on a test he can take it again and again until he does well, and only his highest score is counted. (This system of testing depends on the existence of a very large number of very well written test items.) Each week's work must be completed within the week, but the student has the freedom to choose his study and testing time within this limitation. The end-of-term grade depends on how well a student does above what would be pure chance; 50 percent above the score expected by pure chance leads to a D, 90 percent above pure chance to an A. The commonest grade is now an A, failure has been reduced to less than 10 percent, and enrollment has doubled.

Under certain circumstances, student cooperation can extend even to having students grade their own papers. Ackerman (1971) found that letting students in psychology classes grade their own tests (after having listened to a talk on the evils of cheating) produced no increase in the amount of cheating. The primary advantage of honor grading to the students is the feedback of a greater sense of integrity. Perhaps, under appropriate teaching-learning conditions, in which stress on grades is eliminated, this added sense of integrity will lead to the elimination of cheating.

Self-Paced Evaluation

Keller (1968) designed a course in general psychology in which students move at their own pace, not necessarily finishing a term's work in a single term, perhaps finishing it in less than a term. Lectures and demonstrations are provided to a student only when he has demonstrated that he is ready for them by passing a test—there are 30 of these tests, in addition to a final examination.

A mimeographed list of study questions is given to each student to be used in preparing for a readiness test. Any test in the series of 30 can be taken at any of several times during any week. The student himself chooses both the week and hour he will take a particular test. The test is given and scored by a proctor who has already finished the course. The proctor is assigned to several students for the term and helps each one as necessary. The proctor usually scores and returns the test paper immediately, and discusses the wrong answers, and sometimes a few of the right ones, with the student. This inevitably leads to the proctor becoming a kind of tutor who explains the subject matter and gives advice about further study. Failure to pass a readiness test at any point does not count against a student. A student may be tested as many as 40 to 50 times during one semester; he always gets an opportunity to defend any answer that has been marked wrong, and an opportunity to learn how to make a correct response. One of the benefits of the program has been a more favorable attitude among the students toward tests because of the benefits they receive from taking them.

The Keller system of instruction can be facilitated by the use of a computer (Young, 1974). In an applied mathematics course taught in a similar system at Oakland University in Rochester, Michigan, a computer was used to produce the tests given after each unit of work. In addition to taking the tests, students sometimes used the computer terminals to generate extra problems on which they worked individually or in groups. Young remarks that the computer could also have been used when diagnostic pre-tests were given at the beginning of the course.

Student peers can be used as proctors in this method of instruction. Tosti (1973) used students who were only one unit ahead of the others as tutors in a program of instruction in arithmetic. Peer proctors, also in use in some other adaptations of Keller's method, are selected from the students who received superior grades from the instructor on the first-unit tests. Tosti reports one professor rotates the proctorships so that most of the class get a chance to act as a proctor before the term is ended. Some instructors use students in advanced courses to supervise the peer proctors. As a result of his own experiences and those of others, Tosti recommends the use of peer proctors. He feels that peers take a more enthusiastic interest in their own learning when they have the opportunity to proctor. This enthusiasm extends to their peers as students, too.

Self-paced evaluation has been used with elementary school students as well as college level students (Klausmeier, Sorenson, and Ghatala, 1971).

GRADING: A MEANS OF RECORDING EVALUATION

As we mentioned at the outset of this chapter, there seems to be a great deal of disagreement about the value of testing and other methods of evaluation. Should they be kept? or eliminated? If kept, should they stay as they are or be changed? If they should be changed, how should this be done? We demonstrated, however, that the controversy is not really concerned with the worth of evaluation in itself, for evaluation is a basic part of the teaching-learning process. But these same questions are being asked about grades, the recording of student performance after it has been evaluated. This recording can be done either in terms of a student's achievement of learning objectives (criterion-referenced grading) or in terms of a student's achievement as compared with that of other students (norm-referenced grading).

Most of the controversy has centered around norm-referenced grading. Many educators and psychologists point out that determining a student's grade by comparing him with other students creates an unhealthy and competitive atmosphere. Student motivation should come from learning itself, these critics argue, not from the need to prove to oneself and to others that one is better than one's classmates. The actual recording of grades does perform certain useful functions, however.

Purposes of Grading   Gall and Ward (1974) have commented on the major roles that grades play in American education. The first, and many feel the most important, function of grades is that of formal feedback to the student about his achievement. Without this feedback, the student might find it difficult to decide on his future course of study and, ultimately, his career. Furthermore, some types of grades, such as letter grades, will help the student to see his own achievement in comparison with others. This will help him to compete in the "real" world.

As we mentioned in Chapter 13, teachers are increasingly being held accountable for the level of achievement of their students. This has often led them to develop more clearly defined learning objectives. The record of a student's performance on a criterion-referenced test will show exactly what each student has achieved.

Thus, when used properly, grades do perform valuable functions. What educators need to strive for is a more objective system of grading, one in which competition is not so severe that it results in lowering the ability of students to achieve.

Types of Grading   There are many types of grading frameworks that can be used by teachers. Ahmann and Glock (1971) and Terwilliger (1971) distinguish between grading a student in terms of his *development*, taking into account his ability, background, experience, and so on—and grading a student in absolute terms according to his *achievement*, what he knows now, regardless of his ability and background.

Generally, the teacher must give the student a single grade. This

Many feel that the most important function of grades is that of formal feedback to the student about his achievement.

(Margot S. Granitsas, Photo Researchers)

forces the teacher to choose between these frameworks. One way of changing this is for schools to adopt multiple marking systems, which would take both frameworks into account (Terwilliger, 1971). Thus, the student would receive one grade based on his achievement, and another based on his growth.

Regardless of the framework chosen, grades are frequently reported either by letters or by numbers representing letter equivalents (1 = A, 2 = B, 3 = C, 4 = D, 5 = F). Many educators feel that even though they cannot communicate everything of interest through the use of letter or number grades, such grades are simple, concise, and convenient (Ebel, 1964). Feldmesser (1972) also favors the use of letter grades; they help a college student decide whether he should stay in college and what he should study, and they provide extrinsic motivation for those who may not realize the importance of what they are studying at the time. Grades can, he admits, be misused, and he urges graduate schools to train teachers how to grade objectively.

Many educators feel, however, that the kind of motivation that results from traditional five-point or letter grading is often undesirable. Extreme competition, sometimes leading to cheating, is too often the result.

An alternative to the traditional five-point grading system is that of pass-fail or pass-no credit. This system was originally developed to relieve students of the pressure to compete and to work for a grade as an end in itself. Instead, it was thought, the student would be motivated only by the desire to learn. This system results in added pressure for the teacher, however. The teacher must very clearly define exactly what criteria must be met if the grading is to be fair and objective.

Furthermore, students who have not received traditional grades in college are often at a disadvantage when trying for admission to graduate or professional schools (Stevens, 1973). In such cases, added weight must be given to scores on standardized tests, but these tests are not always accurate measures of student potential and achievement.

A three-point grading system using honors, pass, and fail is a compromise between these two systems. Such a three-point system was compared with the traditional five-point system by undergraduates, graduate students, and faculty members in a study by Goldstein and Tilker (1971). The three-point system was favored because is supposedly encouarged what the authors called creativity, learning, and fairness. On the other hand, the five-point system was seen as giving better feedback and helping students with admission to graduate school. Other universities have tried out variations of all of these. Goldstein and Tilker suggest a dual system in which students could choose the kind of grading system that best suits their needs.

Many other types of grading systems are used in elementary and high schools. Elementary school teachers are frequently required to give grades for other than academic achievement. These teachers often mark a list of character traits and attitudes. This kind of marking often becomes subjective and superficial, however (Ahmann and Glock, 1971). To make such grading meaningful, the teacher must be careful to avoid the "halo effect."

Teachers may also write letters to parents as reports. If the teacher has adequate records of data on which to base such letters, the comments can be helpful. But like a checklist of traits of character and attitudes, these letters may become superficial. Writing truly informative letters takes a great deal of time and thought.

Conferences between parents and teachers are another means of reporting evaluations. Although they too take up considerable time, they can be a good means of communication. Of course, this can only be true if the teacher prepares detailed information in advance of the conference. In addition, many parents are reluctant to attend such conferences. Furthermore, many high school students are opposed to them, because they feel that they, not their parents, should be receiving the feedback from their teachers. And, of course, students do not receive the direct feedback that results from other grading systems (Richardson, 1955).

Problems of Grading: What the Teacher Can Do

Combining data from different kinds of work—tests, homework assignments, reports, laboratory exercises, and so on—can be a problem, because the units of measurement from the different sources (sometimes even from different tests) may not be truly comparable. To overcome this lack of comparability, Ahmann and Glock (1971) suggest a system of weighting, which must be deter-

Conferences between parents and teachers are an important means of reporting evaluations.
(Myron Wood, Photo Researchers)

mined by the teacher in relation to learning objectives. They also suggest using standardized achievement test scores to supplement final grades. But again, these tests may not have been designed with the same objectives that the teacher had in mind.

Green (1963) has outlined problems of grading: Grades may not reflect actual achievement; clear objective criteria for assigning grades are often lacking; the halo effect too often influences grades; teachers are occasionally biased against individuals; there tends to be a sex bias in assigning grades; and grades may be based on insufficient data. To counteract these difficulties, Green suggested collecting sufficient data to increase the teacher's objectivity through frequent testing and different kinds of written assignment.

Holt (1970) is also aware of the shortcomings of grading and has suggested ways to make grading less harmful to elementary school children:

1. Don't fail a child. Holt believes that all children have the ability to learn. Therefore, if a child doesn't achieve, the failure is the teacher's.

2. Base your grades on a cross-section of the child's best work. Holt found that "If I assigned a paper, and a student did badly on it, this only showed that this was the wrong paper for him, where he could not show what ability he had. The remedy was to try to give a wide enough variety of choices and opportunities for writing, reading, and talking so that everyone would have a fairly good chance of showing his best talents."

3. Grade privately—let no one know what mark someone else has

received. This will, of course, help to control competition and the negative effects that result from it.

4. Don't fail a child against his will. This will add to the child's sense of insecurity and lower his level of aspiration. This, in turn, will make learning even more difficult the following year.

5. Don't assume that someone in a class for slow students can't do superior work. This attitude can result in a self-fulfilling prophecy.

Management of School Grades and Records

There has been much controversy over what constitutes appropriate management (that is, collection and maintenance) of student grades and records. Some interesting proposals have been made in the past decade in this regard. Wellington and Wellington (1966) argued that teachers should never have direct access to student records because records prejudice teachers, and students, as we mentioned in Chapter 6, tend to live up to or down to these expectations. In contrast, however, Lawton (1966) maintained that the extra information from previous records can be of considerable help to a teacher in guiding children; she suggested, however, that teachers be given the training to prepare and to use records properly.

The Russell Sage Foundation (1970) published a set of proposed principles for management of school records, which urged that no information be collected about students without the prior informed consent of students and their parents. The Foundation report argued for careful preservation of confidentiality.

A federal law passed in 1974 allows access to school records by all students over the age of 18 and to the parents of students under the age of 18. This law (commonly known as the Buckley amendment) provides practical recourse for the first time to the student whose teachers, counselors, or other school administrators have evaluated his behavior in less than an objective manner. Today it is necessary for school teachers to be prepared to "back up" evaluations with fact—another aspect of teacher accountability.

Grading and Teacher Accountability

As we mentioned earlier in this chapter and in Chapter 13, the teacher is responsible to the community for providing adequate information about student progress and achievement.

But this does not mean that teachers, in order to impress parents, the community, and students themselves, should give good grades regardless of achievement. A teacher who gives good grades does not necessarily teach more or better than one who gives poor grades. Rever and Kojaku found that the average high school grades of college-bound students are on the rise, even though their scores on tests given by American College Testing slipped slightly in English, mathematics, social studies, and natural sciences. They also found that grades were tending to rise for college freshman as well.

Perhaps teachers are increasingly feeling pressure from students for these grades because of the importance that is placed on grades by the students, their parents, future employers, and graduate and professional schools. Coats, Swierenga, and Wickert (1972) found that student perceptions of teacher effectiveness seem to depend mostly on teacher popularity regardless of the quality of their teaching. According to another study (Bryson, 1974), however, college students also tend to like teachers who help them learn.

Just as a teacher should do the best job he can of teaching, he has a responsibility to evaluate and grade to the best of his ability. Some say that education goes on better without formal grading, but Ebel (1964) observes that this is like saying that business can be carried on better if the owner does not keep accounts. The informal procedures for assessment of progress and reporting on it that are sometimes recommended, he continues, differ from formal procedures only in being less systematic—better information cannot be expected from careless and casual procedures than from systematic ones.

It is true that a school that offers nothing but failure to many of its students is doing a bad job. But it is crucial for teachers to realize that the problem is not with the report cards but with the school program itself.

SUMMARY

Classroom evaluation and testing can be an indispensable and integral part of teaching and learning. However, it is quite clear that unless it is adequately understood and used properly it can work to the detriment of the learning process.

A test score may reveal whether or not a student has mastered a unit of instruction (criterion-referenced testing), or it may compare his score with the scores of other members of the group (norm-referenced testing). Although norm-referenced testing tends to create competition, it does provide an incentive to learn. Testing for mastery (criterion-referenced testing), when combined with certain programs of instruction, gives each student a chance to progress at his own pace and to his own ultimate level of achievement. Criterion-referenced testing is especially well adapted to guiding a course of study in which continual information is needed about how a student should next proceed.

A test is reliable if it gives the same scores on repeated testing. It is valid if it measures what it is supposed to measure.

A valid classroom test of achievement is a representative sample of the content of the unit of instruction. It also gives appropriate weight to the different kinds of cognitive behavior expected from students as a result of learning.

Types of written test questions available include essay, short-essay, multiple-choice, true-false, matching, short-answer, and completion.

An important element of criterion-referenced testing is determining the learning objectives.

In competency-based programs of individualized instruction, students can cooperate in planning the progress of study, and pace their own tests.

There are many ways in which to formally record our evaluations, that is, to grade. Each way has its own advantages and problems. Grades will usually reflect either norm-referenced or criterion-referenced forms of measurement. In either case, they provide information about how well students are doing, and assist in decision-making on the part of students, teachers, administrators, and employers.

A teacher has a responsibility to himself, to the community, and to his students to evaluate and record achievement to the best of his ability.

SUGGESTED FOR FURTHER READING

Ahmann, J. S., and Glock, M. D. *Evaluating pupil growth* (4th ed.). Boston: Allyn and Bacon, 1971.
This book is probably the classic source book for all research on classroom evaluation of students. Many of the topics covered in this chapter are more fully discussed in this book. It should help teachers to have a better understanding of the issues involved in testing.

Educational Testing Service. *Evaluation and advisory service series.* Princeton: Educational Testing Service, 1964.
A series of excellent pamphlets. The topics covered include a list of references in educational measurement, selecting an achievement test, principles and procedures, making the classroom test, and short-cut statistics for teacher-made tests. All of these offer easy-to-follow guides. These pamphlets are available from the Educational Testing Service.

Gronlund, N. E. (Ed.) *Readings in measurement and evaluation.* New York: Macmillan, 1968.
Contains articles by authorities in testing on the principles of constructing, selecting, and using tests. The articles are easy to understand for readers without strong backgrounds in statistics.

Wood, D. A. *Test construction.* Columbus, Ohio: Charles E. Merrill, 1960.

Green, J. A. *Teacher-made tests.* New York: Harper & Row, 1963.
Both of these books give excellent guidelines for teachers. Exercises are given on constructing many types of objective and essay tests. These books would be very useful to read before teachers begin to evaluate students.

STANDARDIZED TESTS OF ABILITY AND ACHIEVEMENT

CHAPTER 15

After completing this chapter, the reader should be able to:

1 Identify and describe the basic types of standardized test commonly used in schools; describe the method by which such tests are developed as well as the implications of this procedure for teachers and for students.

2 Identify and interpret correctly the different types of scores produced in the various standardized tests.

3 Define intelligence and relate this definition to the tests designed to measure it.

4 Describe both advantages and disadvantages of using intelligence tests in the schools.

5 Identify the reasons that standardized achievement tests are used in our society, and discuss the relationship between their use in the schools and curriculum development, student achievement, and teacher accountability.

WHAT IS A STANDARDIZED TEST?

In Chapter 14 we discussed the tools of classroom evaluation that teachers can develop themselves. But these tests are sometimes limited, in that classroom teachers are not professional test writers, and they usually do not have the time or facilities available to develop the objectivity in test items that professional test writers are capable of developing. Furthermore, the results of teacher-made tests cannot be used to compare children across the nation or even across a city. Standardized tests were developed for these purposes.

A *standardized test* is one in which the procedures for administering a test and scoring it have been made uniform, or standard. This uniformity makes it possible to compare the scores of students from different parts of the country. A standardized test is written by a test publisher, who produces the test for a national market and provides with it a manual of instructions on administration and scoring. In addition, before releasing the test, the publisher administers it to a sample of the kind of students for whom it is intended; this is done in order to obtain norms—or standards—by which scores on the test may be interpreted.

Types of Standardized Tests

ABILITY TESTS.   Another important and common type of standardized test is the test of ability; that is, a test of potential maximum performance. "We use these when we wish to know how well the person is capable of performing at his best. . . ." (Cronbach, 1970, p. 35). Abilities can be divided into general and specific skills. Tests of general ability are sometimes referred to as *mental tests* or *intelligence tests*. Measures of specialized abilities such as mechanical comprehension, sense of pitch, and finger dexterity also exist.

What are often referred to as *aptitude tests* are really only a special kind of ability test. Aptitude tests are "intended to predict success in a specific occupation or training course" (Cronbach, 1970, p. 38). Examples are tests of engineering aptitude, musical aptitude, aptitude for algebra, and so on. A single aptitude test may include separate sections that measure general mental ability and special abilities. Thus, an engineering aptitude test may have subtests of general mental ability, mechanical reasoning, and spatial reasoning (these last two are subtests of special abilities).

There is an important distinction between ability and achievement tests. "A test is referred to as an achievement test when it is used primarily to examine the person's success in past study, and as an ability test when it is used to forecast his success in some future course or assignment" (Cronbach, 1970, p. 38). In other words, an achievement test looks backward, and an aptitude test looks forward. This does not contradict what we said earlier about the predictive powers of achievement tests, however. The difference is that achievement tests predict future achievement on the basis of present knowledge, that is, already *acquired* skills. What we have referred to as ability and aptitude tests attempt to measure what people think of as *potential*, regardless of present level of scholastic achievement. The difficulties in designing valid measurements of ability, ones that do not actually test environmental factors and therefore acquired ability, will be discussed later in the chapter.

ACHIEVEMENT TESTS.   Many standardized tests are tests of achievement; that is, tests of what has been learned in a school subject. Ahmann and Glock (1971) believe that a teacher can use a standardized achievement test to check that he has been emphasizing the important skills, or, at least, the skills selected by the test designers as important. If the students do poorly on a standardized test, the teacher might ask himself if this means that important knowledge and skills covered by the test have been omitted from the course work. Ahmann and Glock also recommend the use of standardized achievement tests to determine student progress. Progress within a given term can be determined when there are available equivalent forms of the same test, one of which can be given at the beginning of the term (pre-test) and the other at the end (post-test). Interpretations of differences in individual scores must be tentative because of the many extraneous factors, such as mood and health, that can affect them. But if the group does better as a whole, the teacher can assume that progress has been made in the skills measured by the test. Standardized achievement tests can also be used to diagnose individual difficulties in achievement. They can also help to predict whether or not a student will do well in a particular course and then to group students accordingly.

INDIVIDUAL AND GROUP TESTS.   A standardized test may be designed to be administered to only one individual at a time, or it may be designed for groups of any size. When an individual test is given, a trained examiner asks the test taker questions, one by one, or else directs him—by words or gestures—to perform certain tasks; the test taker usually does not have to read the questions, and sometimes he does not need to use language at all. Group tests are usually paper-and-pencil tests, often requiring the test taker to read the questions himself. The advantages of group tests are economy and convenience. The whole class can be tested at once, for instance, and need not be interrupted to take out one child for testing. Furthermore, a trained examiner is usually not needed. Usually a classroom teacher can read the test manual for instructions on giving and scoring a group test. With an individual test, however, a skillful examiner is better able to put the person being tested at ease and therefore make him more likely to do his best. But the primary benefit of individual tests is that they do not have to rely as extensively on language abilities. This is crucial for measuring the abilities of American students who have trouble speaking English at all or who do not speak standard English.

VERBAL AND NONVERBAL TESTS.   A group test that relies heavily on the use of words is an example of a *verbal test*. A *nonverbal test* does not rely as much on words in the questions, but may still use words in giving the test directions. Tests that make use of apparatus— equipment, machinery, materials, implements, and other instruments—also fall into this category. The latter may be called a *non-language* or *performance test*. Such tests are usually individual tests. Nonverbal tests can be used for measuring the general mental ability of anyone who may have a language handicap.

SPEED AND POWER TESTS.   A speed test is made up of a very large number of questions of a uniform level of difficulty. A speed test score depends on the total number of questions the test taker answers correctly in a restricted time period. (There are too many questions for anyone to be able to answer all of them.)

In contrast, a power test is made up of questions of varying degrees of difficulty. Ideally there is no time limit, and scores on the test depend on the ability of the test taker to answer correctly. Giving a test taker unlimited time to answer does not necessarily increase his score on this type of test (Ahmann and Glock, 1971). Therefore, a time limit is often set up, designed to allow a certain percentage of the test takers (usually 90 percent is the minimum) to attempt to answer all questions.

CRITERION-REFERENCED AND NORM-REFERENCED TESTS.   The reader will remember from Chapter 14 that a student's score on a test may be compared with the scores of other people taking the same test. In this case the test is called norm-referenced. Or his score may be based on his achievement of specified learning objectives. Then the test is called criterion-referenced. Although tests are usually designed for either one purpose or the other, sometimes scores from a test can be used either way. By their very nature and purpose, most standardized tests are norm-referenced.

Questions for Thought

How many of the types of tests we have discussed have you taken as a student?

What do you think being a "test-wise" culture has done to our thinking about education?

As with teacher-made tests, the general content to be covered and the students for whom the test is intended must be decided on before constructing a standardized test. For example, the aim may be to produce an achievement test in American history intended for students from the fifth through the eighth grades. A detailed list of the content specifying the percentage of questions to be devoted to subtopics and to different kinds of desired behavior on the part of the test takers must be prepared. In order to construct a test for a wide market, the test publisher must analyze the content of many programs, textbooks, courses of study, and sets of examinations. Some of the writers who produce the items will be specialists in American history; if necessary, the publisher will train them in the techniques of item writing. Other writers will be testing specialists. A different group of both kinds of specialist will edit the items, looking for content errors and technical imperfections in measurement. A much larger pool of items is put together than will be needed in the test; they are tried out on a group of students with similar backgrounds to those for whom the test is intended. This pretesting will reveal whether or not the items discriminate in the right direction (that is, whether or not difficult items tend to be answered correctly by students with high overall scores and incorrectly by students with low overall scores), whether all the choices in a multiple-choice item are working, and how difficult each item is (the properties of a test item were discussed in Chapter 14). The information obtained is then used to choose the items that will be used in the final test. When most of the items chosen are answered correctly by about half the students, a spread of scores results, with total scores all along the line from very low to very high. Ideally, for a norm-referenced test, these scores would fall in the shape of a normal curve, as described in Chapter 14 and Appendix 2.

When the items selected have been assembled as a final test, the test is administered to a second group of students representative of those students for whom the test is intended. This second group is called the *standardization sample*. The process of administering the test to this sample is known as *standardizing the test*. The test is standardized so that norms can be obtained. Norms are information about typical scores—typical, that is, for the kind of students who were sampled.

Standardized tests use a variety of norms, depending on the purpose of the test. One type of norm, percentile rank, tells the percent of scores in the standardization sample falling below a given raw score (number of correct answers on the test). Thus, a student who receives a percentile rank of 80 knows that 80 percent of students in the standardization sample received scores lower than he did. Age or grade norms tell the age or grade level for which a given raw

How Standardized Tests Are Developed

score is typical. (Review Appendix 1 for definitions of typical and average.) Thus, a student receiving a raw score on a standardized achievement test that matches an age norm of 10 is performing as an average 10-year-old. A student whose raw score matches a grade norm of fifth grade, 0 months, is performing at a level comparable to the average fifth grader at the beginning of the school year.

A common score used on standardized tests is the standard score, or z score. A *z score* tells how far from the average a given raw score is. A student whose raw score is above average of the standardization group will receive a positive z score; one whose raw score falls below the average will receive a negative z score.

The most common norms used in interpreting standardized test scores are explained in detail in Appendix 4. It would be useful for the reader to study the descriptions if he plans to make use of standardized testing at any time in his career. Standardized tests typically list norms in the teachers' manual accompanying the test, but the manual does not include definitions of these norms, since it is assumed that they are understood.

Usually when scores on standardized tests are reported to students or to others, corresponding norms rather than raw scores are given. Suppose that a student in the tenth grade got 65 correct answers out of 100 on an achievement test in American literature, and that this is a better score than 90 percent of the tenth-grade students received. To tell the student that his raw score was 65 would be meaningless. Instead we would normally report the percentile rank of 90.

In the manual accompanying the standardized test, the test publisher should describe for each table of norms provided in the test manual the standardization sample of students who were tested in order to arrive at the norms. It is usually not possible, for instance, when testing items intended for the upper years of grade school, to sample all school children in the fifth, sixth, seventh, and eighth grades in the country. In other words, it is usually impossible for a test publisher to arrive at truly universal norms for children. The publisher should, then, define his sample so that the teacher and administrator can see whether it is a suitable one against which to compare their own group of students. It might be possible for the publisher to test fifth-, sixth-, seventh-, and eighth-grade children in the middle-class neighborhoods of several large and scattered cities. Sometimes the publisher will provide several tables of norms for different groups—with one sample, for instance, drawn from middle-class eastern urban schools, one from rural western schools, and so on. Each sample should be clearly described in the manual, and the teacher or administrator must keep in mind while reading the manual that such variables as region, density of population, and socioeconomic status affect the performance that can be expected on a test.

Critics of standardized achievement tests often point to the bias of such tests in favor of white middle-class Americans. Such critics feel that minority group students are underrepresented in the test-development process and, as a result, often have low scores when these tests are used. Defenders of the tests, on the other hand, argue that white middle-class standards, which represent those of the majority, are necessary for comparison of schools and students. The tests, they say, serve as a measure of a minority student's ability to compete with the majority and, perhaps, to join the mainstream. Now the United States government has stepped into the picture, as Theodore Schuchat (1975) reports:

"WITH EDUCATION IN WASHINGTON: RESTANDARDIZATION"

Congress directed the Office of Education to develop an achievement test that would satisfy both viewpoints and could be used to evaluate newly desegregated schools. The OE selected certain reading and mathematics achievement tests for grades 3–5 and then improved their sensitivity, reliability, and validity for students in schools with a minority enrollment of 50 percent or more.

This process of restandardization produced a test battery referenced to two sets of norms. The score of a student or a school can be compared to the norms for students and schools in general and also to norms for minority students and schools with heavy enrollments of minority group students.

Some 9,000 minority group children were tested during the process. To no one's surprise, about 80 percent of elementary school students in general achieved at a higher level than those in the restandardization sample. Nevertheless, now there is a test battery that can be used to evaluate the effect, if any, of the not inconsiderable amount of funds the federal government is providing for improvement of their schooling. (p. 63)

Is this a compromise? A solution? What might the ramifications of "two sets of norms" be? And perhaps, above all, should the federal government assume any role in respect to the complex issues facing American educators today?

Questions for Thought

How often do you think teachers study the manual for the standardized tests they administer in order to see exactly what each score means?

How do you think this affects their ability to interpret the quality of their students' work?

THE RELIABILITY AND VALIDITY OF STANDARDIZED TESTS.   As you will remember from Chapter 14, the reliability of any test is the extent to which it measures consistently. The reliability of a standardized test is estimated by means of a statistic called a *correlation coefficient*. A correlation is a mathematical measure of the degree of relationship, in this case between the score obtained by the same person on two different administrations of the same test. To the extent that the two scores are related, we say that the test is reliable. If the scores are identical, the correlation coefficient is 1, which means that the test is absolutely reliable. (See Appendix 3 for an explanation of the meaning of correlation coefficients.) There are various methods for obtaining a correlation coefficient for a standardized test. All of them naturally involve two lists of scores. The list of scores from one administration of a test can be correlated with a second list of scores from a second administration of the same test to the same students, but this is not usually practical for an educational test. A better way to estimate the reliability of a test is to give two equivalent forms of the same test to the same students, and use the two lists of scores to obtain a correlation coefficient. It is best to allow a short time interval, perhaps a few weeks, between the two testings.

A test may measure reliably, but that does not necessarily mean it is valid. As you will recall from Chapter 14, a valid test is one that measures what it is supposed to measure. If a standardized test is meant for poor urban students, but the standardization sample was drawn from middle-class suburban students, then we would say that the test is invalid, even if the student gets the same score over and over. Using another example, suppose a test is meant to measure ability to add using word problems. The word problems, however, use everyday situations from white middle-class America. The socially disadvantaged student may not be familiar with such situations and therefore may be unable to answer the questions. But this does not mean that he doesn't know how to add. It means only that he is not familiar with white middle-class America.

Content validity, an adequate sampling of the knowledge to be tested, was discussed in Chapter 14 in relation to classroom achievement tests. The same rules for constructing content-valid classroom tests apply to standardized achievement tests. The validity of standardized tests of ability, particularly group tests of ability, is measured in a different way. This is called *predictive validity* (also called *statistical validity* or *empirical validity*). This can best be explained by giving an example: It is common for students to take tests of general mental ability (or scholastic aptitude) late in high school for additional information in their college applications. The test score for each student is used to predict his college gradepoint average. If a student gets a high score on the test, how likely is it that he will have a high college gradepoint average? A correlation coefficient relating test scores and gradepoint averages gives us the answer: The higher the correlation coefficient between student scores on a previous standardized aptitude test and college grades, the more valid that test is to predict future college students' grades.

In some cases, the validity of an ability test is determined by cor-

National standardized tests have become a fact of life for hundreds of thousands of American students—as necessary for movement through the pathways of our schools as the motor car is through urban and rural traffic patterns. Few students realize that these tests are the product of the "General Motors" of its field—the Educational Testing Service. The increased use of these tests has, like the automobile, created problems. It has also raised serious questions of abuse and misuse of unregulated power, which have become the focus of investigations of ETS itself. ETS holds a near-monopoly on "the development of tests which classify candidates for pre-secondary school, secondary school, college, graduate school, business school, and law school" (Brill, 1974, p. 67). For many students, ETS exams serve as vehicles of forward movement; others, however, are carried to a dead end, because low scores deny them access to further education at schools of their choice. For them, the gates are closed. Critics of ETS, in increasing numbers, are today charging that "the way ETS 'aptitude' and 'achievement' tests are evaluated and interpreted is a classic model of unaccountable power" (p. 79).

ETS has a contract "in perpetuity" to produce, consolidate, and administer the SAT, or College Boards, which constitute 42 percent of the annual revenues of ETS and 24 million dollars in income. In fact, says another corporate official, ETS has "outgrown its very name, because 'Educational Testing Service' no longer adequately suggests its range of activites. In recent years, ETS has, for example, designed tests to measure the vocation-related skills of stockbrokers, realtors, automobile mechanics, housing managers, and golf shop pros. ETS has also broadened its horizons at the other end of the age scale and now has tests for pre-schoolers as well" (Rodriquez, 1974, p. 7).

Do we need all these tests? Or is ETS creating a need where none exists in order to justify its existence? These are the kinds of questions that are being asked. Ralph Nader says, "ETS has us all locked into a test that doesn't look for creativity, stamina, motivation, or ethics— which are the four qualities on which man's greatest achievements are based" (Brill, 1974, p. 72). The basic issue, say critics of ETS, is one of regulation of power, not the necessity for some kind of testing procedures or the responsibility with which ETS carries on its functions. One author has put the issue this way:

> . . . regulation would at least fulfill what has to be the most urgent need for change at ETS, that of full disclosure of all aspects of the organization—from finances to test quality to test abuse. With these facts and issues out in the open, we will all be able to see what gatekeeping is like in America—what the profits are and where they go, what the tests mean and what they don't mean, who scores high and who doesn't, and how the tests are used and abused by our educational institutions. Then, we may be able to reach some kind of clear consensus on what gatekeeping *should* be like. For now, all that is clear is that we've got to get some control over the gatekeepers. Testing is just too important to be taken completely on trust. (Brill, 1974, p. 83)

ETS: NATIONAL GATEKEEPER #1

relating scores on that test with some other currently accepted criterion of ability. For example, the validity of most group tests of intelligence is determined by correlating scores on those tests with scores on the most reliable and widely accepted individual test of intelligence, the Stanford-Binet Scale. In this case, the correlation coefficient is a quantitative statement of what is known as the *construct validity* of the test.

Question for Thought

If the validity of a group test of intelligence is determined by correlating scores on this test with those of the Stanford-Binet Scale, how do you think we determine the validity of the accepted criterion, the Stanford-Binet Scale?

Advantages and Disadvantages of Standardized Tests

The use of standardized ability and achievement tests in selecting students for college and graduate and professional schools is well known. A standardized ability test can be used to predict a child's or a class's future achievement. Other uses of standardized ability and achievement tests within the schools will be discussed later in this chapter.

There are two main disadvantages of standardized tests. First, such tests are inflexible and cannot be adapted to special local needs. If local objectives are not covered by a standardized achievement test, the test should not be used (Thorndike and Hagen, 1961), another reason for the teacher to carefully study the manual accompanying the test. Second, even if the objectives of the standardized test are the same as local objectives, the table of norms may not be satisfactory. No matter how satisfactory the table of norms is, for some purposes local norms are needed. For instance, Cronbach (1970) observes that a first grade child who scores at the twentieth percentile when his raw score on a standardized test is compared with national first-grade urban norms may be only at the second percentile in the first grade of a very select school. Of course, the exact opposite may be true for children in socially disadvantaged neighborhoods. A socially disadvantaged student taking the math test described earlier may score at the 90th percentile in his neighborhood, but only at the 50th percentile according to the table of norms. Collecting local norms, therefore, is essential in determining the validity of a test. Furthermore, they are useful in comparing children of similar backgrounds.

Question for Thought

Each school district determines what is to be learned by students living within its boundaries. The detailed aims of education often differ among the schools of a district and even among the classes of one school. How then is a school board to choose appropriate standardized tests?

STANDARDIZED TESTS OF ABILITY: THE IQ TEST

What Is the IQ?

Standardized tests of intelligence have been used for years, but there has always been controversy about what intelligence actually is and how it should be measured. Some psychologists regard intelligence as the ability to adjust to the environment. Others attach a much more specific definition to intelligence—namely, that it is the ability to do academic work. Still others consider intelligence as simply the ability to learn. Finally, some think intelligence can be categorized into separate and discrete abilities to perform specialized tasks. It is this last meaning of intelligence that Spearman (1904) tackled. He noticed that the many different abilities measured by intelligence tests correlate highly with one another. That is, people who do well on some ability tests tend to do well on most; people who do poorly on a few tend to do poorly on most. Spearman explained this evidence by a two-factor theory of intelligence, in which he stated that intelligent behavior depends both on an overall intellectual ability and, in addition, on a large number of specific and separate abilities. Subsequent investigation led another psychologist (Thurstone, 1938) to maintain that Spearman's theory was too simple. Rather than Spearman's single general intellectual ability, Thurstone proposed a number of intellectual factor groups, each one accounting for performance on a set of related tasks. Guilford (1968), on the other hand, holds that intelligence is composed of a large number of totally unrelated abilities.

The idea that intelligence is the ability to adjust to the environment has been expressed by many psychologists, including both Binet and Wechsler, the writers of the two most widely accepted individual tests of intelligence.

A most controversial theory of the origins of intelligence has been widely publicized by Jensen (1969), who suggested that heredity may be more responsible than environment for racial and ethnic differences in tested intelligence. Jensen's theory has been vigorously criticized (Hebb, 1970; Crow, 1969; Bodmer and Cavalli-Sforza, 1970). His critics argue that while it is true that intelligence may be in part due to hereditary influences, there is no way to measure exactly how much, certainly not at the present time. The tools that we have at the present time for measuring intelligence are culturally biased and thus invalid for the very groups that Jensen claims have inferior intelligence as a result of heredity.

How were today's tests developed? Intelligence testing as we know it today grew out of the work of Alfred Binet, a French psychologist. In 1905 Binet developed the first Binet Scale of Intelligence. This early test was designed to identify those children in the Paris schools who, because of apparently lower ability, could not benefit from ordinary instruction and so were to be taken out of regular classes and given a simpler education. In developing his scale, Binet tried many ways of distinguishing the bright children from the dull, and finally arrived at the conclusion that intelligence is "the tendency to take and maintain a definite direction; the capacity to make adaptations for the purpose of attaining a desired end" (Terman, 1916, p. 45). This was the definition that shaped the final scale.

Binet's early test has long since been revised for use in this country. The American revision, known as the Stanford-Binet Scale of Intelligence, uses many items similar in content and form to the early Binet scale. The general purpose of both tests has been the same: to measure differences among children in ability to learn. The latest revision of the Stanford-Binet Scale was published in 1960.

The IQ, or intelligence quotient, obtained from the Stanford-Binet Scale was at first an actual quotient; that is, it was mental age divided by chronological (actual) age and multiplied by 100.

Mental age was obtained by comparing the test taker's raw score with the standardization sample scores typical of different ages; the age that his score matched was called his mental age. Suppose that a child had a mental age of 10. This would mean that the child answered as many questions correctly as the typical 10-year-old in the standardization sample. This mental age would be divided by his chronological age, let us say, of 8 years old. Then the quotient would be multiplied by 100. For this hypothetical child, the IQ was: $10/8 \times 100 = 125$. This type of IQ score is called a *ratio IQ*. In the 1960 revision of the Stanford-Binet Scale, another kind of IQ score was added. This is called a *deviation IQ*. A deviation IQ score is determined by comparing the individual's raw score with only those raw scores of individuals from the standardization sample who are of the same chronological age as the person being tested. For the Stanford-Binet Scale deviation IQ, the average score at each age is arbitrarily set at 100. The student's score is computed by measuring how much above or below the student is as compared to those of his own age, or how much he deviates from the norm.*

Deviation IQs have the advantage of being comparable from age to age. An IQ of, say, 135 means the same thing from age to age, in that it indicates the same degree of superiority relative to the aver-

---

*The distance between the average score and the actual score is divided into 16 point groups. Each group of 16 points is called a standard deviation. Therefore, a child who is one standard deviation above 100, the average score for his age, has an IQ of $100 + 16$, or 116. Appendixes 1 and 2 explain the meaning and use of averages, standard deviations, and the normal curve from which these statistics are derived.

age score for the age of the individual. Ratio IQs were replaced because they varied in meaning from age to age; deviation IQs do not.

The 1960 revision of the Stanford-Binet Scale has 21 levels of questions; 17 of these cover the years from 2 through 14 (some levels covering only six months), and there are four adult levels as well.

At each level the questions form several subtests of different types. The subtests vary widely in content, depending on the age level. For instance, very young test takers are asked to identify objects ("Show me the dolly's hair"); those a little older are asked to trace mazes; vocabulary is tested at all age levels; picture and verbal absurdities are presented, and the person taking the test must explain what is wrong with them (for example, the shadow is going in the wrong direction); the examiner recites a set of digits, and the test taker must say them backward; adults are asked to explain essential differences ("What is the principal difference between work and play?").

The Stanford-Binet Scale is in some ways a test of scholastic ability, and the tests are predominantly verbal, especially at the older age levels. This bias is understandable when one remembers Binet's original purpose in developing the scale: to discriminate among differing levels of ability of children to succeed in school.

The Binet Scale, as we said before, is an individual test. A specially trained examiner records and scores the test takers' responses as they go along. This is necessary because the examiner must know which subtests to present—no one takes them all. An important part of the examiner's job is to establish rapport with the child being tested, so that he will give his full cooperation.

A test that eventually came to rival the Stanford-Binet Scale had its origin in the efforts of David Wechsler. Wechsler was the first to develop an intelligence test giving a deviation IQ. Furthermore, Wechsler felt that the single total score of general mental ability that comes from the Stanford-Binet test did not provide enough information. Wechsler constructed ten or more subtests for each of several age levels, each subtest devoted to one kind of task. Some of the subtests were primarily verbally oriented, yielding what Wechsler termed a *verbal measure* of intelligence; others required little or no verbal ability, yielding what Wechsler termed a *performance measure* of intelligence. One way he used the test was in diagnosis. Wechsler noted that particular patterns of scores corresponded to certain types of intellectual problems.

The Wechsler-Bellevue Intelligence Scale was originally developed in 1939. Wechsler has since updated his original scales and developed the Wechsler Intelligence Scale for Children (WISC) and the Wechsler Adult Intelligence Scale (WAIS). He also developed an additional scale for children from 4 to 6 years of age, the Wechsler Preprimary and Primary Intelligence Scale (WPPIS). In these tests the subtests

This child is demonstrating her ability to remember a design which was presented to her by the examiner as part of the Stanford-Binet test of intelligence.

(Nancy Hays from Monkmeyer)

By observing closely this girl taking the WISC performance subtest on picture arrangement, a trained examiner can make diagnostic inferences about her intellectual performance.

(Nancy Hays from Monkmeyer)

are divided into verbal tests and performance tests. For example, in the WISC the verbal subtests are Information, Comprehension, Arithmetic, Similarities, and Vocabulary; the performance subtests are Block Design, Picture Completion, Picture Arrangement, Object Assembly, Mazes, and Coding. Separate verbal and performance deviation IQs are obtained; there is also a combined total deviation IQ score.

The Wechsler Scales all are individual tests of intelligence. Just as with the Stanford-Binet test, the examiner must keep a record of the test taker's responses and score them as he goes along. The performance subtests are useful with those who for any reason have difficulties with language that make other tests unsuitable. Much attention has been paid to different patterns of response on the verbal and performance subtests, but this kind of analysis has not proved sound and should not be depended upon (Cronbach, 1970). Nevertheless, as with the Stanford-Binet Scale, a trained examiner can make diagnostic inferences about intellectual performance and perhaps even emotional problems by observing how the test taker works. (We repeat, however, that such inferences should be considered in light of the standardization of the test.)

Both the Stanford-Binet and the Wechsler tests are individual tests. There are other individual tests of ability appropriate for special purposes. The Goodenough-Harris Drawing Test, which uses drawing to test general mental ability, can be employed with children from different cultures, even though it is not wholly free of cultural influence (Cronbach, 1970).

In the Peabody Picture Vocabulary Test, the examiner says a

word, and the child being tested points to the right picture. This measuring instrument does not require the child to use language himself, yet tests his knowledge of vocabulary. It is good with the retarded or handicapped, although not very comprehensive (Cronbach, 1970).

Because of the greater reliability, psychologists prefer such individual tests as the Stanford-Binet and the WISC to group tests of general mental ability. But, because they require trained examiners, individual tests are expensive to administer. As a result, most testing of intelligence in the schools is done by means of group tests.

Among the better known group tests are the Lorge-Thorndike Intelligence Tests, for grades 3 through 13, which include both verbal and nonverbal subtests. A Lorge-Thorndike Test can be given quickly — it takes only 62 minutes, plus time for distributing materials and explaining directions. Furthermore, a carefully planned national sample was used to obtain the norms (Cronbach, 1970).

The same child taking both a group and an individual IQ test is not likely to receive exactly the same score. This demonstrates that, as we mentioned before, group and individual tests, by their very nature, test different kinds of abilities. Group tests usually do not eliminate verbal skills entirely, because the person taking the test must write his answer. They are usually timed tests, while individual tests are not.

Question for Thought

Consider all of the theories and definitions of intelligence as well as the different types of intelligence test. Do you think that the following statement has merit: "IQ can be defined simply as what IQ tests test."

Are stable scores obtained from tests of general mental ability? Will one IQ score predict another one, obtained years later?

IQ is not very stable during the first years of life. At first it had been thought that an IQ would remain the same at all ages. It was later discovered, however, that test scores obtained in the first few months of life were not related to scores at the end of the first year (Bayley, 1955). In fact, the correlation is very low between two scores on tests separated by a year or two among infants and young children. Furthermore, it is well established that later intelligence cannot be predicted from test scores in infancy. This is logical in view of the fact that what is a valid test for an infant will not be so for an older child. What is being tested must change; infants do not perform many different tasks, and there are only a few ways to test them. At first, all that can be done is to see whether their senses act as they should when confronted with stimuli. Does a 1-month-old infant look at a dangling ring? Does a sharp sound make him start

The IQ Test as a Predictor of Future Ability

ALTERNATIVE GROUP TESTS OF ABILITY

Although the Lorge-Thorndike Intelligence Tests are the most widely used group tests, there are several alternative group tests of ability available (Cronbach, 1970).

The Culture Fair Intelligence Tests are intended for people from the age of 4 years through college age. They require no language skill, but the scores do reflect cultural influence. "The test has no advantage over the nonverbal sections of tests such as the Lorge-Thorndike" (Cronbach, 1970, p. 277).

The Henmon-Nelson Tests of Mental Ability, meant for the third grade through college, use different item types all mixed together, but with the items increasing in difficulty as the test goes on; this is called a "spiral omnibus pattern" (Cronbach, 1970, p. 279).

The Kuhlmann-Anderson Measure of Academic Potential tests children from kindergarten through the eighth grade; separate verbal and quantitative scores are provided from the seventh grade on, but the difference between the two scores is not usually reliable.

Progressive Matrices is a nonlanguage test that uses abstract drawings to test general intellectual ability, as Spearman defined it, in people from the age of 5½ years through adulthood.

Most private colleges and universities, especially those in the East, belong to the College Entrance Examination Board, and require all applicants for admission to take the College Board's Scholastic Aptitude Test (SAT). An applicant's scores on this test—his verbal score from a subtest made up for the most part of reading comprehension, and his mathematical score from a subtest of mathematical reasoning, reading tables, and such—count heavily in admissions, along with achievement test scores and high school grades.

ACT, the scholastic aptitude test of the American College Testing Program, is taken by applicants to public colleges and universities. ACT is more closely tied than SAT to learning in school—answering the questions requires reading comprehension, reasoning in mathematics and science, scientific judgment, and the ability to use clear and correct language.

The Cooperative School and College Ability Tests (SCAT) and the shorter form, SCAT II, are similar to SAT, but are suitable for the fourth to the twelfth grades.

The Graduate Record Examination (GRE), for college-age adults, is a difficult version of the SAT that is used to select applicants for admission to graduate school.

The Miller Analogies Test, for superior adults, is made up of verbal analogies ("Hot is to warm as cold is to _____"); it is used to select applicants for admission to graduate school.

or blink? At 6 months, motor coordination can be tested. Can the infant pick up a 1-inch cube in easy reach? As time goes on, the development of language can be observed. Does the infant use relatively complex language? Is it meaningful? (Bayley, 1955).

Honzik and his co-workers (1948) studied the IQs of 252 urban children between the ages of 21 months and 18 years. They obtained a correlation between scores at the age of 2 years and scores at the age of 5 years that was only slightly better than what would be expected by pure chance. To some extent, the changes in IQ came from the low reliability of testing in very young children, to some extent from certain technical problems in the study.

These investigators report further dramatic changes: Between the ages of 6 and 18, the IQs of almost 60 percent of the group changed 20 or more points, and the IQs of 9 percent of the group changed 30 or more points. The IQs of only 15 percent of the group changed less than 10 points. Some individuals showed a change of more than 50 points. On the whole, children tended to change in the direction that brought them more in line with the average IQ of people of the same educational and socioeconomic status as their parents.

Some startling case histories are related in this study. One girl went from an IQ of 133 down to an IQ of 77. The investigators give no sufficient explanation of the decrease, but do say this: "She was always overindulged by the mother, who lived to feed her and keep her young, and who was always complaining that her daughter never gave her enough affection" (Honzik, MacFarlane, and Allen, 1948, p. 77).

In contrast, a boy in the study whose score deviated significantly *below* the average raised his IQ to even more of a deviation *above* the average. Honzik et al. (1948) write,

> He is small-statured, thin, with very poor musculature, and presents a history of early ear infections and chronic bronchitis from infancy — headaches (early glasses), stomach pains (appendectomy); he has had three operations and three serious accidents. He has had only one six-month period in his life free of illness. In spite of a frail frame, which has suffered many serious indignities, an early strained family situation, and relatively low mental test scores in his early preschool years, his tested ability steadily increased until 9, from which time he has maintained high and fairly stable scores. (p. 77)

These investigators found, however, that the briefer the interval between testings, and the older the child when the two testings were done, the more likely it was that the IQ score would stay the same, or close to the same.

Cronbach (1970) also observes that IQ scores tend to become more stable with age. Test scores obtained in adolescence have been very closely related, with a correlation of .75 (a correlation of 1 means they are identical) to scores obtained 20 to 40 years later. Nevertheless, as he points out, there are some late bloomers, whose high ability becomes apparent relatively late in life. In general, no matter

THE ART OF TEST TAKING

McCall's is a national magazine aimed at that strata of society known as the middle class. Many important tips are given in its pages on how children (and often their parents) can be helped to cope with current trends. A recent issue, for example, describes how youngsters can overcome "the traumas of test taking" (Chan, 1975). The author goes on to say that it is never too early to begin teaching children how to cope with standardized tests, for "the skills of test taking are really a necessary survival strategy." The most important part of this strategy is making a child more comfortable and confident about taking tests, helping him to understand that tests are not a measure of personal worth.

Teachers can help prepare a student for taking tests by giving elementary classes sample answer sheets to play with, by giving them the required #2 pencils to use on exercises where they practice darkening boxes for the correct answer, and by changing their seating arrangements from time to time. It also helps if, once in a while, the teacher uses the language of the test administrator. It is important that children understand the meaning of such words as "match," "missing," and "identify." One test-taking authority also advocates

"a healthy disrespect for the rules." On reading comprehension tests, where a paragraph of text is followed by a series of questions about it, she warns students to read the questions before reading the test. Don't become too involved in the passage's content, she says. The tests "measure skim-and-match skills more than comprehension." What she recommends is the "whiz-through" technique of test taking. Rather than ponder difficult questions, students should skip them, going back to them only if they have time. (p. 38)

And "prepping" for standardized tests is not simply child's play—as can be seen from the many ads for schools specializing in preparing high school and college students for standardized tests.

(Van Bucher, Photo Researchers)

what the age, Cronbach (1970) recommends that if a decision is to be made about a student on the basis of a test score, only a recent score should be used. Furthermore, he cautions, we should watch out for children who are not used to being tested. Scores on tests improve just with practice in taking tests.

Questions for Thought

If IQs of an individual vary from age to age, what does an IQ test really measure?

Similarly, if you do not know the name of the test used to determine the IQ of an individual, what does a score on that test really mean?

In Chapter 11 we discussed individualizing instruction on the basis of ability. The primary advantage of IQ testing is that it attempts to identify the students with special needs—be they gifted or mentally retarded.

Tests of general mental ability can also be used for diagnosis of learning disabilities, although, as we mentioned in Chapter 11, additional diagnostic procedures are often needed.

But the teacher must keep in mind the limitations of mental tests. It should be remembered that tests are not infallible. IQs do not always remain stable, and the longer the interval since the last testing, the less faith we can put in the score. Tests that require reading will be unfair to a child with a reading difficulty—no matter how intelligent he is, he will not get a high score. Most intelligence tests are heavily verbal and therefore unfair to the child who does not speak English well or has other verbal problems, for they do not demonstrate nonverbal intelligence. In such cases, the only fair test would be a nonverbal or performance test.

Much has been written about the unfairness of intelligence tests to what we have called earlier the "socially disadvantaged." Members of this group are likely to be scholastically handicapped, because, among other reasons, as children they did not learn the skills needed to achieve in today's schools. It is not clear whether—without such skills—intellectual capacities cannot be realized, or whether they are in fact realized, but not in the conventional academic way. In either case, the result is low scores on the verbal intelligence tests that schools too often rely on so heavily. As we have pointed out in Chapter 10, ability grouping using verbally oriented tests in the early grades of public school frequently leads socially disadvantaged children into the lower-ability classes or sections, where they do not receive the kind of intellectual stimulation they need. Thus their history of intellectual failure is perpetuated. This failure promotes continuation of the self-fulfilling prophecy we described in Chapter 10.

This state of affairs has caused a loud outcry against intelligence testing, and in some cities (for example New York), intelligence testing has been forbidden in the schools.

Cronbach (1970) remarks:

> The opposition to tests rests in part on the belief that the test is designed for the white middle-class child, and does not give the slum child a fair chance. The middle-class child is encouraged to develop verbal abilities and to reason critically; such training is much less common in lower-class homes. This does not show the tests to be unfair; abstract and critical reasoning is indispensable for full participation in a complex and technical civilization. But *it justifies our thinking of the low-scoring slum children as culturally handicapped rather than as inferior from birth* [italics added]. (p. 303)

To support his argument, Cronbach quotes two test questions from Davis (1951):

A symphony is to a composer as a book is to what?
paper   sculptor   author   musician   man

A baker goes with bread, like a carpenter goes with what?
a saw   a house   a spoon   a nail   a man

Answering the first question requires knowledge that only advantaged children are likely to have; the second is based on information children of all social strata are equally likely to have. When children were divided into two groups according to socioeconomic status, 81 percent of the advantaged group got the first question right, but only 51 percent of the disadvantaged group did so. In each of the two groups 50 percent got the second question right.

Cronbach concludes, "The critical problem is not one of modifying tests but of inventing educational procedures suitable for children who are prepared neither intellectually nor motivationally for the traditional school" (p. 306).

Many educators agree. Zach (1972) says that our real problem is not the tests themselves but how we use them. Are we going to continue, she asks, to use tests only to make divisions between the fast learners and the slow, or are we going to use them to determine the state of intellectual development a child has reached so that we can use this information to help him develop further?

Furthermore, many argue, a student's test score is meaningful only when compared with norms—but no just comparison is possible unless the norms were drawn from a group similar to the student's own group. Totally culture-free tests do not exist; therefore, a low score on an IQ test should only be considered in light of both the test taker's background and the background of the standardization sample. If a student's cultural and intellectual background differ greatly from that of the standardization sample, comparing his score with the published norms is inappropriate and unfair.

STANDARDIZED TESTS OF ACHIEVEMENT

What Are the Purposes of Standardized Achievement Tests?

Standardized achievement tests exist in profusion—they cover almost every school subject. The public schools rely on them heavily for placement, prediction, and planning. As students now move more and more freely among school systems, this form of standardized measurement is needed for determining which classes the transferring students should be placed in. A standardized achievement test can provide a rough estimate to a teacher of where to begin course work with either an individual or a class. These tests, along with ability tests, provide information needed in counseling individual students. They can be used in comparing different methods of teaching, and they can be used to compare a group with national norms. They have some value in diagnosis of learning problems.

Thorndike and Hagen (1961) recommend still other uses: Standardized achievement tests, they say, can be used to compare achievement with potential for either an individual or a group. They can be used to compare achievement in different subjects. Further, they can be used to compare classes and schools, and to study student growth over time (presumably with equivalent forms being used for pre-test and post-test).

These authors remind us that standardized achievement tests cover the large segments of subject matter and the broad aims common to many schools and are not suitable for evaluating achievement in a limited unit of instruction or judging how well a strictly local learning objective has been accomplished.

Colleges and universities sometimes employ standardized achievement tests, along with standardized ability tests and high school grades, as a means for predicting the college gradepoint averages of applicants for admission.

No matter what the purpose is, in selecting a standardized achievement test a teacher should examine the test manual to see what evidence the publisher presents about the reliability and validity of the test. He should also examine the tables of norms to see if they are appropriate and check the instructions for administration and scoring to determine their practicality. Most importantly, he should examine the test objectives to see if they match his own.

Questions for Thought

Given the fact that standardized tests are used on a regular basis in American schools, has any thought been given as to *who* has the control to decide what goes into these tests (for example, what the specific questions should be)?

Since this is such an important decision in a society where we are so frequently judged by our test scores, do you think that the officials of the corporations responsible for developing these tests should be elected by the people or appointed by their corporations?

One of the most frequent uses of achievement tests is to predict future achievement. Teachers often want to predict the future success of their students — even as early as preschool. One group of tests that attempts to measure prereading achievement is the Metropolitan Readiness Tests (MRT). These tests have been used with moderate success with preschool children to predict what their reading, spelling, and arithmetic achievement will be in the latter part of first grade. Tests like the MRT can be useful in identifying children with learning problems when they first enter school. They can also be used to identify which children should enter school early and which should not. Furthermore, kindergarten programs in reading readiness can be evaluated through the use of pre-test and post-test scores on such tests (Rubin, 1974).

Many of you may remember a battery of achievement tests called The Iowa Tests of Educational Development. These tests have given better prediction of college gradepoint average than the usual scholastic ability test. In fact, these tests have been as useful in predicting future achievement as a combination of high school grades and scholastic ability tests. But, compared with the scholastic ability tests, which take from 45 minutes to 2 hours to administer, the Iowa tests take several hours. (D. Harris, 1940; Science Research Associates, 1957.)

The College Level Examination Program, a set of college achievement tests, is intended for use in "evaluation of independent study for college credit, college equivalency, transition to upper-division studies, curriculum evaluation, and institutional self-study." However, in at least one large southeastern university, when used alone this test was not useful in counseling and guiding college students about the choice of a major or in screening students who might have difficulty as upperclassmen (Goolsby, 1970).

Another study (Burnham and Hewitt, 1971) showed that scores on the College Entrance Examination Board (CEEB) Mathematics Achievement Test were successful in evaluating a student's readiness to pursue college level mathematics and quantitative science work. When used in conjunction with the CEEB test of scholastic verbal ability, these scores were also successful predictors of general academic success.

These last studies have suggested what is well known among measurement specialists—the best prediction of all will most likely be obtained by using a combination of a few good predictors.

Advantages and Disadvantages of Standardized Achievement Tests

Highly reliable and valid standardized achievement tests, just like well-constructed and standardized scholastic ability tests, have much to offer. They are used in placement, planning, and evaluation, for example. They can also be invaluable in diagnosis and in the individualization of instruction.

On the other hand, standardized achievement tests, like standardized IQ tests, are invalid for students whose backgrounds or current school curricula do not match those of the standardization sample. Thus, it is unjust for large groups of students to have their achievement assessed by these exams. In order for a test to be a truly suitable measure, the sample on which the test is standardized

The test-publishing industry, in an effort to eliminate any cultural or linguistic bias against minority children, has translated existing tests, adjusted norms for ethnic subgroups, and attempted to construct tests that are culture-free. Such actions, say two authorities in the field, have resulted in tests that "are of little use to anybody" (DeAvila and Havassy, 1974, p. 72).

Edward DeAvila and Barbara Havassy suggest that test developers consider an alternative assessment model derived from the work of Jean Piaget. Such a model was used, along with standardized achievement and IQ tests, on 1,100 Mexican-American and other children in four southwestern states. Results of the pilot study showed that the four Piagetian stages of cognitive development are exhibited in a developmental progression of performance scores appropriate to each age—regardless of ethnicity. Minority children failed to perform as well as Anglo-Americans on the traditional capacity and achievement measures, but the difference was not one of cognitive inferiority but perhaps a result of poorly designed curriculum, language usage, and so on.

DeAvila and Havassy have also demonstrated that the information provided by the neo-Piagetian approach can be used by administrators and by teachers on a daily basis. To help teachers do this, they designed a computerized system, which:

> at the administrative level . . . provides group statistical data for program evaluation and needs assessment and, at the teacher level, provides classroom recommendations rather than scores.
>
> This system simultaneously takes into account achievement and developmental scores for both the individual child and the child's referent group. It thus becomes possible to determine all of the possible test outcomes and, thereby, to design individual computerized program prescriptions for each child tested. Workshops are then held with the teachers involved to discuss the implementation of these prescriptions. A copy of these recommendations can also be sent to the home so that parents are aware of what the teacher is trying to accomplish with the child and can, with guidance from the teacher, participate in the child's education. (p. 75)

This system, called Program Assessment Pupil Instruction (PAPI), has been used successfully in the four states where the data was gathered. Perhaps soon we will see it applied on a broader scale.

THE TESTING OF MINORITY CHILDREN: A NEO-PIAGETIAN APPROACH

must be similar in all important respects to the population for whom the test is designed.

Because of the stress placed on achievement tests by the community, many teachers find themselves teaching *for* the standardized tests alone. Sometimes they teach for the College Boards. In recent years many colleges have allowed students to practice on the College Boards by taking them in both their junior and senior years of high school, perhaps giving them an unfair advantage.

But by teaching for the standardized tests alone, teachers have given up the right to select what will be taught to their students, and have handed over that right to the test developers. The United States is noted for its insistence on local control of schools as a necessary measure to prevent political control of education. Curriculum has long been selected by the community in which the students live in order to prevent excessive federal control. However, although we have carefully protected ourselves from control by politicians in the field of education, we have inadvertently given much of this control to the testing centers responsible for developing standardized achievement tests. In many cases, the learning objectives of a school or class do not match those of the standardized achievement test in question. When we judge achievement by the scores obtained on such a test, we have abandoned local control.

Standardized tests of achievement can be extremely valuable when they are flexible enough to deal differentially with individual students, aims, and instructional facilities. But invalid tests that force students and teachers into predetermined molds do not achieve these goals.

Standardized Achievement Tests and Accountability

In Chapter 13 we discussed the rising demands for teacher accountability. One way of evaluating a teacher's success is through the use of standardized achievement tests.

Demands for accountability in the educational system have in some cases given rise to specific agreements between groups offering instruction and schools needing services (Lennon, 1971). The group offering instruction is paid on the basis of student achievement, and that achievement is measured by standardized tests. While such contracts may sound efficient, in practice there have been many problems. Stake (1971) has examined the basic difficulties in such contracts. In the first place, curriculum is often narrowed severely; there are many aims in any classroom, and when a teacher or anyone else is asked to make a list of them, many will be left out because they cannot easily be put into words. Those aims that do find their way into the plan are likely to be the ones that are most readily measured. Stake believes that because of this, such aims will take up the lion's share of the questions on any achievement test. Thus, in his opinion, any achievement test is necessarily quite restricted in what it measures; yet under these conditions teaching is limited to what can be measured by achievement tests. Still worse, there was evidence in at least one contract that the instructional group had advance knowledge of which achievement test would be used at the end of the year and limited the teaching to the very questions that were going to be asked. To complicate the situation, payment may depend on the gain scores of the students; that is, a comparison between scores on the test before any learning has taken place and scores on the same test after learning. But gain scores tend to be unreliable, and apparent gains may not necessarily be due to student achievement as a result of a teacher's efforts. Furthermore, contract teaching, because of its very structure, tends to be depersonalized (Stake, 1971).

In view of the prevalent disillusionment with schooling, any efforts to make educators accountable to the public for what they are doing are understandable and even commendable. But the public must at the same time realize the many problems that can result from holding educators accountable.

SUMMARY

A standardized test is one in which the procedures for administering and scoring the test have been made uniform, or standard. Many standardized tests are tests of achievement—of what has been learned in a school subject. Tests of ability are tests of maximum performance. The primary use of an achievement test is to measure success in past study; the primary use of an aptitude test is to predict future success. There are both individual and group tests of ability. Group tests are usually verbal. Individual tests can be either verbal or nonverbal. Other types of tests are speed and power, norm-referenced, and criterion-referenced.

After constructing the final form of a test, the test publisher administers it to a standardization sample. The resulting norms or typical scores for a test are properly used only with students who resemble the standardization sample for that test. For some purposes local norms are needed, and data for them should be collected.

The reliability of a standarized test is best calculated by correlating scores from the administration of two equivalent forms of the test with a time interval of perhaps a few weeks between the two tests. Test scores are worthless if they are not valid measurements—if they don't measure what they are supposed to measure.

There are many theories of intelligence. Some, such as Spearman's, state that there is a general intellectual ability affecting intelligent behavior—general mental ability as well as subcomponents. Others think that intelligence must be broken down into many components. The Stanford-Binet and Wechsler scales are the most prominent individual tests of intelligence. They measure a general intelligence, although Wechsler also breaks IQ scores down to verbal and performance abilities as well. For individuals with language handicaps of any kind, individual nonverbal or performance tests should be used.

Startling cases of large changes in IQ are on record. Although IQ scores tend to become more stable with age, if any decision about a student is to be based on such a score, only a recent testing should be used.

Intelligence tests can be used to identify the retarded and the gifted, to individualize instruction, and to sort children into groups by ability. They can also be used to estimate roughly how much achievement can be expected from a student.

There are standardized achievement tests in existence to cover almost every school subject. These tests can be used to determine where to place transfer students, to estimate where to begin course work with an individual or a group, and (along with ability tests) to provide information needed in counseling and guidance. They can be used in comparing different methods of teaching and in comparing a group with national norms.

Both intelligence tests and achievement tests have some use in diagnosis of individual difficulties in learning, although often other techniques of diagnosis must be used as well.

Buros, O. K. (Ed.) *The seventh mental measurements yearbook.* Highland Park, N. J.: Gryphon Press, 1972.

This volume and those that precede it are essential references for critical reviews of all published tests in many different areas. Buros' manuals and the test manual for each particular test are two excellent sources of information on standardized testing.

Cronbach, L. J. *Essentials of psychological testing* (3rd ed.). New York: Harper & Row, 1970.

Cronbach's comprehensive book on standardized testing, which explains how to evaluate tests and what the scores mean, is a reference book for the teacher in all issues relating to standardized evaluation.

Lyman, H. B. *Test scores and what they mean.* Englewood Cliffs, N.J.: Prentice-Hall, 1963.

This is an easy-to-read guide to understanding standardized test scores. The basic attributes of a test as well as types of tests and scores are explained. The section on statistics should be considered a nice complement to the appendixes in this textbook.

Tyler, L. E. (Ed.) *Intelligence: Some recurring issues.* New York: Van Nostrand Reinhold, 1969.

This excellent book of readings contains many classic articles on the nature of intelligence and intelligence testing. Different theories of intelligence and critics of evaluating intelligence are included.

Young, M. *The rise of the meritocracy.* Harmondsworth, England: Penguin Books, 1958.

The rise of the meritocracy is a "psychological science fiction" that describes what the author feels to be the overemphasis on intelligence testing in our culture. It is essentially an essay on education and equality that should be read and enjoyed by most people concerned with education.

APPENDIXES

APPENDIX 1: AVERAGES

After preparing a test and giving it to a class, the classroom teacher needs to know the average score. In addition, teachers often need to know the average scores on standardized tests. But what does "average" mean?

Suppose these are grades on a spelling test of 10 words given to a small class: 3, 10, 8, 3, 7, 5.
The sum of these scores is 36. There are 6 children in the class. If we divide the sum of the scores (36) by the number of children in the class (6), we get

$$36 \div 6 = 6$$

We can say that 6 is the average score on this test in this class. This kind of average has a special name. It is called the *arithmetic mean*. Usually, the *arithmetic mean* is shortened to simply the *mean*. The mean is the sum of all scores divided by the number of scores.

The formula for the mean is:

$$\text{Mean} = \frac{\text{Sum of scores}}{\text{Number of scores}}$$

The mean score is important on many standardized tests.

There are other kinds of average besides the mean. Under certain circumstances, the mean is not the best kind of average to use. Consider these scores of children in a small class: 7, 4, 11, 9, 94.
The mean score for this test equals 125 divided by 5, or 25. But 25 is not a very typical score for this group. How many children in this class got a score equal to or greater than 25? Only one—the child who got a 94. The next highest score is 11. All the children except one had scores that were considerably lower than 25. Because one

score is markedly different from the others, the mean score here gives a distorted idea of the average.

Whenever one or a few scores in a small group are much higher or much lower than the rest of the scores, the mean will not represent a typical score. These few extreme scores are called *outliers*. Outliers are a problem only when the group is small. When there are outliers, we need a different sort of measure of the average.

Let us use the same scores listed in the last example and arrange them in order from high to low: 94, 11, 9, 7, 4. The midpoint is 9. This is the score that falls at the exact middle of the group of scores. The midpoint is also an average. This kind of average is called *the median*.

The median has a value equal to or larger than half of the scores and equal to or smaller than half of the scores.

Let us look at another example: 7, 4, 7, 11, 5, 94. If we arrange these scores in order from high to low, they look like this: 94, 11, 7, 7, 5, 4. Here the median is 7. This number is equal to or larger than half of the scores and equal to or smaller than the other half.

Suppose that in the last set of scores the second 7 had been an 8. The two middle scores would have been 7 and 8. When there is an even number of scores, and the two middle scores are not the same, take the two middle scores and split the difference between them to get the median. Here the median is 7.5. (Notice that no one actually got a score of 7.5. Note that the median and the mean scores do not have to be scores that students actually receive, but they *can* be.)

Because it is not influenced by a few extreme scores at one end of a small group, the median is of special value when outliers occur. For this reason it is used in educational research when the sample being studied is small. In addition, because it reflects the typical scores, the median is used a great deal in interpreting the scores on standardized tests. For both these reasons it is of value to the classroom teacher.

A third kind of average is called the *mode*. The mode is the score that occurs most frequently in the total number of scores. In this set of scores (7, 8, 4, 9, 3, 3) the mode is 3; it occurs more often than any other score. The mode is useful in classroom testing, standardized testing, and educational research, but is less frequently used than the other two averages because unless there is a sufficiently large sample, it might not appear at all. In some cases there may be more than one mode, which also makes it a less useful description of average in small classes. (The mode, of course, is always an actual score, one obtained by at least two people.)

In reading research reports it is important to remember that these measures of the average—the mean, the median, and the mode— often give different results for the same set of scores. This is why there are sometimes arguments about the true average of a set of figures. For more about the subject, and about similar statistical confusions, see *How to Lie with Statistics,* by Darrell Huff and Irving Geis (1954).

APPENDIX 2: THE NORMAL CURVE AND OTHER FREQUENCY DISTRIBUTIONS

Suppose we were to select a number of people at random and group them according to their IQ scores. We could then make up a table like this:

IQ Score	Number of People
60	0
70	3
80	7
90	10
100	14
110	16
120	17
130	11
140	5
150	0

This table shows the IQ scores and the number of people who got each score. A set of scores along with the number of people who got each score is called a *distribution.*

A distribution can be plotted on a graph or displayed in a table. Figure A-1 is the graph that corresponds to the above table. The baseline on this graph shows IQ scores. The vertical axis at the left shows number of people, or *frequency.* Each point on the graph can be read downward to the base line to discover the IQ score that it stands for. Then it can be read across to the vertical axis to discover the number of people that got that score. For instance, the graph shows that the IQ score of 120 was obtained by 17 people.

Notice that the line connecting the points on the graph has been brought down to the baseline on both the left and right ends. This has produced a closed geometrical figure like a triangle.

Let us imagine that, instead of obtaining IQ scores for 83 people, as before, we had done so for a much larger number of people. Let us suppose further that we had successfully measured very slight differences in IQ. The angular lines between each point of the triangle would then be very short. Eventually, if the number of people measured were large enough, the lines between each point would become invisible. The lines would blend into a smooth curve, shown in Figure A-2.

This is the normal curve. Another term for it is the *normal distribution.* The normal distribution is extremely important in psychology; when social scientists measure a trait in a large number of people the resulting distribution is often normal, or approximately normal,

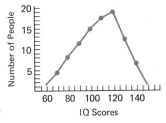

Figure A-1

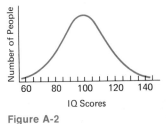

Figure A-2

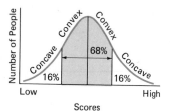

Figure A-3

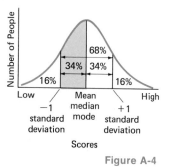

Figure A-4

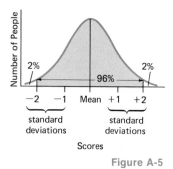

Figure A-5

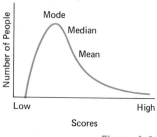

Figure A-6

provided that the number of people used is large enough.

The normal curve is symmetrical—the left and right halves are mirror images of each other.

The mean, the median, and the mode all have the same value in a normal distribution.

The normal curve never quite meets the base line on either side, but continues in what we call the *asymtote*. This is to show that—in theory, at least—there is no limit on how low or high the scores can be in normal distribution.

In the normal distribution we know the percentage of scores that will fall under each part of the curve. If two vertical lines are drawn from the base line to the two points where the curve changes slope from convex to concave, then 68 percent of the total area under the curve is cut off, as shown in Figure A-3.

The distance along the base line from the center of the distribution to one or the other of the solid lines perpendicular to the base is called a *standard deviation*. It is shown in Figure A-4.

We have just defined the standard deviation as a distance measured along the base line. We could also say that it is a measurement of score distance.

Since the mean, the median, and the mode cut the normal distribution in half, 34 percent (half of 68 percent) of the scores fall between the mean and the point that represents one standard deviation *above* the mean. Thirty-four percent of the scores fall between the mean and the point that represents one standard deviation *below* the mean. (We speak of *plus* one standard deviation and *minus* one standard deviation from the mean.)

If we double the distance along the base line that represents one standard deviation, we then include two standard deviations, as in Figure A-5. In this figure we see that 96 percent of the scores in a normal distribution fall between the point two standard deviations above the mean and the point two standard deviations below the mean. In addition, statisticians working with the normal curve have drawn up tables giving the percentages of scores that fall above or below a point any fractional number of standard deviations from the mean. These tables have important uses in the interpretation of research. They will be discussed in Appendix 4.

Not all distributions are normal. Sometimes a distribution that otherwise would be approximately normal will not look normal because too few people were used in gathering the data. Sometimes there are other reasons. Figure A-6, for instance, shows the curve for a classroom test that was too difficult for the class. This is an example of what we call a *skewed distribution*. The scores have piled up at the low end of the base line—not many students did well on this test. If a test is too easy for a class, the curve will be skewed in the opposite direction. Figure A-7 shows this kind of curve.

Notice that in these skewed distributions the mode, the median, and the mean do not have the same value. On the difficult test the median is lower than the mean; on the easy test the median is higher than the mean.

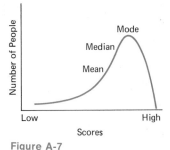

Figure A-7

APPENDIX 3: CORRELATION

Suppose that we were to make a list of all the children in a particular class and write each child's height and weight after his name. We would then have a list of names with two numbers linked to each name. Of course, as children grow taller they tend to weigh more. Therefore there would be some tendency for the larger weight numbers to be related to the larger height numbers—but the relationship would not be perfect. For instance, some of the taller children would be heavy, but some would be skinny; this fact would cause some irregularity in the relationship of height to weight. It might be useful to have some way of measuring the degree of relationship between the two sets of numbers in order to see just how strong the relationship is.

The relationship of sets of numbers is called *correlation*. Correlation is a mathematical measure of the degree of relation between two sets of numbers when the two sets are so linked to the same group of people that we can think of the numbers in pairs. In our case height and weight are paired for each child. We will not discuss the mathematical formula used in obtaining correlations, but we will discuss some of their properties, so that the reader will understand their meaning when he comes across them in research reports.

The number used as a measure of correlation is referred to as a *correlation coefficient*. It is usually a decimal fraction between 0 and +1 or −1. From the fact that we can observe (simply by looking at the pairs of numbers) that there is an association between weight and height, we know that in our case the correlation coefficient could not be 0. It would be 0 or close to 0 only if there were no relation between height and weight, no tendency for greater heights to go with greater weights or lesser heights with lesser weights. Our correlation coefficient could not be +1, either. It would be +1 only if there were a perfect correlation between height and weight—if the tallest child always weighed the most, the second tallest child always weighed the second most, the third tallest child always weighed the third most, and so on in orderly fashion throughout the entire class.

Negative correlations also exist. We can guess that among college students, the number of hours spent watching television will be negatively correlated with grades on tests. The students who watch the *most* probably will tend to get *lower* grades. A list might be made of the names of students in a particular class, the number of hours of television they watched, and each student's average test grade for a given period of time. A correlation coefficient might be calculated for the paired numbers. If our guess about the effect of watching television is correct, then the correlation coefficient will be negative. This time it will be a decimal falling somewhere between 0 and −1.

In judging the strength of the correlation between two sets of numbers we are guided only by the absolute value of the correlation coefficient. The sign—whether it is plus or minus—does not tell us anything about the strength of the relationship. A correlation coefficient of either +0.90 or −0.90 is very substantial, one of either +0.70 or −0.70 is fair, and one of +0.30 or −0.30 is usually quite low.

People often assume when two sets of numbers are highly correlated that the underlying relation must be one of cause and effect, but this is not necessarily so. It is extremely important never to assume a cause-effect relationship from a high correlation alone. In one amusing study of large American cities, a substantial positive correlation was found between birth rate and the amount of street paving—more babies were born in those months when more street paving was done.

Even when we feel more confident that cause and effect underlie correlation, we can never be certain of which was cause, which effect. The incidence of smoking among grammar school children has been found to be positively correlated with low grades. Does this happen because smoking causes low grades? Or do the factors that produce cigarette smoking in young children (such as lack of adult attention) lead also to low grades? We can never tell from a correlation alone.

The possibility of outside influences on correlation should not be ignored.

APPENDIX 4: SCORES OFTEN USED ON STANDARDIZED TESTS

The reader should study Appendixes 1 and 2 before reading this appendix.

A percentile rank tells us the percentage of scores below a given score. If a test score of 65 has a percentile rank of 80, this means that 80 percent of the people who took the test got a score of less than 65. We can also say that anyone who got a score of 65 was at the 80th percentile. (The reader who has read Appendix 1 will realize that the median is the 50th percentile.)

Percentile ranks are frequently used by publishers of standardized tests in reporting scores. They are easy to understand, and they make it possible to compare scores on different tests.

Age norms and grade norms are percentile ranks, too. The norm or typical score for an age is the 50th percentile, or median for that age. Well-meaning but uninformed people sometimes urge that every pupil in a community be brought up to what is called "grade level" or "grade norm." If every pupil in the country were brought up to grade level, the grade level itself would of course change!

Age norms and grade norms are also used by publishers of standardized tests. So is another kind of score—the z score or standard score. In order to discover the meaning of z scores, let us consider the distribution of scores on a hypothetical test. The distribution of scores has a mean of 80. We want to make a value statement about a score of 85 on this test. This score is 5 points above the mean. On this hypothetical test the distance of one standard deviation from the mean also is 5 points (standard deviations were explained in Appendix 2). Therefore, we can say that a raw score (the number of correct answers) of 85 is one standard deviation above the mean—we call a score given in terms of numbers of standard deviations a z score. A raw score of 85 on this test is thus equivalent to a z score of +1.

Suppose that on the same test someone has a raw score of 62. This is 18 points below the mean of 80. Since one standard deviation on this test is 5 points, this raw score is 3.6 standard deviations below the mean ($18 \div 5 = 3.6$). We say that a raw score of 62 is equivalent to a z score of −3.6.

A z score tells how many standard deviations from the mean a given raw score has fallen. Positive z scores are above the mean; negative z scores are below the mean.

The use of z scores makes it possible to compare scores from different tests because all scores describe performance in the same terms, that is, the amount of deviation from the mean.

The use of z scores sometimes requires using unwieldy decimals. In such cases, z scores can be transformed to less confusing numbers.

A well-known type of transformation is that used by the College Board. Since the College Board figures z scores on its Scholastic Aptitude Test to two decimal places, multiplying all the z scores by 100 gets rid of the decimal points (a z score of +1.43 becomes +143). College Board scores have a normal distribution (see Appendix 2), so, practically speaking, virtually all scores fall between the z scores of −3.00 and +3.00. After multiplication to get rid of the decimal points, these z scores equal −300 and +300. In order to get rid of the minus signs, 500 is added to these already multiplied scores. The mean (which is equivalent to a z score of 0) is now 500.* Virtually all students receive scores between 200 and 800. We have seen that a score of 600 on the College Board Scholastic Aptitude Test must be one standard deviation above the mean. Because the scores have a

*Because the population of students applying to college has changed since the College Board Scholastic Aptitude Test was normed, the mean has now sunk to below 500.

normal distribution, such a score equals or surpasses 84 percent of the population, as the reader will remember from Appendix 2; thus it is a good score. Any score in the 700s is very good; such scores surpass 96 percent or more of the population who take the test.

The reader can see that the College Board standard scores have a mean of 500 and a standard deviation of 100. Other systems of transformation have produced other well-known types of standard score. The Wechsler Adult Intelligence Scale (discussed in Chapter 15) has a mean of 100 and a standard deviation of 15, so that a score of 85 on the WAIS indicates a z score of −1; it surpasses only 16 percent of the population (intelligence is believed to be normally distributed). The Stanford-Binet test (also discussed in Chapter 15) has a mean of 100 and a standard deviation of 16. A score of 140 on the Stanford-Binet test is the equivalent of a z score of +2.5; tables of the normal curve tell us that this score surpasses 99.4 percent of the population.

In interpreting a score on a standardized test, a teacher should keep in mind that no test is perfectly reliable. The test manual may report a measure called the *standard error* of the test. Knowledge of the standard error, which is calculated from the reliability of the test as well as from other figures, helps a teacher to remember this and adjust for it. Assume that the standard error on a certain test is reported as 6 points. This means that if a student could retake the test the chances are good (about 7 out of 10) that the new score would fall in the range between 6 points below and 6 points above the old score. If he got a score of 78 the first time, the chances are 7 out of 10 that his score would fall between 71 and 85 the second time. But there are about 3 chances in 10 that his second score would differ even more widely from his first one—that it would fall somewhere below 71 or somewhere above 85 on the second test.

APPENDIX 5: A SIMPLE ITEM ANALYSIS THAT THE TEACHER CAN USE

The *validity* of a test depends on whether or not it measures what it is supposed to measure. In an achievement test, a particular question is a valid measure of student achievement when it discriminates between those students who have learned whatever behavior is being tested and those who have not. If a question is so easy that all students answer it correctly, or so difficult that no one gets it right, then it is not useful for discriminating between those students who have achieved an instructional goal and those who have not.

It is useful for the classroom teacher to be able to determine whether any particular test item (test question) is doing its job of discriminating between those who have learned the material and those who have not. Garrett (1965) devised a simple test-item analysis for calculating this important evaluative index. He called a test item's power of discrimination its validity index. This index, also called the index of discrimination, can easily be calculated by the teacher in the following manner:

Step 1. Rank all the test papers from low to high. Take the top quarter and the bottom quarter and put them aside for analysis. If there are 100 students in the class, set aside the 25 best papers and the 25 worst papers. (If there are less than 50 students in the class, set aside a larger proportion, such as the top third and the bottom third.)

Step 2. Count the number of students in the top quarter who answered the first test item correctly. Then do the same for the bottom quarter.

Step 3. Fill in the following formula.

Index of discrimination =

$$\frac{\text{\# right in top quarter} - \text{\# right in bottom quarter}}{\text{total \# in top quarter}}$$

Suppose that there are 30 students in the top quarter and that all of them answered the test item correctly. Suppose also that there are 30 students in the bottom quarter and that 10 of them answered the test item correctly.

$$\text{Index of discrimination} = \frac{30 - 10}{30} = \frac{20}{30} = .67$$

Thus, the index of discrimination of the first test item equals .67. The validity of a particular test item can range from +1 to −1. An item is completely valid (index of +1) when all the students in the top quarter get it right and all the students in the bottom quarter get it wrong. It is completely invalid (index of −1) when the opposite situation occurs.

The teacher can go through a test item by item, repeating steps 2 and 3 of the process above, to determine the validity of the whole test.

GLOSSARY

ability grouping the grouping of students in a particular grade into homogenous classes based on IQ and reading achievement scores.

ability tests tests of maximum performance, used to find out how well the person is capable of performing.

acceleration a school program in which a gifted student can skip one or more grades and progress more rapidly through school.

accommodation according to Piaget, a cognitive process that occurs when we add a new activity to what we already know, or modify an old behavior.

achievement motivation a persistent attempt to achieve what is thought to be excellence.

achievement-oriented an enduring personality characteristic in which the individual is predisposed toward success and relatively unconcerned with failure.

achievement tests tests of what has been learned in a school subject.

acquisition the process of obtaining new information that can be used to either replace or refine something known previously, the first step in learning, according to Bruner.

adaptation the intellectual activity, according to Piaget, by which we can alter the ways we deal with the environment, either by changing ourselves (accommodation) or changing the environment (assimilation).

aggression quarrelsome or attacking behavior that may be self-assertive, self-protective, or hostile to oneself or others.

analysis breaking down an entity into its component parts, a middle level in Bloom's taxonomy.

anxiety an internal fear response that has generalized from the original feared stimulus to many stimuli.

application the ability to solve problems that are similar in principle, but different in form from those seen previously; a middle level in Bloom's taxonomy.

aptitude test a special kind of ability test intended to predict success in a specific occupation or training course.

assimilation part of the Piagetian process of adaptation. Assimilation occurs when new objects are treated in the same way familiar objects are treated.

associationism a psychological theory that explains behavior in terms of stimulus and response, based on the premise that people naturally tend to associate their behavior with stimuli in the environment.

attention the process of selecting information from the environment and the ability to attend to stimulation changes as a result of development.

attitudes hypothetical constructs that are not directly observable but are used to account for observed behavior.

avoidance learning a type of classical conditioning in which the subject learns to make a response after the presentation of a stimulus in order to avoid some unpleasant occurrence.

behavior a collection of stimulus-response associations, according to associationist theorists; a meaningful product of perceptual change due to interactions between the individual and his environment, according to the cognitive-field theorists.

behavior management the process of taking conscious and active control of the environment by rewarding desirable behavior and ignoring or punishing undesirable behavior.

black English a dialect of English very different from the formal middle-class "standard English" of the schools.

branching programmed instruction routes each student individually, depending on his responses at preselected choice points.

capabilities the precise behaviors the teacher wants a student to master; the objectives of a lesson, according to Gagné.

chaining higher-order learning in which the subject learns to make a series of responses in a specified order before reinforcement occurs.

circular reactions Piaget's term for the repetitious actions performed by babies for the sake of the action itself or to observe the results of an action.

classical conditioning the procedure in which a subject learns to respond to a new stimulus by associating it with a stimulus that elicited the desired response automatically. In classical conditioning the response occurs *after* a stimulus is presented.

code emphasis in reading instruction children are taught to "sound out" what they are reading in their earliest reading instruction.

cognitive development the development of thought processes; a spontaneous process that occurs as a function of total development.

competence motivation White's idea that an individual has an intrinsic need to deal effectively with the environment.

competency-based instruction a type of instruction that is geared toward achieving specific learning objectives.

comprehension the ability to identify or restate information in a form that is not an exact replica of the original; the school level of cognitive learning, according to Bloom's taxonomy.

computer-assisted instruction (CAI) the computer itself instructs the students and prescribes learning materials on an individual basis.

computer-managed instruction (CMI) the computer assists teachers and students in planning and record keeping, but does not instruct students.

concept an abstraction or idea that permits the learner to classify a variety of related phenomena into a convenient, meaningful category.

concrete operations according to Piaget, the stage of cognitive development from around 7 to 11 years of age, at which a child has the ability to deal with concrete objects in a logical fashion.

conservation according to Piaget, the cognitive ability of children in the concrete operations stage to realize that an object remains constant or the same regardless of its changes in form.

consequence the term used in precision teaching for a reinforcer such as a gold star or being leader in the line.

content validity a measure of the representativeness of the sample of knowledge that the test is intended to measure.

construct validity the validity of a test, determined by correlating scores on that test with some other currently accepted criterion measure for that area.

contiguity the temporal (time) relationship between a stimulus and a response.

continuous reinforcement reinforcement follows every response and leads to a regular pattern of responding.

contract teaching agreements between groups offering instruction and schools needing such services. The group offering instruction is paid in proportion to student achievement on standardized tests.

control group the group that is compared with the experimental group but does not receive the treatment that the experimental group does.

correlation a mathematical measure of the degree of relationship. Correlations do *not* indicate cause-and-effect relationships.

criterion-referenced testing measures whether or not a student has mastered specified learning objectives. This type of testing does not tell the student how he did in relation to other students.

cybernetic theories of memory a group of theories that compare the functioning of the human brain with similar processes in a computer.

deductive method of teaching this method involves presenting concepts by verbal definition and description, for example, lecturing.

delayed reinforcement reinforcement that occurs after a period of time has elapsed since the behavior was exhibited.

depression a problem behavior related to anxiety. Clinical symptoms include psychomotor retardation, sadness, hopelessness, and suicidal ideas or threats.

deschooling Illich's idea to eliminate the need for schools, placing learning in the community through individual interactions.

developmental stage the characterization of various age levels according to specific traits and behaviors.

developmental task term used by Havighurst to describe the age-related, culture-bound activities a person must learn for successful adjustment.

deviation IQ score the type of IQ score currently used on the Stanford-Binet and Wechsler tests. The deviation IQ score is determined by comparing the individual's raw score with those raw scores of people from the standardization sample who are of the same chronological age.

differentiation the process of responding differently to two or more similar stimuli. Differentiation is a fundamental aspect of perceptual learning, according to E. J. Gibson.

direct teacher talk the category in Flander's interaction analysis that includes explaining information, giving directions, and scolding.

discovery teaching a teaching method endorsed by Bruner that requires rearranging the subject matter structure so that the learner is able to go beyond the evidence presented to newly gained insights.

discrimination the process in learning whereby an individual responds in a certain way to one set of circumstances and in a different way to another, similar set of circumstances. Discrimination occurs when two or more stimuli are responded to differentially.

distributive justice Piaget's term for older children's way of deciding rewards and punishments on the basis of fairness of treatment.

drive the internal state or compulsion that generates activity. Drive is inferred from measurable circumstances.

drive strength the amount of energizing behavior or the measure of a drive.

dyslexia a type of learning disability characterized by language difficulties, particularly in reading.

economy the amount of information a person must learn and remember in order to understand a subject. The larger the amount, the less the economy. Bruner uses the term in relation to the structure of a subject.

efficacy White's term for competence. The goal of such behavior is getting to know what the environment is all about.

egocentric speech undirected speech, according to Piaget; not aimed at others for the purposes of communication.

egocentrism the inability of a child to see viewpoints (either in perception or in conception) other than his own, according to Piaget.

enactive mode according to Bruner, the most basic way of representing the environment. The enactive mode is a set of actions appropriate for achieving a certain result.

encoding the process that enables people to reduce or abbreviate the amount of information stored for a particular item.

enrichment programs programs that allow gifted children to remain in regular classrooms but still receive the extra stimulation and challenge they need.

epilepsy a neurological disorder characterized by *grand mal* and *petit mal* seizures. During a *grand mal* seizure the person loses consciousness, twitches convulsively, and may even lapse into a coma. *Petit mal* seizures are less severe and may cause the individual to lose motor control temporarily.

equilibration the transforming process in Piaget's cognitive developmental theory which goes from simpler to more complex conceptual thinking.

equilibrium the balance between assimilation and accommodation as a function of a person's level of cognitive development, according to Piaget.

essay test requires the student to organize material and write the answer in a sentence form. This test is graded subjectively.

evaluation (1) indication of whether or not a person's work meets the specified criterion, or a comparison with someone else's work. (2) Ability to evaluate is the most complex type of learning, according to Bloom's taxonomy, and the final step of the learning process, according to Bruner. (3) Evaluation is the process of checking whether the acquired information has been manipulated appropriately.

exploratory drive the intrinsic human need to explore whatever is novel or unfamiliar, according to Berlyne.

extended family a household unit consisting of parents, children, and close relatives living together.

extinction the process in operant conditioning in which a nonreinforced behavior will gradually occur less and less frequently and eventually return to the rate of occurrence before conditioning was first begun.

extrinsic motivation doing something for the sole purpose of an external reward without any inherent reinforcement.

fading theory of forgetting the representation of items in the memory, called traces, gradually fade with time and forgetting occurs.

failure-oriented an enduring personality characteristic in which the individual is concerned more with his possible failures than with his successes.

figure-ground perception according to Gestalt psychologists, perception of an object (figure) as clearly standing out from its background (ground).

fixed schedule of reinforcement reinforcement is given according to a consistent and set pattern. Both interval and ratio schedules may be fixed schedules.

foreign hull the term Lewin used to describe those things in a person's external environment that do not affect his behavior.

formal operations Piaget's last stage of cognitive development, which is characterized by the ability to use formal or abstract logic and reason through the use of hypothesis.

formative evaluation a type of evaluation used to improve instruction or to diagnose student weaknesses while the course is being taught.

functional invariants intellectual functions, such as organization and adaptation, that do not change with development, according to Piaget's theory of intelligence.

generalization the process in learning whereby an individual responds in an identical way to two or more separate stimuli. Generalization also occurs when a particular stimulus evokes responses that are similar or related to the desired response. (See also **stimulus generalization** and **response generalization**.)

generative grammar system of rules and principles governing the relationships between sound and meaning.

gestalt the German term meaning form, shape, or configuration.

grades the recording of student performance after it has been evaluated.

graphemes the printed symbols in an alphabet.

group reinforcement reinforcing a group for their collective behavior rather than individual behavior. The Soviet Union uses group reinforcement in its schools.

group standardized tests tests that many people can take at one time. Group tests are usually paper and pencil tests, often requiring the use of language and reading.

hierarchy of needs according to Maslow, there are five hierarchical types of needs: physiological, safety, love and belonging, esteem, and self-actualization.

homeostasis the tendency of individuals to resist deviation from an optimally steady state. People act to reduce their needs so as to maintain a steady or balanced internal state of being.

hyperactivity a child who is hyperactive is characteristically overactive, restless, excitable, impulsive, and seems never to sit still. Hyperactivity may also be seen as a learning disability.

iconic mode Bruner's term for a pictorial representation that stands for a concept without fully defining it.

identification more than imitation of a model, a cognitive process in which a person adopts for himself the standards of the model by which he can judge his own behavior. Identification requires internalization.

identity the personality factor that makes each person unique.

identity diffusion Erikson's term for the lack of a clear answer to the question, "Who am I?"

imitation occurs when children's behavior very closely matches the behavior of other people in certain situations.

immanent justice Piaget's term for young children's belief that punishment is a natural consequence and must follow when they have done something wrong.

immediate feedback immediate knowledge of results or correctness of a response; often serves as reinforcement in learning.

index of discrimination the degree to which a question discriminates between high scorers and low scorers. Items discriminate in the right direction when questions are answered correctly by more high scorers than low scorers.

indirect teacher talk the category in Flander's interaction analysis that includes praise, asking questions, and clarifying ideas.

individual standardized tests tests in which the trained examiner asks the test taker questions, one by one, or directs him to perform tasks. The test taker usually does not have to read the questions.

individualized instruction offers special individualized plans of study based on the individual's needs, abilities, and interests. Individualized instruction is often individually paced.

inductive method of teaching consists of presenting a series of positive and negative instances of a concept and allowing the learner to make inferences from the invariant attributes. This is similar to Bruner's "discovery" approach.

information-processing theories of memory. (See **cybernetic theories of memory.**)

Initial Teaching Alphabet (ITA) an artificial, printed English language, in which there is a one-to-one phoneme-grapheme relationship. Used for the purposes of early reading instruction.

insight a form of discovery learning in which the end results are finding a solution that works and developing an understanding as to why it works. One may achieve insight when there is a reorganization or transformation of stimuli. It can be both a product and a process.

instrumental conditioning. (See **operant conditioning.**)

intelligence tests mental tests of general ability.

interaction analysis a system developed by Flanders to help teachers assess the patterns of interaction in their classes. Verbal communications are broken down into several categories and a frequency count of each is made based upon classroom observations.

interference theory of forgetting new and old learning compete and interfere with one another.

intermittent schedule of reinforcement reinforcement given on the basis of a specified number of responses (ratio) or a specified amount of time after the last reinforcement (interval).

interval schedule of reinforcement reinforcement that depends on the amount of time that has elapsed since the previous reinforcement.

intelligence quotient (IQ) the ratio of mental age divided by chronological (actual) age, multiplied by 100.

intervening variable a theoretical construct that cannot be observed but is used to explain behavior. The presence of an intervening variable is inferred by performance.

intrinsic motivation the reward in a task is intrinsic to the behavior itself, without need for external reinforcers.

intuition immediate apprehension or cognition, according to Bruner. Intuitive thinking is characterized by the development of hunches and hypotheses, by perceptions that seem to appear suddenly and dramatically.

knowledge the simplest type of learning, according to Bloom's taxonomy. Knowledge includes rote memory. One may have knowledge without comprehension or understanding.

law of closure the Gestalt principle that closed figures are more stable (remembered better) than open figures.

law of continuation the Gestalt principle that the way in which the first part of a stimulus is perceived determines how a continuation of that stimulus is perceived.

law of effect E. L. Thorndike's principle that the associative bond is strengthened or weakened, depending on whether a satisfier (reward) or an annoyer (punishment) follows a response. (See also **truncated law of effect.**)

laws of organization Gestalt principles used to explain the basic understanding of how individuals perceive their environment.

law of Prägnanz the Gestalt organizational principle for both perception and learning. This law includes four separate laws: similarity, proximity, continuation, and closure. We tend to perceive objects as more simple, regular, and complete than they actually are.

law of proximity the Gestalt principle that stimuli occurring close to each other are perceived as belonging together.

law of similarity the Gestalt principle that stimuli similar in nature are perceived as belonging together.

learning the process whereby the perceptual field is organized, according to Gestalt psychologists. A relatively permanent change in behavior as a result of reinforced practice, according to associationist psychologists.

learning disability categorizes the problems of individuals who may be termed slow learners but actually have normal or above-average intelligence. These people have different kinds of problems, involving reading ability, memory, concentration, motor ability, and disruptive behavior.

learning-environmental theories of development theories that explain cognitive development through focusing directly on the environmental stimulation and learning experiences that are possible.

learning objectives instructional objectives that describe in behavioral terms what the student should be able to do, the conditions under which the task is to be performed, and the criterion for acceptable performance.

learning styles different ways in which people process information in the course of learning, including individual preferences in both perceptual organization and conceptual categorization. Also called cognitive styles.

level of aspiration the individual's expectation of his own future success or failure, based upon his evaluation of his past performance and his desire to perform better in the future.

life space Lewin's term for psychological field, the total psychological world in which a person lives. Incorporates events and ideas relating to the person's past, present, and future.

linear programmed instruction the questions in a lesson are arranged in a single line from simple to complex; all students answer the same questions in the same order.

long-term memory a permanent memory store of almost unlimited capacity. Stores information only after it has been processed or rehearsed.

Lorge-Thorndike Intelligence Test widely used, reliable group test of intelligence for children that includes both verbal and nonverbal subtests.

mainstreaming the incorporation of students with special needs into regular classes.

maintenance systems the economic, political, and social structures necessary to uphold a society.

manipulation drive an independent but nonphysiological drive to investigate and control the environment. Harlow believes that this drive is independent because it is not associated with any primary drives.

maturation the development of the body, regardless of outside influences.

meaning emphasis in reading instruction attention given in early reading instruction to semantics, or the meaning of words, rather than the sounds of the letters.

meaningfulness measures of meaningfulness include number of associations, familiarity, and frequency of use. The more meaningful something is, the better it will be retained.

memory traces structural changes in the nervous system that are associated with learning.

mental age obtained by comparing the test taker's raw score with the typical age of the standardization sample who obtained the same raw score.

mental combinations Piaget's term for the child's ability to represent to himself the outcome of actions before he makes them.

mentally retarded those individuals who are significantly deficient in both thinking capacity and behavioral adaptation to society. The four classifications of retardation are (in order of decreasing intelligence): the educable, trainable, severely, and profoundly retarded.

mnemonics special strategies for rote memorization, such as associating one word with another, associating words with geographical locations, or forming a sentence using words formed from the first letters of the terms to be remembered.

mode of representation Bruner's term for the basic method by which people understand and make use of their environment. The three modes are enactive, iconic, and symbolic.

modeling a process in which children exhibit symbolic equivalents of observed behavior, not exact replications. Children generalize their behavior to situations other than the exact ones observed.

modular instruction individualized instruction programs structured around separate sequential units of study known as modules. Students play an active role in their own learning with modular instruction.

molar behaviors common-sense units larger than individual stimuli and responses; used by Tolman in analyzing behavior.

Montessori method an instructional program within a planned environment; emphasizes action, sensorimotor materials, self-learning, and self-reinforcement or feedback.

morality aspect of personality that includes the development and expression of conscience, or the internalization of values accepted by society.

morality of constraint Piaget's term for young children's morality, in which parental and other authority figures' decisions are accepted as moral absolutes. It is based on unilateral respect.

morality of cooperation Piaget's term for a more mature basis of morality, which grows out of mutual respect. The individual is personally responsible for his own actions.

morpheme any word or part of a word that conveys meaning and cannot be divided into a smaller form conveying meaning.

motivation the internal factors that cause a person to act, the goals or purposes underlying an individual's behavior. Motivation includes both energizing and directional properties.

motor learning taxonomy a classification scheme of motor skills based on subject matter, developed by Merrill. The five different motor skills he identified include physical education, communication, fine arts, language, and vocational skills.

movement theory most learned behavior involves movement of one kind or another. Motor behavior is the major channel through which cognitive and affective behavior become apparent to oneself and others.

multiple-mothering or multiple-caretaking the child-rearing practice whereby the child is cared for, to a large extent, by more than one mother or more than one primary caretaker.

need a requirement that must be met by an organism for optimal adjustment to the environment.

negative reinforcer reinforcer that is meant to increase the frequency of escape behavior. Negative reinforcers are effective only when there is an opportunity to escape and the opportunity is obvious to the person.

negative transfer the interference of learning in one area with learning in another area.

neutral stimulus a stimulus that by itself would be incapable of eliciting a response. Through repeated associations with unconditioned stimuli, neutral stimuli themselves elicit a response and become conditioned stimuli.

nongraded classrooms a heterogeneous age grouping of students, based on the premise that children of the same age are capable of learning the same things.

nonverbal test test that is completely without words; usually administered individually.

norm-referenced testing used to compare students' scores within a group.

normal curve the distribution of a human trait when measured in sufficiently large numbers of people. The normal curve is a symmetrical, bell-shaped curve.

normal distribution a statistical, hypothetical distribution based on an infinitely large population.

norms information about typical scores for the kinds of students who made up the standardization sample. Norms can be percentile ranks or age or grade norms.

nuclear family a household unit consisting of two parents and their offspring.

objective tests tests requiring the student to write a short answer or to choose the correct answer. Multiple-choice, true-false, matching items, short answer, and completion questions are examples of objective tests.

the open classroom (1) a nontraditional approach to teaching in which the room is divided into functional areas for specific subjects (learning resource centers). The students work individually or in small groups. Children have a great deal of say in determining their own learning. (2) An underlying flexible attitude toward education with an informal style of teaching and individualized instruction.

operant conditioning the process of modifying behavior by reinforcers; involves responses that occur before any stimulus is presented.

operants behaviors that request (or make) a change in the environment.

operant strength the strength of the response, such as the increase in the number of bar-pressings.

organization the intellectual activity, according to Piaget, whereby we arrange and systematize perceptual and cognitive data into units and patterns that have meaning for us.

overgeneralization generalization to such an extent that it distorts reality.

overlearning learning that continues after material appears to be learned and remembered. Overlearning reduces forgetting, especially of factual material.

parallel play play in which preschool children perform the same activities at the same time, aware of one another but independently of one another.

peer group people of about the same age and status in a society or neighborhood.

peer teaching the educational process in which children work together and teach each other.

percentile rank a statistic telling the percent of scores in the standardization sample falling below a certain given raw score.

perception sensation, as it is given meaning through the learning experiences of the developing mind.

perceptual field also known as *psychological world*, the term cognitive-field theorists use to describe the meaning of an individual's perception at any given moment.

perceptual learning an increase in one's ability to extract meaningful and relevant information from one's environment as a result of practice and experience, according to E. J. Gibson.

performance tests tests that use apparatus such as equipment, machinery, materials, implements, and other instruments. They are also called nonlanguage tests. They may measure both general and specialized abilities.

phonetics the system of teaching reading in which letters are the basic units, beginning with instruction in how to sound or pronounce various letters.

positive reinforcers stimuli that follow operant behavior and increase its frequency.

positive transfer occurs when learning in one activity facilitates learning in a new or similar activity.

power the term Bruner used to describe the value of the material being learned in terms of its applicability.

power tests tests composed of questions of varying degrees of difficulty. The score on a power test depends on the ability of the test taker to answer the questions correctly.

precision teaching a behavior management program of individualized instruction that emphasizes monitoring of a child's performance, which is clearly pinpointed and charted on daily progress records.

predictive validity a measure of the ability of a test to predict future success in a field or in a school. Predictive validity is also called *statistical validity* or *empirical validity*.

Premack principle allows child to select his own reinforcers; teachers use school activities that the students enjoy as reinforcers.

preoperational stage Piaget's second stage of development occurring between the ages of 2 to 7 years old. Children learn to use language effectively during this stage, however, their thought is still very egocentric.

primary needs those requirements that must be met in order for the organism to survive, such as the need for food or water.

primary reinforcers stimuli that are of prime importance to the physical survival of the organism such as food and water.

proactive inhibition occurs when prior learning interferes with the ability to remember new learning.

problem behaviors behaviors exhibited as a result of poor personal and social adjustments to the environment.

programmed instruction an active learning process in which students are constantly asked questions as they progress through the unit. The material is presented in a progressive, stepwise order of difficulty. Immediate feedback as to the correctness of the answers is given.

prohibition learning a type of learned behavior that occurs together with the identification process. A child is taught certain "don'ts" by parents and other models.

purposive behaviorism Tolman's term to explain that all organisms are goal-seeking and that behavior cannot properly be understood without considering the purpose behind the behavior.

psychological reality one's perceptions of the physical sensations one receives. Psychological reality may or may not accurately interpret physical reality; yet it is thought of as real by the individual.

psychological world. (See **perceptual field.**)

punishment the administration of an aversive stimulus for the purpose of inhibiting the preceding response.

Pygmalion effect the term given to the self-fulfilling prophecy by Rosenthal and Jacobson. Middle-class teachers' negative expectations of disadvantaged children may contribute strongly to failure in the schools due to their own self-evaluations and reduced performance.

ratio schedule reinforcement is given only after the subject makes a specified number of desired responses.

raw score the number of correct answers attained by an individual on a test.

recall a fairly insensitive method of measuring remembering that requires the student to remember as much information as possible with only a minimum number of cues or suggestions as to the correct answer.

reception teaching/learning a method of teaching in which the material is presented in more or less final form to the student. The student learns the information in that form without greatly transforming it; his learning is guided closely by the teacher.

recognition a measure of remembering in which many cues are given. The multiple-choice question is the most frequently used type of recognition question.

reduction of uncertainty the reinforcing aspect of learning, according to E. J. Gibson's perceptual learning theory. It helps the student to transform what would otherwise be confusion into meaningful stimulation.

reinforcer stimulus that increases the future probability of a particular response occurring.

relativism the term cognitive-field therapists use to explain how new perceptions develop (by relating to the new sensation, integrating it with other material with which one is already familiar, and perceiving it in relation to past experience).

relearning the most sensitive measure of remembering, in which one measures the number of trials needed to learn material at a later date and compares that number to the original number of trials needed to learn the material.

reliability one of the most important criteria for a good test. A test is reliable if it gives the same scores on repeated testing.

remembering the retention of information after learning has taken place; the availability of previously learned information.

repression a psychoanalytic explanation for forgetting. We push painful experiences out of our consciousness as a way of preserving our self-esteem.

respondent conditioning. (See **classical conditioning**.)

response generalization occurs when a particular stimulus evokes responses that are similar or related to the desired response.

retroactive inhibition interference in which subsequent learning interferes with earlier learning.

role playing when people assume other or new roles and portray these in common situations.

schedule of reinforcement the manner or rate in which reinforcers are given following a subject's responses. The schedule of reinforcement helps to determine the strength of the response or operant strength.

school phobia reluctance or refusal to go to school, usually as a result of an extreme fear about some aspect of the school situation; a common school-related anxiety.

secondary needs requirements that are not needed for survival but that optimize a person's adjustment to a complex learned, social, and physical environment. Secondary needs develop from association with primary needs.

secondary reinforcers stimuli that in themselves are not rewarding but come to be rewarding when they are associated with primary reinforcers. Secondary reinforcers, such as approval or money, are created by the process of conditioning.

self-concept, self-image the unified mental picture every individual has of himself. Includes self-evaluation, a self-enhancing aspect.

self-esteem an individual's attitude regarding his own worth as a person.

self-management of contingencies rewarding oneself after one has achieved certain previously determined subgoals.

self-paced evaluation a method of evaluation in which students move at their own pace and are evaluated when they believe they are ready. The Keller plan was based on self-paced evaluation.

sensorimotor stage Piaget's earliest stage of cognitive development, usually from birth to about 2 years old. This is an action-oriented stage, which occurs prior to the development of language.

sensory information storage an extremely short-lived memory storage, it refers to our perception of the world through our senses.

sex-role identification the way in which children learn how to feel and act the role of a particular sex. Parental rewards, imitation, and modeling contribute to sex-role identification.

shaping the process of conditioning in which successive reinforcements are given for closer approaches to the desired behavior. At first any improvement is reinforced; later, only more correct or more precise responses are reinforced.

short-term memory material that is stored as an immediate and direct interpretation of sensory stimuli. This memory is short-lived and of limited capacity.

socialization the learning process whereby a child learns the behaviors, ideas, attitudes, and values that are socially acceptable in his culture.

socialized speech speech directed toward communication, according to Piaget.

speed test a type of test that is made up of a very large number of questions of a uniform level of difficulty. A speed test score depends on the total number of questions the test taker answers correctly in a restricted time period.

spiral curriculum Bruner's concept in which there is a logical progression from the simple to the complex in the structural representation of the subject matter.

stage-dependent theories the developmental process is seen in terms of a sequence of maturational stages that occur in a fixed and predictable order.

standard score. (See **z score**.)

standardization sample the group of people given the final version of a standardized test. This sample should be representative of those people for whom the test is intended. Norms are obtained from the standardization sample.

standardized test a test in which the procedures for administering and scoring the test have been made uniform or standard.

Stanford-Binet Intelligence Test the most reliable and widely accepted individually administered, standardized test of intelligence currently in use.

stimulus generalization the same response is made to two or more stimuli.

summative evaluation a type of evaluation done at the end of a course to assign grades or to measure the success of the instruction.

superstitious behavior a response or series of responses that occur before reinforcement but yet do not have any relationship to the reinforcement. There is no causal link between the behavior and the reinforcement.

symbolic mode according to Bruner, the most advanced mode of representation, because it provides a means of going beyond what is immediately perceptible in a situation. Language plays a major role in the symbolic mode.

synthesis the ability to combine knowledge, skills, ideas, and experiences to create a new and original product. A most complex type of learning in the cognitive domain, according to Bloom.

taxonomy of objectives an instructional plan for determining what general class or category of behavior is desired in a given situation; gives the full possible range of objectives that are available in a learning situation.

teacher accountability the idea that the teacher, not the student, is ultimately responsible for what and how much a student learns.

teaching machines instructional devices that students can operate and then be reinforced depending on the appropriateness of their response.

team teaching a variety of teaching techniques in which a number of teachers share responsibility for teaching students and subject materials.

theory of generalized principles Judd's idea that transfer is based upon an understanding of the principle underlying two or more activities. Understanding a general principle makes it possible to interrelate and interpret a whole body of varied experiences.

theory of identical elements E. L. Thorndike's belief that transfer occurs only within a restricted range of conditions. Transfer occurs to the extent that two activities share composite elements.

token economy immediate reinforcement for a desired response is given in the form of some sort of token. After a number of tokens have been accumulated the child can cash them in for a desired object or privilege.

topological diagram a cognitive map or way to depict visually the significant elements in a person's life space, according to Lewinian theory.

traces. (See **memory traces.**)

transfer the application of knowledge from one area to another.

transfer of learning the process that occurs whenever the existence of a previously established habit has an influence upon the acquisition, performance, or relearning of a second habit.

transformation the manipulation of information to make it fit new situations; the second step of the learning process, according to Bruner.

transformational grammar the contemporary approach to linguistics developed by Noam Chomsky. Sentences are constructed and related to one another by means of underlying syntactical rules called *transformations*.

transposition the Gestalt term for application of learned solutions to new situations or the transfer of training.

truncated law of effect E. L. Thorndike's revised law of effect: although satisfiers always strengthen the bond between the stimulus and the response, annoyers (punishment) do not necessarily weaken it—they may have little effect upon it at all.

unconditioned response an automatic response. When bright light is directed toward someone's eyes, that person automatically blinks. The blink is an unconditioned response.

unconditioned stimulus a stimulus, such as noise, light, etc., that produces a response without learning having to take place.

valence the approach or avoidance tendency of an individual to a particular place, object, or situation, according to Lewinian theory.

validity one of the important criteria for a good test. A test has validity if it measures what it is designed to measure.

variable schedule of reinforcement the average number (ratio) or average time period (interval) of responses, rather than a specific number of responses or specific time period, determines the reinforcement schedule.

vector a moving force going in a specified direction; in a topological diagram Lewin used an arrow to show direction and strength of the force.

verbal tests tests that rely on the use of words in the questions or directions. Group tests are usually verbal tests.

Wechsler Intelligence Scales individual, standardized intelligence tests for children and adults that yield both a verbal and a performance subscore and a total deviation IQ score.

withdrawal a problem behavior characterized by shyness, fear, secretiveness, apathy, daydreaming, and isolation.

Zeigarnik effect recalling an incomplete task more readily than a completed one due to motivation.

z score or standard score a statistic that tells how far from the average a given raw score is. Z scores may be positive (raw score above the average), negative (raw score below the average), or zero (raw score the same as the average of the standardization group).

REFERENCES
AND
AUTHOR INDEX

The numbers in **boldface** at the end of each reference indicate the pages in this text where the works are cited.

Ackerman, P. D. The effects of honor-grading on students' test scores. *American Educational Research Journal*, 1971, *8*, 321–333. **488**

Adkins, A. Testing: Alternative to grading. *Educational Leadership*, January 1975, pp. 271–273. **482**

Ahlstrom, K. G. *Motivation and achievement*. Uppsala: Institute of Education, Uppsala University, 1957. **214**

Ahmann, J. S., & Glock, M. D. *Evaluating pupil growth* (4th ed.). Boston: Allyn & Bacon, 1971. **484, 490, 492, 499, 500**

Ainsworth, M. D. S. *Infancy in Uganda*. Baltimore: Johns Hopkins University Press, 1967. **20, 21, 22**

Airasian, P. W. The role of mastery learning. In J. H. Block, *Mastery learning*. New York: Holt, Rinehart & Winston, 1971. **485**

Allender, J. S. A radical psychology of learning. In M. L. Silberman, J. S. Allender, & J. M. Yanoff (Eds.), *The psychology of open teaching and learning*. Boston: Little, Brown, 1972. **313**

Allender, J. S. *A radical psychology of learning*. Book in preparation 1974. **451**

Alper, T. G. Achievement motivation in college women. *American Psychologist*, 1974, *29*, 194–203. **212**

Alschuler, A. S. *How to increase motivation through climate and structure* (Achievement Motivation Development Project Working Paper No. 8). Cambridge: Harvard University Graduate School of Education, 1968. **196**

American Federation of Teachers, AFL-CIO. *Academic freedom and the rights of faculty* (Position paper). Unpublished manuscript, n.d. (Available from author, 1012 14th St., N. W., Washington D.C. 20005) **443**

Amidon E. J. & Flanders N. *The role of the teacher in the classroom* (Rev ed.). Minneapolis: Association for Productive Teaching 1967. **455**

Amidon, E. J., & Giammatteo, M. The verbal behavior of superior teachers. *Elementary School Journal*, 1965, *65*, 283–285. **453**

Anderson, E. M. *The disabled schoolchild*. London: Methuen, 1973. **390**

Anderson, N. World war on hunger called must. *Pittsburgh Press*, October 6, 1974, p. A-24. **189**

Anderson, R. C. Learning in discussions: A resume of the authoritarian-democratic studies. *Harvard Educational Review*, 1959, *29*, 201–215. **451**

Anderson, R. P. *The child with learning disabilities and guidance*. Boston: Houghton Mifflin, 1970. **386**

Andrews, T. G., & Cronbach, L. J. Transfer of training. In W. S. Munroe (Ed.), *Encyclopedia of educational research* (2nd ed.). New York: Macmillan, 1950, **298, 301**

Angell, G. W., & Troyer, M. E. A new self-scoring test device for improving instruction. *School and Society*, 1948, *67*, pp. 84–85. **467**

Animals go to Northgate school. *Pittsburgh Press*, March 4, 1975, p. 9. **290**

Aronson, E. The need for achievement as measured by graphic expression. In J. W. Atkinson (Ed.), *Motives in fantasy, action, and society*. Princeton: Van Nostrand, 1958. **194**

Assignment: Assertion. *Time*, May 19, 1975, p. 65. **441**

Association for Education of the Visually Handicapped. *A look at the child*. Philadelphia: Author, 1970. (ERIC Document Reproduction Service No. ED 084 738) **398**

Atkinson, J. W. (Ed.) *Motives in fantasy, action, and society*. Princeton: Van Nostrand, 1958. **211**

Ausubel, D. P. *Theory and problems of adolescent development*. New York: Grune & Stratton, 1954. **92**

Ausubel, D. P. *The psychology of meaningful verbal learning*. New York: Grune & Stratton, 1963. **180**

Ausubel, D. P. *Learning theory and classroom practice* (Bulletin No. 1). Toronto: Ontario Institute for Studies in Education, 1967. **180**

Ausubel, D. P. *Educational psychology*. New York: Holt, Rinehart & Winston, 1968. **152, 153, 154, 180, 260, 301**

Ausubel, D. P., & Robinson, F. G. *School learning: An introduction to education psychology*. New York: Holt, Rinehart & Winston, 1969. **180**

Ausubel, D. P., & Sullivan, E. V. *Theory and problems of child development* (2nd ed.). New York: Grune & Stratton, 1970. **180**

Bachrach, A., Candland, D., & Gibson, J. Group reinforcement of individual response experiments in verbal behavior. In I. Berg & B. Bass (Eds.), *Conformity and deviation*. New York: Harper & Brothers, 1961. **119**

Back, K. W. *Beyond words: The story of sensitivity training and the encounter movement*. New York: Russell Sage Foundation, 1972. **430**

Back to basics in the schools. *Newsweek*, October 21, 1974, pp. 87–88 ff. **174**

Bahrick, H. P., Bahrick, P. O., & Wittlinger, R. P. Long-term memory. *Psychology Today*, December 1974, pp. 50–56. **271**

Bailyn, L. Mass media and children. *Psychological Monographs*, 1959, *73* (1, Whole No. 471). **33**

Bandura, A. Behavioral psychotherapy. *Scientific American*, March 1967, pp. 78–86. **430**

Bandura, A. Social-learning theory of identificatory processes. In D. A. Goslin (Ed.), *Handbook of socialization theory and research*. Chicago: Rand McNally, 1969. **34**

Bandura, A., & Harris, M. B. Modification of syntactic style. *Journal of Experimental Child Psychology*, 1966, *4*, 341–352. **240**

Bandura, A., & McDonald, F. J. Influence of social reinforcement and the behavior of models in shaping children's moral judgments. *Journal of Abnormal and Social Psychology*, 1963, *67*, 274–281. **85**

Bandura, A., Ross, D., & Ross, S. A. Imitation of film-mediated aggressive models. *Journal of Abnormal and Social Psychology*, 1963, *66*, 3–11. **34**

Banks, J. A. Imperatives in ethnic minority education. *Phi Delta Kappan*, 1972, *53*, 266–269. **363**

Banta, T. J. The preschool in action. In R. K. Parker (Ed.), *Exploring early childhood programs*. Boston: Allyn & Bacon, 1972. **308**

Baratz, J. C. A bi-dialectal task for determining language proficiency in economically disadvantaged Negro children. *Child Development*, 1969, *40*, 889–901. **358**

Barber, T. X., Calverley, D. S., Forgione, A., McPeake, J. D., Chaves, J. F., & Bowen, B. Five attempts to replicate the experimenter bias effect. *Journal of Consulting and Clinical Psychology*, 1969, *33*, 1–6. **210**

Barber, T. X., & Silver, M. J. Fact, fiction, and the experimenter bias effect. *Psychological Bulletin Monograph*, 1968, *70*(6, Pt. 2), 1–29. **210**

Bard, B. Pills for learning. *McCall's*, August 1974, p. 49. **387**

Barro, S. M. An approach to developing accountability measures for the public schools. *Phi Delta Kappan*, 1970, *52*, 196–205. **455**

Bartholomew, B. R. Teachers' instructional problems, 1974. *Today's Education*, September 1974, pp. 78–80. **445**

Bartlett, F. C. *Thinking*. New York: Basic Books, 1968. **154**

Bayley, N. On the growth of intelligence. *American Psychologist*, 1955, *10*, 805–818. **512**

Bayuk, Z. The case for elitism. *Clearing House*, 1972, *46*, 506–507. **394**

Bechterev, V. M. [*General principles of human reflexology*] (E. Murphy & W. Murphy, trans.). New York: International Publishers, 1928. **110**

Beilen, H. Teachers' and clinicians' attitudes toward the behavior problems of children. *Child Development*, 1959, *30*, 9–25. **411**

Bereiter, C., & Engelmann, S. *Teaching disadvantaged children in the preschool*. Englewood Cliffs, N.J.: Prentice-Hall, 1966. **68**

Bereiter, C., & Engelmann, S. An academically oriented preschool for disadvantaged children. In *Psychology and Early Childhood Education*. Toronto: Ontario Institute for Studies in Education, 1968. **368, 369**

Berko, J. The child's learning of English morphology. *Word*, 1958, *14*, 150–177. **239**

Berlyne, D. E. Conflict and information-theory variables as determinants of human perceptual curiosity. *Journal of Experimental Psychology*, 1957, *53*, 399–404. **198**

Berlyne, D. E. Notes on intrinsic motivation and intrinsic reward in relation to instruction. In J. S. Bruner (Ed.), *Learning about learning* (Cooperative Research Monograph No. 15). Washington, D.C.: U.S. Department of Health, Education, and Welfare, Office of Education, 1966. **218, 219**

Bernard, H. W. *Child development and learning*. Boston: Allyn & Bacon, 1973. **242, 245, 247, 250, 260, 356, 384, 406, 407, 408, 415, 417**

Bernauer, M., & Jackson, J. H. Review of school psychology for 1973. *Professional Psychology*, 1974, *5*, 155–165. **391, 393**

Bernstein, B. Some sociological determinants of perception. *British Journal of Sociology*, 1958, *9*, 159–174. **46**

Bernstein, B. Language and social class. *British Journal of Sociology*, 1960, *11*, 271–276. **63**

Berryman, C., & Perry, B. *A manual for teachers of learning disabled children*. Bristol City, Tenn.: Bristol City Board of Education, 1974. (ERIC Document Reproduction Service No. ED 085 958) **383**

Bettelheim, B. *The children of the dream*. New York: Macmillan, 1969. **20, 203**

Bias is charged in book rejection. *New York Times*, November 10, 1974, p. 53. **439**

Bigge, M. L. *Learning theories for teachers* (2nd ed). New York: Harper & Row, 1964. **129, 135, 145, 146, 147, 152, 153, 157, 160, 179, 218, 279, 285, 292, 296, 434**

Bijou, S. W., & Baer, D. M. *Child development* (Vol. 1). New York: Appleton-Century-Crofts, 1961. **57**

Biller, H. B. Father absence, maternal encouragement, and sex-role development in kindergarten-age boys. *Child Development*, 1969, *40*, 539–546. **24, 25**

Birch, J. Special education for exceptional children through regular school personnel and programs. In M. C. Reynolds & M. D. Davis (Eds.), *Exceptional children in regular classrooms*. Minneapolis: University of Minnesota Press, 1971. **391**

Blakeslee, S. Challenge for the very bright: A "college for kids". *New York Times*, May 21, 1975, p. 39. **396**

Blank, M., & Solomon, F. A tutorial language program to develop abstract thinking in socially disadvantaged preschool children. *Child Development*, 1968, *39*, 379–389. **63**

Bloom, B. S. *Stability and change in human characteristics*. New York: Wiley, 1964. **61**

Bloom, B. S., Englehart, M. D., Furst, E. J., & Krathwohl, D. R. *A taxonomy of educational objectives* (Handbook 1). New York: David McKay, 1956. **251**

Bloomfield, L. *Language*. New York: Holt, 1933. **241**

Blumberg, P. Achievement and affiliation motivation in women as a function of verbal stimulus cue and college major. Unpublished M. A. thesis, University of Pittsburgh, 1974. (a) **211**

Blumberg, P. *Play as it is reflective and imitative of a culture*. Unpublished manuscript, University of Pittsburgh, 1974. (b) **33**

Bodmer, W. F., & Cavalli-Sforza, L. L. Intelligence and race. *Scientific American*, October 1970, pp. 19–30. **507**

Bogatz, G. A., & Ball, S. *The second year of Sesame Street* (Vol. 1). Princeton: Educational Testing Service, November 1971. **68, 369**

Bonehead English. *Time*, November 11, 1974, p. 106. **174**

Borinsky, M. E. *Provision of instruction to handicapped pupils in local public schools, Spring 1970*. Washington, D.C.: National Center for Educational Statistics, 1973. (ERIC Document Reproduction Service No. ED 087 169) **389**

Bower, E. M., & Lambert, N. M. *In-school screening of children with emotional handicaps*. Princeton: Educational Testing Service, 1961. **428**

Bower, G. H. A multicomponent theory of the memory trace. In K. W. Spence & J. T. Spence (Eds.), *The psychology of learning and motivation* (Vol. 1). New York: Academic Press, 1967. **277**

Bower, G. H. Analysis of a mnemonic devise. *American Scientist*, 1970, *58*, 496–510. **287**

Bowerman, C. E., & Kinch, J. W. Changes in family and peer orientation of children between the 4th and 10th grades. *Social Forces*, 1959, *37*, 206–211. **91**

Bowlby, J. *Attachment.* New York: Basic Books, 1969. **21**

Bradbury, W. An agony of learning. *Life,* October 6, 1972, pp. 57–58 ff. **383**

Breyer, N. L., Lapp, B., Calchera, D., & McCarthy, J. F. An integrated approach to pupil personnel services. *Psychology in the Schools,* 1974, *11,* 174–182. **392**

Brill, S. The secrecy behind the college boards. *New York Magazine,* October 7, 1974, pp. 67–83. **505**

Brock, M., Lambert, W., & Tucher, G. *Cognitive and attitudinal consequences of bilingual schooling: The St. Lambert project through grade 6.* Unpublished manuscript, McGill University, 1973. **358**

Brod, R. L. *The computer as an authority figure* (Technical Report No. 29). Stanford: Stanford Center for Research and Development in Teaching, Stanford University, August 1972. **325**

Brody, J. E. More coeds find less guilt in sex. *New York Times,* December 30, 1967, p. 1. **424**

Bronfenbrenner, U. Some familial antecedents of responsibility and leadership in adolescents. In L. Petrullo & B. M. Bass (Eds.), *Leadership and interpersonal behavior.* New York: Holt, Rinehart & Winston, 1961. **87**

Bronfenbrenner, U. Soviet methods of character education. *American Psychologist,* 1962, *17,* 550–564. **85**

Bronfenbrenner, U. The dream of the kibbutz. *Saturday Review,* September 20, 1969, pp. 72–73 ff. **20**

Bronfenbrenner, U. *Two worlds of childhood: U.S. and U.S.S.R.* New York: Basic Books, 1970. **26, 27, 32, 40, 79, 85, 90, 130**

Bronfenbrenner, U. The roots of alienation. In U. Bronfenbrenner (Ed.), *Influences on human development.* Hinsdale, Ill.: Dryden, 1972. **99**

Brooks, H. Piano lessons: Striking a new chord. *McCall's,* August 1974, p. 48. **282**

Brown, R., & Fraser, C. The acquisition of syntax. In U. Bellugi & R. Brown (Eds.), *The acquisition of language.* Monographs of the Society for Research in Child Development, 1964, *29,* 43–79. **239**

Brozan, N. Film and TV violence: A nursery school takes a stand. *New York Times,* June 3, 1975, p. 28. **34**

Bruininks, R. H., & Rynders, J. E. Alternatives to special class placement for the educable mentally retarded. In Meyer, Vergasons & Whelan (Eds.), *Strategies for teaching exceptional children.* Denver: Lowe, 1972. **391**

Bruner, J. S. Learning and thinking. *Harvard Educational Review,* 1959, *29,* 184–192. **165, 167**

Bruner, J. S. *The process of education.* New York: Vintage, 1960. **56, 162, 164, 168, 169, 171, 172, 173, 174, 178, 179**

Bruner, J. S. *On knowing: Essays for the left hand.* Cambridge: Belknap Press, 1962. **177**

Bruner, J. S. The course of cognitive growth. *American Psychologist,* 1964, *19,* 1–15. **47, 165**

Bruner, J. S. The growth of the mind. *American Psychologist,* 1965, *20,* 1007–1017. **167**

Bruner, J. S. *Toward a theory of instruction.* Cambridge: Harvard University Press, 1966. **162, 165, 166, 167, 178, 179**

Bruner, J. S. Child development: Play is serious business. *Psychology Today,* January 1975, pp. 81–83. **48**

Bruner, J. S., Olver, R. R., Greenfield, P. M., & others. *Studies in cognitive growth.* New York: Wiley, 1966. **62**

Bryson, R. Teacher evaluations and student learning. *Journal of Educational Research,* 1974, *68,* 12–14. **495**

Burnham, P. S., & Hewitt, B. A. Advanced placement scores: Their predictive validity. *Educational and Psychological Measurement,* 1971, *31,* 939–945. **518**

Busk, P. L., Ford, R. C., & Schulman, J. L. Effects of schools' racial composition on the self-concept of black and white students. *Journal of Educational Research,* 1973, *67,* 57–63. **361**

Byalick, R., & Bersoff, D. N. Reinforcement practices of black and white teachers in integrated classrooms. *Journal of Educational Psychology,* 1974, *66,* 473–480. **453**

Caldwell, B. M. The fourth dimension in early childhood education. In R. D. Hess & R. M. Bear (Eds.), *Early education.* Chicago: Aldine, 1968. **67, 366**

Cameron, N. A. *Personality development and psychopathology.* Boston: Houghton Mifflin, 1963. **420**

Campbell, S. B., Douglas, V. I., & Morgenstern, G. Cognitive styles in hyperactive children and the effect of methylphenidate. *Journal of Child Psychology & Psychiatry,* 1971, *12,* 55–67. **418**

Carlson, J. S. Children's probability judgments as related to age, intelligence, socio-economic level, and sex. *Human Development,* 1969, *12,* 192–203. **55**

Carpenter, A. M., & Rogers, J. Harlem Prep: An alternative system. In R. Gross & P. Osterman (Eds.), *High school.* New York: Simon & Schuster, 1971. **336**

Carroll, J. B. Words, meanings & concepts. *Harvard Educational Review,* 1964, *34,* 178–202. **244, 245**

Castaneda, A., Palermo, D. S., & McCandless, B. R. Complex learning and performance as a function of anxiety in children and task difficulty. *Child Development,* 1956, *27,* 327–332. **203**

Caudill, W., & Weinstein, H. Maternal care & infant behavior in Japan and America. *Psychiatry,* 1969, *32,* 12–43. **12**

Cazden, C. The Electric Company turns-on to reading. *Harvard Graduate School of Education Bulletin,* Spring 1972, *16,* pp. 2–3. **312**

Central Advisory Council for Education. *Children and their primary schools* (Vols. 1 & 2). London: Her Majesty's Stationery Office, 1967. **313, 390, 394**

Chall, J. S. *Learning to read: The great debate.* New York: McGraw-Hill, 1967. **226**

Chan, J. The art of test taking. *McCall's,* April 1975, p. 38. **514**

Child, I. L., & Whiting, J. W. M. Determinants of level of aspiration. *Journal of Abnormal and Social Psychology,* 1949, *44,* 303–314. **208**

Choice in Quincy. *Time,* March 10, 1975, p. 73. **338**

Chomsky, C. *The acquisition of syntax in children from five to ten.* Cambridge: M.I.T. Press, 1969. **239**

Chomsky, N. *Syntactic structures.* The Hague: Mouton, 1957. **238**

Chomsky, N. Language and the mind. *Psychology Today,* February 1968, pp. 48–51 ff. **239**

Ciccone, D. S. Massed and distributed item repetition in verbal discrimination learning. *Journal of Experimental Psychology,* 1973, *101,* 396–397. **269**

Cicirelli, V., & others. *The impact of Head Start: An evaluation of the effects of Head Start on children's cognitive and affective development.* The report of a study undertaken by Westinghouse Learning Corporation and Ohio University under DED contract B 89–4536, Washington, D.C., 1969. **68, 367**

Citizens' Board of Inquiry into Hunger and Malnutrition in the U.S. *Hunger U.S.A.* (A report). Boston: Beacon, 1968. **352, 353**

Claiborn, W. L. Expectancy effects in the classroom. *Journal of Educational Psychology,* 1969, *60,* 377–383. **210**

Clark, D. H. (Ed.). *The psychology of education.* New York: Free Press, 1967. **327, 328, 423, 424**

Clark, K. *An appendix to a possible reality.* New York: Metropolitan Applied Research Center, 1970. **5**

Clarke-Stewart, K. A. Interactions between mothers and their young children. *Monographs of the Society for Research in Child Development*, 1973, 38(6–7, Serial No. 153). **21, 22**

Clifford, J. O. Kids check out pets at library. *Pittsburgh Press*, April 27, 1975, p. E-1. **314**

Clifford, M. M., Cleary, T. A., Walster, G. W. Effects of emphasizing competition in classroom-testing procedures. *Journal of Educational Research*, 1972, 65, 234–238. **214**

Closed-circuit sight. *Human Behavior*, February 1975, p. 30. **381**

Coats, W. D., Swierenga, L., & Wickert, J. Student perceptions of teachers. *Journal of Educational Research*, 1972, 65, 357–360. **495**

Cogan, M. L. The behavior of teachers and the productive behavior of their pupils. *Journal of Experimental Education*, 1958, 27, 89–124. **453**

Cohen, A. The Culver City Spanish Immersion Program: The first two years. *Modern Language Journal*, 1974, 58, 95–103. **358**

Cohen, A. L., & Filipczak, J. *A new learning environment*. San Francisco: Jossey-Bass, 1971. **212**

Cohen, M. A., & Martin, G. L. Applying precision teaching to academic assessment. *Teaching Exceptional Children*, 1971, 3, 147–150. **398**

Cohen, P. S., & Cohen, L. R. Computer generated tests for a student paced course. *Educational Technology*, March 1973, pp. 18–19. **489**

Coleman, J. *The adolescent society*. New York: Free Press, 1961. **92**

Coleman, J. *The psychopathology of adolescence*. New York: Grune & Stratton, 1970. **75**

Coleman, J. & Broen, W. E., Jr. *Abnormal psychology and modern life* (4th ed.). Glenview, Ill.: Scott, Foresman, 1972. **406**

Coles, R. Like it is in the alley. *Daedalus*, 1968, 97, 1315–1330. **350**

Coltheart, M. (Ed.). *Readings in cognitive psychology*. Toronto: Holt, Rinehart & Winston of Canada, 1972. **287**

Coming of age in communist China. *Newsweek*, February 21, 1972, pp. 44–46. **30**

Cook, T. W., Morrison, S. H., & Stacy, C. L. Whole and part learning in a visually perceived maze. *Journal of Genetic Psychology*, 1935, 47, 218–232. **280**

Cooley, W. W., & Glaser, R. The computer and individualized instruction. *Science*, 1969, 166, 574–579. **322**

Cooper, J. A. Application of the consultant role to parent-teacher management of school avoidance behavior. *Psychology in the Schools*, 1973, 10, 259–262. **430**

Coopersmith, S. *The antecedents of self-esteem*. San Francisco: Freeman, 1967. **89**

Coopersmith, S. Studies in self-esteem. *Scientific American*, February 1968, pp. 96–100 ff. **412**

Costanzo, P. R., & Shaw, M. E. Conformity as a function of age level. *Child Development*, 1966, 37, 967–975. **91**

Cottle, T. J. The White House conference on children. *Saturday Review*, February 20, 1971, 56–57 f. **97**

Cowen, E. L., Gardner, E. A., & Zax, M. (Eds.). *Emergent approaches to mental health problems*. New York: Appleton-Century-Crofts, 1967. **411**

Craig, R. C. *The transfer value of guided learning*. New York: Teachers College, Columbia University, 1953. **303**

Crawford, J. (Ed.). *CORD national research training manual* (2nd ed.). Monmouth, Oregon: Training Research Division of the Oregon State System of Higher Education, 1969. **259**

Cromie, W. J. Your speech may mirror your emotions. *The Pittsburgh Press Roto*, March 16, 1975, p. 16. **237**

Cronbach, L. J. How can instruction be adapted to individual differences? In R. M. Gagné (Ed.), *Learning and individual differences*. New York: Merrill, 1967. **319**

Cronbach, L. J. *Essentials of psychological testing* (3rd ed.). New York: Harper & Row, 1970. **498, 506, 510, 511, 512, 513, 514, 515**

Crow, J. F. Genetic theories and influences. *Harvard Educational Review*, 1969, 39, 301–309. **507**

Crowder, N. A. Intrinsically programmed teaching devices. *Invitational Conference on Testing Problems, Proceedings*, October 31, 1959, pp. 40–52. **135**

Cruickshank, W. M., Junkala, J. B., & Paul, J. L. *The preparation of teachers of brain-injured children*. Syracuse: Syracuse University Press, 1968. **397**

Cusimano, V. J. The test as a teaching and learning tool. *American Biology Teacher*, March 1975, pp. 176 f. **474**

Dale, P. S. *Language development*. Hinsdale, Ill.: Dryden, 1972. **237, 241, 242, 364**

Davis. A. Socio-economic influences upon children's learning. *Understanding the Child*, 1951, 20, 10–16. **516**

Davis, A. Cultural factors in remediation. *Educational Horizons*, 1965, 43, 231–251. **359**

Davis, R., & Buchwald, A. M. An exploration of somatic response patterns. *Journal of Comparative and Physiological Psychology*, 1957, 50, 44–52. **198**

Davis, R., Sutherland, N. S., & Judd, B. R. Information content in recognition and recall. *Journal of Experimental Psychology*, 1961, 61, 422–429. **288**

Day Care? In France, it's a science. *New York Times*, December 20, 1970, Section 2, p. 18. **30**

Day, W. F., & Mowrer, O. H. Beyond bondage and regimentation. (Review of *Beyond freedom and dignity*, by B. F. Skinner). *Contemporary Psychology*, 1972, 17, 465–472. **141**

DeAvila, E. A., & Havassy, B. The testing of minority children: A neo-Piagetian approach. *Today's Education*, November-December 1974, pp. 72–75. **519**

DeCecco, J. P., & Crawford, W. R. *The psychology of learning and instruction: Educational psychology* (2nd ed.). Englewood Cliffs, N.J.: Prentice-Hall, 1974. **120, 133, 136, 235, 236, 238, 239, 244, 250, 254, 260**

DeGroat, A. F., & Thompson, G. G. A study of the distribution of teacher approval and disapproval among sixth-grade pupils. *Journal of Experimental Education*, 1949, 18, 57–75. **453**

Dennison, G. *The lives of children*. New York: Vintage, 1969. **362**

Devereux, E. C., Shouval, R., Bronfenbrenner, U., Rodgers, R. R., Kav-Venaki, S., Kiely, E., & Karson, E. Socialization practices of parents, teachers, and peers in Israel: The kibbutz versus the city. *Child Development*, 1974, 45, 269–281. **18**

Divorce course. *Time*, December 2, 1974, p. 92. **84**

Divorky, D. Assault on privacy. *Intellectual Digest*, February 1974, pp. 38–39. **444**

Dodd, C. A., Jones, G. A., & Lamb, C. E. Diagnosis and remediation of pupil errors. *School Science and Mathematics*, March 1975, pp. 270–276. **467**

Domino, G. Interactive effects of achievement orientation and teaching style on academic achievement. *Journal of Educational Psychology*, 1971, 62, 427–431. **437**

Donegan, D. Unpublished manuscript. 1973. **356**

Dorros, S., & Browne, J. R. What you can do now. *Today's Education*, January 1973, pp. 41–42. **442**

Dorsey, M. F., & Hopkins, L. T. The influence of attitude upon transfer. *Journal of Educational Psychology*, 1930, 21, 410–417. **298**

Douvan, E., & Adelson, J. B. *The adolescent experience.* New York: Wiley, 1966. **92**

Doyal, G. T., & Friedman, R. J. Anxiety in children: Some observations for the school psychologist. *Psychology in the Schools,* 1974, *11,* 161–164. **420**

Doyle, W., & Redwine, J. McN. Effect of intent-action discrepancy and student performance feedback on teacher behavior change. *Journal of Educational Psychology,* 1974, *66,* 750–755. **455**

Dubois, M. E. *Developmental learning in urban areas: An overview of learning disorders for Detroit teachers.* Bay City, Mich.: Bay-Arneac Intermediate School District, 1974. (ERIC Document Reproduction Service No. ED 081 160) **397**

Dunaway, J. How to cut discipline problems in half. *Today's Education,* September-October 1974, pp. 75–77. **453**

Dwyer, F. M. *A guide for improving visualized instruction.* State College Pa.: Learning Services, 1972. **166**

Dyk, R. B., & Witkin, H. A. Family experiences related to the development of differentiation in children. *Child Development,* 1965, *36,* 21–55. **211**

Ebbinghaus, H. [*Memory: A contribution to experimental psychology*] (H. A. Ruger & C. E. Bussenius, trans.). New York: Teachers College, Columbia University, 1913. (Originally published, 1885.) **269, 289**

Ebel, R. L. The relation of testing programs to educational goals. In W. G. Findley (Ed.), *The impact and improvement of school testing programs* (62nd Yearbook of the National Society for the Study of Education, Part 2). Chicago: University of Chicago Press, 1963. **254**

Ebel, R. L. Should school marks be abolished? *Michigan Journal of Secondary Education,* 1964, *6,* 12–18. **491, 495**

Ebel, R. L. Behavioral objectives. *Phi Delta Kappan,* 1970, *52,* 171–173. **254**

Ebel, R. L. Criterion-referenced measurements. *School Review,* 1971, *79,* 282–288. **486**

Ebel, R. L. Command of knowledge should be the primary objective of education. In H. D. Thornburg (Ed.), *School learning and instruction.* Monterey, Calif.: Brooks-Cole, 1973. **174**

Eisner, E. W. Emerging models for educational evaluation. *School Review,* 1972, *80,* 573–590. **488**

Elkind, D. Children's conceptions of brother and sister: Piaget replication study V. *Journal of Genetic Psychology,* 1962, *100,* 129–136. **55**

Ellingson, C., & Cass, J. Teaching the dyslexic child: New hope for non-readers. *Saturday Review,* April 16, 1966, pp. 82–85 f. **384**

Ellis, H. C. *The transfer of learning.* New York: Macmillan, 1967. **291, 297**

Ellis, H. C. *Fundamentals of human learning and cognition.* Dubuque, Iowa: William C. Brown, 1972. **268, 278, 284, 290, 297, 299**

Enterprise: Cheating, Inc. *Newsweek,* March 20, 1972, pp. 89–90. **470**

Erikson, E. H. Identity and the life cycle: Selected papers. *Psychological Issues,* 1959, *1* (1). **200**

Erikson, E. H. *Childhood and society.* New York: Norton, 1963. **74, 76**

Erikson, E. H. *Identity: Youth and crisis.* New York: Norton, 1968. **74, 76, 96**

Ervin-Tripp, S. Language and thought. In S. Tax (Ed.), *Horizons of Anthropology.* Chicago: Aldine, 1964. **235**

Esbensen, T. Writing instructional objectives. *Phi Delta Kappan,* 1967, *48,* 246–247. **257**

Estes, W. K. *Learning theory and mental development.* New York: Academic Press, 1970. **147**

Evaluation and Advisory Service. *Short-cut statistics for teacher-made tests.* Princeton, N.J.: Educational Testing Service, 1964. **483**

Fairchild, T. N. An analysis of the services performed by a school psychologist in an urban area. *Psychology in the Schools,* 1974, *11,* 275–281. **391**

Farrell, E. J. Performance contracting. *English Journal,* 1972, *61,* 560–564. **457**

Feather, N. T. Persistence at a difficult task with alternative task of intermediate difficulty. *Journal of Abnormal and Social Psychology,* 1963, *66,* 604–609. **195**

Featherstone, J. *Schools where children learn.* New York: Liveright, 1971. **313, 315, 317**

Feingold, B. F. *Introduction to clinical allergy.* Springfield, Ill.: Charles C. Thomas, 1973. **419**

Feingold, B. F. *Why your child is hyperactive.* New York: Random House, 1975. **43**

Feldhusen, J. F., & Treffinger, D. J. Psychological background and rationale for instructional design. *Educational Technology,* October 1971, pp. 21–24. **250**

Feldmesser, R. A. The positive functions of grades. *Educational Record,* 1972, *53,* 66–72. **491**

Felker, D. W. *Building positive self-concepts.* Minneapolis: Burgess, 1974. **94**

Ferster, C. B., & Perrott, M. C. *Behavior principles.* New York: Appleton-Century-Crofts, 1968. **327**

Feshbach, N. D. Cross-cultural studies of teaching styles in four-year-olds and their mothers. In A. D. Pick (Ed.), *Minnesota Symposium on Child Psychology* (Vol. 7). Minneapolis: University of Minnesota Press, 1972. **126**

Festinger, L., & Carlsmith, J. M. Cognitive consequences of forced compliance. *Journal of Abnormal and Social Psychology,* 1959, *58,* 203–210. **248**

Fields, C. M. Students' rights versus confidential files. *Chronicle of Higher Education,* October 7, 1974, pp. 1 f. (a) **443**

Fields, C. M. 2,000 guideline critics. *Chronicle of Higher Education,* October 21, 1974, p. 7. (b) **440**

Finding out what teachers need and want. *Today's Education,* October 1972, pp. 31–35. **443**

Findley, W. G., & Bryan, M. M. *Ability grouping: 1970.* Athens: Center for Educational Improvement, University of Georgia, 1970. **395**

Fine, M. J., Nesbitt, J. A., & Tyler, M. M. Analysis of a failing attempt at behavior modification. *Journal of Learning Disabilities,* 1974, *7,* 70–75. **430**

Fisher, R. J. *Learning how to learn.* New York: Harcourt Brace Jovanovich, 1972. **315, 316, 442**

Fitts, P. M. Factors in complex skill training. In R. Glaser (Ed.), *Training research and education.* Pittsburgh: University of Pittsburgh Press, 1962. **233, 234**

Flanders, N. A. Intent, action and feedback: A preparation for teaching. *Journal of Teacher Education,* 1963, *14,* 251–260. **453, 455**

Flanders, N. A. *Analyzing teaching behavior.* Reading, Mass: Addison-Wesley, 1970. **455**

Flanders, N. A., & Havumaki, S. Group compliance to dominative teacher influence. *Human Relations,* 1960, *13,* 67–82. **451**

Flanders, N. A., Morrison, B. M., & Brode, E. L. Changes in pupil attitudes during the school year. *Journal of Educational Psychology,* 1968, *59,* 334–338. **249**

Flanders, N. A., & Simon, A. Teacher effectiveness. In R. L. Ebel (Ed.), *Encyclopedia of educational research* (4th ed.). New York: Macmillan, 1969. **455**

Flavell, J. H. *The developmental psychology of Jean Piaget.* Princeton: Van Nostrand, 1963. **51, 54, 80, 81**

Fleming, E. S., & Anttonen, R. G. Teacher expectancy or My Fair Lady. *American Educational Research Journal,* 1971, *8,* 241–252. **210**

Florida State Department of Education, Division of Elementary and Secondary Education. *District procedures for providing special education for exceptional students: 1974 guidelines* (Vol. 2). Tallahassee, Fla.: Author, 1974. (ERIC Document Reproduction Service No. ED 087 164) **386, 388**

Follman, J., Lowe, A. J., & Miller, W. Graphics variables and reliability and level of essay grades. *American Educational Research Journal,* 1971, *8,* 365–373. **483**

Fondy, A. The "merit pay" mirage. Pittsburgh: Pittsburgh Federation of Teachers, AFT, AFL-CIO, June 1973. **459**

Fontana, G. L. J. An investigation into the dynamics of achievement motivation in women. (Doctoral dissertation, University of Michigan, 1970). *Dissertation Abstracts International,* 1971, *32B,* 1821B. (University Microfilms No. 71–23, 754) **211**

Frank, G. H. The role of the family in the development of psychopathology. *Psychological Bulletin,* 1965, *64,* 191–205. **42**

Franklin, B. A. The Appalachian creekers: Literally, a world apart. *New York Times,* October 27, 1974, p. 10. **439**

Fraser, S. E., & Hawkins, J. N. Chinese education: Revolution and development. *Phi Delta Kappan,* 1972, *53,* 487–500. **435**

Freud, A. [*The ego and the mechanisms of defence.*] (C. Baines, trans.). London: Hogarth, 1937. **78**

Freud, A., & Burlingham, D. T. *War and children.* New York: International Universities Press, 1943. **23**

Freud, A., & Burlingham, D. T. *Infants without families.* New York: International Universities Press, 1944. **23**

Freud, S. [*The basic writings of Sigmund Freud*] (A. A. Brill, Ed. & trans.). New York: Modern Library, 1938. **76**

Freud, S. [*An outline of psychoanalysis.*] (J. Strachey, trans.). New York: Norton, 1949. **96**

Freyberg, J. T. Increasing children's fantasies. *Psychology Today,* February 1975, pp. 63–64. **216**

Frieder, B. Motivator: Least developed of teacher roles. *Educational Technology,* February 1970, pp. 28–36. **221**

Friedman, R. J., & Doyal, G. T. Depression in children. *Psychology in the Schools,* 1974, *11,* 19–23. **422**

Friedrich, L. K., & Stein, A. H. Aggressive and prosocial television programs and the natural behavior of preschool children. *Monographs of the Society for Research in Child Development,* 1973, *38*(4, Serial No. 151). **34**

Fries, C. C. *Linguistics and reading.* New York: Holt, Rinehart & Winston, 1963. **241**

From a student—William (Mannix) Smith. In J. Bremer & M. von Moschzisker (Eds.), *The school without walls: Philadelphia's Parkway Program.* New York: Holt, Rinehart & Winston, 1971. **335**

Frostig, M., & Maslow, P. *Learning problems in the classroom.* New York: Grune & Stratton, 1973. **386**

Fuchs, E. How teachers learn to help children fail. In J. McV. Hunt (Ed.), *Human intelligence.* New Brunswick, N.J.: Transaction Books, 1972. **360**

Furth, H. *Piaget for teachers.* Englewood Cliffs, N.J.: Prentice-Hall, 1970. **69**

Furth, H. G., Youniss, J., & Ross, B. M. Children's utilization of logical symbols. *Developmental Psychology,* 1970, *3,* 36–57. **55**

Gagné, R. M. The analysis of instructional objectives for the design of instruction. In R. Glaser (Ed.), *Teaching machines and programmed learning. II: Data and directions.* Washington, D.C.: National Education Association, 1965. (a) **250**

Gagné, R. M. Educational objectives and human performance. In J. D. Krumboltz (Ed.), *Learning and the educational process.* Chicago: Rand McNally, 1965. (b) **254, 255, 256**

Gagné, R. M. The learning of concepts. *School Review,* 1965, *73,* 187–196. (c) **242, 243, 244, 246**

Gagné, R. M. Contributions of learning to human development. *Psychological Review,* 1968, *75,* 177–191. **56**

Gagné, R. M. Context, isolation, and interference effects on the retention of fact. *Journal of Educational Psychology,* 1969, *60,* 408–414. **280**

Gagné, R. M. *The conditions of learning* (2nd ed.). New York: Holt, Rinehart & Winston, 1970. **111, 182, 236, 242, 246, 281, 307**

Gagné, R. M. *Essentials of learning for instruction.* Hinsdale, Ill.: Dryden, 1974. **255**

Gagné, R. M., & Briggs, L. J. *Principles of instructional design.* New York: Holt, Rinehart & Winston, 1974. **250, 319, 320, 323, 327**

Gall, M. D., & Ward, B. A. *Critical issues in educational psychology.* Boston: Little, Brown, 1974. **456, 457, 490**

Galloway, C. Precision parents and the development of retarded behavior. In J. B. Jordan & L. S. Robbins (Eds.), *Let's try doing something else kind of thing: Behavioral principles and the exceptional child.* Arlington, Va.: Council for Exceptional Children, 1972. **398, 401**

Gallup, G. H. Fourth annual Gallup poll of public attitudes toward education. *Phi Delta Kappan,* 1972, *54,* 33–46. **458**

Gardner, J. W. The relation of certain personality variables to level of aspiration. *Journal of Psychology,* 1940, *9,* 191–206. **196**

Garrett, H. E. *Testing for teachers.* New York: American Book, 1965. **532**

Garskof, B. E., Garskof, M. H., & Faragher, J. M. The child care community: A model for development of indigenous resources to meet day care needs. *Proceedings of the 81st Annual Convention of the American Psychological Association,* 1973, *8,* 959–960. **32**

Genshaft, J. L., & Hirst, M. Language differences between black children and white children. *Developmental Psychology,* 1974, *10,* 451–456. **358**

Gentile, A. M. A working model of skill acquisition with application to teaching. *Quest,* 1972, *17,* 1–23. **230, 231, 232**

Georgiady, N. P., & Romano, L. G. Ulcerville, U.S.A. *Educational Leadership,* December 1971, pp. 269–272. **470**

Gerbner, G. Drama: Trends & symbolic violence in television functions. In G. A. Comstock & E. A. Rubenstein (Eds.), *Television and social behavior: Media content and control.* Washington, D.C.: U.S. Government Printing Office, 1972. **34**

Gesell, A. L., & Amatruda, C. S. *Developmental diagnosis: Normal and abnormal child development* (2nd ed.) New York: Hoeber, 1947. **49**

Getzels, J. W. Conflict and role behavior in the educational setting. In W. W. Charters, Jr. & N. L. Gage (Eds.), *Readings in the social psychology of education.* Boston: Allyn & Bacon, 1963. **435**

Gewirtz, H. B., & Gewirtz, J. L. Caretaking settings, background events and behavior differences in four Israeli child-rearing environments. In I. J. Gordon (Ed.), *Readings in research in developmental psychology.* Glenview, Ill.: Scott, Foresman, 1971. **18**

Gibson, E. J. Learning to read. *Science,* 1965, *148,* 1066–1072. **70, 225, 226**

Gibson, E. J. Perceptual learning in educational situations. In R. M. Gagné & W. J. Gephart (Eds.), *Learning research and school subjects.* Itasca, Ill.: Peacock, 1968. **225, 226**

Gibson, E. J. *Principles of perceptual learning and development.* New York: Appleton-Century-Crofts, 1969. **175, 176**

Gibson, E. J. The development of perception as an adaptive process. *American Scientist,* 1970, *58,* 98–107. **176**

Gibson, E. J., Pick, A., Osser, H., & Hammond, M. The role of grapheme-phoneme correspondence in the perception of words. *American Journal of Psychology,* 1962, *75,* 554–570. **225**

Gibson, J. T. *Educational psychology* (2nd ed.). New York: Appleton-Century-Crofts, 1972. **201, 225, 242, 313, 315, 316, 317, 319, 352**

Gibson, J. T. *Experiencing the inner city.* New York: Harper & Row, 1973. (a) **3**

Gibson, J. T. *Principles of instruction.* Pittsburgh: University of Pittsburgh Press, 1973. (b) **316**

Gibson, J. T. *Goals of educational psychology in teacher preparation.* Paper presented the meeting of the American Educational Research Association, Washington, D.C., March 1975. **1**

Ginott, H. G. *Between parent and child.* New York: Macmillan, 1965. **15**

Gladis, M. Grade differences in transfer as a function of the time interval between learning tasks. *Journal of Educational Psychology,* 1960, *51,* 191–194. **303**

Glaser, R. Psychology and instructional technology. In R. Glaser (Ed.), *Training research and education.* Pittsburgh: University of Pittsburgh Press, 1962. **486**

Glaser, R. Concept learning and concept teaching. In R. M. Gagné & W. J. Gephart (Eds.), *Learning research and school subjects.* Itasca, Ill.: Peacock, 1968. **242, 244, 245**

Glaser, R., & Resnick, L. B. Instructional psychology. *Annual Review of Psychology,* 1972, *23,* 207–276. **61, 134, 225, 280**

Glass, G. V. The many faces of "educational accountability." *Phi Delta Kappan,* 1972, *53,* 636–639. **456**

Glass, G. V., & Stanley, J. C. *Statistical methods in education and psychology.* Englewood Cliffs, N.J.: Prentice-Hall, 1970. **379**

Goldberg, C. Some effects of fear of failure in the academic setting. *Journal of Psychology,* 1973, *84,* 323–331. **217**

Goldstein, K. M., & Tilker, H. A. Attitudes toward A-B-C-D-F and honors-pass-fail grading systems. *Journal of Educational Research,* 1971, *65,* 99–100. **492**

Golick, M. *A parents' guide to learning problems.* Montreal, Quebec: Association for Children with Learning Disabilities, 1970. **387**

Goolsby, T. M., Jr. The validity of the college level examinations programs' tests for use at the college sophomore level. *Educational and Psychological Measurement,* 1970, *30,* 375–380. **518**

Gores, H. B. Schools in the 70's. *National Association of Secondary School Principals Bulletin,* May 1970, *54,* 134–138. **317**

Grade-School Philosophers. *Time,* November 18, 1974, p. 74. **62**

Graubard, A. The free school movement. *Harvard Educational Review,* 1972, *42,* 351–373. **330, 331, 339**

Gray, F., Graubard, P. S., & Rosenberg, H. Little brother is changing you. *Psychology Today,* March 1974, pp. 42–46. **131**

Green, J. A. *Teacher-made tests.* New York: Harper & Row, 1963. **493**

Green, R. L. The black quest for higher education. *Personnel and Guidance Journal,* 1969, *47,* 905–911. **374**

Green, R. L., Smith, E., & Schweitzer, J. H. Busing and the multiracial classroom. *Phi Delta Kappan,* 1972, *53,* 543–547. **438**

Greeno, J. G., James, C. T., & DaPolito, F. J. A cognitive interpretation of negative transfer and forgetting of paired associates. *Journal of Verbal Learning and Verbal Behavior,* 1971, *10,* 331–345. **302**

Grier, W. H., & Cobbs, P. M. *Black rage.* New York: Basic Books, 1968. **415**

Grimes, J. W., & Allinsmith, W. Compulsivity, anxiety, and school achievement. *Merrill-Palmer Quarterly,* 1961, *7,* 247–271. **203**

Gronlund, N. E. *Preparing criterion-referenced tests for classroom instruction.* New York: Macmillan, 1973. **485, 487**

Gross, B., & Gross, R. A little bit of chaos. *Saturday Review,* May 16, 1970, pp. 71–73 ff. **69, 313, 315, 316**

Gross, R., & Osterman, P. (Eds.). *High school.* New York: Simon & Schuster, 1971. **410**

Guilford, J. P. The structure of intellect. *Psychological Bulletin,* 1956, *53,* 267–293. **154**

Guilford, J. P. Intelligence has three facets. *Science,* 1968, *160,* 615–620. **507**

Gullotta, T. P. Teacher attitudes toward the moderately disturbed child. *Exceptional Children,* 1974, *41,* 49–50. **412**

Guthrie, E. R. *The psychology of learning* (Rev. ed.). New York: Harper & Brothers, 1952. **109**

Haan, N. Moral redefinition in families as the critical aspect of the generational gap. *Youth and Society,* 1971, *2,* 259–283. **97**

Hackett, R. In praise of praise. *American Education,* March 1975, pp. 11–15. **427**

Hagen, J. W., & Hale, G. H. The development of attention in children. In A. D. Pick (Ed.), *Minnesota Symposia on Child Psychology* (Vol. 7). Minneapolis: University of Minnesota Press, 1972. **261**

Hales, L. W., Bain, P. T., & Rand, L. P. The pass-fail option. *Journal of Educational Research,* 1973, *66,* 295–298. **217**

Hall, C. S., & Lindzey, G. *Theories of personality.* New York: Wiley, 1957. **76**

Hall, J. W., & Pressley, G. M. *Free recall and recognition memory in young children.* Paper presented at the Annual Meeting of the Psychonomic Society, St. Louis, November 1973. **289**

Hall, K. A. Computer-assisted instruction. *Phi Delta Kappan,* 1971, *52,* 628–631. **322**

Hall, R. V., Axelrod, S., Foundopoulos, M., Shellman, J., Campbell, R. A., & Cranston, S. S. The effective use of punishment to modify behavior in the classroom. *Educational Technology,* April 1971, pp. 24–26. **119**

Hallahan, D. P., Kauffman, J. M., & Ball, D. W. Selective attention and cognitive tempo of low achieving and high achieving sixth grade males. *Perceptual and Motor Skills,* 1973, *36,* 579–583. **262**

Hamblen, A. A. *Investigation to determine the extent to which the effect of the study of Latin upon a knowledge of English derivatives can be increased by conscious adaptation of content and method to the attainment of this objective.* Philadelphia: University of Pennsylvania Press, 1925. **295**

Hamm, N. H., & Hoving, K. L. Conformity of children in an ambiguous perceptual situation. *Child Development,* 1969, *40,* 773–784. **91**

Harari, H., & McDavid, J. W. Name stereotypes and teachers' expectations. *Journal of Educational Psychology,* 1973, *65,* 222–225. **437**

Harlow, H. F. The formation of learning sets. *Psychological Review,* 1949, *56,* 51–65. **244, 299**

Harlow, H. F. The nature of love. *American Psychologist,* 1958, *13,* 673–685. **22**

Harlow, H. F., & Harlow, M. K. Learning to love. *American Scientist,* 1966, *54,* 244–272. **22**

Harlow, H. F., Harlow, M. K., & Meyer, D. R. Learning

motivated by a manipulation drive. *Journal of Experimental Psychology*, 1950, *40*, 228–234. **198, 218**

Harlow, H. F., & Zimmermann, R. R. Affectional responses in the infant monkey. *Science*, 1959, *130*, 421–432. **22**

Harper, R. A. *Psychoanalysis and psychotherapy*. New York: Jason Aronson, 1974. **430, 431**

Harrington, C., & Whiting, J. W. M. Socialization process and personality. In F. L. K. Hsu (Ed.), *Psychological anthropology* (2nd ed.). Cambridge, Mass.: Schenkman, 1972. **12, 17**

Harris, D. Factors affecting college grades: A review of the literature, 1930–1937. *Psychological Bulletin*, 1940, 37, 125–166. **518**

Harris, D. V., & Reese, J. *A comparative study of the influence of six techniques in modifying undesirable behavior in adolescents*. Paper presented at the meeting of the Southwestern Psychological Association, 1969. **126**

Harris, T. G. To know why men do what they do: A conversation with David C. McClelland. *Psychology Today*, January 1971, pp. 35–39 ff. **197**

Harrison, M. *Instant reading: The story of the initial teaching alphabet*. London: Pitman, 1964. **241**

Hart, V. *Multi-handicapped: The king of challengers*. Paper presented at the Biennial Conference of the Association for the Education of the Visually Handicapped, 1972. **392**

Hartley, E. L., & Hartley, R. E. *Fundamentals of social psychology*. New York: Knopf, 1952. **12**

Hartman, C. L. Describing behavior: Search for an alternative to grading. *Educational Leadership*, January 1975, pp. 274–277. **467**

Hartshorne, H., & May, M. A. *Studies in the organization of character*. New York: Macmillan, 1930. **92**

Hartup, W. W. Peer interaction and social organization. In P. H. Mussen (Ed.), *Carmichael's manual of child psychology* (3rd. ed.) (Vol. 2). New York: Wiley, 1970. **40**

Harvey, J. C., & Holmes, C. H. Busing and school desegregation. *Phi Delta Kappan*, 1972, *53*, 540–542. **438**

Haslerud, G. M., & Meyers, S. The transfer value of given and individually derived principles. *Journal of Educational Psychology*, 1958, *49*, 293–298. **296**

Hassett, J. D., & Weisberg, A. *Open education*. Englewood Cliffs, N.J.: Prentice-Hall, 1972. **315, 316**

Havemann, E. Alternatives to analysis. *Playboy*, November 1969. **431**

Havighurst, R. J. *Developmental tasks and education* (2nd ed.). New York: Longmans, Green, 1952. **70**

Havighurst, R. J. *Human development and education*. New York: Longmans, Green, 1953. **405**

Havighurst, R. J. Minority subcultures and the law of effect. *American Psychologist*, 1970, 25, 313–322. **350, 359**

Heathers, G. Grouping. In R. L. Ebel (Ed.), *Encyclopedia of educational research* (4th ed.). New York: Macmillan, 1969. **394, 395**

Hebb, D. O. On the nature of fear. *Psychological Review*, 1946, *53*, 259–276. **202**

Hebb, D. O. A return to Jensen and his social science critics. *American Psychologist*, 1970, 25, 568. **507**

Hechinger, G., & Hechinger, F. M. The corporal punishment debate, updated. *New York Times Magazine*, October 6, 1974, pp. 84 ff. **452**

Henry, J. Attitude organization in elementary school classrooms. *American Journal of Orthopsychiatry*, 1957, 27, 117–133. **450**

Henry, J. Of achievement, hope, and time in poverty. In J. McV. Hunt (Ed.), *Human intelligence*. New Brunswick, N.J.: Transaction Books, 1972. **363**

Hentoff, N. A parent-teacher's view of corporal punishment. *Today's Education*, May 1973, pp. 18–21 f. **452**

Hess, R., & Shipman, V. *Parents as teachers: How lower class and middle class mothers teach*. Urbana: University of Illinois, 1967. (ERIC Document Reproduction Service No. ED 025–301) **63, 64**

Hetherington, E. M. Effects of paternal absence on sex-typed behaviors in Negro and White preadolescent males. *Journal of Personality and Social Psychology*, 1966, 4, 87–91. **25**

Hewett, F. M. Teaching speech to an autistic child through operant conditioning. *American Journal of Orthopsychiatry*, 1965, *35*, 927–936. **402**

Hilgard, E. R., & Bower, G. H. *Theories of learning* (4th ed.). Englewood Cliffs, N.J.: Prentice-Hall, 1975. **116, 118, 136, 148, 154, 155, 156, 272**

Hill, W. F. *Learning: A survey of psychological interpretations*. San Francisco: Chandler, 1971. **109, 122, 149, 150, 152, 154, 155, 156, 158**

Hoffman, M. L. Homosexuality. *Today's Education*, November 1970, pp. 46–48. (a) **424**

Hoffman, M. L. Moral development. In P. H. Mussen (Ed.), *Carmichael's manual of child psychology* (3rd ed.) (Vol. 2). New York: Wiley, 1970. (b) **40**

Hoffman, M. L., & Saltzstein, H. D. Parent discipline and the child's moral development. *Journal of Personality and Social Psychology*, 1967, *5*, 45–57. **81**

Holland, J. G. *Design and use of a teaching machine program*. Paper presented at the meeting of the American Psychological Association, Chicago, 1960. **138**

Holland, J. G. *Behavior modification for prisoners, patients, and other people as a prescription for the planned society*. Paper presented at the meeting of the Eastern Psychological Association, Philadelphia, April 1974. **141**

Holstein, C. E. *The relation of children's moral judgment level to that of their parents and to communication patterns in the family*. Paper presented at the Biennial Meeting of the Society for Research in Child Development, Santa Monica, Calif., 1969. **86**

Holt, J. *What do I do Monday?* New York: Dutton, 1970. **493**

Holzman, P. S., & Klein, G. S. Cognitive system principles of leveling and sharpening: Individual differences in assimilation effects in visual time-error. *Journal of Psychology*, 1954, *37*, 105–122. **262**

Honkavaara, S. Organization process in perception as a measure of intelligence. *Journal of Psychology*, 1958, *46*, 3-12. **176**

Honzik, M. P., MacFarlane, J. W., & Allen, L. The stability of mental test performance between two and eighteen years. *Journal of Experimental Education*, 1948, *17*, 309–324. **513**

Horner, M. S. Toward an understanding of achievement-related conflicts in women. *Journal of Social Issues*, 1972, *28*(2) 157–175. **211**

Hottleman, G. D. Collective bargaining and the emerging profession. *Today's Education*, December 1972, pp. 49–50. **447**

House, B. J. Discrimination of symmetrical and asymmetrical dot patterns by retardates. *Journal of Experimental Child Psychology*, 1966, *3*, 377–389. **176**

Houts, P. S., & Entwisle, D. R. Academic achievement effort among females. *Journal of Counseling Psychology*, 1968, *15*, 284–286. **211**

Hoving, K. L., Hamm, N., & Galvin, P. Social influence as a function of stimulus ambiguity at three age levels. *Developmental Psychology*, 1969, *1*, 631–636. **91**

Howe, F. Sexism, racism, and the education of women. *Today's Education*, May 1973, pp. 47–48. **442**

Howsam, R. B. Some basic concepts. *Today's Education*, April 1972, pp. 35–40. **457**

Hraba, J., & Grant, G. Black is beautiful: A reexamination of racial preference and identification. *Journal of Personality & Social Psychology*, 1970, *16*, 398–402. **360**

Hsu, T. C., & Carlson, M. *Oakleaf school project: Computer-assisted achievement testing.* Pittsburgh: Learning Research and Development Center, University of Pittsburgh, February 1972. **486**

Huck, S., & Bounds, W. Essay grades: An interaction between graders' handwriting clarity and the neatness of examination papers. *American Educational Research Journal.* 1972, *9*, 279–283. **483**

Huff, D., & Geis, I. *How to lie with statistics.* New York: Norton, 1954. **526**

Hulse, S. H., Deese, J. E., & Egeth, H. *The psychology of learning* (4th ed.). New York: McGraw-Hill, 1975. **268**

Hunt, J. McV. *Development and the educational enterprise.* Paper delivered at the college of Education at Hofstra University, Hempstead, N.Y., November 15, 1973. **59**

Hunter, M. C. The role of physical education in child development and learning. In H. D. Behrens & G. Maynard (Eds.), *The changing child.* Glenview, Ill.: Scott, Foresman, 1972. **230**

Hurlock, E. B. Experimental investigations of childhood play. In R. E. Herron & B. Sutton-Smith (Eds.), *Child's play.* New York: Wiley, 1971. **33**

Husen, T. *International study of achievement in mathematics* (Vol. 2). Uppsala, Sweden: Almquist and Wiksells, 1967. **396**

Hyram, G. H. *Socio-psychological concepts related to teaching the culturally disadvantaged.* New York: Pageant-Poseidon, 1972. **374**

If you want to give up cigarettes. New York: American Cancer Society, 1970. **132**

Illich, I. *Deschooling society.* New York: Harper & Row, 1971. **333, 334**

Instamatic therapy. Human Behavior, February 1973, p. 30. **413**

Israel, B. Success grows in Brooklyn. *Audiovisual Instruction,* December 1969, pp. 40–42. **317**

Jackson, P. W. *The teacher and the machine.* Pittsburgh: University of Pittsburgh Press, 1968. **320, 325**

Jacobs, C., & Eaton, C. Sexism in the elementary school. *Today's Education,* December 1972, pp. 20–22. **440**

Jacoby, S. Who raises Russia's children? *Saturday Review,* August 21, 1971, pp. 40–43 f. **27, 28**

James, W. *Principles of psychology.* New York: Holt, 1890. **292**

Jason, L., Clarfield, S., & Cowen, E. L. Preventative intervention with young disadvantaged children. *American Journal of Community Psychology,* 1973, *1*(1), 50–61. **365**

Jenkins, J. G., & Dallenbach, K. M. Oblivescence during sleep and waking. *American Journal of Psychology,* 1924, *35*, 605–612. **273**

Jensen, A. How much can we boost IQ and scholastic achievement? *Harvard Educational Review,* 1969, *39*, 1–123. **507**

Jensen, D. D. Toward efficient, effective and humane instruction in large classes: Student scheduled involvement in films, discussions and computer generated repeatable tests. *Educational Technology,* March 1973, pp. 28–29. **488**

Jerman, M. Computers, instruction, and the curriculum. In R. W. Burns & G. D. Brooks (Eds.), *Curriculum design in a changing society.* Englewood Cliffs, N.J.: Educational Technology Publications, 1970. **322**

Johnson, E. C. Precision teaching helps children learn. *Teaching Exceptional Children,* 1971, *3*, 106–110. **328**

Johnson, N. J. A. *Four steps to precision teaching.* Unpublished manuscript, Western Illinois University, 1973. **328, 329, 369, 371, 372, 373**

Johnson, R. C. A study of children's moral judgments. *Child Development,* 1962, *33*, 327–354. **86**

Johnston, J. E. Effects of imagery on learning the volleyball pass. (Doctoral dissertation, Temple University, 1971). *Dissertation Abstracts International,* 1972, *32A*, 772A. (University Microfilms No. 71–19, 985) **233**

Jones, R. L. Labels and stigma in special education. *Exceptional Children,* 1972, *38*, 553–564. **389, 390**

José, J., & Cody, J. J. Teacher-pupil interaction as it relates to attempted changes in teacher expectancy of academic ability and achievement. *American Educational Research Journal,* 1971, *8*, 39–49. **210**

Journard, S. M. *The transparent self.* New York: Van Nostrand-Reinhold, 1971. **406**

Judd, C. The relation of special training to general intelligence. *Educational Review,* 1908, *36*, 28–42. **4, 294**

Judd, C. H. *Educational psychology.* New York: Houghton Mifflin, 1939. **294**

Kagan, J. The concept of identification. *Psychological Review,* 1958, *65*, 296–305. **78, 79**

Kagan, J. Reflection-impulsivity. *Journal of Abnormal Psychology,* 1966, *71*, 17–24. **262**

Kagan, J. *Personality development.* New York: Harcourt Brace Jovanovich, 1971. **408**

Kagan, J., & Moss, H. A. The stability of passive and dependent behavior from childhood through adulthood. *Child Development,* 1960, *31*, 577–591. **75**

Kagan, J., Moss, H. A., & Siegel, I. E. Psychological significance of styles of conceptualization. In J. C. Wright & J. Kagan (Eds.), Basic cognitive processes in children. *Monographs of the Society for Research in Child Development,* 1963, *28*(2, Serial No. 86). **260**

Kamii, C. An application of Piaget's theory to the conceptualization of a preschool curriculum. In R. K. Parker (Ed.), *Exploring early childhood programs.* Boston: Allyn & Bacon, 1972. **67**

Kamii, C. K., & Radin, N. L. Class differences in the socialization practices of Negro mothers. *Journal of Marriage and the Family,* 1967, *29*, 302–310. **36**

Karagianis, L. D., & Merricks, D. L. (Eds.). *Where the action is: Teaching exceptional children.* St. John's, Newfoundland: Memorial University, 1973. (ERIC Document Reproduction Service No. ED 084 764) **380, 381, 382, 389, 390, 399, 401**

Karnes, M. B., Teska, J. A., Hodgins, A. S., & Badger, E. D. Educational intervention at home by mothers of disadvantaged infants. *Child Development,* 1970, *41*, 925–935. **364**

Karnes, M. B., Zehrbach, R. R., & Jones, G. R. *The culturally disadvantaged student and guidance.* Boston: Houghton Mifflin, 1971. **354**

Kaufman, B. A love letter to a dead teacher. *Today's Education,* March-April 1975, pp. 20–23. **454**

Keller, F. S. Goodby, teacher. . . . *Journal of Applied Behavior Analysis,* 1968, *1*, 79–89. **488**

Keogh, B. K., Tchir, C., & Windeguth-Behn, A. Teachers' perceptions of educationally high-risk children. *Journal of Learning Disabilities,* 1974, *7*, 367–374. **412**

Keyserling, M. D. *Windows on day care.* New York: National Council of Jewish Women, 1972. **30, 31, 32, 364**

King, S., & Frignac, D. *Teaching objectives for the emotionally handicapped.* Phoenix, Arizona: Creighton School District No. 14, 1973. (ERIC Document Reproduction Service No. ED 081 144) **426**

Kinkade, K. Commune: A Walden Two experiment. *Psychology Today,* January 1973, pp. 35–42 ff. **141**

Kintsch, W. *Learning, memory, and conceptual processes.* New York: Wiley, 1970. **269**

Klaus, D. J. *Instructional innovation and individualization.* Pittsburgh: American Institutes for Research, 1971. **60, 319, 321, 322, 324**

Klausmeier, H. J., & Ripple, R. E. Effects of accelerating bright older pupils from second to fourth grade. *Journal of Educational Psychology,* 1962, *53,* 93–100. **395**

Klausmeier, H. J., Sorenson, J. S., & Ghatala, E. S. Individually guided motivation. *Elementary School Journal,* 1971, *71,* 339–350. **489**

Klein, G. S., Gardner, R. W., & Schlesinger, H. J. Tolerance for unrealistic experiences. *British Journal of Psychology,* 1962, *53,* 41–55. **262**

Klein, R. D., & Schuler, C. F. *Increasing academic performance through the contingent use of self-evaluation.* Paper presented at the Annual Meeting of the American Educational Research Association, Chicago, April 1974. **208**

Kleinmuntz, B. *Essentials of abnormal psychology.* New York: Harper & Row, 1974. **417**

Koffka, K. *Principles of Gestalt psychology.* New York: Harcourt, Brace, 1935. **148**

Kohl, H. R. *The open classroom.* New York: Vintage, 1969. **316, 317**

Kohlberg, L. The development of children's orientation toward a moral order: Sequence in the development of moral thought. *Vita Humana,* 1963, *6,* 11–33. **82, 83**

Kohlberg, L. Development of moral character and moral ideology. In M. L. Hoffman & L. W. Hoffman (Eds.), *Review of child development research* (Vol. 1). New York: Russell Sage Foundation, 1964. **82, 83**

Kohlberg, L. Stages of moral development as a basis for moral education. In C. M. Beck, B. S. Crittenden & E. V. Sullivan (Eds.), *Moral Education.* Toronto: University of Toronto Press, 1971. **85**

Köhler, W. [*The mentality of apes*] (E. Winter, trans.). New York: Harcourt, Brace, 1925. **153**

Kotz, N. *Let them eat promises: The politics of hunger in America.* Englewood Cliffs, N.J.: Prentice-Hall, 1969. **353**

Kounin, J. S. *Discipline and group management in classrooms.* New York: Holt, Rinehart & Winston, 1970. **207**

Kounin, J. S., & Gump, P. V. The comparative influence of punitive and nonpunitive teachers upon children's concepts of school misconduct. *Journal of Educational Psychology,* 1961, *52,* 44–49. **452**

Krathwohl, D. R. The taxonomy of educational objectives. In C. M. Lindvall (Ed.), *Defining educational objectives.* Pittsburgh: University of Pittsburgh Press, 1964. **251**

Krathwohl, D. R., Bloom, B. S., & Masia, B. B. *A taxonomy of educational objectives* (Handbook 2). New York: David McKay, 1964. **251**

Kryspin, W. J., & Feldhusen, J. F. *Analyzing verbal classroom interaction.* Minneapolis: Burgess, 1974. (a) **455**

Kryspin, W. J., & Feldhusen, J. F. *Writing Behavioral Objectives.* Minneapolis: Burgess, 1974. (b) **283**

Kuhlen, R. G. Needs, perceived need satisfaction opportunities, and satisfaction with occupation. *Journal of Applied Psychology,* 1963, *47,* 56–64. **461**

Lambert, W. E. *Language, psychology, and culture: Essays by Wallace E. Lambert* (A. S. Dil, Ed.). Stanford: Stanford University Press, 1972. **358**

Lambert, W. W., Triandis, L. M., & Wolf, M. Some correlates of beliefs in the malevolence and benevolence of supernatural beings. *Journal of Abnormal and Social Psychology,* 1959, *58,* 162–169. **17**

Landis, J. T. The trauma of children when parents divorce. *Marriage and Family Living,* 1960, *22,* 7–13. **408**

Langdon, J. S. Court rules girls can compete with boys in PIAA. *Pittsburgh Press,* March 19, 1975, p. 1. **234**

Lawton, E. Should teachers see student records? Yes. *National Education Association Journal,* October 1966, pp. 35–37. **494**

Leacock, E. B. *Teaching and learning in city schools.* New York: Basic Books, 1969. **210**

Lecky, P. *Self-consistency: A theory of personality.* New York: Island Press, 1945. **88**

Leinhardt, G. *A training program for selected teacher functions.* Pittsburgh: Learning Research and Development Center, University of Pittsburgh, 1973. **320**

Lennon, R. T. *Accountability and performance contracting.* Paper presented at the Annual Meeting of the American Educational Research Association, New York, February, 1971. **520**

Lessinger, L. M. The powerful notion of accountability in education. *Journal of Secondary Education,* 1970, *45,* 339–347. **455, 456, 457**

Levenson, D. Make phys ed fit. *Teacher,* February 1975, pp. 58–60 ff. **234**

Levine, S., Chevalier, J. A., & Korchin, S. J. The effects of early shock and handling on later avoidance learning. *Journal of Personality,* 1956, *24,* 475–493. **203**

Levy, B. Do teachers sell girls short? *Today's Education,* December 1972, pp. 27–29. **440, 442**

Lewin, K. [*A dynamic theory of personality*] (D. K. Adams & K. E. Zener, trans.). New York: McGraw-Hill, 1935. **156**

Lewin, K. [*Principles of topological psychology*] (F. Heider & G. M. Heider, trans.). New York: McGraw-Hill, 1936. **156**

Lewin, K. *Field theory in social science.* New York: Harper & Brothers, 1951. **156**

Lewin, K. Studies in group decision. In D. Cartwright & A. Zander (Eds.), *Group dynamics: Research and theory.* Evanston, Ill.: Row, Peterson, 1953. **451**

Lewis, O. The culture of poverty. *Scientific American,* October 1966, pp. 19–25. **350**

Lewis, W. W. Project RE-ED: Educational intervention in discordant child rearing systems. In E. L. Cowen, E. A. Gardner & M. Zax (Eds.), *Emergent approaches to mental health problems.* New York: Appleton-Century-Crofts, 1967. **425**

Lindsay, P. H., & Norman, D. A. *Human information processing.* New York: Academic Press, 1972. **269, 270, 272**

Lindvall, C. M., & Bolvin, J. O. The role of the teacher in individually prescribed instruction. *Educational Technology,* February 1970, pp. 37–41. **320**

Little, J. K. Results of use of machines for testing and for drill upon learning in educational psychology. *Journal of Experimental Education,* 1934, *3,* 45–49. **466**

Loftus, E. Reconstructing memory. *Psychology Today,* December 1974, pp. 116–119. **275**

Long, N. J., Morse, W. C., & Newman, R. G. *Conflict in the classroom: The education of emotionally disturbed children* (2nd ed.). Belmont, Calif.: Wadsworth, 1971, **408**

Lovell, K., & Ogilvie, E. A study of the conservation of substance in the Junior School child. *British Journal of Educational Psychology,* 1960, *30,* 109–118. **55**

Lowe, W. T. *Structure and the social studies.* Ithaca: Cornell University Press, 1969. **164, 167, 169, 173**

Lowell, J. *Dear folks.* New York: Putnam's, 1960. **53**

Luria, A. K. Towards the problem of the historical nature of psychological processes. *International Journal of Psychology,* 1971, *6,* 259–272. **57**

Lynn, D. B. *The father: His role in child development.* Monterey, Calif.: Brooks-Cole, 1974. **16**

Maccoby, E. *Sex differences revisited, myth and reality.* Address presented at the Annual Meeting of the American Educational Research Association, Chicago, 1974. **36, 37**

Madden, P. C. Skinner and the open classroom. *School Review,* 1972, *81,* 100–107. **317**

Madsen, C. K., & Madsen, C. H., Jr. You are already using behavior modification. In *Annual Readings in Psychology 73–74*. Guilford, Conn: Dushkin, 1973. **128**

Maehr, M. L., & Sjogren, D. D. Atkinson's theory of achievement motivation: First step toward a theory of academic motivation? *Review of Educational Research*, 1971, *41*, 143–161. **194, 195, 209**

Mager, R. F. *Preparing instructional objectives*. Belmont, Calif.: Fearon, 1962. **256**

Margolin, E. *Sociocultural elements in early childhood education*. New York: Macmillan, 1974. **15, 20, 37, 39**

Markle, S. M., & Tiemann, P. W. Problems of conceptual learning. *British Journal of Educational Technology*, 1970, *1*, 52–62. **244, 246, 247**

Marshall, J. C. Composition errors and essay examination grades re-examined. *American Educational Research Journal*, 1967, *4*, 375–385. **483**

Marshall, J. C., & Powers, J. M. Writing neatness, composition errors, and essay grades. *Journal of Educational Measurement*, 1969, *6*, 97–101. **483**

Marwit, S. J., Marwit, K. L., & Boswell, J. J. Negro children's use of nonstandard grammar. *Journal of Educational Psychology*, 1972, *63*, 218–224. **358**

Marx, M. Some suggestions for the conceptual and theoretical analysis of complex intervening variables in problem-solving behavior. *Journal of General Psychology*, 1958, *58*, 115–128. **154**

Marx, M. (Ed.). *Learning: Theories*. New York: Macmillan, 1970. **146**

Marx, M., & Tombaugh, T. *Motivation*. San Francisco: Chandler, 1967. **187, 188, 215**

Maslow, A. H. A theory of human motivation. *Psychological Review*, 1943, *50*, 370–396. **189, 190, 191**

Maslow, A. H. *Motivation and personality*. New York: Harper & Brothers, 1954. **189, 192**

Maslow, A. H. *Toward a psychology of being* (2nd ed.). Princeton: Van Nostrand-Reinhold, 1968. **189, 190**

Maslow, A. H. *Farther reaches of human nature*. New York: Viking Press, 1971. **205**

Mattsson, K. D. Personality traits associated with effective teaching in rural and urban secondary schools. *Journal of Educational Psychology*, 1974, *66*, 123–128. **449**

McCandless, B. R. *Adolescents: Behavior and development*. Hinsdale, Ill.: Dryden, 1970. **92**

McCandless, B. R., & Evans, E. D. *Children and Youth: Psychosocial development*. Hinsdale, Ill.: Dryden, 1973. **40**

McCauley, B. L., Cornbush, S. M., & Scott, W. R. *Evaluation and authority in alternative schools and public schools* (Technical Report No. 23). Stanford: Stanford Center for Research and Development in Teaching, Stanford University, June 1972. **331, 333**

McClelland, D. C. Toward a theory of motive acquisition. *American Psychologist*, 1965, *20*, 321–333. **193**

McClelland, D. C. What is the effect of achievement motivation training in the schools? *Teachers College Record*, 1972, *74*, 129–145. **193, 206, 207**

McClelland, D. C., Atkinson, J. W., Clark, R. A., & Lowell, E. L. *The achievement motive*. New York: Appleton-Century-Crofts, 1953. **193, 211**

McConnell, T. R. (Ed.). *The psychology of learning* (41st Yearbook of the National Society for the Study of Education). Chicago: University of Chicago Press, 1942. **161**

McCord, W., McCord, J., & Howard, A. Familial correlates of aggression in nondelinquent male children. *Journal of Abnormal and Social Psychology*, 1961, *62*, 79–93. **417**

McCullough, C. M. Implications of research on children's concepts. *Reading Teacher*, 1960, *13*, 100–107. **247**

McDonald, P. Media offer new charting possibilities. *Teaching Exceptional Children*, 1971, *3*, 151. **398**

McFeatters, A. Debate stalls over TV ads for children. *Pittsburgh Press*, 1974. **140**

McGeogh, J. A., & Irion, A. L. *The psychology of human learning*. New York: David McKay, 1956. **289**

McKenna, B. H. Teacher evaluation. *Today's Education*, February 1973, pp. 55–56. **458, 459**

McNeill, D. *The acquisition of language*. New York: Harper & Row, 1970. **240**

Mead, M. A cultural anthropologist's approach to maternal deprivation. In *Deprivation of maternal care* (Public Health Paper No. 14). Geneva: World Health Organization, 1962. **203**

Mecklenburger, J. A., & Wilson, J. A. Learning C.O.D.: Can the schools buy success? *Saturday Review*, September 18, 1971, pp. 62–65. **456, 457**

Memphis City School System. *Report for diffusion: Project CLUE, Memphis component*. Memphis, Tenn.: Author, 1974. (ERIC Document Reproduction Service No. ED 083 773) **397**

Merrill, M. D. Necessary psychological conditions for defining instructional outcomes. *Educational Technology*, August 1971, pp. 34–39. (a) **250, 251**

Merrill, M. D. Psychomotor and memorization behavior. In M. D. Merrill (Ed.), *Instructional design*. Englewood Cliffs, N.J.: Prentice-Hall, 1971. (b) **228, 230**

Merrill, M. D. Psychomotor taxonomies, classifications and instructional theory. In R. N. Singer (Ed.), *The psychomotor domain*. Philadelphia: Lea & Febiger, 1972, 385–414. **227, 251**

Messick, S. *The criterion problem in the evaluation of instruction*. Princeton, N.J.: Educational Testing Service, 1969. **260**

Messick, S. The criterion problem in the evaluation of instruction. In M. C. Wittrock & D. E. Wiley (Eds.), *The evaluation of instruction: Issues and problems*. New York: Holt, Rinehart & Winston, 1970. **261, 262, 263**

Metric measuring: What it is and how it will affect you. *Good Housekeeping*, June 1974, p. 6. **302**

The metrics are coming! The metrics are coming! *Changing Times*, May 1974, pp. 33–34. **302**

Michigan State Department of Education, Division of Special Education. *Careers in special education*. Lansing, Mich.: Author, July 1971. (ERIC Document Reproduction Service No. ED 081 165) **392**

Michigan State Department of Education, Division of Special Education. *Where special education fits in*. Lansing, Mich.: Author, 1973. (ERIC Document Reproduction Service No. ED 082 386) **391, 392**

Miles, D. T., & Robinson, R. E. Behavioral objectives: An even closer look. *Educational Technology*, June 1971, pp. 39–44. **255**

Milgram, S. Behavioral study of obedience. *Journal of Abnormal and Social Psychology*, 1963, *67*, 371–378. **93**

Miller, A. Learning miniature linguistic systems. *Journal of General Psychology*, 1973, *89*, 15–25. **278**

Miller, D. J., Cohen, L. B., & Hill, K. T. A methodological investigation of Piaget's theory of object concept development in the sensory-motor period. *Journal of Experimental Child Psychology*, 1970, *9*, 59–85. **55**

Miller, D. R., & Swanson, G. E. *The changing American parent*. New York: Wiley, 1958. **87**

Miller, D. R., & Swanson, G. E. *Inner conflict and defense*. New York: Holt, Rinehart & Winston, 1960. **87**

Miller, G. A. The magical number seven, plus or minus two: Some limits on our capacity for processing information. *Psychological Review*, 1956, *63*, 81–97. **164**

Miller, G. A., Galanter, E., & Pribram, K. *Plans and the struc-*

ture of behavior. New York: Holt, Rinehart & Winston, 1960. **287**

Miller, N. E. Studies of fear as an acquirable drive: I. Fear as motivation and fear-reduction as reinforcement in the learning of new responses. *Journal of Experimental Psychology,* 1948, *38,* 89–101. **201**

Montague, E. K. The role of anxiety in serial rote learning. *Journal of Experimental Psychology,* 1953, *45,* 91–96. **203**

Montessori, M. *The Montessori method* (Rev. ed.). New York: Schocken Books, 1964. (Originally published, 1909.) **66**

Montessori, M. [*The absorbent mind*] (C. A. Claremont, trans.). New York: Holt, Rinehart & Winston, 1967. **309**

Montgomery County Student Alliance. Wanted: A humane education. In R. Gross & P. Osterman (Eds.), *High School.* New York: Simon & Schuster, 1971. **410**

Moore, B. Getting into education the better way. *The Pitt News,* September 30, 1974, p. 7. **339**

Moore, O. K. Autotelic responsive environments and exceptional children. In O. J. Harvey (Ed.), *Experience, structure and adaptability.* New York: Springer, 1966. **324**

Moore, O. K., & Anderson, A. R. The responsive environments project. In R. D. Hess & R. M. Bear (Eds.), *Early education.* Chicago: Aldine, 1968. **324**

Moore, O. K., & Anderson, A. R. Some principles for the design of clarifying educational environments. In D. A. Goslin (Ed.), *Handbook of socialization theory and research.* Chicago: Rand McNally, 1969. **219, 324**

Morrison, B. M. The reactions of external and internal pupils to patterns of teacher behavior. (Doctoral dissertation, University of Michigan, 1966). *Dissertation Abstracts,* 1967, *27A,* 2072A. (University Microfilms No. 66–14, 560) **249**

Mosby, R. S. *A seminar for teachers of the culturally disadvantaged.* New York: Pageant-Poseidon, 1971. **362**

Moulds, H. To grade or not to grade: A futile question. *Intellect,* Summer 1974, *102,* 501–504. **124**

Mouly, G. J. *Psychology for effective teaching* (3rd. ed.). New York: Holt, Rinehart & Winston, 1973. **98**

Mowrer, O. H. *Learning theory & personality dynamics: Selected papers.* New York: Ronald Press, 1950. **78**

The mural message. *Time,* April 7, 1975, p. 79. **355**

Narang, H. L. Characteristics of a remedial teacher. In L. D. Karagianis & D. L. Merricks (Eds.), *Where the action is: Teaching exceptional children.* St. John's, Newfoundland: Memorial University, 1973. (ERIC Document Reproduction Service No. ED 084 764) **398**

National Education Association, Division of Instruction and Professional Development. *Accountability.* Washington, D. C.: Author, December 1972. (ERIC Document Reproduction Service No. ED 077 894).\ **457**

Nations, J. E. *Caring for individual differences in reading through non-grading.* Lecture at the Seattle Public Schools, May 13, 1967. **260**

Neill, A. S. *Summerhill: A radical approach to child rearing.* New York: Hart, 1960. **333**

New tool: Reinforcement for good work. *Psychology Today,* April 1972, pp. 68–69. **141**

Nimnicht, G. P., & Brown, E. The parent-child toy library programme. *British Journal of Educational Technology,* 1972, *3,* 75–81. **365**

1980: Target date for metric conversion in U.S. *Publishers Weekly,* November 25, 1974, pp. 12–13. **302**

Nugent, F. A. School counselors, psychologists, and social workers. *Psychology in the Schools,* 1973, *10,* 327–333. **429**

Olson, M. N. Ways to achieve quality in school classrooms. *Phi Delta Kappan,* 1971, *53,* 63–65. **263**

Osborn, J. Teaching a teaching language to disadvantaged children. In M. A. Brottman (Ed.), Language remediation for the disadvantaged preschool child. *Monographs of the Society for Research in Child Development,* 1968, *33*(8, Serial No. 124). **369**

Osgood, C. E. *Method and theory in experimental psychology.* New York: Oxford University Press, 1953. **272**

Overing, R. L. R., & Travers, R. M. W. Effect upon transfer of variations in training conditions. *Journal of Educational Psychology,* 1966, *57,* 179–188. **300**

Ozanam. Information booklet, n.d. (Available from Ozanam Cultural Center, 1833 Wylie Avenue, Pittsburgh, Pa. 15219). **361**

Palardy, J. M. What teachers believe–what children achieve. *Elementary School Journal,* 1969, *69,* 370–374. **437**

Palermo, D. S., & Molfese, D. L. Language acquisition from age five onward. *Psychological Bulletin,* 1972, *78,* 409–428. **239**

Pankopf, J. *Free learning environment program* (Year end report, 1972–1973). Pittsburgh: Washington Education Center, Pittsburgh Public Schools, 1974. **337**

Parker, H. C. Contingency management and concomitant changes in elementary-school students' self-concepts. *Psychology in the Schools,* 1974, *11,* 70–79. **426**

Pavlov, I. P. [*Conditioned reflexes*] (G. V. Anrep, Ed. & trans.). London: Oxford University Press, 1927. **109**

Pearl, A. There is nothing more loco than loco parentis. *Phi Delta Kappan,* 1972, *53,* 629–631. **449**

Pearlin, L. I., Yarrow, M. R., & Scarr, H. A. Unintended effects of parental aspirations: The case of children's cheating. *American Journal of Sociology,* 1967, *73,* 73–83. **90**

Pedrini, B. C., & Pedrini, D. T. *Special education.* 1973. (ERIC Document Reproduction Service No. ED 085 927) **389, 390, 399**

Perkins, H. V. Factors influencing change in children's self-concepts. *Child Development,* 1958, *29,* 221–230. **75**

Pettigrew, T. F. The measurement and correlates of category width as a cognitive variable. *Journal of Personality,* 1958, *26,* 532–544. **263**

Pettigrew, T. F. On busing and race relations. *Today's Education,* November-December, 1973, p. 37. **438**

Phillips, D. We have a successful tool now–Let's use it. In J. B. Jordan & L. S. Robbins (Eds.), *Let's try doing something else kind of thing: Behavioral principles and the exceptional child.* Arlington, Va.: Council for Exceptional Children, 1972. **398, 399, 401**

Piaget, J. [*The moral judgment of the child*] (M. Gabain, trans.). New York: Free Press, 1965. (Originally published, 1933.) **79**

Piaget, J. [*The origins of intelligence in children*] (M. Cook, trans.). New York: International Universities Press, 1952. (Originally published, 1936.) **49**

Piaget, J. [*The psychology of intelligence*] (M. Percy & D. E. Berlyne, trans.). London: Routledge & Kegan Paul, 1950. **49**

Piaget, J. Development and learning. In R. E. Ripple & V. N. Rockcastle (Eds.), *Piaget rediscovered.* Ithaca, N.Y.: School of Education, Cornell University, 1964. **54**

Piaget, J. [*Six psychological studies*] (A. Tenzer, trans.). New York: Random House, 1967. **200, 201**

Piaget, J. [Intellectual evolution from adolescence to adulthood] (J. Bliss & H. Furth, trans.). *Human Development,* 1972, *15,* 1-12. **61**

Pines, M. *Revolution in learning.* New York: Harper & Row, 1967. **317**

Pitman, J., & St. John, J. *Alphabets and reading.* New York: Pitman, 1969. **241**

Popham, W. J. *Probing the validity of arguments against behavioral goals*. Paper presented at the Annual Meeting of the American Educational Research Association, Chicago, February 1968. **254, 255**

Popham, W. J. *Criterion-referenced instruction*. Belmont, Calif.: Fearon, 1973. **487**

Popham, W. J. Teacher evaluation and domain-referenced measurement. *Educational Technology*, June 1974, pp. 35–37. **486**

Precision teaching in perspective: An interview with Ogden R. Lindsley. *Teaching Exceptional Children*, 1971, *3*, 114–119. **328**

Premack, D. Toward empirical behavior laws: I. Positive reinforcement. *Psychological Review*, 1959, *66*, 219–233. **130**

Pressey, S. L. A third and fourth contribution toward the coming "industrial revolution" in education. *School and Society*, 1932, *36*, 668–672. **466**

Prince, R. *A study of the relationships between individual values and administrative effectiveness in the school situation*. Unpublished doctoral dissertation, University of Chicago, 1957. **435**

Pronko, N. H. On learning to play the violin at the age of four without tears. *Psychology Today*, May 1969, pp. 52–53 ff. **229**

Proscura, E. V. [The role of teaching in the formation of seriation actions in pre-school children.] *Voprosy Psychologee*, 1969, *15*, 37–45. (I. Z. Holowinsky, Seriation actions in pre-school children. *Journal of Learning Disabliities*, 1970, *3*, 34–45.) **55**

Rabinow, B. *The training and supervision of teaching of emotionally disturbed children*. Albany: University of the State of New York, State Department of Education, Bureau of Teacher Education, 1964. **397**

Radolf, A. The robot who teaches in the Bronx. *PTA Magazine*, June 1974, pp. 28–29. **323**

Rafferty, M. An analysis of Summerhill–Con. In *Summerhill: For and against*. New York: Hart, 1970. **333**

Ramella, R. The anatomy of discipline: Should punishment be corporal? *PTA Magazine*, June 1973, pp. 24–27. **127**

Ramsay, D. L., & Solomon, L. M. *Simulations in dermatology*. New York: Appleton-Century-Crofts, 1974.

Rappaport, S. R., & McNary, S. R. Teacher effectivenesss for children with learning disorders. In L. D. Karagianis & D. L. Merricks (Eds.), *Where the action is: Teaching exceptional children*. St. John's, Newfoundland: Memorial University, 1973. (ERIC Document Reproduction Service No. ED 084 764) **397**

Rathbone, C. H. Examining the open education classroom. *School Review*, 1972, *80*, 521–549. **314, 315**

Rebelsky, F. G., Allinsmith, W., & Grinder, R. E. Resistance to temptation and sex differences in children's use of fantasy confession. *Child Development*, 1963, *34*, 955–962. **86**

Redl, F., & Wattenberg, W. W. *Mental hygiene in teaching* (2nd ed.). New York: Harcourt, Brace, 1959. **452**

Reese, H. W. & Lipsitt, L. P. (Eds.). *Experimental child psychology*. New York: Academic Press, 1970. **78, 92**

Reilly, D. H. A conceptual model for school psychology. *Psychology in the Schools*, 1974, *11*, 165–170. **391**

Reiss, I. L. America's sex standards–How and why they're changing. *Trans-action*, 1968, *5*, 26–32. **92**

Reissman, F. Styles of learning. *National Education Association Journal*, March 1966, pp. 15–17. **260**

Resnick, L. B. *Teacher behavior in an informal British infant school*. Pittsburgh: Learning Research and Development Center, University of Pittsburgh, 1971. **313**

Resnik, H. Parkway: A school without walls. In R. Gross & P. Osterman (Eds.), *High school*. New York: Simon & Schuster, 1971. **334**

Rheingold, H. L. The modification of social responsiveness in institutional babies. *Monographs of the Society for Research in Child Development*, 1956, 22(2, Serial No. 63). **19**

Rheingold, H. L., & Bayley, N. The later effects of an experimental modification of mothering. *Child Development*, 1959, *30*, 363–372. **23**

Rhine, R. J., & Silun, B. A. Acquisition and change of a concept attitude as a function of consistency of reinforcement. *Journal of Experimental Psychology*, 1958, *55*, 524–529. **248**

Rhodes, W. C. Curriculum and disordered behavior. *Exceptional Children*, 1963, *30*, 61–66. **425, 426**

Rhodes, W. C. *The emotionally disturbed student and guidance*. Boston: Houghton Mifflin, 1970. **429**

Richardson, S. K. How do children feel about reports to parents? *California Journal of Elementary Education*, 1955, *24*, 98–111. **492**

Riessman, F. The "Helper" therapy principle. *Social Work*, 1965, *10*(2), 27–32. **330**

Roberts, J. M., & Sutton-Smith, B. Child training and game involvement. *Ethnology*, 1962, *1*, 166–185. **33**

Roberts, J. M., & Sutton-Smith, B. Cross-cultural correlates of games of chance. *Behavior Science Notes*, 1966, *3*, 131–144. **33**

Robinson, M. R. E. Helping the adolescent with learning problems. In J. Elkins (Ed.), *The identification and treatment of children with learning disabilities*. Brisbane, Australia: Queensland University, Schonell Educational Research Centre, 1973 ((ERIC Document Reproduction Service No. ED 087 146) **386**

Roden, A. H. & Hapkiewicz, W. G. Respondent learning and classroom practice. In R. D. Klein, W. G. Hapkiewicz & A. H. Roden (Eds.), *Behavior modification in educational settings*. Springfield, Ill.: Charles C Thomas, 1973. **125**

Rodriguez, E. Inside ETS: Or the plot to multiple-choice us from cradle to grave. *Washington Monthly*, March 1974, pp. 5–12. **505**

Rogers, C. Forget you are a teacher. *Instructor*, August-September 1971, *81*, 65–66. **436**

Rogers, C. R. *Client-centered therapy*. Boston: Houghton Mifflin, 1951. **88**

Rosen, B. C. Conflicting group membership. *American Sociological Review*, 1955, *20*, 155–161. **92**

Rosen, B. C., & D'Andrade, R. The psychosocial origins of achievement motivation. *Sociometry*, 1959, *22*, 185–218. **211**

Rosenberg, M. J. Cognitive reorganization in response to the hypnotic reversal of attitudinal affect. *Journal of Personality*, 1960, *28*, 39–63. **248**

Rosenham, D. The kindnesses of children. *Young Children*, 1969, *25*, 30–44. **40**

Rosenshine, B., & McGaw, B. Issues in assessing teacher accountability in public education. *Phi Delta Kappan*, 1972, *53*, 640–643. **455, 459**

Rosensweet, A. Head Start wears off. *Pittsburgh Post Gazette*, February 24, 1971, Section 2, p. 24. **68**

Rosenthal, R., & Jacobson, L. Teachers' expectancies: Determinants of pupils' IQ gains. *Psychological Reports*, 1966, *19*, 115–118. **436**

Rosenthal, R., & Jacobson, L. *Pygmalion in the classroom*. New York: Holt, Rinehart & Winston, 1968. **210, 360**

Rothbart, M., Dalfen, S., & Barrett, R. Effects of teacher's expectancy on student-teacher interaction. *Journal of Educational Psychology*, 1971, *62*, 49–54. **210**

Rubin, R. A. Preschool application of the Metropolitan Readiness Tests: Validity, reliability, and preschool norms. *Educational and Psychological Measurement*, 1974, *34*, 417–422. **518**

Ruddell, R. B., & Graves, B. W. Socioethnic status and the language achievement of first-grade children. *Elementary English*, May 1968. **357**

Rush, G. P. Visual grouping in relation to age. *Archives Psychology*, 1937, *31*(Whole No. 217). **176**

Russell, J. D. *Modular instruction.* Minneapolis: Burgess, 1974. **327**

Russell Sage Foundation. *Guidelines for the collection, maintenance, and dissemination of pupil records.* New York: Author, 1970. **494**

Ryans, D. G. *Characteristics of teachers.* Washington, D.C.: American Council on Education, 1960. **453**

Ryans, D. G. Some relationships between pupil behavior and certain teacher characteristics. *Journal of Educational Psychology*, 1961, *52*, 82–90. **362, 448**

Sage, W. Classrooms for the autistic child. *Human Behavior*, March 1975, pp. 39–42. **400**

Sarason, J. G. *Abnormal psychology.* New York: Appleton-Century-Crofts, 1972. **409, 414**

Schaefer, E. S. Parents as educators. In W. W. Hartup (Ed.), *The young child: Reviews of research* (Vol. 2). Washington, D.C.: National Association for the Education of Young Children, 1972. **64, 365**

Scheerer, M. Problem-solving. *Scientific American*, April 1963, pp. 118–128. **152**

Schimmel, D. To speak out freely: Do teachers have the right? *Phi Delta Kappan*, 1972, *54*, 258–260. **442, 443**

Schneir, W., & Schneir, M. The joy of learning in the open corridor. *New York Times Magazine*, April 4, 1971, pp. 30 ff. **317**

Schuchat, T. With education in Washington. *Educational Digest*, May 1975, p. 63. **503**

Science Research Associates. *Using the Iowa Tests of Educational Development for college planning.* Chicago: Author, 1957. **518**

Scott, W. A. Attitude change through reward of verbal behavior. *Journal of Abnormal and Social Psychology*, 1957, *55*, 72–75. **248**

Sears, R. R., Maccoby, E. E., & Levin, H. *Patterns of childrearing.* Evanston, Ill.: Row, Peterson, 1957. **14, 35, 87**

Selcer, R. J., & Hilton, I. R. Cultural differences in the acquisition of sex roles. *Proceedings of the Annual Convention of the American Psychological Association*, 1972, 7 (Part 1), 91–92. **37**

Senior Scholastic, May 8, 1972, pp. 4–8. **470**

Sex bias. *New York Teacher*, September 15, 1974, p. 24. **440, 441**

Seymour, D. Z. Black children, black speech. *Commonweal*, November 19, 1971, pp. 175–178. **357, 359**

Shaw, M. E. Some motivational factors in cooperation and competition. *Journal of Personality*, 1958, *26*, 155–169. **214**

Shellow, R., Schamp, J. R., Liebow, E., & Unger, E. Suburban runaways of the 1960's. *Monographs of the Society for Research in Child Development*, 1967, *32*(3, Serial No. 111). **98, 423, 424**

Shenker, I. "Chomsky is difficult to please." "Chomsky is easy to please." "Chomsky is certain to please." *Horizon*, Spring 1971, pp. 104–109. **236, 238, 239**

Shore, A. L. Confirmation of expectancy and changes in teachers' evaluations of student behavior. (Doctoral dissertation, University of Southern California, 1969). *Dissertation Abstracts International*, 1969, *30A*, 1878A. (University Microfilms No. 69–19, 402) **210**

Shulman, L. S. Psychological controversies in the teaching of science and mathematics. *Science Teacher*, September 1968, pp. 34–38 ff. **168, 182**

Shumsky, A. *In search of teaching style.* New York: Appleton-Century-Crofts, 1968. **261, 262**

Sigel, I. E. The Piagetian system and the world of education. In D. Elkind & J. Flavell (Eds.), *Studies in cognitive development.* New York: Oxford University Press, 1969. **61**

Silberberg, N. E., & Silberberg, M. C. Myths in remedial education. In L. D. Karagianis & D. L. Merricks (Eds.), *Where the action is: Teaching exceptional children.* St. John's, Newfoundland: Memorial University, 1973. (ERIC Document Reproduction Service No. ED 084 764) **394**

Simon, H. A. On the development of the processor. In S. Farnham-Diggory (Ed.), *Information processing in children.* New York: Academic Press, 1972. **270**

Simpson, D. D., & Nelson, A. L. Attention training through breathing control to modify hyperactivity. *Journal of Learning Disabilities*, 1974, *7*, 274–283. **419**

Sinowitz, B. E. School integration and the teacher. *Today's Education*, May 1973, pp. 30–33. (a) **438**

Sinowitz, B. E. The teacher's right to privacy. *Today's Education*, November–December 1973, pp. 89–90 f. (b) **442**

Skinner, B. F. "Superstition" in the pigeon. *Journal of Experimental Psychology*, 1948, *38*, 168–172. (a) **122**

Skinner, B. F. *Walden II.* New York: Macmillan, 1948. (b) **140**

Skinner, B. F. *Contingency management in the classroom.* Paper presented at Western Washington State College, October 2, 1969. **131, 133**

Skinner, B. F. *Beyond freedom and dignity.* New York: Knopf, 1971. **139, 142**

Skinner, B. F. (Ed.) *Cumulative record* (3rd ed.). New York: Appleton-Century-Crofts, 1972. **321**

Skinner's utopia: Panacea or path to hell? *Time*, September 20, 1971, pp. 47–53. **139**

Sloan, W. The Lincoln-Oseretsky motor development scale. *Genetic Psychology Monographs*, 1955, *51*, 183–252. **234**

Slobin, D. I. *Psycholinguistics.* Glenview, Ill.: Scott, Foresman, 1971. **237, 239**

Smart, M. S., & Smart, R. C. *Children: Development and relationships* (2nd ed.). New York: Macmillan, 1972. **39, 40, 42**

Smedslund, J. Educational psychology. *Annual Review of Psychology*, 1964, *15*, 251–276. **180**

Snadowsky, A. (Ed.). *Child and adolescent development.* New York: Free Press, 1973. **86**

Snapp, M., McNeil, D. C., & Haug, D. Development of in-school psychoeducational services for emotionally disturbed children. *Psychology in the Schools*, 1973, *10*, 392–396. **428**

Snider, A. J. Hyperactivity. *Pittsburgh Press*, July 1, 1974, p. 13. **43**

Solzhenitsyn, A. I. [*The Gulag archipelago.*] (T. P. Whitney, trans.). New York: Harper & Row, 1973. **189**

Spearman, C. "General intelligence," objectively determined and measured. *American Journal of Psychology*, 1904, *15*, 201–293. **507**

Spence, K. W. Anxiety (drive) level and performance in eyelid conditioning. *Psychological Bulletin*, 1964, *61*, 129–139. **303**

Sperry, L. (Ed.). *Learning performance and individual differences.* Glenview, Ill.: Scott, Foresman, 1972. **262**

Spiro, M. E., & D'Andrade, R. G. A cross-cultural study of some supernatural beliefs. *American Anthropologist*, 1958, *60*, 456–466. **17**

Spitz, H. H. Effects of symmetry on the reproduction of dot patterns by mental retardates and equal MA normals. *American Journal of Mental Deficiency*, 1964, *69*, 101–106. **176**

Spitz, R. A. Hospitalism: An inquiry into the genesis of psychiatric conditions in early childhood. *Psychoanalytic Study of the Child*, 1945, *1*, 53–74. **23**

Spitz, R. A. Hospitalism: A follow-up report. *Psychoanalytic Study of the Child*, 1946, 2, 113–117. **23**

Stake, R. E. Testing hazards in performance contracting. *Phi Delta Kappan*, 1971, *52*, 583–589. **520, 521**

Stanley, J. C. Accelerating the educational progress of intellectually gifted youths. *Educational Psychologist*, 1973, *10*, 133–146. **395, 396**

Starlin, C. Peers and precision. *Teaching Exceptional Children*, 1971, *3*, 129–132 ff. **398, 399**

Starnes, R. "Johnny" proves he can read. *Pittsburgh Press*, April 7, 1975, p. 23. **363**

Stearns, K., & Swenson, S. H. The resource teacher: An alternative to special class placement. *Viewpoints*, 1973, *49*, 11. **390**

Steinberg, T. *Educational television.* Unpublished manuscript, University of Pittsburgh, October 1974. **310, 312**

Stevens, E. I. Grading systems and student mobility. *Educational Record*, 1973, *54*, 308–312. **492**

Stewart, M. A. Hyperactive children. *Scientific American*, April 1970, pp. 94–99. **418**

Stillwell, L. Students slip, but grades rise. *Pittsburgh Press*, July 15, 1974, p. 19. **494**

Strickland, D. S. Black is beautiful vs. white is right. *Elementary English*, 1972, *49*, 220–223. **358**

Strong, C. H. Motivation related to performance on physical fitness tests. *Research Quarterly*, 1963, *34*, 197–207. **214**

Suing for not learning. *Time*, March 3, 1975, p. 73. **457**

Sutton-Smith, B. Children at play. *Natural History*, December 1971, pp. 54–59. **33**

Taylor, J. A. The relationship of anxiety to the conditioned eyelid response. *Journal of Experimental Psychology*, 1951, *41*, 81–92. **203**

Templeton, I. Class size. *Educational Management Review Series*, 1972, *8*, 1–7. **263**

Terman, L. M. *The measurement of intelligence.* Boston: Houghton Mifflin, 1916. **508**

Terrell, G., Jr., Durkin, K., & Wiesley, M. Social class and the nature of the incentive in discrimination learning. *Journal of Abnormal and Social Psychology*, 1959, *59*, 270–272. **220**

Terwilliger, J. S. *Assigning grades to students.* Glenview, Ill.: Scott, Foresman, 1971. **469, 490, 491**

Thompson, M., Brassell, W. R., Persons, S., Tucker, R., & Rollins, H. Contingency management in the schools. *American Educational Research Journal*, 1974, *11*, 19–28. **142**

Thompson, N. L., Jr., & McCandless, B. R. IT score variations by instructional style. *Child Development*, 1970, *41*, 425–436. **36**

Thornburg, H. D. (Ed.). *School learning and instruction.* Monterey, Calif.: Brooks-Cole, 1973. **295, 301, 302**

Thorndike, E. L. Animal intelligence. *Psychological Review Monograph Supplement*, 1898, *2* (4, Whole No. 8). **112**

Thorndike, E. L. *Educational psychology* (Vol. 1). New York: Teachers College, Columbia University, 1913. **111**

Thorndike, E. L. Mental discipline in high school studies. *Journal of Educational Psychology*, 1924, *15*, 83–98. **292, 293**

Thorndike, E. L. *The fundamentals of learning.* New York: Teachers College, Columbia University, 1932. **112**

Thorndike, R. L. (Review of *Pygmalion in the classroom* by R. Rosenthal & L. Jacobson). *American Educational Research Journal*, 1968, *5*, 708–711. **210**

Thorndike, R. L., & Hagen, E. *Measurement and eveleauation in psychology and education* (2nd ed.). New York: Wiley, 1961. **506, 517**

Those books are restored in West Virginia. *New York Times*, November 10, 1974, Section 4, p. 9. **439**

Thurstone, L. L. Primary mental abilities. *Psychometric Monographs*, 1938, No. 1. **507**

Toddler logic: New findings. *Society*, September 1974, pp. 10 f. **168**

Toffler, A. *Future Shock.* New York: Random House, 1970. **5, 88, 413**

Tolman, E. C. *Purposive behavior in animals and men.* New York: Century, 1932. **185**

Tolman, E. C. A psychological model. In T. Parsons & E. A. Shils (Eds.), *Toward a general theory of action.* Cambridge: Harvard University Press, 1951. **185**

Tolor, A. Evaluation of perceived teacher effectiveness. *Journal of Educational Psychology*, 1973, *64*, 98–104. **459**

Tolor, A., Scarpetti, W. L., & Lane, P. A. Teachers' attitudes toward children's behavior revisited. *Journal of Educational Psychology*, 1967, *58*, 175–180. **411**

Torrance, E. P. Explorations in creative thinking. *Education*, 1960, *81*, 216–220. **214**

Tosti, D. T. The peer-proctor in individualized programs. *Educational Technology*, August 1973, pp. 29–30. **489**

Townsend, J. *Learning strategies and tactics.* Pittsburgh: University of Pittsburgh, September 1974. **339, 340**

Travers, J. *Learning: Analysis and application* (2nd. ed.). New York: David McKay, 1972. **146, 151, 161, 180, 231, 233, 234, 296**

Travers, R. M. W. *Essentials of learning* (2nd ed.). New York: Macmillan, 1967. **126, 154, 158, 160, 161, 188, 190, 205, 216, 235, 242, 244, 245, 246, 247, 249, 277, 286, 293**

Tulkin, S. R. An analysis of the concept of cultural deprivation. *Developmental Psychology*, 1972, *6*, 326–339. **351**

Tulving, E. Episodic and semantic memory. In E. Tulving & W. Donaldson (Eds.), *Organization of memory.* New York: Academic Press, 1972. **277**

Tyler, L. E. *The work of the counselor* (3rd ed.). New York: Appleton-Century-Crofts, 1969. **391**

Tyler, R. W. Some persistent questions on the defining of objectives. In C. M. Lindvall (Ed.), *Defining educational objectives.* Pittsburgh: University of Pittsburgh Press, 1964. **255**

Ullmann, L. P., & Krasner, L. *A psychological approach to abnormal behavior.* Englewood Cliffs, N.J.: Prentice-Hall, 1969. **379**

Underwood, B. J. Forgetting. *Scientific American*, March 1964, pp. 91–99. **269**

Urevick, S. J. Ability grouping: Why is it undemocratic? *Clearing House*, 1965, *39*, 530–532. **394, 395**

U.S. Department of Health, Education, and Welfare. *The health of children. I. The world that greets the infant.* Washington, D.C.: U.S. Government Printing Office, 1970. **353**

Vail, E. O. What will it be? Reading or machismo and soul? *Clearing House*, 1970, *45*, 92–96. **358**

Van Brunt, H. L. (Review of *Children of crisis* [Vols. 2 & 3] by R. Coles). *Saturday Review*, April 8, 1972, p. 69–72. **351**

Vargas, J. S. *Writing worthwhile behavioral objectives.* New York: Harper & Row, 1972. **250, 253, 256, 257, 258**

Vaughn, J. An experimental study of competition. *Journal of Applied Psychology*, 1936, *20*, 1–15. **214**

Veroff, J., Wilcox, S., & Atkinson, J. W. The achievement motive in high school and college age women. *Journal of Abnormal and Social Psychology*, 1953, *48*, 108–119. **211**

Vincent, W. S. *Further clarification of the class size question* (IAR Research Bulletin 9). New York: Institute of Administrative Research, Columbia University, November 1968. **263**

Vygotsky, L. S. [Thought and language] (E. Hanfmann & G. Vakar, trans.). Cambridge: M.I.T. Press, 1962. (Originally published, 1934.) **47, 57**

Waldfogel, S., Coolidge, J. C., & Hahn, P. B. The development, meaning, and management of school phobia. *American Journal of Orthopsychiatry*, 1957, 27, 754–780. **420, 422**

Walker, S., III. Drugging the American child: We're too cavalier about hyperactivity. *Psychology Today*, December 1974, pp. 43–48. **43**

Warburton, F. W., & Southgate, V. *I.T.A.: An independent evaluation.* London: Murray & Chambers, 1969. **241**

Waters, C. R. Thank God something has finally reached Him. *TV Guide*, January 19, 1974, pp. 6–9. **311**

Watson, J. B. Psychology as the behaviorist views it. *Psychological Review*, 1913, 20, 158–177. **47**

Watson, J. B. *Psychology from the standpoint of a behaviorist.* Philadelphia: Lippincott, 1919. **108**

Watson, J. B., & Rayner, R. Conditioned emotional reactions. *Journal of Experimental Psychology*, 1920, 3, 1–14. **201**

Wax, M. L. *Indian education in eastern Oklahoma* (Research contract report No. O.E. 6-10-260 and B. I. A. No. 5-0565-2-12-1). Washington, D.C.: U.S. Office of Education, 1969. **359**

Weinberger, G., Leventhal, T., & Beckman, G. The management of a chronic school phobic through the use of consultation with school personnel. *Psychology in the Schools*, 1973, 10, 83–88. **421**

Wellington, J., and Wellington, C.B. Should teachers see student records? No. *National Education Association Journal*, October 1966, pp. 35–37. **494**

Wertheimer, M. *Productive thinking* (Rev. ed.). New York: Harper & Brothers, 1959. **155, 156**

White, R. W. Motivation reconsidered. *Psychological Review*, 1959, 66, 297–333. **197**

Whiting, B. *Six cultures.* New York: Wiley, 1963. **12**

Whiting, B., & Child, I. *Child training and personality.* New Haven: Yale University Press, 1953. **12**

Whiting, J. W. M. Sorcery, sin, and the superego: A cross-cultural study of some mechanisms of social control. In M. R. Jones (Ed.), *Nebraska Symposium on Motivation* (Vol. 7). Lincoln: University of Nebraska Press, 1959. **17**

Whiting, J. W. M. Socialization process and personality. In F. L. K. Hsu (Ed.), *Psychological anthropology.* Homewood, Ill.: Dorsey Press, 1961. **17**

Wickman, E. *Children's behavior & teachers' attitudes.* New York: Commonwealth Fund, 1928. **411**

Wicks, L. E. Teacher evaluation. *Today's Education*, March 1973, pp. 42–43. **460**

Wight, A. R. Beyond behavioral objectives. *Educational Technology*, July 1972, pp. 9–14. **254**

Wilson, C. H. The case against merit pay. *Saturday Review*, January 20, 1962, pp. 44 ff. **460**

Winett, R. A., & Winkler, R. C. Current behavior modification in the classroom: Be still, be quiet, be docile. *Journal of Applied Behavioral Analysis*, 1972, 5, 499–504. **142**

Winterbottom, M. R. The relation of need for achievement to learning experiences in independence and mastery. In J. W. Atkinson (Ed.), *Motives in fantasy, action and society.* Princeton: Van Nostrand, 1958. **211**

Wise, H. D. How teachers can promote equality. *Today's Education*, March-April 1974, p. 75. **442**

Witkin, H. A., Dyk, R. B., Paterson, H. F., Goodenough, D. R., & Karp, S. A. *Psychological differentiation.* New York: Wiley, 1962. **262**

Witkin, H. A., Goodenough, D. R., & Karp, S. A. Stability of cognitive style from childhood to young adulthood. *Journal of Personality and Social Psychology*, 1967, 7, 291–300. **262**

Woestehoff, E. S. *Students with reading disabilities and guidance.* Boston: Houghton Mifflin, 1970. **394**

Wolfson, B. J. *Pupil and teacher roles in individualized instruction.* Chicago: University of Chicago Press, 1968. **319**

Wood, G. Organizational processes and free recall. In E. Tulving & W. Donaldson (Eds.), *Organization of memory.* New York: Academic Press, 1972. **277**

Wulf, F. [Tendencies in figural variation.] In W. D. Ellis (Ed. and trans.), *A source book of Gestalt psychology.* New York: Harcourt, Brace, 1938. (Translated and condensed from *Psychol. Forsch.*, 1922, 1, 333–373) **150**

Yalom, I. D., & Lieberman, M. A. A study of encounter group casualties. *Archives of General Psychology*, 1971, 25, 16–30. **431**

Yarrow, L. J. Separation from parents during early childhood. In M. L. Hoffman & L. W. Hoffman (Eds.), *Review of child development research* (Vol. 1). New York: Russell Sage Foundation, 1964. **203**

Yerkes, R. M. *Chimpanzees· A laboratory colony.* New Haven: Yale University Press, 1943. **154**

Young, B. J. Imagine you're the parent of a deaf-blind child. In J. B. Jordan & L. S. Robbins (Eds.), *Let's try doing something else kind of thing: Behavioral principles and the exceptional child.* Arlington, Va.: Council for Exceptional Children, 1972. **401**

Young, J. I., & Van Mondfrans, A. P. Psychological implications of competency-based education. *Educational Technology*, November 1972, pp. 15–18. **217, 220**

Young, K. C. Using a computer to help implement the Keller method of instruction. *Educational Technology*, October 1974, pp. 53–55. **489**

Zach, L. The IQ debate. *Today's Education*, September 1972, pp. 40–43 ff. **516**

Zarembka, D. Introductory remarks presented at the Pittsburgh Council on Public Education Conference on Alternative Secondary Education, Pittsburgh, April 1974. **339**

Zax, M., & Cowen, E. L. *Abnormal psychology.* New York: Holt, Rinehart & Winston, 1972. **424**

Zimbardo, P. G., Pilkonis, P. A., & Norwood, R. M. The social disease called shyness. *Psychology Today*, May 1975, pp. 69–72. **416**

Zimiles, H. Preventive aspects of school experience. In E. L. Cowen, E. A. Gardner & M. Zax (Eds.), *Emergent approaches to mental health problems.* New York: Appleton-Century-Crofts, 1967. **409**

Photo Credits

Cover photo by Paul Fusco/Magnum

Chapter opening photos: 1 Ellen Kirouac / 2 Rene Burri, Magnum / 3 Mamie Harmon / 4 Rogers, Monkmeyer / 5 Robin Gibson, Alternative Curriculum / 6 Rohn Engh, Photo Researchers / 7 Hanna Schreiber, Rapho/Photo Researchers / 8 Cornell Capa, Magnum / 9 Nancy Hays, Monkmeyer / 10 J. Paul Kirouac / 11 United Press International / 12 Sherry Suris, Rapho/Photo Researchers / 13 Fritz Menle, Photo Researchers / 14 James Foote, Photo Researchers / 15 Van Bucher, Photo Researchers

Acknowledgments

p. 53	Excerpts from pp. 41, 43 reprinted by permission of G. P. Putnam's Sons from *Dear Folks* by Juliet Lowell. Copyright © 1960 by Juliet Lowell.
p. 64	R. Hess and V. Shipman, *Parents as Teachers: How Lower Class and Middle Class Mothers Teach*, 1967. ERIC Clearinghouse on Early Childhood Education, University of Illinois. Reprinted by permission.
p. 69	B. Gross and R. Gross, "A Little Bit of Chaos," *Saturday Review*, May 16, 1970. Copyright © 1970 by Saturday Review/World. Reprinted by permission.
p. 82	Table from L. Kohlberg, "The Development of Children's Orientation Toward a Moral Order: 1) Sequence in the Development of Moral Thought," *Vita Humana*, 1963, 6, 11–33. Published by S. Karger AG, Basel.
p. 111	R. M. Gagné, *The Conditions of Learning* (2nd ed.), 1970, Figure 2. Published by Holt, Rinehart & Winston. Reprinted by permission.
p. 132	American Cancer Society, Inc., *If You Want to Give Up Cigarettes*, 1970.
p. 227	Figure from M. D. Merrill, "Psychomotor Taxonomies, Classifications and Instructional Theory." In R. N. Singer (Ed.), *The Psychomotor Domain: Movement Behavior*, 1972, pp. 385–415. Published by Lea & Febiger.
p. 239	R. Brown and C. Fraser, "The Acquisition of Syntax." In U. Bellugi and R. Brown (Eds.), *The Acquisition of Language, Monographs of The Society for Research in Child Development*, 1964, 29 (serial no. 92), Figure 1, p. 46. Copyright © 1964 by The Society for Research in Child Development.
pp. 246, 293	Excerpts from R. M. W. Travers, *Essentials of Learning*, pp. 138–141, 239–240. Published by Macmillan Publishing Co., Inc. Copyright © 1963, 1967, 1972 by Robert M. W. Travers. Reprinted by permission.
pp. 251–252	Excerpts from B. S. Bloom, M. D. Englehart, E. J. Furst, and D. R. Krathwohl, *A Taxonomy of Educational Objectives*. Handbook 1: The Cognitive Domain, pp. 201–207. Copyright © 1956 by the David McKay Co., Inc. Reprinted with permission of the publishers.
p. 257	Excerpts from J. S. Vargas, *Writing Worthwhile Behavioral Objectives*, pp. 119, 121, 123, 130. Copyright © 1972 by Julie S. Vargas. Reprinted by permission of Harper & Row, Publishers, Inc.
p. 259	C. F. Paulson and F. G. Nelson, "Behavioral Objectives." In J. Crawford (Ed.), *CORD National Research Training Manual*, 1969, p. 80. Monmouth, Oregon, Teaching Research Division of the Oregon State System of Higher Education.
p. 275	E. Loftus, "Reconstructing Memory," *Psychology Today*, December 1974, pp. 116–119. Reprinted by permission.
p. 324	Cartoon by Sidney Harris in *Saturday Review*, September 21, 1974, p. 49.
p. 335	J. Bremer and M. von Moschzisker (Eds.), *The School Without Walls: Philadelphia's Parkway Program*, 1971, pp. 189–191. Published by Holt, Rinehart & Winston. Reprinted by permission.
p. 338	"Choice in Quincy," *Time*, March 10, 1975, p. 73. Copyright © 1975 by Time, Inc. Reprinted by permission.
p. 369	Table from J. Osborn, "Teaching a Teaching Language to Disadvantaged Children." In M. A. Brottman (Ed.), *Language Remediation for the Disadvantaged Preschool Child, Monographs of the Society for Research in Child Development*, 1968, 33 (serial no. 124), Table 1, p. 47. Copyright © 1968 by The Society for Research in Child Development, Inc. Reprinted by permission.
pp. 369–372	Excerpts from N. J. A. Johnson, *Four Steps to Precision Teaching: A Workbook for Teachers and Aides*. Unpublished manuscript. Reprinted by permission of the author.
p. 421	G. Weinberger, T. Leventhal, G. Beckman, "The Management of a Chronic School Phobic Through the Use of Consultation with School Personnel," *Psychology in the Schools*, 1973, 10, 83–88. Reprinted by permission.
p. 430	J. A. Cooper, "Application of the Consultant Role to Parent-Teacher Management of School Avoidance Behavior," *Psychology in the Schools*, 1973, 10, 259–269. Reprinted by permission.
p. 454	Excerpt from Bel Kaufman, "A Love Letter to a Dead Teacher," *Today's Education* (March–April, 1975), 20–23. Reprinted by permission.
p. 458	Table from B. H. McKenna, "Teacher Evaluation," *Today's Education*, February 1973, p. 55. Reprinted by permission.
p. 505	S. Brill, "The Secrecy Behind the College Boards," *New York*, October 7, 1974, p. 83. Copyright © 1974 by the NYM Corporation. Reprinted by permission.

SUBJECT INDEX

Ability grouping, 394–95
Ability tests, 498, 506, 507–16
Abstractions, 53, 54, 63, 85, 242–43
Academies, street, 332–33
Acceleration, 395–96
Accommodation, 51, 56, 58, 60
Accountability, teacher, 445, 455–60, 494–95
Achievement, classroom, teacher behavior and, 433–61
Achievement motivation, 193–96, 197; development of, 205–208; sex differences and, 210–12
Achievement tests, 498–99, 501, 502, 503, 516–21
Acquisition: of information, 171; of language, 62
Adaptability, disadvantaged children and, 356
Adaptation, 49, 50, 51
Adolescence, 74–100, 422; problem behavior during, 422–24
Aggression, 34–35, 36, 40–41, 417–18
Aides, paraprofessional, 329
Aids, visual, 321
Alcohol, 97, 423
Alienation, 95, 98, 100, 355, 414, 415
Alternative Curriculum, 339–40
Altruism, 40
Ambivalence, 97
American Federation of Teachers, 446
Analysis, 252, 262
Analytic reasoning, 172
Anger, 40–41, 422
Annoyers, 111, 112
Anomie, 415
Anxiety, 78, 79, 118, 120, 125–27, 188, 262, 408, 450; as a drive, 201–203; chronic, 420; learning and, 203; reduction of, 216–18; severe, 420–22
Aptitude tests, 498, 512
Arithmetic mean, 523
"Ask-and-Guess Test," 214
Aspiration, level of, 196; increasing, 208–210
Assertiveness, 441
Assimilation, 51, 56, 58, 60
Associational meaning of words, 235
Associationism, 108, 185, 271–74, 278
Athletics, participation of girls in, 234
Attachment, 39
Attention span, 261
Attitude learning, 247–49; planning objectives for, 253–54
Attitudes: of disadvantaged children, 354–55; teachers, toward problem behaviors, 425–26
Audiologists, 392
Audiovisual devices, 321
Auditory handicaps, 380–82, 386, 401
Autistic children, 400
Autotelic activity, 324
Averages, 523–25
Avoidance learning, 110

Behavior: aggressive, 34–35, 36, 417–18; antisocial, 43; associationist theories, 107–43; average, 405; control of, 139–43; desirable, selecting, 129; disadvantaged children and, 354–55; disruptive, dealing with, 133; effect of reinforcement on,

Behavior (cont.)
126; hyperactive, 43, 383, 388, 407, 418–19, 420, 427; management of, 128–34, 141–43, 328; means-end, 52; molar, 185; problem, 384, 390, 404–32; purposeful aspect of, 147, 185; science of, 139–43; sex-typed, 36–38; shaping of, 181, 197; socialization and, 12, 38–43; superstitious, 122–23; terminal, 250; undesirable, 133; well-adjusted, 407
Behavior modification, 113, 126, 131, 132, 141, 400, 426–27
Behavioral technology, 140–41
Behaviorism, 108
Belonging, need for sense of, 190, 204
Bereiter-Engelmann program, 242, 367–69
Bilingual Education Act, 358
Binet Scale of Intelligence, 508, 509
Blindness, see Visual handicaps
Branching programming, 135
Breakfast programs, 363
Bribes, reinforcers as, 130–31
Busing, 437–39

Caldwell's children's center, 366
Capacity for independent work, 261
Caretaking systems, 16–21; multiple, 18–21
Censorship, schools and, 439
Chance, learning and, 154–55
Character training, school and, 92–94
Chaining, 122–23
Cheating, 90, 470
Child-centered preschool programs, 63
Child-rearing practices, 12, 13–22, 87–91; games and, 33; household structure and, 16–17; kibbutz and, 18–20; religion and, 17; sex differences in achievement motivation and, 211; socialization process and, 408; socioeconomic status and, 35–36; studies of, 14, 87, 203
China, preschool education in, 29–30
Circular (repetitive) reactions, 52
Class size, 263
Classical (respondent) conditioning, 109–11, 113, 125–26, 132
Classifications, use of, 263
Classroom: applications of cognitive-field theories to, 175–82; atmosphere of, 134; behavior management in, 128–34; increasing motivation in, 203–21; nongraded, 327–28; open, 69, 313–18; overcrowded, 443–44
Closure, law of, 149–50, 276
Cognition: theories of language and, 47–48; Tolman's view of, 186
Cognitive development, 45–71, 168–71, 200–201; Bruner's views of, 168–71; curriculum and, 56, 60–61; increasing, Montessori method and, 307–10; language and, 46–49, 62–63; learning-environmental approaches to, 61–64; parental role in, 63; planning for, 58–70; stage-dependent approaches to, 58–61; stages of, 49, 50–54, 55, 56, 169, 201; theories of, 49–58
Cognitive map, 158
Cognitive processes, 46
Cognitive-field theories, 145–48, 185; applications of, to the classroom, 175–82; differentiated from associationist theories, 147–48, 154; foundations of, 146–47
Collective bargaining, 447

College Level Examination Program, 518
Communication skills, 228. *See also* Language
Community liaison, 429
Community participation, 3, 99, 100
Compensatory programs, older students and, 373–75
Competence motivation, 197–98
Competency, 218
Competition: as reinforcer, 130; as source of motivation, 212–14; reinforcement of, 450
Completion tests, 476
Comprehension, 251–52
Computers, instructional use of, 321–25, 398
Concept learning, 242–47; economy and, 166; foundations of, 244–45
Concepts, 242–43; abstract, 243; concrete, 242–43; formation of, 243, 262; principles distinguished from, 243–44; teaching, 242–47
Concrete operations stage (cognitive development), 53, 169
Conditioning: classical (respondent), 109–11, 113, 125–26, 132; operant (instrumental), 113–25, 126–28, 132, 201, 346
Conflicts, adolescent, 96, 97
Conformity, 39, 80, 83; peer group, 91
Conservation, 54, 171
Content validity (tests), 504
Contiguity factor (learning), 109
Continuation, law of, 149
Contracts, student-teacher, 221
Controversial issues, teachers and, 437–42
Cooperation, 40; stimulating, 130
Cooperative planning, students and, 488
Cooperative School and College Ability Tests, 512
Correlation, 527–28
Correlation coefficient, 503–504, 527
Co-teaching, 325–26
Counseling, 391; individual, 429
Creativity, 251, 252, 263, 378; as goal of teacher, 214–15, 216
Crisis intervention, 429
Criterion-referenced testing, 468, 484–87, 500
Culture: effects of, on socialization, 35–38; motivational indoctrination and, 197; peer group and, 32–33; play and, 32–33; socialization and, 12, 13
Culture Fair Intelligence Tests, 512
Curriculum: cognitive development and, 56, 60–61; discovery teaching and, 178–79; elementary school, 69–70; motivation and, 220–21; movement theory and planning of, 230; preschool, 67; spiral, 171, 177–78, 279; stage-dependent, 67; structure of, 279–81
Cybernetic theory, 276

Day-care centers, 30–32, 65–66, 100
Daydreaming, 133, 380, 415, 416
Deafness, *see* Hard-of-hearing children
Deduction, 168, 245
Defensive identification, 78
Delinquency, 97–98, 140
Dependence, field, 262
Dependency, 39
Depression, 422
Deprivation, effects of parental, 22–25
Deschooling, 333–34
Desegregation, school, 437–38
Development: cognitive, 45–71, 168–71, 200–201; definition of, 8; emotional, speech and, 237; generalizations about, 8; identity, 76–79, 87–95; independence and, 16, 17, 38; individual differences and, 86; kinds of, 8; learning-environmental approach to, 9, 10, 56–58, 61–64, 78–79, 85–86; moral, 74, 75, 79, 80, 81, 82–95; personality, 13, 14, 16, 17, 21–22, 75, 76, 87; socialization and, 11–44; stage-dependent approach to,

8–9, 10, 49–56, 58–61, 76–78, 79–85; value, 79–87
Developmental tasks, 9, 405–406, 407
Diagnostic teaching, 467
Diagram, topological, 158–60
Dialects, 242
Differences, individual, *see* Individual differences
Differentiation, 175
Discipline: classroom, 128–34; mental, doctrine of, 291, 292, 293; parental, 81, 87
Discovery learning and teaching, 177–82, 245; curriculum planning and, 178–79; evaluation of, 180–82; practical implementation of, 179–80; reinforcement and, 178
Discrimination, 121, 176, 236, 262, 263, 299
Diseases, disabling, 382
Disequilibrium, 200, 201
Distractibility, 262
Distribution, 525; normal, 525–26; skewed, 526–27
Divorce, effect on children, 408
Doodling, 194
Drive-reduction theory, 188
Drive strength, 187–88
Drives, 185, 187; exploratory, 198, 218–20; fear and anxiety as, 201–203; functional role of, 187; manipulation, 198
Dropouts, school, 98
Drug abuse, 96–97, 423

Economy: structure of a subject and, 165–66; token, 130
Edison Responsive Environment, 323–24
Education: by choice, 338; China and, 29–30; competency-based, 217–18, 220; higher, alternative instructional designs for, 339–41; implications of topological theory for, 161–62; individualized, 60; kibbutz, 28–29; modular, 319, 326–27; nongraded, 327–28; objectives of, 61, 162, 174, 182, 191, 250, 425; open classroom, 69, 313–18; physical, 226, 227, 228; role of punishment in, 112; Soviet, 26–28, 329–30; special, for handicapped students, 399–402; vocational, 228. *See also* Preschool education programs; Schools
Educational Testing Service, 505
Effect, law of, 111–12, 113; truncated law of, 112
Egocentric reasoning, 53
Electric Company, The, 312
Electronic data processing equipment, 324
Emotional development, speech and, 237
Emotional handicaps, 384, 388, 401–402, 404–32
Enactive mode of representation, 165, 169
Encoding, 277
Encounter groups, 430–31
England, open classroom in, 314–15
Enrichment programs, 396–97
Environment: factor in problem behavior, 408–15; learning, 219–20, 276; linguistic, 46
Epilepsy, 382
Equilibration, 52, 60
Equilibrium, 51–52, 188; need for, 200–201
Error, standard, 530
Escape response, 115, 116, 126
Essay tests, 473, 475; improving, 483–84
Esteem needs, 190, 205
Evaluation, 171, 252, 463–522; classroom learning, 465–96; free school movement, 337–39; importance of, 3; of individualized instruction, 320; of discovery teaching, 180–82; of tests, 471–72, 477; of open classroom, 317–18; self-, 88, 89, 208, 354; self-paced, 488–89; testing as means of, 466–72. *See also* Grading; Testing; Tests
Exchange games, 48
Expectations, 196, 208, 209–10, 262, 330; teacher, 360
Exploratory drive, 198, 218–20
Extended family, 13, 16, 17, 18, 20, 21, 88

External Studies Program, 340–41
Extinction, 119–20, 131, 201, 274

Fading theory (forgetting), 272
Familiarity of material, importance of, 278–79
Family: extended, 13, 16, 17, 18, 20, 21, 88; as factor in problem behavior, 408–409; influence on child's development of identity and values, 87–91; nuclear, 13, 17, 18, 19, 21; socialization and, 13–25
Family therapy, 431
Father: child-rearing role of, 15–16; effects of child's deprivation of, 24–25; influence on child's behavior, 408. *See also* Parents
Fear, 41–42; as a drive, 201–203
Feedback, learning and, 166–67, 205, 219, 228, 230, 283, 319, 327
Femininity, 36, 424
Field dependence, 262
Field independence, 262
Field trips, 290
Figure-ground perception, 150–51
Fine arts, 228
Fixation, 152
Fixed-solution problems, 154
Foreign hull, 158, 162
Forgetting, 149–50, 268, 269; fading theory, 272; theories concerning, 271–77
Formal operations stage (cognitive development), 54, 58, 169
Free school movement, 330–39; evaluation of, 337–39
Freedom, myth of, 139
Freedoms, personal: of students, 443; of teachers, 442–43
"Future shock," 414

Games: child-training patterns and, 33; exchange, 48; "story," 372
Generalized principles, theory of, 294–96
Generalizations, 121; meaningful, development of, 301; response, 121; stimulus, 121
"Generation gap," 96
Geometry, 172–73
Gestalt psychology, 146–47, 148–62
Gifted students, 378, 385; college-level courses for, 396; identifying, 388–89; special classes for, 399–400; special programs for, 394–97
Goals, 185, 186, 187, 220–21, 425, 426; free school movement, 337–38. *See also* Objectives
Goodenough-Harris Drawing Test, 510
Grading, 124, 125, 468–69, 489–95; purposes of, 490; types of, 490–92
Graduate Record Examination, 512
Grammar, transformational, 238
Graphemes, 241
Growth, *see* Development
Group reinforcement, 130, 329; as source of motivation, 212
Group trading, teaching and, 326
Grouping: ability, 394–95; of students, 263–64

Habits: bad, behavior modification and, 132; study, 284–85
Handicapped children, 378, 379–84; auditory, 380–82, 386, 401; emotionally, 384, 388, 401; gifted students as, 378, 385; identifying, 385–88; mainstreaming and, 389–95, 397, 399; mental retardation, 378, 380, 381, 382–83, 386, 401; neurologically, 382; physically, 382, 386, 402; special classes for, 399; special programs and services for, 393–94, 401–402; supportive services for, 391–93; visually, 380, 381, 401
Hard-of-hearing children, 380–82; identifying, 386; special programs and services for, 401
Harlem Prep, 336–37, 339

Head Start, 58, 68, 242, 366–67
Health: mental, 406; of disadvantaged children, 352–54
Hearing handicaps, 380–82, 401; identifying, 386
Henmon-Nelson Tests of Mental Ability, 512
Hierarchical teaching, 325
Homeostasis, 188, 200
Homosexuality, 424
Hyperactive behavior, 43, 383, 388, 407, 418–19, 420, 427
Hypotheses, 54, 104, 172, 214; testing, 179

Iconic mode of representation, 165, 169
Identical elements, theory of, 293–94
Identification, 78–79; defensive, 78; with the aggressor, 78
Identity: definition of, 199; development theories, 76–79; need for, 199–200; negative, 200; planning for development of, 87–95; positive ego, 76–77; search for, 74–75, 199; sex typing and, 36–38; sexual, 424
Identity crisis, 77
Identity diffusion, 77
Imaginativeness, 216
Imitation, 34–35, 78
Impulsivity, 262
Independence: development of, 16, 17, 38; field, 262
Independent work, capacity for, 261
Individual differences, 3, 4, 346–461; concept learning and, 247; development and, 86; in positive transfer ability, 303; learning styles and, 264; motor skills and, 234–35; recognition of, 260. *See also* Handicapped children
Individualized instruction, *see* Instruction, individualized
Inductive method, 245
Indulgence, infant, 16–17
Inferiority, sense of, 191
Information: computers and, 321; retrieval of, 277; sequencing of, learning and, 166–67; storage of, 268, 270, 276–77; transfer of, 155, 167–68, 171
Information-processing approach, 276
Inhibition: proactive, 273, 291; retroactive, 273, 291
Initial Teaching Alphabet, 241
Insight, 152–53; as product and process, 153–54; Bruner's views on, 171–73; development of, 154; fixation as enemy of, 152; "magic moment" of, 173; test for, 155
Insight learning, 152–53, 154, 162; chance and, 154–55
Insincerity, 205
Instruction: alternative designs for, 306–43; competency-based, 484–87; computer-assisted, 322–25, 398; computer-managed, 322; direct, preschool programs and, 68; individualized, 60, 220, 263, 318–20, 321, 322, 323, 324, 326–27, 398; modular, 319, 326–27; programmed, 134–39
Instructional planning, 255–56
Intelligence quotient, 508
Intelligence quotient tests, 507–16; advantages of, 515–16; disadvantages of, 515–16; as predictor of future ability, 511–14
Intelligence tests, 498, 507–16
Interference: learning and, 272–74, 277, 301–303; reducing effects of, 281
Intervention programs: early childhood, 364–73; parent-child, 364–65; problem children and, 429–31
Intuition, 162, 171, 172, 173
Intuitive stage (intellectual development), 52
Intuitive thinking, 163, 171–73
Iowa Tests of Educational Development, 518
IQ, *see* Intelligence quotient
Israel: child-rearing practices in, 18–20; kibbutz education in, 28–29

Jealousy, 41
"Job-jumper," 202
Justice, 80–81

Kibbutz: child-rearing practices, 18–20; education, 28–29
Knowledge, 251, 253; transfer of, 155, 167–68, 171, 268–69, 289–303
Kuhlmann-Anderson Measure of Academic Potential, 512

Language, 59; acquisition of, 62; as a productive system, 236–37; disadvantaged children and, 357–59; learning, 235–42; of music, 229; play and, 48; relationship between cognitive development and, 46–49; theories of, 47–48
Leadership: authoritarian, 451; effective, factors in, 448–49; poorly used, problems stemming from, 449–52; punitive, 451–52; teachers and, 448–55
Learned techniques, 48
Learning, 104; associationist theory in, 125–28; attitude, 247–49, 253–54; avoidance, 110; Bruner's theories of, 162–75; chance and, 154–55; classroom, evaluation of, 465–96; concept, 166, 242–47; contiguity factor in, 109; definition of, 8, 104; disabilities, 383–84, 386–88, 401; discovery, 177–82, 245; discrimination, 236; environment for, 219–20, 276; feedback and, 166–67, 205, 219, 228, 230, 283, 319, 327; Gestalt theories of, 148–62; higher-order, operant conditioning and, 120–22; how to learn, 299; increasing, in the classroom, 203–21; insight, 152–53, 154, 162; intellectual development and, 56; interference and, 272–74; language, 235–42; listening and, 229; meaningful, 278; motivation and, 163–64; motor, 226–35; objectives of, 249–58; outcomes of, 249–58; over-, 281–82, 286, 300; perceptual, 224–26; principle, 244; process of, 171; prohibition, 78; rate of, 261; reception, 180–81; relationship between anxiety and, 203; research concerning, 105; satisfaction of needs and, 204–205; sequencing of information and, 166–67; signal, 111, steps in, 171; stimulus-response approach, 108; styles of, 259–64; theories of, 104, 105; topological or vector theory of, 156–61; transfer of, 155, 167–68, 171, 268–69, 289–303; types of, 224–49. See also Relearning
Learning-environmental approach (development), 9, 10, 56–58, 61–64, 78–79, 85–86
Lewinian field theory, 156–61
"Liberation schools," 333
Library: pet, 314; toy, 365
"Life adjustment" courses, 84
Life space, 157–62
Linear programming, 135
Linguistic environment, 46
Linguistics, 237–39, 240, 242
Linguists, 238
Listening, learning and, 229
Loci method (remembering), 287
Lorge-Thorndike Intelligence Tests, 511, 512
Love, need for, 190, 204
Lying, 80, 82

Mainstreaming, 389–95, 397, 399, 407, 424–25
Maintenance systems, 12, 16
Malnutrition, 352, 353
Management, behavior, see Modification, behavior
Manipulation drive, 198
Map, cognitive, 158
Masculinity, 36, 424
Matching, 54, 58, 59, 85; peer, 334
Maternal deprivation, effects of, 21–24
Maternal leave, teachers and, 444–45
Maturation, defined, 8, 49
Mean, 523, 526, 527
Meaningful material, importance of, 269, 278–79, 301–302
Median, 524, 526, 527
Memory, 262; increasing, 277–89; long-term, 270, 271, 277–89; measuring methods, 287–89; reconstructing, 275; short-term, 270, 277; theories concerning, 271–77; types of, 269–71. See also Remembering

Memory traces, 272
Mental combinations, 52
Mental discipline, doctrine of, 291, 292, 293
Mental health, 406
Mental retardation, 378, 380, 381, 382–83, 385, 386; special programs and services for, 401
Mental tests, 498, 507–16
Merit pay, teachers and, 459–60
Metric system, 302
Metropolitan Readiness Tests, 517–18
Miller Analogies Test, 512
Mnemonics, 287
Mobilization for Youth, 330
Mode, 524, 526, 527
Model building, 33
Modification, behavior, 128–34, 141–43, 328
Modular individualized instruction, 319, 326–27
Modules, 319, 327
Molecular bits, 185
Monitoring, 328
Montessori method (teaching), 66–67, 307–10
Morality: cooperative, 81; development of, 74, 75, 79, 80, 82–95; stages of, 82–84; types of, 81
Mother: characteristics of, and child's personality development, 21; child-rearing role of, 14, 15, 16, 21; child's cognitive development and, 63–64; child's deprivation of, 22–24; influence of, on child's behavior, 408. See also Parents
Mothering, multiple, 18
Mother-substitute, characteristics of, child's personality development and, 21
Motivation, 52, 129, 147–48, 184–222; achievement, 193–96, 197, 205–208, 21C–12; competence, 197–98; competition as source of, 212–14; curriculum planning for, 220–21; extrinsic, 220; fear and anxiety as source of, 201–203; group reinforcement as source of, 212–14; increasing, in classroom, 203–21; intrinsic, 218–19; kinds of, 197, 218–20; learning and, 163–64; Piaget's concept of, 200; theories of forgetting, 274–76; theory of, 185–203
Motor learning, 226–35; basic principles of, 228, 230; individual differences and, 234–35; movement theory and, 230; practice and, 233–34; taxonomy of, based on subject matter, 227–28; teacher's role in, 230–33
Movement theory, 230
Multiple-choice tests, 475–76
Multiple mothering, 18
Music, 229, 282

Needs: belonging, 190; definition of, 186; equilibrium, 200–201; esteem, 190; identity, 199–200; love, 190; Maslow's hierarchy of, learning and, 204–205; nutritional, 204; physiological, 189; primary, 186, 187; safety, 189, 204; secondary, 186, 187; self-actualization, 191; special, children with, 377–403
Neurological handicaps, 382
Neuroses, 42
Nongraded classroom, 327–28
Non-language tests, 500
Nonverbal tests, 500
Normal curve, 379, 405, 468–69, 501, 525–26
Normal distribution, 525–26
Norm-referenced tests, 469–70, 472, 500, 501
Nuclear family, 13, 17, 18, 19, 21
Nutritional needs, 204

Obedience training, 93–94
"Object concept," 52
Objective tests, 475–77; improving, 477–83
Objectives: educational, 61, 162, 174, 182, 191, 250, 425; learning, 249–58. See also Goals
Occupational therapists, 392

Open classroom, 69, 313–18; evaluation of, 317–18; in England, 314–15; in United States, 315–17

Operant (instrumental) conditioning, 113–25, 126–28, 132, 201, 346; components of, 114–15; higher-order learning and, 120–22

Operant strength, 114, 119

Operation Upgrade, 369–73

Oral recitation, 283–84, 286

Oral tests, 476–77

Organization, 49, 50, 51; information storage and, 277; laws of, 148, 276, 279

Orthopedic handicaps, 382

Outliers, 524

Overgeneralization, 121–22

Overlearning, 281–82, 286, 300

Pairing, 110, 111, 113

Panic reaction, 420

Paranoia, 414–15

Paraprofessional aides, 329

Parental deprivation, effects of, 22–25

Parent-centered programs, 63 – 64

Parents: adolescent conflicts and, 96, 97; child-rearing practices, 12, 13–22; discipline by, 81, 87; effects of child's deprivation of, 22–25; influence on child's behavior, 408; of children with special needs, 392–93; overprotective, 39, 89. *See also* Father; Mother

Parent-teacher cooperative elementary schools, 331–32

Parkway School, 334–36

Participation, community, 3

Paternal deprivation, effects of, 24–25

Pay, merit, teachers and, 459–60

Peabody Picture Vocabulary Test, 510

Peer group: adolescence and, 422; influence of, 32–33, 91–92; socialization and, 32–33

Peer matching, 334

Peer teaching, 329–30

Percentile rank, 501, 528

Perception, 145–48, 262; developmental differences in, 175–76; figure-ground, 150–51

Perceptual learning, 224–26

Perceptual skills, teaching of, 175

Performance, student: measuring, 328; teacher and, 362–63

Performance tests, 500

Personality: child-rearing practices and, 408; development of, 13, 14, 16, 17, 21–22, 75, 76, 87; poorly adjusted, 406; problems, 404–32; well-adjusted, 405, 406

Philosophy, elementary school class in, 62

Phobia, school, 420–22

Phonemes, 240

Physical education, 226, 227, 228

Physical handicaps, 382, 385, 402; identifying, 386

Physical therapists, 392

Physicians, 392

Physiological needs, 189

Pickering v. Board of Education, 442–43

Pittsburgh Free Learning Environment, 337

Planning, cooperative, students and, 488

Play: acquisition of language through, 48; imitative, 32; model, 33; parallel, 32; patterns of, disadvantaged children and, 362; role, 32, 33; socialization and, 32–33

Plowden Report, 313

Policy-making, school, teachers and, 445

Positive ego identity, 76–77

Poverty, 355, 356

Power of material being learned, 166

Power tests, 500

Practice: learning and, 233–34, 282; problem-solving and, 299–300

Prägnanz, law of, 148

Precision teaching, 328–29

Preconceptual stage (cognitive development), 52

Predictive validity (tests), 504

Prejudice, problem behavior and, 414–15

Premack principle, 130

Preoperational stage (cognitive development), 52, 169

Preschool education programs: alternative instructional designs for, 307–12; child-centered, 63; Chinese, 29–30; compensatory, 58, 63, 65; curriculum and, 67; day-care centers and, 30–32; direct instruction and, 68; disadvantaged children and, 65, 68, 364–69; kibbutz, 28–29; Montessori method, 66–67; parent-centered, 63–64; reasons for, 65–66; socialization and, 25–32; Soviet, 26–28; television and, 310–12

Pre-testing, 501

Principle learning, 244

Principles: concepts distinguished from, 243–44; generalized, theory of, 294–96; psychological, 2, 5

Proactive inhibition, 273

Problem behavior, 384, 390, 404–32; adolescence and, 422–24; behavior modification and, 426–27; common forms of, 415–24; factors related to, 408–15; group-centered approaches to, 430–31; handling, 130, 424–31; intervention programs, 428–31; teacher attitude toward, 425–26

Problem-solving, 154, 155, 172; concept learning and, 242–47; practice in, 299–300

Productive thinking, 155–56

Program Assessment Pupil Instruction, 519

Programmed instruction, 134–39

Progressive matrices, 512

Prohibition learning, 78

Project PLAN, 60, 319–20, 322–23, 326

Proximity, law of, 149

Psycholinguists, 238

Psychological field, 157, 161

Psychological principles, applying, 2, 5

Psychological reality, 145

Psychological services, 391, 428–29

Psychological world, 146, 147

Psychologists, school, 428–29

Punishment, 84, 111, 112, 116, 117, 118, 120, 126, 139–40, 407, 408, 417, 451–52; corporal, 127–28; disadvantaged children and, 359; fear of, 202

Pygmalion effect, 210, 360

Racism, 354

Randsight, 381

Readiness, 230, 262; learning, 162, 169–70; reading, 70, 225

Reading, 70, 175, 225–26, 311, 312, 335, 363; Bereiter-Engelmann program and, 242, 367–69; disadvantaged children and, 242; Operation Upgrade and, 369–73; readiness for, 70, 225; remedial classes and, 393–94; role of teacher and, 240–42

"Reading is FUNdamental" program, 363

Reality, psychological, 145

Reasoning: analytic, 172; deductive, 168; egocentric, 53. *See also* Thinking

Recall, 287–88

Reception learning, 180–81

Recitation, oral, 283–84, 286

Recognition method of measuring memory, 288–89

Record keeping, schools and, 444, 494

Reduction of uncertainty, 176

Reference services: to educational objects, 334; to professional educators, 334

Reflectivity, 262

Reflexive stage (cognitive development), 52

Reforms, educational, 306–43

Reinforcement, 86, 113–25, 132–33, 176, 228, 328; as bribe,

Reinforcement (cont.)
130–31; continuous, 123; delayed, 128; discovery teaching and, 178; effects of, 126–28; group, 130, 212, 329; intermittent, 123; negative, 115–20, 126–27, 128; of competition, 450; of docility, 450; positive, 115, 117, 119, 120, 126, 130, 221; primary, 114–15; schedules of, 123–25; secondary, 114–15

Reinforcers, 113–25, 346; as bribes, 130–31; generalized, 133; negative, 115–20; positive, 115, 117, 119, 120, 140; primary, 114; proper, selection of, 129–33; reduction of uncertainty as, 176; secondary, 114–15; social, 133

Relativism, 145

Relearning, 289

Religion, child-rearing practices and, 17

Remedial classes, 393–94

Remembering, 268, 269; methods for measuring, 287–89; theories concerning, 271–77. See also Memory

Representation, modes of, 165, 169

Representational meaning of words, 235

Repression, 275–76

Research: about learning, 105; applied, 105; basic, 105; educational, 2, 5

Resource rooms, 399

Respect, need for, 190

Response, 111–12, 113; conditioned, 109, 110, 111; escape, 115, 116, 126; unconditioned, 109, 110, 111

Response mode, 260

Retardation, see Mental retardation

Retention, see Memory; Remembering

Retroactive inhibition, 273

Reward, 84, 111, 112, 113, 114, 121, 129, 218, 407, 408; disadvantaged children and, 359; external (extrinsic), 220; student-teacher contracts and, 221; token economy and, 130

Rivalry, 41; sibling, 41

Role playing, 32, 33

Runaways, 98, 407, 416–17, 423–24

Russia, education in, 26–28, 329–30

Safety needs, 189, 204

Satisfiers, 111, 112

Schedules, reinforcement, 123–25

Schizophrenia, 42

Scholastic Aptitude Test, 512

School phobia, 420–22

Schools: alternative instructional designs for, 306–43; as factor in problem behavior, 409–13; censorship and, 439; character training role of, 92–94; desegregation issue and, 437–38; free, 330–39; "inverse of," 333; "liberation," 333; Montessori, 307–10; record keeping and, 444, 494; sex bias in, 440–42; special, for handicapped children, 401–402

Scores, standardized test, 528–30

Self-actualization, 191, 192, 205, 405

Self-concept, 88, 95; of disadvantaged children, 354–55

Self-control, 38

Self-esteem, 88–90, 99, 330, 360, 361; influence of school on, 94

Self-evaluation, 88, 89, 208; of disadvantaged children, 354

Self-fulfilling prophecy, 210, 360

Self-image, 88; of disadvantaged children, 354, 357, 360–62; positive, promoting, 360–62

Self-reliance, development of, 38

Self-respect, 190, 205

Sensitivity training, 430–31

Sensorimotor stage (cognitive development), 52, 58

Sensory information storage, 270

Sesame Street, 68–69, 310–12, 369

Sex bias, schools and, 440–42

Sex differences: achievement motivation and, 210–12; motor skills and, 235

Sex-role identification, 36

Sex typing, 36–38

Sexuality, 424

Shaping, 120–21, 129, 131

Short-answer tests, 476

Shyness, 416

Sibling rivalry, 41

Signal learning, 111

Similarity, law of, 148–49

Skewed distribution, 526–27

Skills: communication, 228; fine arts, 228; motor, development of, 226–35; perceptual, teaching of, 175; teaching, 1–5; vocational, 228

Skinner box, 113, 119

"Slow learners," 383–84

Social-emotional handicaps, 384, 388, 401–402

Social stress, 413–14

Social workers, school, 392, 429

Socialization, 11–44, 408; behavior and, 12, 38–42; behavior disturbances and, 42–43; defined, 12; effects of culture on, 35–38; family and, 13–25; importance of, 46; peer group and, 32–33; play and, 32–33; preschool education programs and, 25–32; private enterprise in, 38; process of, 12; socioeconomic status and, 35–36; television and, 33–34; variables influencing, 13

Socially disadvantaged children, adaptability, 356; attitudes of 354–55; behavior of, 354–55; defined, 350–52; educational television and, 310–11, 369; effect of rewards and punishments on, 359; health of, 352–54; language difficulties of, 357–59; meaningful material and, 278–79; Montessori method and, 308–10; Operation Upgrade and, 369–73; preschool programs and, 65, 68, 364–69; reading and, 242; self-image of, 354, 357, 360–62; teacher expectations and, 360; teaching, 349–76

Society: adolescents and, 98–100; as factor in problem behavior, 413–15; deceptive image of, 98; developmental tasks and, 9; socialization and, 12

Socioeconomic status: problem behavior and, 414; socialization and, 35–36

Soviet educational system, 26–28, 329–30

Special needs, children with, 377–403; identifying, 385–89; problem behaviors, 404–32; programming for, 389–402

Special services, director of, 392

Specificity in perceptual learning, 175

Speech, 47; defects, hard-of-hearing children and, 380–82; delayed, 381; emotional development and, 237

Speech correctionists, 392

Speed tests, 500

Spelling, 242

Stage-dependent approach (development), 8–9, 10, 49–56, 58–61, 76–78, 79–85

Stammering, 381

Standard Daily Behavior Chart, 328, 329

Standard deviation, 526

Standard error, 530

Standardization sample, 501

Standardized tests, 497–522; of ability, 507–16; of achievement, 516–21; advantages of, 506; definition of, 498; development of, 501–506; disadvantages of, 506; reliability of, 503–506; scores used on, 528–30; types of, 498–500; validity of, 503–506

Stanford-Binet Scale of Intelligence, 508–509, 510, 511, 530

Statistical validity (tests), 504

Stereotypes, 122

Stimulus, 111–12, 113; conditioned, 109, 110, 111, 125; unconditioned, 109, 110, 111, 125

Stimulus-response approach, 108

"Story game," 372

Street academies, 332-33
Stress, social, 413–14
Strikes, teachers', 447
Structure of a subject, 162, 164–67, 177
Student-teacher contracts, 221
Students, personal freedoms of, 443
Study habits, 284–85
Study sessions, spacing and timing of, 285–86
Stuttering, 381
Subculture, adolescent, 75
Subject, structure of a, 162, 164–67, 177
Subject-matter content, importance of, 2
Summerhill, 333
Superstitious behavior, 122–23
Supportive services, 391–93, 428–29
Symbolic mode of representation, 165, 169
Synthesis, 252

"Talking Typewriter," 323–24
Teacher-preparation programs, 3
Teachers: accountability of, 445, 455–60, 494–95; as human beings, 437–48; as leaders, 448–55; attitude toward problem behaviors, 425–26; behavior modification of, by children, 131; behavior of, and classroom achievement, 433–61; community participation and, 437; controversial issues and, 437–42; creativity as goal of, 214–15, 216; "helping," 428–29; importance of, 436–37; interactions between students and, 453–55; major dissatisfactions of, 443–46; maternity leave policies and, 444–45; merit pay and, 459–60; perceptions of students, 411–13; personal freedoms of, 442–43; policy-making and, 445; "resource," 397; role conflict in, 434–36; role in teaching children to read, 240–42; role in teaching motor skills, 230–33; roles of, 434–37; sex bias and, 440–42; strikes and, 447; successful, 1–5, 397; tenure system and, 459; unionization and, 446–47
Teaching: Bruner's view on problems of, 174–75; coordinate, 325–26; diagnostic, 467; disadvantaged children, 349–76; discovery method of, 177–82, 245; hierarchical, 325; innovations in, 306–43; major dissatisfactions with, 443–46; Montessori method of, 307–10; of perceptual skills, 175; paraprofessional, 329; peer, 329–30; precision, 328–29; team, 325–26; therapeutic approaches to, 397–98; trading groups and, 326
Teaching-learning process, 2–4, 5
Teaching-learning units (TLU's), 60
Teaching machines, 135, 136, 321
Team teaching, 325–26
Techniques, learned, 48
Technology: behavioral, use of, 140–41; use of, in classroom instruction, 320–25; visually handicapped aided by, 381
Television: commercial, as learning resource, 311; educational, 68–69, 310–12, 321, 369; instructional, 310; socialization and, 33–34
Tenure system, 459
Terminal behavior, 250
Test taking, art of, 514
Testing: alternative approaches to, 484–89; criterion-referenced, 468, 484–87, 500; as a learning experience, 482; as means of evaluation, 466–72; norm-referenced, 469–70, 472, 500; purposes of, 466–69; social implications of, 469
Tests: ability, 498, 506, 507–16; achievement, 498–99, 501, 502, 503, 516–21; aptitude, 498, 512; completion, 476; criterion-referenced, 468, 484–87, 500; essay, 473, 475, 483–

Tests (cont.)
84; evaluation of, 471–72, 477; good, criteria of, 471–72; group, 499, 511, 512; improving, 477–84; individual, 499–500, 509, 510; intelligence, 498, 507–16; mental, 498; multiple-choice, 475–76; non-language, 500; nonverbal, 500; norm-referenced, 469–70, 472, 500, 501; objective, 475–83; oral, 476–77; performance, 500; power, 500; short-answer, 476; speed, 500; standardized, 497–522; standardizing, 501; as teaching and learning tools, 474; true-false, 476; types of, 473–77; validity of, 472, 503–506, 530–31; verbal, 500
Therapy: family, 431; problem children and, 429–31
Thinking: analytic, 172; convergent, 154; creative, 214, 216; divergent, 154; intuitive, 163, 171–73; pattern of, 260; productive, 155–56; programmed instruction and, 136. *See also* Reasoning
Thought, 46, 47
Thought processes, development of, *see* Cognitive development
Toilet training, 17
Token economy, 130
Topological diagram, 158–60
Toy library, 365
Trading groups, teaching and, 326
Training: character, school and, 92–94; obedience, 93–94; sensitivity, 430–31; transfer of, 155, 167–68, 171, 268–69, 289–303
Transfer of learning, 155, 167–68, 171, 268–69, 289–303; defined, 289; development of concept of, 291–93; general, 299–300; negative, 291, 301–303; positive, 290–91, 296–303; theories of, 293–96
Transformational grammar, 238
Transposition, 155
Trial and error, 52, 112, 155
Trips, field, 290
True-false tests, 476
Truncated law of effect, 112
Trust, 39–40

Uncertainty, reduction of, 176
Unionization, teachers and, 446–47
Upward Bound, 374

Valence, 159; negative, 159, 160
Validity of tests, 472, 503–506, 530–31
Values, 74; development theories of, 79–87; planning for development of, 87–95
Vector theory, 159–61
Verbal tests, 500
Violence, 417; exposure to, 34–35
Visual aids, 321
Visual handicaps, 380, 381, 401
Vocation, choosing a, 94–95
Vocational education, 228

Wechsler Adult Intelligence Scale, 509, 530
Wechsler-Bellevue Intelligence Scale, 509
Wechsler Intelligence Scale for Children, 509, 511
Wechsler PrePrimary and Primary Intelligence Scale, 509
Withdrawal, 355, 407, 414, 415–17, 422
Working conditions, dissatisfaction of teachers with, 443

Z score, 502, 509
Zeigarnik effect, 275